The Libertine Colony

A JOHN HOPE FRANKLIN CENTER BOOK

The LIBERTINE COLONY

Creolization in the Early French Caribbean

Doris Garraway

DUKE UNIVERSITY PRESS

Durham and London 2005

© 2005 Duke University Press

All rights reserved

Printed in the United States of America

on acid-free paper ⊗

Designed by Amy Ruth Buchanan

Typeset in Adobe Caslon by

Tseng Information Systems, Inc.

Library of Congress Cataloging-

in-Publication Data appear on the

last printed page of this book.

In loving memory of
Michael O. Garraway
and Paolo Palezzato

Contents

Illustrations

Preface

At the time I began this project, the bicentennial anniversary of the Haitian Revolution had reminded the world of the "horrors of Saint-Domingue," the most brutal slave colony in history, out of which arose the most radical liberation movement of the so-called "Age of Revolutions." Still, little scholarly attention had been devoted to the cultures of slavery of Old Regime France and, in particular, the texts and literary representations produced about them. While this may not seem surprising, given the historic suppression of colonialism and slavery in Western historiography and humanistic disciplines, more remarkable was that a certain silence around colonial slavery persisted in the very subdiscipline whose mission it was to promote the study of colonial legacies and non-European traditions in the humanities—postcolonial studies. Equally striking to me was that the burgeoning subfield of francophone Caribbean studies demonstrated considerable disregard for early colonial narratives and cultural history, despite the critical interest of literary specialists in theories of creolization that describe the emergence of syncretic cultural forms on the plantation. I soon discovered, however, that there were important reasons for these silences. For a literary scholar, it is immediately far more gratifying to read novels of slavery and colonialism written by postcolonial writers committed to reimagining the subversiveness, resistance, and intelligence of captive peoples than to confront the missionary relations, colonial histories, legal codes, travel literature, novels, and political treatises that represent the same people in quite different terms. At the same time, few of the categories and concepts current in postcolonial studies are useful in a discussion of the Old Regime cultures

of slavery in which the "other" was not native and there was so little ambivalence involved in the process of commodifying the human individual.

As I read on, however, I became convinced that these reasons were not
sufficient cause to leave the serious study of French writing on the Caribbean to other disciplines. I felt that, not only were these neglected colonial
texts fascinating in their own right, but that a literary analysis of them would
have profound implications for some of the most difficult and contentious
issues in Caribbean studies, while at the same time opening up new perspectives on modern francophone Caribbean literature and on early modern French literature and popular culture. In working with this corpus, the
issues that concerned me were not limited to the rhetorical and ideological
characteristics of the texts themselves or the ways in which they portrayed
the power relation between the colony and the metropole. I also sought
to identify which stories the published narrative record told or suppressed
about the cultural, social, and sexual dynamics of colonialism and slavery
in French territories, and the ways in which these dynamics changed over
the course of the seventeenth and eighteenth centuries. That broad focus
required a reconsideration of the object of literary analysis and the limits
and possibilities of textual critique in a historical frame. In my view, the
particular contribution of literary criticism to the study of cultures lies in
its ability to go where historians often do not tread; on the basis of a close
reading of a particular text, image, or anecdote, to imagine, as Joan Dayan
has put it, what cannot be verified; to posit what could never have been
documented in any historical archive; to recover the fantasies, beliefs, mentalities, and silences in which the desires and anxieties of historical subjects
may be lodged; to consider, furthermore, the ways in which a text's form
and structure provide as much insight into the cultural conditions of its
production as the manifest narrative it contains. In addition to supplement-
ing and in some cases questioning dominant historical and anthropological
understandings of early French Caribbean cultures, I therefore endeavored
to produce a study of the first French colonial literature from the Caribbean
region.

This book thus represents a historically situated literary interpretation of
selected texts that provide insights into the process whereby radically different ethnic and national groups were coerced into coexistence and structured
in social relations of domination based on race. In particular, my analyses
shed light on the relationship between the cultural transformation and hybridization of transplanted populations and the emergence of borders of
violence between them. In contrast to theorists of creolization who celebrate

the cultural and biological synthesis of different groups without examining the violent antagonisms across which such processes were negotiated, I seek to understand how the violence and desires enacted by the settler minority were instrumental in shaping Creole cultural forms, colonial racial ideologies, and the legal means by which the white elite established its hegemony in the Old Regime Caribbean.

Central to my inquiry is the concept of libertinage, through which writers continually defined the Caribbean as a space of spiritual, social, and moral deviance. While tracing this critique in accounts of cross-cultural encounters, piracy, colonial domesticity, occult practices and beliefs, slavery, and miscegenation written by representatives of the colonizing culture, I intervene in a number of debates about the cultural workings of colonialism and slavery in the Americas. These debates pertain to the representational value of European ethnographic accounts of Amerindian peoples, the social and cultural meanings of piratical violence and plantation agriculture, the relation between missionary ideology and the law of slavery, and the creolization of spirit beliefs. Most importantly, I ask how the concept of colonial libertinage might be expanded and redeployed to describe the impact of gender and sexuality on white elite racial discourses, political identity, and social practices in French Caribbean slave societies. My study of the narrative sources convinced me of the centrality of desire and sexuality to ideologies of racial domination espoused by members of the white elite over the course of the eighteenth century, ideologies which had their corollary in scenes of subjection and legal regimes of exclusion directed against free nonwhites. To illustrate this proposition, I develop an alternative understanding of libertinage as a sexual economy that undergirded exploitative power relations among whites, free people of color, and slaves. Drawing on literary and psychoanalytic criticism, historical research, and my own textual analyses, my theory of a "libertine colony" posits a relationship between white elite sexual engagements (coerced and consensual) with nonwhite women, slave and free, and the extreme segregationist regime that reached its apogee in the exceptionally brutal slave society of late-eighteenth-century Saint-Domingue.

Based on an analysis of legal and narrative discourses, I argue that, over time, elite white colonials imagined their relation to free nonwhites and slaves through a metaphor of illegitimate filiation. While rooted in the knowledge of the sexual relations that linked individuals across ethno-social groupings in the slave colony, this image offered the white elite a means of repressing its involvement in interracial libertinage by projecting the burden of culpability and punishment onto both slave women and the growing class of free people of color, deemed the immoral carriers of a primal sin. Racially discriminatory legislation therefore became the primary mechanism by which the white elite attempted to control, manage, and suppress the social and economic consequences of interracial sexual relations. The ironic effect of such discrimination was to discipline indirectly white libertinage, while at the same time leaving elite men free to pursue their interracial desires with impunity, thus reinforcing white sexual hegemony in the colony. Close analysis of the fantasies inherent in narratives of race and reproduction produced in the libertine colony demonstrates, furthermore, the fundamentally incestuous structure of white colonial desire, a structure that arguably manifested itself on the plantation and in the discursive and legal persecution of free people of color in Saint-Domingue. The "libertine colony" thesis thus offers a means of understanding the centrality of desire and sexuality to notions of white Creole identity and political legitimacy in Saint-Domingue, as well as the concrete effects of such desires; in particular, their role in creating precisely those segregationist measures that were intended to erect an untransgressible social barrier between whites, free nonwhites, and slaves in Saint-Domingue.

* * *

This book began as a doctoral thesis at Duke University, and I am deeply grateful to my advisors, Philip Stewart and Michèle Longino, for allowing me the freedom to pursue research that challenged and expanded the categories of early modern French and francophone Caribbean literature in often unpredictable ways. I am also grateful to Walter Mignolo, Sibylle Fischer, Jean Jonassaint, Toril Moi, and Nicole Jacques-Chaquin for the suggestions, criticisms, and encouragement they offered in the early stages of the project's development.

At Northwestern University the project grew and matured, and I owe a considerable debt to the people who have nurtured that growth. In the department of French and Italian, I would like to thank Bernadette Fort, Jane Winston, Sylvie Romanowski, Jean Mainil, and Scott Durham for their valuable feedback on various portions of the manuscript. Michal Ginsburg and Bill Paden provided critical professional support and guidance during their successive tenures as department chair. I would also like to thank those historians at Northwestern who have been enthusiastic interlocutors on the subjects of my research. Tessie Liu, Sarah Maza, Peter Carroll, Stephanie McCurry, and Martha Biondi commented on various chapter drafts. I am grateful to Mary Weismantel and Jorge Coronado for sharing their expertise on anthropological theory and colonial Latin American studies, respectively. I would also like to acknowledge the students in my courses at Northwestern who have been patient and engaged discussants of some of the topics presented in this book.

Numerous individuals beyond Northwestern have offered the intellectual companionship and moral support without which this project would not have been possible. I am especially grateful to Joan Dayan for the inspiration, expertise, and encouragement she has offered since I first discovered her spellbinding scholarship on Saint-Domingue and Haiti. Many thanks are also due to Carina Johnson, Carroll Smith Rosenberg, Tim Reiss, Srinivas Aravamudan, Arlene Keizer, and Stephanie Camp for commenting on chapter drafts. Over the past several years I have had various opportunities to present my work in progress in the form of lectures, workshops, and conference papers. I would like to thank Carroll Smith Rosenberg, Christine Clark-Evans, Downing Thomas, Michèle Longino, Jerome Branche, Elizabeth Monasterios, Françoise Lionnet, Philip Stewart, Byron Wells, and Peter Reiss for inviting me to their events. I am also grateful to the two anonymous readers from Duke University Press for their comments on and enthusiasm for the manuscript; to my copy editor Janet Opdyke for her able assistance; and to Ken Wissoker for believing in the project. My editor Mark Mastromarino expertly ushered the manuscript through production. For help with some translations in chapters 1 and 2, I thank Brad Reichek and Fran Hutchins, and for assistance with the index, Nancy Zibman.

Research for this book could not have been completed without the financial assistance I have received from several sources. Initial research in France was supported by grants from Duke University's Center for European Studies and Department of Romance Studies, and the Ford Foundation. I am especially grateful to the Alice Berline Kaplan Center for the Humanities at Northwestern University for awarding me a fellowship in 2002–03, which provided me the time necessary to expand my research and write most of the final manuscript. I also thank the staff of Northwestern's Interlibrary Loan Service, the McCormick Library of Special Collections, and the Newberry Library for their research assistance. An earlier version of the first half of chapter 3 appeared as "Material Bodies, Spiritual Worlds: Ideologies of the Occult and Regimes of Discipline in the Colonial French Caribbean," in *Interpreting Colonialism*, edited by Byron R. Wells and Philip Stewart, a special issue of *Studies on Voltaire and the Eighteenth Century* 2004, no. 9: 260–83; and a segment of chapter 5, entitled "Race,

Reproduction and Family Romance in Moreau de Saint-Méry's *Description . . . de la partie francaise de l'isle Saint-Domingue*," was published in *Eighteenth-Century Studies* 38.2 (2005): 227–46. I thank the publishers of these journals for their permission to reuse this material. All translations from texts in French are mine unless otherwise indicated. With the exception of citations to modern editions, I have retained the original spellings of titles of primary sources.

Finally, I owe an incalculable debt to the family members and loved ones who have expressed unwavering confidence in me and interest in my work. My deepest gratitude goes to Annie Marie Garraway, Levi Alexander Garraway, and Isla Garraway Shavelle for giving me strength and courage. I am also very thankful for the steady and enthusiastic support offered by Mamadou Bâ. Most of all, I would like to acknowledge the two people in my life who most motivated and encouraged my endeavors in this project, but who, tragically, did not live to see its final form. This book is dedicated to the memory of my father, Michael Oliver Garraway, who first inspired and will forever remain present in my words, my thoughts, and my imagination. It is also dedicated to the memory of Paolo Palezzato, who for years listened to and supported my thinking on every subject treated here, and who taught me the meaning of intellectual honesty, ethical conviction, and love.

Introduction *Creolization in the Old Regime*

This is a study of published narrative sources from the French Caribbean from the inception of colonization in the 1640s until the onset
of the Haitian Revolution in the 1790s. My goal in reading these sources is
to contribute to the study of cultural contact, exchange, and social transformation, which resulted in the rise of one of the most profitable yet brutal slave societies in history. I believe that literary criticism and theoretical
interpretive methodologies offer crucial insights into some of the most fascinating yet elusive questions encountered by writers and scholars on the
historical Caribbean. How are cultural traits and belief systems shared between individuals and groups in social relations of domination? What are
the relationships between cultural interaction and boundary crossing, on
one hand, and the construction and maintenance of repressive regimes enforced by exclusions and violence, on the other? Alternatively, at what point
do exchanges, desires, and intimacies across the boundary of power subvert
regimes of violence and at what point do they encourage, reinforce, or even
produce them? In posing these questions, I focus on a productive paradox
in recent theories of creolization, namely, the notion that a common culture may be constructed in a social system marked by asymmetrical power
relations and the threat of violence. By attending to the power dynamics
governing the development of Creole societies, I examine the ways in which
social conflicts inherent in slavery and a racialized social structure impacted
processes of cultural syncretism. Most importantly, I call attention to what
has often been masked or misapprehended in discussions of both creolization and colonial slavery: the role of desire and sexuality alongside violence

in shaping Creole society. Far from being mitigating factors in structures of oppression, desire and sexuality contributed in fundamental ways to practices and ideologies of domination in the colonial French Caribbean.

Descriptive writings on the Old Regime French Caribbean were first published soon after the creation of the second state-sponsored trading company in 1635 and continued until the fall of French Saint-Domingue in the late 1790s. Throughout this time span, colonial narratives changed significantly in subject matter, authorship, and ideological orientation. From this corpus, I have made selections based on the ethnographic interest of texts and their reception and influence. These include missionary histories and relations written to provide superiors, donors, the company administration, and the French reading public with information on the colonies. In the seventeenth century, missionaries Jean-Baptiste Du Tertre, Raymond Breton, Jean-Baptiste Labat, and a score of minor writers documented the history, customs, and morals of the three main population groups in the colonies: Island Caribs, French settlers, and captive Africans. In the same time period, there appeared what I call narratives of adventure and transgression. Writers such as the pirate Alexandre Oexmelin and the libertine Pierre-Corneille Blessebois operated outside the official civil and religious power structure and offered a more satirical and sensational portrait of the colonies as a space of piracy, violence, libertinage, and creolized spirit beliefs. In the eighteenth century, a number of travel narratives were influenced by the new Enlightenment philosophy. Works by Baron Wimpffen and Girod de Chantrans, for example, provided documentary information mixed with scathing criticisms of colonial slave societies, which they viewed as moral and economic dystopias. Yet concomitant with the escalation of colonial wealth and the slave trade the eighteenth century saw the publication of numerous procolonial descriptions and treatises on slavery and administration, including works by Hiliard d'Auberteuil, Moreau de Saint-Méry, and Émilien Petit. These texts offer valuable insight into the dynamics and mentalities of colonial slavery and the consolidation of white racial hegemony in the French Caribbean. While most of these narratives are nonfictional, my corpus also includes the first colonial novel written in French, *Le Zombi du Grand-Pérou*, published in 1696 by Blessebois. In addition, I analyze the earliest linguistic description of the Carib language, Raymond Breton's encyclopedic bilingual dictionary of 1665. Throughout the study, I examine the Code noir and other laws that codified slavery and racialized power relations. In particular, legal discourses on miscegenation and racial discrimination indicate the extent to which the products of cultural exchange and race mixture were subject to legal control by colonial authorities.

Part of the intent of the project is to provide historically contextualized interpretations of many little-known works on the Old Regime Caribbean colonies. It must be said, however, that to read these texts is to enter into a corpus and a world largely disavowed, forgotten, or silenced by scholars and readers in France and the French Caribbean. For Édouard Glissant, the roots of this forgetting in his native Martinique are deep and reflect the ideological conditioning of the metropole, under whose influence the Caribbean people live, he argues, in a collective amnesia regarding their ancestral bondage and their material conditions of dependency in the present.[1] Michel-Rolph Trouillot attributes what he calls the "silencing" of French colonial slavery to French historiography's continuous evasion of colonialism in the Old Regime, as well as its suppression of the revolution that almost ended slavery in all French territories and inexorably changed the course of French colonialism.[2] For Louis Sala-Molins, the history of denial began with the Enlightenment avoidance of colonial slavery, and it has continued to this day, to judge from state commemorations of the bicentennial of the French Revolution, where, as Sala-Molins points out, little mention was made of colonial slavery, the Haitian Revolution, or the momentary abolition of slavery brought by the National Convention in 1794.[3] An examination of the circumstances and progressive enactment of this forgetting—what I call historical abjection—will suggest both the challenges and the urgency of rereading Old Regime colonial narratives.

On Memory and Forgetting

By the time Jacques Bouton published the first missionary relation from the Caribbean colonies in 1640, French readers had developed a distinct taste for travel literature from the Americas.[4] French writings largely followed the tradition of sixteenth- and seventeenth-century narratives from colonial Spanish America and New France, whose pages were rich with natural historical and ethnographic information. Works by Lopez de Gómara, Garcilaso de la Vega, and Bartolomé de Las Casas went through numerous French editions from the sixteenth century to the eighteenth.[5] Among the best-known early French publications on the New World are those documenting the establishment of colonies in South America, such as André Thevet's *Les Singularitez de la France Antarctique* (1557) and Jean de Léry's more polemical *Histoire d'un voyage fait en terre du Brésil* (1578). When French attempts to settle the Brazilian littoral and other points along the Atlantic coast faltered, Canada emerged as the center of French colonial activity in the seventeenth century, as evidenced by the published works of Cartier, Champlain, Lescarbot, and the priest Gabriel Sagard.[6] In the following century, however, Canada was overtaken in geopolitical importance by the Antilles, a fact that is reflected in the number of published works on the island colonies. Whereas in the seventeenth century the total number of books on the French Caribbean did not exceed several dozen, this number increased to over three hundred in the eighteenth century, thus signaling the new centrality of the Caribbean to the Old Regime colonial empire.[7]

The fact that few of these works were popular successes in France is due in large part to the late date at which colonial slavery became a topic of interest for metropolitan readers and writers. For much of the eighteenth century, the fiction of American exoticism was concerned with pastoral utopian settings or representations of idyllic natives, *not* slavery.[8] Some Caribbean texts were popularized through multivolume compilations such as Buffon's *Histoire naturelle* (1749–67), Prévost's *Histoire des voyages* (1746–59) and the *Encyclopédie* (1751–65), and they influenced the anthropological thinking of Enlightenment philosophes such as Rousseau.[9] Yet colonial slavery had little impact on French literature until the mid–eighteenth century, with the publication of Montesquieu's *De l'Esprit des lois* (1748), which contained a satirical critique of contemporary rationales for the slave trade, and Pierre Antoine de Laplace's enormously successful theatrical adaptation of the English writer Aphra Behn's antislavery novel, *Oroonoko* (1688), published in 1745. Behn's novel was one of the nine most frequently read English novels in France at midcentury, and it went through seven editions by 1800.[10] In the second half of the eighteenth century, the colonies were at the center of growing debates about the economic viability of slave labor, humanitarian objections to the slave system, the feasibility of monopolistic trade restrictions, and the significance of American expansion for the well-being of Europe. Hence we find some antislavery sentiment in the writings of such Enlightenment luminaries as Condorcet, Raynal, Diderot, Montesquieu, Mirabeau, and Prévost. The plight of heroic slaves was imagined in poetry, plays, novels, and the genre of harangue, or prosopopoeia, in which black characters, most often men, were fictively ventriloquized by European sympathizers. These appeared most notably in Prévost's *Le pour et contre* (1735), in the novel *Ziméo* (1773) by the minor philosophe Jean-François de Saint-Lambert, and most importantly in Raynal's *Histoire des deux Indes* (1770, 1774, 1780), the third edition of which was secretly edited by Diderot, who inserted numerous inflammatory passages critical of colonial slavery. With its detailed historical descriptions of the Caribbean colonies, notably Saint-Domingue, this work constituted the most radical critique of colonialism to emerge from Enlightenment France.[11] Finally, physiocratic inquiry into the issue of slavery appeared in political and economic tracts and philosophical forums such as the physiocratic journal *Ephémérides du citoyen*, founded in 1765 by the Abbé Baudeau and edited by Du Pont de Nemours.[12]

Yet, even as French metropolitan writers engaged with the issue of colonial slavery, they arguably repressed the specifics of France's own interests in and practice of it in the Caribbean colonies. Much of the so-called antislavery literature was situated not in the French Caribbean but in Surinam (Voltaire, *Candide*; Laplace, *Oronoko*), Spanish America (Montesquieu, *De l'esprit des lois*), and Jamaica (Saint-Lambert, *Ziméo*; Prévost, *Le pour et contre*).[13] In an astute critique of the eighteenth-century literary obsession with an eroticized Orient, Madeleine Dobie rightly maintains that French writers masked the magnitude of French interests in slavery in its own Atlantic colonies by transposing the problem of slavery to the oriental context.[14] Furthermore, as many have argued, philosophical contestations of slavery and the colonial system usually led to reformist arguments or contradictory positions rather than endorsements of actual abolition.[15] Beneath the rhetoric lay the assumption that slavery could not be immediately discarded and that colonial commerce and industry had nonetheless contributed to the benefit of mankind. Thus, in Condorcet's *Réflexions sur l'esclavage des nègres*, written under the pseudonym "Schwartz," the author advocated a complicated scheme of gradual abolition so as to "train" slaves for freedom.[16] And, while Raynal is often heralded as an antislavery hero, his famous *Histoire des deux Indes* was followed in 1785 with the *Essai sur l'administration de St.-Domingue*,[17] in which he defended slavery on the basis of the legendary argument that enslaved Africans were better off living in a progressive civilization.[18] Perhaps the most famous example of flawed antislavery concerns the revolutionary organization La société des amis des noirs, founded in 1787 by Brissot. Condorcet served as president, and its members, drawn from the social elite, included Lafayette, Volney, Mirabeau, and Abbé Grégoire. The society publicized abuses of the slave trade and advocated its abolition. It did not, however, advocate the immediate emancipation of the slaves. Likewise, its support for ending the slave trade was premised on an imperialist program of European expansion into Africa whereby Africans would be made to work for Europeans on their own soil. During the revolutions in France and Saint-Domingue, members of the society fought for mulatto rights to the detriment of the cause of freedom for slaves, and by the time the National Convention passed the abolition decree of 1794 the society had almost completely disbanded and none of its members had taken an active role.[19]

The repression of colonial slavery and its narrative corpus only increased after the Haitian Revolution, though within a new geopolitical landscape. Whereas French Enlightenment antislavery proved inadequate to the cause of emancipation, nineteenth-century political upheavals resulted in the re-establishment of slavery and the Code noir, followed by a legislative act of abolition by the provisional government of the Second Republic in 1848. The loss of Saint-Domingue and the massacre by former slaves of the remaining white French residents in 1804 greatly undermined abolitionist fervor while reducing France's interest in and dependence on slavery and the slave trade, as French imperial power turned its attention to Egypt, Algeria, and sub-Saharan Africa.[20] The 1848 act of abolition and its accompanying ideological discourse of republicanism signaled the official disavowal of slavery. The proclamation by the French commissioner Louis Thomas Husson to Martinican slaves in 1848 cast the abolition as the good news of an enlightened republic free from monarchical despotism in all its guises.[21] Official French history of slave emancipation in French territories has since championed the antislavery activist Victor Schoelcher and the Second Republic as its heroes and reinvented the Enlightenment as the source of revolutionary values driving republican abolitionism.[22] According to this narrative, the abolition of slavery represented the achievement of the liberal ideals of the philosophes and a definitive break with the past crimes of an unenlightened, despotic monarchy. Slavery became, in the words of Françoise Vergès, the "*secret de famille*" that was repressed "for the sake of reconciliation."[23] Furthermore, by forgetting slavery France proclaimed itself the harbinger of the Enlightenment values that could "civilize" Africans on their own soil, thus laying the ideological groundwork for nineteenth-century imperialist expansion.[24]

This suppression of Old Regime colonialism and slavery is nonetheless surprising given the enormous economic significance of the Antilles for France. In terms of material rewards, the Caribbean plantation system represented by far the most successful colonial venture of the Old Regime. Yet it was founded on what was by far the most brutal experiment in social engineering and physical repression ever engaged in by France. The initial consolidation of the territory required decades of territorial warfare with the islands' indigenous inhabitants, the Caribs. From 1626 to 1664, the islands of Saint-Christophe, Guadeloupe, Martinique, and the western half of Hispaniola (later known as Saint-Domingue), as well as several adjoining islands and their dependencies, all came under French rule. Following the initiative of the privateering explorers Pierre d'Esnambuc and Urbain de Roissey, Richelieu backed the creation of the first colonies, which were first administered through successive incarnations of the trading company established for that purpose. In 1674, the company was definitively liquidated and the colonies were brought under direct royal rule as provinces of France itself. Settled by impoverished noblemen, traders, missionaries, farmers, bondsmen, vagabonds, women, and, most importantly, captive Africans and their descendants, the islands grew into profitable plantation enclaves producing large quantities of tobacco and sugar by the latter part of the seventeenth century. Channeled back to France according to a monopolistic policy that later became known as the Exclusif, these products and the ensuing trade in humans mapped out a triangular shipping route between Europe, Africa, and the Caribbean. France's monopolistic colonial policies were perfected under Richelieu's renowned successor and the minister of the royal navy, Colbert. He regarded the development of overseas trade as the most important foundation for the regeneration of French commerce, the navy, and the merchant marine.[25]

All kinds of domestic French industries grew rich supplying the colonies and slave trade, including textiles, distilleries, manufactures, and shipbuilding. This industrial clamor contributed greatly to the growth of the merchant and marine bourgeoisie, first in Norman and Breton ports such as Le Havre, Dieppe, Nantes, Rochefort, and Saint-Malo. In the late seventeenth century, as the northern ports were increasingly tied up in wartime naval activities with England, the southern cities of La Rochelle, Bordeaux, and Marseilles benefited from colonial trade. Even more remarkable, however, was the productivity of the island colonies themselves, as they were able to supply both the French and European demand for tropical commodities. Though small in territory, the Caribbean colonies far exceeded French possessions in North America in their capacity to generate wealth using slave labor. As early as 1685, the French Antilles ranked second in world sugar production. War would hardly break this trend. Several international conflicts raged in the Caribbean seas in the seventeenth and eighteenth centuries, involving England, France, Spain, and Holland. When in 1763 the Treaty of Paris was signed ending the Seven Years' War, Great Britain claimed Canada from France but returned Martinique, Guadeloupe, and Saint-Domingue to France. Western Louisiana had been sold in 1762 to the king of Spain, an ally in the conflict. Despite this seemingly disproportionate loss of land, Choiseul, the French foreign minister, deemed the treaty a victory in that it secured the most profitable colonial domains, the key to further colonial expansion. In the eighteenth century, the Caribbean islands were the most prized colonial possessions in the Western Hemisphere.[26]

By 1789, the runaway success of the French Caribbean colonies had reached its outer limit. The single island of Saint-Domingue was the world's largest producer of sugar and was considered by some the most valuable province of France. Likewise, this island dominates the historical imagination of eighteenth-century French colonialism, for it best encapsulates the horrific contradictions plaguing the Old Regime's colonial project. The colony originated on the small island of Tortuga off the northwestern coast as a loose settlement of pirates, buccaneers, and vagabonds, who for many years resisted the imposition of colonial authority. Only in 1697 did the Treaty of Ryswick officially annex the western side of the island to the French state. Yet, although the island was a latecomer to the plantation sugar economy already established in Martinique and Guadeloupe, Saint-Domingue's explosive growth during the first three decades of the eighteenth century led France to assume a dominant position in the world's sugar market. Between 1686 and 1720, the population of slaves in the Lesser Antilles quadrupled, while in Saint-Domingue their numbers increased fourteen times.[27] By midcentury, the single island of Saint-Domingue was producing more sugar for France than all of the British islands did for England.[28] Despite international tensions in the region, sugar production continued to escalate due to the obsessive reliance on slave laborers brought into the colony by the thousands and the development of irrigation technologies that allowed arid plains to be made over into new plantations. Added to this was a boom in coffee production after 1760. This new source of profitability, met largely by the class of free people of color in Saint-Domingue, was responsible for the agricultural development of the mountains.[29] Thus, at the close of the eighteenth century Saint-Domingue was indisputably the richest colony in the world, providing France with untold wealth from imported and reexported colonial goods.[30]

In 1792, the colonial lobby of the National Assembly maintained that prior to the revolution over 40 percent of French commerce with foreign powers derived from reexported colonial goods. This colonial system in turn supplied labor to six million French people throughout the kingdom.[31] At the same time, however, the system that supported the French labor market literally consumed hundreds of thousands of captive Africans and their descendants. They were brought to the colonies in such escalating numbers that in the last decade of French colonial rule in Saint-Domingue the proportion of slaves to colonists was greater than ten to one. Modern population figures on this period put the total population of the colony at approximately 500,000 persons: 30,000 whites, an equal number of free nonwhites, and over 400,000 slaves.[32] In the last two decades of French rule, the slave population increased twofold due to an escalation in slave trade activity, not natural reproduction. Thus, an extraordinarily brutal form of slavery underwrote French commercial success in the eighteenth century at the very moment when the philosophes were proclaiming the rights of man. Their so-called antislavery writings did precious little for the people who were sacrificed to the colonial system.

Still, the predominant view of the French Enlightenment was long purified of its imperial sympathies and complicities. The Age of Enlightenment has been upheld in French culture as progressive, antislavery, cultural relativist, and even primitivist with regard to writings by luminaries such as Rousseau, Diderot, Raynal, Voltaire, and Montesquieu.[33] It is no wonder that, at the end of the nineteenth century, the first historian of the social aspects of colonial slavery, Lucien Peytraud, lamented that historical scholarship had thus far favored the achievement of French abolition over the discussion of slaves in history.[34] Breaking with the tradition of studying only the military, political, or economic dimensions of colonialism, Peytraud and Pierre de Vaissière were the first historians to make use of narrative sources from the Old Regime colonies, while Jacques de Dampierre compiled the first critical study of published sources on the Antilles.[35] Yet, whereas historians regarded this material as a vital source of information about slavery as a social system, scholars of French literature have shown considerably less interest in these texts. Since the appearance in 1931 of Gilbert Chinard's in-depth study of several colonial narratives in relation to what he called the "American imaginary" of French literature, most literary research on French colonialism, slavery, antislavery discourse, or early anthropology has concerned metropolitan French literary, scientific, or philosophical texts, thus leaving the narratives of Caribbean colonialism largely unexamined.

By contrast, it is in the study of the French Caribbean itself that early modern colonial writings have been explored more deeply, a fact that points to the importance of the politics of location in the remembrance of colonial legacies. Understandably, however, literary historians of the region have registered uncertainty about how to place colonial writings in relation to the oppositional poetics of Caribbean writers of color, who championed the end of racism and colonial domination. If we consider two literary histories, *La Transgression des couleurs* by Roger Toumson and *Les Écrivains français et les Antilles* by Régis Antoine, the methodological difficulty becomes obvious. As Toumson's title suggests, he conceives the identifying feature of the history of francophone Caribbean literature as the subversive emergence of Afro-Caribbean contestations of colonialist literary forms, tropes, and ideologies. Toumson thus identifies Caribbean literary traditions in terms of a racial binary—"la littérature blanche et la littérature nègre"—seen to inherit the vision of the world of the colonizer and colonized, respectively.[36] Antoine, on the other hand, distances himself from the formative phase of Afro-Caribbean literary consciousness by choosing as an endpoint to his study the year 1932, the date of the appearance of the periodicals *L'Etudiant Noir* and *Légitime Défense*. His title—*Les Écrivains français et les Antilles: Des premiers Pères blancs aux surréalistes noirs*—suggests that he considers both white and black writers to be "French," even as he maintains a distinction between the French national identity and the islands themselves. In his preface, the author avoids the tensions among race, place, and national identification by conflating the French nationality with the use of the French language: "We therefore took into consideration all the French literary texts . . . that speak of the Antilles."[37] Yet the very scope of the work represents a certain drawback from the perspective of this study, for the literary historical approach limits the degree to which, through the work of interpretation, the author may contribute to or challenge dominant understandings of the historical, social, and cultural phenomena treated by these texts. In contrast, Joan Dayan's *Haiti, History, and the Gods* demonstrates the advantages of abandoning strict disciplinary methodologies in examining colonial writings.[38] Through the critical practice she calls "literary fieldwork," Dayan engages the literary and spiritual archive of French colonialism in late Saint-Domingue as well as that of nineteenth-century Haiti, thus offering a penetrating interpretation of the culture, history, and memory of the island nation as it has been constructed both within Haiti and by outside observers.

Toward a Historicist Literary Interpretation

My interest in this corpus of forgotten narratives from the early French Caribbean is compelled in part by the move in postcolonial studies to reread the narrative archive of colonialism for evidence of the ways in which European accounts of the non-European world enabled the progressive deployment of colonial and imperial power. Yet my approach and objectives differ substantially from that project. Dissenting from what have become conventional and often limiting orthodoxies about the relation between discourse and colonial power, I maintain that the mere deconstruction of colonialist categories, stereotypes, and ideologies only further centers the history of Western imperialism and confines the scholar to a critique of representation that presumes the hegemony it seeks to expose. Instead I believe that any critique of colonial texts has inescapable ramifications for the ways in which both scholars and living communities understand and create new narratives about the past, understandings that are not limited to the abstract structures of colonial domination but include the formation of cultures and societies. This is especially true in cases such as the Caribbean, where, as Peter Hulme has noted, the only remaining evidence of the past is often the very European texts that constitute the discourse of colonialism.[39] If, for Hulme, there is little hope of contesting the European narratives through recourse to some alternative evidence, what he calls the "protocols for critique" may very well lead to a new appreciation of what these narratives say about colonial dynamics and cultural shifts. To examine further the relation between literary and cultural historical interpretation, we may review briefly the terms in which poststructuralist and postcolonial literary critics have redefined their objects of analysis.

The rise of literary and theoretical approaches to colonialism must be seen in the context of poststructuralism's attack on the limits of Western epistemologies and structures of knowledge, among them historicism. As Robert Young has shown, colonial discourse analysis has participated in a larger project aimed at exposing the ways in which the presumed universal validity of those epistemologies was an effect of an "ontological imperialism," whose corollary was the actual subjugation of alternative cultures and systems of knowledge through imperialism.[40] Historicism epitomized the linkages between structures of knowledge and forms of domination, for, taken in its Hegelian sense, History was a unifying, totalizing discourse that assimilated non-European cultures, peoples, and forms of difference into one universal story, whose beginning, center, and endpoint was the West. This position is echoed in much postcolonial criticism. The late Edward Said viewed historicism as the basis of orientalism, which he attacked for its self-validating tendencies and what he considered to be an avoidance of its own relationship with European imperialism.[41] Similarly, Gayatry Spivak has pointed out the ways in which historical narratives depend on multiple and strategic silences, exclusions, and marginalizations, suggesting that the work of criticism is not to recover an alternative viewpoint or historical narrative but rather to chart the "itinerary of the silencing."[42]

Suspicious of revisionist histories and counternarratives of colonialism as themselves based on nationalist essentialisms and a nostalgia for lost origins, postcolonial theorists have attempted to dismantle colonial histories and discourses through theoretical analysis and deconstruction. Critics of this approach charge that colonial discourse analysis relies on a set of ahistorical, overreaching suppositions that reduce all of Western knowledge and representation to its instrumentality in colonialist expansion, thus tacitly assuming the unchallenged efficacy of European imperial power around the globe.[43] Said, despite his Foudauldian bent, considered fifteen hundred years of Western discourse on the "Orient" to be a unified discursive formation that produced an object for Western domination and control.[44] Yet, whereas Said traced the institutions, disciplines, and discourses in which "orientalist" knowledge developed over time, critics such as Homi Bhabha have invoked transhistorical theoretical concepts to critique colonialism as a discursive system. In his psychoanalytic framework, singular abstractions such as "the colonial subject," "ambivalence," "mimicry" and "hybridity" pose a serious impediment to thinking through variations in colonial discourses and their effects in different times and places.[45] In general, the very concept of "colonial discourse" itself condemns much of the analysis to tautology, since critics define the object in terms identical to the arguments made about it. The designation almost always prejudges the discourse it seeks to critique as that which, either by design or effect, produces non-Europeans as denigrated, domesticated others of a Western imperial self.

From the perspective of this study, the most troubling historical blind spot resulting from postcolonial theory's concentration on nineteenth-century imperialisms and the attendant fetishization of the category of "native/colonized" is its almost complete neglect of one of the most important features of early modern European colonialism—colonial slavery in the Americas. The exclusion of slavery and slave societies from most recent "theories" of colonial discourse raises many questions about the kinds of issues this subdiscipline is willing to raise and why. Why does the cultural critique of colonialism eschew those cultures forged on the basis of relations of domination obtaining from two or more transplanted populations? What happens in cases in which the native is eliminated and deep settler colonialism persists with imported populations of exploitable labor, extracted from both the colonial center and a third peripheral site of encounter, exchange, and coercion? How do such conditions affect the way colonial discourse constructs its object and the stories it has to tell? The presence of slave societies is one of the unifying traits of the colonial cultures of the Americas, dating from the first modern European colonial enterprise in the fifteenth century. While slave societies have informed much thinking about the relationship between race and class oppression, specifically in the development of capitalist power relations, the postcolonial theorists have largely stayed out of the debate.[46]

In one of the most forceful critiques of postcolonial theory's flight from history, Benita Parry has argued that postcolonial criticism's refusal to provide any account of change, discontinuity, and social conflict homogenizes the many states of imperialism and "obliterate[s] the role of the native as historical subject."[47] Although recent work on eighteenth-century colonialisms attends to many of these issues, there remains a significant methodological chasm between the project of contextualizing historically the discourses under study and that of providing interpretations of the cultural or social dynamics of colonialism through the analysis of those discourses. Alternatively, when cultural or historical claims are advanced, they often do not concern specific areas of colonial influence but rather broad structural relationships between Europe and the non-European world. Madeleine Dobie's study of literary representations of the Orient laments the failure of previous studies to assess "the historical evolution of French colonial policy and the changing interplay between this policy and the literary sphere."[48] While she justifiably departs from the tendency to couple eighteenth-century French orientalism with an undifferentiated concept of "colonial discourse," her contextualizations mainly relate to French domestic politics, aesthetic movements, and colonial policies toward the Orient. Srinivas Aravamudan, on the other hand, takes up the question of subaltern agency in European cultural texts pertaining to a range of geographic regions and political relationships between Europeans and non-Europeans.[49] However, since many of the works he analyzes do not concern actual colonies (or if they do they represent derivative or fictional discourses about them), his larger claims concern what might be called the global imagination of Enlightenment Europe rather than the eighteenth-century colonies themselves. In a more radical attempt to merge colonial discourse studies with historical interpretation, Ann McClintock arrives at a "situated psychoanalysis . . . that is simultaneously a psychoanalytically informed history."[50] Rejecting the textualist mode of literary scholarship, McClintock deals with what she considers to be "the more demanding historical task of interrogating the social practices, economic conditions, and psychoanalytic dynamics that motivate and constrain human desire, action and power."[51] Yet, given McClintock's interest in the relation between imperialism, industrial capital, and categories of race, class, and gender in the nineteenth- and early-twentieth-century British empire, her methodology ultimately leads her to make broad claims about the role of imperialism in the formation of Western industrial modernity rather than to analyze in depth the dynamics of a particular colonial locale.

By contrast, what motivates this study of French colonial narratives is neither a concern with early modern French imperial power writ large nor a deep interest in studying colonialist representations for their own sake. I am compelled, rather, by the role literary analysis has to play in reinterpreting narrative sources that in some cases constitute the only surviving written account of peoples and cultures of the colonial French Caribbean at particular points in time. My aim is both to contribute to the literary history of a region best known for its postcolonial literatures and to interrogate the cultural, sexual, and racial dynamics of emerging slave societies by exploring representations produced by the colonizing culture itself. If I willingly tread on the unstable ground that lies between "history" and "representation," it is because I wish to blur the distinction between them. In this respect, I defer to the poststructuralist claim that no narrative bears a privileged relation to "reality" and that the very idea of referentiality or representation fails to recognize the role of narrative itself in constituting the reality it pretends only to describe. This is not to say that there are no events, materialities, or feelings in human experience, but rather that they are always constructed in and mediated through language, most often in a narrative structure that, as Roland Barthes reminds us, derives from myth and imposes certain meanings and constraints intrinsic to the form on what then becomes knowable as "reality" or "the past."[52] Whereas narrative sources are the stories told by contemporary actors about their lives, experiences, and beliefs, historical discourse builds new narratives by deducing from the former what it considers to be the truest or most plausible stories about the events they describe. As Hayden White has argued, traditional historiography has maintained the assumption that narrative offers a simulacrum of the structure and processes of "real" events and that the significations of narrative accord with the imagined historical referent.[53]

Of course, the other and perhaps more difficult lesson of poststructuralism is that, in the words of Spivak, "we cannot but narrate," and thus we are forever caught within the epistemological and linguistic structures that we critique.[54] The challenge, then, is to forge a critical practice that takes this into account. Literary scholars such as Peter Hulme have managed the radical antifoundationalism of poststructuralist thought by professing not a transcendental truth but rather a subjective or provisional one informed by the political agenda of the present. In this respect, they acknowledge that their stories are not entirely representative of the pasts to which they ostensibly refer. I would add to that the claim that, if the past is only knowable as a succession of narratives, then the work of interpreting those stories becomes a central, if not *the* central, task of scholars who concern themselves with it. By interpretation, I do not mean the distillation of "truth" from "falsity" but rather the critical analysis of extant narratives; their truth claims; the conditions of their production; their allegorical, rhetorical, and formal features; and the latent and manifest meanings of the stories they tell. I therefore part company with some poststructuralist critics of colonialism by assuming that texts exist in contexts (cultural, economic, social, or political) that are in many cases evidenced by the texts themselves. In addition, authors are critical to my project both as personages in the stories they recount and as writing subjects operating in a discursive field they reflect and at times challenge.

In these respects, I share some of the contentions of New Historicist criticism, notably the belief in the "mutual embededness" of art and history and the idea that it is possible to treat "all of the written and visual traces of a particular culture as a mutually intelligible network of signs."[55] New Historicists approach texts previously considered nonliterary or noncanonical and illuminate the "cultural matrix" out of which representations emerge. However, I differ from the response offered by Stephen Greenblatt and Catherine Gallagher to the most challenging and productive attack on historicist criticism, namely, the suggestion that the application of literary interpretive strategies to nonliterary objects leads critics to aestheticize culture or, in the worst case, to "endorse as aesthetically gratifying every miserable, oppressive structure and every violent action of the past."[56] I formulate the problem in relation to Arun Mukherjee's critique of postcolonial criticism, which, in her view, leaves scholars only one discursive position: "We are forever forced to interrogate European discourse, of only one particular kind; the ones that degrade and deny our humanity."[57] How and why do we read sources that denigrate and offend our humanity? What are the goals of reading nonliterary narratives of domination with a literary interpretive methodology? What Gallagher and Greenblatt implicitly suggest, and what I have discovered, is that what has been kept out of the canon reflects the most disavowed aspects of a culture, what it must expel, or, in

Julia Kristeva's terms, abject, in order to create an image of itself and its past consistent with its ruling ideology.[58] In Western liberal discourse, slavery is either repressed or treated as a kind of refuse that has been dutifully shed in order to universalize liberal ideologies of freedom, individuality, and the rights to property, even as each of these ideas developed in parallel with and were arguably informed by contrary notions of bondage, nonpersonhood, and property in persons.

Gallagher's and Greenblatt's response to the question of how to avoid aestheticizing the cultural is to retreat to the canon, the interpretation of "the writers we love," as what is truly in question, what really stands to gain from serious attention to "culture." The intent, they argue, has not been to "leave works of literature behind" but to "venture out to unfamiliar cultural texts," so that "these texts—often marginal, odd, fragmentary, unexpected, and crude—could in turn begin to interact in interesting ways with the intimately familiar works of the literary canon."[59] Yet recourse to the canon as the justification for cultural work eschews the more interesting and radical challenge New Historicism poses to both literature and history, that is, the idea that reading cultures as texts means that some of our conclusions will concern peoples and cultures as well as texts. This is especially true in the case of slavery, in which there are no "great" works of literature and in which the entire system constitutes the abject that has been expelled from the colonizer's cultural memory. Whereas many postcolonial critics have essentially adopted the New Historicist approach by invoking colonialism and slavery as a lens through which to reread the "greats"— Montesquieu, Diderot, Raynal, Voltaire—I have chosen to study these abjected systems as cultures in themselves. While demonstrating the interest of certain works individually and in relation to metropolitan discourses of witchcraft, magic, libertinage, nobility, and race, for example, I am equally concerned to situate them within the environment in which they emerged, and to use my literary training to say something about that context as I read it in the texts. There are many questions about cultures that historians do not or cannot ask and literary scholars can. In my view, literary interpretive strategies offer the most powerful means of probing the ideas, beliefs, power relations, anxieties, and fantasies of a society through the partial accounts left in its cultural narratives. The goal is not to aestheticize the abject but to serve memory by refusing to forget or to accept uncritically inherited accounts of the past.

The contours of this project thus reveal my fascination with origins. The mixed cultures and societies of the New World offer rather precise circumstances of origin, and we refuse to acknowledge them at our peril. Origins here are not a fetish on which to found claims of truth or authenticity but rather a point from which to gain an understanding of culture as a process of change. In this sense, historicity functions as an antidote to cultural fundamentalisms of all kinds. The particular availability of origins in the Caribbean is also reflected in my openness to Freudian psychoanalysis and its idea of primary repression, which becomes especially important when discussing the sexual aspects of racial slavery. Otherwise I employ a range of tools that literary and cultural theory bring to bear on these texts, together with the widest possible awareness of subsequent narratives (historical, literary, or anthropological) about the early French Caribbean. In this respect, my approach is inspired by the work of Peter Hulme, Joan Dayan, and Françoise Vergès.[60] Like them, I refuse to limit myself to a critique of representation, or even ideology, as though there is something outside of representation that is the province of History alone. I contend that literary interpretation of narrative discourse produces forms of truth that are theoretical in nature, that is, whose explanatory potential derives not from a presumption of fact but rather from the critic's ability to make meaning from the analysis of a set of discourses in their relation to one another.

Creolization in the Old Regime

In maintaining that no narrative has a privileged relation to something like "reality," I analyze a range of genres, both nonfictional and fictional, as every source offers insight into the values and dynamics of the culture in which it was produced. The questions I ask of the corpus address blind spots in prevailing explanations of the cultures of slavery offered by theorists, historians, novelists, and literary scholars. A key concept framing this study is the idea of "creolization," which scholars commonly invoke, alongside notions of mestizaje and hybridity, to describe processes of fusion and syncretism between radically different cultures and ethnicities. Due to the speed, intensity, and violence of the migratory movements and cultural flows that characterized the development of colonialism and racial slavery in the Caribbean islands, many critics and scholars regard the region as a paradigm for the cross-cultural contacts, transformation, and heterogeneity that have come to typify a globalized, postcolonial world. Yet the generalized espousal of creolization theory has arguably obscured the local specificity of the concept and its different valences in anglophone and francophone Caribbean cultural theory.

On one hand, the term *creolization* refers to what many consider to be a cultural nationalist view of Caribbean social history formulated by anglophone West Indian intellectuals in direct refutation of prevailing notions of the Caribbean colonies in British imperial historiography. Building on the idea of cross-cultural transfer defined by the sociologist Fernando Ortiz as "transculturation," the Jamaican historian Kamau Brathwaite's notion of creolization conceives of the plantation as a transformative, productive space, not just for tropical exports but also for cultures and languages. Following Ortiz's emphasis on the mutual exchange of culture between groups, where each is both active and passive, impacted by and influencing the other in the dynamic production of a new, derivative culture, Brathwaite sees creolization as a "cultural action—material, psychological and spiritual—based upon the stimulus/response of individuals within the society to their environment and—as white/black, culturally discrete groups—to each other."[61] During a time of Caribbean nationalisms and independences, "creolization" and the corollary notion of "creole society" were meant to oppose the prevalent assumption among British colonial historians that Jamaican society was, as Brathwaite puts it, merely "a declining appendage of Great Britain [whose] internal structure and body was, at best, a parody of the metropolitan, at worst, a disorganized, debased and uncreative polity."[62] In contrast, Brathwaite's theory stresses the importance of integration and change within and across groups in a stratified power dichotomy.[63] While on one hand this adaptation led newcomers to adopt behaviors and attitudes linked to their new position with respect to the other group in the racial hierarchy—racial prejudice for whites and socialization into plantation labor and Afro-Creole forms of recreation for slaves—Brathwaite's theory also conceives of cultural flows and influences between groups, such as the slaves' imitation of white culture and privilege and the impact of black Creole linguistic and cultural forms on white Creole speech, tastes, and styles of dance.

Departing from Brathwaite's historical analysis and interest in social relations, francophone Caribbean cultural theorists have emphasized the Creole language as a paradigm for other forms of cultural exchange between groups in the region. Creolization is thus a process of cultural transformation productive of new ways of thinking, knowing, and imagining that diverge from colonialist epistemologies and exclusionary identity formations based in fixed notions of race, language, and nation. Important here is the idea that linguistic and cultural creation was instrumental as a practice of resistance for slaves. Building on Édouard Glissant's notion of orality as the privileged site of collective memory,[64] the *créoliste* writers Raphaël Confiant, Patrick Chamoiseau, and Jean Bernabé locate Caribbean literary agency in the sonorities of the slave, the silences of the maroon, and the orality of the Creole storyteller. Their view of creolization highlights the complex dialectic between violence and accommodation marking social relations on the plantation: "For three centuries, the islands . . . proved to be the real forges of a new humanity, where languages, races, religions, customs, ways of being from all over the world were brutally uprooted and transplanted in an environment where they had to reinvent life."[65]

While their theory remains intimately tied to a historical consciousness of colonial fusions and hybridities, the créolistes follow Glissant in privileging literature over history as the discourse best able to represent the creolizing process. Like many Caribbean writers, Glissant sees history as unable to speak to a populace whose collective memory has been repeatedly erased by the brutality of colonialism and the manipulations of official ideologies and whose lived experience is constantly defamiliarized by the globalizing consumer culture to which it increasingly aspires. In a society that has been abused by prejudicial and partial accounts of the past, history as a discourse is associated with colonial ideologies. For Glissant, the role of the writer is to articulate a relation between present and past, what he calls "a prophetic vision of the past."[66] Similarly, Derek Walcott, who views history as problematic in the Caribbean, writes that "what has mattered is the loss of history, the amnesia of the races, what has become necessary is imagination, imagination as necessity, as invention."[67] In addition to rejecting official history, the créoliste writers question the ability of colonial texts to represent the creolization process: "In its propaganda, self-censorship, colonial apologias, and heavy, almost mathematical deployment of information, the writing of the record (*registre*) clamors with more literary silence than even the smallest stone engraved by the Savages."[68] The writer of "*créolité*" thus writes over and against "la Chronique coloniale," proclaiming literature to be the privileged site of the restitution of Creole identities and the tradition of the *conteur créole*.[69]

Yet, creolization theory raises pressing questions about the very colonial histories rejected by the créolistes. These relate to the very term *créole*, which they claim as a cultural signifier. In Martinique and Guadeloupe today, *créole* refers to an "*enracinement local*," in counterdistinction to exterior reference points for cultural identity.[70] However, the use of this term to valorize an identity distinct from that of "Africa" or "Europe" has a long history within colonialist discourse. The word *créole*, in French, originates from the Hispano-Portuguese terms "*criollo/crioulo*," which originally referred to both blacks and whites born in the colonial Americas.[71] The colonial missionary writers Du Tertre and Labat used the term to mean simply "born in the colonies," a designation used for both the master and servile classes.[72] From the revolutionary period on, the word *créole* developed a more restricted usage, referring only to whites by the nineteenth century. This meaning becomes solidified in the *Dictionnaire Littré*, for example, where *créole* is defined as "homme blanc, femme blanche, originaire des colonies."[73] The fact that today the *Petit Robert* retains the primary meaning of *créole* as a "person of the white race, born in the tropical colonies, notably the Antilles," indicates the persistence of the term's racial connotation in France. This meaning also points to the double contestation inherent in its reappropriation by contemporary writers to oppose divisive notions of racial difference. A return to the historical record thus reveals an ironic continuity with postcolonial meanings applied to the term *créole*.

My adoption of the term *creolization* to refer to cross-cultural negotiations within and between ethnic groups in the Caribbean is in fact conditional on the critical investigation of the literary traces and narratives left by colonial writers who witnessed, described, and produced their experiences in discourse. Rather than taking creolization as a stable signifier whose objective historical referent is knowable through historical research or imaginative reconstruction, I collapse the study of creolization onto the study of representations of colonial cultures and societies. Brathwaite began that project, but his own readings were often burdened by a positivist attempt to lay out the precise parameters and components of Creole society, which led him to reproduce unwittingly the same style of ethnographic inventory prevalent in colonial discourse. Furthermore, as Chris Bongie has argued, Brathwaite does not call into question the existence of culturally distinct groups he defines as white and black and links to "cultural bases" in Europe and Africa, thus betraying an essentialist belief in the presence of precolonial identities that converge in the creolization process. Yet, while cautioning against notions of autonomous culture that underlie theories of cultural fusion and hybridity, we must bear in mind the historical processes of colonization and enslavement whereby internally diverse populations from different parts of the world were structured into rigidly defined socio-ethnic blocks primarily on the basis of color. When creolization theorists err on the side of essentialism, it is, I would contend, because they momentarily naturalize these historically constructed colonial social or ethnic categories (African/black slaves, European/white colonists, Island Caribs, etc.) as distinct cultures that contribute to a Creole mosaic of culture, elements of which are shared by all groups in the colonies. Whereas this narrative is meant to overturn the discriminatory logic of colonial discourse by positing the cultural interrelatedness of different groups in the colonial hierarchy, it has the effect of masking the specific mechanisms of violence and segregation meant to keep colonial populations artificially separated and contained along lines of race and class. As Nigel Bolland has argued, the integrationist, synthetic logic of creolization theories tends to neglect the structural contradictions and social conflicts of the plantation. Although the French créolistes gesture to the "brutal entry into contact" and "nonharmonious mixing" of peoples and cultures, they nonetheless imagine the "transactional aggregate" of cultural elements as having the power to transcend and subvert relations of force by creating a "kaleidoscopic totality." What gets left out is a consideration of how the cultural flows both within and between diverse groups were impacted by the violence of plantation slavery.[74]

Since the French narrative sources I analyze were produced almost exclusively from the perspective of those in power, the view of creolization I distill mainly concerns the colonizing group, while suggesting the kinds of exchanges, negotiations, and resistances that took place within and between the Carib, slave, and free colored populations. My inquiry also responds to the inadequacies of creolization theories on the question of the relation between the evolution of shared cultural forms and social antagonisms in French colonial slave societies. Several important questions arise from the resultant ambiguity: How did culture cross boundaries of power and violence? In what ways were Creole syncretisms and fusions instigated by specific practices of domination, and how did the process of cultural exchange itself impact those practices? Whose culture was being exchanged with whom, and under what circumstances? Finally, were syncretisms and forms of integration always liberatory for the subalterns, or did they just as often serve the interests of the colonizing group?

Nowhere are these questions more pressing than in relation to the issues of gender, sexuality, and desire which occupy an important place in colonial narratives but have often been underexplored in male-authored Caribbean cultural theory. Whereas the creolization thesis conceives of cultural flows in the presence of relations of domination, sexuality is viewed as enabling greater integration through miscegenation.[75] In Brathwaite's brief consideration of the subject, sexuality contributes to the creolization process by binding members of radically opposed social groups biologically,

socially, and culturally: "It was in the intimate area of sexual relationships that the greatest damage was done to white creole apartheid policy
and where the most significant—and lasting—inter-cultural creolization
took place."[76] For Brathwaite, the biological product of miscegenation—
the colored population—provided a sort of social cement to further integrate society. Francophone writers are far less explicit about the roles of gender and sexuality, tending to invoke *métissage* only to pass immediately to
its metaphorical rather than literal meaning. For Édouard Glissant, métissage refers to the "encounter with the Other," one step along the way to the
full complexity of creolization, defined as a "métissage without limits."[77]
Glissant thus moves away from negative images of the métis formulated
in what he calls "traditional literature."[78] Likewise, Chamoiseau, Confiant,
and Bernabé reject the ideology of racial naming in favor of the linguistic
metaphor for cultural fusion: "In multiracial societies such as ours, it seems
urgent that we drop the usual racial distinctions and return to the habit of
calling our countryman by the only term that suits him: Creole."[79]

The problem is that by setting aside issues of gender and sexuality, or by
viewing them as mitigating factors in an otherwise brutal system of domination and subordination, these writers overlook the ways in which certain
sexual practices contributed to and reinforced those very power structures.[80]
This contention relates in many respects to the first black American feminist
critique of male historians' avoidance of the sexual exploitation of female
slaves in the antebellum United States. Repudiating decades of historical
research by male scholars whom they considered to have downplayed the
reality of sexual violence, portrayed slave women as complicitous, or cast
sexual relationships as benevolent expressions of white male desire, black
feminist critics such as Angela Davis and bell hooks redefined sexuality between master and slave in terms of rape. As such, sex became a "weapon of
domination," an "institutionalized form of terrorism" through which male
slaveholders exploited the bodies of female captives, degendered them with
respect to Euro-American codes of femininity, and "extinguished [their]
will to resist."[81] In a moderated formulation, Hortense Spillers has questioned whether " 'sexuality' as a term of implied relationship and desire is . . .
appropriate, manageable, or accurate to any of the familial arrangements
under a system of enslavement, from the master's family to the captive
enclave."[82]

I am committed to evaluating slavery as a system of sexual domination,
but my perspective is closer to that of Saidiya Hartman, Joan Dayan, and
Arlette Gautier, who regard desire as an unavoidable component of the

violence that structured gendered relations of power between masters and slaves.[83] Far from being irrelevant in a system in which slaveholders claimed right of access to the bodies they "possessed," desire was a function of power that deeply impacted practices and ideologies of domination. The question then becomes who desired and what were the uses, parameters, and consequences of those desires and their pursuit, both real and imagined? In her discussion of nineteenth-century antebellum slave law, Hartman analyzes "the dynamics of enjoyment in a context in which joy and domination and use and violence could not be separated."[84] In her view, desire and seduction are strategies of mastery as well as terms in a logic that celebrates the surrender and perfect submission of the enslaved.[85] Arlette Gautier and Joan Dayan offer subtle discussions of the conditions under which sex, desire, and love were possible, and for whom, in Old Regime French Caribbean slave societies. For Gautier, desire existed only for the master, who constituted the female slave as an object of his desire, unable to refuse herself.[86] Similarly, Dayan has analyzed what she calls the "cult of desire" in late-eighteenth-century Saint-Domingue, whereby white men were consumed with frenetic passions for slaves and especially free women of color. "No matter how degrading, how despotic the effects of slavery," she writes, "there remained a place for love, a kind of excrescence from the everyday oppression and torture, an experience that could be named and claimed by the 'civilized' agents of an odious institution."[87]

This insistence on "loving" their slaves coexisted with the most extreme performances of terror, thus raising the question of the role of desire and sexuality in strategies of denial that undergirded the masters' sense of legitimacy. On the other hand, the frequency with which masters imagined frenetic passions to reside in the slave women they subjugated and abused suggests as well their desire for sexual hegemony in the Gramscian sense, that is, a kind of power accrued through the consent of the subordinated group.[88] To examine the relation between the masters' sexual practices and the ideologies and practices of racial domination under slavery, I embrace the psychoanalytical valences of the term *desire*. Moving beyond issues of attraction and seduction, white colonial sexuality may thus be placed in relation to individual psychology, the emotions, gender identity, filial relations, and the unconscious, all of which had a formative role in shaping individual displays of mastery, as well as the imaginary justifications for structures of racial rule in the colonies.[89] Drawing on carefully selected concepts in Freudian theory in my analysis of colonial narratives, I show that libidinal dynamics were both legible on the surface of colonial relationships and activated fantasies, displacements, wishes, and fears in the white colonial unconscious that were no less central to the functioning of a brutal regime. Especially important here is the notion of fantasy, by which I mean the imaginary or unconscious fulfillment of a desire that is otherwise prohibited by reality or social norms. In classical psychoanalytic theory, fantasies are linked to reality in that they block out shameful memories or unpleasurable aspects of experience, and they can also play a formative or structuring role in a subject's life, behavior, and actions.[90] As I will argue, interracial sexual fantasies were the primary means through which white men legitimated their desired social and racial supremacy while at the same time repressing the brutality and sexual violence of racial slavery. At various points in my analysis, I place legal codes and discriminations enacted in the colony under scrutiny as themselves symptomatic of often unacknowledged desires, anxieties, and fantasies among the colonial elite. Finally, desire as a concept allows, in certain cases, for the careful redistribution of agency across the power dichotomy, such that slave women and free women of color may be viewed as agents and negotiators of desire, as well as victims of sexual violence.

The Libertine Colony

Through the concept of "libertinage," the second half of this book examines the roles of desire and sexuality in mediating colonial power relations. Interestingly, the earliest appearance of the word *libertine* was in the context of a slave society, that of ancient Rome. Its etymological roots go back to the Latin *libertinus*, meaning "freed slave." Roman law opposed this concept to *ingenuus*, or "free man," but the true opposite of a libertine was a slave. In sixteenth- and seventeenth-century France, the word referred to religious disbelief, a refusal to submit to religious authority, and immorality. Thus, the first literary movement by that name embraced an *esprit critique* characterized by skepticism, epicurism, and a critique of religious belief and dogma. This literary revolt took a philosophical turn with the emergence of *libertinage érudit*, a movement concerned with sensualist philosophy and empiricism. By the eighteenth century, this style of thought came to be known simply as "philosophy," whereas *libertinage*, while retaining the meaning of irreligion, referred mainly to the refusal of conventional sexual morality and the unbridled pursuit of sensual pleasures. The accompanying literature celebrated gallantry and eroticism, attacked transcendental ethics, and advanced earlier inquiries into materialist philosophy.[91]

When deployed by representatives of church and state, *libertine* and *libertinage* were almost always used to identify and proscribe practices that threatened royal power and religious authority. The title of this study, *The Libertine Colony*, refers on one hand to a central anxiety in colonial texts concerning the nature of the creolization process. From the inception of colonization to its apex in the late eighteenth century, missionaries, writers, and travelers consistently invoked the terms *libertine* and *libertinage* to describe the colonies as a space of immorality, religious heresy, violence, and sexual license. The discourse of libertinage was largely a reaction to what observers considered to be threatening and uncontrollable about the creolizing process as French emigrants reacted and accommodated to the cultural difference of native Caribs and imported Africans while spontaneously fashioning new identities outside the bounds of traditional authority, morality, and social codes. As early as 1640, the Jesuit missionary Jacques Bouton expressed his shock at the nearly complete lack of religious supervision on the island of Martinique: "With respect to morals, our Frenchmen are like a people almost completely abandoned by spiritual assistance, without Mass, priests, preachers, or sacraments, in too great a state of license, liberty, and impunity." [92] While Bouton limited most of his criticisms to religious deviants and protestants—"heretics, a handful of libertines and atheists, slow-witted and brutish minds"—other early missionaries openly criticized sexual immorality in the colonies. [93] For Du Tertre, both religious and sexual indiscretions had led to the bad reputation of the colonies in France, a reputation he claimed was no longer merited: "Although the licentious life of some of the first settlers [*habitants*] has disgraced the Islands and made them known as a land of libertinage and impiety, I can truthfully attest that God has so greatly blessed the zeal and work of the missionaries, that one will soon find as much virtue and piety there as in France." [94] Yet Du Tertre's self-interested optimism was belied by later observers and colonial officials, who almost universally decried the lack of public decency in the colonies. Among the most contentious and volatile issues in colonial history, sexual libertinage took many forms, from the traffic in Indian and European women and the taking of African slaves as wives and concubines to sordid attacks and sexual indulgences on the plantation and the libidinal excesses in colonial cities, where free women of color rivaled their white competitors for the richest white men.

In invoking the term *libertinage*, I intend not only to trace the discourse through which colonial writers criticized religious, moral, and social indiscipline in the Caribbean but to propose an alternative understanding of the centrality of desire and sexuality to the ideologies and practices of domination in Creole society. In this respect, I reconceive libertinage not merely as the moral deviance of particular colonial subjects but rather as a libidinal economy undergirding exploitative power relations among whites, free nonwhites, and slaves in the colonies. This understanding of libertinage relates to the literary tradition insofar as, in the libertine imagination, desire and sexuality were detached from sentiment and instrumentalized within gendered relations of power. Most famously, writers such as Crébillon and Laclos portrayed figures of a declining aristocracy, male and female, competing among themselves for pleasure, influence, and social prestige through an endless cycle of seduction, manipulation, and abandonment.[95] Voluntarily sequestered in the castle, boudoir, or monastery, fictional libertines are supremely idle, filling their time by deploying desire and pleasure to satisfy their vanity, greed, and desire for power. Critics have repeatedly made the connection between the pleasure principle and the will to power in libertine fiction, in some cases characterizing the erotic situation as a form of slavery.[96] In Peter Brooks's classic interpretation of Laclos's *Dangerous Liaisons*, eroticism among the leisure class gives rise to a conception of the group as a closed order of social conformity, "a society which has given exclusive value to games of domination and control, pursuit and enslavement, which can, in human logic, find their outcome only in the erotic relationship."[97] The Marquis de Sade in particular insisted on the mutually reinforcing relation between exploitative social relations and libertinage and broadened the parameters of the social to include relations between different classes. Yet, what is fascinating is that Sade's most horrific scenarios of terror and pleasure may have in fact been inspired by the French colonial slave societies of his time. Joan Dayan first drew attention to stunning parallels between the Sadean imaginary and colonial reality when she placed *The 120 Days of Sodom* and *Juliette* in the context of planter discourse and the infamous Code noir. As she argues, Sade's literary imaginary was fundamentally shaped by his reading of colonial discourses and histories: "Sade brought the plantation hell and its excesses into enlightenment Europe. . . . The debauchery and unbridled tyranny of Sade's libertines have their sources in the emblematic Creole planters, dedicated to the heady interests of pleasure, greed, and abandon."[98]

The correspondence between the Sadean imaginary and practices of colonial subjection may be further inferred from Marcel Hénaff's analysis of *The 120 Days* as a scintillating critique of both aristocratic privilege and protoindustrial regimes of labor exploitation.[99] Though Hénaff reads mainly through a Marxist, structuralist framework, with no reference to colonialism, he reveals the author's deep insights into the relations among desire, power, and domination, thus enabling provocative comparisons with the social order of slavery. For Hénaff, Sadean libertinage functions as a highly rationalized system of exploitation in which the jouissance of the one is based on the pain of the others. In Sade's libertine factory, the primary product is pleasure itself, "fabricated" through the expenditure of proletarian bodies for the benefit of the aging libertine *maître* and his coterie of aristocrats. The master's wealth and membership in the nobility afford him an immense store of political and economic capital with which to secure an endlessly renewable sexual labor force, comprised of anonymous individuals selected for their diverse domestic and erotic tasks. In Hénaff's analysis of "the libertine proletariat," what becomes abundantly apparent is the ease with which arbitrary social relations of domination are mediated through libidinal means. In the Sadean imaginary, extreme power inequities between the nobility and their social subalterns are enacted and indeed enforced through the domination of the latter as bodies in the service of libertinage. Writes Hénaff, "Silling tells the dirty little secret about this mode of production: that masters of capital, through the factory system, become masters of bodies as well, and that the sexual exploitation of these bodies is the only logical conclusion of their industrial explotiation."[100]

In some respects, Hénaff's reading of Sade is useful as an analytic model for thinking through the role of desire in colonial practices of domination, for only in a slave colony were the extreme scenarios envisioned by the author possible. Yet Sade's theoretical insight alone cannot account for the political and social dimensions of libertinage in the French Caribbean, where the great majority of human beings were held in perpetual bondage, sexual agency was attributed to more than one class and gender, and, as I shall argue, the reproductive consequences of informal sexual relationships greatly impacted the discourse on libertinage and the emergent social order, as well as white attitudes toward racial and gender differences. These complicating factors are evident from the testimony of contemporary travelers and colonists, who never failed to comment on one of the most shocking aspects of Creole society—the prevalence of interracial libertinage amid a system of extreme segregation based on race. Nowhere was this more apparent than in Saint-Domingue, the largest and most "prosperous" of France's sugar-producing colonies, where, according to a late-eighteenth-century Swiss traveler, Girod de Chantrans, libertinage was the main diversion and principle topic of conversation among whites after their own self-interests.[101] From the inception of the plantation economy, colonial authorities frequently denounced relations of concubinage between whites and slave women, which were discouraged by the Code noir.[102] The repeated legislation passed in the eighteenth century to reiterate this law, combined with continuous denunciations by colonial officials and writers, indicates the persistence of the practice. For Baron de Wimpffen, who visited the island in the last three years before the onset of the Saint-Domingue revolution, concubinage posed one of the greatest threats to the health and survival of the white Creole populace: "Let us have morals in Saint Domingue; let the colonists, spent by villainous libertinage, instead of these black concubines—livid, yellowed, bruised—who besot and cheat them, marry women of their color, and soon enough this country will offer, to the eye of the observer, a completely different countenance."[103]

While the lack of white women during the early history of the colony surely contributed to its culture of interracial concubinage, this is an insufficient explanation for the later persistence of interracial liaisons in late-eighteenth-century Saint-Domingue, which exceeded concubinage to include various kinds of sexual relationships and intimate encounters, both coerced and consensual.[104] Numerous colonial narratives attest to the emergence of a veritable cult of the free mulatto woman in the eighteenth-century French Caribbean. She was deemed superior in charms, intelligence, and sexual savoir faire to white women, thus leading white men to shun women of their own race in favor of colored lovers and concubines. Whereas in the Sadean imagination libertinage was synonymous with a social relation of subjugation in which the master extracted pleasure from the other, eighteenth-century colonial representations of libertinage were much more varied in their attributions of sexual power and moral indiscretion. Despite the social relations of race, which placed women of color in a doubly subordinate position vis-à-vis white men in the island, colonial writers and observers cast interracial libertinage less as the libidinal expression of white hegemony or the abuse of the weak than as a political strategy whereby women of color accrued agency and control over whites. The usual eighteenth-century distinction between libertinage and love—sex and sentiment—was thus apparent in the widespread notion that libertinage constituted the only political weapon for those condemned by their color to live a debased existence in the shadow of white supremacy. The colonist Dubuisson, for example, decried women of color as "objects of unbridled debauchery who can inspire love and all of its frenzy, but who will never be capable of the delicate emotions of a tender heart." Pleasure in Saint-Domingue was only physical, limited, he contended, to the "lascivious caresses of these women, destined by the blemish of their birth and the color of their skin, for the dishonorable life of a woman of pleasure."[105] For Girod de Chantrans, mulatto women displaced their white female rivals through a combination of nature and culture: "These women, naturally more lascivious than European women, and pleased by their influence over White men, have, in an attempt to retain it, mustered all of the voluptuousness in their power. . . . Shamelessly wanton, they have easily acquired a decided superiority in the realm of libertinage."[106] Hilliard d'Auberteuil, a colonial lawyer and critic of immorality in Saint-Domingue, assessed the relative power of mulatto women in even more symbolic terms. They had, he maintained, arrogated to themselves a veritable *empire* over white men, founded on libertinage.[107] The colonial discourse of libertinage thus displaced much of the stigma and responsibility for the material extravagance, luxury, and debauchery of the colonies onto free women of color, at once celebrated and vilified as peons of pleasure, dedicated to cultivating the erotic excess to which "nature" predisposed them. Similarly, black slave women were designated as sexual savages ready to manipulate their white masters in their own self-interest.

Implicit in this rhetoric of libertinage was the idea that interracial intimacy was subversive to the colonial social order. Wimpffen, for one, derided colonists for what he considered to be sexual self-sabotage: "The colonist, who would blush with shame to work with his Negress, does not blush to live with her in a degree of intimacy that necessarily establishes relations of equality between them, which precedent challenges in vain."[108] In raising the specter of relations of equality in the sexual as well as sentimental relations between whites and nonwhites, the colonial discourse on libertinage referenced the rigid caste system, which divided the society into slaves, free people of color, and whites. By the late eighteenth century, the colony of Saint-Domingue had one of the largest populations of free people of color in the Caribbean, with its proportion of the total free population far exceeding those of other French and English islands.[109] Over time, colonial courts and the royal administration subjected this group to a severe regime of legal apartheid and social dispossession that stripped them of all social privileges and political rights. Believed to have derived mainly from interracial libertinage on the plantation, free people of color (also known as mulattoes or freedmen) constituted a racially and socially diverse class made up of freed slaves and their descendants. As successful and highly educated planters, skilled laborers, business owners, slaveholders, and military leaders, the free colored population held substantial economic power, had strong roots in the colony, and by the end of the century owned as many as one-third of all slaves.[110] As such, members of the free colored elite aspired to join the ruling class of whites and desired access to titles of nobility, political offices, and full civil and political rights. Throughout the eighteenth century, the colonial order in Saint-Domingue responded with an increasingly stringent segregative order founded on notions of racial purity. Barred from the legal and medical professions, free people of color were forbidden to wear luxurious attire, use the names of whites, gather for celebrations, sit at the same table with whites, go to Europe, and even play European games. In addition, mulattoes were coerced into special units of the colonial militia charged with the pursuit of runaway slaves, internal policing, and the general defense of the colony. And, whereas in the seventeenth century and the early eighteenth there were no restrictions on interracial marriage, the second half of the century saw a proliferation of social penalties against whites who committed the misdeed of mésalliance (marrying a nonwhite person). The irony of such legal discrimination in the presence of unbridled sexual libertinage was not lost on Baron Wimpffen, who remarked sardonically that the social abjection of free people of color "prevents them from cultivating with whites relationships close enough not for sleeping together, but for eating at the same table."[111]

In *Haiti, History, and the Gods,* Joan Dayan offers a riveting description of the colonial contest for love and luxury in Saint-Domingue, in particular the ways in which a system of terror gave rise to the most tumultuous passions and public displays of lust, envy, and love. Building on these insights, my theory of libertinage establishes a relation between the two most distinctive and seemingly contradictory features of Creole society—the extreme racial segregation and discrimination that resulted in a rigid three-tiered caste system, on one hand, and interracial intimacies and boundary crossing, both coerced and consensual, on the other. Rather than viewing the coincidence of racially exclusionary law and interracial libertinage as a contradiction, I consider these phenomena to be mutually reinforcing and constitutive of the system of white supremacy and racial domination that shaped French slave societies. Several questions motivate this inquiry. What roles did gender and sexuality play in regimes of bodily discipline and racial repression? In what ways did the law of exclusion respond to the phenomena of colonial desire, libertinage, and métissage? How much did white supremacist ideologies accommodate colonial practices of interracial desire, sexuality, and reproduction, and how much did they repress them? My point in retaining the disparaging term *libertinage* is to stress that whatever their affective dimensions, these relationships were overdetermined by the broader system of racial subjugation and gender oppression in the colony and in turn impacted it. While many historians accept that slavery involved a system of sexual domination, there has been little attempt to analyze the specific discourses, fantasies, and mentalities underlying interracial sexual practices and much less to relate these to the logics of racial discrimination and segregation that characterized slave societies in the Caribbean.[112]

Central to my analysis is the signal irony of a repressive tripartite racial caste system in which the middle group is considered by the ruling caste (white) to be the result of sexual union with the inferior caste (black). I argue that such prejudice implicated the ruling class itself and in particular its role in the biological reproduction of colonial society. Laws of exclusion, by restricting the political, economic, and social opportunities of free people of color, also functioned to displace anxiety about the conditions of their production—interracial sexuality, and libertinage—away from the white minority. At the same time, the colonial regime of racial exclusion enabled the white elite and colonial administration to suppress the multiple ties—sexual, emotional, affective, and filial—that bound them to the subordinated classes, both slaves and free people of color. My argument is based on an interpretation of the languages, discourses, and rhetoric through which sexual libertinage was articulated, together with ideas about racial difference, throughout colonial history. This has meant abandoning certain assumptions that underlie descriptive accounts of legal discrimination against free people of color in French slave societies. Whereas historians often attribute the systematized racial prejudice in the French colonies to whites' fears about the threat free nonwhites posed to their supremacy, social scientists have analyzed it as the inevitable response to the mulatto's subversion of the socioracial binary between black slaves and white masters that collapses racial difference onto social status (black = slave, white = free).[113] Jean-Luc Bonniol, after Yvan Debbasch, suggests that prejudice represented whites' mode of reacting against the internal threat posed by mulattoes to the Manichaean order of racial slavery, thus revealing the contradictions posed by the practice of manumission, on one hand, and métissage on the other. Writes Bonniol: "This model of biracial slavery is marred by two internal contradictions, leading to the appearance of a third term, unexpected at the start and destabilizing the initial structure"[114]

In my view, this argument goes awry in supposing a stable Manichaean order of race and status that preexisted métissage and that it in turn upset. In contrast, I suggest that métissage and the consolidation of racial determinism within slavery occurred simultaneously and thus fundamentally influenced ideologies of race and status that evolved within and have since been largely accepted as natural to that institution.[115] My perspective is informed by Robert Young's insight into the relation between nineteenth-century scientific racism and fantasies of libidinal boundary crossing. Young argues that insofar as theories of racial difference stood or fell on the basis of claims about the fertility of the product of interracial union, debates about race "focussed explicitly on the issue of sexuality and the issue of sexual unions between whites and blacks."[116] Polygenetic propositions that collapsed "race" into species thus belied an obsession with interracial sex and hybridity, what Young calls "colonial desire." I expand on Young's analysis by considering the reproductive implications of colonial desire in a slave society. The emergence of ideas of racial difference in the French slave colonies contributed to the formation of juridically actionable categories of exclusion that over time enabled the emergence of a tripartite racial caste society. I argue that this process of exclusion and the resultant social condition of the colonial mixed-race population represent the response by colonial authorities to interracial libertinage. In particular, it represents their attempt to control and manage the consequences of sexual relationships between free Europeans and captive Africans and later between whites and nonwhites, slave and free. Taken together, the coexistence of segregationism and libertinage typifies a critical ambivalence in the colonies between whites' obsession with and disavowal of interracial sexual union.[117]

My first contention, therefore, is that the coincidence of unbridled interracial libertinage and an extreme segregationist regime reflected both the extent of white anxieties about interracial sex and the efforts of colonial authorities to punish, displace, and suppress such practices. Reading legal and narrative discourses of miscegenation, I trace the emergence of racial prejudice and discrimination against persons of mixed race to a central ambiguity in official discourse as to the licitness or illicitness of sex between slaves and free people. I argue that discriminatory legislation figured free people of color as the illegitimate children of white men and slave women and functioned to displace onto them the anxieties of the dominant class about interracial libertinage. Making illegitimate children taboo meant not only defining them in terms of immorality, concupiscence, and sexual savagery; it also meant making them forbidden, untouchable, and unclean, capable of polluting white society if allowed any elite social privileges, political offices, or conjugal ties to whites. In Saint-Domingue, the very word *mulatto* became synonymous with notions of illegitimacy and immorality, which in turn justified the treatment of the entire class of free people of color as tabooed objects of social reprobation. The stereotype of the mulatto woman voluptuary is symptomatic of the mechanisms of displacement and repression whereby whites both acknowledged colonial desire and libertinage and displaced it onto the interracial other. What is fascinating is the radical circularity of this system of desire and exclusion, for the very exclusionary measures that indirectly punished the unbridled libertinage also enabled its continuance through the legal impunity of desiring white men. The astonishing "truth" of the libertine colony is that the law of exclusion ensured both the sexual and political hegemony of white men.

My second contention concerns the specific fantasies through which the white elite configured their sexual and racial dominance in highly allegorical ethnographic accounts of colonial society. Central here is the invariable conflict between sexual libertinage and the phenomenon of interracial reproduction, which, regardless of its causes, both benefited whites and posed a threat to their rule. This ambivalence is apparent in the ways in which they figured colonial society in terms of a metaphor of filiation. I argue that in the libertine colony the identity and sense of political legitimacy of the white elite depended on an imaginary conception of colonial society as an interracial family. Whereas in the case of exclusionary legislation the implicit narrative of filiation functioned to displace the taboo of métissage onto the class of free people of color considered to derive from it, in the late eighteenth century many whites in positions of authority actively and openly embraced familial metaphors of the social order in order to capitalize ideologically on colonial libertinage and its reproductive effects. This was arguably a response to the drastic demographic imbalances of late-eighteenth-century Saint-Domingue, as whites began to view free coloreds as their only protection against the mass of slaves. Imaginary constructions of the filial or libidinal relation between ethno-classes thus functioned as fantasies that enabled the white elite to deny relations of force, coercion, and violence between masters and slaves and to naturalize its political authority over subjugated classes on the island. Essential to this fantasy was the suggestion that white men could control the reproductive implications of their libidinal relations with nonwhite women, slave and free. In colonial ethnographies and racial taxonomies, white men were cast as the symbolic fathers of both the slaves and free people of color, capable of producing the latter through their sexual commerce with slave women. In the work of Moreau de Saint-Méry and others, slave women were positioned as the sexual sub-ordinates of white men and the mothers of slaves as well as free people of color.

Moreau's text suggests as well the incestuous underpinnings of white Creole ideologies of desire and reproduction in French Caribbean slave societies. I argue that Moreau's racial theory is representative of a larger fantasy informing colonial slavery in the Caribbean and elsewhere, which is a fantasy of incestuous family romance. In a society in which white men placed themselves in the position of symbolic fathers of all the races, and biological fathers of free people of color in particular, while at the same time erecting a cult of desire around mixed-race women and fantasizing their effective sterility, the structure of interracial desire was decidedly incestuous. The question thus arises as to the importance of incest as an acknowledged or repressed sexual narrative of racial slavery in Saint-Domingue and the extent to which incestuous fantasies impacted the discourses and practices of desire and subjection in the colony. Drawing on psychoanalysis, anthropology, libertine fiction, and literary research on slave societies, I theorize the role of incest in the sexual order of racial slavery, while testing the limitations of available scholarly understandings of incest and its prohibition.

* * *

Although the theory of the libertine colony is articulated in the last three chapters of the book, all chapters address the various valences of the term *libertinage* invoked by writers and observers to characterize creolization in the early French Caribbean. The organization of the book is both thematic and chronological and reflects the shifting relations between French settlers and the three other main population groups in the Caribbean—Island Caribs, African captives, and free people of color—over time. Through a historically contextualized interpretation of narrative sources, I examine these relations around specific topics that represent especially productive points of exchange and/or subjection at particular junctures in colonial history such as religion, culture, race, and slavery.

The first chapter concerns seventeenth-century missionary representations of the encounter between French settlers and the indigenous people present at the time of colonization, the Island Caribs. Here I depart from the tendency to critique early modern colonial narratives either as self-referential constructions of the French cultural imaginary or as ideologically coded misrepresentations of the colonial other. The challenge in reading early colonial accounts is to see what they reveal, wittingly and unwittingly, about French attitudes toward the relation, or border, between the French and the Caribs at a specific time and place. In particular, I analyze the tension in missionary narratives between representations of violence toward and desire for the other, that is, between stories of war and the ideology of conversion and incorporation of the Caribs into the French social body. Through readings of the missionaries Du Tertre, Breton, the protestant Rochefort, and a host of minor writers, I argue that the border of violence is discernible in the kinds of information recorded about the Caribs and that this representation in turn suggests the kinds of exchanges—cultural, linguistic, material, and religious—that took place between the French and the Caribs. Yet, whereas the border is always implied in French representations of the Caribs, it is itself fundamentally unrepresentable except in the remarkable genre of the dictionary, which escapes the logic of incorporation that absorbs the other into the time and story of the same. Drawing on the theories of Mikhail Bakhtin and Emmanuel Levinas, I examine Raymond Breton's *Dictionnaire français-caraïbe* as the quintessential border text, one that offers the possibility of nonhegemonic readings of colonial encounters.

Chapter 2 deals with the representation of creolization among whites of different ethnic and class origins, whose migration to the colonies resulted in dramatic changes on the levels of culture and social identification. Narratives by the pirate writer Alexandre-Olivier Oexmelin and the Dominican missionaries Du Tertre and Labat suggest the extent to which colonial settlers resisted the social order imagined by colonial authorities and representatives of the church. Anarchy, piracy, irreligion, and social travesty were only some of the behaviors writers attempted to both describe and disparage. Through the concept of "white noble savagery," I theorize the seemingly contradictory impulse among colonists toward lawlessness, libertinage, and freedom from social norms, on one hand, and a desire for social promotion and class ascension on the other. I read the two most diametrically opposed social activities in the seventeenth-century Caribbean— piracy and plantation agriculture—as fundamentally similar performances of nobility and aristocratic privilege denied to the lower classes in France. Finally, I relate the tendency toward social travesty, reinvention, and cross-dressing in the colonies to the parallel move by writers and colonial authorities to regulate colonial access to social rewards and noble status. Narratives written from the perspective of colonial authority counteract the varied and unstable colonial performances of nobility with an ideology of production, domesticity, and military service to the king.

In chapter 3, I explore the colonial spirit world on the basis of repeated associations in narrative sources among supernatural beliefs, violence, and sensuality. The central contention here is that narratives of the spirit world serve as allegories of relationships found in the material world. Through the concept of "colonial demonology," I first consider the ways in which missionaries such as Du Tertre, Breton, and Labat adapted early modern discourses of witchcraft to describe the unfamiliar beliefs and spiritual practices of Caribs and Africans. Beginning with an examination of the figure of the suffering, abused body in missionary narratives, discourses of salvation and colonial slave law, I move on to a libertine rewriting of demonology's obsession with the body to exploit its erotic subtext. The first colonial novel in French, *Le Zombi du Grand-Pérou*, satirizes white colonial spirit beliefs as both creolized and dedicated to the interests of sexual libertinage. In this respect, the novel offers insight into the relationship between regimes of bodily discipline and libertine sexual practices. I show that, through the figure of the "*zombi*," Pierre-Corneille Blessebois documents the syncretic nature of white colonial beliefs while at the same time exposing the ease with which the colonial elite transformed modalities of colonial violence into libertine fantasies of desire.

Chapters 4 and 5 constitute a detailed analysis of the libertine colony, that is, the system of desire and exclusion whereby the white male elite secured a position of sexual and political hegemony. Chapter 4 deals with the relationship among desire, miscegenation, and the law as seen in legal codes and narrative discourses in the seventeenth and eighteenth centuries. More specifically, I argue that the presence of a family metaphor at the heart of the juridical discourse of race prejudice suggests that the development of a caste society in the Caribbean colonies reflected an attempt by whites to manage the many consequences (political, biological, affective) of interracial libertinage in the interest of white supremacy. Drawing on Freud's notion of taboo, I show that, although the law originally declared sex between free men and slave women to be a crime, colonial authorities gradually shifted responsibility and the burden of punishment onto both slave women and, importantly, their mulatto offspring. Colonial discourse and the law thus transferred the stigma of immorality, forbidden interracial desires, and pathological sexuality onto the growing population of mixed-race persons, leaving the desiring white male subjects free from legal retribution. In addition, as free people of color were legally assigned second-class status below the white elite, antimanumission laws proliferated, thus shutting down avenues for black female entitlement. Reading exclusionary measures against works by Hilliard d'Auberteuil, Girod de Chantrans, Baron Wimpffen, and others, I argue that these laws displaced anxiety about white involvement in continuing relations of métissage, which bound members of different colors and social stations while at the same time ensuring that no social rewards devolved to free people of color or slaves. Late-eighteenth-century representations of the mulatto woman served this system by projecting onto her the debauchery, luxury, and excess that marked the libertine colony in the minds of colonials and travelers alike. In this sense, I show that segregationism was driven largely by the efforts of colonial authorities to repress white libertinage and control its social effects.

In chapter 5, I build on the thesis of the libertine colony by exploring the relation between interracial libertinage and white Creole identity in the work of the most important colonial writer and Creole political figure of the eighteenth century, Moreau de Saint-Méry. An Enlightenment thinker, lawyer, colonial historian, political activist, and author of the massive *Description . . . de la partie française de l'isle Saint-Domingue*, published in 1797, Moreau self-consciously represented his voice and that of the white elite of Saint-Domingue. In examining the ethnographic portion of this work and its extensive racial taxonomy, I argue that narratives of sexuality, reproduction, and filiation functioned in the colonial imagination to veil relations of force, coercion, and violence between social castes and to naturalize white authority over those whom they subordinated. Thus, in Moreau's ethnographic portrait of colonial society, Creole identity is collapsed onto the idea of métissage and the entire social edifice of colonial society is viewed through a metaphor of desire and filiation. Moving on to the racial taxonomy, I contend that the racial text is a privileged site for the inscription of covert or unconscious fantasies of desire and reproduction, as well as the invariable conflict in the white Creole imagination between the desire for sexual hegemony and the fear of proliferating numbers of free people of color. In my interpretation, Moreau's reproductive hypothesis solves the dilemma by revising Enlightenment notions of race and fertility. Through the figure of the sterile mulatto woman, Moreau fantasizes an end to the "rule of consequence"—reproduction—even as he exposes the incestuous underpinning of the structures of interracial desire in colonial discourse. While white Creole men vest their authority in their sexual power and the corollary idea of symbolic (if not biological) paternity over subordinate classes, at the same time they greatly eroticize their "daughters," those stereotypical mulatto voluptuaries who dominate colonial fantasies. I argue that the entire pattern of desire and sexuality in colonial representations is essentially incestuous and raises questions about the ability of slave societies to uphold the incest taboo. Drawing on anthropological, pyschoanalytical, and libertine representations of incest, I propose a theory of incestuous "family romance" in Saint-Domingue through which to reinterpret mechanisms of exclusion and social control in late-eighteenth-century Saint-Domingue.

Chapter One   *Border of Violence, Border of Desire:*

The French and the Island Caribs

To speak of the Caribs poses a difficulty for students of colonialism in the region known also by that name. Although the term *Carib* is claimed today by the last descendants of indigenous people living on the island of Dominica, it refers to the first and arguably the most destructive instance of cross-cultural misapprehension that marked the encounter between Europeans and Amerindians in the New World. For most anthropologists and ethnohistorians working today, it is not at all clear to what extent anything like a "Carib" ethnicity or group identity existed in the Lesser Antilles before the seventeenth century, when indigenous people themselves began using the term as an ethnic self-ascription.[1] What is certain is that the term *Carib* and its early variants, *Caniba* and *Canibal*, were imposed on a culturally unfamiliar group by Christopher Columbus and his chroniclers. In time, the term and its accompanying stereotype became central to an ideologically charged ethnic map through which Europeans validated their colonial ambitions in the region.

The political nature of the ethnic ascription Carib was already evident in the publications documenting Columbus's voyages to the New World (see figure 1). In his journal, Columbus compared those he called Caribes or Canibales unfavorably to his hosts on Hispaniola, whom he perceived as peaceful, timorous, and willfully subservient to the Spanish.[2] Based on his professed understanding of the entirely foreign language spoken by his native guides, Columbus declared the Caribes/Canibales to be a monstrous race of men who made war on their neighbors and ate them. Yet Columbus was initially skeptical about the charge of anthropophagy among the Caribes, since he assumed they were soldiers of the "Khan" of Cathay in the Asia of his imagination. His acceptance of the accusation was prompted not by eyewitness confirmation but rather by the only reported instance in which he was attacked by Indians. When describing a hostile encounter with a group on the coast of Hispaniola, he asserted that those people were "without doubt . . . those of *Carib* and that they would eat men," thus collapsing their hostility with the still unproven allegation of anthropophagy.[3] The circumstances of this determination foreshadow the future basis for ethnic distinctions in the Spanish Caribbean: resistance or accommodation to the Spanish. Those Indians who submitted to Christianity and acquiesced to Spanish demands for gold were considered vassals of the Crown, legally free though subject to royal authority. Carib, on the other hand, became a generic label for Indians deemed hostile to Christians. Allegedly identifiable by a conflation of undesirable traits, including anthropophagy and aggressiveness toward the Spanish, they were subject to legal enslavement.

Over time, the geographical boundaries of the Carib/non-Carib distinction shifted considerably. Initially limited to the Lesser Antilles, where Spanish royal edicts authorized the enslavement of "Caribs" resistant to Christianity, the ethnic map was revised when slave armadas encountered resistance in the smaller islands. As slavers expanded into the discovered territories of Venezuela and the Guyanas in response to an increased colonial demand for labor, the simple accusation of anthropophagy sufficed to identify a group as Carib. This led to indiscriminate slaving throughout the Spanish Main. In 1520, the Crown moved to regulate this slave trade by redefining as Carib those territories uninhabited by Christians whose populations had engaged in armed resistance against the Spanish. No longer an ethnic ascription limited to the Antilles, the term *Carib* was applied in the islands and on the mainland to make political distinctions between tractable and resistant populations.[4]

The strategic nature of the Carib stereotype notwithstanding, those living in the Lesser Antilles did retaliate against Spanish incursions and slave raids in their territory. In addition to defeating at least one attempt by the Spanish to colonize Guadeloupe, "Caribs" were repeatedly accused of attacking the Spanish colonies in the Greater Antilles.[5] Yet one of the most remarkable consequences of this instance of ethnic stereotyping was the impact it had on the ethnic identities and affiliations on the ground, literally setting the terms within which resistance took place. If the warlike Carib identity was invented to serve Spanish colonial imperatives, in time it was appropriated by the islanders themselves. Some groups struck up strategic alliances with the Spanish by denouncing others as Caribs, knowing full

1. "Christophe Colomb descend à terre, & prend possession de l'Isle Guana-hani," in Pierre-François-Xavier de Charlevoix, *Histoire de l'isle espagnole, ou de S. Domingue*, Paris, 1730–31. (Reproduced courtesy of the McCormick Library of Special Collections, Northwestern University Library.)

well the consequences of doing so.[6] By the seventeenth century, however, in-digenous peoples began to use the term *Carib* to describe themselves, a fact that is amply demonstrated in the French ethnographic record.[7] When the French arrived in the Caribbean, they encountered people whose 130-year battle with European interests had predisposed them to identify with their "given" name and its warrior connotation, if only to repel further European conquests in the region.

Creolization and cultural exchange between French settlers and Island Caribs thus raises the vexing question of the border. Unlike subjugated Africans, who were forced to live with European colonists, sharing the same physical, cultural, and even domestic environment, Island Caribs and French settlers did not live in the same communities. The Caribs' very group identity was based on a historic refusal to submit to European colonists on their own territory. The French colonizing companies approached the islands of the Lesser Antilles with a view toward the production of to-bacco, an activity in which the Caribs would have little part given their notorious resistance to enslavement. The Caribs were never colonized by the French; rather, they were repeatedly displaced and their numbers di-minished through a series of bloody conflicts in the first several decades of colonization. Beginning in Saint-Christophe, where French privateers and buccaneers joined forces with the English to drive out the Caribs, territorial warfare increased in the 1630s as the French expanded to sur-rounding islands. In Guadeloupe, starving and desperate French settlers planned an all-out attack on the Caribs, provoking a four-year struggle. From the neighboring island of Dominica, Caribs launched guerrilla-style raids against the fledgling colony before losing the island to the French. The story in Martinique was no less bloody; an initially warm welcome by Caribs turned violent when the French constructed a fort. In the ensuing conflict, Caribs were defeated by massive artillery and cannon fire and withdrew to the eastern half of the island. Following a brief period of peace in the 1640s, hostilities between the two parties were reignited when individual gover-nors led a second wave of expansion. Perhaps the most devastating episode was Du Parquet's possession of Grenada, which led to a mass Carib suicide at the site of the eponymously named "*morne des sauteurs.*"[8]

The story of French-Carib contacts was thus one of a moving border that shifted across space so as to reduce Caribs, finally, to the islands of Saint-Vincent and Dominica.[9] Yet, despite the recurrent hostilities that marked the first contacts with European colonists, the border was not imperme-able to exchanges and contacts of various kinds. The particular ambiguity

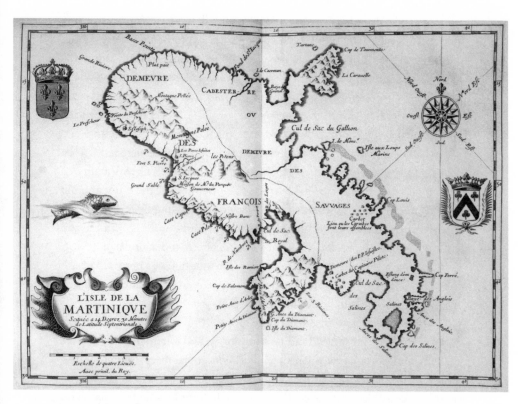

2. "L'Isle de la Martinique," in Jean-Baptiste Du Tertre, *Histoire générale des Antilles habitées par les François*, Paris, 1667–71. (Reproduced courtesy of the McCormick Library of Special Collections, Northwestern University Library.)

of the French-Carib border is strikingly apparent on a map of Martinique produced for Du Tertre's 1667 edition of the *Histoire générale des Antilles habitées par les François* (see figure 2). The map represents the island of Martinique, drawn with a line separating the "Territory of the Savages" from the "Territory of the French." The border is not sharp but broken, a fact that makes the map a fitting visual allegory for the instability and porousness of the boundary between the French and the indigenous peoples. As a border of conquest, the dotted line is equivocal. It signifies a boundary that is not fixed but indeterminate, tentative, and contested. An imagined limit to the French territorial presence on the island, the broken line marks a frontier that would move with future French expansion. Du Tertre himself reported that by the end of 1658 the French had driven out the remaining Caribs in Martinique, thus claiming the entire island for themselves.[10] Just as importantly, however, the dotted line denotes the permeability of the interstitial zone—that is, its porousness to exchanges—of all kinds, which became important to the livelihood of both communities. Interactions between the French and the Caribs included the movement of people, ideas, commodities, culture, and language, as well as the creative reconstruction and adaptation of various elements according to the needs of emergent or displaced communities. In addition to ensuring the survival of several French settlements, such an open border was central to the ideology of French missionary colonialism, which was based on the pledge to Christianize the Caribs and assimilate them into the French state. The particular permeability of the French-Carib border is evidenced in the richness of the ethnographic information produced by French missionaries. Surpassing Spanish and English writings in amount and quality, French accounts are still considered by anthropologists to provide the most valuable observations on Island Carib culture, language, and society. The broken line thus figures a border of desire as well as a border of war; it is a site of exchange rather than merely a delimitation of what is to be excluded.

Too often border studies have transformed the border into a placeless metaphor for the presumed fluidity, complexity, and heterogeneity of postmodern and postcolonial identities. The border has been figured as the site of a liberating transculturation, a refusal of essentialized notions of bounded identities, and the production of subaltern knowledges that contest the hegemony of rational modernity.[11] The implication is that borders accrue significance only from the perspective of the subaltern, or only in the aftermath of colonialism, a view that forecloses important questions as to how actual borders were produced in the imagination of the colonizing power. Theories of creolization, on the other hand, while assuming the cross-pollination of cultures and languages between disparate groups from the inception of the colonial presence, have only recently considered the Amerindian contribution to Creole societies. Thus far, they have not accounted for the specificities of cultural flows across borders marked by militarized violence.[12] In this chapter, I explore colonial representations of the border in order to better understand the kinds of exchanges (missionary, linguistic, commercial, or ethnographic), migrations, and power dynamics, that characterized early French-Carib contacts. Scenes of encounters between the French and the Caribs offer insight into the values and meanings that the French attached to the intercultural border. In particular, narrative representations of cultural encounters reveal a central tension between the missionary assimilationist ideal and the repressive effects of territorial appropriation on indigenous peoples.

I begin by examining the ideological foundations of colonialism outlined in the documents that established the first commercial companies. These project the incorporation of Island Caribs into the French social body through the logic of reciprocity and religious conversion. I then analyze Jean-Baptiste Du Tertre's history of the French Antilles, which provided the first comprehensive account of the bloody settlement of the three main islands under French control. I argue that in his representation of violence and the emergence of territorial boundaries between French and Caribs, Du Tertre reconciles the failure of reciprocity with a providential narrative of French colonialism. Turning to ethnographic writings on Caribs, I show that stories of Carib origins, as well as scenes of peacetime exchange, serve to sublimate missionary anxiety over the failure of incorporation and the continued violence of the colonial encounter. In particular, I analyze the work of Raymond Breton, arguably the most important colonial ethnographer of Island Caribs, who lived for many years in Dominica and produced an encyclopedic dictionary of the Carib language. I argue that the Carib language becomes a surrogate object through which the missionary imagined the incorporation of the Carib other. At the same time, the dictionary stands as an unexplored source of discourse by speaking Carib subjects, who both acquiesced to and contested the French colonial desire for their land and language. Although relations of desire and violence influenced the kinds of information produced about Caribs in French colonial narratives, the border between Caribs and the French eluded representation except in the dictionary, where Caribs appeared as speaking subjects.

Fictions of Reciprocity

The French colonial enterprise in the Caribbean was born of a peculiar alliance of private, state, and church interests. The first royal trading companies were founded in response to proposals by the Norman naval captain and corsair Pierre d'Esnambuc to establish a colony on the island of Saint Christopher. An avid privateer on the Spanish Main, d'Esnambuc conceived of the idea after a shipwreck led him and his privateering companion Urbain du Roissey to take refuge on the island. There they discovered a small number of English colonists, who were successfully producing tobacco. Impressed by the commercial potential of the crop, and undeterred by the potential for hostilities with the native population, d'Esnambuc set off for France in 1625 to present a proposal for colonization to the king and Cardinal Richelieu. He arrived at an opportune moment, for Richelieu had recently been named grand master of navigation and commerce. After several failed colonial ventures, he was committed to restoring French naval power and commerce abroad by forming colonies in the New World. Richelieu enthusiastically endorsed d'Esnambuc's venture, and in 1626 the Compagnie de Saint-Christophe was established, with the cardinal as its largest shareholder.[13]

From its inception, the company's attitude toward the indigenous population was ambiguous. There is no question that the French expected staunch resistance from the people of the Lesser Antilles. Since the sixteenth century, Spanish travel accounts had depicted Caribs as hostile man-eaters whose ferocity in war was enhanced by their use of poisoned arrows. Even before making his proposal before Richelieu, d'Esnambuc and an English captain named Warner had effectively driven the Caribs from the island. In theory, however, seventeenth-century colonialism was based as much on a policy of engagement with indigenous populations as it was on territorial acquisition and cultivation. Reacting against the presumed barbarousness of Spanish conquistadors, and in recognition of the historic resistance of Caribbean peoples, the French did not view native peoples as a necessary source of labor power. Instead they had a vested interest in gaining native favor so as to appropriate local knowledge of the land and its resources, create a hospitable environment for colonial recruits from France, and enable military alliances against rival European colonizers. Hence there emerged in France what Philip Boucher has called an independent colonial theory based on the union of colonization and evangelization.[14] The Christian mission became the official strategy by means of which French officials and the company leadership legitimated colonialism and pursued a policy of "friendship" with the natives.

This position comes through clearly in the documents that established the Compagnie de Saint-Christophe. Rather than viewing the natives as adversaries across a boundary of violence and exclusion, company directors imagined a scene of reciprocity, conversion, and assimilation of the other into the French social body. In the Acts of Association of the company, the directors authorized its agents to "inhabit and people the islands of Saint-Christopher, Barbados, and others situated off the coast of Peru, from the eleventh to the eighteenth degree from the equator, which are not possessed by Christian princes." The notion of possession is crucial here, for the document implicitly called into question the existence of autochtonous populations, the extent to which they may be said legitimately to possess the islands they inhabit, and the potential for hostilities caused by French settlement of the land. These questions were only indirectly addressed by the professed goals of colonization, which were "as much as to instruct the inhabitants in the Catholic, Apostolic, and Roman Religion as to trade and traffic in the precious metals and commodities which may be gathered and taken from the said islands and from those of the surrounding areas."[15]

The ideological implications of this representation may be productively explored through Marcel Mauss's theory of reciprocity in nonviolent social relations. For Mauss, exchange is the very precondition for peace between two social entities. The most primitive form of social contract, exchange is based on the hidden rule of hospitality whereby any gift received must be graciously reciprocated. By professing the first aim of colonization to be the Christianization of the native "inhabitants," company officials recognized the existence of indigenous peoples only insofar as they were recipients of a gift, which in Mauss's theory implies a fundamental obligation to reciprocate.[16] The French exploitation of island resources was thus inscribed under the sign of exchange; it appeared less as an imposition on foreign lands and peoples than as a form of compensation for the gift of faith. This fiction of reciprocity was all the more explicit in the text of Richelieu's commission, with the difference that the order of exchange was reversed. The preamble presents the Christian mission as a direct response to the eventual discovery of tropical commodities and precious metals:

> [The Lords and Captains d'Enambuc and du Rossey] have seen and judged the air there to be very mild and temperate and the land fertile and profitable, from which could be obtained a number of useful commodities to maintain the life of men. The Indians living on the said islands have even informed them that there are mines of gold and silver. This would have given them reason to populate the island with a number of Frenchmen in order to instruct the inhabitants in the Catholic, Apostolic and Roman Religion, and to plant there the Christian faith for the glory of God and the honor of the king, under whose authority and power they would desire the said inhabitants to live and keep the islands subject to his Majesty. (12)

Here the apparently contradictory explanation of colonial goals makes sense only as a sublimation of overt territorial motives through a fiction of reciprocity. The pledge of missionary intent expresses the wish for a more just exchange with the natives, here recognized as freely yielding knowledge of precious gems and fertile soil. Even the metaphorical language expresses this longing for reciprocity: as if to replenish the precious metals and crops extracted from the land for sale abroad, the faith will be *planted*.[17]

What the missionary colonial ideology concealed was the unequal nature of the exchange and the likelihood of its failure. No sooner does Richelieu identify Indians as gracious objects of missionary desire than he approves of canons for their control: "The said Lords d'Esnambuc and du Rossey would have constructed and built two Forts and Ports on the island of Saint-Christopher . . . and left canons and other war munitions for their defense and protection as much against the Indian inhabitants of the said islands as all others who would undertake to drive them out from there" (12). The significance of reciprocity in the narrative of missionary colonialism, then, is that it suppressed the possibility for violence and the creation of dangerous border zones in the colonies. As a model of cross-cultural relations, fictions of reciprocity constructed indigenous peoples as perfectible subjects of Christianity whose conversion would ally them to the French cause. The fullest expression of this vision emerged in the charter for the second colonial company, founded in 1635 on the heels of the failing Compagnie de Saint-Christophe. This company aimed to expand French colonization to islands beyond Saint Christopher and increase the population of French settlers. In addition, company directors extended to converted Indians the right of French naturalization (49). When Christianity conferred French nationality on converted natives, the Christian mission became a vehicle for the incorporation of natives into the French social body.[18] The effect was to suppress the border of violence between the French and the natives.

Such fantasies of assimilation were not borne out by the missionary experience in the Caribbean. The first missionaries commissioned for service in the West Indies complained of a deadly struggle for survival in a tropical hell. Though avid defenders of the colonial enterprise, they were at times vocally critical of what they perceived as the company's greedy neglect of settlers, whose repeated calls for assistance fell on the deaf ears of impatient investors, who insisted on returns before replenishing supplies. The fallacy of missionary colonial ideology was exposed in practice, as it became apparent that the administration's main goal was not in fact to provide liberal missionary support for the islands and that where this was offered it was primarily intended for the colonists and not for the indigenous population. The first chartered colony at Saint Christopher progressed without an organized religious contingent for ten years.[19] When the company was restructured with designs to expand the Antillean colonies into surrounding islands, Louis XIII and Richelieu recruited missionaries from the Capuchin and Dominican orders. Jesuits were later recruited for service on Martinique. Yet the missionary ranks were severely decimated by the ills of the crossing and the various afflictions of arrival, exacerbated by faulty planning and a lack of supplies. The case of the Dominicans in Guadeloupe was the most highly publicized disaster; of the missionaries who traveled there at the inception of the colony between 1635 and 1640, half died within a few years, and several others returned complaining of the unbearable conditions and lack of aid. Writing in 1654, Father Du Tertre expressed shock that any missionaries survived there at all: "I am shocked a thousand times over that in the last nineteen years, of the eleven missionaries who have resided there for however brief a stay, only seven have died, considering the misfortunes that we have had to endure."[20] When replacements were not forthcoming, the islands would remain with few spiritual laborers for years on end. The burden of policing the French settlers, who were frequently accused of being libertines, heretics, and protestants, was the primary concern, as Jacques Bouton, a founder of the Jesuit mission in Martinique, lamented: "It is no less necessary, and pleasing to God, to prevent former Christians from becoming Savages than to entice Savages into becoming Christians."[21]

Perhaps the most important barrier to the evangelical project was the nature of the colonization itself: the French did not conquer the Caribs, but they took Carib land, a fact that led to irrepressible wars of resistance led by Caribs, who took refuge in Dominica and Saint-Vincent from the 1630s through the 1650s. The work of the mission thus always required the crossing of a territorial border, which was often opposed by colonial governors concerned about the risk of violence. Hence suspicion and discord arose between some missionaries and the secular leadership on the islands. The Dominican Mathias DuPuis, for one, looked angrily on governors who prohibited the work of evangelization: "They betray the glory of the blood of the son of God, since they prevent it from being laid on the poor souls who groan under the devil's tyranny."[22] The Catholic mission thus functioned sporadically, upheld by exceptionally courageous priests such as Raymond Breton, who spent years on end alone within Carib communities.

Jean-Baptiste Du Tertre: Writing Violence

In addition to ministering to colonists and Christianizing the natives, missionaries in the seventeenth-century Caribbean were responsible for publicizing colonialism and the evangelical mission for a metropolitan readership. This included company directors, shareholders, officers of the royal administration, religious superiors, and any members of the public enticed by the prospect of emigrating to the New World.[23] It is perhaps ironic that those whose mission entailed the establishment of reciprocity and peaceful ties with natives would be charged with telling the history of missionary failure, colonial violence, and the emergence of a militarized border between the French and the Caribs. In so doing, missionaries created the foundational stories of French colonial origins that would shape contemporary attitudes toward Caribs as well as future perceptions of the roots of conflict between the two groups.

Especially noteworthy in this regard is Jean-Baptiste Du Tertre, the author of two of the earliest general histories of the French Caribbean. Born in Calais in 1610, Du Tertre served in the Dutch army and navy before being ordained as a Dominican in 1635. That same year, four Dominican missionaries, including Raymond Breton, departed for Guadeloupe at the request of Richelieu and members of the new Company of the Islands of America. Due to the ill preparedness of the expedition, disease, and famine, only Father Breton remained after five years. To relieve him, Du Tertre traveled to Guadeloupe in 1640 with two other missionaries during that island's grueling war with the Indians. Returning briefly to France in 1642 to request aid for the mission, Du Tertre remained in Guadeloupe until political differences with the governor forced him to leave in 1647. Back in France, he circulated his historical manuscript among friends and supporters such as the illustrious Achilles de Harlay, chief financial administrator of the company and longtime counselor to the king. According to his preface of 1654, Du Tertre resolved to publish the work following the mysterious disappearance of one early draft. His *Histoire générale des isles de Christophe, de la Guadeloupe, et le Martinique et autres* appeared in 1654 (see figure 3). Four years later César de Rochefort's *Histoire naturelle et morale des iles Antilles de l'Amérique* was published anonymously in Rotterdam and thereafter carried the stigma of plagiarism from Du Tertre's lost copy. Accusing Rochefort of inauthenticity and misrepresentation, Du Tertre produced an expanded second edition of his work based on research carried out during his final visit to the colonies in 1656–57. Published from 1667 to 1671, the *Histoire générale des Antilles habitées par les François* became a reference for all subsequent historians of the French Caribbean.[24]

Du Tertre's colonial historiography is defined both by its scope and methodological rigor. Whereas previous writers had published partial accounts of historical events or missionary projects on single islands, Du Tertre covered

3. Frontispiece, Jean-Baptiste Du Tertre, *Histoire générale des Antilles habitées par les François*, Paris, 1667–71. (Reproduced courtesy of the McCormick Library of Special Collections, Northwestern University Library.)

all islands under French control using a range of sources including unpublished manuscripts, ecclesiastical and state records, official correspondence, and private memoirs. Until the mid–twentieth century, the *Histoire générale des Antilles habitées des François* was considered by some scholars to be the most authoritative history available of the early French Caribbean. Yet the earlier historical narrative is arguably more interesting on the level of style and narrative. The 1654 edition conformed to the genre of humanist history, which deemphasized historical precision in favor of rhetorical and thematic embellishment. As in a novel, humanist history illustrated the motivations of typed characters, thus presenting history as a basis for moral instruction.[25] Du Tertre's choice of genre was well suited to the task of representing for the first time the emergence of the border of violence between the French and the Caribs. Refusing to hide the extent of colonial crimes and misfortunes, the author promised instead to provide "a complete account of all that is commendable there without any exaggeration and of all the misdeeds without concealment, which is a rather rare thing in the majority of Authors who have written about the Americas until now."[26] What is fascinating is that Du Tertre managed to reconcile a story of French colonial abuses and missionary failure with a procolonial, promissionary stance by telling history like a morality tale in which the French colonists are challenged, judged, and disciplined by the deity whom they serve. Rather than being a blight on French memory, the history of territorial warfare and suffering is cast as a process of sin, repentance, and redemption whereby French settlers show themselves worthy of being God's chosen people in the New World.

What is immediately apparent from Du Tertre's text is the legitimizing power of the Christian mission for the history of French colonialism. The author justifies the French contestation of Spanish territorial rights to the New World as divine retribution against the Spaniards, who had savagely perverted their evangelical mission: "God inspired the French to inhabit such a rich part of the world, which He seems to have denied to this ambitious nation that has shown itself unworthy of it due to the horrible cruelties it has visited upon the Indians" (3). Du Tertre's providential narrative is informed by the writings of a fellow Dominican friar, Bartolomé de Las Casas, who a century earlier had denounced the Spanish for allegedly massacring Indians in the New World. Throughout the sixteenth and seventeenth centuries, rival Europeans popularized what became known as the Black Legend, a propaganda campaign that charged Spain with the decimation of the Indians and rejected the exclusivity of Spanish rights to the New World.[27] Yet, as Du Tertre himself acknowledges, the French tenure in the Caribbean was not without massacre and barbarism. The difference, he contends, is that the French have been duly punished: "God behaved toward the French as he had toward the Israelites in the desert, leaving not a single crime unpunished. For, it is certain that all those who have soaked their hands in the blood of these poor innocents have expiated their massacre through the loss of their lives or their possessions" (4). In evoking the Old Testament as an allegory for the ultimate justice of colonialism, Du Tertre relies on the notion of expiation, according to which colonial history is a trial between God and his people, who pay a heavy price for barbarous acts. Likewise, the author portrays the immense adversity experienced by arriving settlers as tribulations exacted by an angry deity.

Du Tertre divides his history into three main chapters, each telling the story of one of the first three colonies at Saint Christopher, Guadeloupe, and Martinique. Nowhere is the logic of expiation more apparent than in the case of Guadeloupe. This island was settled by two entrepreneurs, Charles Liénard Sieur de l'Olive and Jean Duplessis, who in 1635 received commissions directly from Richelieu to found a colony there. From the beginning, the expedition encountered huge difficulties, which threatened the very survival of the colony. Du Tertre explains that, having neglected to stop at the populous English colony of Barbados to take on provisions, they arrived in Guadeloupe having only a two months' supply of food. The ensuing famine greatly contributed to the misery of the indentured servants, already oppressed by the backbreaking and insalubrious labor of clearing land in a foreign climate under the command of ruthless masters. In Du Tertre's account, what might have relieved the settlers' hunger was trade with the indigenous people, whom he calls "savages" and who generously supplied the French with island fish and produce when they came to trade. These ties are destroyed, however, by French insecurities, stoked by their jealousy of the Indian bounty. When a skirmish leads to the cessation of Carib visits, the now desperate colonists conceive a plan to wipe them out: "In one word, they concluded that it was necessary to kill all the Savages, take their women and children, and seize their possessions" (37).

Du Tertre's story draws on two previous Dominican accounts of the settlement of Guadeloupe, each of which emphasized the role of French jealousy and starvation in precipitating the offensive against the Caribs.[28] He follows most closely the manuscript relation of Raymond Breton, who witnessed these events and directly opposed the principal proponent of massacre, Sieur de l'Olive. In Du Tertre's account, L'Olive is the prototype of the barbaric conquistador, who, having seized power after the death of Du

Plessis, galvanizes an army of settlers in pursuit of Carib gardens. Suspicious of French intentions, the Caribs evacuate their homes in advance, burning their plantations behind them. This leaves L'Olive without an outlet for his aggression until he encounters an old Carib man and his sons, the last to evacuate the area. When one son defies L'Olive's demand to call back fleeing Carib women, a scene of hyperbolic cruelty ensues: "Monsieur de L'Olive was so incensed that he had the old man tied up and put in his row boat with one of his sons, whom they stabbed immediately in his presence. Then, they turned to the father, who had been left stunned by such horrible cruelty, and after stabbing him all over his body with their knives and swords, they threw him all tied up into the sea head first. But, as this good man was in robust health for his age he still made some feeble attempts to save himself, untied one hand and swam toward the boat begging for mercy. . . . Instead of helping him, and with unbelievable cruelty and unstoppable rage, they struck him over the head with the oars" (42). Here the representation of colonial rage is reinforced through the idea of the *bon sauvage*. The old man, described as "more than one hundred and twenty years old," stands as a stereotypical symbol of the robust health and longevity of the Caribs so admired by Europeans. His slaughter at the hands of the French dramatizes the battered sovereignty of a proud and ancient people, savagely massacred in the presence of their young by putatively "civilized" foes. Du Tertre writes that the French "returned from Fort Saint Peter, their hands red with the blood of these innocents, and their souls blackened by this massacre" (44).

This is neither the first nor the worst French massacre of Caribs re-counted in Du Tertre's history. A more substantial event takes place in Saint Christopher, where the French, acting, the reader is told, on an advance warning of pending Carib aggression, carry out a devastating attack: "In one single night they stabbed them all while they were sleeping in their beds, ex-cepting none but some of the more beautiful of the women to assuage their brutal passions" (7). In the case of Guadeloupe, however, the French pay for their accumulated crimes through a prolonged and intense conflict with Caribs. Du Tertre's critique of colonial savagery at Guadeloupe sets up the Indians as legitimate avengers in a divine plan to punish the French for colo-nial sin: "God, who leaves nothing unpunished, soon began to make them feel the punishment called for by such crimes, for the savages resolved to make war against our inhabitants and to avenge by the venom of their arrows the outrages that they had received from them" (45). From the neighboring island of Dominica, the Caribs wage a four-year guerrilla war that leaves scores of French settlers dead or wounded. Significantly, the author portrays this show of force not as an attempt to contest the French incursion but rather as a punishment designed to force the colonist's atonement before the Christian God. Invoking the deity as a historical personage, Du Tertre casts the Caribs as divine agents exacting a hefty penalty for French injustice.

Throughout the hostilities with the Caribs, the narrator's attention remains focused on the French, who are portrayed as paying for their sins with an almost unspeakable decline of body and soul: "The famine was so severe that we saw some of them eating the excrement of their fellows and others feeding on grass like beasts. Sometimes they wandered off into the forest to find something to eat and gave up their souls for lack of food. We found a number of them eaten by dogs, who were as famished as their masters, and perhaps more so" (47–48). Du Tertre unflinchingly depicts the civilized colonizer's nearly total deterioration into bestiality. Suffering a moral and physical abjection of almost unrepresentable proportions, the French are preyed on by animals. With mortality rates at 75 percent, some willingly flee to the Indians, where they are well treated. In the end, the desolation of the community is reflected in the symbolic decline of its commander, L'Olive, who falls ill, struck with insanity and blindness. Yet, remarkably, the pitiful destitution to which the colonists are reduced is ultimately assuaged by the promise of expiation. L'Olive's dignity is restored by divine grace, as he repents and is redeemed on his deathbed. His redemption stands as an example of God's forgiveness of the community of chosen ones, who have paid for their sins: "So many misfortunes were more than sufficient to lift the hearts and eyes of our French men towards the one who only punishes so that his mercy may be implored" (49). War with the natives thus serves to solidify further the French pact with their Christian God. The arrival of a new governor, Aubert, brings about new diplomatic efforts with the natives, and a peace is declared in 1640. For Du Tertre, the colony's survival is proof of heavenly mercy and the ultimate justice of the colonial mission: "It was reestablished from its own ruins against all hope" (2).

For all the care Du Tertre takes in rationalizing French crimes as duly expiated through a process of prolonged warfare and suffering, the text nonetheless exhibits considerable anxiety about the question of massacre, anxiety that cannot be entirely contained by the providential narrative of history. Massacre, one of the most recurrent themes in the text, is the crime of crimes, and its expiation requires suffering and death. As we have seen, Du Tertre attributes the decline of Spanish legitimacy in the colonies to their ruthless massacre of native peoples. Everywhere in this text, the border between French and Caribs is haunted by the memory of massacre, a fact with particular importance for the work of the mission. In a later chapter on "savage manners," Du Tertre confesses that the Caribs' memory of massacre constitutes the most serious impediment to evangelization. This memory lives on in the oldest among them—"eyewitnesses of the extreme cruelties that the Christians visited upon them and their fathers"—and leads Caribs to detest the very word *Christian*: "They hold the name 'Christian' in such horror that it is the most atrocious reproach that they can make to another man" (460).[29] Evidently, a history of massacre also informed the French missionary view of Caribs. Describing the commission given by Richelieu to the Dominican religious order to supply the colony of Guadeloupe with missionaries, Du Tertre recognizes those of his order who had ministered to the Caribs on that island since the time of the discoveries. Quoting a panegyric in Latin from the Dominican archives, he mentions a dozen missionaries, most of whom are of Castilian descent, who in his words "have soaked the soil of Guadeloupe with the blood they spilt in preaching the Gospel to the Barbarians living there" (29). The most important single massacre dates from 1604, when six priests were killed "by arrow wounds" (30).

Du Tertre himself expresses profound regret over the failure of evangelization: "We asked God for nothing with greater earnestness and we wished for nothing else more fervently as it was what our mission intended" (61). The only purely evangelical expedition recounted in the text is nearly impeded by the secular leadership. After peace is declared in Guadeloupe, the Father de la Mare, superior of the Dominicans, plans to send Raymond Breton and another missionary to Dominica to "diligently find out and inquire into what was left to do among the Savages" (63). When the governor general forbids the visit, fearful that "an accident could befall them which could renew the hostilities," the missionaries proceed covertly. Du Tertre represents them as heroes persevering amid threats of impending destruction: "[The devil] spoke to the Savages through the mouths of their *Rioches* (which are a kind of marmoset made of cotton) and gave them the false impression that the French had no other intention than to subject them to the same treatment that they had inflicted on the rest of the islands, where these foreign nations always insinuated themselves modestly, and having increased in numbers little by little, robbed them of their possessions, driven them away from their patrimony, and deprived them of their land" (63). In the end, the missionaries are saved by a Carib leader, who dissuades his people from their aggression. Yet Du Tertre's account of Amerindian dispossession resounds strongly with his earlier critique of Spain's historic mistreatment of Amerindians, which was repeated, he alleges, in important ways by the French. The theme of massacre and dispossession thus occupies the textual unconscious of Du Tertre's history as a repressed narrative of French colonialism in the Caribbean.

This is particularly apparent when Du Tertre invokes the devil to explain Carib apprehensions regarding the French settlers.[30] Despite Du Tertre's sensitivity to the plight of the Caribs, he explains their fear of massacre not as a rational response to past historical events but as a diabolical ruse designed to turn them against the Christians. Thus, in Saint Christopher the Caribs are inspired by the "spirit of lies" to believe that "those foreign nations had only landed on the Island in order to massacre them cruelly, as they had killed their ancestors in all the lands that they occupy" (6). They immediately formulate a plan to get rid of the French. Ironically, however, Du Tertre's historical plot supports the putatively diabolical prediction, for the Carib threat becomes the colonists' pretext for mass murder, thus clearing the way for the settlement of the island. Later, desperate French settlers in Guadeloupe vow to massacre the Caribs and take their food, this time without any threat of impending aggression. If the irony appears to be lost on Du Tertre, it is because the author desperately needs the narrative of diabolical intervention to reject a more damning interpretation of French Caribbean history, that is, that there is little difference, ultimately, between the French and other European colonizers where the Caribs are concerned. Despite the grandest principles of missionary ideology, the commercial aims and violent methods of French colonialism posed a fundamental threat to its fulfillment.

There is one point in the narrative where this possibility unabashedly comes to light. Neither God nor the devil makes an appearance in the last chapter on the settlement of Martinique except as a conceit. After recounting the relative success of settlers in avoiding the mistakes of the past regarding provisions and defense, the author blames Indian intolerance for the disruption of the peace. In putative self-defense, colonists unload their superior artillery on an army of Caribs, which Du Tertre describes as producing "such an uncommon carnage of these Savages that these poor people fled, believing that all the Maboyas of France had come out of the mouths of the cannons to destroy them. Since that time they have not dared to attack the French" (72). With the Gods of France raining terror on the Indians, the colonists seize their best lands and begin extensive settlement of the island.

Ethnography and Carib Identity at the Border

By the 1640s, the French and the Caribs were thus living in a border zone, a space marked by boundaries between ethnic or national groups. These borders had emerged out of a history of violence, massacre, and peacemaking whereby Europeans established permanent colonies in the Caribbean. Martinique, with its borderline down the middle, was exceptional in this respect. The other borders were marked by the sea as Europeans claimed entire islands for their own domains. For most of the seventeenth century, Dominica and Saint-Vincent belonged to the Caribs.[31] The remaining islands in the eastern Caribbean chain were targeted for colonization by the French, English, and Dutch, such that by the end of the seventeenth century the indigenous peoples had been almost entirely eliminated from the region. For Du Tertre, the Carib-French border zone was so fraught with violence and the memory of violence that it required a providential narrative of expiation in order to make it compatible with the ideology of missionary colonialism. What is fascinating is the formative impact that the border had on the kinds of ethnographic information produced about Caribs in French texts, as well as on the evolving identity of the people so described.

Narratives from the seventeenth-century French colonization of the Antilles are the sources on "Island Caribs" (distinct from the Caribs of South America) most highly praised by anthropologists and ethnohistorians. Published and manuscript journals, relations, histories, and descriptions by Raymond Breton, Jean-Baptiste Du Tertre, and César de Rochefort constitute the core of an ethnographic corpus enhanced by the narratives of a score of lesser-known travelers such as Bouton, Pelleprat, Dupuis, and La Borde. Although they sometimes followed and incorporated the observations of Spanish historians such as Oviedo, Herrera, and Acosta, French authors provided unusually rich and detailed impressions of the Amerindian cultures they encountered. Anthropologist Neil Whitehead has called the French missionaries pioneers in ethnographic writing on Caribs, and Louis Allaire has stressed the primacy of French sources: "Essentially, what anthropologists and historians know today of Island Carib culture, language, and society is based almost entirely on these documents."[32]

Still, the French ethnographic corpus has not escaped the charge, leveled against much European colonial writing, of "inventing" the native Caribbean, either by projecting a familiar European cultural imaginary onto an unfamiliar cultural reality or by defining resistant indigenous peoples in ways that would justify their unhindered conquest by European colonial powers.[33] By questioning the rhetorical and narrative strategies through which ethnography constructed a domain of truth about its object, literary scholars in particular have challenged the referentiality of early modern colonial narratives.[34] Nowhere has the truth value of European accounts been more suspect than in colonial reports of Carib origins and ethnic differences in the Caribbean prior to European intervention. As we have seen, Christopher Columbus first described the native Caribbean in terms of two warring tribes, one tractable and the other intractable. In time, this picture evolved into a historical explanation of the origins of the "Carib" peoples that portrayed them as conquerors of a more peaceful group. For Peter Hulme, the dualist picture of the native Caribbean justified the European colonizers as "gallantly and unselfseekingly taking upon themselves the task of protecting the docile by removing the intruders."[35] I would argue that, rather than implicitly allying colonists with the more peaceful natives, French stories of Carib origins offer striking allegories of the colonial border zone itself. French ethnographers discredited their own colonial foes by projecting onto them the very ambitions of conquest they otherwise denied in the French. In this sense, colonial discourse on the native Caribbean may be read as a projection of French anxiety about the border of violence between the French and the Caribs.

One of the most unusual accounts of Carib origins was produced by César de Rochefort, author of the anonymously published *Histoire naturelle et morale des iles Antilles de l'Amérique* (1658; see figure 4).[36] Rochefort was a French protestant minister who traveled to the Antilles in the 1640s and based much of his book on memoirs supplied to him by contemporary travelers and the governor general, Poincy.[37] His controversial story of Carib origins draws on the account of an English traveler named Bristock, who traced this group to the Florida plains. The story begins with a restless people called the Cofachite, who desire the fertile lands of their southern neighbors, the Apalachites. In a successful military offensive, they seize territory at the foot of the Appalachian mountains and negotiate a peaceful coexistence with the Apalachites, who share their land and resources, granting the Cofachites full rights as members of the Appalachian kingdom on the condition that they recognize their sovereign and embrace his solar religion. Given the name Caraïbe, which supposedly means "sudden arrival," "foreigner," or "valiant man" in the Appalachian language, the newcomers never wholly accept the sun worship required of them by the treaty.[38] Offended by this deceit, the Appalachian priests devise an alternative strategy to seduce the Caribs into full submission. They invite the Caribs to partici-

4. Frontispiece, César de Rochefort, *Histoire naturelle et morale des iles Antilles de l'Amérique*, Rotterdam, 1658. (Photograph courtesy of the Newberry Library.)

pate in a ceremony of feasts, celebrations, and gift giving accompanying a sun worship pilgrimage. From chief to commoner, all the Caribs are showered with presents and favors in a carnival of festivities and feasting. Only after the Apalachites have given over almost all of their wealth do they again invite the Caribs to either fully adopt their religion and recognize their sovereign rule or face military action. Some Caribs, won over by the generosity of their hosts, acquiesce and assimilate fully to Appalachian political and spiritual authority. Those in the leadership, however, balk at the thought of submitting to foreign rule and religion: "[They] said . . . that they did not wish to disgrace their reputation and the glory of all their previous victories by submitting to a shameful peace, which would make them subjects of the Appalachians under the pretext of religion. They said that they were born free and left the peace of their births and brought themselves to a better land by the valor of their arms and that they had to defend forever this precious liberty and sacrifice their own blood for it, if necessary."[39] Unwilling to be lured into submission by the material largesse of Appalachian priests, these Caribs split from their brethren and hold on to their freedom, announced as an inalienable truth of character. Migrating south, they become the original inhabitants of some vacant islands in the Caribbean Sea.

Rochefort's thesis was criticized by many of his contemporaries and has been discounted by modern research.[40] However, the story inscribes the defining stereotype of the native Island Carib as fiercely independent and impervious to missionary invitations. In addition, this narrative of Carib origins exposes the gift as a ruse of power designed to manipulate an adversary. While professing disinterested generosity, the Apalachites' gift of faith and material rewards communicates the desire of the giver for something even more valuable than the thing offered—total submission to Apalachite political and spiritual authority. By underscoring the function of the gift in the exercise of proselytism, Rochefort's historical anecdote about Carib origins appears as an allegory of missionary colonialism. The story may also be read as an explanatory anecdote for the military intransigence and religious intractability that etched the Caribs in the imaginations of generations of European writers, missionaries, and travelers. Fearless colonizers on the move in search of more fertile lands, they are uncompromising before even the most lavish of bribes. Refusing to bow before a foreign god and king, they repudiate the debt entailed by material expressions of missionary desire and brace themselves for war, the unavoidable consequence of not returning the gift. This characterization presents as historical destiny the missionary failure in the French Caribbean and the colonial Americas more generally, upsetting in the process the founding fantasy of European colonialism.

The figuration of Caribs as colonizers was common in French stories of Carib origins. In general, Caribs were characterized by their reviled practice of anthropophagy and fierce, warlike demeanor in opposition to a more peaceful group, usually called the Arawak. In the most familiar and influential version of the story, the Caribs are said to have exterminated and cannibalized Arawakan men, taking their women as wives as they made their way up the island chain from South America.[41] This explanation was first offered by Raymond Breton in the highly influential manuscript most likely written with the Dominican superior, Father Jacquinot. The first chapter, "De l'origine et humeurs des Sauvages," recounts the Caribs' own story of a founding father, Callinago, who came to Dominica from the southern continent and populated the island with his family. Deeming this a "fable," Breton instead portrays the Caribs as ruthless colonizers from the continent who conquered the islands, taking peaceful mountain-dwelling peoples as their slaves: "Many Frenchmen believe that there were other inhabitants on these Islands before the Caribs and that they were driven away. This is based on the fact (a certainty according to the Savages) that on some islands there are still some of these people who have withdrawn into the mountains, are white like the French, and have long beards."[42] This conquest narrative of Carib origins portrays Caribs as themselves having questionable title to the lands from which they had been displaced by Christian colonization. Native oral testimony may well have been adjusted to accommodate the story, as evidenced from an important discrepancy between the two existing versions of the manuscripts. Whereas one version states, "Our Caribs say that according to a sure tradition among them they were the first to inhabit the islands and those who live in the mountains were their slaves," the other contains the correction, "that they killed the Arawaks, the first inhabitants of the Islands."[43] In the chapter on warfare, Breton describes the Arawaks as the Caribs' primary adversary: "They have an implacable hatred of the Arawaks . . . and eat the males and make the women into slaves."[44] With some slight variation, this is the story that appeared in missionary accounts by Pelleprat, Du Puis, and Du Tertre.[45]

Through the tropes of massacre and cannibalism, Breton projects onto the Caribs a particularly gruesome version of the history of conquest that so troubled French missionary efforts in the region.[46] Similarly, in descriptions of Carib warfare early colonial writers displaced the border of violence between the Caribs and the French onto the native Caribbean. Despite the fact that the French repeatedly battled the Caribs in the first decades of settlement, as is recounted in the historical narratives of colonial texts, colonial ethnographies of Carib warfare systematically privilege the Caribs' hostility toward other Amerindian nations. In Breton's chapter, "De leurs guerres, ennemys et armes," the Caribs' war harangues, guerrilla attacks, and cannibal feasts are reserved for the Arawaks, followed by the Spanish and the English.[47] Often, however, the repressed French adversary returns in the situations described. In Breton's story of Carib origins, the author describes the Arawak as being "white like the French," as though they are a foil for the French in the colonial unconscious. The Jesuit Jacques Bouton identifies the Caribs' primary enemy as the Calibis, even as he goes on to recount what are clearly French firearms and tactics: "They are in continual movement to escape the effects of the firearms and because they can see the lit fuse of our muskets, they easily avoid the fuses by throwing themselves to the ground . . . but they greatly fear our rifles because they cannot see them being lit and they say that it is the *maboïa*, that is, the devil, who sets fire to them."[48] Du Tertre rather conspicuously excludes the French from the Caribs' foes in his ethnographic narrative, as is clear from his account of the Caribs' scorch and burn strategy: "Finally the fire reaches the *Carbet*, in which their enemies (that is to say Savages and not Europeans) stay to be burned rather than to give themselves up to the mercy of those Anthropophages."[49] The only writers who diverge from this strategy of silencing are Rochefort and Chevillard. In his chapter "Des guerres des Caraibes," Rochefort privileges Carib-Arawak hostility but mentions the war in Grenada, which claimed hundreds of French and Carib lives.[50] Chevillard actually justifies Carib animosity toward the French, who he claims "took their land, killed their parents, and . . . massacred their friends."[51]

The priority French writers gave to intertribal animosity is in part an effect of their desire to represent the Caribs as they were prior to European intervention. Rochefort regretted the corrupting influence of Europeans, claiming that the most authentic Caribs were to be found in Saint-Vincent: "Among our Caribs, those who have had less contact with Europeans, such as those of Saint-Vincent, are more strict observers of their old customs than are, for example, those of Martinique or those of Dominica, who frequent us more often."[52] Yet the notion of native authenticity itself repressed the reality of the colonial border and the relation it instilled between natives and colonial powers. As Johannes Fabian has argued, by assigning to conquered populations a different *time* through rhetorical devices of sequencing and distancing colonial writers could avoid acknowledging the violence of displacement, as well as the extent to which the history of colonial contact irremediably impacted the indigenous peoples, thus destroying their putative "original state."[53] Indeed, as though to create the effect of cultural purity, colonial writers separated the historical narrative of French colonialism from the ethnographic chapters on "savage manners." In most texts, the two discourses differ significantly in their style and rhetoric; whereas history is written in the past tense and identifies specific actors and contexts, the ethnographic discourse is in the present tense and often omits details in favor of generalizations. In these chapters, French colonial writers privileged what they insisted were the Caribs' ancient rivalries, as opposed to the ongoing hostilities with the French. Essential to this picture of the native Caribbean was the battle between Caribs and Arawaks.

This dualist model of conflictual relations survived for more than three centuries, dominating the writings of the two most important modern anthropologists of the native Caribbean, Irving Rouse and Douglas Taylor. Most historians of the French Caribbean still accept its logic.[54] They do so based on the "proof" most often cited in support of the conquest thesis—the presence of a sex-based linguistic dimorphism among Island Caribs. French colonial ethnographers recorded that women and men spoke different languages, whose characteristics reflected different origins, and that there existed, furthermore, special registers for war harangues and other ritual speech.[55] The standard explanation of these differences is that a Kariña-speaking group from South America conquered an Arawakan-speaking group but kept their women, whose language was ultimately adopted by the offspring and the evolving society.[56] Remnants of the male Kariña language survived in some ritual speech and in the name of the group, Kallinago. Yet scholars have recently disputed this story of conquest and sexual possession. As Peter Hulme has argued, the dualist narrative of the native Caribbean in many ways perpetuates the original colonialist dichotomy between tractable and resistant populations, noble and ignoble savages, first applied to the indigenous populations by Columbus.[57] Ethnohistorians and anthropologists now cite numerous other plausible causes for the linguistic dimorphism, including the possibility that, as Neil Whitehead has argued, "the men's jargon was added to the total linguistic repertoire of the Island Carib during the process of deep social and cultural change and reorientation that the colonial system induced." In a fascinating hypothesis, Whitehead sees Island Carib identity itself as an "ideological event" related to a process of shared tribalization and militarization in response to the expanding European colonial states in the Caribbean and on the South American mainland.[58]

What is remarkable is the impact that colonial stereotyping had on the ethnic picture it set out to define. More than being a mere ideological falsification in the colonial narrative arsenal, the widely diffused stereotype of the fierce Carib shaped the self-definition of the indigenous people themselves, who gradually adopted the ethnic term *Carib*. Raymond Breton's *Dictionaire caraibe-françois* indicates that the word *Caraibe* (Carib) was a European linguistic construct, since the term is not contained within the Carib language volume. Rather, the self-ascriptions *Callínago/Calíponan* designate the indigenous peoples in their own language. Breton defines the male variant *Callínago* as follows: "This is the true name of our island Caribs. They are those cannibals and *Anthropophages* whom the Spanish complained so often that they could not vanquish, and who devoured a prodigious number of them and their allies."[59] The passage both acknowledges *Caraibe* to be a foreign term and clings to the very stereotypes that identify the people so defined as irrepressibly resistant barbarians. Yet the writings of Dominican missionaries contain numerous transcriptions of speaking natives identifying themselves as Caraibe.[60] Rochefort discussed the question at length in his *Histoire*, noting the particular pride with which indigenous peoples used the term: "Not only do all of these people call themselves Caraibe but in addition they glorify in it and turn it to their advantage."[61] Rochefort insisted that they adopted the term only when communicating with foreigners and vehemently refused to be identified by its corollary meanings of "savage," and "cannibal." What remained was the connotation of fearless valor: "They take great pleasure in being called Caraibe because this is a name which seems to them to be glorious, indicating their courage and their generosity."[62] To resolve the contradiction of a beleaguered people taking the name of their enemies, Rochefort concluded that the word must be Amerindian in origin. In so doing, he evaded the more compelling hypothesis of a border identity created in part by European colonizers and eventually appropriated by Caribs themselves as they launched an organized resistance against the expansion of permanent European settlements. It is as though Caribs drew inspiration from their reputation for indomitable independence, a reputation that in turn aided a process of ethnic consolidation in the region. Operable on both sides, Carib identity was a construction of the border zone. As such, we may consider this term to be the original word in the first pidgin language born of cross-cultural dialogue between Amerindians and Europeans in the New World.[63]

Thus far we have examined the impact of the border of violence on French perceptions of the indigenous population and on the relations between the two groups more generally. Yet the border of peace was equally if not more determinant of French-native relations than the border of blood. Consonant with Mauss's theory, peace was signified not merely by the cessation of hostilities but also by the crossing of borders through trade and other forms of exchange highly desired by both parties. According to most colonial histories, the four-year guerrilla war in Guadeloupe ended in a ritual of exchange when the French governor visited Dominica bearing gifts and invited the Caribs to come to Guadeloupe. As Du Tertre put it, the Caribs recommenced their "old visits, . . . not without great gain for the inhabitants because in addition to feeding almost the entire island with tortoises, pigs, lizards, cured fish, and the fruit of the region they brought a number of handsome tortoise shells, some beds made of cotton, and a great many small items from a booty that they had brought back from their defeat of the English, all of which they gave to us as trinkets."[64] Yet peacetime exchange involved not only commodities but also names and people. According to Breton, in Carib culture the name was a near sacred word, which could normally not be uttered in the presence of its holder.[65] To tell another one's name and to offer it for their taking was thus akin to offering one's greatest possession. Similarly, Rochefort attested that Caribs took the names of their hosts "as proof of their great affection and inviolable friendship."[66] Breton maintained that in the Carib language friendship and trade were expressed by the same word, a friend being defined as one with whom one is accustomed to trading.[67] The exchange of names thus signified the reestablishment of material exchanges between the French and the Caribs. The French also asked for Carib children as "hostages," a request that was supposedly granted by Caribs on the condition of reciprocity.[68]

If Caribs often visited the French islands in times of peace, the opposite was also true, to judge from enthusiastic reports of Carib hospitality toward the French (see figure 5). Pacifique de Provins, a Capuchin priest who toured Dominica in 1645, gave this account of his reception: "We stayed fifteen days . . . visiting the whole length of the island, coming ashore every day and conversing with the savages either in the boat (where they came to see us in crowds, bringing all sorts of fruits and possessions and where they exchanged a number of objects with the men of my lord, the governor) or in

5. "Visite des sauvages aux François," in Du Tertre, *Histoire générale des Antilles habitées par les François*, Paris, 1667–71. (Reproduced courtesy of the McCormick Library of Special Collections, Northwestern University Library.)

their own houses where we ate and slept with them and were received with great compassion."[69] According to Rochefort, Caribs greeted friendly visitors in their boats, brought them safely to shore and on to the Carbet, or public square, to be welcomed by the whole community. After being offered a bed and island refreshments, guests were invited to an elaborate meal and tour of the village: "The Caribs lead you around in their homes and in their gardens; show you their arms, their curiosities, and their baubles; and offer gifts of fruit or some small crafts."[70]

In some cases, Carib generosity extended to intelligence on political or military matters. The French had the habit of cultivating privileged relations with various Carib chiefs so as to obtain information and favor in the event of conflict.[71] Bouton explains that in Martinique the French depended on a Carib named Pilote: "Pilot always had a particular affection for them, helping them when they were in need, giving them warning of the plans of other savages, and working for peace as much as he could. Some believe that without him the French would not have been able to house and maintain themselves on the island. He still continues these services, haranguing before the council of the savages on behalf of the French, and revealing to us the secrets of their assemblies."[72] According to Bouton, Pilot and the Caribs offered the French governor, Du Parquet, the ultimate form of hospitality, literally making him over as one of their own: "They received him like they would a man of honor, painted his body, styled his hair in their manner, made him dance like them, and did everything they could to demonstrate their affection for him."[73]

Although colonial accounts are often laconic regarding the nature and impact of cultural interaction between the Caribs and the French, what is clear is that French colonists were forced by necessity to learn from Amerindians how to adapt to local conditions and produce food in the tropics.[74] In the first edition of his history, Du Tertre wrote of the stranded Frenchmen on the island of Saint Christopher, who prior to D'Esnambuc's arrival resided in "great peace" with the "Savages," "living upon the provisions which they freely furnished them."[75] A similar acculturation occurred in the arena of material culture, to judge from Father Bouton's account of Martinique in the first five years: "Due partly to the poverty of the settlers [*habitants*], partly to the lack of craftsmen, and . . . the lack of necessity to better cover oneself . . . we neglected these commodities in order to content ourselves with huts, in the manner of the Savages, made of reeds or wooden stakes and covered with palm tree leaves, reeds, and other things."[76] In the early years, the French appear thus as apprentices of the Caribs in island lifestyles and agriculture. Bouton described the lopsided nature of this dependency: "Our savage Caribs live in comfort without needing to go amongst the French to seek their assistance, or to ask them to come live with them. They say that it is we who are in need of them, since we have come into their lands."[77] According to narrative sources, the French used Carib beds and handicrafts; produced and ate Carib foods such as manioc, cassava bread, and various plants, fish, and crustaceans; drank the Carib brew, *oüicou*; adopted Carib agricultural and cooking methods; and relied on some Carib antidotes for island illnesses.[78] In exchange for such provisions, the Caribs gained access to European products that were useful in traditional agriculture and the construction of canoes. By the time the French established colonies in the Caribbean, the Caribs had become reliant on the Spanish trade in metal manufactures such as tools, knives, and axes, as well as alcohol, all of which they later obtained from the French along with some clothing and weaponry. In addition, colonial writers repeatedly describe the exchange of inexpensive glass beads, mirrors, and the like, what the French called *des bagatelles* (trifles). The French tried hard but failed to fabricate a rare metal from the continent called *calloücouli*, which was treasured by Indians for its luster, purity, and resistance to rust.[79]

Remarkably, however, despite the various secular contexts in which peacetime exchange occurred, representations of this exchange were often determined by the writers' experience of missionary failure. Missionaries were the most fervent advocates for peace between the French and the natives, since only in peacetime could the ideological justification for colonialism be enacted and souls saved. For Chevillard, a Dominican missionary to Guadeloupe, peace was "the only way to convert these wretched Idolators and the sole means to work amongst them in their lands for their salvation."[80] Here peace is literally figured as a passage across the border into the territory of the other. Yet, if the border of peace held the most promise for missionary work, it was also the true space of missionary failure. Missionaries themselves offered several reasons for their lack of success, both material and political. Missing among them, however, is an account of the tenuous relation between evangelization and practices of commercial exchange. What is, however, apparent from the narrative record is that not only was missionary ideology predicated on an idea of reciprocity but the missionaries themselves relied on structures of trade between the French and the Caribs to perform the work of conversion.

Missionaries often described their own practice in the very language of exchange and mercantilism that governed secular ventures in the colonies.

After spending two months in Martinique in 1640, Father Bouton envisioned profits for his mission: "If the merchants can harvest temporal commodities from this island and others there may be hope for a triple harvest for those who deal in souls [*font le negoce des ames*]."[81] The caveat was that the priest would restrict his efforts to ministering to wayward French, whom he claimed were at risk of falling victim to savage ways. Father Pelleprat offered rosier claims of missionary success but suggested that his converts were mainly African slaves. He nonetheless described the role of gifts in the work of conversion: "We use every means to win them over to God. . . . We insinuate ourselves in their minds by giving presents; an *Agnus Dei*, an image, or a medallion are sometimes more effective than a long sermon."[82] Either by design or by necessity, missionaries were drawn into similar dealings with the Caribs. They used European goods as material representations of the kingdom of God and as evidence of the glory of the Christian nation, France, and its houses of worship. Most importantly, material objects were instrumental as enticements for the unbelieving. The trouble came in the confusion of different codes of valuation between the commercial and spiritual, on one hand, and the French and Caribs on the other.

Ultimately, the interaction of spiritual work with material exchange posed problems for the missionary endeavor, a fact that is clear from the various meanings attached to the material objects in circulation and to the Caribs who possessed them. For the anthropologist William Pietz, cross-cultural exchange involves precisely this entanglement of incompatible systems of value through which objects are invested with conflicting meanings.[83] In colonial narratives, missionary failure often appears as a breakdown of reciprocity, whereby the material gifts do not yield the desired spiritual return. Natives do not so much refuse the faith as feign acceptance of Catholic habits and beliefs in order to reap the material reward of the gift or, in Du Tertre's words, "take from us what they need. . . . No Savage who receives the baptism in exchange for a small knife or some other trinket will hesitate to scorn this beloved sacrament if we refuse him the slightest thing."[84] In his historical narrative, the author recalls a disappointing encounter with a Carib during the exchange rituals marking the end of the long war at Guadeloupe: "The first of the Savages who set foot on land made straight for me as if he had known me for a long time and, taking my hand, he made a sign of the cross on my sleeve and kissed it several times. He asked me in Spanish for a rosary and when I inquired as to what he wished to do with it, he responded that he wanted to pray to God; although, in fact, he had no other intention than to wear it around his neck . . . and parade about in it." [85] Here the rosary as decorous ornament straddles two systems of value, one spiritual and the other material. For the missionary, the Indian's mimicry signifies a deceitful profanation of the symbolic worth of a religious object of worship. The author links the incident to the frequency of "converted" Caribs' return to their own ways following from an *excess* of freedom, intractable even by means of slavery.

Yet, many writers remarked that natives adopted European clothing to signal respect and fidelity to French authority. Telling the same story of the Carib man who approached Du Tertre, Rochefort notes that he wore a habit when visiting the governor of Guadeloupe "to make himself more commendable." [86] Similarly, Father Bouton described Pilot's habit of wearing a hat when calling on the governor, "to show that he loved and esteemed the French." [87] In his second edition's ethnographic chapters, Du Tertre radicalized this theme of submissive mimicry, representing natives as subordinated to the French due to their materialism and covetous attachment to European commodities. Du Tertre has been a major reference in debates about the noble savage idea in French literature. Gilbert Chinard credited him with outlining the rudiments of natural savage virtue, showing the Indians great sympathy despite the fact that his evangelical mission among them failed. [88] In fact, only a partial reading of his chapter "Des Sauvages en général" would give this impression. Although Du Tertre champions natural Indian virtues as superior to the sins of the unrepentant colonists, he greatly depreciates the Carib character as demonstrated in their contacts with Europeans. If anything, Du Tertre's originality thus lies in his clever *subversion* of the bon sauvage trope, a fact that must be placed in the context of his own experience of failed missionary exchange. By portraying natives as essentially corrupted by the material objects they attempt to appropriate or mimic, Du Tertre represents exchange as a form of peaceful conquest that brings about the fall of natural man.

The author initially lauds the tropical paradise and the peoples within it. Rather than the dry, desolate, and overheated wasteland deemed uninhabitable by medieval cosmology, the torrid zone is the theater of man's original innocence and perfection. Wishing to usher his readers into the age of transatlantic travel, Du Tertre refutes the myth of the savage brute bound up in fantastic images from Mediterranean teratology. The New World holds no such monstrous race but rather reasonable men who may even surpass those of the Old in natural dignity and virtue. They enjoy perfect freedom and equality, having no distinctions of superiority or private property among them. They scorn frivolity and wear no clothing. The essential virtue of the

Indian shines through in his flawless physique: an attractive body, strong, well-proportioned, and robust. Indian male beauty seemingly exemplifies the physical ideals of the colonizer himself. Wrinkles and gray hairs are scarce, even among the oldest of them, who reach 120 years of age. Phenotypic difference from a European standard is explained as an effect not of nature but of culture. The image of the native is thus resolutely consonant with the ideal European self, with one exception: "Only their leathery coloring distinguishes them from us; for their skin is tawny like the color of olives, and even the whites of their eyes contain this color."[89]

This positive description destabilizes received notions of savagery and alludes instead to an Edenic innocence. In a striking illustration accompanying the second edition, an Indian couple appears under a papaya tree with ripe fruit hanging deliciously within their reach (see figure 6). The male is adorned with bows and arrows and carries a decorated staff, while the woman is dressed in a beaded belt, necklaces, and ornamental bands around the arms and knees. She performs a gesture of modesty by covering her privates with a leafy branch. Gazing at her partner, the woman reaches out her hand, curiously empty below the voluptuous fruits on the tree. The allusion to the tree of knowledge cannot be missed. Yet, in Du Tertre's colonial imaginary, Indian woman is not a temptress, a fact that suggests a lack of iniquity among natives generally. This scene of Edenic innocence implies naive vulnerability and the risk of corruption from without, precisely through European intervention. Du Tertre's biblical subtext meets colonial history by inscribing the colonial encounter as the fall of savage man: "[The Savages] reason well and with as much subtlety as is possible for those who have no concept of writing and who have not been cultivated [polis] by the human sciences, which often fill us with malice, even as they refine us. I can truly say that if the Savages are more ignorant than us, they are much less vicious; in fact, they know no other malice than what the French teach them."[90] Central here is the familiar claim that interference with native "savagery" leads to its corruption into true savagery, and that the European subject is the source of this mutation.

Du Tertre thus subverts the topos of Christian conversion through which the European arrival in the New World was a means of *saving* the Indians. In this tropical paradise natives do not need the French and even find them ridiculous. Indians laugh at the European habit of taking a stroll, "which they consider to be one of the greatest stupidities that they have yet observed in us." Yet in a cunning reversal of the joke Du Tertre reinscribes a

6. Carib man and woman, in Jean-Baptiste Du Tertre, *Histoire générale des Antilles habitées par les François*, Paris, 1670–71. (Reproduced courtesy of the McCormick Library of Special Collections, Northwestern University Library.)

power imbalance between colonist and native. The trope of mimicry discredits native integrity, as it is through uncritical imitation that natives imbibe vice and the sin of pride: "They presume to stand up for their honor but they are only imitating us."[91] The author recounts one Indian's willing imitation of an ennobling accessory among colonists: the tie. According to Du Tertre, a native elder named Amichon was so impressed by this accessory that he adorned himself in the same way. But, finding only a piece of a canoe sail to wrap around his neck, he became the object of derision for colonists and the narrator alike: "He came to Gaudeloupe in this attire, where he became a laughingstock to all those who saw him. I inquired in all seriousness why he was dressed in this fashion and he responded with a grave and serious tone that it was like his Friend du Parquet."[92] Du Tertre chooses his characters strategically; du Parquet, governor of Martinique, emerges as a praised model not only for the French on the island but also for the leadership of the Indian peoples from Dominica, the most important stronghold of native resistance in the region. The proper noun *Amichon* is steeped in symbolism, recalling a legend of native royalty. Elsewhere, the author reveals the word to be a geographical term for the place of origin of Indian chiefs. More significantly, Rochefort's text refers to Amichon as an honorable Indian captain chosen to lead an ambassadorial expedition to Guadeloupe to confirm the peace of 1640.[93]

If mimicry exposes natives to French mockery, Du Tertre reveals the true forbidden fruit to be the European commodity. Abandoning the tropes of the noble savage and the corrupt colonist, the author disparages natives for prostrating themselves before the lowliest of goods: "But in truth, whatever great wish they may have to be honorable, they have no point of honor that they will not trample in the interest of a little knife, a grain of crystal, a glass of wine, or some 'burning belly' [*brusle ventre*] (this is what they call spirits)."[94] Here Indian honor can be quantified and equated with the trivial value of material objects, which dupe and subjugate by virtue of the fact that they are coveted. Du Tertre represents a mimetic native, who, rather than deceiving missionaries through his strategic performance of conversion, dupes himself by coveting mystifying objects of European industry. In this way, the missionary transforms savage avarice into a self-destructive vulnerability. The source of missionary failure becomes the seed of colonial victory. The meaning of peacetime contact with the Caribs is encapsulated in the material fetish, which provokes the fall of natural man.

Raymond Breton: Language and Desire in the Border Zone

Aside from rituals of commerce, the most essential form of peacetime exchange between the French and the Caribs was communication itself, through languages both foreign and familiar. Critic Eric Cheyfitz's provocative claim that "translation was . . . the central act of European colonization and imperialism in the Americas" points to the efforts of Europeans to communicate with natives and learn from them all kinds of information about their environment and themselves, some of which ended up in the pages of colonial historiography.[95] Modern ethnography, too, has been described as a hermeneutic process of translation whereby the foreign is made familiar.[96] Yet, as many literary scholars have shown, colonial literature often effaced the communicative process of exchanging linguistic knowledge with non-Europeans, thus leaving an impression of unproblematic translatability and transparency of language.[97] This criticism is echoed by modern anthropologists, who challenge the discipline's suppression of the intersubjective dialogue and translation essential to ethnographic knowledge production. For Dennis Tedlock, anthropology is "ana-logical" because it involves the replacement of native discourse with that of the observer, as contrasted with the dialogical talking back and forth of the fieldwork situation. The fact that native speech was, until recently, almost taboo in academic ethnography suggests for Tedlock a reluctance to represent the relationship between the author and the peoples under study.[98]

Not surprisingly, most French colonial histories silenced natives as transmitters of knowledge. With the exception of references to Carib myths of origin, or, in the case of Rochefort, anticolonial passages culled from older European colonial sources, natives are more often than not presented as mute objects of an ethnographic gaze.[99] French colonial writers nonetheless fetishized native language by collecting, transcribing, and translating it in print. The phenomenon was generalized throughout the colonial Americas, to judge from the numerous vocabularies, dictionaries, and grammars of native languages published in Europe from the sixteenth century onward.[100] These two seemingly contradictory preoccupations — the ethnographic description of silenced native peoples and the translation of native speech and language — converge in the extraordinary bilingual dictionary published by the Dominican missionary Raymond Breton in 1665. Based on the author's experience among the Caribs of Dominica during the second decade of French colonization, the *Dictionaire caraïbe-françois, Meslé de quantité de remarques historiques pour l'esclaircissement de la langue* is commonly recognized as the most comprehensive linguistic description of the Carib language ever produced.[101] Yet, as its title suggests, Breton bridges the distinction between linguistic and cultural descriptions by organizing extensive ethnographic commentary on the basis of the Carib lexicon. Comprised of over six thousand words and phrases, the dictionary offers both literal translations and lengthy narrative explanations of particular words, ideas, and expressions within the context of Carib cultural practices and contacts with the French. In the many cases in which lexical equivalents do not exist, the narrative translations signal a certain untranslatable excess of Carib difference, thus giving the dictionary the quality of an encyclopedia of ethnographic information organized on the basis of the Carib lexicon.

It is possible to view Breton's dictionary as an example of the colonization of native languages whereby Europeans appropriated native symbolic systems and subsumed native knowledges in the interests of colonial hegemony and the Christian mission.[102] I would contend, however, that such a claim would foreclose a set of far more fascinating questions regarding the relation between the dictionary and the intercultural border zone from which it emerged. Based on the author's own experience of radical displacement, observation, and language learning among the Caribs, the dictionary attempts the transgression of boundaries and the bridging of linguistic and cultural difference. Yet, through its hybrid form (part dictionary, part ethnography) and varied content, Breton's dictionary represents and itself instantiates the dialogical complexities of the border zone, as well as the failures of the French language and colonial authority in the face of it. Especially significant here is the dictionary's incorporation of thousands of instances of Carib speech. By representing natives as speaking subjects in their own language, Breton explodes the univocal logic of colonial ethnography and exposes the multiple contexts of his interaction with the Caribs. In this respect, the dictionary may be read as a polyphonic text in which a diversity of voices constantly dialogizes the author's narrative authority, thus ironically undermining the epistemological pretension of ethnographic histories to reduce the other to the status of an object to be comprehended. This struggle extends to the explanatory sections that provide ethnographic, personal, and historical narratives on both French and native subjects. While various aspects of the dictionary inscribe native agency in the production of colonial knowledge, the most significant irony lies in the importance of language learning as a vehicle for missionary desire. The fetishism of Carib language was a product of Raymond Breton's fervent commitment to the evangelizing of the natives, a commitment easily displaced onto the goal of language acquisition itself.

The linguistic situation in the seventeenth-century Antilles was exceedingly complex. In addition to the different regional dialects introduced to the colonies by the French, the colonists used what Breton called a "language of the islands," which likely refers to a set of colonial neologisms and expressions traded between various groups. In the preface to the dictionary, Breton explains: "In the history I let my spelling slip and spoke like a Burgundian, such as I am, and I often used the language of the islands, although it offends the refinements of the French language" (xi). In the face of radical linguistic alterity and the task of translation, Breton here becomes conscious of his own linguistic specificity with respect to French, while at the same time suggesting the indispensability of the new colonial lexicon for the task of describing the Antilles. By this time, there also existed a pidgin trading language, which was used between transient Europeans and indigenous peoples of the Caribbean and may have overlapped somewhat with the island language. In his manuscripts, Breton described this as a "gibberish [baragouïn] or corrupted language that they spoke with us, which is Spanish, French and Carib all mixed together."[103] Rochefort relates that the Caribs knew this "bastardized language" as well as a simple variety of French.[104] Colonial writers commonly used these idioms to stereotype native speech in phrases signifying reciprocity or acquiescence. The Dominican missionary Father Chevillard, anxious to proclaim success in evangelization, represented Carib converts saying, "Father, . . . me want be good Christian for the great Captain, the God of the Christians."[105] In Du Tertre's portrayal of L'Olive's vicious attack on the old Carib man, the victim protests ruefully: "O Jacques, France very angry, be killing Caribs," a phrase that shows Spanish influence.[106] Yet, if these representations affirmed a notion of Caribs as feeble-minded mimic men, they only thinly masked the much greater linguistic ineptitude of the French colonists. By almost all accounts, Carib facility with the French language far outmatched French abilities in Carib languages. César de Rochefort praised the Carib language for its beauty and difficulty: "Whatever advantages our natural mental faculties or our pleasant pronunciation should afford us in pronouncing their language, they nevertheless learn ours more easily than we learn theirs."[107] Rochefort suggested, furthermore, that the Caribs resisted sharing their language with the French lest their war secrets be discovered.

The Carib language thus remained an elusive object of desire, especially for those missionaries who believed that true acceptance of Christianity was possible only in a language understood by the convert. Based on the idea of the gift of faith, and ritualized in the act of baptism, the ideology of Christian redemption was above all a fantasy of consummation with the native peoples, who were to be saved, perfected, and joined to the French social body. Breton was born in 1609 and began his formal religious training at the age of sixteen. He was chosen to accompany the first company-sponsored expedition to Guadeloupe in 1635. His three missionary companions returned to France in protest over the destitute conditions, leaving him to work alone among the hundreds of dying colonists for almost three years. Arriving with the second contingent of missionaries to Guadeloupe, Du Tertre gave a heartrending account of Breton's own suffering: "He was reduced to such misery that he was covered only by a tattered habit of linen-cloth. . . . He was in such great need of all things and suffered such grievous afflictions that I asked myself a thousand times how a mortal man could have endured so much without dying."[108] Following the conclusion of peace with the Caribs, the Dominican Pere de la Mare sent Breton to Dominica to pursue the work of evangelization. He lived intermittently among the Caribs over a period of twelve years, carrying out the extensive ethnographic and linguistic research that earned him great renown among all subsequent French missionaries to the Antilles. The results of Breton's investigations included the dictionary, followed in 1666 by the French-Carib version, a Carib translation of the Catechism, published in 1664, and a grammar, which appeared in 1667. Breton was also the source of the manuscript *Relation de l'île de la Guadeloupe*, which was signed by Father Jacquinot, as well as a shorter Latin version of the same.[109]

Du Tertre and Rochefort not only borrowed from Breton's manuscripts on all aspects of colonial history and island Carib cultures, but they mythologized his sojourn in Dominica as a heroic odyssey among a diabolical horde. Yet such an idealization was tempered by the acknowledgment of missionary failure in many French narratives from the colonial Caribbean. Writers invoked Breton as the most dedicated of Dominican missionaries, as though to repress the paltry results of Christian evangelism among natives generally. Likewise, Breton's obsession with the Carib language represents the sublimation of his own anxiety of missionary failure. In the preface to the dictionary, missionary success is less proclaimed than promised to future missionaries, as Breton viewed language as the last frontier of the souls of Indians. Addressing himself to his fellow Dominican priests, he writes: "You with these great talents, solid doctrine, and the burning zeal with which God favored you, me with these inanimate words . . . will set the souls of these poor infidels on fire, enlighten their minds with the truths of the Roman Catholic Church, and guide their lives according to the teachings of the Christian Gospel" (vii). For Breton, language acquisition and translation both replace and defer the dreamed-of conversion. Language becomes the vehicle through which to transmit Christian ideas, thus effectuating the incorporation of the other into the religion of the same. Yet, while conversion required that natives acculturate to French religious custom, the work of translation called for the French writer's total immersion in native culture. Breton founds his authority on this sacrificial experience of crossing borders, living with Caribs, and extricating their language through a delicate and painful negotiation: "You will never imagine the trouble I had in stealing [*dérober*] these words from the mouths of the Savages . . . , how much time I spent being a Savage among them, retired on a sandy shore, trying to win their good graces, and waiting for a rare and extraordinary moment of convenience" (vii). Language here is viewed as a treasured and protected object that may be acquired only by theft, such thievery being justified, Breton seems to suggest, by the greater gift of faith.

Breton's persona here approximates that of the participant observer in modern ethnography. As James Clifford explains: "Participant observation obliges its practitioners to experience, at a bodily as well as an intellectual level the vicissitudes of translation. It requires arduous language learning, some degree of direct involvement and conversation, and often a derangement of personal and cultural expectations."[110] Yet, if the missionary justifies his seizure of Carib language with an image of his own "becoming savage," this appropriation is effective only in the act of translation, where French words could be seen to overlay or stand for the Carib. To judge from much colonial discourse on Amerindian languages, the process of equivalence would not pose a challenge, for European languages were thought to be far superior to Amerindian ones in their lexical breadth and capacity to capture mood, abstract concepts, and metaphors.[111] Breton himself claims that this lack impeded his translation of the Catechism.[112] In the preface addressed to his fellow Dominican missionaries, the author appears apologetic for the apparent incommensurability between Carib and French: "This dictionary will not be filled as you might wish, for I can only communicate what the Savages taught me. They did not teach me what they did not know, and they do not know what they cannot see, and what they have no use for. They know how to say 'I understand,' 'I want,' but not 'understanding,' 'wish,' 'memory.' Nor do they have words for the other interior sensations, spiritual and celestial things, the liberal arts, most of the mechanical arts, and terms such as 'government' (*police*), 'justice,' 'religion,' 'vice,' 'virtue,' 'wealth,' 'poverty,' 'civility,' and 'incivility' . . . and other things which are unknown to them" (iv–v).

But the dictionary project challenged the lexical breadth of the colonizer's tongue, testing its ability to name elements in the contested territories of the Americas. Until Linnaeus proposed a universal vocabulary capable of classifying all known species on a comparative grid, it was the language of the indigenous peoples that held the desired totality of terms with which to apprehend the New World. The historian Jean Petitjean Roget estimates that by 1640 approximately one-third of European natural historical terminology was directly derived from the Carib language.[113] Breton's collection of Carib botanical and animal terminology amounts to more than double the number of species recorded in Rochefort's natural historical compilation. The particularities of the Carib language required, however, that Breton diverge from the model of the Latin dictionary, which organized nouns and infinitive verbs in alphabetical sequence. On one hand, Breton often classifies proper nouns under the heading of a general class, such as trees, fish, and island toponyms. Because all Carib verbs began with *A*, he classifies them by the imperative and third-person forms, contracted with various pronominal subjects. Breton explains that this format also served to illustrate the conjugation of various tenses of verbs in affirmative and negative forms (x). Thus, many phrases appear that, following from a common lexical element repeated in different examples, create the effect of a dialogic exchange between anonymous speakers.

While the author provides French lexical equivalents wherever possible, the dictionary is considerably augmented by what he calls "historical" discourse which provides extensive commentary on Carib terms and customs (see figure 7). This was apparently in response to a suggestion by a Jesuit priest that he "shed light upon the words of the Savages" (xi). Yet the question of "history" raises the issue of who the subjects of history are in the colonial text. In fact, the translations not only explain Carib practices but represent French colonists and missionaries as subjects in history, sharing, challenging, or appropriating this knowledge. In addition, the dictionary includes a fragmented discourse of colonial history that suggests the contest between the French and the Caribs over territory, resources, and souls. In my analysis, I distinguish three narratives imbricated throughout Breton's dictionary: the narratives of ethnography, missionary memoir, and colonial history.

The narrative of ethnography dominates Breton's dictionary, as he pro-

7. Pages from Raymond Breton, *Dictionaire caraibe-françois*, Auxerre, 1665. (Photograph courtesy of the Newberry Library.)

vides detailed descriptions of the Carib material culture, customs, and beliefs that he experienced firsthand. Surpassing mere definition, these explanatory translations verge on the encyclopedic, specifically regarding Carib social relations, warfare, spirituality, botanical knowledge, and cultural life. In many cases, they remain an important source for modern anthropological research on Island Caribs. For example, when explaining the word *iuenematobou*, meaning "my firstborn, the occasion for my fast," Breton expounds on what was for the French one of the most distinctive male rituals in Carib society, later known as *la couvade*: "The Savages observe the fast fairly often, particularly just after a death in the family, the arrival of their firstborn children, and the capture of an enemy. Ordinarily, they spend the first five days without food or drink and the four following days they take a drink made from boiled cassava" (373).[114] The translation of the phrase *Kayani ali*, he has a wife, he is married," occasions an explanation of the Carib kinship system, whereby girls are destined from birth for a maternal cousin. The marriage ceremony consists of their first meal together: "She is led by her father and mother to the groom's habitation, where she brings him his dinner on a *matoutou* and sits with him on the ground to eat. And they say, '*poulíarou lone*,' which means they are married" (268–69). Other entries provide enlightening details on Carib perceptions of time and space. Translating the word meaning "sun," *Huéyou*, Breton notes: "The Caribs have no clocks, nor any conception of hours. Where we would say, 'What time is it?' they say, *állia huéyou báo?* which means 'where is the sun?' If it is nine o'clock they would say, *ignouráali*, 'it is quite high'; if it is after noon, they would say *tabaláali* 'it is turning'; at four o'clock, *ínhouti-kéili*, 'it is not yet too late,' etc." (263). Breton includes numerous accounts of Carib pastimes and leisure activities, such as the phenomenon called *attataóbaca*, translated as "the wave pushes forward," which resembles surfing: "The children of the Caribs, either to teach themselves to swim, or to get used to the sea's currents, or for their amusement, take small planks [of wood] on which they lie down and let themselves go. Some are taken by the waves that push them from behind into the mouths of the rivers. Others who are stronger go out into the river current and get upon the waves of the sea, which are tall and frightful where the two waters meet. . . . To see them in the waves, some with head down and feet up, others feet down and almost standing, is amusing, though we would shudder with fear. This is the meaning of these two words" (314–15).

While dispensing ethnographic information, the author's remarks frequently rehearse common tropes of the noble and ignoble savage. Breton celebrates Carib modesty and sexual restraint despite their relative nudity. Marveling at their frugal reliance on tropical nature, he idealizes them as proto-Christians: "The Savages are sufficiently lacking to be on the level of the Christian monks . . . , for they possess neither gold nor silver and they carry neither purse, nor wallet, habit or staff. They do not even have the means to acquire them" (316). Yet the Caribs appear somewhat less saintly when the topic of warfare is broached. In his translation of *Caíman huétoucounou. boüic kchéne*, "to war!"[115] Breton explains their guerrilla style of fighting, use of flaming arrows, and the taking of prisoners, a subject that occasions an oblique suggestion of Carib cannibalism: "If [the prisoners] are large [the Caribs] starve them, because they eat no fat, and then they kill them" (375). Especially compelling are the author's descriptions of island plants, with hundreds of references to their medicinal and chemical properties. According to Breton, the leaves, bark, and juices of plants and trees are used to treat stomachaches, fever, pox, nausea, lice, toothaches, ulcers, bleeding, the pain of childbirth, and other discomforts. In one case,

Breton describes how Caribs catch fish out of rivers with the aid of a plant called *conámi*: "You attach it to a pebble and then dip it into still water, and the fish who smell it actually jump out of the water and die. Then, you take and eat them without the slightest inconvenience" (177). Explaining the word meaning "famine," the author maintains that, in contrast to the French, Caribs could never suffer it due to their practice of maintaining stores of food in caves and reserve gardens tended in the mountains. The author's own feelings about Carib eating habits are ambivalent, however. Discussing the preparation of the alcoholic beverage, *ouïcou*, Breton describes the women's practice of chewing the manioc to aid the fermentation process: "This is quite disgusting, though, notwithstanding, it makes it much better" (117).

The dictionary's "translations" of botanical diversity thus catalog remarkable secrets of the Caribbean landscape, in some cases unlocking the key to Carib survival and demonstrating the trust gained by Breton among his hosts. What is fascinating, however, is the extent to which the discursive translations relay ethnographic information about the *French* experience of creolization and adaptation to tropical nature. This is especially apparent in the descriptions of over fifty species of trees following the Carib term *hué-hue*, or "wood, tree." On the *Iácarcachi* tree, which the French called "red mahogany," Breton includes both French and Carib use values: "The French construct frames for the roofs of their houses out of it, the Savages use it for their canoes, and the joiners (*menuisiers*) do with it what they will" (253). The produce of the *Matállou* tree is especially convenient for both groups: "On the Islands the dishes hang from the trees, for the *callebassiers* produce many things. . . . The smallest are used by the French to put powder in and by the Savages to hold their black makeup" (254–55).[116] In numerous instances, the dictionary documents the Carib origins of foods and material practices that supported French subsistence in the Antilles. In the passage that defines the root vegetable manioc, by far the most important staple in the Caribbean, Breton includes a description of both Carib and French agricultural methods (328).[117]

Not only do the dictionary translations reflect French practices in the islands, they reveal manifold evidence of the Caribs' attempts to translate in reverse, naming and appropriating objects, species, and customs introduced to the colonies by the French and other Europeans. Breton records, for example, Carib words for the kinds of people who came after A.D.1492, including Christians (*Balánagle*, a word closely related to the name of the sea, *Balánna*), and blacks/Moors (*tibouloüe*). Also present are Carib terms for crops brought to the islands by the Europeans, such as sugarcane. Recording the word *caniche*, Breton explains: "It seems that the Caribs take this plant as well as its name from the Spanish. If they bring animals to the island for a drink when their boats pass, all the more reason to feed them cane; in fact the Caribs bring them this commodity when they are docked at bay" (250). Just as interesting are descriptions of European trade objects fancied by the Caribs, such as *cachourou*: "These are small beads of white glass, round like little pearls, that one brings from Venice. . . . [T]he Savages are very curious about them, stringing them on little cords. They then wrap them to a thickness of three fingers from shoulder to elbow, and around their wrists in place of bracelets. They show up well against their red skin" (100). As these examples show, the dictionary complicates the simple opposition of self and other supposed by the dictionary form itself. The culture Breton is translating has already been affected by his own, such that the dictionary translates Carib words that are in some sense prior translations of European objects and practices.

Similarly, Breton includes his personal experience in the explanatory passages, thereby announcing the narrative of missionary memoir. This self-referential dimension records the author's personal crossing of boundaries between the French and Carib communities, as well as his efforts to Christianize the natives. Breton emerged as a trusted border figure within the Carib community. On more than one occasion, he acted as their interpreter, communicating their grievances to the governor, Houel, in Guadeloupe (415), and he remained unwavering in his opposition to colonial wars. The dictionary entry for the word *inchiakêtoni*, translated as "a letter or some other parcel," indicates how Breton kept abreast of colonial events during his expeditions to Dominica: "The Savages freely brought me letters from Guadeloupe because they believed that they spoke to me and that I had a God like their *Boyez*, who gave me notice of everything in the letter" (300). Scattered throughout the dictionary are fragments of sacred speech invariably used in Breton's missionary endeavors, such as "Jesus Christ died for our sins" (64). In the explanatory definition of *boyé*, a kind of shaman, Breton proclaims the power of the rosary to prevent the daughter of a Carib chief from coming under the influence of this figure (286–87). Often, however, Breton fashions himself as a martyr on the verge of oblivion, suggesting that his proselytizing actions were met with violent retaliation on the part of the Caribs. Defining the Carib self-ascription *Callínago*, he provides an ironic commentary on the stereotype of Carib cannibalism and aggressiveness: "In my case I have not had occasion to complain of their cruelty. On the contrary, I would freely complain of their gentleness in my regard (Oh, the sweet cruelty of being ground up, devoured, and torn apart for a dispute over God!)" (105). This fantasy of engulfment by brutal savages may have been, in the realm of Christian symbolics, more glorious than the plain and simple truth of failure and vulnerability. Recounting his time in Dominica, Breton includes a startling admission of the poor results of his spiritual labors over twelve years: "I have baptized only four people, three of which died soon thereafter. I dared not attempt any further [baptisms] because I could not conceive of ways to maintain them in the beliefs which I tried to instill in them" (414–15).

Given his lack of success as a missionary, Breton's research into the Carib language takes on an even greater significance; the dictionary project emerges as a fetish onto which the author displaces his desire to gain more souls for the Christian faith. Many translated fragments point to Breton's *apprentissage* of language and culture next to his Carib tutors, such as the phrases "what is this called?" (313), "correct my speech," (163), and "familiarize me with your language" (134).[118] Others point to Breton's hurried transcription of all that he was learning: "I am going to make haste, to hurry to write."[119] There is even a Carib word translated as "dictionary" (313). Yet another phrase suggests that language acquisition actually surpasses conversion as the primary motivation for Breton's protracted stay in Dominica: "I will return from Dominica when I know the language so well that I will no longer be able to forget it" (417).[120]

Breton's explanation of the Carib word for "writer" offers an especially revealing commentary on the meaning of writing in the colonial contact zone:

> *Aboulétouti, Abouletácati,* Writer, painter. The Caribs are neither one nor the other. As for the former, they know not how to read or write. Because, however, they believe themselves to be knowledgeable in painting and dabble in it from time to time, they believe that the two resemble one another. Thus, they use the word for their paintbrush to name the quill [*plume à écrire*] and the word for painting to refer to writing. When they must go to a feast, a man will stand up straight and a woman will begin to trace lines from his shoulders to his backside, filling his back, arms and the chest with images [*fantaisies*] that are not disagreeable. However, I admired the patience of the man who must stay upright for twelve hours more than the paintings. The women draw on their beds

and their gourds as well, though painters would have reason to contest their quality. (89)

Initially translating the Carib words as "painter" and "writer," the author proceeds to deny this semantic equivalence, proclaiming instead the profound *lack* of letters in Carib cultures. What the passage reveals, then, is not that Caribs are writers but that Breton was a writer in an oral culture, where his hosts rationalized his unfamiliar practice by naming it after their own tradition of graphic representation—body painting. The author reflects admirably on the sensual inscription of a tattoo on a man's back, only to subtly disavow his pleasure, suggesting the inadequacy of painting with respect to his own writerly sign system. His writing instrument, the quill, stands out in the text as a metonym for Breton himself. The comparison between painting and writing reveals Breton's anxiety about being an object of curiosity among Caribs, misrecognized and misnamed by them. In this respect, the passage evokes a kind of combat of names and denominatives between members of radically different societies. Breton subtly protests his own enclosure as an object within the Carib language by the very people he is attempting to circumscribe and define in writing.

The self-referentiality of Breton's dictionary is heightened by the narrative of colonial history, in which the French take center stage as colonial power relations are disclosed in the text. In the passage on *Calloúcouli*, a valued gemstone from South America, Breton writes: "It is a metal that we sent to France to study and fabricate, but to no purpose. Our Savages always discerned the fraud; even silver and gold do not equal it. . . . It is the richest of their gems" (106). This surprising admittance of the seizure and counterfeiting of the *Calloúcouli* suggests that colonials liberally exploited their knowledge of Carib beliefs and material culture for their own advantage. Even more fascinating is the extent to which the French entirely displace the Caribs as ethnographic subjects, especially when agriculture and colonial export commodities are discussed. In the translation for the word *Obogne*, meaning "habitation," Breton eschews Carib land-use practices and recounts instead the history of colonial land grants and the progressive peopling of the islands by the French (393). Similarly, Breton defines the tobacco plant, *Iouli*—described elsewhere in the dictionary as having particular cultural and social significance within Carib society—exclusively in terms of its cultivation and exchange in a French colonial economy: "It is the currency of the islands. It is said that a pound of bread, a quantity of wine, or a cask of lard is worth so many pounds of tobacco"

(309). Here, the impersonal "one" discloses the collective French subject whose appearance throughout the ethnographic narrative signals the re-insertion of colonial interests and colonial history within the description of Carib culture.

The extent to which the dictionary both records and itself instantiates the colonial contestation for proprietorship and control over tropical land-scapes is nowhere more apparent than in the passages referring to Carib toponyms for islands in the Caribbean archipelago. At issue is the found-ing gesture of European colonialism in the Americas, which is the power to name the "discovered" territories. Anne McClintock has described the urge to name in terms of patriarchal anxiety about the origin of entities found and born and the desire to lay a secure claim on that origin.[121] In some sense, the very presence of French translations for Carib toponyms represents a discursive rehearsal of the colonial takeover, negating in language the ter-ritorial claims of the other, which had been annulled through military con-quest. Classified alphabetically after the term *Oúbao*, meaning "island," the Carib names for the entire archipelago are followed by narrative "transla-tions" recounting each island's discovery and settlement by Europeans. The entry for *Ioüanacaéra* evokes the formalities of possession in Martinique: "Mssrs., our Governors de l'Olive and du Plessis have orders from the Lords to inhabit it. This is why they took possession of it and planted the Fleur de Lys there. The Reverend Fathers Pellican and Griffon set up the cross there" (412). On *Caloucaéra*, translated as *la Gardeloupe*, the historical pas-sage silences the bloody war that lasted several years between the Caribs and the French. Instead, the passage begins: "It is one of the largest and most beautiful of all those that the French possess in the Islands of the Americas" (410). Caribs are mentioned only in the historical narratives for the islands of Dominica and Saint-Vincent, where the French had achieved only par-tial influence and the Caribs organized an irrepressible war of resistance. By reverting to stories of colonial origins, the toponym translations naturalize the discursive and physical displacement of the Caribs by the French.

Through its imbrication of ethnographic, personal, and historical nar-rative, the dictionary simulates mastery over the Carib language and terri-tories, thereby enclosing the Carib people within a self-referential colonial discourse. Yet through the voiced effect of its many phrases the dictionary ironically subverts this display of colonial mastery. Alongside the author's narrative, whose purpose is to orient the reader's interpretations, the dic-tionary comprises thousands of examples of Carib speech which appear as anonymous quotations and sometimes as series of dialogues or exchanges between interlocutors. Mikhail Bakhtin's theory of dialogism in narrative discourse allows for a provocative reading of these dispersed phrases. Bakhtin was critical of literary genres dominated by a single, authoritative, narrative voice identifiable as that of the author/narrator that effectively subordinates other discourses and ideologies. In Bakhtin's theory of the polyphonic novel, meaning is constructed not by a narrator, who monologically interprets, explains, or describes the speech of the characters, but rather by the friction of the dialogue, such that "the characters' discourse is never entirely subsumed and remains free and open (as does the discourse of the author himself)." Thus in Bakhtin's interpretation of the novels of Dostoyevsky the author resolves the plot of the novel but the characters' discourse remains "internally incomplete and unresolved."[122] In many ways, the dictionary resembles a narrative in which the unnamed speakers of the Carib tongue are like characters whose speech conveys the dialogism entailed by the crossing of cultural and linguistic borders. Although Breton attempts to fix the meanings of Carib speech with extensive commentary and interpretation, much of which betrays particularly colonial motivations and strategies for taking possession of island territories and resources, his authority is impinged upon by their voices. The dictionary thus reveals the extent to which, as David Murray explains, "every utterance is the product of the interaction between speakers and . . . of the broader context of the whole complex social situation in which the utterance emerges."[123] Whereas in a novel the multiplicity of voices and discourses—what Bakhtin calls "heteroglossia"—enacts a struggle for influence within an author's imaginary construction of characters in a society, the dictionary represents a diverse and discontinuous set of exchanges, encounters, and dialogues in which the positions of the observer and the observed, subject and object, are in constant flux. Every linguistic fragment calls up a context— some likely occurring between Caribs, others suggesting the presence of the linguistic, cultural, and geographic border between the Caribs and the French—and many words and phrases respond in some sense to another, even as the reader is left to wonder who may have spoken them in each case and how much the author may have intervened to reconstruct the collected language.

This dialogism leaves the reader free to interpret at will the meanings, speakers, and contexts of suspended language and to imagine the reciprocity of contacts so often lost or suppressed in colonial histories. Several quotations evoke the struggle for island territories.

- chakímain nhánhanum iouloumaìna balánanagle, *The Savages of the Island of Saint Vincent have driven back the Christians.*[124]
- ábana-lic iénrou oúbaonhábou callinágoium akímpa-keínum, *There remains only one Island from which the Savages have not been driven away.* (121)[125]
- Káoulío ucati oüakáera oüaoüária, *They are taking our land from us.* (47)[126]
- Tibámêboule cátou hókoya oüaoüária, *You populate more than we do.* (381)[127]
- acamátêti likia, *He is a pirate who takes away the Caribs and puts them in chains.* (9)[128]
- amanle toubaokê aickeu, *Come live on this island.*[129]
- toubaokay ao aioüíelam, *I lived here before you.* (416)[130]

Other voices evoke the consolidation of Carib group identity.

- koumoúlicou nhányem amonchéentium oúbao, *The Caribs who come from other islands are people of our nation.* (313)[131]
- itara nikibélam! *Why are our people so miserable!* (332)[132]

What is fascinating is the potential of the dictionary as dialogic text to produce nonhegemonic representations of the colonial border zone. Especially compelling is the way in which Breton's presence as an uninvited observer of the Caribs is seemingly interrogated by anonymous speaking subjects.

- cat-ábo yéntibou yéte? *What brings you here? On what business, for what reason?*[133]
- Nábo-yéntina ... *I am here to see you.* (112)[134]

Here Carib speakers are subjects in language and the colonial encounter, leaving Breton in the vulnerable position of object of their gaze. What is more, several quotations call into question the linguist's task of learning and recording the Carib language. These voices impart a powerful irony in the dictionary, suggesting the very impossibility of translation.

- chéoüallayénrou enétapa bómpti timále huéolam càchi enétapanoúbali héolam, *You are as ignorant and badly versed in our language as I am in yours.* (137)[135]
- Ménega omêtou oüariángonnê ... *Our languages do not resemble each other, our words bear no relation to each other.* (209)[136]
- Mabaketacátiba néolam, *do not mimic* [contrefais] *my speech.* (2)[137]

Thus, the image of the counterfeit returns as a defining trope in the dictionary, this time as the Caribs' interpretation of Breton's attempts to decipher and transcribe their language.

In breaking out of the monologic, normative discourse of colonial histories and ethnographies, Breton's text unwittingly avoids a particular relation to the other built on what Emmanuel Levinas calls "comprehension" or the reduction of the "other's" alterity with the aim of incorporating or enclosing it within the thought concept of the "same."[138] For Levinas, the only ethical relation is the one that respects the alterity of the other and does not try to assimilate it or divest it of its difference. Opposing the discourse of history as that which enacts the violent assimilation of the other through the logic of identification whereby every object is at once apprehended and incorporated into the same, Levinas proposes language as the only respectful form of relation with the other. Only in conversation does the other remain intact and separate from the same, thus escaping totalization as an object of the same's story. The guarantee of this ethical relation is not merely the speech of the other but its ability to pose the question to the same, thus calling the same into question. The point, therefore, is not to remain the same in the presence of another but to be changed by the conversation and forced to justify oneself in relation to the other: "The strangeness of the Other, his irreducibility to the I, to my thoughts and my possessions, is precisely accomplished as a calling into question of my spontaneity, as ethics."[139]

The irony in Breton's case is that his recourse to the dictionary form was a conscious attempt to take the language of the other and complete an evangelical mission, thus enabling the assimilation of the Caribs into the French social body through conversion and baptism. As an expression of the missionary desire to know and unite with the other, Breton's narrative passages attempt to subsume the Caribs into his point of view and explain their difference, thus domesticating it. For Levinas, this totalizing relation of "comprehension" mimics a will to power too often expressed by means of violence and war. In dialogue, however, an entirely different relation to the other is represented, one that reinstitutes the border as irreducible difference through the question.[140] The Caribs' question disrupts Breton and the French settlers' self-certainty as historical subjects in the space of the other, as well as their assumed position of epistemological sovereignty. In challenging the terms and objectives of the French presence and the missionary's attempt to take their language, the Carib voices subvert the dictionary's will to knowledge together with the colonizing intent of its author. Yet, even as they represent native resistance to the missionary and colonial project, contestations such as these best signify Breton's ultimate achievement of language acquisition and intercultural communication.

The dictionary thus succeeds more than any other text in representing the border of difference, that is, the juxtaposition of subjectivities, languages, and temporalities that can neither be synthesized nor assumed to be totally incommensurable. From speech acts dispersed randomly throughout the dictionary, combined with the author's explanations of Carib words and phrases, the colonial border zone emerges as a space of linguistic exchange and confrontation. While the dictionary structure erects the essentialist binary between languages and cultures, the text deconstructs that same dichotomy, telling stories of its subversion. In addition to problematizing the act of translation, the narrative passages and voiced phrases demonstrate the kinds of transculturation and creolization that had a profound effect on the missionary-ethnographer, French settlers, and the Caribs. It would seem, then, that the bilingual dictionary as a genre offers far more subtle representations of intercultural contact than contemporary narrative sources. What is fascinating is that Breton's work approximates in many ways recent approaches in postmodern ethnography, in which the major challenge has been to bring an intersubjective dimension to the ethnographic encounter. Emphasizing the dialogic element of ethnographic research, Stephen A. Tyler imagines a postmodern ethnography as the inscription of free voice, "in one of its ideal forms, . . . a polyphonic text, none of whose participants would have the final word in the form of a framing story or encompassing synthesis. . . . It might just be the dialogue itself."[141] At the same time, Breton's dictionary stands as the radical model for the trend in postrealist ethnography to structure ethnographic analysis around the contextual exegesis of native concepts.[142] This is none other than the translation and explanation of native language. Yet, while the dictionary represents Breton's effective conquest of the native language as a surrogate for the Carib soul, the author cannot avoid representing Caribs as subjects in language. In this, he cedes power in the colonial encounter, for, as Frantz Fanon has written, "to speak is to exist absolutely for the other."[143] The dictionary discourse thus provides an ironic counterpoint to Shakespeare's classic legend of Caliban and Prospero, in which Caliban curses after being taught the colonizer's language. In Breton's case, it is in the *taking* of the Carib language that the colonist inscribes Carib resistance, thus allowing the Carib, if not to "curse" at least to question.

* * *

I began this chapter by posing two related questions: how does culture cross a border of violence, and how did French colonial writers represent the border between the French and the Caribs and its crossing? As we have seen, much of what little we know of cultural and material exchanges between the French and the Caribs was delivered to us by those most deeply invested in an open border—the missionaries. Missionaries bore the ideological burden of colonialism, since in principle the justice of the entire enterprise vis-à-vis the autochtonous population was predicated on their success. The missionary ideology promoted a notion of peaceful incorporation of the other into the French social body, even as French colonial officials liberally pursued policies at odds with that goal. Likewise, the double failure of early colonialism—ongoing violence with Caribs and the lack of missionary success—was felt most strongly by the missionaries and greatly impacted their perceptions and stories of contacts with the Caribs. Du Tertre balanced his role as propagandist and missionary by framing colonial failures within a providential narrative that ultimately absolved the French of sin. In their ethnographic descriptions, colonial missionaries displaced the border of violence onto the native Caribbean, thereby repressing its existence in the colonial present and projecting the image of conquistador onto the Caribs. Alternatively, scenes of border crossing and exchange became the very means by which writers expressed their anxieties over the lack of reciprocity in their own encounters with Caribs. Yet the most revealing text of the border is the one that disrupts the authority of the missionary messenger and dialogizes the message with thousands of Carib voices. As Breton's *Dictionnaire caraïbe-françois* demonstrates, dictionaries offer largely uncharted representations of intercultural contact that exceed the univocal, monologic perspective of narrative histories and ethnographies, thus allowing for non-hegemonic readings of colonial borders. In the dialogic dictionary, the other cannot be totally subsumed by the categories, concepts, and points of view of the same; on the contrary, it is the same that struggles to "comprehend" the language, categories, and culture of the other. In Breton's text, there is a space for the autonomy of the Caribs in their difference, a difference that asserts itself in the narrative passages and especially in the phrases of spoken language in which cross-cultural communication takes place. What we learn is the extent to which both Carib and French colonial culture, language, and society were fundamentally remade by the contacts, both violent and peaceful, between them.

Chapter Two   *Domestication and*
                                  the White Noble Savage

Who were the French who settled in the Antilles? What distinguished them as "Creole" and what ensured their "Frenchness" and loyalty to the metropole? How was creolization in the settler populace represented in colonial literature? These questions point to a central anxiety in seventeenth-century narratives about the colonies, which is the need to both *describe* and *prescribe* codes of conduct, civility, and culture for French immigrants to the Caribbean. While creolization entailed the effective indigenization of Europeans in the tropical landscape alongside Africans and Caribs, it also involved the encounter of diverse ethnic and regional identities from within the French nation, such that Provençaux, Bretons, Aquitains, and Normans of all ranks began a process of cultural synthesis even as they embarked on the ship of colonial transfer. Just as importantly, creolization entailed the reorientation of culture and values within a capitalist system based on the exploitation of slave labor by an entrepreneurial class.[1] Yet these changes were synonymous with the rise of unlicensed nonstate violence, social indiscipline, and a spirit of frontier independence, all of which would prove a challenge to metropolitan authority in the region. In the seventeenth and eighteenth centuries, narrative sources bore witness to the ways in which pirates, wanderers, rogues, and libertines claimed the colonial space for themselves, defying the cultural and social norms of Old Regime France as well as the new dictates of settlement, agricultural production, and commerce. The challenge for writers was to represent insurgent or undisciplined elements of colonial society while downplaying the threat they posed to the colonial enterprise and social order. They did so by constructing a figure I will call the white noble savage.

The official story of French colonialism begins, ironically, with the colonization not of native Caribs but of the itinerant European and French nationals who were surviving on the fringes of English, Dutch, and Spanish territories in an illicit search for Spanish plunder and New World riches. The first colonist of the French Antilles, Pierre Belain d'Esnambuc, had similar ambitions, with the difference that his were authorized by the Crown. An experienced privateer, and former navy captain with access to royal patronage, he was also a minor nobleman seeking to restore his own personal fortunes through repeated expeditions to the Caribbean islands. Every history of the French West Indies since that of Jacques Bouton in 1640 tells of his accidental landing on the island of Saint-Christophe in 1625 after battling a Spanish galleon of superior force.[2] Finding a group of Frenchmen living alongside a fledgling English settlement led by Captain Thomas Warner, d'Esnambuc stayed on, repaired his ship, and surveyed the lush island and its tobacco fields, which were tended by the English. Jean-Baptiste Du Tertre insists on the enthusiastic reception of the shipwrecked noblemen by the scattered white men, who longed for enterprising leaders of like temperament: "He met on this island twenty-five or thirty Frenchmen, who had taken refuge there at different times and for different reasons, maintaining themselves in peace with the Savages, and living off the provisions that [the Savages] very generously gave them. The arrival of Monsieur Desnambuc and his men gave them much consolation. They lived with him for seven or eight months, loving him like a father and honoring him as their chief."[3] This scene of genesis, renewal, and paternalism represents the founding fiction of French colonization in the West Indies. Building on the idea of a discovered settlement of wayward refugees—quite possibly the legendary buccaneers and pirates of ill repute living outside the law—the narrative transforms them into lost children desiring to be saved, reformed, and domesticated by d'Esnambuc, a founding father "inspired by God, who had chosen him as the Father of the settlers [habitants]." Upon his return to France, d'Esnambuc would obtain an audience with Richelieu himself and propose the development of a tobacco-producing colony at Saint-Christophe, the first permanent French settlement in the Caribbean. Thus, in the French colonial myth of origin, the original narrative of encounter occurs not with Indians but with rugged whites, whom d'Esnambuc identified as a population of exploitable labor.[4] This group, along with lower-class engagés, migrants, reckless planters, and some nobility—indeed, much of the white population—would be continually cast by writers in the mold of noble savagery.

The meanings I attach to the term *white noble savage* both draw and differ from those commonly associated with the myth of the noble savage Indian due to the specific valences of "nobility" I wish to emphasize in reference to transplanted Europeans. The very notion of noble savagery has provoked debate among scholars in the humanities and social sciences, who have questioned the thematic consistency of that myth, its origins and attribution to particular writers, and, most importantly, the term *noble savage* itself, which appears in none of the primary sources usually associated with the myth.[5] The problem is in part one of translation, for *noble savage* has been the accepted English equivalent of the French *bon sauvage* despite significant differences in meaning between the two expressions. Both phrases refer to stylized representations of non-European peoples as paragons of natural virtue, innocence, and freedom, but they vary in their polemical significance. The French usage suggests a simple judgment of moral worth, while the English phrase invokes highly charged ideas about class and nobility, thus making an implicit commentary on Europeans themselves. For Hayden White, the ironic dissonance of the oxymoron *noble savage* works to destabilize assumptions associated with both terms. By implicitly characterizing nobility as "savage," White claims, the phrase both undermines nobility and confers it on all of humanity, criticizing in the process the European idea of nobility tied to genetic inheritance.[6] Yet, as Ter Ellington has noted, in the early modern period this expression almost never appeared in any of the texts most often associated with it. The only contemporary writer known to have actually used the phrase "noble savage" in reference to Indians did so in order to justify both native virtue and a particular form of European dominance. In his analysis of Marc Lescarbot's *Histoire de la Nouvelle France* (1609), Ellington shows that the French writer interprets native charity, hospitality, ideas of justice, and hunting practices through the lens of aristocratic values so as to claim that "the savages are truly noble."[7] As Ellington explains, Lescarbot aimed not to idealize the "savage" but to argue for the preservation (as opposed to extermination) of the conquered people in a new age of European dominance.[8]

If the expression "noble savage" has proved misleading as a category through which to analyze European accounts of non-Europeans, it is ironically compelling when applied to European subjects themselves. Like the concept of the "noble savage," the phrase "white noble savage" never appeared in any of the sources I will analyze; it is, rather, a critical construct through which I explore the ideological problem of representing French colonial subjects for a metropolitan readership. By inserting the racial modifier *white*, I distinguish this figure from the noble savage Indian and suggest the beginnings of a racialized sensibility, resulting in the gradual homogenization of the French colonial populace. In retaining the expression "noble savage," I explore the points of tension between writers' accounts of libertinage, savagery, and social travesty among colonial recruits and settlers, on one hand, and portraits of moral virtue, social respectability, and economic prosperity on the other. I argue that writers attempted to discipline the radical violence and social ambiguity of colonial life by framing it within a narrative of social uplift better suited to the goal of defending the colonial project and attracting new recruits.[9] To a large extent, this narrative reflected the contemporary manipulation of social hierarchies by the royal administration in order to achieve the aims of colonial expansion. It was mercantilist ambition that drove Richelieu to erode one of the most symbolic distinctions between the aristocracy and the bourgeoisie—participation in commerce. Not only were privileges and letters of nobility conferred on the commoners who operated the largest ships in the merchant marine,[10] or headed up small settlements in the early stages of colonization,[11] nobles themselves were encouraged to engage in colonial commerce in defiance of the long-standing rule of derogation.[12] Richelieu relaxed that rule in full knowledge that the seas and coasts of the Caribbean were already scattered with gentlemen such as d'Esnambuc, who were seeking to restore their fortunes through plunder and pillage on the Spanish Main. Within the colonies, authorities offered social entitlements, privileges, and in some cases letters of nobility to persons whose entrepreneurial pursuits or military prowess—including piratical endeavors—advanced the interests of France. By applying the trope of nobility, figuratively and literally, to white colonials, colonial writers thus sought to publicize the socially transformative effects of life in the tropics. The discourse of white noble savagery refashioned pirates into heroes in the service of the king and elevated the bourgeois values of production and commerce alongside older aristocratic notions of virtue, valor, and heredity as bases for social distinction. Yet such narratives could not erase entirely the scandal of white libertinage, social travesty, and resistance to landed colonialism. As colonials performed their real or imagined nobility through vestimentary display, invented names, and ownership of land and slaves, writers balanced a narrative of social ascent with a critique of what often appeared as the unauthorized usurpation of nobility.

The chapter begins with Alexandre Olivier Oexmelin, whose account of piracy around Tortuga, Saint-Domingue, and the Spanish Main immediately became an international bestseller. Oexmelin's book focuses on the most subversive class of settlers, those buccaneers, freebooters, and pirates whose villainous roguery at sea both shadowed and in some respects made possible the sedentary planter lifestyles pursued on land. While acknowledging the significance of piracy as a collective, international, and democratizing revolt against the ideology of mercantile colonialism, I place greater emphasis on the violence through which its practitioners performed that revolt. Through Oexmelin, I read piracy as the unauthorized performance of the kind of unrestrained savagery and warfare previously reserved for the nobility of the sword in late medieval and Renaissance France. In the literary account, the uninhibited cruelty and destruction of piracy is alternatively disdained as criminal and sensationalized as reflecting an admirable intrepidity and noble valor. At the same time, Oexmelin's history represents the primary means by which the piratical movement was contained and ultimately defeated—that is, through social promotion and the recuperation of pirates into the apparatus of state colonialism. By documenting the rise of pirates, buccaneers, and filibusters to respectable positions in government and the royal navy, Oexmelin's story of the repression of pirates becomes one of their symbolic ennoblement for the glory of the absolutist king.

In the second part of the chapter, I examine the representation of white creolization and landed settlement in the works of two Dominican missionaries, Jean-Baptiste Du Tertre and Jean-Baptiste Labat, who provided comprehensive views of a burgeoning Creole culture based on cultivation and commerce. While both writers downplay social liminality through a narrative of progress and respectability, they also expose the kinds of spontaneous self-fashioning and fabricated privilege through which settlers performed a simulacrum of nobility. Du Tertre draws on his ecclesiastical authority to prescribe a model of colonial domesticity based on religion, agriculture, and commerce. In so doing, he raises important questions about the nature of colonial authority and its ability to intervene in the otherwise haphazard reorientation of social, cultural, and gender norms among colonial settlers. Labat adds complexity to this analysis by considering the relationship between white settlers and the colonial environment. The author's exhaustive account of his own naturalization in the Caribbean through exploration, industry, and social ascension demonstrates the ways in which colonial subjects attempted to master their environment while at the same time being radically transformed by it. In scrutinizing the social history of the colonial upper crust against the background of generalized class indeterminacy, however, Labat highlights the ambiguities associated with the rise from "savagery" to a simulacrum of "nobility."

8. "Carte des Isles de l'Amérique," in Pierre-François-Xavier de Charlevoix, *Histoire de l'isle espagnole, ou de S. Domingue,* Paris, 1730–31. (Reproduced courtesy of the McCormick Library of Special Collections, Northwestern University Library.)

Piracy, Transnationalism, and Insurgency in the Caribbean Sea

To think of the French colonial enterprise in relation to piracy is to imagine simultaneously its origins and its antithesis. The legendary myth of origins surrounding the fateful landing of Pierre Belain d'Esnambuc on the island of Saint-Christophe makes a hero out of a Norman privateer who founded a state-backed colony of tobacco planters that would become an extension of France itself. In predicating the beginnings of colonialism on the end of piracy, the story encapsulates the course of colonial history. Piracy was the condition of possibility for a colonialism that would forever identify itself in counterdistinction to piracy. Piracy often contravened Colbert's policy of monopoly mercantilism, and the nomadism, errancy, and intemperance of the pirates was diametrically opposed to the state's ideal of landed settlement and agricultural production. Yet what happened in the Caribbean during the first century of colonization greatly impacted the ability of the French to establish a colonial presence there.

Since the reign of King Francis I, piracy had been endorsed by northern European heads of state in contestation of Spain's claims to be sole proprietor of American territories and exploitable ressources.[13] Privateering was the form of piracy legitimated by a commission of war authorizing a private captain and his crew to plunder at sea in a monarch's name and keep the profits.[14] As the Spanish colonization effort moved from the greater Antillean islands to mainland conquests of Mexico and Peru, ships bringing wealth back to Europe became open targets for privateers from France, England, and Holland. French attacks achieved spectacular success, one of the earliest being the 1523 capture of Spanish ships carrying the stolen treasures of the Aztec city Tenochtitlan off the coast of the Azores by Jean d'Ango, a wealthy ship owner from Dieppe. This feat attracted many more daring servants, sailors, soldiers, déclassé nobles, petit bourgeois *révoltés*, and castaways seeking their fortunes in the Caribbean beginning in the 1530s. The Reformation contributed significantly to the growth of piracy, as it provided further reason for northern Europeans to revolt against the Spanish abroad. Throughout the sixteenth century, privateers carried out devastating raids on New World port cities identified as enemy territory. In 1555, the French privateer Jacques de Sores captured Havana and burned it to the ground, a feat that announced the pirates' potential to act as a military force in conflicts abroad. Even when the Treaty of Vervins was signed in 1598, ending French and Spanish hostilities in Europe, it did not extend to the American territories, containing, rather, the signature clause of piracy—"no peace beyond the line"—in reference to the longitudinal line located at the Azores.

The French state's tolerance of piracy was evidenced by the protections it afforded the pirates themselves, who received automatic title to their goods following the payment of high duties. French ports along the English Channel benefited enormously from the trade in Spanish booty and their close proximity to Dutch ports and likewise produced noteworthy pirates from the class of former sailors and soldiers. Yet the very nature of piracy favored a rebellious spirit and aggressive opportunism that tended to defy strictly national fidelities. Pirates operated as a formidable but loose confraternity of mainly French, English, and Dutch men, who mixed freely, knew each other's languages, and sailed for whoever would provide the necessary protection. Alternatively, they would go without a commission. In either case, the state was powerless to exercise control over those it authorized to use force beyond its borders.[15] The legends of Olonnais, Morgan, Montauban, Roc, and others sensationalized by Alexandre Olivier Oexmelin in his *Histoire des aventuriers flibustiers qui se sont signalés dans les Indes* were made with the support of international crews and not always with the sanction of any national government.[16] Unauthorized nonstate piracy was inevitable, as pirates acted first and foremost for themselves, building their lives and a unique social culture out of the precariousness of constant sea travel, combat, and the quest for riches.

We have several terms with which to designate this transnational sea culture. Like the English, the French terminology distinguished between state-sponsored and rogue piracy. According to the 1694 *Dictionnaire de l'Académie*, the word *pirate* in French referred to someone engaging in unlicensed theft and pillage on the high seas, as opposed to *corsaire*, which referred to a pirate sailing with a state commission. Another common equivalent of *pirate* was *coureur de mer* (sea rover). Oexmelin's French editors preferred *aventurier* (adventurer), defined in the 1694 dictionary as a sort of soldier of fortune who voluntarily seeks adventure in battle while avoiding the less glorious duties of the regular army. Like other terms for piracy, this word carried the figural meaning of *libertinage*—"those who, without being in love with any woman, try to gain the good graces of all women"—and was also a derogatory term meaning "he who has no fortune, and who attempts to establish himself through adventure."[17] In the title of Oexmelin's 1699 edition, the word *aventurier* was qualified with *flibustier* for precision. This word derives from the Dutch *vryjbuiter*, meaning "he who freely takes booty."[18] Over time, *flibustier* (filibuster) became roughly equivalent to *boucanier* (buccaneer), which refers specifically to hunters of wild cattle in the Caribbean.[19] The term originated from the Amerindian-derived French word for the native style of barbecue, *boucan*. This was a process of slow grilling, smoking, and drying of meat, which could be so preserved for several months.[20] Disparate groups of these men constituted the earliest northern European settlers of the Caribbean, supplying pirate outposts or simply surviving shipwrecks by hunting the cattle and feral pigs on islands abandoned by the Spanish. Pirates, filibusters, and coureurs de mer maintained a symbiotic collaboration with buccaneers on land, sharing an amphibian lifestyle that eventually made their names interchangeable.[21] They coalesced around two strongholds: Jamaica for the English; and Tortuga, just off the northern coast of Hispaniola, which was used by both the English and French. From these and other bases, Caribbean pirates grew into a flexible and responsive social organization.

Characterized by an aggressive and adaptive individualism, the piratical commonwealth constituted a parallel society in the Caribbean that strongly impacted the success of the colonies. Piratical theft supplied fledgling settlements with provisions and luxury goods at a time when French monopoly practices often failed to meet their commercial needs. In addition to being itself a colonizing force in Tortuga and Saint-Domingue, piracy represented an indispensable defensive resource for the colonies.[22] Yet the association of piracy and buccaneering with social anarchy, vice, heresy, and nonproductivity continued even as pirates were revered for their brash talents. In the first edition of his history, Du Tertre indicted the prodigality of the French Caribbean's first white inhabitants, whom he conceived as an international pack of heretics, ex-convicts, castaways, and libertines. He complained that as soon as they "had won a little booty, they would withdraw to their native countries . . . such that in this way they always took whatever they could from the land without bothering to cultivate or improve it."[23] This is none other than the pirate ethic of plunder and abandonment. Du Tertre later described buccaneering as "the most hideous, troublesome, perilous, and . . . roguish life that could ever be imagined in this world." He stressed, furthermore, their animal-like existence, culinary crudeness, vagrancy, shabby dress, and filth, observing that "when they return from the hunt to the grill [*boucan*], you would think they were the vilest of butcher's valets, having spent eight days in the slaughterhouse without bathing."[24] The eating of raw meat was enough to prove their savagery, as the hunters' most prized meal was reputed to be the fresh marrow sucked from the bones of their prey. This was the American incarnation of the European wild man, the bestial man who ate raw flesh and drank blood, incommunicable and unsociable except when he descended on weary travelers at night to ruthlessly rob them.[25] It was a lifestyle with political consequences, for Du Tertre characterized the first white inhabitants of Tortuga as "a colony that will refuse to submit to the Church, the king, and the company."[26] In Du Tertre's myth of colonial origins, however, unrepentant piracy and buccaneering constitute the shadowy chaos from which God created the first colonies, which, he assures the reader, have since been inhabited by "honorable people": "Almost all of the common people live there with great liberty; virtue is highly esteemed, and the vicious and wicked are hated by all."[27]

This affirmation of the moral virtue of colonists reflects Du Tertre's desire to impose a disciplinary regime rather than an observation of fact. The demise of piracy coincided with the annexation of the colonies to the royal domain in 1674. The expansion of royal control over colonial affairs led to the growth of institutions such as the Church, colonial militia, civil adminis-

1. *Tortue fuisant son trou pour pondre.*   3. *Verre de la Tortue.* 155 5. *Rosinier.* 156 7. *Arras* 3. 161.   9. *Chasse des poissons volans* 112. 11. *Festu en cul ou oiseau du tropique.* 156 13. *Crabier*
2. *Comme on la retourne.* p. 227.   4. *Courbaril* p. 163.   6. *Fic d'Inde.* 8. *Peroquets.* 161 10. *Fregate.* p. 165.   12. *Flamant.* 251.   14. *Grand gosier.* p. 171.
p. 225.   Le Clerc f.

9. Tortoise hunting, in Jean-Baptiste Du Tertre, *Histoire générale des Antilles habitées par les François*, Paris, 1667–71. (Reproduced courtesy of the McCormick Library of Special Collections, Northwestern University Library.)

tration, and, most importantly, the justice system, which on each island was composed of a judge and the *conseil souverain*, or high court. The establishment of criminal justice and the construction of prisons provided the material means by which to impound persons or groups deemed dangerous to society.[28] Buccaneers and pirates became a nuisance to state power when in the late seventeenth century tensions with Spain subsided and France consolidated its control over Tortuga and Saint-Domingue, islands the pirates called home. Their populations had long been considered a menace to organized colonial commerce, and they adamantly resisted the planter lifestyle encouraged by the Crown. Furthermore, piracy offered a refuge for revolted engagés, those white maroons who fled the brutality of the master-slave relationship for a more equitable apprenticeship at sea. As early as 1670, the population of Saint-Domingue successfully revolted against the policies of religious exclusion and commercial monopoly imposed by the French trading company. The revolt led to special exceptions for Saint-Domingue and the colony's enduring spirit of independence.[29] Yet their unique culture of buccaneering and piracy would not long survive the seventeenth century.

Through royal orders, arrests, inducements to attract buccaneers to establish homes, and the Crown's discontinuance of the policy of militarizing pirates in conflicts abroad, piracy was slowly eradicated, not, however, before some of the most renowned buccaneers were propelled to the highest offices in the royal administration to carry out the suppression of their brethren.[30] It is an irony that would have its counterpart in literature.

Ode to the White Savage: Oexmelin's Buccaneer Republic

In 1666, the vessel *Saint-Jean* arrived at Port Margot on the island of Hispaniola, with a cargo of engagés from Le Havre. Soon it was approached by a fearsome welcome party. Recalling the moment, one of the ship's passengers would write: "A canoe with six men came toward us, which caused much astonishment among most of our Frenchmen who had never left France. For clothing they had only a short linen coat and breeches that covered just half of their thighs. One had to see them up close to know if this clothing was made of linen or not, so soaked it was in blood. They had a swarthy complexion and their hair was bristly and knotted; all of them had long beards and wore a purse of crocodile skin on their belts, in which they carried four knives and a bayonet" (18–19). The description calls up a certain stereotype of savagery in its emphasis on the men's relative lack of dress, dark skin, long and unkempt hair, and the blood of an animal stained on the body. Yet what made these men truly extraordinary was that they were white Europeans, an image of what was to become of many of the ship's naive passengers. "We knew that they were buccaneers. In what follows, I will give a singular description of them, because I, too, was one" (19). With these words, the buccaneer pirate Alexandre Olivier Oexmelin introduces the heroes of his renowned narrative history of this most legendary of social strata in the seventeenth-century Caribbean.

The *Histoire des aventuriers*, first published in Holland in 1678, became an international print sensation, appearing in five European languages and many more editions by the end of the seventeenth century alone. The earliest narrative account of buccaneering in the Caribbean, Oexmelin's text captivated the French public and arguably inaugurated the vogue of pirate literature in eighteenth-century England.[31] The book is equally remarkable for its staying power. An indispensable narrative source for modern historians of seventeenth-century buccaneer piracy, the work has remained in print through numerous editions, new translations, and adaptations in English, French, and Spanish.[32] Yet surprisingly little is known about the life of the writer outside of the extraordinary events relayed in the narrative. His French nationality and place of birth at Honfleur were established only in 1933. Six years later a medical student named Henri Pignet published an unsubstantiated and highly fallacious thesis on Oexmelin that has adversely affected subsequent scholarship on him.[33] What is certain is that he was a native of Honfleur, who in 1666 signed an *engagement* for three years to the Compagnie des Indes Occidentales. On May 2 of that same year, he embarked on the *Saint-Jean* bound for Saint-Domingue. In his book, Oexmelin attests to having experienced the worst of indentured servitude before becoming a surgeon aboard filibuster expeditions beginning in 1668. Although in 1672 he traveled back to Europe, where he obtained his surgeon's license in 1679, the author returned to the Caribbean several times before the expanded French edition of his work appeared in 1699.[34]

What is fascinating about Oexmelin as a literary figure is that the international editorial history of his narrative mirrors in reverse the author's transnational piratical exploits. Whereas Oexmelin himself sailed under the flags of many a nation against the Spanish, his text immediately became a valuable object of international pillage, as country after country produced unauthorized and substantially revised versions. With the original manuscript lost, we have only a strange configuration of incompatible editions, evidence of the international competition between editors and translators to remake the story and its author in their own national images.[35] While the Dutch edition of 1678 overtly endorsed the activities of Dutch interlopers in the Caribbean Sea, the very title of the Spanish translation of 1681—*Piratas de la America, y luz à la defensa de las costas de Indias Occidentales*—indicates the editor's primary concern to allay Spain's fears about defending its empire against the pirates, in particular Henry Morgan, whose cruelties were more strongly condemned than in the Dutch version. When in 1684 both the Dutch and Spanish editions were translated into English, the translators revised the text to promote the glory of Morgan. Praising Oexmelin for faithfully rendering the "true English valor," they called on the English people to emulate the courageous patriotism of Englishmen on the Spanish Main.[36] This renationalization of pirates and the pirate narrative entailed important changes to the text, the most blatant being the "correction" of Oexmelin by Thomas Malthus, the English publisher of the Dutch edition. The biases of other nations could only be rectified, he argued, by putting the narrative to the "test" of unnamed gentlemen "who had resided many years in those parts" and "were pleased to correct, purge and reform it of many abuses and mistakes, wherewith this account was sullied."[37]

With the appearance of the first French edition of Oexmelin's text in 1686, a new nationalization was at play (see figure 10). The editor, a certain Frontignières, explains that he was directed to work on Oexmelin's memoirs by a "person of importance," who found them "quite excellent [*fort curieux*]."[38] This was most likely Jean II, Duc d'Estrées, vice admiral and marshal of France, the second highest ranking member in the French army. D'Estrées frequently led royal fleets on expeditions to the Caribbean, and he appears in the French edition as a beneficent authority who comes to the aid of Morgan and his pirate crew. According to Frontignières, d'Estrées was familiar with the manuscript, having commanded Oexmelin to "give him an account of the details of his voyages."[39] Both figures influenced the contents of the French edition, for substantial changes reflect state colonial interests. The title, *Histoire des aventuriers qui se sont signalez dans les Indes . . . avec la vie, les moeurs, les coûtumes des habitans de Saint Domingue . . .* [History of the Adventurers Who Have Distinguished Themselves in the Indies . . . with the Lives, Morals, and Customs of the Inhabitants of Saint-Domingue . . .], frames the text as a sort of natural and moral history of the colony of Saint-Domingue, now officially joined to the French domain. Likewise, the editor added two chapters copied from Du Tertre's *Histoire générale des Antilles* describing the emergence of the colony at Tortuga and its eventual governance by the Compagnie des Indes Occidentales. Several of the more salacious chapters were either plagiarized or completely invented, including the piratical exploits of Montbars and Bras-de-Fer.[40] Most important, however, is the ideological tone of the work. In the epistle to the Directeur de la Caisse des Consignations, the French editor presents Oexmelin's text as an ode to the powers of absolutism over obedient subjects abroad: "You will observe that there, as elsewhere, he commands fear and love, and he reigns and triumphs. In a word, he is everywhere Louis the Great"[41] Thus, the transnational adventurers were reinvented as the "conquerors" of Tortuga for France, effectively filling the symbolic mold of the Spanish conquistador and English sea captains. Oexmelin himself underwent a radical transformation. Remarking on his lack of formal education or high birth, the editor nonetheless endowed him with the status of an *honnête homme* (honest man), a form of honorary nobility: "It seems, however, that this author has a bit of both [good birth and education], if one pays attention to common sense, and has a certain liberty of a noble man that governs his writing."[42] In exchange for submitting his narrative to royal authority, Oexmelin was himself remade in the image of the king and the state.

The publishing history of Oexmelin's text thus demonstrates the irre-

10. Frontispiece, in Alexandre-Olivier Oexmelin, *Histoire des avanturiers*, Paris, 1686. (Photograph reproduced courtesy Newberry Library.)

sistible appeal of pirate narratives, not only for the public but for the state actors who proceeded to "pirate" the text through the authorized or unauthorized appropriation of its subversive meanings. The French nationalization of Oexmelin did not stop with the 1686 edition; an expanded edition appeared in 1699 with new changes, "corrections," and chapters on piratical interventions since the 1670s. The most important of these detailed the massive siege of Carthagena in which pirates joined the French navy in a devastating campaign against the Spanish city. It is unlikely that Oexmelin personally oversaw the revision of his text. The preface by Frontignières indicates that the author was "obligated" to return to America, and the text was prepared with the collaboration of a certain Abbé Bertrand. The editors transformed the text into a sort of compilation with the addition of passages from private *mémoires* and other published sources.[43] Although the 1699 edition is the rarest and possibly the least "authentic" of Oexmelin's editions in French, it is the most clearly allied to the ideological objectives of state colonialism. It is also the version best known to modern readers. Reprinted in 1744, it has become the standard reference for modern scholars owing to Bertrand Guégan's widely available version of 1930.[44] Based on this edition, I would like to explore Oexmelin's history as an ethnography of the white colonial outcast—the white maroons, buccaneers, and rogue filibusters who operated on the fringe of state colonialism. In invoking the name Oexmelin, I refer not to an autonomous author but rather to the authorial function, which was occupied by Oexmelin and his French editors in response to concrete political and ideological objectives. While sensationalizing the barbarity of piratical culture so as to exploit its value on the literary market, the narrative transforms the image of the savage pirate into that of the pirate statesman. Oexmelin thus figures the pirate as a sort of white noble savage whose unregenerate roguery is forgiven, co-opted, and rewarded by state power.

Beginning with a personal account of Oexmelin's crossing and sale as an engagé, the *Histoire des aventuriers* includes a general history and description of the French colonies at Tortuga and Saint-Domingue, followed by a description of the buccaneers and an account of the author's own distinctly American rise from indentured servitude to adventure as a surgeon aboard pirate fleets. The latter half of the work recounts the mythical expeditions of pirate giants with legendary nicknames such as Roc, Bras-de-fer, and the Exterminateur. The author links their skills to the landed nomadism of buccaneers: "I wanted to show that the most famous adventurers train with them in their lands. . . . One could say that they serve their apprenticeship in the country, in the forests, and on animals in order to deliver masterful blows [*faire ensuite des coups de maître*] on the sea, in the cities, and against men" (77). Anticipating the criticism of those unwilling to take the stories as truth, the author Oexmelin mocks these readers with this caution: "I do not advise these gentlemen to read about the lives of pirates, where everything is extraordinary" (143). The narrative veracity is based on Oexmelin's credibility as an eyewitness and his candor in revealing instances in which he relies on the testimony of others. Of his unique perspective, Oexmelin remarks: "One may find it surprising that although so many authors have written of America, I still thought it necessary to do so. He should be more surprised that having been an indentured servant, a settler [*habitant*], and pirate, I did not say much more" (77).

Oexmelin here refers to the division of labor that evolved historically into three distinct classes: the buccaneer hunters, the pirates, and the planters, called *habitants*. Their partnership founded a viable commerce, attracting English and Dutch settlers and French ships to trade in commodities such as cowhides, pork, Spanish treasures, tobacco, produce, and silverware. The author describes the buccaneer profession as "one of the roughest one can do in life" (60). Traveling into the bush in groups of ten to twelve matelots accompanied by servants and a pack of dogs, the buccaneer hoard descends on unsuspecting cattle, which are killed and skinned on the spot. At night, they dine on beef, practice shooting, and sleep in tents. The greatest travail comes in carrying a bloody hide on one's back for several miles of rough terrain. Such arduous labor strengthened the survival instinct among these men, as illustrated by the anecdote of a young arrival who faints after a near fatal assault by his master. Waking up later in isolation, he wanders the island for months, surviving on random hunts and eventually assembling a herd of dogs and pigs. When he finally reunites with a pack of buccaneers, he becomes one of the most notorious, though never again regaining his taste for cooked meat: "It gave him such a stomach ache that when he skinned a wild boar, he could not stop himself from eating a piece raw" (64). Undoubtedly, for the author the Saint-Domingue buccaneers were among the wildest men on earth, far more so than the Spanish who literally hunted them. He chides the comparatively polite manners of Spanish thugs as a sign of frivolity: "They prepare their food with more delicacy and never eat their meat without bread. . . . They are also infinitely more clean in their attire, and insist on having white linens" (67).

Yet when buccaneers are compared to Amerindians the stereotype of unregenerate white savagery is subtly disrupted. Oexmelin's portrayal of Indians equivocates between animosity and admiration. On one hand, Oexmelin relays images of ignoble Indian savages and delights in their near extinction. Describing the Spanish-dominated eastern side of Hispaniola, the pirate narrator turns archaeologist as he tells of the skeletal remains of Indians found in caverns, evidence of the Spanish extermination. Oexmelin approves of such treatment, suggesting that the Indians are inhuman cannibals who ingest slave women as well as infamous pirates such as Olonnais. When first defining the term *boucan*, the author is quick to note that while the buccaneers are named for an Indian cultural element they are in no way as savage as the Indians, for the buccaneers "did to animals what the Indians do to men" (55). The cannibal trope thus functions to assert a critical difference separating buccaneers from the *true* savages.

Elsewhere, however, the subversiveness of the cannibal mystique and its associated "savagery" are reserved for the European wild men alone. At one point, a group of abandoned pirates is so hungry as to contemplate the taboo act: "If they had found some savages, they were resolved to kill some of them for food, for they had been eating only grass and leaves" (142). In the end, they find friendly Indians who offer food. Oexmelin expresses sympathy for those Indians, with whom he seeks an alliance, for example, the *indios bravos*, so named because of their valor in resisting the Spanish: "Thus the Indians have their customs which are different from ours, but should not therefore seem ridiculous to us" (305). The similarities outweigh the differences in ways Oexmelin is perhaps less prepared to admit. Although the pirates fashion themselves as defenders of the Indians against the evil Spanish, by performing their own brand of frontier belligerence they essentially usurp the Indians' role as indomitable savages countering Spanish greed.

Oexmelin's talents as a participant-observer of buccaneer culture derive in part from the fact that he never considered himself truly to belong in the ranks of the pirates and therefore sustained a sense of judgmental indignation at their practices. His account of his arrival on Saint-Domingue tells of his rude entry into the system of indentured servitude, being sold for the sum of thirty écus. The departing governor had picked him out of the pack of disembarked engagés as one who would never survive such slavery and wished to take him back to France, "judging from my face that if I encountered a bad master I would never be able to withstand the hardships of the country; but the Sieur de la Vie already had retained me" (20). The Sieur de la Vie belonged to the class of habitants to which Oexmelin devotes one chapter and much bitterness. Formerly buccaneers or engagés in Tortuga, the first habitants migrated to the coastal mainland to establish plantations.

A social structure was built from the quasi-formal masculine marriage practice known as *matelotage*, described by Oexmelin as the voluntary union of two men for the purposes of sharing resources and buying servants. The settlement of Saint-Domingue progressed in stages, from the coast to the interior, where tobacco was cultivated on small plantations. The most established settlers acquired servants and an overseer, who in the worst cases enforced order "like a galley master over his slaves [*forçats*]" (74). Oexmelin's own story reemerges against this picture as he describes his eventual escape. Caught accepting food from the governor after nearly starving, he is held in a dungeon for several days. Later appealing to a priest for help, he recuperates and is transferred by the governor to a well-known surgeon to serve out his term of servitude. From there, the author receives permission to join a filibuster expedition to practice his trade on the high seas.

Oexmelin attributes the rise of filibuster piracy to the institution of state-backed company colonialism by Britain and France, which threatened the livelihood of existing merchants and traders: "Such that people who had begun to establish themselves in this country for trade, seeing that they had nothing left to do, abandoned everything and chose to rove the high seas, looking always to rob the Spanish" (79). The historian Charles Frostin distinguishes this practice with the term *la petite flibuste*, meaning a small-scale mix of contraband and piracy, as opposed to *la grande flibuste*, meaning state-sponsored pirate warfare.[45] Naming themselves the Brothers of the Coast, they constituted a parallel social order that afforded members a greater degree of autonomy than was possible within the strict labor hierarchies of company colonialism. Piracy was a haven for revolted engagés and merchant seamen, hence the almost religious dedication to a fraternal egalitarianism, shared power, and noncoercive forms of authority. Oexmelin thoroughly describes the sort of rogue democracy they formulated on the basis of group consensus under a chosen leader, usually the most respected or authoritative pirate among them. Alternatively, the captain was he who had captured the boat on which the group sailed, since the buccaneer pirates stole of necessity all that is required to launch an expedition, sometimes graduating from a small canoe to a highjacked Spanish military vessel. The captain could be deposed at any time for abusing his power, since mistreatment was hotly resented by the buccaneers.

For each expedition, selected matelots would work out an agreement with the captain, called the *chasse-partie*, stipulating how the spoils would be distributed and injuries indemnified. In the chasse-partie included in the text, the surgeon receives special compensation for his medicine cabinet and expertise. Yet, in the case of an unsuccessful expedition entailing physical injury, compensation comes in the form not of money or material goods but of people. This reflects the prevalence of slaves as cargo recovered from conquered ships and transformed into currency as they moved across the boundary between colonial commerce and piratical robbery. For the loss of an eye, a pirate crewman could receive one hundred écus or one slave. Arms and legs were valued at two slaves, and so on. Otherwise, crewman were bound to one another through contracts of matelotage, here a specific form of marriage testament stating a line of inheritance: "They sign an agreement in the form of a will; this document stipulates that if one of them should die, the other has the right to all of his belongings" (84). These agreements superseded all bonds with women, who were introduced more as servants than equal partners. Women, if found, would serve both matelots: "When two among them find a beautiful woman, to avoid any dispute over her, they flip a coin [*jettent à croix-pile*] to see who will marry her. The winner marries her, but his comrade is always welcome at the house" (85).[46]

For all the apparent order that the author documents among the filibusters, Oexmelin refuses to sanction what he perceives to be a barbaric and anarchical antisociability. As intrepid and unstoppable bandits motivated by the ephemeral pleasures of material gain, the buccaneers alternate between feast and famine, riches and poverty, glory and shame: "The success of their undertakings seems to justify their temerity, but nothing can excuse their barbarity. It would be preferable if they were as diligent in observing the laws that maintain order among men as they are faithful in observing the laws they establish among themselves" (81). Scholars typically characterize the piratical social organization as a quasi-proletarian revolt against the interests of the maritime bourgeoisie and royal administration. According to this view, piracy represents criminality on a massive scale, and an organized attack on merchant property, international commerce, and all forms of traditional authority. Following Eric Hobsbawm, Marcus Rediker considers piracy a sort of "social banditry," defined as an "endemic peasant protest against oppression and poverty: a cry for vengeance on the rich and the oppressors."[47] Similarly, for Janice Thomson piracy is "not simply or always an economic crime—the theft of private property. It was also a political act—a protest against the obvious use of state institutions to defend property and discipline labor."[48] I would contend, however, that these perspectives on piratical revolt are insufficient to explain the immediate and uninhibited use of violence it entailed. For an absolutist, centralized state that had constituted itself precisely by imposing controls on the release of affect and the use of force by its subjects, piracy and buccaneering represented an open and unbridled seizure of power on the geographical margins of state sovereignty.[49] What is more, piracy unleashed forms of aggressiveness that were previously the exclusive privilege of the warrior nobility of the Middle Ages, coinciding with its powers as a secular ruling class. As Norbert Elias has argued, rapine, murder, and devastation were socially permissible pleasures for the knight, reflecting both his elite social position and the lesser threshold of "affect control" that characterized the medieval period.[50] Thus, rather than acting solely as democratically minded proletarians who liberated themselves from repressive social organizations, pirates deliberately seized power and glory through behaviors that mimicked older forms of aristocratic violence, warfare, and privilege.

This point becomes clearer if we recall the close relationship between class status and the use of violence in medieval and early modern Europe. In this period, fighting was not only universally recognized as a nobleman's exclusive industry and raison d'être, but it was a pleasure and a joy, as recounted in epic literature and legend. The noble had a duty to fight and cultivated a love for the raw violence of warfare as a "theater for the exercise of virtue."[51] Yet nobles were just as easily motivated by the lure of adventure, conquest, and pillage for the sake of gain. Critics complained that often this violence degenerated into illegitimate brigandage and vandalism, as knights indiscriminately robbed the innocent and the powerless, compounding their gains by ransoming captives. In the eighteenth century, French Enlightenment writers and historians commonly attacked the nobility for what they called "feudal anarchy," an excessive militarism that bordered on the criminal, involving rape, pillage, and indiscriminate violence against commoners.[52]

All of these behaviors were magnified in the extreme in the piratical ventures recounted by Oexmelin. Pirate and buccaneer forces routinely fashioned themselves into vigilante armies, placing entire cities under siege for weeks of combat, villainy, destruction, and raiding, with or without a commission. Practicing *la grande flibuste*, they overwhelmed their enemies on the Spanish Main by force and wit. Such was the case in the account of Olonnais's ravenous search for wealth on the coast of Venezuela. After literally massacring a Spanish garrison on the island of Oruba, Olonnais takes Maracaïbo with little resistance. On learning that its residents had fled to nearby Gibraltar with the city's treasures, his troops pillage the town for six weeks and burn it to the ground. Back in Maracaïbo, he demands from residents an enormous ransom to save that city from destruction by fire, all the while raiding it for every treasure it contains in a devastating act of robbery. Not sparing the most sacred structures, his men delight in the trappings of divine worship: "The pirates (*aventuriers*) demolished churches and brought the ornaments, paintings, icons, sculptures, bells, and even the crosses from the bell towers, to the island of Tortuga, where they decided they would build a chapel." For the pirates, mass ruin and violence become both the means of acquiring wealth and an end in themselves, since the pleasure of criminality is as enticing as the booty. Captain Morgan's expeditions epitomize the piratical war on riches, as he habitually terrorizes "bourgeois" individuals in order to seize their wealth. In Maracaïbo, Morgan's men repeatedly torture and burn a wealthy Portuguese man and hang another from his genitals until they confess to having hidden their wealth (223–24), the discovery of which sets off five weeks of pillage and destruction. Murder, however, is usually limited to Spanish soldiers. Oexmelin recounts piratical cruelties in lurid detail, displaying a surgeon's fascination with gore. The infamous filibuster known as Roc is among the most vicious: "He was barbarous enough to put several of them [the Spanish] on the spit and roast them over a fire" (99). However, equal treatment is expected on each side. After taking prisoners from a Spanish galleon and killing the injured, Olonnais learns that these soldiers had planned to murder every last buccaneer in the event of a conflict. He promptly assassinates them in a horrible manner: "He opened the hatch and ordered the Spanish to come out one by one. As soon as they came up, he beheaded them with his saber" (109).

Although pirates often triumphed militarily by the sheer force of their numbers, the pirate narrative depends on stories of against-the-odds bravery and underdog heroism, some of which historians consider to be fantastic. Yet, compared to that of the warriors of old, who proclaimed a higher cause or derived legitimacy from nobility itself, piratical violence appeared to be particularly illegitimate and gratuitous. Stories of treachery thus served a justificatory function. Piratical savagery may have been motivated by greed alone, but the booty appeared as somehow *earned* when the pirates exposed themselves to unbelievable odds and dangers to acquire it. Oexmelin explains that "the most precious things in the world cost them no more than the effort spent to take them, and when they have, they think that they own them legitimately" (80). In this sense, piracy follows the logic of gambling, whereby the higher the odds the greater the rewards. Alternatively, the harder the fight the more there is to gain: "The most courageous . . . fancied that if the Spanish put up a good fight, it was a sure sign that there was great booty to be had" (252). Known to be fearless in the worst of circumstances—"brave, determined and intrepid, no dangers or hardships can stop them in their raids"—pirates are even willing to maximize risk as a means of forcing themselves into an all-out struggle for life and victory. When initiating an attack on a large Spanish galleon, Olonnais orders his own ship to be sunk "in order to oblige his men to do everything to prevail" (79). His raid of Gibraltar is especially onerous, as the captain has no choice but to rush a Spanish firing squad, condemning those on the front lines to a certain death in order to secure victory for the rest (119). The rewards were among the most notorious in the history of Caribbean piracy. Yet no pirate struggle was more dramatic than that of Morgan's second expedition to Panama, a rich way station for Peruvian gold. According to Oexmelin, sixteen hundred men on twenty-four boats departed with Morgan, who carried a commission from the governor general of Jamaica. The expedition took a horrific turn when the adventurers were forced to approach the city by land, charging through a swampy wasteland devoid of provisions. Their suffering was more than compensated, however, for after marching for nine days without food from Santa Cruz to Panama the men brought the city to its knees and burned it to the ground. The sacking of Panama made captain Morgan a celebrity throughout Europe and the New World.

Not surprisingly, piratical ventures often thwarted the goals of merchant capital and company colonialism. Rather than investing in productive ventures on land, piratical wealth supported the emergence of a veritable pleasure industry in the Caribbean. Dedicating a chapter to the pirates' pastimes after a round of pillage, Oexmelin describes Port-Royal, Jamaica, and Saint-Domingue as capitals of sin: "We were astonished at the site of them loaded with huge sacks of silver on their shoulders or their heads, or carrying all they could on their backs or in their arms" (178). Making the rounds between the cabaret, bordello, merchant storehouses, and gambling house, they depart dejected and spent, "as wasted and destroyed from their debauchery and indulgence as they had been from the deprivation and hardships of their raids" (178). According to Oexmelin, pirates sanction such inveterate waste and pillage with a fatalistic ethos: "Exposed as we are to infinite dangers, our destiny is quite different from that of other men. Alive today, dead tomorrow, what good is it to us to hoard or set up house? We are more concerned to live life than to save up in order to maintain it" (179). Evidently, the rhetoric of victimhood and necessity was more conducive to heroism than the narrative of self-imposed risk, spontaneous aggression, and transnational gambling. This fatalism subtly obscures the fact that, far from being a product of conditions beyond their control, the pirates' high-risk lifestyle was chosen and supported by their breathtaking waste of resources.

In this sense, pirates liberally threw off the conventions of what Elias would call "affect control" to embrace a life of social savagery and violence on the margins of the known European world. Such a revolt achieves its full significance only if we consider that, far from being lower-class insurgents, many of the most illustrious pirate captains were members of the bourgeoisie and the nobility. Numerous bourgeois men ventured to the colonial frontier to acquire fame, fortune, and an unparalleled degree of power through the use of force. What this space offered was the freedom to perform modes of war, aristocratic heroism and "wildness" that were increasingly implausible in France, where the power over force and coercion was increasingly shifting from the nobility to the state. Only in the colonies could the sons of nobles and the bourgeoisie step outside the law and become the law, thus recalling the nobility's former right to glory and terror. The most prominent members of this international pack of white men gone wild included figures such as Roc, Morgan, Montbars, and Ogeron, whose high social status translated into a distinct talent for savagery. Roc, the son of Dutch merchants in Brazil who emigrated to the Antilles, personifies the figure of the polyglot multinational wild man (see figure 11). He reputedly spoke Dutch, Portuguese, French, English, and Spanish, as well as several Indian languages, a talent that helped him deceive his opponents. Oexmelin describes him thus: "He is manly and robust, of medium height, but solid and upright. His face is wider than it is long, with rather large eyebrows and eyes and a proud but cheerful countenance. He is skilled in handling all types of Indian and European arms, is as good a captain as he is a brave soldier, but terribly given to debauchery. He always walks with an unsheathed saber in hand, and if, by some misfortune, someone should quarrel with him over the smallest thing, he makes nothing of cutting him through or bashing in his head" (99).

The cavalier yet murderous use of the sword and overindulgence in libertinage appear to secure, rather than sabotage, the adventurer's prestige. A similar mix of attributes is apparent in the portrait of Montbars, "the Exterminator." Monbars was of high birth and had been raised with all the amenities of a gentleman. Yet he proved to be among the most ruthless avengers in the West Indies. Oexmelin writes, "I remember seeing him when I was passing through Honduras. He was lively, alert, and full of fire, as are all the Gascons. He was tall, upright, and solid, with a noble, martial air and tawny complexion. As for his eyes, it is difficult to describe their shape

ROCK. BRASILIANO

11. Portrait, 1684, of "Rock Brasiliano," in A. O. Exquemeling, *The Buccaneers of America*, London, 1893. (Reproduced courtesy of the McCormick Library of Special Collections, Northwestern University Library.)

and color: his thick, black eyebrows joined in an arch, almost completely covering them so that they appear to be hidden under a dark canopy. It is easy to see that a man built like this can only be terrible" (313). By emphasizing the grandeur of the Gascon noble in all his physicality, Oexmelin suggests that true nobles can be the best savages. Far from being contradictory, nobility (both social and metaphorical) and savagery appear as mutually affirming, ironic cognates of one another, insofar as they valorize an intrepid spirit and imposing demeanor. Both of these traits are foregrounded in the corresponding portraits of the pirates. Although pirates habitually carried pistols and battles were almost always decided through gun and cannon fire, the portraits in Oexmelin's text consistently present the more virtuous symbol of the sword to signify piratical valiance and skill at fighting.[53] In early modern France, only nobles and soldiers had the privilege of carrying a sword.[54]

Indeed, for all its defiance of traditional authority and democratic leanings, piracy embodied the memory of a class of noblemen whose style of warfare was vanishing in Europe. Yet by performing such extreme acts of violence on a global stage, pirates were not merely expressing their own desires for social ascendancy and noble status at home. Pirates claimed the right to violence while balking at the supposedly noble virtues of selflessness, love of country, and loyalty to the king. In this respect, they were self-consciously mocking all social norms and their associated hierarchies from a position on the margins of state authority. This did not, however, result in any real subversion of the oppressive binaries and power structure that opposed racialized subalterns or native peoples to colonial Europeans. For, despite the pirates' clear hostility to the forms of labor coercion and exploitation undergirding state colonialism, they opportunistically took advantage of oppositions of colonizer and colonized in their encounters with Indians and slaves. In other respects, piracy represented in the extreme the ethos of colonialism itself, that is, a search for profit in which conventional morality and social structures are radically undermined. What elevated the pirate, transformed him into a hero, and made his story worth telling was both the sensational, uninhibited violence of his expeditions and the booty itself, the ultimate goal for which all social laws were flouted. A different form of exploitation from that of agricultural ventures based on slave labor, piracy nonetheless exposed the colonial space as one in which opportunism and the courage to plunder replaced aristocratic essence as the basis for wealth, social status, and power. If piracy was subversive to colonial interests, it was because it operated outside the channels through which the state and maritime bourgeoisie regulated colonial labor, production, and commerce.[55]

When pirates were made into subjects for popular reading, however, the piratical challenge to state colonialism was diffused through the language of valor and heroism. In Oexmelin's text, pirates emerge as veritable military heroes worthy of the reader's awe and admiration. Words such as *courage, valor, ardor,* and *bravery* shape the reader's appreciation of battle scenes, notwithstanding the author's frank denunciation of *barbarism, cruelty, laziness,* and *waste.* By relating piracy to more socially acceptable forms of honorable warfare, the literary text advanced the interests of the state, which desired to reform pirates into responsible soldiers and settlers. These ideological motivations are apparent in the plot of the historical narrative recounting the gradual imposition of royal control over the rebellious pirates at Tortuga and Saint-Domingue. Central to this transition was the state's promotion of former pirates to high posts within the French colonial administration, as though only they could effectively colonize the "men of the coast" (*les gens de la côte*).[56] De Cussy, the governor of Tortuga, articulates this strategy when he entices a group of filibusters to leave the life of brigandage: "I exhort you all to abandon such enterprises and I promise to repay you with every high office imaginable, and to find for each of you work befitting your merit and condition" (331). Most symbolic of the domestication of pirates is the social rise of Ogeron, who was appointed governor

of Saint-Domingue by the newly founded Compagnie des Indes Occidentales in 1664. A minor nobleman from Anjou Province, Ogeron had himself
sailed as a buccaneer and fortune hunter before being promoted to lead the
colony and enforce Louis XIV's policy of repressing piracy. In Oexmelin's
text, Ogeron appears as a skilled and well-loved leader capable of reconcil-
ing company demands with pirate individualism.[57] He builds the colony's
population through the importation of women and families and encourages
buccaneers to cultivate plantations, all the while remaining supportive of
limited piratical expeditions.[58]

The last expedition recounted in the work announces a new era of state
regulation of pirate warfare. In the year 1697, France was concluding the
Nine Years' War against England, Holland, and Spain. Warfare in the
Caribbean had twice led to the destruction of Cap Français, and in retaliation the ex-buccaneer governor, Du Casse, prepared an army of pirates to
cooperate with royal forces. The 1697 mission to Carthagena, the main port
for Spanish treasure fleets sailing from Peru, was the last great buccaneering raid, with the largest booty in the history of French piracy. Du Casse
assembled a joint force of sixteen hundred buccaneers and slaves to fight
alongside nine royal frigates commanded by Baron de Pointis. The implication was that, though buccaneers were a devastating force in themselves,
nothing could be more invincible than their collaboration with the royal
navy, "the glory of the arms of France." Such a venture required the repression of piratical insurgence and a clear show of deference to French royal
authority, both of which are secured by Du Casse's forceful pronounce-
ment of the king's will: "He reprimanded the pirates and told them of the
king's intention to maintain strict discipline in the army. The pirates demonstrated by their submission the deep respect they had for His Majesty"
(342). The reign of absolutism over the rebel buccaneers is the ideology that
closes the book and provides its most cogent message. Pirates are useful
when restrained by order: "The ferocity of their spirit went together well
with the mildness [*douceur*] of the organized troops." In congratulating the
buccaneers for their courageous service, in particular their skill in opening a
path through savage terrain for the regular army, Oexmelin envisions their
prowess as an arm of Louis XIV: "So many extraordinary events are the
product of the powerful genius of only one prince, but one superior to all
others in power, reason, and generosity" (363).[59]

Oexmelin's narrative of the transnational pirate republic combines many
tropes suffusing the European imagination of the Americas: savagery, cannibalism, conquest, valor, heresy, unrestricted consumption, and lawless-

ness. Most importantly, the *Histoire des aventuriers* portrays the colonies as a space in which transient Europeans perform fantasies of decivilization in the New World and are then welcomed back home. Although piratical violence may only be concerned with immediate gain, the text seems to say, the destiny of pirates is just as often to serve the king and receive compensation for their sacrifices in the form of social prestige and high office. Oexmelin attests to the existence of many ex-pirates in high positions who will no longer speak of their pasts: "They would perhaps be angry if it was known that they had been freebooters; although in practicing that profession they had acted admirably on thousands of occasions, which deserve to be reported. I think, however, that they do not mind being exposed, because since that time, their actions have been just as admirable, but more honorable and useful for their country, for they have drawn their swords only in the service of their prince" (144). Like those pirate wild men recuperated into the fold of the state, Oexmelin reinvents himself as a man of letters, domesticated, recivilized, and uniquely qualified to tell the story of the white savage, the original but endangered subject of colonialism in Saint-Domingue.[60] The literary text thus contributes to the state's work of social repression and cultural exclusion both in the colonies and at home. Piracy is transformed from what Norbert Elias would call an "active form of aggression," which directly threatened state interests, into a passive object of voyeuristic pleasure.[61] The *Histoire des aventuriers* offered French subjects of all social ranks an imaginary ground of transgression—distanced in both time and space—onto which they could project their own desires for savagery and aggression without threatening the prerogatives of the absolutist state. At the same time, piracy was the condition of possibility for the landed culture of the Antilles that Du Tertre and Labat would call Creole.

Colonizing the Colonizer: Du Tertre's
Narrative of Colonial Domesticity

As Oexmelin's account suggests, perhaps the most subversive aspect of piracy lay in the pirates' tacit assertion that all was rapine in the colonies, first and foremost the abusive system of indentured servitude from which many pirates had liberated themselves. Through self-righteous displays of cruelty and violence, pirates balked at what passed for social order in the colonies, exposing the fragility of colonial authority and effecting the collapse of might into right. Against this background of violence, social instability, and resistance to traditional authority, missionaries such as Du Tertre and Labat wrote their own histories of the colonies, complete with detailed ethnographic portraits of white creolization. The colonial ideologies they espoused were largely a response to the performance of social freedom by whites themselves. While this included piratical villainy, just as important was the reinvention of class and culture around the economic system of the plantation. For prospective colonists, the Caribbean colonies promised access to one of the most sought-after marks of nobility, the landed estate. Yet, whereas the aristocratic lifestyle in France excluded commerce, its colonial variant was consubstantial with capitalist enterprise, commodified labor, and for-profit production.[62] In this sense, the plantation represented a strange anachronism, a travesty of feudal privilege created in the service of profitability and capital accumulation. The socialization process of settlers was similarly fraught with contradiction. Colonists borrowed liberally from the symbolics of aristocratic rank, appropriating traditional marks of nobility such as arms, luxurious attire, elongated names, and landed estates, even as their mode of production ran directly counter to the noble ethos. In their accounts of white settlers, missionaries struggled to account for the dramatic and spontaneous reorientation of social life that colonialism entailed.

Du Tertre and Labat clearly favored the bourgeois values of private enterprise, hard work, and investment over false claims of nobility and wasteful shows of wealth. Yet, as Du Tertre himself found, any discussion of "les Français dans les Colonies" was controversial in a colony in which the inhabitants so deeply resented inquiries into their social origins. In his first edition, Du Tertre opened his chapter on the subject by affirming the colony's progress from a previous state of disarray, libertinage, and ill repute:

> It is true that, like all the other colonies, our French colonies were made up of all kinds of people gathered from every nation. They were of every condition and age, and different in religion and morals. I confess as well that there were some impious men, atheists, and libertines, who, after having made enough of a fortune to be at ease for the rest of their lives, came to dine in the ports and harbours of France, where their debauchery and scandalous actions discredited the islands and their inhabitants. But I truthfully attest that I have always noticed several good families there, as well as honorable men who feared God and maintained their virtue steadfast. Almost all of the common people live there with great liberty; virtue is highly esteemed and the vicious and wicked are hated by all. They attend church with much devotion and practice the

sacraments as normal. In a word, Christianity is as strongly established there as it is in France. (466)

In the passage, the author describes a putatively past state of the colony as one in which the heterogeneity of morals and origins was detrimental to the birth of an ordered society. The very idea that people of all "nations" would live together appears to be as threatening as their reputed impiety, libertinage, and inveterate search for wealth. The evocation of the traveling nouveau riche who flaunts his wealth back in France is one that would haunt more than one colonial writer attempting to describe the colony as a place worthy of home and local pride rather than a space of plunder and transgression. In the end, the author has no recourse but to affirm the hegemony of a Christian morality strong enough to homogenize a pluralistic society, suggesting a utopian view of the colony that polices itself.

Yet Christianity as a disciplinary, colonizing regime proved to be at odds with a changing structure of secular governance in the islands, which shifted between company and private seigniorial rule over the first fifty years of settlement. Du Tertre's two histories chronicle these changes, often venturing to critique the colonial leadership for fostering the very "heresy" and lax morals the missionaries had set out to eradicate. His 1654 edition was published following the failure of two trading companies—the Compagnie de Saint-Christophe and the Compagnie des Isles de l'Amérique, the latter of which folded in 1648. Founded by royal charter, these enterprises derived revenue from their monopoly of trade in resalable commodities from the colonies—mainly tobacco—as well as the taxation of settlers. In return, they were expected to meet the commercial needs of the colonies, provide leadership and defense, and sponsor their expansion. Never successful in fulfilling these obligations, both companies eventually succumbed to financial difficulties due to the slow pace of agricultural development in French territories coupled with a sharp decline in tobacco prices. In the late 1640s, the islands were sold to their respective colonial governors.[63] In the first-edition history, Du Tertre was highly critical of the companies, claiming that they withheld needed victual and other support on the pretext that the colonists should first provide yield for sale. In contrast, private ownership appeared to offer the colonies a measure of independence: "They now have a Lord present, who, by treating the land as his own and the inhabitants as his good and true subjects, will undoubtedly be more sincerely loved and respectfully honored by them" (469).

By the time Du Tertre published the second edition, *Histoire générale des*

Antilles habitées par les François, Colbert had assumed control of maritime affairs in France and founded La Compagnie des Indes Occidentales.[64] By forcing a sale to buy back the islands from the private governors, the minister brought an end to the seigniorial era. Du Tertre's second-edition history reflects positively on this change. Revising his earlier critique of company rule, the author praised the early history of company colonialism as a golden age of "aristocratic" rule. In contrast, he now viewed the period of private ownership as quasi totalitarian: "The governors were absolute masters. . . . With the same authority with which they received whomever they wanted in their islands, they banished those who did not please them." (2:416). Du Tertre's polemic highlights the power disputes between missionaries carrying the moral legitimacy of the enterprise and the governors, whose political and administrative authority often directly thwarted missionary aims. The case of Philippe de Lonvilliers de Poincy is especially interesting, for he aspired to a particular form of imperial power and grandeur that had been almost wholly absent from the paltry beginnings of the colonization. In his capacity as governor general residing in Saint-Christophe, Poincy was responsible for extending French control over fourteen additional islands.[65] Most sensational was his importation of an army of workers—carpenters, locksmiths, brick makers, and masons—to construct an extravagant neoclassical chateau (see figure 12). The building was situated on a mountaintop and surrounded by manicured gardens, tree-lined alleys, and a chapel.[66] Du Tertre denounced Poincy's arrogance, in particular the governor's repeated defiance of royal orders to step down from power and his repression of anyone who opposed his rule: "Henceforth he was concerned only to maintain power by fear and by force" (1:169).

As though in response to the self-indulgence and abuse of power that private ownership entailed, Du Tertre's second-edition history emphasized colonial submission to the absolute monarch. A biblical allegory undergirds the author's account of the birth of colonial society; as in the Creation, the colonies were pulled out of nothingness by the pains of men and the glory of the Sun King: "We owe it to our triumphant monarch, who like a shining sun sends his rays to these faraway countries by the care he takes to maintain them in peace and tranquility [*repos*], and to bring forth from there an abundance of all kinds of goods" (2:397). This vision of colonial order entailed agricultural production, the repression of Indian resistance, and a steady flow of trade with the mother country. The question remained, however, as to who made up the majority of the population. For even as Du Tertre imposed a vision of moral order and discipline on colonial reality, he

Paysage d'une partie de l'Ile de S. Christofle, auec un Crayon du Chasteau de Mr. le General.

1. Le Chasteau. 2. Le Jardin. 3. La Basse cour. 4. La Chapelle et les Offices. 5. Les Escuries. 6. La Tour des munitions. 7. La Ville d'Angele

12. The chateau of General Philippe de Lonvilliers de Poincy, governor of Saint Christopher, in César de Rochefort, *Histoire naturelle et morale des iles Antilles de l'Amérique*, Rotterdam, 1681. (Photograph reproduced courtesy of the Newberry Library.)

could not ignore the reordering of social life and values that colonialism entailed, nor the abuses inherent in a hierarchized productive order dependent largely on indentured or permanent servitude.

In the section of the *Histoire générale des Antilles* entitled "Mes voyages aux Antilles, mes retours en France . . . ," themes of illness, madness, and decay structure the author's account of crossing from the port at Dieppe to the Antilles in 1640. So loaded is the ship with cargo—evidence of the first priority for colonial investors—that the more than two hundred passengers "of all ages, nations and religions" can hardly find room for themselves and slowly experience the loss of their moral, social, and mental moorings (2:40). Physically and culturally heterogeneous, none are exempt from the physical hardships of the crossing, which included a scarcity of provisions and "the intolerable stench of ships filled with the sick, sleeping on top of each other amidst filth and excrement." The only respite from such misery is the carnivalesque ritual that marks the ship's passage through the Tropic of Cancer. In this scene, the mariners lead the passengers through a sort of pastiche of Christian baptism by dunking each of them several times in ocean water. Presiding over the ceremony are the ship's crew, disguised in a most extraordinary fashion: "All the ship's officers dress as grotesquely and foolishly as possible. Most of them are armed with tridents, harpoons, and other marine instruments. Others take up razors, cauldrons, dripping pans, and similar cooking utensils. They smear their faces with the black residue from the bottom of kettles, making themselves so hideous and ugly that one would take them for real demons" (2:42). Surprisingly, Du Tertre excuses the ritual as a form of baptism signifying the passengers' courageous entry into the tropics, another world of sorts, where, according to legend and Saint Augustine's conviction, man could not survive.[67] The scene arguably reflects particularly racial anxieties regarding the torrid zone and its potential to bring about monstrous bodily transformations, such as the blackening of the skin, madness, and death, in Europeans. As though in celebration of a safe passage, the ceremony concludes with cathartic festivities described by the author as "excessive rejoicing and debauchery" (2:43).[68]

Themes of sickness, madness, and social confusion reappear in Du Tertre's account of his second voyage to the islands. Describing a stopover on the Spanish-dominated island of Madeira, off the coast of Africa, the author worries that the consumption of wine may compound the effects of the climate on the passengers. Again at sea, he remarks at length on the dementia that seems to overtake them, revealing the sea to be a space of madness and liminality:

> We had not gone a hundred leagues when the most reasonable among us began to lose hope and become hypochondriacs, without even having a fever. In this state, our whole crew was worthy of laughter and pity at the same time. Some were imagining death lurking over their shoulder and struggled day and night to rid themselves of this burden. Others spent their time by rolling barrels on the deck. Still others were convinced they were kings and treated everyone else as ambassadors and princes. In the end each man had a different occupation. This strange illness lasted three weeks, during which time there were never more than two or three reasonable people on board the ship, whom God kept safe to prevent the others from throwing themselves into the sea, and to hold onto the rudder. For without this the smallest gust of wind certainly would have frightened us. If anyone had encountered us in this pitiful state, he would have believed us to be a transmigration from the hospitals of Paris to the West Indies. (2:54)

Divorced from all social reality outside the ship itself and traveling in a time-less, unending ocean toward an unknown world, the travelers experience a loss of all boundaries—between life and death, sanity and insanity, health and sickness, rich and poor, noble and nonnoble.[69] Oscillating uncontrol-lably between fear of death and delusions of grandeur, they feign illness, hallucinate, and perform rituals of social travesty, reimagining themselves as royalty. Here, Du Tertre draws on the European tradition associating the sea with folly, melancholy, and a loss of stable attachments to God and coun-try. By comparing the vessel of colonial crossing to a hospital, he conjures as well the image of the "ship of fools," in which madmen were received and committed to an errant existence.[70] The author includes himself among those few passengers whose reason is protected by the divine, as though to keep the entire ship from drifting into mental and spatial oblivion.

Yet, while the ship of fools is a central figure for the liminality of sea travel, the trope of the hospital signifies the social meanings of the colonial crossing. By the mid–seventeenth century, the principal function of French hospitals was to house, feed, and contain destitute persons, who presented themselves willingly or were forcibly committed by the police.[71] As reposi-tories of the unemployed and socially dysfunctional, the hospitals of Paris were an important source of immigrants to the colonies.[72] The literal and figural valences of the hospital image become all the more transparent in the author's account of arrival: "At the cry of 'Land!' " all of the sick came out of the ship's hold like the dead risen from the grave. Immediately all the pas-sengers began throwing off their old, tattered rags from the crossing . . . and began to shave, wash, make up, and straighten themselves, parading their finest possessions to go on land, as if they were getting married. We wit-nessed a hospital transformed into a court, and a troop of beggars ennobled in an instant" (2:44). For the starving, meager, half-moribund hopefuls dis-embarking onto a space of newness, arrival represents an almost miracu-lous experience of rebirth, deliverance, and self-fashioning. In addition to being healed of their sickness and despair, the French urban poor assume the power of travesty and the freedom to reinvent themselves. Du Tertre's use of *ennobled* gestures to the social significance of dress in a society situ-ated entirely outside the bounds of traditional mechanisms for determining and policing class boundaries.

In his chapter "Les habitants des Antilles," Du Tertre prescribes a set of values that would channel popular desires for social reinvention toward the economic goals of the colonial enterprise. Essential to this narrative is a notion of colonial domesticity conceived entirely in terms of the social organization of plantation agriculture, one that encompasses the almost exclusively masculine roots of French colonization. The author proposes a double vision of family—one based on marriage and another on *matelotage*, a term deriving from the word *matelot* (sailor), which in its colonial usage referred to the cohabitation of two men. This domestic relation underscores the homosocial character of piracy and male indentured servitude, that is, the extent to which survival on the colonial frontier depended on intense, intimate bonds between men.[73] These male-male relationships were not necessarily synonymous with homosexual desire. Rather, coupling fit into the cycle of upward mobility and labor renewal. Du Tertre explains that once a European servant's contract with his master expired, he would join efforts with another freed servant, and together they would clear a plot of land and begin their own plantation with the purchase of indentured servants and slaves. While emphasizing that matelotage was meant to be provisional— each partner was in a sense awaiting a wife with whom to found a tradi- tional family—Du Tertre admits that matelots would often stay together in the presence of a woman, so strong was the homosocial bond. The au- thor defends this unusual domestic arrangement by stressing its formative role in the emergence of Creole society: "All the best families on the islands started this way" (2:426).

Indeed, the system of indentured servitude was at least as old as the first company expedition and was reformed by d'Esnambuc when in 1633 workers threatened sedition against their masters, protesting their protracted terms of labor. D'Esnambuc established a three-year standard, such that the ser- vants, or engagés, were henceforth known as "the thirty-six months."[74] En- gagés were often from the lower classes but not always. One of the earliest accounts of the Antilles was written by Guillaume Coppier, an engagé and son of a notary in Lyon who sailed from Le Havre in 1627 on a ship carry- ing six hundred passengers.[75] In the first decades of settlement, the trade in engagés was a veritable business due to the extreme shortage of labor in the colonies. Throughout the seventeenth century, the Crown actively encouraged the institution of indentured servitude to counterbalance the demographic and social consequences of slavery.[76] Yet administrators and missionary writers decried the systematic abuse of recruits, many of whom were of higher birth than their masters. In 1680, Lieutenant General Du Blénac gave a candid account of the violence: "The treatment of the inden- tured servants makes one tremble. . . . It is unbelievable. I would have to be enraged to beat my horse or my dog in that way. Every day I see some whose bodies are covered with abscesses from the force of the blows."[77] Such brutality led to sedition and revolt, especially in Saint-Domingue, where, as we have seen, engagés frequently joined bands of marauders, buccaneers, and pirates in the hills and at sea.[78] Du Tertre deplored the bad treatment of engagés as "the only thing that appears grievous [*fascheux*] to me" about island life (2:448). He denounced in particular the ship's captains who seduced their prey at the ports of Dieppe, Le Havre, Saint-Malo, and La Rochelle: "Captains who took part in this abominable trade quite often cajoled poor students and sons of good birth, making them believe a thousand wonders about the country where they would be reduced to slavery" (2:437).[79] In one case, a captain seized two hundred such underage recruits and sold them to the English in Barbados; all of them reportedly died.

It is not surprising, therefore, that for all the stability matelotage brought to indentured servants, Du Tertre portrays European women as the indispensable catalyst for the emergence of a social order. In his narrative of colonial origins, there was once a land of disparate, nomadic brutes, who made their living trading pelts, raiding ships, producing crops, and the like, until God brought French women to domesticate them. Women had the effect of tying them to a sedentary, landed existence, creating social bonds, and enabling the biological reproduction of the settler class: "Marriage made the men settle down. By fathering many children who have no knowledge of France, they strengthened the Colonies and established a very pleasant and agreeable way of life there" (2:443). As Jean Bernabé has argued, the importance of reproduction in the colony for emergent Creole societies was that it established a new autochtonous population that could claim *jus soli*, or the right to the land through birth in the territory.[80] Yet Du Tertre's notion of family encompassed much more than the biological kin; the family was conceived as a unit of production encompassing all levels of the labor hierarchy. Writes Du Tertre: "Families of married people are usually composed of three kinds of people: the masters, the French servants, and the slaves" (2:427). In seventeenth-century France, the word *family* referred both to a notion of lineage linked to the concept of "nobility of race" and an idea of the household, which included kin and domestics living under the same roof.[81] Du Tertre's usage recalls as well the notion of the patriarchal family in the Old Testament scriptures and ancient Rome, where *family* referred to "the collection of slaves and freed slaves attached to a married couple."[82] Most importantly, Du Tertre's colonial family is synonymous with production itself, since the author makes no distinction between private and work space: "Each family of a little importance made up a kind of Hamlet, for besides the principal cabin [*case*] where they lived, there were many other small buildings close together, in the center of which stood the large tobacco house" (2:429).

The specificity of Du Tertre's colonial patriarchy, however, is that it was founded almost entirely through the commoditization of persons. Most members of the family were either hired or bought outright by the male, including wives, so scarce were white women in the mid–seventeenth century.[83] Men avid for conjugal pleasures and domestic comforts essentially purchased women as indentured servants and "freed" them in marriage. According to Du Tertre, the practice of amassing women from in and around Paris began around 1640. Originally led by company officials, the trade in women later fell under the control of female lords such as Madame de la Fayolle, who ran the 1643 shipment of young girls from France and fashioned herself as a legendary godmother of the colonies: "It was by the means of the love trade [ces commerces d'amour] that she made her reputation in the Islands. With her proud and lively temper, she established such an empire that she practically ruled the commanders" (1:228).[84] Du Tertre maintained an ambivalent attitude toward women, whom he viewed both as guarantors of male salvation and proponents of a dangerous form of social travesty. In describing the female auction, he is less critical of male avarice than of the pretension of lower class women to mask their social origins, reinventing themselves as "noble" in the process: "The women had hardly come to shore when they would run all at once to the market and to love. They often did not examine their birth, virtue, or beauty, and two days after their arrival they would marry them without knowing them, for almost none of these affected women [precieuses] failed to boast of good connections in France. Whatever the case, the husband dressed her as sumptuously as he could, and thought himself blessed to have gotten her at this price" (2:428). For Du Tertre, women represent a fraudulent drain on male resources, contaminating the island with vanity and luxury. Adorned in fine fabrics, satin and tapestry, women literally exhibited the fruits of their husbands' labors, thus giving rise to a popular saying that "the Islands were hell for the Frenchmen and heaven for their wives" (2:446).

Du Tertre's response to women indicates the author's struggle to fully accept the radical reinvention of social life that colonialism entailed. On one hand, he embraces the recalibration of status among whites based on wealth: "There is no difference, between noble or nonnoble among the inhabitants; he who owns the most is the most respected" (2:445). Du Tertre views this social leavening positively, pointing out both the opportunities for obtaining land and a plantation and the infectious sense of camaraderie that binds the community of white settlers across cultural, regional, and social differences. Forged in the moment of arrival, when droves of inhabitants rush to welcome incoming passengers at the ports, hospitality emerges as the privileged mode of colonial social contact. Yet in Du Tertre's account, despite the obsolescence of hereditary aristocracy in the colonies, colonials have an extreme taste for luxury in dress: "They are especially taken with beautiful linens, and because most do not wear doublets, they have fine shirts of Dutch linen with extraordinarily long neckties. Their stockings are trimmed at the top with fine cloth, embroidered with fine silver or gold lace, or laden with ruffles. The officers are usually richly dressed and have a particular taste for plumes of feathers and shoulder belts, for which they spare no expense" (2:445). Such adornment in dress was especially extravagant at a time when the royal government was acting to protect noble appearance and limit the merging of conditions through sumptuary laws.[85] Du Tertre thus anticipates a concern with colonial luxury and sartorial elegance that would explode in the following century. Yet, whereas luxury typified both men's and women's dress in the colonies, Du Tertre attributes a particular predilection for nobility to female society. While reaping the profits of male labor, women are portrayed as appropriating aristocratic airs unbefitting their low social origins. In Du Tertre's account, the most affluent women fashion themselves as a leisure class. Although all white men are armed as soldiers, their wives derive from this an undue sense of privilege, as though elevated to the nobility: "They believe that [their husbands'] condition as soldiers means that they deserve to be treated as gentlewomen" (2:446). The author complains, furthermore, that the women hold "court" around the governor's wife as though in the presence of royalty.

Ultimately, Du Tertre's critique of women discloses a larger anxiety about the breakdown of Old Regime social hierarchies in the colonies, one that has less to do with women's vanity than the difficulty of intervening in the creolization process. What is subversive to the missionary is not that the formerly poor can become rich but that the poor may misrepresent themselves as social elites, thus reducing social rank to a matter of performance and display. Ultimately, the conundrum derived from the central contradiction of colonialism itself, in that it functioned as an anachronistic simulacrum of the noble estate achieved through commercial means and toward commercial ends. Though immersed in for-profit production for a European market, the white planter class exploited slave society to command a semblance of precapitalist aristocratic privilege. The case of women was all the more subversive, since by cross-dressing as courtiers they implicitly contested Du

Tertre's own model of colonial domesticity, which celebrated the values of virtue, simplicity, piety, and reproduction. Du Tertre complained, "Most of the fathers and mothers raise their daughters with too much liberty; for this reason they lack the reserve and modesty of our French girls, as well as many other things they ought to know, such as how to work with needle-point, linens, washing, and such." (2:447). In criticizing young women for not being modest enough, the passage also foreshadows the denunciation of white female libertinage that would reach fruition in the novella by Pierre-Corneille Blessebois.[86]

Father Labat's Colonial Conquest

What is striking in Du Tertre's figuration of colonial domesticity is the distanced manner of description, as though the author, while he was an eye-witness to what he describes, nonetheless remains outside of it. By contrast, the most famous work on the colonial French Caribbean was produced by a missionary who wrote in the style of a diarist, demonstrating through his very experience the social and cultural change occurring in his midst. Critics have described Jean-Baptiste Labat as legendary, irrepressible, arrogant, Rabelaisian, and fully secularized. Although his oeuvre of published travel narratives spans several continents in its referential breadth, he is best known for the *Nouveau voyage aux isles de l'Amerique*.[87] The eight volumes comprising the expanded edition of 1742 have been read for more than two centuries, as Labat was the most prolific informant on the French Caribbean to publish in the eighteenth century. Abbé Prévost relied on his text to write the history and natural descriptions of the French Antilles in volume 15 of his geographic encyclopedia, *Histoire générale des voyages*. Noting Labat's unique style, however, Prévost voiced this complaint: "In the extreme variety of his Descriptions, portraits [*peintures*], characters, and reflections, he lacks a little order, such that it is even impossible to give him the benefit of the doubt."[88] It is a criticism that Labat himself anticipated in the preface to the first edition of 1722. Dismissing the idea that his work should follow a methodical organization—"that I should arrange things in such a way that each species was found under its genus"—the author embraces a more ambulatory style expressive of subjective experiences that he apparently recorded in a journal: "I preferred to follow my Journal and write things in the way that I saw, learned, or did them." (1:18). The central organizing principle is chronology, as the writer tells a story inclusive of the entire twelve years of his Caribbean sojourn. To this are added liberal digressions on a variety of topics, such that the resulting text is heterogeneous and unwieldy: technical, historical, anecdotal, satirical, documentary, and impressionistic all at once. A consummate diarist, Labat wrote of tropical nature, industry, and society in miniaturist detail. Salient portraits of diverse colonial characters such as clergy, planters, prisoners, indentured servants, slaves, pirates, and Caribs are laced with painstaking descriptions of the appearance and behavior of all manner of island species, down to the last termite.

The most dominant subject of the work, however, is Labat himself. Born in Paris in 1663, this Dominican priest and former professor of philosophy and mathematics volunteered to leave the convent at the Rue Saint-Honoré for the colonies in order to replace deceased missionaries on Martinique. Arriving in 1693, he was assigned to the small parish of Macouba and charged with reviving the debilitated grounds and managing a sugar plantation.[89] Labat's journey coincided with the height of the sugar revolution in the Caribbean. By the 1660s, sugar had become the chief industry in the Lesser Antilles, and by 1685 French territories ranked second in world sugar production after those of the English.[90] Labat became extremely active in improving sugar production techniques in the French colonies, contributing to the design and operation of sugar mills and refineries. As he developed a reputation as a knowledgeable manager, engineer, and architect, he also directed the construction of church properties, a Freemason lodge, water mills, forts, and defenses. His many successes brought him notoriety among the clergy and the secular administration, and Labat quickly ascended the ranks of the Dominican leadership to assume the role of acting superior and finally superior at Martinique. His enormous ego and unstoppable ambition brought about his downfall, however, for he eventually became known in official circles as a "man of wit, but impudent and impassioned," and a "meddler."[91] An obstinate overachiever, Labat was at the same time convinced that he was not sufficiently appreciated by the royal authorities. As his relationships with members of the church and colonial administration soured, he was sent to France, ostensibly on official business. Later the authorities refused him readmittance to the colonies and forbade him to correspond with anyone there.[92] He spent several years in Italy as an inquisitorial judge before returning to France, where he began his career as a travel writer. Labat produced numerous works on America, Africa, Europe, and the East Indies, most of which were compilations based on the private journals of other travelers.[93] Apart from his work on the West Indies, only *Voyages en Espagne et en Italie* (Paris, 1730) was based on his own writings. The *Nouveau*

Voyage was published in two editions, in 1722 and 1742, the latter appearing four years after the author's death.[94]

As though in response to the dishonor of his virtual expulsion from the colonies, Labat's narrative is marked by an egotistical, self-justificatory anxiety, as he insists on his influence and the value of his expertise in almost all matters. He justifies the excessive documentation of his own projects, scientific insights, and opinions through a profession of civic duty: "A writer must not withhold anything known to him that could be useful to his nation" (1:150). By attending to his individual judgments and physical and emotional reactions to his environment, however, Labat presented the colony and himself as consubstantial. The relationship between autobiography and the narrative of the islands is suggested in the book's frontispiece, which displays a mise en abyme of the author's portrait held against a colonial landscape (see figure 13). Father Labat is shown in his priest's cloak and hood, his frame engraved with the date of his death in 1738. A muscular, nearly naked black man happily bears the weight of the priest's image, holding the portrait in one hand as he gestures to the image with the other. The identity of this personage is rendered ambiguous due to his feathered garment and black skin. Yet his placement and expression indicate the ideological nature of the visual and narrative texts of the *Voyage*. Behind him lies a fertile landscape containing houses, roads, and tropical animals, with a boat approaching in the open sea. It is a picture of an orderly colonial nature turned to productive purposes. At the base of the image appears an inscription declaring Labat's conformity with the French classical aesthetic and in particular his talent for instructing the reader and mixing "the pleasing and the useful." The implication of this montage is that Labat does not exist outside the colony and the colony exists because of him. The book, then, is the textual representation of both.

In this respect, Labat's narrative stands as a firsthand account of what I will call "indigenization" or the process of becoming "native" to the colonial environment. Whereas Du Tertre emphasized birth in the colony as a means of securing Creole belonging and greatly depreciated the tendency of colonials to "go wild," Labat endorses the idea that one may become "native" to a place without being born there. He represents colonization as fundamentally driven by Europeans' desire to overcome the foreignness of the landscape by transforming it, mastering it, and forcibly remaking it so as to feel at home in it. At the same time, indigenization for Labat cannot be disassociated from upward mobility in the colonies, for the author was in search of social as well as economic returns. More generally, Labat reveals

13. Frontispiece, in Jean-Baptiste Labat, *Nouveau voyage aux isles de l'Amérique*, 1742. (Reproduced courtesy of the Rare Book, Manuscript, and Special Collections Library, Duke University.)

the extent to which the French immigrants underwent a dramatic change as they adapted to each other, the tropical environment, and the near total absence in the colonies of traditional codes of conduct regulating social, civil, and cultural life.

Labat's personal and figural conquest of tropical nature occurs through a process of acclimation that transforms his tastes, habits, and physical constitution. At the outset, he experiences the passage into the "New World" as a deconstruction and reconstruction of the body, which is besieged by a strange and dangerous malady. He begins his voyage in a state of physical precariousness, falling so seriously ill that he feigns his recovery so as to be allowed on the ship. Though he recovers one month later at sea, another disease would await him on the other side of the ocean. Among Labat's first impressions of the islands is the sight of the terrible *mal de Siam*, or bubonic plague, ravaging a fellow missionary. He describes the drastic effect of this illness in gruesome detail, though not without wit: "What was convenient about this illness was that it carried off its victims in very little time, six or seven days at most and it was over" (1:55). Throughout the text, scenes of suffering from the plague recur to represent the danger and lack of salubrity of the colonial environment for transplanted Europeans. Said to have been brought on a ship that originated in Siam and having passed through Brazil, the illness ravaged newcomers in the Caribbean for more than seven years. Labat recounts the horrific deaths of a clergyman whose body turned black and spurted blood from all sides and a young arrival at Fort Royal who body progressively darkened and atrophied until he was lifeless. But the fact that Labat himself is struck by the illness twice and recovers both times suggests his growing hardiness and physical adaptation to colonial life. He spares the reader no detail of his bout with the plague, filling his text with descriptions of his convulsions and bodily discoloration.

Labat's ability to survive the worst of island afflictions is complemented by his frank delight with island cuisines quite unknown to the French palate. Eating is a resounding theme in the text; Labat's itinerary revolves around the table, the locus of dialogue, conviviality, and the study of island characters of all ranks. In an account of island gastronomy, Labat shows himself to have an insatiable taste for such island delicacies as turtle, manioc bread, and fermented beverages made in the manner of the Caribs. Most surprising is Labat's taste for island fauna. Of baked turtle, he exclaims: "Never have I eaten anything so appetizing and flavorful" (1:99). Describing his stop in Saint-Christophe on a voyage to Saint-Domingue, he recounts the pastime of hunting wild monkeys, culminating in their consumption at the dinner table: "It is true that I felt a certain revulsion when I first saw what resembled the heads of four small children in the soup, but as soon as I tasted it, I easily moved beyond this consideration and continued to eat it with pleasure" (4:14). That Labat would so enthusiastically describe this culinary experience as something close to cannibalism is telling of his willingness to embrace difference and be changed by it. His adventurous appetite even leads him to roast the worms found in the trunks of palm trees, called *vers de palmistes* (palm worms): "They are very good to eat and quite delicate once one has overcome the revulsion one ordinarily feels for eating worms, especially when they are seen alive" (1:213). The literal ingestion and incorporation of island curiosities by the author are symbolic of his gradual indigenization into island landscapes.

The same may be said of Labat's sustained appetite for construction, invention, and experimentation in nature. In the course of the narrative, the landscape shifts from being an adversary to a beneficent host that yields its secrets to the missionary naturalist. Upon first arriving in Martinique, Labat views the environment as untamed, hostile, and wild: "I could not marvel enough at how we had come to live on this Island. To me it appeared to be nothing but an hideous mountain dotted [*entrecoupée*] with precipices. Nothing gave me pleasure save the green one sees everywhere, which seemed novel and agreeable to me, considering the season we were in" (1:51). From within this nature of gigantic altitudes and unruly vegetation, Labat initiates the work of indigenization by researching, observing, and exposing himself physically to hundreds of species of animals and insects (see figure 14). In turn, he takes pleasure in the power of nature to act on him, inexorably altering his tastes, emotions, and view of the world. When describing turtles, for example, he recounts not only the different varieties but how to catch them, including a humorous description of his attempt to ride on the back of a tortoise: "It is the roughest of carriages" (1:160). While in Guadeloupe, he embarks on field trips to investigate the volcanic properties of the island's mountaintops and underwater geysers. Discovering a profusion of boiling water currents just off the beach, he attempts to boil an egg, later discovering the source of the sulfur. The same zeal for experimentation and research motivates the author's detailed disquisitions on the insect world. On the subject of termites, he meticulously describes their behavior, recounting how he deliberately poked at their hut to learn how they almost instantaneously rebuild the damage (1:399). Especially symbolic is his ascent, accompanied by several slaves, to a sulfur spring (*la souffrière*) atop the mountain Piton, an event that represents a full transformation from

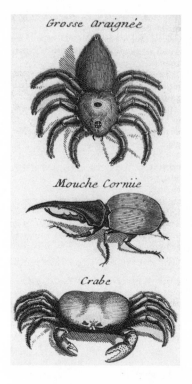

Grosse Araignée

Mouche Cornüe

Crabe

14. Engraving of invertebrates, in Jean-Baptiste Labat, *Nouveau voyage aux isles de l'Amérique*, Paris, 1722. (Reproduced courtesy of the McCormick Library of Special Collections, Northwestern University Library.)

his original distaste for the rugged mountain heights of the islands. The excursion represents his effective conquest of the island and its perils, a feat seemingly rewarded by the panoramic vista from its highest point. Noting its precarious position and the dangerous craters surrounding it, Labat extols the dramatic beauty of the view: "We could see Dominica, the Saints, Grande Terre and Marie Galante, as if we were above them. When we were higher up we could see clearly Martinique, Monsarat, Nieves, and other neighboring islands. I do not believe there is a more beautiful point of view on earth" (1:412).

Labat's interest in island nature is largely channeled toward his ambitions to transform it through cultivation and industry. By the time he arrived in the Caribbean, the clergy no longer operated independent of the colonial economy of for-profit production. Gone were the days when the companies supplied missionaries with an annual allowance for the material outfitting of the church and land for subsistence agriculture. As successive companies faced financial ruin, missionaries were obliged to produce export crops such as sugar and tobacco in exchange for manufactures and food.[95] Labat vigorously defends this involvement in production and commerce as necessary for the survival of the religious orders, yet it is clear that his own ambitions were at stake. The desire to improve island technologies and infrastructure all but superseded the care of souls as the driving motivation behind Labat's colonial mission. Indeed, the author regarded the depressed condition of the Dominican plantation at Fond St.-Jacques as a personal opportunity: "All of these buildings were as dilapidated on the outside as they were badly furnished on the inside. . . . Besides, our house was in debt by approximately seven hundred thousand pounds of sugar and had no more credit. . . . Such was the state of our affairs in Martinique upon my arrival there. We will see the difference upon my departure in 1705" (1:72–73).

In recognizing the industrial aspects of sugar production, Sydney Mintz first suggested what scholars of empire now argue vehemently: that the colonies represented a space not only for the importation of European commodities but for the development of modes of production and social control that foreshadowed and in many cases directly informed the growth of industrial power on European soil.[96] Labat pondered seriously the sugar revolution sweeping the French Caribbean islands as one that would irrevocably affect their demographics, landscape, and culture. Although sugar farmers enjoyed the most wealth and prestige of all cultivators, due in large part to the exorbitant capital investment required to process cane, Labat remained ambivalent about the demographic trends accompanying the rise of sugar production. His greatest concern was that a majority slave population would threaten island identity and security. In contrast, he associates tobacco and its culture of matelotage with colonial origins: "It was the free trade in tobacco that attracted this multitude of vessels from all nations and such a prodigious number of settlers" (3:333). In addition to shifting colonial demographics, sugar farming resulted in massive deforestation of the islands, a theme that recurs in the literature of late-eighteenth-century visitors to Saint-Domingue. Land was cleared of indigenous forests not only to make room for the cane fields but also to provide fuel for the massive cauldrons used in refining. Labat attributes the increase of houses made of masonry to the scarcity of wood in the islands (2:294). Throughout his text, he insists on the need to diversify colonial agriculture and explore new markets, suggesting that the production of tea, coffee, and even olives would be less devastating to the landscape.

Yet, despite Labat's critique of sugar as a crop, his text is replete with the narrative and pictorial evidence of its takeover. He integrates technical discourse on the agricultural and industrial aspects of sugar production into a personal memoir and general history of the islands destined for a

15. "Sucrerie," in Jean-Baptiste Du Tertre, *Histoire générale des Antilles habitées par les François*. Paris, 1667–71. (Reproduced courtesy of the McCormick Library of Special Collections, Northwestern University Library.)

wide readership. This was a significant departure from the work of Du Tertre, for example, who almost completely avoided the specifics of colonial production even when treating the subjects of slave labor, commerce, and the family. In the *Histoire générale des Antilles*, colonial industries were portrayed through idealized, allegorical illustrations of the industrial process. In an image entitled "Sucrerie," the structures of sugar production—the mill, boiling house, and slave quarters—are embedded within a pastoral landscape of tropical trees and plants (see figure 15). The key at the bottom of the image negates the historical contingency and social constructedness of sugar production, presenting the industrial process and the social system that drives it as entirely natural to the Caribbean landscape. Man-made components of the plantation are classified with species of exotic flora as though there is no difference in kind between nature and machine. In contrast, Labat's treatise on sugar occupies more than half of the second volume of the *Nouveau voyage*. In addition to analyzing the costs of maintaining slaves, the types of personnel needed to oversee their work, and the protocol for growing cane, Labat describes how best to design a sugar plantation. The plantation is for Labat a built environment, the very construction of which reflects a desire to exploit the environment for maximum productivity. In particular, he devotes considerable attention to the mechanics of

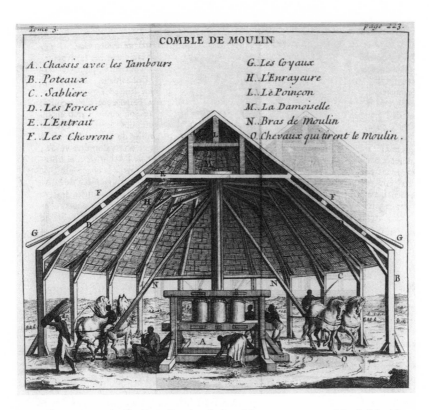

Tome 3.   *Page 223.*

COMBLE DE MOULIN

A..*Chassis avec les Tambours*   G..*Les Coyaux*
B..*Poteaux*   H..*L'Enrayeure*
C..*Sabliere*   L..*Lè Poinçon*
D..*Les Forces*   M..*La Damoiselle*
E..*L'Entrait*   N..*Bras de moulin*
F..*Les Chevrons*   O..*Chevaux qui tirent le moulin .*

16. "Comble de moulin," in Jean-Baptiste Labat, *Nouveau voyage aux isles de l'Amérique,* 1742. (Reproduced courtesy of the McCormick Library of Special Collections, Northwestern University Library.)

the pressing process required of sugarcane before its juice can be refined into a usable product. With technical illustrations almost completely devoid of aesthetic or allegorical content, the author tirelessly analyzes the merits and disadvantages of three types of sugar mill, all the while exhibiting his expertise in physics, hydraulics, and engineering (see figure 16). He features lengthy descriptions of his own inventions, which include a sugar press and a more wood-conserving, energy-efficient sugar boiling system (2:221–22).

What is particularly striking in Labat's industrial exposé is the way in which it figures humans as both driving and driven by the machinery. Labat offered unusually detailed descriptions of the slaves, exposing their working conditions with a mix of pity and pride. For Labat, their oppressive workload is proof that the colonial sugar factory is one of the premier industries of his time: "Whatever one might say about the iron forges, the glass factories, and other industries, it is certain that none is more harsh than a sugar factory. The former require no more than twelve hours of work instead of the eighteen hours per day at a sugar factory; and from the six hours they have to sleep, one must subtract time to eat, and often time to go looking for crabs, for there are many settlers who are satisfied to give only manioc flour to their slaves" (2:194). In this configuration of factory labor, slaves are made to conform to the pace of the machine or be consumed by it. With an air of nonchalance, Labat relates the horror stories of slaves who fall out of sync with their mechanistic roles, only to be maimed or even executed in the press itself. Such "accidents" are to be controlled through the social manipulation of labor. The author prescribes the use of a black overseer and denounces gallantry and seduction between white servants and slave women as a threat to the industrial process. He recommends, furthermore, that slaves be given extra food at dinner in order to increase their ability to withstand intense fatigue. Yet, despite the author's plan to transform humans into indefatigable units of production, religion remains prominent as the legitimating ideology behind plantation management. Labat calls for regular prayers before dawn and the baptism of new slaves, reminding the master that he is "father of his slaves" and "Christian": "These two qualities should inspire in him sentiments of justice, reason, gentleness, and moderation for them such that he would never demand something by force and the threat of punishment when he can obtain it with gentleness" (2:297).

The detailed attention given to slavery and the industrial process in the *Nouveau voyage* is matched by an unprecedented account of the social history of the seventeenth-century French Caribbean. Departing from Du Tertre's moralist focus on colonial domesticity, Labat presents intimate historical and genealogical portraits of the diverse inhabitants of Martinique and Guadeloupe, often using information from the personal memoirs and journals of private individuals. On one hand, the focus on family history serves to document the emergence of a "Creole" society. The term itself appears frequently throughout the narrative, defined as "born in the country" (1:79). Yet in chronicling the history of legendary families the author is equally concerned to publicize sensational stories of social ascent and enrichment, even at the cost of exposing the ignoble roots of "noble" colonials. On the heels of Oexmelin's salute to the white renegades who rose to fame, fortune, and distinction from a past of seaborne villainy, Labat scrutinizes the sometimes feeble beginnings of some of the more prominent families on land. In the preface of 1742, the author explains: "Some people have complained about my speaking about their origins, as if I intended to make others there look down upon them. I never had this thought. On the contrary, I believed I was honoring them, for it is a real and true honor to rise to the most respectable offices and even to the nobility that the King himself, who is always just, has conferred on them in recognition of their service and fidelity" (1:20). Labat's comments suggest the deep and persistent discomfort associated with social promotion among those colonials who hid their origins so as to project an image of inherited privilege and stable rank. In advocating that colonists embrace their recent social ascent, Labat calls for a revised notion of nobility, one better suited to the fast fortunes and capitalist ethos of a burgeoning plantation society. This is the ideology of the parvenu, which challenged notions of innate status and nobility of blood.[97] By arguing that nobility is a just reward for hard work and talent, Labat presents the colonies as a meritocracy in which elite status is a consequence of hard work and distinguished service to the king.[98]

The island genealogies tell the story of many such sensational success stories. In the author's account of crossing to the New World, his journal documents the lives and characters of the crew members with interest and humor, such as the pirate captain Sieur Kercoue, whose life recalls that of Oexmelin. Leaving Dieppe as an engagé—"he ran away from his father's home"—he was sold to a buccaneer, lived as one, and then went on to piracy (1:45). In later chapters, Labat outlines the trajectories of engagés such as Lozol, la Boissière, and Sieur Verrier. The latter was a Gascon merchant, who, following his marriage to a Creole woman, established sugar and coffee plantations: "With all of this, he was not among the richest. But although we remembered having seen him as an engagé, his good humor and joyful manner made us want to have him on all the assemblies, and it was always a pleasure to go to his home" (1:95). The most remarkable story of a rise to riches is that of a certain Monsieur Roy, who, having arrived as an engagé, became the owner of several plantations with upward of eight hundred slaves (1:121). The acquisition of titles of nobility in the colonies often followed from military achievements, a fact that corroborates the social rise of the fighting pirates. Labat describes at length the exploits of the Buc family of Martinique, members of which battled the Caribs and the English. Their military service over two generations earned them letters of nobility from the king (1:240–41).

Yet, even as the author celebrates the colonies as a space of social transformation and economic opportunity, he displays a certain ambivalence toward the pretensions of the colonial nouveaux riches: "I could make a long list of those who, having come here as engagés or the servants of Buccaneers, are now such big Lords that they can hardly make one step without being in a six-horse carriage" (1:93). The chapters on colonial manufactures and trade speak of the colony's indomitable taste for luxury merchandise: "Everything that is used for clothing, furniture, household ornaments, and especially women's finery, is sold expensively and quickly" (2:327). Even books play a part in the social performance of privilege: "Although our Creoles and other residents [*habitants*] have not degenerated from their ancestral valor, they are still given to the tastes of the rest of the world. They want to seem knowledgeable, they all read, or want to appear to have read. . . . Women are getting into it too, and instead of keeping to their spinning wheels and spindles, they read thick books and pretend to be knowledgeable" (2:329–30).[99] Against the background of faked social distinction, Labat delighted in the ways of the poorest whites on the island. Of a certain M. Lietard, the most destitute white man in the book, Labat writes: "The simplicity of the golden age was reflected in this capital officer's appearance. His feet and legs were covered with the socks and shoes he had brought from his mother's womb. The few white hairs on his head were covered with a straw hat and the rest of his body with a shirt and underpants of good home spun linen. Despite this shabby garb, Monsieur Lietard did not lack wit, good sense and courage" (1:387). Even as Labat encourages colonials to aspire to noble status, it is in the simple poverty of the *petit blanc* that he invests his greatest admiration. The discourse of the noble savage encompasses the entire population of native-born white Creoles, who are invested with the physical robustness once reserved for idealized Caribs: "They are all perfectly well made, and this is common to all Creoles of French and British America, where it is as rare to find hunchbacks, men who are blind in one eye, and cripples, as it is common to see such men in Europe" (4:18).

Of all colonial characters, however, Labat was most fascinated by the filibusters and buccaneers of Saint-Domingue. That he has been called the "pirate's priest" is due to his frequent service to them at sea, saying the Mass and administering the sacraments. In exchange, he gladly accepted any church-related plunder they brought back from rich Spanish ports: "Our Pirates [*Flibustiers*] . . . took over the upkeep of our Churches at no cost to them or us. In fact, by pillaging villages and seizing vessels, they have always been extremely careful to set aside whatever they thought would be suitable for churches" (2:328). What signals the widespread allure of buccaneer lifestyles is the co-optation by the colonial elite of the buccaneer cookout in a pastiche of a putatively uncivilized practice. In a chapter on the subject of the *boucan de cochon*, Labat meticulously re-creates the scene of the buccaneer barbecue with a group of planters. Each guest is given a chore in the preparation of the meal according to the strictest code of compliance with buccaneer rusticity, "the buccaneer order." Even the hunt is reproduced, as guests depart into the woods to add wild game to the main dish of barbecued pork and are called back with two gunshots. For the meal, guests are seated on the ground and no metallic instruments or utensils are allowed, as they would "spoil the buccaneer manners that we seem to want to imitate in this meal" (3:189). Using leaves as napkins and tablecloths, Labat's party enjoys a menu of meat and bread (a minor infraction of buccaneer practice) and extols the virtues of primitivism: "It was in these innocent pleasures that we spent the day so joyously" (3:190).

That the author brings twenty slaves to enact a scene of rustic "innocence" makes the ritual a hyberbolic moment of social boundary construction. In staging scenes of decivilization imputed to white "savages," slave owners affirm both their difference from and desire for the internal other of colonialism. It is only by performing a ritual crossing of the boundary between "noble" and "savage" that white elites both establish and confirm that boundary's existence. At the same time, they self-consciously transform white savagery into a ground for "innocent" amusement, a gesture that both appropriates and trivializes the buccaneer's radical challenge to colonial authority. Buccaneer culture here represents a romantic refuge from the slave-owning lifestyles that alienated colonists—some of whom were former buccaneers—from labor and the land. Likewise, the buccaneer picnic allows for a ritual simulation of "roughing it" in the colony, recalling the frontier culture abandoned by the *grands blancs*, the wealthy white planters, for a simulacrum of nobility on the plantation.

* * *

My investigation has focused on representations of two seemingly opposed social behaviors characterizing colonialism in the seventeenth-century French Caribbean, piracy and plantation agriculture. Despite their contrary aims and means, piracy and plantation society both offered the French the opportunity to mimic forms of power and privilege that were traditionally the sole domain of the French aristocracy. Piracy, while it did entail a significant move toward modern ideals of egalitarianism and collective governance, is far more compelling as a decentralized and transnational regime of force comparable only to the warrior nobility of medieval times. In Oexmelin's account, pirates are romanticized not for their democratic sociability but for the wanton destruction, uninhibited cruelty, and thievery they visited on their enemies, all of which represented the seizure of power in the extreme. Of course, in mimicking the old noble prerogative of force, pillage, and "savagery," pirates also subverted it, for, lacking the strong codes of honor, sacrifice, and service to country on which traditional nobles publicly justified themselves, they instead demonstrated the new basis for status in the colonies—self-interest and profit. It is in this sense that they coincided with the planters. The activity of plantation agriculture offered its own appeal to colonists interested in bettering their social condition, for it enabled them to mimic the aristocratic ideal of the landed estate complete with servants and workers. Yet plantation slavery represented as much an abandonment of noble ideals as an imitation of the material aspect of aristocratic privilege. The capitalist cultivation of land for personal gain clearly ran counter to the noble ethos of honor, duty, and selflessness. The institution of slavery represented a new level of degradation in European social relations of production, thus fundamentally perverting the ideology of mutual obligation that ordered relations between a lord and his peasants.[100]

In their accounts of colonial culture and society, writers confronted this massive confusion of social roles and conditions by attempting to domesticate the "savage" or politically threatening aspects of mimetic nobility. What is fascinating is that, in so reforming social disorder and travesty, writers presented a modern ideal of social relations in which force was monopolized by a state authority, status was based on wealth, and persons fashioned their outward appearance to reflect a desired rather than a fixed or inherited social status. For Oexmelin, what was most useful and subversive about piracy was its unauthorized use of violence. The last French edition of his text represents the virtual colonization of piracy in the interests of the state, reforming pirates in the mold of soldiers and statesmen, a move that reflected the modern emergence of state armies and the absorption of the nobility into the ranks of military leadership and government. Du Tertre reacted to the colonial experience of social and cultural disorientation by proposing a program of moral values true to his role as a religious authority. His ideal of colonial domesticity accommodated the practices of slavery and commercial agriculture and attempted to curb social subversion by orienting colonial values toward cultivation, home, and family. In the process, he articulated a program of patriarchal values that identified women with the vices of luxury and unauthorized social impersonation. Labat, on the other hand, went much further in adapting to and validating the new bases for rank and status being expressed in the colonies. As the most secular of the seventeenth-century colonial missionary writers, and the one most deeply involved in the material development of the island, the institution of slavery, and the cultivation of sugar for financial profit, Labat was himself a model of the very kind of social mobility and confusion of categories that typified many subjects of his travel narrative. This is equally apparent in his vision of colonial creolization, which is based on a subject's transformation in nature, as well as his mastery over it. Labat suggests that this very process must be valued and rewarded in the social sphere. Although he mocks the colonial obsession with faking a higher social condition, he nonetheless recommends that social achievement and ascension itself be considered a valid basis for claims of high social status. Labat thus demonstrates the many ways in which colonialism contributed to the dissolution of traditional hierarchies of status and class in the Old Regime.

Chapter Three *Creolization and the Spirit World:*
Demons, Violence, and the Body

Although the Old Regime French colonial project is best characterized
by a conquest of territory for settlement and agricultural exploitation,
it was no less imagined as a conquest of the soul. Throughout the seventeenth century, themes of spirits, gods, and the occult were powerful sub-
strates in French missionary representations of the Caribbean, such that
religion preceded race as the original discourse of difference marking the
cultural other in colonial context and defining French colonial identities
in the process. By invoking the idea of a spirit world, I refer to the intan-
gible, supernatural ground of referentiality for the religious practices, spiritual beliefs, and rituals of magic held by all groups in contact: Europeans,
Island Caribs, and Africans. In the process of colonization and enslavement, Christians ascribed to non-European occult forms the power of evil
symbolized in the Christian devil. The colonization of the New World was
coincident with the peak of witch hysteria in France and most of Europe,
from the early fifteenth century to the mid-seventeenth. Given that in late
medieval and Renaissance Europe an obsession with evil and demoniacal
forces had led ecclesiastics and theologians to fear the spread of the devil's
empire, the continents and islands of the Americas appeared to missionaries
as bastions of unmitigated diabolical influence.[1] The parallel was marked
by a phenomenon of intertextuality. In Europe, the massive repression of
witches was made possible by the discursive body of knowledge called demonology—the science of demons—which described demoniacal witchcraft through treatises, manifestos, trial transcriptions, and literary works.[2]
Likewise, in attempting to describe, define, and repress the magical and
spiritual practices of Indians and Africans, missionaries drew on early mod-

ern European conceptions of witchcraft and diabolism to create a new discourse, which I call colonial demonology.

Rather than simply comparing French colonial demonology with the large body of early modern European demonological literature, I will here explore the relation between colonial interpretations of the non-European spirit world and the rhetoric of the Christian mission insofar as both of these articulate a discourse on the body, specifically the suffering body. The centrality of this theme in Christian writings is perhaps not surprising, since, as Elaine Scarry has shown in her reading of the Old Testament scriptures, the figure of the wounded, mutable body is the primary means by which God's invisible presence, so often denied—or, as she puts it, "disbelieved in"—is signified and verified in the sacred text. Bodily pain is directly correlated with a divine cause, and the human species becomes a "canvas" on which "God's power of alteration continually re-manifest[s] itself."[3] Scarry goes on to argue that in the New Testament scriptures the relation between the divinity and the human body is radically overturned through the appearance of God in the flesh as Christ and the subjection of the fleshly God to the very rituals of pain and suffering previously inflicted on humans. In this case, the human body in the text signifies the divinity's supreme power through scenes, not of suffering, but rather of recovery and healing mediated by Jesus. Still, the symbolism of Christ's bodily sacrifice remained central to mysticism and the medieval church, as adherents performed their religious devotion through the "exercise" of the body in torturous rituals of flagellation.[4] During the inquisition and European witch craze, religious and civil authorities used violence and torture as a means of liberating the body and soul from the demon or heretical disposition.[5] In the French Caribbean, however, the encounter of spirit worlds led missionaries to produce new discourses designed to subordinate the bodies and souls of subjugated populations in concert with the specifically *secular* goals of conquest, settlement, and agricultural production. Seventeenth-century colonial narratives offer fundamental insights into the way in which missionaries defined the body of the other in relation to the immaterial world of spirit, thus underwriting particular forms of discipline and coercion inflicted on the bodies of enslaved persons in the name of Christianity. The point is especially significant given that the problem of forced labor and brutality toward Africans was often suppressed in seventeenth-century French colonial writing. In many cases, it is only with respect to the spirit world that writers represented violence against slaves.

In this chapter, I examine concepts of religion, spirits, violence, and sensual affliction that circulated in French narratives and legal discourse in the Caribbean in the seventeenth century and the early eighteenth. My intention is both to underscore the relationship between these themes and to demonstrate how narratives about the spirit world offered missionaries and secular writers an imaginary ground on which to rationalize colonial violence in the material world. Central to my investigation is the figure of the body in pain, a foundational and recurrent trope of spiritual and material conquest on the colonial frontier. While this trope first appeared as a symbol for Carib and African subservience to diabolical forces, it was also deployed by the discourse of the Christian mission in reference to actual slaves in the colonies. Writers consistently invoked ideologies of the occult in order to justify regimes of bodily discipline in the French colonies. The evidence of this powerful relationship lies in a remarkable paradox sustained in colonial discourse: Violence done to the body of the other is both attributed to the devil and claimed as the right of Christians.

This exploration of the relation between the colonial spiritual imaginary and the politics of the body occasions as well a look at the historical conditions of possibility for religious syncretism across colonial populations. For, contrary to the image of Christian influence and authority projected in missionary narratives, the French colonial populace was not immune to ideas of spirit they attributed to Caribs and Africans. Seventeenth-century colonial narratives suggest that not only did colonial knowledge of the non-European occult influence ideologies of slavery and coercion, but it also contributed to an evolving praxis of colonial witchcraft and magic. In this respect, I conceive the creolization of the colonial spirit world as both the European imposition of Christian beliefs and demonological understandings onto the non-European occult and, as importantly, the recombination of occult beliefs and rites across all populations in contact.

I begin by reading seventeenth-century representations of native Carib religion as a cult of the devil, paying particular attention to the body as a site of spiritual mediation through cannibalism, dismemberment, and slavery. By attributing to the Carib deity the power to brutalize his victims, missionary writers both justified the colonial presence and represented the Christian mission as an extreme act of devotion in which they wagered their own bodies for the glory of their God. Yet, whereas the missionary discourse of colonial demonology figured native religion as a form of slavery unto the devil, the Christian rationale for the slave trade turned this relationship on its head. That is, as ideologies of spirit possession confronted the realities of physical possession in the colonies, the body in pain emerged as a fetish for colonial regimes of discipline. To illustrate this transformation, I explore the dichotomy of body and soul in the Code noir, the first set of laws regulating African slavery in the French colonies, promulgated by Louis XIV in 1685. This is followed by an examination of the interrelated themes of body and spirit in Father Jean-Baptiste Labat's exhaustive *Nouveau Voyage aux isles de l'Amérique*, published in 1742. As an advocate for the conversion of slaves, Labat exhibits the uncanny ease with which slaves' suffering bodies were interpreted according to contrary logics of salvation and damnation and were forced to resolve through pain the paradoxes of Christian discipline.

In the second half of the chapter, I turn to the first colonial novel in French, *Le Zombi du Grand-Pérou, ou la comtesse de Cocagne*, by Pierre-Corneille Blessebois, to examine the ways in which a libertine convict rewrites demonology's obsession with the body. Drawing on a number of familiar tropes within demonological lore to create a story of feigned magic and libertinage, this remarkable work of 1697 portrays the white French and Creole elite as obsessed by both European witchcraft and a creolized spirit entity known as a *zombi*. In addition to exploring the possible origins and meanings of the zombi trope in the context of late-seventeenth-century Guadeloupe, I argue that Blessebois imaginatively recasts witchcraft and magic as a convenient pretext for the pleasures of the libertine body. Blessebois transposes both fantasies of spiritual violence and the realities of corporeal violence in the Caribbean into figures for colonial libertinage, identifying colonial femininity as the locus of threat, deviance, and diabolism. In so doing, he offers a satirical perspective on the relations among religion, witchcraft, libertinage, and criminality in a burgeoning slave society.

The Devil and the Savage

When French missionaries described the indigenous cultures of the Caribbean, they deployed a demonological paradigm in order to represent the inscrutable reaches of the colonial spirit world, whose conquest was essential to their authority. In practice, however, the French Catholic mission in the Caribbean was beset by serious problems owing to a lack of personnel and a consequent lack of confidence by the missionaries themselves, who blamed the trading companies for privileging material over spiritual profits. Missionary writers complained of the immediate challenge of policing the religion of the French settlers, whom they frequently derided as libertines and heretics. Yet the most important barrier to the evangelical enterprise was the nature of colonization itself. The French did not conquer the Caribs; they took Carib land, a fact that led to irrepressible wars of resistance led by Caribs who took refuge in Dominica and Saint-Vincent from the 1630s through the 1650s. While Caribs and the French interacted extensively through commercial and diplomatic relations, they rarely coexisted in the same communities. Subsequently, the Catholic mission functioned sporadically, upheld by exceptionally courageous priests such as Raymond Breton, who spent years on end alone within Carib enclaves. This spiritual labor was all but fruitless. As Jean-Baptiste Du Tertre explained in his *Histoire générale des Antilles*, "In thirty-five years, all the missionaries together have perhaps not won over for God twenty adult savages, even though they have sacrificed themselves to their instruction, and some of them have gone to live with these cannibals."[6]

The nearly complete failure of the Catholic mission among the Caribs may explain in part the missionary writers' hostile response to the natives and their beliefs, as well as the relative uniformity of information they produced about them. Five colonial writers—Raymond Breton, Jean-Baptiste Du Tertre, Pierre Pelleprat, Sieur de la Borde, and César de Rochefort—offered particularly salient representations of religion and the spirit world among Carib Indians. All traveled in the Caribbean and published narratives of their experiences in the first half century of colonization.[7] Their writings span a variety of styles and genres, including histories, chronicles, treatises, and even a dictionary, documenting all aspects of the French colonization of the Caribbean. While the various circumstances of their travel and patronage make for considerable differences in perspective in their narratives, these writers developed a common discourse on the Carib spirit world that reflected predominant ideas about witchcraft in European demonology. In transposing these conceptions to the colonial context, missionary writers instrumentalized them within a discourse of religious authority.

Whether or not Caribs had a religion at all was usually the opening question in ethnographic chapters on the subject. The responses reflected a Christian worldview in which the spirit world was irreconcilably divided between good and evil, symbolized by God and the devil, respectively, and where Carib divinities were drawn mainly from the latter. In general, Caribs were said to recognize a panoply of gods, usually referred to as devils, each of which corresponded to a shaman, called a *boyé*, whose duty it was to call on the divinity in times of need. In most accounts, Caribs sought spiritual guidance in order to prepare for war or summon a cure for illness. The god

Maboya was considered to be the evil spirit who exerted the greatest power over the Caribs, and the name was also deployed as a generic word meaning "god" or "spirit." Missionaries were sometimes inconsistent in their naming of evil spirits, however, and some noted the existence of benevolent deities as well. In his 1654 account, Du Tertre identified Maboya with the Christian devil and referred to another high spirit of evil as Yris. He also made passing reference to a good deity, Chemin, who lived in the sky but whom the Caribs had, in his view, foolishly rejected: "They take no account of him, and say that he must be left alone because he is good and he does not send them hurricanes."[8] For Du Tertre, the idea that the Caribs would pay the benevolent god no allegiance confirms his initial belief that they are essentially sorcerers, who, through a "servile fear and not for love, . . . do some works for the devil."[9] Following Du Tertre, Rochefort also noted the existence of good spirits, called Chemÿn or Icheïri, and explained that the two names reflect the linguistic dimorphism in Carib languages between men and women. In Breton's Carib-French dictionary, the word *chemign* is translated as "God, my god."[10] However, in his narrative passages Breton makes no mention of benevolent spirits and identifies all Carib divinities with the generic *dieu*, *diable*, or *maboya*.

This confusion and inconsistency regarding the names of spirits may reflect the possibility that, as Stephen D. Glazier contends, "Gods' names conferred power and were not readily shared with others."[11] Just as importantly, French missionaries' attempts to identify and categorize Carib gods registered anxiety about the power of the non-Christian occult. In some sense, these anxieties are comparable to those articulated by European demonologists of the previous century regarding the reality or illusion of diabolical forces. Was the power of the devil to be admitted in the realm of the possible or was the very belief in devils, magic, and sorcery itself heretical and the witch hunt an expression of religious fanaticism? At the height of the witch craze in France, this debate had crystallized around the two contrasting viewpoints offered by Johann Weyer and Jean Bodin. Weyer, a Lutheran physician, in his *De Praestigiis Daemonum* (1563), questioned the validity of beliefs about witches. He reconfigured states of trance, possession, and hysteria as medical disorders stemming from illnesses of the imagination. For Weyer, the devil only had the power to deceive the so-called witches, who in their weak mental state were vulnerable to him. Bodin, in *La Démonomanie des sorciers* (1580), on the other hand, argued that evil spirits were natural and their spells had an objective reality. A Carmelite monk, professor of Roman law, and trial judge, Bodin advanced a legal definition of a witch as someone who, knowing God's law, tries to bring about some act by recourse to the devil. A strong believer in the most extravagant phantasms in demonology, he urged a strict legal procedure for condemning suspects and extremely brutal treatment of them. In response to Weyer's more lenient position, Bodin practically accused anyone who questioned the reality of demons and witches of themselves being in league with the devil.[12]

French missionaries to the Caribbean were often equivocal in their attribution of power to the Carib spirit world. On one hand, they conceived the power of Maboya as a reign of diabolical terror over the imaginations of the Indians, who in turn propitiated the god with food offerings in hopes of avoiding natural disaster or physical injury. They frequently ridiculed the Caribs' belief in the ability of the spectral Maboya to consume perishable offerings, heal the sick, and perform other services. Du Tertre described Carib rites as "childish nonsense [*badineries enfantines*]" and condemned them as sorcery: "Speaking rationally, all the obligations that the *Ichéiris*, as well as the *Maboyas*, require of them through their *Boyés*, are more like lively imitations of what happens at the witches' Sabbath than acts of a veritable religion."[13] Denying any real powers to the spirit of evil, Du Tertre contends that the maboyas maintain followers only through deception and artifice. In the case of curing the sick, he judges that "the poor patient is healed more by imagination than in effect, and is more enchanted than disabused."[14] Yet at the same time missionaries repeatedly figured the Carib body as manipulated and traversed by the devil through rituals of spirit possession, copulation, and transvection, the spectral state of flying. As in the discourse of European witchcraft, women were most often conceived as the victims of such diabolical intervention. In his *Relations*, Breton affirmed that "the devils even enter into the bodies of men to speak through their mouths," but he gives an example of a devil who spoke through the mouth of a woman asleep in her bed, who subsequently had no recollection of the occurrence.[15] Similarly, Du Tertre recounted a story he claims was originally relayed to another missionary by a native shaman, that of a god who entered the body of a Carib woman, spoke through her mouth, and transported her to the cosmos: "He had taken her several times up above the Sun, without being dazzled by the bright rays of light, . . . [and] that he had seen beautiful uninhabited lands." Interpreting such information in a demonological frame, Du Tertre concluded: "The Gods of the Savages are Devils, since they enter into the bodies of women and speak through their mouths."[16] Du Tertre also believed in the power of evil spells enacted between persons by means of the bones of the dead, causing illness and eventual death.

Given the missionaries' equation of the god Maboya with the Christian devil, and their fervent belief in his power to infiltrate and displace the bodies of the Caribs, it is perhaps not surprising that they attributed to Maboya himself a remarkably powerful presence with certain material effects. This entity's ability to appear in spectral form was never questioned, and the missionaries produced captivating scenes of the ceremonial conjuration of Maboya by the boyés. Describing them as "these ministers of Satan," Du Tertre portrays the nocturnal invocation of a maboya in a dark, closed space. In the account, the boyé prepares food offerings and then summons the god with tobacco smoke: "and immediately the Devil or Maboya arrives, as though falling from the top of the hut, and snapping his fingers. Being interrogated there, he responds in a clear and distinct voice to all that is asked of him."[17] The devil and his shaman proceed to perform healing rites by touching, massaging, and sucking the victim's afflicted body part. One wonders how Du Tertre could have given such a vivid description of the god's apparition, since no native informant mediates his comments. Indeed, the Jesuit La Borde emphasized that the Caribs' sacred ritual excluded all "suspicious persons," suggesting that Christians were kept out.[18]

In his account of the conjuration, Raymond Breton addressed the problem of the witness more directly and attributed an even greater materiality to the Carib deity. His most poignant observations on Carib religiosity appear in the dictionary entry for the Carib phrase meaning "The boyé sings to make his gods descend."[19] First describing the boyé's invocation of the god with offerings, song, and tobacco smoke, which cause the deity to drop down like a "sack of flour," Breton tells of his own attempted infiltration of the rite armed with a torch and Christian fetish objects intended to dispel the power of the evil spirit. Surprisingly, Breton admits to never having had the courage to share his Christian rites with the Caribs, instead performing them in secret, "because I was alone among them, and . . . I dared not say the mass before them." The ensuing narrative depicts Breton's intervention as an almost mystical encounter between the forces of good and evil, Christianity and diabolism. His very approach sends shock waves through the ritual in progress, provoking the unforeseen wrath of a Carib goddess: "Being near, I heard their supposed goddess (it was a woman who was a boyé and consequently a goddess, as is common) not only fall backwards, but cry, scream and have a mad fit for almost one quarter of an hour, until I stopped. The Savages who heard it with me were so astonished that they did not know where they were. I withdrew, since God had not inspired me to do any more, being well assured that this was a true devil, the *boyée* a magician, and her song her pact, which I never would have wanted to hear nor write."[20] Breton conflates shaman and god; for him, the woman boyé is the devil since she acts as an intercessor. What is fascinating is that the devil is heard but not seen. In this sense, Breton's scene of encounter with the devil recalls the representational conventions of Judeo-Christian narratives in which the deity is portrayed only as a bodiless voice.[21] Reconstructing the goddess's unfathomable fury based on what he claims to have heard, Breton affirms that he has witnessed the devil, with whom the Caribs have sealed an ominous pact.

Breton's strategic mise en scène of the talking spirit had an even stronger significance for the missionary discourse of colonial demonology, insofar as it objectified the body as a site of contestation between gods. Whereas the military and commercial colonial encounter occurred on the terrain of the Caribbean islands, the spiritual encounter was repeatedly mediated by the human body, conceived as a living territory, a house for the soul to be claimed by the divine. Breton held the demonological conviction that the devil posed a lethal menace to believers in Christ, threatening their very bodies as a means of shaking their faith. Although he refused to inscribe the words of the boyé's song, he does record the Carib goddess's insults. The angry divinity cries out orders to her followers, presaging the priest's oblivion: "Hurry, hurry, tie him up, lest he escape from me, so that I may eat him, head, shoulders, feet, even his excrement; that I may grind him, reduce him to a pulp, and swallow him."[22] The graphic nature of the threat—Breton is simultaneously pulverized, dismembered, and boiled down—is exemplary of the way in which missionaries depicted their own engulfment by diabolical forces through the trope of cannibalism, thus enacting the ritual dismemberment and consumption of the Christian body by the devil or his human worshipers.

Aside from being a staple of popular European and antique myths of wild men of faraway lands, the trope of cannibalism had a discursive history with which the missionaries would have been especially familiar. Cannibal themes were characteristic of European demonology, as witches were commonly accused of ingesting fetuses and cadavers. The perversity of this kind of food ritual partakes of demonology's conception of the witches' Sabbath as a negative simulacrum of the Christian mass; cannibalism is the diabolical inverse of the Eucharist, the magical body and blood of Christ.[23] In French narratives from the Caribbean, however, cannibalism was most commonly represented as occurring between warring Indian groups on account of vengeance, thus outside of a religious context. Arawaks were reputed to be the most common victims of Caribs, and their body parts were fetishized in the course of colonial narratives. Indeed, the odd foot or arm appears front and center in otherwise unremarkable passages describing Carib feasts of war. In one passage from Du Tertre the feminized witch trope returns as the cannibal scene devolves into a disquisition on the lewd tastes of Carib women: "Above all, it is a prodigious and astounding thing to see the mania, or rather the rage, of the women eating the flesh of their enemies, because they chew, gnaw, and press it between their teeth, and are so afraid to lose any of it, that they lick the grease from sticks."[24]

That Du Tertre would depict such indelicacies in lurid detail raises questions about the extent to which cannibalistic pleasures were a fantasy of missionary writers such as him. Du Tertre insistently projected his own cannibalization at the hands of Caribs, a ritual that carried meanings both spiritual and secular. On one hand, the scenario of Caribs eating Europeans is cast in terms of a contest of the flesh in which the French are the most delectable: "I have heard them say several times that of all the Christians, the French were the best and the most delicate; but that the Spanish were so tough that they had trouble eating them."[25] More than an attack on the Spanish, the passage represents a displacement of colonial desire for sensual consummation with the other. To be eaten and incorporated by Caribs, especially Carib women, is announced as a privilege, suggesting even a fantasy of desire. Paradoxically, however, the allegory of attraction between Caribs and the French is suspended where missionaries themselves are concerned. Recounting a story of the alleged killing and cannibalization of a French missionary following a Carib attack on Saint-Christophe, Du Tertre explains that afterward the Indians were struck by illness and most died: "Since that time, they have no longer wanted to eat Christians, contenting themselves with killing and leaving them." Here Du Tertre co-opts cannibalism, the most notorious stereotype about the native Caribbean, in order to present a particular narrative of Christian martyrdom. The lethal nature of the Christian body symbolizes divine justice; even when dismembered and consumed, the missionary body retains the power of the Christian god.[26]

Whereas violence inflicted on the body of the French was often framed within a narrative of Christian martyrdom, the discourse of missionary demonology consistently depicted the Carib body as brutalized by its own god. Missionaries explained this violence as a state of slavery in which the supposed devil terrorized his servants, leading them with fear and literally beating their bodies. The metaphor of servitude before the devil was not foreign to colonial representations of New World religions. One century earlier, Jean de Léry had propagated the notion that the South American Indians were tormented by their god, causing them to cry out in desperation.[27] Similarly, missionaries to the French Caribbean represented the Maboya as an executioner who left deep scars on his victims in order to ensure his power over them. The Jesuit Bouton, the first chronicler of Martinique, made a brief but salient mention of this treatment: "The devil, whom they call maboya, beats them sometimes to the death."[28] Du Tertre provided a more ample explanation: "This Maboya does not cease to worry them, beat them, and treat them with a frightening severity so as to keep them in fear, such that the apprehension of his rigors ensures their respect and submission. I have seen several who wore marks and bruises larger than a hand on their arms and shoulders, which came from the blows that this Maboya had given them."[29] In the passage, the devil exerts his influence through both psychological and physical tortures, inscribing through violence the visible trace of his presence on the bodies of his Carib victims. Whereas European demonological lore maintained that the devil's mark was a spot of unexplained numbness hidden on the body of a witch, often assumed to be within the sexual organs, in colonial descriptions of Caribs only pain and physical injury signified the devil's relation to his followers. The devil's pursuit was one of brutality and abuse, not seduction.[30]

The trope of the beating devil appeared in nearly every narrative account of Carib religion. While variations on the story questioned the objective reality of the corporeal violence, they retained the trope as a frightening scene conjured in the victim's imagination or dream state. Breton, for one, adamantly refuted the idea that the devil physically beat the Caribs: "For in all the nineteen years that I conversed with them, never have I seen or heard the Savages say anything like that." He attributed the delusions of bodily assault to a combination of extreme melancholia and the Caribs' bad sleeping posture, which produced "smoke in the mind that causes them terrible, black dreams as though they were in Maboya's hold, or he was taking them away."[31] Both Breton and La Borde wrote that these reveries caused the Caribs to cry out in the night in fear.[32] Rochefort, though acknowledging the melancholia argument, attested that both French and English sources concurred in their assessments of the reality of the beating devil: "The Devil effectively beats them, and . . . they often show on their bodies visible marks of the blows they received from him."[33] Thus, through the trope of the beating devil, both real and imaginary, early colonial writers figured the body in pain as the symbol of domination and physical possession by the spirit of evil. According to the view that the devil maintained his followers in strict obedience through pain and wounding, slavery became the central metaphor through which they understood Amerindian religiosity. This idea clearly served the interests of missionary colonialism, for missionaries conceived of Christian baptism as a means of divine liberation from diabolical servitude. The touch of the Christian savior, mediated by the hand of the missionary, would eradicate the devil's power to both hurt and redeem his followers. Hence Rochefort confidently declared that Caribs could not be mistreated by the devil in the presence of a Christian and that baptism offered the best protection against his wrath: "Once the holy sacrament is bestowed on the savages, the devil no longer beats or abuses them for the rest of their lives."[34]

Body and Soul in the Code Noir

Pierre Pelleprat, a Jesuit missionary to Martinique in the 1640s, added new significance to the notion of the beating devil by extending its power over both Caribs and Africans insofar as they were slaves of the French. His comments appear in the chapter entitled "De l'instruction des Nègres et des Sauvages esclaves" in his *Relation des missions des PP. de la Compagnie de Jésus*, in which he outlines the traffic in slaves, including their origins, price, and strategies for attracting them to the Christian faith. In some sense, Pelleprat's narrative reflects the general failure of the mission among Amerindian populations, such that the most likely converts were slaves taken in war or traded throughout the Caribbean, perhaps not even of Island Carib origin. Like other missionaries, he attributed the appeal of Christian salvation to the beating devil, "who reduces several of them to the happy necessity of having themselves baptised to avoid the persecution of such a cruel enemy."[35] Yet the fact that Pelleprat referred to Africans who labored under the whip represents a significant departure from the exclusively Carib focus in other contemporary writings. Although Pelleprat arrived in Martinique at a time when the slave population was increasing and tobacco production reaching its peak, it is only when discussing the beating devil that he acknowledges the wounding of the slaves' body, signaled by the sound of blows and visible scars.[36] What is more, Pelleprat maintains that physical abuse by the devil is ultimately good for the slaves and sanctioned by the Christian god: "Those who stay with them often hear the sound of the blows he inflicts upon them, and this cannot be an illusion, because not only do they wear the scars, they are sometimes made sick from them. I can hardly believe that the devil, who works so hard to steal a soul from God, would want to continue a treatment that makes him lose so many unless he was constrained to do so. But, whether the providence of God orders or allows it, these poor people benefit greatly from it."[37]

The idea that the Christian god approves the devil's brutality as a means of attracting them to the Christian faith amounts to a justification of violence done to the bodies of slaves, one that had added significance in the context of slavery. The question thus arises as to whether Pelleprat used the beating devil trope as a legitimating allegory of violence toward slaves or as a means by which to sublimate his knowledge of Christian brutality in the colonies. Although these questions are ultimately unanswerable, Pelleprat suggests the extent to which the beating devil could be valorized in the service of the Christian mission and demonstrates the possibility of a close association between the ideas of servitude to the devil and actual slavery to Christians. In this respect, his narrative foreshadows what would become the dominant Christian ideology of the slave trade, which openly embraced the suffering of slaves as a path to salvation. Whereas Pelleprat invoked the devil as a torturer whose abuse drives slaves to baptism, colonial power would soon codify the dispensation of violence as a duty of the Christian regime itself.

From its inception, representatives of the clergy had rationalized the enslavement of Africans as a forced and sustained induction into Christianity and an enduring, rigorous punishment for idolatry. The slave trade was first justified as a means of salvation by Pope Nicolas V, who in 1454 officially authorized the trade for the king of Portugal.[38] Two and a half centuries later, Father Labat claimed that this argument alone convinced Louis XIII to allow slavery in the French colonies: "We showed him that it was the only means to inspire the cult of the true God in the Africans, draw them out from idolatry, and make them persevere until death in the Christian religion that we would have them embrace."[39] A notion of reciprocity subtends the argument, implying that African bodies may be sacrificed to pay for the soul's redemption. Most missionary writers applied this rationale in the French colonies. Pelleprat assured his readers that Africans, in their slavery, enjoyed the freedom of the children of God. Noting their physical depravity on his arrival in the colonies, the author comments: "You would think that they are devils emerging from hell. They are nonetheless souls redeemed [*rachetées*] with the blood of the Son of God, and treasures of the islands; a man is considered wealthy in this country if he has twenty-five or thirty slaves."[40] The conflation of spiritual and material indicators of worth is telling; simultaneously redeemed to join the ranks of Christian salvation and turned over as commodities at the colonial outpost, Africans are conceived in terms of body and soul. As an embodiment of this dualism, the slave mediates between two contrary systems of value that collude in the colonial enterprise. Du Tertre was another fervent advocate of the exchange of the body for spiritual redemption. While expressing deep pity for African slaves and deploring their condition as beasts of burden, he nonetheless argues for the perfectibility of Africans in this state: "Their servitude is the principle of their happiness, and . . . their disgrace is the cause of their salvation, since the faith that they embrace in the islands enables them to know God, to love him and to serve him."[41]

What is clear in these assertions is that missionaries equated metaphorical servitude qua devotion with the physical service exacted from Africans in the colonies. Abandoning their prior fixation on the horrors of the beating devil, escapable only through conversion to Christianity, missionaries now openly endorsed the idea of the beating Christian as a means of winning Africans for Christ. They did so by exploiting the homology between metaphorical service to the Christian God and real slavery to Christian colonists. Thus, in missionary ideology the African inducted into slavery is simultaneously converted into a Christian and a beast of burden; the capture of the soul is transacted through the theft and dispossession of the body. Nowhere was this principle better illustrated than in the 1685 Code noir, which was promulgated under Louis XIV by Colbert in order to regulate the practice of slavery in the French colonies. With breathtaking ease, this document effected a rhetorical transformation of humans into movable objects (*meubles*), nonpersons in the law. As Louis Sala-Molins has shown, the legislators of the Code introduced the word *slave* in the preamble without definition or qualification, affirming simply the king's intent, first, to assist his "subjects" in "maintaining the discipline of the Catholic, Roman, Apostolic Church" and, second, to "regulate that which concerns the state and quality of the slaves."[42] With the latter phrase, the king approved, and by his proxy gave divine sanction to, a practice that had been going on unregulated since the inception of colonization. At the same time, he enjoined his subjects henceforth to conform to royal law in all matters concerning human property.

Yet what is striking about the rhetoric of the Code is that it fails to dehumanize, except by making humanity itself a legal offense. The law circumscribes every aspect of slaves' existence in a series of articles that reflect in reverse the values of personhood held by the masters. This is perhaps most apparent where matters of marriage and reproduction are concerned, since the Code subjected family formation to the logic of capital gain. While slaves could marry with consent of the masters (articles 10–11), children born to slave women were to inherit the status of the mother following the rule of "*partus sequitur ventrem*," thus becoming the property of her master (articles 13–14). Furthermore, insofar as the master had the right to sell separately members of a slave family once the children reached puberty (article 47), slave law transformed the slaves into what Orlando Patterson has called genealogical isolates, with no power to maintain ties with ancestors and no claims on their own offspring.[43] In addition, the Code reduced slaves' social existence by outlawing gatherings of slaves from more than one plantation (articles 16–17) and denied them any form of economic autonomy. Article 24 curtailed slaves' ability to produce goods for sale or barter by forbidding masters to "allow slaves to work a certain day of the week for their own account." Forbidden to sell sugarcane, the product of their labor (article 18), they were barred from selling any other goods without the express permission of the master (article 19). The Code thus targeted the popular slave markets, centers in which slaves bartered the fruits of the subsistence gardens they maintained in addition to their regular duties.[44] Commodities themselves, slaves could not be party to any transaction, nor could they own anything, as proclaimed in article 28: "We declare slaves to be unable to have anything that does not belong to their master; and all that comes to them by industry or by the liberality of other people . . . to be acquired in full propriety by their master."[45] Finally, the Code deprived slaves any legal or political existence whatsoever. Recognized only in their condition as dependent bodies and perfectible souls, they were barred from all offices and public functions, and were rendered juridically nonexistent, unable to testify formally at any civil or criminal legal proceeding (article 30). The extent of their legal subjection is summarized in articles 44–55, which declare them to be "movable property" and regulate their circulation among creditors, debtors, buyers, sellers, and inheritors.

Although the text of the Code reiterates the status of slaves as things depersonalized in the law, it nonetheless explodes with contradiction, owing largely to the strange and enduring ambivalence between the legal effort to degrade slaves' indubitable humanity and the need to represent such dispossession as motivated not by self-interest or metaphysical evil but rather by Christian charity, solicitude, and compassion. The Code never explicitly explains the reasons for or methods of acquiring slaves and introducing them into the colonies. Following article 1, which establishes the exclusivity of the Christian faith, article 2 calls for all slaves to be "baptized and instructed in the Catholic, apostolic and roman religion" and provides specific instructions for doing so: "We enjoin residents [*habitants*] who will buy newly arrived negroes to inform the governor and intendant of the said islands in no more than eight days, on pain of arbitrary fine; and they will give the necessary orders to have them instructed and baptized at a convenient time." In describing slaves as commodities, the Code presents slavery not as something imposed as a social penalty for some specific fault or condition (prisoner of war or debtor status, inherent sin, and civilizational inferiority were several previous justifications for slavery) but rather a condition following from a purely commercial exchange.[46] At the same time, the Code legitimates such a transaction through the rhetoric of Christian salvation. The opening phrase of the preamble asserts the consubstantiality of royal and divine authority by defining the colonial populace as "people that divine providence has placed under our dominion." By claiming both to maintain Catholic discipline and to regulate slavery, framers of the Code explicitly frame slavery itself as a Christian institution conforming to the will of God. Similarly, by barring non-Catholics from serving as commanders or overseers of slaves (article 4), the Code designates those invested with the authority to hurt slaves as spiritual custodians of those in their possession. In addition, the Code contains harsh provisions against non-Catholics in the colonies, thus anticipating the revocation of the Edict of Nantes only months later. Renewing the royal edict of 1615, which expelled Jews and non-Christians from the French kingdom (article 1), the Code banned the public exercise of any non-Catholic religion (article 3) and ordered the strict observance of the Sabbath and Catholic holidays (article 6). Non-Catholics were barred from legal marriages (article 8).

Religion thus functioned as a strategy of inclusion through which the Crown attempted to incorporate the slave into the colonial social order. On the basis of the slave's status as a Christian subject, the Code invested him or her with certain rights, including marriage with the consent of the master. By the same token, masters had obligations to the slave as both a redeemable soul and a dependent body. These obligations appear to conflate the demands of Christian morality with colonial self-interest. Masters were enjoined to care for old and disabled slaves, feed and clothe the healthy, and refrain from giving them liquor as a means of sustenance (articles 22–27). The sustenance they were required to provide was, however, exceedingly limited. Each week adults were to be fed "two and a half pots of manioc flour or three cassavas weighing at least two and a half pounds each, or equivalent things, with two pounds of salted beef and three pounds of fish or like things in pro-portion" (article 22). A certain imprecision in the designation of foods and amounts pervades the article, seemingly presaging the near ineffectiveness of the law. Within the terms of the Code, however, the slave was required to be satisfied and to obey in return. The narrative of salvation was predi-cated on a logic of reciprocity; in exchange for perpetual submission, the enslaved person would receive the baptismal rite, religious guidance, a few scraps of food and clothing, and the hope of emancipation.[47]

Yet the instruction typically received by slaves in matters of religion was at best an indoctrination into the propaganda of domination and at worst a perverted approximation of rituals nearly forgotten by the French. By the mid-eighteenth century, "true" Christianity would be seen as inimical to the maintenance of slavery, as a potential conveyor of ideas of equality, sal-vation, and justice.[48] In the framework of the Code noir, religion thus comes close to what Homi Bhabha has called "mimicry" or a failed simulacrum of an idea or ideology, which, when deployed in the colonial context, is de-graded and alienated from its prior meaning. The Code noir "produces a knowledge of Christianity as a form of social control," one that threatens and ultimately makes a mockery of the original it imitates.[49] In the French Caribbean, this subversion was no less than total, transforming Christianity into a vehicle for the permanent servitude of the body. The Code's pre-scription of religious exclusivity would facilitate as well the destruction of the African spirit world so valuable to transported persons, who initially lacked social institutions, kinship organizations, and the physical strength necessary to resist slavery by other means.

Yet what is fascinating about the Code is the way in which it carries within it an implicit knowledge of the radical incommensurability of the exchange it offers slaves. For at the heart of the document are a series of articles forecasting not only the failure of the assumed pact of reciprocity but also the captives' refusal to be dehumanized and their persistent attempts to circumvent slavery's mandate of abjection so as ultimately to challenge the system itself. Following the articles legislating religion, domestic life, economic and political dispossession, and the masters' obligations to slaves comes a story of resistance and the dispensation of pain. In articles 33–38, the captives do not consent to being enslaved, branded, malnourished, and brutalized; in response, they find food, strike their masters, and run away. Framers of the Code viewed such acts not in terms of survival but rather in terms of criminality and threat. What is more, the legislators appear to honor this criminality by designating the deviant slave as a person and subject capable of being held responsible to the state before the law. As Joan Dayan puts it, "the slave is recognized as having a will only insofar as it is perverted."[50] Indeed, whereas articles 30–31 announce slaves' juridical inexistence except as property of the master, article 32 proclaims that slaves may be prosecuted as freed persons: "Slaves may be pursued criminally without there being a need to inform the master, except in case of complicity; and the said slaves will be judged . . . with the same formalities as free persons."[51] Furthermore, by representing the slave almost exclusively in terms of terror and threat, the Code seems more concerned with protecting the master from the slave than vice versa. As a fully endowed object of legal retribution for crimes against slavery, the slave may be brutalized or put to death. Thus, in article 33 the slave appears as an aggressor toward his master: "The slave who will have struck his master, his mistress or his mistress' husband or their children with contusion or the drawing of blood, or on the face, will be put to death." In the next article, the slave perpetrates violence toward all free people generally: "And as for excesses and violent blows [*voies de fait*] that will be committed by the slaves against free people, we wish that they be severely punished, even by death if the occasion warrants it." The unauthorized seizure of the master's property also carries severe penalties. Article 36 declares the theft of large livestock to be punishable by death, whereas the taking of small livestock and produce "will be punished according to the quality of the theft, by judges who will be able, if there be occasion, to condemn them to be beaten with rods by the executor of high justice, and branded with a fleur-de-lis."

Even in its hesitations, this article reveals what is most shocking about the Code noir, which is its determination to mark and mutilate the body of the slave as a sign of royal and divine authority. Even in its attempt to limit the power of masters to abuse slaves, the Code clarifies the range of terrors sanctioned by the law. Article 42 reads: "When they believe that their slaves will have deserved it, masters may only chain them and beat them with cords; we forbid them to torture them, or to mutilate any of their members, on pain of confiscation of the slaves and criminal prosecution of the master." Clearly, chaining and beating were not considered torture, despite the fact that the article imposed no limits on those forms of punishment. Nor were mutilation and dismemberment outlawed. On the contrary, the Code invested this power in the courts. The penalty for running away was most severe: "The fugitive who will have escaped for one month counting from the day his master denounces him before the law, will have his ears cut off and will be branded with a fleur-de-lis on one shoulder; if he repeats the offense for another month counting again from the day of denunciation, he will be hamstrung and branded with the fleur-de-lis on the other shoulder; and the third time he will be put to death" (article 38). Christianity thus provided no protection against mutilations and beatings performed in the name of justice to enforce the subjection of the slave. Pain and dismemberment became rather the primary means of establishing the authority of the colonial regime. In this respect, the Code noir, written in large part to promulgate Christianity for the slaves, retained all that previously had been imputed to the devil in the demonological reading of the colonial spirit world. Christian discipline sanctioned the legal dismemberment of the body. The invariable contradictions therein would not dishonor the system but would further degrade the slave. Article 14 admits in unapologetic terms the unreliability of the Code's rhetorical commitment to the work of conversion. Providing guidelines on the burial of slaves, the article reads: "Masters will be enjoined to have their baptized slaves placed in holy ground in cemeteries destined for this effect; and as regards those who will die without receiving baptism, they will be buried at night in some field bordering the place where they will have deceased."

Father Labat: Spirits, Violence, and the Body

Thus far, we have witnessed a critical shift in seventeenth-century missionary conceptions of the relation between the non-European spirit world and the pained, suffering body. Missionaries first portrayed violence and beatings to the body, both real and imagined, as the devil's means of coercing and maintaining his tyranny over the Caribs, a view that presented the evangelical mission as a benevolent act of deliverance. With the codification of the enslavement of Africans, however, this logic was entirely reversed, such that the beating devil was replaced with the beating Christian and violence was converted into a means of ensuring the care of souls and the love of Christ. In this sense, missionaries openly justified the physical subjection of Africans through the narrative of Christian salvation. Perpetual servitude, coercion, and violence to the body were seen not only as a good and necessary means of inducting Africans into Christianity but also as the right and duty of Christians in the colonies, ordained by the king in his capacity as representative of the divine. A question thus arises: What happened to the devil when the Christians appropriated his monopoly on beatings and violence?

Father Jean-Baptiste Labat's four-volume *Nouveau voyage aux isles de l'Amérique*, published in 1742, offers the most complete narrative panorama of colonial culture of the late seventeenth century and includes several remarkable scenes detailing the colonial encounter with the African spirit world. Labat was himself a slave owner, and he is best known as a secularized priest, a man of action impassioned as much by industry, commerce, and invention as the care of souls.[52] Still, his self-justificatory narrative placed great emphasis on his functions as a parish priest and church official, documenting the administration of daily rites and sacraments as well as the affairs of the church throughout the French possessions. On his spiritual surveillance of slaves, Labat was adamant: "I had occasion to commend myself for the exactitude of my parishioners on this article."[53] In his journal, Labat engaged the slave population with a deeply personal and ambivalent narrative. The author both confessed the beauty he saw in slaves and their culture and described in the first person the purchase of slaves and his own unabashed violence toward them. The *Nouveau voyage* naturalized slavery in the colonies, making no apology for the institution or its brutality; both appeared rather as regular features of the colonial *pittoresque*.

Nowhere was this violence more acute than with respect to African infractions on the domain of the spirit, which Labat vociferously guarded for himself and other representatives of the Catholic clergy. He applied the discourse of colonial demonology to African practices of magic, demonstrating the persistence of colonial beliefs in the occult supernatural at the beginning of the eighteenth century, when the European witch craze was undeniably in decline. In France, the gradual wane of witch hysteria was marked by the 1670 reprieve of twelve witches at Rouen by Louis XIV, followed by a royal edict of July 1682, which reclassified witchcraft according to older rubrics of "superstitious practices" and "pretended magic." The document targeted two practitioners of the occult—"seducers" and "poisoners"—suggesting that the crime in question was either one of imposture that takes advantage of ignorant or credulous individuals or one of illicit alchemy and the use of poison outside sanctioned professions.[54] Labat made reference several times to the growing skepticism toward witchcraft but retained a firm belief in African powers over the supernatural: "I know that there are many people who regard as purely imaginary, and as ridiculous tales or falsities, all that is related about witches and their pacts with the devil. . . . I am also persuaded that there are some facts of a very certain truth" (1:286). Labat claimed that almost all adult Africans were either witches or possessed some knowledge of "magic, sorcery and poison" (2:395). He recommended that special care be taken to identify and exorcize African "witches" before baptism, believing that their powers of evil would be enhanced once they were Christian (4:322).

Yet anxiety over African occultism had just as much to do with traditional forms of medicine and knowledge of plants. In Saint Christopher, for example, the Superior Council in 1686 endorsed distinctions proposed by the Jesuit missionary Moreau between four occult practitioners. Sorcerers were defined as those who, through a pact with the devil, obtain the power to perform extraordinary magical feats. The three remaining categories pertained to witch doctors, including those who combine sorcery with unnatural drugs in cooperation with the devil; *jongleurs* or mere charlatans; and, finally, those who heal with simple natural remedies.[55] These distinctions reflect the tendency for colonial authorities to co-opt the slaves' knowledge of "white magic" for healing purposes. Whereas convicted sorcerers could be condemned by the courts, benign practices classified under the last category were encouraged to treat illness within the slave community. One law in Saint Christopher specified that African techniques of healing and medicine were permissible in the presence of the master.

Labat's narrative reveals that in Martinique and Guadeloupe as well certain blacks were identified and authorized to treat slaves who suffered from an illness or had been injured in an accident. In his lengthy chapter on sugar production, Labat points out the role of women in the medical care of slaves: "One assigns the care of the sick to some wise and intelligent negresse who serves them diligently" (2:286–87). Elsewhere he writes approvingly of the care given to a slave bitten by a poisonous snake by a black man who professed to make a living by his practice of natural medicine. Expressing interest in the secret antidote, the author is disappointed: "He declined to tell me the names of all the herbs that went into the composition of his remedy because this secret helped him earn a living, and he did not want to make it public" (1:92). Labat nonetheless records in indirect style the advice of this African healer, noting in detail as much as is revealed to him of the protocol for treating a venomous bite. In this sense, Labat's memoirs encapsulate a range of colonial knowledges that lay outside the boundaries of European medicine and industry so as to preserve secret slave remedies for the colonial record.[56] Other examples of "white magic" recorded by the author include powers over the natural environment. In one case, Labat tells the story of a young African boy who fulfills his master's wish for rainfall. Performing incantatory rites with the aid of a few oranges and tree branches, the boy succeeds in bringing a light rain that lasts one hour and is entirely circumscribed by his master's small plot of land (1:247).

Yet, despite the apparent permissiveness of the law toward benign magic and occult forms of healing, popular hysteria over the origins of such powers and the potential malice to which they could be put sometimes resulted in brutal acts of recrimination by colonial authorities. Sorcery and magic were indistinguishable from medicine insofar as they relied on the consultation and conjuring of spirits and the casting of spells to determine events, effect change, or inflict malice. Planters feared sedition, resistance, and retaliation by means of supernatural or magical practices, particularly poisoning. Although the Code noir is silent on the question, a royal ordinance of 1724 punished poisonings by hanging.[57] Labat himself makes reference to cases of poisonings of slaves in Martinique in 1696 and 1698 and reports the burning at the stake of slave "sorcerers."

Thus, colonial authorities both feared and revered African slaves for their knowledge of the spirit world. Labat's stories of magic and sorcery show the covert power of spells proven effective despite the intervention of colonial authority.[58] Indeed, much of the narrative interest of such episodes lies in precisely the sensational effects of spirits conjured by slaves, as though better to justify physical retaliation against them. In particular, the slave ship emerges as a mythic site for the consolidation of African occult forms. Labat explains that the young rainmaker's talent was learned during the middle passage: "He says that some Blacks from his country taught it to him during the crossing" (1:247). Another example concerns a French slave ship bound for the Caribbean in 1696. Based on the transcript of the confessions of witnesses to the event, Labat recounts the story of a woman accused of using sorcery to forestall the ship's advance for nearly two months, causing shortages and death among its human cargo. When the captain and surgeon resort to violence to discourage her intentions, the woman turns her powers against them, threatening to devour the heart of the surgeon. He so dies a few days later: "They opened him, and found his noble parts dried up like parchment." Fearing further retribution, the captain appeases the woman by releasing her from the ship: "He resolved to treat her gently, and made her the most beautiful promises in the world, providing that she cease her witchcraft. They negotiated and agreed that they would set her back on land with two or three others that she would name, and she promised to allow the boat to leave" (2:396).

Here Labat plays with the irony of the slave traders' capitulation before the power of the African supernatural, commanded by a sorcerer with power over the seas. But this spiritual power is had at the expense of the woman's body, which is declared insensitive to the pain of torture. Early modern demonologists and trial judges often maintained that a sure proof of witchcraft was the accused witch's ability to withstand great pain with little evidence of suffering, for they believed that the devil himself enabled this insensitivity so as to protect his devotees from persecution. While the devil's mark was described as a particular spot of numbness on the body, the devil was generally seen as having power over his followers' every sensation. As Pierre de Lancre wrote, "He makes them see that he can render them insensitive, make them feel good and evil when it pleases him, and in this way he also persuades them that he is the true master of their misfortune and their happiness, and that they can expect it only from him."[59] This demonological myth had added meaning in the context of the Atlantic slave trade. Recounting the black woman sorcerer's punishment, Labat explains, "The captain had the accused negress seized, attached to a canon and whipped very severely in order to draw out the confession. As it seemed that she did not feel the blows, the surgeon general of the ship believed that the loblolly boy [*prévôt*] was not beating her vigorously enough. He took one end of the cord and applied a few blows with all his might. Even more than before, the negress acted like she felt no pain." It would seem that for the speaker as well as for the Europeans in the scene, the woman's resistance is explicable only as evidence of her commerce with the devil. In a manner reminiscent of European witch trials, the ship's crew uses torture to evoke an admission or prove guilt by the supposed insensitivity of the body, an assumption with potentially devastating consequences for Africans on slave ships. Given that Africans traded in the colonial marketplace were valued primarily as bodies with little regard for their capacity for feeling, the demonological supposition of insensitivity predisposed slaves to excessive rituals of violence meant to extirpate demons as well as instill colonial discipline.

Father Labat reveled in such explosive rites of violence, many of which he claimed to have performed himself. Another example constitutes perhaps the best-known passage from Labat's immense work and deserves ample quotation and commentary here. In it, one of Labat's slaves is afflicted with a strange illness untreatable by French surgeons and black healers alike. Against her master's wishes, she receives a visit from a black shaman, who, with the aid of fetish symbols and incantations, consults a spirit to determine her fate. The response provokes great sadness and crying from the woman and her loved ones present at the ritual. Spying from a safe distance, Labat allows the scene to unfurl before bursting in to impose his authority.

I took the *marmouset* [figurine, or fetish], the incense holder, the sack and all the implements, and I asked the negress why she was crying: she responded that the devil had said that she would die in four days, and that she had heard the voice come from the little figure. The other blacks affirmed the same thing. To disabuse them, I told them that it was the black who had spoken by mimicking his voice, and that if the devil had been present to respond to him, he would have warned him that I was at the door to seize him. However, I had the sorcerer tied and dealt about three hundred blows of the whip which skinned him from the shoulders to the knees. He cried in desperation and our blacks asked me to show favor towards him, but I told them that sorcerers feel no pain, and that his cries were to mock me. I brought a chair, put the marmouset before him, and told him to pray that the devil deliver him from my hands, or carry off his body. As he did neither, I continued to have him whipped, to good profit. Our blacks who were gathered together trembled and told me that the devil would kill me, and so prejudiced were they by this foolish imagination that I could not dissuade them from it, no matter what I told them. Finally, to show them that I feared neither the devil nor witches, I spit on the figurine and stomped on it, even though I really wanted to keep it, and I shattered the incense holder and the rest of the implements. I started a fire, burned all the sorcerer's rags, and had the bits of the statue smashed and the ashes and dust thrown into the stream. That appeared to reassure our blacks a bit. I had the sorcerer placed in irons after being washed with a *pimentade*, that is, a brine containing crushed peppers and lemons. This causes horrible pain in those flayed by the whip, but it is a rather sure remedy against the gangrene that would not fail to attack the wounds. I also had all those who were in the assembly thrashed so as to teach them not to be so curious next time.

What was troublesome in this adventure was that the negress in effect died the fourth day, either because her imagination had been struck by the devil's response, or because he had truly known that her infirmity would take her in that time. Worst come to worst, I took care to have her confessed and had the consolation of seeing her die as a good Christian, and very repentant of the faults she had committed. (1:248–49)

In this astonishing scene, Labat presents the recurrent paradox between reality and illusion, belief and skepticism, in colonial representations of the occult. By interceding for the slave woman by means of African occult practices, the shaman poses a direct threat to Labat's spiritual authority.

Yet Labat himself clearly believes in the powers of the devil and the non-European occult, a fact that he willingly discloses to the reader. This adds a powerful irony to the scene, in which Labat performs an appallingly brutal extirpation on the shaman and destroys his ritual implements as though in order to reaffirm his religious authority. Before his slaves, he maintains the appearance of skepticism about their powers by subscribing to the demonological mythology of witches' insensitivity to pain and enthusiastically directing his black henchmen to carry out the devastating beatings. In the process, he posits an explicit analogy between body and fetish object: both must be destroyed in order to prove his disbelief in the spirit of evil. As if his unrelenting whip and stomping feet are not enough, he deploys invective and the rhetoric of the inquisition, mocking and ridiculing the adherent's faith in the devil. The irony of the story is that in the end Labat confesses the truth of the shaman's presage, thereby reconfirming his belief in the slaves' actual communication with the devil. This final credulity lends value to the story as worthy to be told, proof that "there truly are people who have commerce with the devil, and who make use of him in many things."

There is a further irony in Labat's excited performance of exorcism by torture, in that he borrows a technique from the Caribs, whose rituals of scarification tested the body's resistance to pain. What Labat refers to as a pimentade was in fact described by seventeenth-century ethnographers as a rite of passage marking important moments in the lives of Carib men such as their initiation as soldiers and the birth of a child. Pierced all over with the sharp teeth of a fish known as an *agouti*, the men were then treated with a searing solution of fermented peppers, which intensified the pain of their wounds while also preventing infection.[60] Du Tertre was particularly impressed by this and other examples of the Caribs' capacity for suffering, seeing it as evidence of their potential as Christians: such a sacrifice of the body could only mean a tenacity of soul.[61] Similarly, the body in pain is a recurrent obsession in Labat's memoirs, and it is most often attached to thematics of the spirit world.[62] In some instances, the author's discourse of demonology attributes a diabolical cause to the suffering of slaves. Cases of suicide, epileptic fits, and emaciated appearance are attributed to possession and chastisement by the devil, not to the suffering of Africans and their acts of resistance (2:322). But this explanation was not as successful for African slaves as it was for the Caribs because for slaves violence was ideologically justified as part of the solution rather than part of the problem. Instead Labat transforms the black body into a paradoxical fetish for colonial authority, an object that was revered insofar as the colonial project engineered its demolition in labor, torture, and rites of absolution. Labat often portrays black slaves as deriving pleasure from violence to their bodies in rituals of masochistic subservience and Christian devotion. One scene depicts the system of tutelage between veteran and newly arrived slaves to ensure the latter's instruction in the Catechism. The violence between master and slave is reproduced in the rapport between a "godfather" (*parrain*) and his pupil, who graciously receives floggings for faults of recitation: "He gave him blows of the whip on the shoulders, for which she then thanked him and kissed his feet" (2:399). In another instance, Labat describes a stopover in the Cape Verde Islands during which two clergymen, Fathers Beaumont and Boulogne, undertake the burial of a deceased colleague, Father Recolet. On the island of Saint-Yague, they unexpectedly encounter a black priest officiating at the parish church. Following this representation of black solemnity and decorum, the author juxtaposes an enigmatic black figure dressed in a white robe and hood who beats himself with a studded whip during the funeral procession: "His shoulders were naked, and in his hand he had a huge whip of cords, strewn with iron bosses [*molettes*]. He began to whip himself, rather moderately at first, but when his flesh heated up he went at it with all his strength, and in a few moments we saw blood streaming from everywhere" (3:98).

This haunting image of a Christian black man's self-flagellation recalls a medieval imaginary of sacred rites of painful penance and inscribes the body in pain as an aestheticized rendition of the Passion of Christ. Because of the suffering body, the black is worthy of the white robe. More importantly, however, the image projects a colonial fantasy of slaves' resistance to pain as evidence of a durable body and stoic disposition. Describing the character and physique of the coastal West Africans who make up the colonial slave population, Labat departs from the demonological explanation for numbness to pain. He glorifies not the insensitivity of the body but the tenacity of the soul: "We cannot say that it comes from insensitivity, because they have very delicate skin, and very strong feelings, but from a certain grandeur of the soul and an intrepidity that makes them scorn pain, dangers, even death. I have seen some broken alive without letting out the slightest cry. We burned one at Fort Royal in Martinique, without him saying anything. After he was attached to the stake, he asked for a bit of lit tobacco which was placed in his mouth, and he was still smoking it when his legs had already burst from the violence of the fire" (2:411). Here Labat pays homage to the defiant black whose uncanny power derives from a fearless embrace of death as he is sacrificed at the stake. While fixating on the delicacy of his skin, the author is careful to note the depth of sentiment that makes the suffering slave more than just a body. But far from indicting the torturers this affirmation of black nobility of spirit only further legitimates the apparatus of colonial discipline; the dying black body and noble soul are fetish objects to behold, created by colonial power.[63] Thus, Labat, who so readily defends Christian authority by destroying African fetish symbols and beating the bodies of slaves, himself fetishizes the black noble savage in colonial spectacles of punishment. Ultimately, Labat was protective of the sole right of whites and "justice" to inflict death on African slaves by any means. He attributed slave suicides not to a nobility of soul but to "black melancholy," which was said to afflict blacks and unmarried white Creole women alike, and their "foolish imagination," which he claimed led them to believe that in death they would return to their native land.[64]

Pierre-Corneille Blessebois and the Libertine Burlesque

As we have seen, missionaries used colonial demonology to define native Carib and African occult practices and to attack the legitimacy of those beliefs through a specifically Christian interpretation of spirits and the supernatural. Yet in stigmatizing the non-European occult the discourse of colonial demonology raises questions as to the missionaries' ability to police the spirit world of colonials themselves. The proclamation of the Code noir in 1685 indicated the Crown's desire to purge the colonial social body of non-Catholic beliefs. Yet, although the law openly targeted Protestantism and Judaism, magic and popular witchcraft were much less closely monitored in the colonies. Narrative sources suggest that French settlers were rarely the object of legal proceedings involving charges of witchcraft. Du Tertre recounts only one witch trial, which occurred in Martinique in 1657, ten years after the establishment of a colonial tribunal. Following the procedure outlined in demonological manuals, the judges tested the accused witch for proof of commerce with the devil by placing her in irons and throwing her, bound and tied, into a river to see if she would float. In the end, she was condemned to die by fire. According to Du Tertre, the punishment was opposed by many on the island: "Everyone blamed the judge's procedure and the missionaries complained to the Governor that it was contrary to French custom and had dangerous consequences."[65] One wonders whether the danger missionaries feared was a regression into a European-style witch-hunt that could have implicated a large proportion of the colonial population, which was isolated physically and culturally from the church.

Missionaries were not, however, the only ones to produce accounts of the colonial Caribbean, its culture, and its religious practices. In the late seventeenth century, they were joined by an engagé by the name of Pierre-Corneille Blessebois, who spent three years in Guadeloupe, leaving his mark in 1690 as a convicted criminal. On returning to Europe, Blessebois published a burlesque tableau of the underside of the colony, where illicit desires and beliefs reigned supreme. Hailed by Guillaume Apollinaire as the first colonial novel, *Le Zombi du Grand-Pérou, ou la comtesse de Cocagne* appeared in 1697 and contained stories untold by missionary chroniclers.[66] Pierre-Corneille Blessebois was an incorrigible, flamboyant libertine who had already published several satirical works by the time he departed for the Antilles. Appearing between 1676 and 1679, they included a comedy, lascivious stories, and novels such as the best known of his works, *Le Rut ou la pudeur éteinte*. For Blessebois, literature fulfilled a documentary function much like travel writing, closely mirroring his life and social milieu. His life in turn offers a lesson on the fascinating relationship among libertinage, criminality, witchcraft, and colonialism in the seventeenth century.

Born Paul Alexis Blessebois in Verneuil, Normandy, around 1646, he was the protestant son of a tax collector from the lower nobility and a wellborn woman, Madeleine Gautier, who ran a local thread factory.[67] As a young man, he changed his name to Pierre-Corneille, a gesture that indicates less his admiration for the dramatist than a taste for ironic imposture and libertine burlesque. Indeed, his life would be a self-conscious mockery of all that Corneille represented. Blessebois thrived on criminality and libertinage in life as well as art. His literary career began in the town of Alençon, where he studied, lived as a seducer, and produced a licentious work, *Le Parc d'Alençon*, which exposed the love lives of local notables. In 1670, he became a wanted criminal. He and his younger brother had set fire to their mother's house in an effort to escape an audit of royal finances that would have implicated his deceased father's accounts. While his brother managed to escape, Blessebois was arrested and charged for the crime. From his prison cell in Alençon, he entertained several lovers and gained the favor of a woman of high birth, Marthe le Hayer, who fell deeply in love with him. By promising to marry her, Blessebois used her money and family connections to get himself out of prison. Once free, he continued his libertine pursuits and disappeared with her dowry. He was again imprisoned in 1672 when she pressed charges. Released one year afterward, he roamed Verneuil and La Haye, pursuing women and writing the occasional licentious tale, most notably *Le Rut ou la pudeur éteinte* (1676), which ruthlessly defamed Marthe le Hayer.

After studying in Leiden, Holland, Blessebois served in the Dutch navy and the French army before landing a third prison sentence in 1678 for assaulting the wife and daughter of a wigmaker. This time, however, he attempted to barter his release by claiming knowledge of the Affaire des Poisons, which was being investigated by the Parisian Police Commissioner at the time. The investigation had begun in 1677 with the discovery of an anonymous note announcing the imminent poisoning of the king and the dauphin. Within a few months' time, the authorities uncovered evidence of a vast industry in black magic dominated by a conjurer and maker of poisons and aphrodisiacs, Madame Montvoisin, also known as La Voisin. She had amassed a formidable following, including one of Louis XIV's own mistresses, the marquise de Montespan, who sought to eliminate her rivals with the aid of magic and poison, as well as the performance of black masses in La Voisin's home. In the course of four years, the investigation riveted the Parisian upper class and led to hundreds of interrogations and the creation of a secret tribunal in what became known as the Chambre ardente because it was draped in black and lit with torches.[68] Although Blessebois's testimony turned out to be useless, the fact that he feigned knowledge of this case is telling of the society he may have frequented and his predilection for stories of black magic and sorcery. Evidently, however, he found it difficult to stay out of prison by any means, magical or otherwise. After his release in 1679, he was again incriminated for desertion from the royal navy. The penalty was severe; in 1681, the Council of War at Rochefort condemned Blessebois to the galleys "in perpetuity." Blessebois was later declared an invalid, but when Michel Begon, the former intendant of Martinique, was named intendant of the galleys, he was shipped off with an entire contingent of invalids to Basse-Terre, Guadeloupe.

There is some question among scholars as to whether on his arrival in 1686 Blessebois was purchased as an engagé or had enough money to avoid the heavy labor otherwise required to pay for his passage.[69] What is certain is that he ended up on the sugar estate of Dupont, one of the most prosperous planters in the early history of Guadeloupe. The parish registry at Capesterre records Blessebois as having abjured his protestant faith in 1687, perhaps on account of the 1685 edict. The other official trace of Blessebois's whereabouts is a trial launched against him from 1688 to 1690 by the *conseil souverain*, or high court, of Guadeloupe, whose verdict of 1690 condemned him to "publicly acknowledge the crime by appearing half-naked, torch in hand before the Church and the palace door, asking pardon from God, the King and Justice, on pain of being hung and strangled on the second offense."[70] The verdict was given in the defendant's absence, as Blessebois was once again on the run, perhaps on his way back to Europe, where *Le Zombi du Grand-Pérou* was published in 1697.

The story is narrated in the first person by a certain "Monsieur de C——", who tells of the circumstances leading to his condemnation as a sorcerer by the tribunal in Guadeloupe. Through a narrative of vindication, or *plaidoyer*, he offers a biting satire of colonial society as licentious, credulous, and possessed by its own belief in zombis.[71] The main focus of his ridicule is the comtesse de Cocagne, the mistress of the Marquis du Grand-Pérou, on whose sugar plantation the narrator temporarily resides. A married woman from the planter class with a reputation for debauchery, the comtesse is hopelessly devoted to the Marquis du Grand-Pérou despite his abusive and dismissive attitude toward her. Having learned of the narrator's supposed expertise in magic and sorcery, she begs him to make her invisible so that she may torment the marquis at night until he honors his promise to marry her. At first denying any knowledge of magic or witchcraft, the narrator senses that he may have something to gain by leading her to believe that he can turn her into a "zombi." He procures sexual favors from the comtesse in exchange for his supposedly supernatural assistance, which is in fact no more than an inventive ruse. Yet so convinced is the comtesse of her own invisibility that she makes two nighttime raids on the marquis's bedroom, violently attacking anyone in sight. Soon she becomes addicted to the power of the spirit world she believes to have infiltrated through the narrator's powers, using her zombi persona to carry out vendettas against anyone with whom she has a grudge. As her violent exploits become known throughout the island, public opinion turns against Monsieur de C——, who is believed to propagate a true practice of witchcraft. The story ends with the fate of Monsieur de C—— in suspension, as he is held in the depths of a chateau in Basse-Terre.

Published anonymously, *Le Zombi du Grand-Pérou* was attributed to Blessebois only in 1829, when the critic Charles Nodier established his authorship on the basis of clues to his name within the text itself and similarities in style and subject matter with Blessebois's other published works.[72] Once it was attributed to Blessebois, the text generated an increase in scholarly interest in him. However, criticism on *Le Zombi* focused mainly on what the bibliophile Pierre Louÿs called "*la clef du* Zombi," or the French colonial archives. Supposing the novel to be a roman à clef, Louÿs and a fellow bibliophile, Louis Loviot, became rivals in their efforts to research the historical identities of all the characters, the results of which were summarized in the 1927 biography of Blessebois by Frédéric Lachèvre.[73] According to Lachèvre, the marquis du Grand-Pérou was none other than Charles Dupont, who owned vast domains in Basse-Terre. A river named Grand-Pérou ran through his property, hence the title of Blessebois's novel. The Dupont workforce included a white servant called La Forêt, who appears so named in Blessebois's text, and more than thirty black slaves of all ages and both sexes. Most sensational was the historical counterpart of the comtesse de Cocagne, identified as Mademoiselle Félicité-Françoise-Antoinette de Lespinay. The daughter of a squire, the Sieur de Famier, and Françoise de Chollet, Lespinay had a notoriously bad reputation in Guadeloupe. She lived on a property called Cocagne nearby that of Charles Dupont's, and after a series of scandalous affairs set her sights on marrying him. Many details on Lespinay's life were divulged in a memoir by the intendant general, Monsieur Dumaitz, on the subject of her ill-fated marriage to a white domestic.[74] Alleged to have had liaisons with a black slave that ended in the murder of her own mulatto newborn, Lespinay had two other illegitimate children and was forced into a marriage with the father before nullifying it a few years later. She was described by the intendant as "known for her lewd temperament" and presumably sought Blessebois's help to win over the marquis.[75] At this point, however, critics have often turned to the novel itself for further details on the real lives and intrigues of the historical personages, often at the expense of literary interpretation.

Approaching the text as literature, the reader is struck by its generic and stylistic features, which combine modes of dramatic monologue, theater, and narrative. The story is told alternately in verse and prose and resembles a play with its heavy use of direct quotation connected by sparse narration. The verse passages parody the function of a Greek chorus, expressing the narrator's often satirical insights and interpretations of the action in the story. The stylistic complexity of Blessebois's colonial novel is mirrored on the level of genre, as the story resembles both an erotic and a libertine novel. According to Raymond Trousson, the erotic novel represents the satisfaction of sexual pleasures forbidden by social, moral, and religious codes through scenes that upset the *bienséances*, or standards of decency, of conventional literary genres.[76] *Le Zombi* certainly deploys an erotic poetics in its unabashed figuration of the heroine, the comtesse de Cocagne, in consummate pursuit of sexual adventure and willingly prostrating herself to the desires of her suitors. Yet, because Blessebois focuses less on scenes of sexual satisfaction than the conditions of its fulfillment through ruse and artifice, he may be considered both a forerunner of the eighteenth-century libertine novelist and a holdover of seventeenth-century modes of libertinage, which were not necessarily always concerned with sex. Blessebois's work bears perhaps the greatest resemblance to that of marginalized libertine writers such as Théophile de Viau, Cyrano de Bergerac, and Charles Coypeau d'Assoucy, whose flamboyant, irreverent, and generically ambiguous works brought public condemnation in the early to middle seventeenth century. As Joan Dejean has shown, these freethinking libertines dramatized their heroes' and their own victimization at the hands of an unjust society, compelling readers to identify with their plight, pity them, and hence sympathize with their views. They excelled at mythologizing their own position as alienated underdogs and self-made scapegoats "because their favorite mode of writing was defensive."[77] Likewise, Blessebois glorifies in the denunciation and ostracism of a society in which he can find no place but whose fanaticism and false pretenses he is therefore especially qualified to unmask. In the process, he displays the tantalizing mix of fact and fiction, autobiography and literature, that has led critics to take his novel as a historical document.

Blessebois restyled his life in his literature, consistently dramatizing his own amorous adventures and intrigues through a satirical lens intended to defame the lover(s) in question. In the case of Le Zombi, the author wielded the plume to excoriate his former lover, mock the libertine lifestyles of the planter milieu, and defend himself against the charges brought against him. Blessebois thus stands in stark contrast to missionaries, who wrote of colonial culture with the aim of ennobling it for skeptical superiors and potential donors to the colonial cause. They critiqued culture mainly from a religious point of view and often with a politicized rhetoric that attributed wrongs to politics or company error, ultimately vindicating the missionary project in the islands. Blessebois was part of a wave of secular writers such as the buccaneer Alexandre Oexmelin, and to a lesser extent Father Labat, who exploited the colonial scene and its libertine reputation for their own self-interest. No longer a space for settlement, domestication, and salvation, the colony is for Blessebois a site of personal adventure, sexual excess, and spiritual transgression. In fact, his text may be read as an ironic response to the fascination with religion and the spirit world exhibited in missionary accounts and satirized in his own work, notably in his mise en scène of the zombi trope. What changes in Blessebois is that it is colonials themselves whose unorthodox spirit beliefs are amplified and shown to be creolized at the same time as their sexual indulgences are thrown into dramatic relief. As a representation of syncretic religious practices, the text thus raises important questions and provides some compelling insights into the kinds of mixing and matching of diverse belief systems that characterized the colonial Caribbean, as well as the particular meanings attached to the word *zombi* in late-seventeenth-century Guadeloupe. In addition, through the narrator's satirical treatment of colonial beliefs, values, and his own moral shortcomings, the text provides a unique perspective on the construction of morality in the early French Caribbean. What, we may ask, is the nature of evil in a world in which conventional religion sanctions slavery and is profaned in favor of a fleshly libertinism, where bodies are owned, abused, and subjected to an earthly economy of capital gain and sexual excess?

Creolizing the Spirit World

At the core of Blessebois's tale is the conceit of the narrator, a former galley slave and engagé named Monsieur de C——, who has a reputation for witchcraft and cons his love object, the comtesse, into thinking she has tapped into his magical powers so as to sleep with her. Like the nobility in the famed Affaire des Poisons, the comtesse relies on him to help her to recapture the Marquis du Grand-Pérou and brutalize anyone who objects to their affair. We first learn of the narrator's supposed art through the comtesse's impassioned entreaties requesting his assistance. According to the comtesse, Monsieur de C——'s reputation for witchcraft was born on the galley ships, where he subsisted on the income he earned through his commerce with the devil, "the black angel." Extoling this rumored supernatural talent, she exclaims: "Good and evil are equally at your command. . . . You are a magician, you hold the devil subordinate to your orders" (23). Yet if the comtesse places unshakable faith in his powers over the devil, her wish is to access a specifically creolized spirit world, one that both encompasses and exceeds the early modern imaginary of demoniacal witchcraft. Indeed, the comtesse desires to become invisible so as to frighten the marquis in his bed by "doing the zombi [*faire le zombi*]." Just what it means for a white Creole woman to "do" or become a zombi is one of the most compelling interpretive dilemmas posed by the text, all the more fascinating considering that Blessebois's work may very well contain the earliest appearance of the word *zombi* in any European language.[78]

Anthropologists link the historical emergence of zombi beliefs in the francophone Caribbean to diasporic slave cultures that retained African ideas of spiritual dispossession, witchcraft, and sorcery. In Haiti, the zombi is a body without a soul made to work for the sorcerer, or *houngan*, who induces a deathlike state and later raises the body from the grave with the aid of magical spells and/or hallucinatory drugs. The zombi then becomes a body devoid of life, moving mechanically, without emotion or individual will.[79] A second, less well understood meaning of the word *zombi* in Haiti refers not to the body but to the captured soul, which may be stored in its invisible state as a form of protection, good luck, or occult power. The idea that through sorcery souls may be captured and humans reduced to slavery exists throughout West and Central Africa, the latter notion occurring frequently in the context of real or imagined labor exploitation suggestive of European influence, slavery, or colonialism. Anthropological research on the origins of the Haitian zombi has revealed a set of corresponding beliefs, none of which can be ascribed historical precedence over the others, but all of which suggest that witchcraft supplied a culturally acceptable explanation for slavery and colonialism's deleterious effect on African peoples and social organization.[80] In the Creole of the lesser Antilles, however, the term *zombi* is commonly defined as "phantom," "ghost," or "errant soul" and refers more specifically to malevolent yet largely invisible nocturnal spirits.[81] In his study of Antillean magic, the anthropologist Eugène Revert relates several anecdotes demonstrating that his Caribbean subjects feared zombis particularly for their power to haunt houses, shake physical structures, and even attack people.[82] These notions correlate in important ways with the meanings that come through in Blessebois's novel, a work that has not been considered in social science scholarship on the Caribbean spirit world.[83]

The meaning of the term *zombi* in Blessebois's text is never clearly explained but is suggested in the description of the comtesse's plan to attack the marquis in a spectral form. In communicating to the narrator, Monsieur de C——, her wish for his supernatural assistance, she pleads: "I ask of you only the favor of making me invisible for just one night. Are you so callous to refuse a young woman that you find sometimes pretty, and will I be the only unfortunate lover who will not benefit from your sublime knowledge?" (24–25). Later the narrator encounters the marquis, his host, whom he describes as dejected because he has just lost "the best of his negroes." As though to cheer him up, the narrator divulges the comtesse's request: "I told him about the conversation I had with his mistress, and her desire to do the zombi to frighten him and get him to lay his hand on his conscience" (25). One wonders what would have been so ridiculous about the comtesse's wish. Was it simply the desire to become a zombi, considered as something fanciful or nonexistent, or was there something about the comtesse that precluded her passage into the invisible world? The marquis's reaction suggests that the transformation simply could not happen except in her imagination: "At first he thought it would be good to have her come in our room so as to laugh at her foolish indulgence [*sa facilité*], but after a little reflection, he put the matter off until his return from Grande-Terre" (25–26). Similarly, the character mockingly named *prince étranger* is so tickled by the prospect of the comtesse imitating a zombi that he wishes to join in the joke: "He eagerly bid me to let him play whatever part I wanted in this comedy" (26).

When the comtesse finally assures herself of the narrator's complicity and dares to act as a zombi, her behavior and the reactions she provokes in the other characters only enhance the mystery of the zombi concept. On the night of her first apparition, the marquis is absent and the narrator stages the event with the help of the prince étranger. The comtesse enters the room in a violent rage, literally beating the prince and other unsuspecting characters.

> First, she took big steps, then furiously jolted the windows in our room, struck us one after the other and moved around so much that the good man La Forest, who was below, was overcome with fright and asked me several times what was the matter. The prince étranger and I responded that we were being beaten, but that we could not see anyone. The marquis's engagé said the same, and the poor boy was not lying, for he hid in his bed with such care as to show the zombi that he would have wanted to be invisible himself. Finally, the comtesse de Cocagne, after having played all kinds of evil little tricks on the prince étranger, threw him so skillfully from his bed onto the floor that the hall trembled as if struck by lightning and we ran downstairs, the engagé and I, with as much speed as if the most dreadful death were upon us (27).

While the comtesse attacks the prince étranger, the engagé and La Forest sustain the greatest shock, since they believe her invasion to be a true case of spirit terror. For La Forest, who could hear the evidence of the supposed zombi from below the bedroom, this would mark another in a long line of encounters with an actual zombi of the river Grand-Pérou. Unable to sleep, the characters tell stories of these apparitions: "We all spent the night together talking about the zombis' love for the Grand-Pérou, and the good man La Forest declared that they had returned in over thirty forms since he had lived there" (28). In these scenes, the zombi accrues meaning as a frightful spirit entity in the colonial imagination, one that is believed to shape-shift, or metamorphose, in myriad ways. Most striking about the comtesse's imitation of the zombi is her brutality and destructiveness. Her violent outrage only increases during her second apparition a few nights later. So severe is this attack that La Forest sustains injuries to his arm and leg and nearly dies.

In representing colonial whites as believing in and, in the case of the comtesse, attempting to infiltrate the spirit world, the text raises questions as to the combination of cultural elements that could have contributed to this notion of a zombi. The magician's power to become invisible is a cliché in various early modern European traditions of magic. The enchanted ring of Solomon, a figure referred to frequently in the narrative, was said to give this power, and Faust used secret incantations to do the trick.[84] In the demonological imaginary, witches were believed to "disappear" or shape-shift in order to be transported to the Sabbath by the devil, and tormenting, bewitching, or possessing others were modes of terror attributed to the devil or his followers.[85] Yet the particular powers attached to the zombi motif in Blessebois are distinct from those of European traditions and arguably bear the imprint of other belief systems, not least because of the zombi name. In anthropological research, the first suggested French derivation, *les ombres*, has largely been eclipsed by a range of terms from African languages, including the Angolan word *nvumbi*, or "body without a soul," and *ndzumbi*, meaning "corpse" in the Mitsogho language of Gabon. The Kikongo word *mvumbi* means "inner, invisible man" or "soul." It is also the word for a corpse that, not yet emptied of its blood, still retains the soul.[86] Two other African terms are especially compelling for the case under study, not only for their phonetic resemblance to the word *zombi* but also because they are drawn from the African languages spoken by the two most prominent groups in the colonial French Caribbean, and their meanings exhibit parallels with Blessebois's zombi motif.[87] Max-Auguste Dufrénot has shown that the term *zombi* closely approximates the word *zanbibi*, meaning "night bogeyman" in the Ewe language spoken by the Aja-Fon ethnic group from Dahomey (modern Benin), Nigeria, Togo, and Ghana. *Zanbibi* is the combination of *zan*, meaning "night," and *bibi*, meaning "ghost, bogeyman," and is used in modern Benin to frighten children into behaving.[88] Another possible African derivation is the word, *nzambi*, from the Kikongo language spoken widely in the western Congo Basin, the second main point of origin of slaves in the Caribbean. Although the word may at times refer to humans, alive or dead, it is because they are conceived as being made in the image of Nzambi, the invisible and omniscient creator god in the Kongo religion. The god of last resort, with absolute power over natural phenomena,

Nzambi is consulted only after all other spiritual and fetishistic rituals to achieve justice or revenge have been exhausted. Nzambi visits destruction on the homes and villages of his followers' adversaries.[89]

Thus, at least three distinct occult systems present in the colonial Caribbean (European, Aja-Fon, and Kongo) could have interacted to produce the idea of a destructive night specter so central to Blessebois's text. To these, we must add the Carib spirit entity that inspired both the greatest awe and horror in seventeenth-century missionary accounts when figured as the beating devil. Blessebois's story also suggests that when whites attempted to harness the terrible powers of the zombi by transforming their bodies into spirits it was through European codes of sorcery. In order to infiltrate the invisible world, the comtesse turns to the French narrator, a former engagé from mainland France who is reputed to have a knowledge of witchcraft. In some sense, Blessebois's text corroborates the close association between indentured servitude and witchcraft. In the islands of Guadeloupe and Martinique, the word *engagé*, creolized as *gens gagés*, has historically referred to those who entered into pacts with the devil to accrue power, wealth, and/or love in the material world. The powers of engagés are varied and recall popular beliefs surrounding early modern European witchcraft. In addition to being able to fly to nighttime meetings, where diabolical festivities are performed, they have the power of metamorphosis, the ability to change into the animal of their choice so as to perform various maleficent acts.[90] This connection may represent more than a mere metaphorical association between selling one's body to the master and selling one's soul to the spirit of evil. Most engagés were drawn from the lower and peasant classes of Brittany, Normandy, Poitou and Aquitaine, which have been credited with transporting to the colonies popular traditions of magic and witchcraft.[91] Thus, the assumption of Monsieur de C——'s familiarity with the European occult, as a former engagé, might seem appropriate. If he chooses to mock that assumption, it is in part because he represents himself as a sort of mistaken engagé, a misplaced poet whose true class identity comes through in his subtle and ironic subversion of popular beliefs in a narrative full of learned references and allusions.

Blessebois's narrator is not, however, the only source of European occult knowledge in the story. The comtesse herself demonstrates an awareness of the malevolent act of *envoûtement*, whereby evil spells are transmitted through the intermediary of wax figurines. Explains the narrator, "she told me that when her mother was living she would sometimes read a magic book . . . and she fancied it so much that she would have made herself very famous if she had not been kept from it. . . . In particular, she spoke to me about a certain wax figure that represented an enemy and through which one could invisibly avenge oneself against the original at will" (35). In bringing her own ideas of witchcraft to the narrator, the comtesse takes charge of their relationship. She demands, in effect, that he model the wax figure of her next intended victim, the marquis's mother, who opposes a possible marriage between her and the marquis. The comtesse wastes no time in mutilating the small wax figurine, which she then places within a Carib basket in hopes that its human original will be so destroyed.

Playing with the Devil: Demonology and Eros

Beatings, dismemberment, and torture are recurrent themes in colonial representations of the spirit world. Whereas missionaries sought to justify the corporeal violence of colonialism by recourse to the narrative of Christian salvation, white colonials are shown in Blessebois's text to perform violence on each other via a spiritual connection with the god of evil. The ultimate objective is not the violence in itself but rather the fulfillment of libertine passions. On one hand, the comtesse exploits the occult as a means of winning back her lover and making him her husband. Yet it is the narrator who, by pretending to possess diabolical powers, achieves the most libertine rewards. In the story, the relationship of reciprocity between the narrator and the comtesse, where sex is exchanged for occult power, reenacts the infamous pact sealed over the body of the witch. Beginning with a kiss, her sensual paybacks increase with each spirit apparition, until finally she submits to being his sexual slave: "Dispose of your servant at the mercy of your desires," she urges (45).

Blessebois's play on the sensual subtext of occult beliefs is not limited to European demonology; he does the same with colonial spirit beliefs, reinterpreting the colonial trope of zombification through the lens of libertinage. In this case, the comtesse is not the perpetrator but the believing victim of such abuse. In order to quell her increasingly ardent desire to inhabit the spirit world, the narrator tells her to lay nude outdoors in the shadow of the night with her eyes shut tightly so as to be carried away by the spirits he calls zombis de ronde. Cautioning her against being duped by them—"the spirits are evil, they will seduce you if you are credulous"—the narrator departs, leaving the comtesse to be molested by the Vicomte du Carbet and the Baron du Marigot. They take advantage of her posture and delirium to satisfy their own desires. Later recounting the scene to the narrator, the comtesse exclaims: "They placed a chaplet in my arms and they fleeced me, pricked my buttocks and even whipped me with branches" (49). That she should be sexually mishandled and beaten points up the author's subversive use of the spirit world to stage a scene of carnal pleasure and pain. One can hardly miss the import of this image in a colonial context in which spirit beliefs mirrored the daily reality of corporeal brutality. By fusing the image of the beating zombi and the whipping master in a libertine frame, Blessebois links tropes of the spirit world to colonial eros, demonstrating one hundred years before Sade that the power to inflict pain could be readily transformed into a libertine fantasy of desire.[92]

Of course, what enables the narrator to exploit colonial spirit beliefs for his own libertine purposes is his own ability to fool the comtesse into thinking he has access to the devil's powers. But so powerful is her superstition and craving for supernatural agency that she cannot detect even the most obvious signs of his imposture. Through the comtesse, Blessebois dramatizes the power of illusion to compel belief in the credulous. Thus, the narrator's repeated denials of supernatural talent—"Stop fooling yourself, . . . I swear by the earth and the sky / That I know not the god who makes us love / Except in your beautiful eyes" (24)—go unheeded. The real magic in the story is not a supernatural power held by the narrator but rather his talent for deception and make-believe through artifice, disguise, and invention. It is also a function of the comtesse's obsession with devils, zombis, and the spirit world, as well as her ardent desire to reclaim her lover. During the comtesse's first rampage as an invisible spirit, the narrator and his accomplice, the prince étranger, fake their horror, screaming that they are being attacked but can see no one. Later, the narrator describes the sight of the monstrous spirit with a richly intertextual image: "It has snakes for hair, / The body is like a harpy, / And it carries in its impious paw / The Chimera full of fire" (28). On discovering the wax figurine of the marquis's mother violently desecrated, he feigns knowledge of the illness of her "original." Finally, when the comtesse desires to see the face and feel the breath of the evil spirit behind the narrator's feigned powers, he presents her with a candle filled with gunpowder, which produces smoke when lit: "It was then that she truly believed in me and that she would invite me to perform miracles where I was blind as a mole" (40).

In these respects, the narrator's performance recalls the demonological trope of the devil as an illusionist who uses lies, deception, and seduction to delude his victims into thinking they have changed shape, are able to fly, or possess other supernatural powers.[93] This figure also suggests Blessebois's affinity with the tradition of the burlesque, or "comic," novel, which incorporated themes of illusion and charlatanism to parodic effect. In Charles Sorel's *Le Berger extravagant* (1627–28), for example, the protagonist fantasizes his transformation into a shepherd so as to live out the pastoral adventures of his favorite novel, *L'Astrée*. He is maintained in this belief by his friends, who act as though they take him seriously, all the while mocking him, as well as the illusions of pastoral literature.[94] The figure of charlatan appeared in seventeenth-century libertine works such as Sorel's *Histoire comique de Francion* (1623) and D'Assoucy's *Aventures* (1677). Joan Dejean has shown that sorcerers, magicians, and alchemists were preferred figures of difference through which these writers figured their desired persecution. Though manifestly not sorcerers and in fact deeply critical of the occult, libertine heroes nonetheless borrowed the persona and, like Blessebois, were complicit in their own condemnation by deliberately deceiving other characters through illusion.[95] If, as Dejean maintains, such exploits demonstrate the "nascent libertine desire to be the other," they also parody the tradition of demonology.[96] When Blessebois pretends to be a sorcerer, the devil's supposed power becomes the libertine's joke. No longer the master illusionist, the devil becomes the perfect mask for the libertine's search for derision and the pleasures of the flesh.

With each illusion of magic and scene of violence, the narrator finds himself incriminated by the colonial society at large, which quickly spreads word of his collusion with the devil. La Forest's injuries are cause for a widespread alarm: "The rumor mill of Cabesse-Terre . . . had made this news known before sunrise. . . . Some were informed enough to judge that the Zombi of Grand-Pérou could only be the comtesse de Cocagne under my auspices" (31). The comtesse's growing infatuation with envoûtement only increases the narrator's anxiety: "This secret will be known, they will declare war on me, / And I will be considered a sorcerer" (36). This awareness of the impending allegations against him haunts the story from beginning to end. If the work is a narrative of vindication, it is an ironic one, for the narrator exonerates himself from the charge of witchcraft only by taking responsibility for inciting the accusation. The author's point, therefore, is to illustrate how even a simulacrum of magic accrues legitimacy in a credulous society, in which the true culprits are the colonists themselves. The comtesse's second zombi apparition is especially emblematic of what we might call colonial irrationality and superstition, for she remains unseen even though fleeing in view of all: "Before the eyes of so many she could hide! / I imagine that, without consulting the oracle, / Faith finds no obstacle; / It can transplant the hardest rock, / And it was faith that performed this great miracle" (30).

The theme of colonial "faith" and superstition reappears in the narrator's account of his departure from Basse-Terre and his trek over land and mountain with the aid of several sympathetic characters. At Trois-Rivières, his host, Cadot, warns of the island's motives for prosecuting him for witchcraft: "The bad state of your present fortune makes me fear that they were using a pretext to make you a criminal and that slander, which spares no one, will poison the innocence of your will and make you responsible for public conduct" (54–55). If the narrator is being so viciously attacked through public rumor and the civil courts, Cadot seems to say, it is because his poverty makes him an easy scapegoat for the diabolical indulgences of the entire colonial populace. Their obsession with the devil becomes apparent in the fantasmatic nature of the accusations various persons make against him. The character Florimond recounts to the narrator all that the islanders believe, warning: "You would not die innocent if all that they say were true" (58–59). The accusations resemble a litany of demonological images of metamorphosis or shape-shifting. In the minds of colonials, the comtesse takes the form of a bull, an ass, a bird, and a sow, demonstrating the sexually predatory and destructive nature associated with devil worship. Seducing men, fornicating with demons, torching sugar mills, or dancing around a symbolic goat as though at a witches' Sabbath, the comtesse's many incarnations are born of whites' fear of and fascination with the colonial spirit world.

It would seem, then, that in addition to staging witchcraft as a scene of seduction Blessebois satirizes the mechanism of panic, fantasy, and scapegoating behind false accusations of witchcraft, both in the colonies and in Europe. This is apparent in the vague aphorisms through which the narrator champions the plight of the poor: "Each slanderer poisons / the cause of the indigent man: / It is enough that he has no money / To be whatever one suspects him to be" (55). Here the narrator announces his tribulation as one of poverty against riches, thus indicting the colonial elite for making an example of him for indiscretions that typify the whole of colonial society, including those of libertinage: "What did I do that the entire island has not done?" (57). Yet even as he condemns witch hysteria as a prurient form of persecuting the weak and indigent the narrator does not let go of his own belief in the devil. On the contrary, he exploits demonological discourse in order to extricate himself from the one "crime" he *did* commit, libertinage.

What is fascinating is that, in so opportunistically reengaging the belief system he otherwise derides, the narrator theorizes colonial evil as a kind of diabolical femininity. Blessebois both acknowledges and forgives the narrator's moral turpitude by figuring colonial women as the embodiment of sexual immorality, Satanism, servitude, and violence.

Nowhere is this more apparent than in the scandalous parody of a love poem that opens the novella. Entitled "Portrait de La Comtesse de Cocagne: Vers irréguliers," the poem enumerates the comtesse's dubious bodily attractions as seen from the rear as though in a state of coitus. Her body mediates the narrator's reflections on the cause of libidinous desires, which are rooted in a corrupt soul. Enumerating her body parts, the narrator establishes a relationship between physiognomy and morality in the comtesse. Her forehead lacks "virtue" and "the desired modesty" (15). Her eyes are like those of a sow because "she leads a similar lifestyle." Even her nose reveals an interior corruption: "One considers it to bear witness / To the unhappy state to which her soul is reduced" (16). In comparing the comtesse to such animals as sows, cows, and the generic "beast," the narrator suggests that, despite her whiteness—the "lovely ivory body" against which the author contrasts his depraved soul—her very humanity is compromised by her sexual rapaciousness. If the comtesse "would rather spend a year in purgatory than one night alone in her bed," it is not for lack of love of the devil. On the contrary, her sexual infidelity is literally willed by the demon: "It is the spirit of malice that gave you to the Marquis du Grand-Pérou; the prudent women builds and uplifts her household, and you, who are senseless, you destroy not only your own, but you make your neighbor's house teeter on its foundation" (22).

Blessebois's representation of the lascivious comtesse is consonant with misogynist assumptions underlying early modern demonology. If Christ was protected from evil and the devil by his masculinity and rationality, femininity, it was presumed, offered the devil an impressionable imagination and fleshy sensuality through which he could literally inseminate the world with evil.[97] In many respects, however, demonological lore positioned women less as the victims than the agents of satanic eros. This is especially apparent in Pierre de Lancre's fantastically prurient treatise on witchcraft in the Basque region of Southwest France, *Tableau de l'inconstance des mauvais anges et démons*, which conceives the witches' Sabbath as a massive orgy. Although De Lancre repeatedly affirms that copulation with devils involved pain and suffering akin to that of childbirth, he attests that witches found pleasure in such pain as integral to the "pleasant stay and delicious amusement" through which they freely explored their desires.[98] The association between aggressive female sexuality and Satanism was exploited by burlesque, libertine, and satirical writers of early-seventeenth-century France, who infused their misogynistic verse with a strong dose of devil lore. As Marianne Closson has shown, the grotesque eroticism of the Sabbath offered male writers such as Pierre Motin and the Sieur de Sigogne a new arsenal of imagery through which to attack, degrade, and ridicule female sexuality, all the while celebrating violence toward women.[99] Blessebois draws on this tradition and transforms it by tailoring his misogyny to the vulgarities of colonialism in seventeenth-century Guadeloupe. Although slaves are conspicuously absent from the story as characters, slavery itself overdetermines the representation of diabolical white femininity and libertinage. In the opening poem, the comtesse is not only figuratively dismembered and compared to a beast; she is described as an item of property, albeit with little exchange value. If her breast is a "household good that one draws upon at will," her bare feet are so caked with dirt as to be literally worth nothing: "I wouldn't even give two coins for them." An attractive Creole, she is missing the indispensable feminine virtues of "chastity, virtue, and modesty." Her nature, repeatedly characterized as mad, senseless, and inconstant, originates in her heart and enslaves her body, which is figuratively placed in "irons": "Her madness is linked to her weak heart, / Her heart communicates it to her wretched soul; / Her soul spreads it in huge waves around her, / And forges irons for her dangerous body; / Her body obeys like a slave, / And this slave is so brutish / Before God, that it hates and bullies, / That it hurts itself when playing around" (19). Her greatest power, however, is that of sexual temptress. The narrator repeatedly depicts his own unrepentant libertinage—"my readiness to surrender to desires of the flesh"—as a weakness known to all men, and surreptitiously exploited by the devil. Placing himself among the ranks of such infamously duped biblical figures as Adam, Lot, David, and Solomon, he concludes that it is man's fate to "bite the fatal apple" and "burn with love for women" (53).

The comtesse de Cocagne thus emerges as the primary agent through which the demon may submerge, engulf, and possess his male victims. In this sense, she becomes a convenient scapegoat through which to redeem libertines such as Monsieur de C——: "This prostituted woman / Has in her dangerous transports / Taken the life of the strongest men; / The island is all infatuated with her. / The terrible and ugly angel / Uses her like a bait / To lose our feeble souls" (46). By so readily embracing the logic of demonology to explain the follies of colonial libertinage, the narrator extricates not only himself but the rest of the elite white male population from the burden of moral guilt in the practice that he otherwise satirizes. In general, the theme of imposture and false pretense is not limited to the narrator's pretended magic but extends to most of the characters whose names parody whites' habit of reinventing themselves as nobility on settling in the colonies. There is hardly a character in the story who lacks a title or an article, yet the names themselves bespeak fabricated privilege and ambiguity of place. The names Marquis du Grand-Pérou, Baron du Marigot (Carib for "swamp"), and comtesse de Cocagne, for example, call up conflicting images of paradise and misery. The title of the work layers two heavily symbolic place names—Pérou, which was at the time a vague geographic appellation for the discovered territories in South America, and *cocagne*, a French term for an imaginary or mythical place where all is plentiful and good—both of which prove to be ironic overestimations of the colonial environment, thus parodying the tendency of colonists and colonial propagandists to exaggerate the richness and opportunities of colonial life. Indeed, these characters' pretended nobility is comically compromised by their material poverty and lack of social institutions other than slavery. The comtesse goes barefoot, *à la créole*, and serves tadpoles to her houseguests. The only forms of entertainment in the story are church, libertinage, and feasting, which are actually combined in a manner not unlike that of the imaginary witches' Sabbath. Indeed, whereas the narrator relies on a notion of the Christian devil to excuse his sexual indulgences, the story also makes plain the blasphemous perversion of Christianity in the colonies, the casual ease with which all that was holy was profaned or eroticized. In a grotesque travesty of Christian piety, Sunday mass is followed by an evening of unrestrained debauchery—*un amour éthiopien*—where, as the narrator explains, "most of the principal residents were present, and whoever wanted to mix whites with blacks could satisfy himself undisturbed" (43).

Yet, even as Blessebois exposes the shocking interface of colonial spirituality and libertinage, no real critique of that behavior is possible outside a misogynist framework. The orgy is attributed to the pagan gods Bacchus and Venus and excused as being "reasonable": "Never was Bacchus more reasonable, / Never did less furor in an excess of wine / poison the joy and peace of a table" (43). And if the narrator willingly compares his mistress to the devil he reserves for himself a parodic likeness to God or at least a Christ-like figure wrongly accused and scapegoated by a credulous, idolatrous, and materialistic society. For the cause of his condemnation is not his weakness before the force of passion but rather the effects of magic he allegedly caused through the comtesse, coupled with his marginal social condition. The story maintains not only the narrator's innocence but figures his impending sacrifice as payment for the iniquity of his accusers. Rendered responsible for "public conduct," the narrator walks up the mountain called Le Dos d'Ane to the place of condemnation in a scene reminiscent of Christ's walk to meet his accusers. Blessebois does not fail to seize the moment for another sardonic aside: "Ah, why are you not, o cruel mountain, / As sweet to come down and easy to mount as the comtesse de Cocagne?" (276). When his friend and sympathizer, Florimond, presses him to turn back and save himself from the death penalty likely to follow his trial, Monsieur de C—— responds like a martyr: "But there is nothing supernatural in my productions; there is only foolishness and indiscretion, and I do not fear false witnesses" (60). The story ends with his arrival in Basse-Terre, where he is immediately seized and taken to "the dirtiest and deepest dungeon in the castle."

In so derisively portraying the comtesse de Cocagne as a figure for colonial evil, the author undoubtedly gave voice to popular misogyny toward white colonial women in the seventeenth-century French Caribbean. Literally imported to the colonies to serve the interests of colonial reproduction, domesticity, and morality, they were despised for the libertine proclivities they ostensibly brought with them. However, whereas missionaries effectively transformed Christianity into a moral justification for slavery, Blessebois suggests that colonials on the ground forced Christianity and its discourse of demonology to accommodate libertinage. In the text, moral good is reducible to the accumulation and consumption of bodies, both economically and sexually. Similarly, Blessebois's use of demonological allusions in his representation of diabolical femininity enables him to remain a victim at his lover's expense. Yet this libertine text represents much more than the hero's descent into infamy and the dungeon; it also unmasks colonial society's deepest anxieties. If unrestrained libertinage provokes neither moral outrage nor panic among colonials, sorcerers and zombis do. For those colonials who condemn the narrator on the basis of rumors about his works, the terror of occult forces lies in their power to attack the property and bodies of colonials who habitually occupy the role of beating master in the material world of colonial slavery. Blessebois's tale shows us the case of a white colonial woman, repressed by a misogynistic society, who attempts to retaliate through spiritual means. What the text leaves conspicuously unspoken is the degree to which captive Africans participated in the deployment of the *zombi du Grand-Pérou* so as to reverse the course of colonial violence or inflict destruction and terror on the colony. Slavery nonetheless overdetermines the significance of the zombi trope. In addition to the many ways in which Blessebois signals the embeddedness of his primary characters in a system of human bondage, he suggests that whites were not immune to the powers of the creolized spirit world; they perceived themselves as both agents and victims within it. In a society in which slavery itself was sanctioned as a moral right, evil could be none other than the subjection of the master's body to the corporal torments suffered by slaves.

* * *

As this chapter has shown, spirits and violence were constantly linked in narratives of the seventeenth-century French Caribbean. Colonial demonology was, as I describe it, a set of beliefs and practices used to categorize, understand, and explain the non-European spirit world in terms of European ideas about devils, witches, magicians, and sorcerers. At the same time, French writers altered, expanded, and instrumentalized that rhetoric in order to respond to the particularities of non-European spirit beliefs and to facilitate the success of the mission and French colonialism generally. Through the stories they told about non-European spirits and gods, French colonial writers allegorized relationships of coercion and rationalized colonial violence in the material world. Whereas initially the body was conceived as the ground on which the wars of spirits were waged, with the establishment of slavery violence became a viable means by which to enforce and maintain captives' compliance with a Christian disciplinary regime. Both the missionaries and the French Crown justified slavery as a path toward Christian salvation. In the case of Father Labat and the Code noir, the narratives of spiritual redemption and lived experience collapsed into one another, such that the slave's bodily desecration became a sign of salvation and a fetish for its earthly cause in colonialism. Blessebois's novel took the interface between spirits and the body in a different direction, exploiting the repressed erotic subtext of demonology's obsession with the body. In portraying the creolized spirit world as a palimpsest of tropes of mixed cultural origin (figures of transvection, shape-shifting, copulation with the demon, and most importantly the spectral beating zombi), Blessebois's text forces the modern reader to reexamine assumptions about the meanings and derivation of zombi beliefs in the Caribbean. At the same time, Blessebois portrays colonials as eager to transform both Christian and occult spiritual practices into pretexts for libertine pleasures, thus reducing morality to the uninhibited consumption of bodies white and black.

While this exploration has focused entirely on what French colonial authorities had to say about themselves and the spirit world, its conclusions invite reflection on the ways in which Afro-diasporic religions have preserved the legacy of colonial slavery. The idea that religious discourses and practices function as cultural allegories of material history is confirmed by surviving religious beliefs in contemporary Haiti. Many aspects of Haitian Vaudou and magic retain fantastically vivid symbols of the physical violence and spiritual alienation imposed under colonial slavery. Take, for instance, the figure of the Haitian zombi, the image of the living dead, a corpse resurrected by means of magic to perform functions for the houngan, or witch doctor, who has captured its soul. Scholars have interpreted the zombi motif as a symbolic transposition of the helpless horror of the slave, coerced into robotic service for the master as though a body without a mind. As the Swiss ethnologist Alfred Métraux explained in his classic study, *Le Vaudou haïtien*: "The zombi is a beast of burden exploited mercilessly by his master who forces him to toil in his fields, crushes him with work, and whips him at the slightest pretext, while feeding him on the blandest of diets. The life of the zombi, on the mythical level, is similar to that of old slaves of Saint-Domingue."[100] More recently, the literary scholars Joan Dayan and Richard Burton have identified covert anti-colonial narratives in Caribbean rituals of possession. As Joan Dayan argues, "The lwa most often invoked by today's vodou practitioners do not go back to Africa; rather, they were responses to the institution of slavery, to its peculiar brand of sensuous domination."[101]

Yet there is another example that strikes even closer to the heart of my inquiry. The legend and legacy of Father Labat has endured for nearly three centuries in the French Caribbean, where he is still read by many Martinicans who relish his exactitude and taste for savory anecdotes of early colonial cultures. Historians also continue to read Labat as a reference on the history and geography of the French Caribbean, often taking his word for fact. Yet the Creole descendants of slaves have preserved his legend in the very realm of spirit he so brutally opposed. So renowned was the author's reign of cruelty over the slaves that he has survived in memory as a spirit condemned to wander in the hills as punishment for the sins he committed. Labat has also been interred in the spiritual archive as a form of devil or malevolent spirit, thus giving rise to popular phrases such as "Father Labat is going to get you," which are used to frighten naughty children.[102] It is difficult to conceive of a more powerful answer to the age-old colonial discourses that subjected Africans to competing and paradoxical regimes of beating devils and Christians. Whereas colonialism maintained this contradiction as a fiction of ideology, the spiritual imaginary of Creole folklore resolved it in the irredeemable ghost of Father Labat. The spirit world thus remains a privileged symbolic terrain on which to reinterpret the terror-ridden legacy of colonialism in the material world.

Chapter Four *The Libertine Colony:*

Desire, Miscegenation, and the Law

Among the sentimental tales produced in the Caribbean and popularized in Europe in the eighteenth century, none is better known than that of Inkle, an English adventurer, and Yarico, an Indian maiden. Scholars have traced this story's print origins to a narrative published by Richard Ligon in 1657 entitled *A True and Exact History of the Island of Barbados.*[1] In a chapter describing Indians, Ligon tells the story of a young Englishmen who docks on the Spanish Main in search of food and drink. When an Indian attack compels him to seek shelter in the tropical forest, he is surprised by a beautiful Indian woman, who falls in love with him at first sight. She pampers and protects him until he can safely return to his ship, where, to her horror, the young man promptly betrays her loving sacrifice by selling her as a slave. Taken up by the English journalist Richard Steele in 1711, the story became a raging success throughout Europe, appearing in numerous theatrical, operatic, and prose editions in the course of the eighteenth century.

This tale of love, betrayal, miscegenation, and slavery seemed to strike a blow to the European colonial establishment and was incorporated strategically in abolitionist literature. In betraying Yarico, Inkle emerges unmistakably as an exploitative, greedy opportunist poised to plunder and abandon native bodies and lands. Yet the politics of pity inherent in such a reading served largely to reinforce colonial fantasies of expanding European hegemony in the New World. As the late Suzanne Zantop argued, in arousing sympathy for the abandoned Yarico, the story called on European readers to identify with Yarico's desire for him and to wish that a nobler sense of duty would establish a lasting bond, thereby legitimating the colonial takeover it would imply. Thus, the love match fantasy represented less a critique of European colonialism than a condemnation of European irresponsibility and lack of commitment both to the love object and to the conquered land.[2] If, however, we consider that the love affair stops when métissage would have begun, and when the presence of offspring would have complicated the duties and sentimental obligations of the colonizer, the narrative of benign invasion of fertile lands (woman / native country) poses a different kind of threat for Inkle. In the most popular version of the Inkle and Yarico tale, published by Richard Steele in 1711, Yarico's pregnancy becomes the very means by which her value is increased in the eyes of European slave traders.[3]

In the French Caribbean, a similar story offered an even more shocking resolution to the question of métissage. In the 1617 edition of Jean Mocquet's *Voyages en Afrique, Asie, Indes orientales et occidentales*, the legend of Inkle and Yarico appeared as an isolated anecdote concluding the author's account of his peregrinations in the Amazon and the Lesser Antilles.[4] Mocquet tells the story of an English captain he met in the arid islands of the lower Caribbean Sea. The lone survivor of a tragic shipwreck off the coast of Mexico, the Englishman fortuitously encounters a young native woman, and the two fall in love. She devotes herself to his safekeeping and sustenance, serving as his faithful guide and interpreter, and he promises to make her his wife. Directed by his compass, the two arrive in Canada after three years of travel, during which time they have a child. When they finally come upon an English fishing vessel, the young man enthusiastically rejoins his countrymen, but, being ashamed to show his naked Indian lover, he refuses her entry, saying only that "she was a savage, and one needn't take any account of her." Horrified by his brutal inconstancy, the Indian woman promptly cleaves her child in two, tossing one half to the departing vessel and taking the other with her "to go back home at the mercy of fortune, full of grief and inconsolable sadness."[5]

Although the two protagonists are not named, Mocquet's narrative unites many elements of the Inkle and Yarico myth and is arguably an early version.[6] Yet the theme of infanticide clearly distinguishes it from that appearing in Ligon's *History*, making it a more complicated allegory for early colonial encounters with Caribs. Most compelling is the fact that this is the only published narrative of miscegenation between whites and Caribs to emerge from the French Caribbean. There is a way in which reciprocity structures the order of infamy and taboo in the story. The final act of infanticide, violating the laws of sentiment and maternity, is itself a response to Inkle's inconstancy and violation of the laws of hospitality.[7] As a fierce, vengeful savage, Yarico provokes both pity and horror in the reader. It is no accident that the male protagonist is an Englishman, reflecting the long-standing rivalry between the French and English and the tendency for French texts to vilify the latter. Yet the tragic outcome may nonetheless reflect a certain taboo of miscegenation in the early French Caribbean. Even as it divides responsibility for the act between colonialist exploitation and native "savagery," the story represents an archetypal failure of miscegenation to produce progeny of mixed race. It is on the body of the offspring that the parents' differences are settled. The child is rejected and destroyed, symbolically cut in half, as though to signify the impossibility of synthesis, union, and the peaceful resolution of differences between Europeans and native Caribs.[8]

In French representations of the early settlement and colonization of the Caribbean islands, anxiety about miscegenation remained but was displaced onto the problem of sexual immorality among settler men. No longer shipwrecked innocents engaging in an uncoerced colonial romance, the colonizers became, in the narratives of missionaries, rogue libertines anxious to satisfy carnal desires. The charge of libertinage emerged in descriptions of French sexual attacks on Carib and English women and figured prominently in the missionary critique of all vices of "irreligion" afflicting those colonists whose adventures took them outside the margins of the traditional authority of church and state. Natives were, from this perspective, paragons of moral purity. In his *Histoire générale des Antilles*, Du Tertre contrasted their sexual chastity before marriage with the colonists' concupiscence in violent sexual conquests.[9] Raymond Breton's dictionary offered further clues to French attitudes toward Carib sexuality. Translating the phrase *Eúnapa leoubátali* as "his face blushes with modesty," Breton commented on Caribs' sexual virtue in light of their near nudity: "Far from doing indecent actions before the world like brutes (as some, perhaps more brutish than they, would want to believe), I would say to their glory and to the confusion of the Christians, that I have never seen them commit any dishonest action in public [*devant le monde*]."[10]

By the late seventeenth century, however, sensational accounts of sexual encounters between Indian women and white men were almost entirely displaced by what was becoming a far more prevalent and politically sensitive case of miscegenation between whites and Africans.[11] Instances of interracial libertinage ranged from whites' taking of African slaves as concubines to sordid attacks on the plantation and the luxurious indulgences in colonial cities, where free women of color rivaled their white competitors for the richest men, as well as accumulating a great deal of wealth themselves. In every instance, the libidinal was politicized, as colonial authorities attempted to manage interracial libertinage and, as importantly, its reproductive consequences. Indeed, Mocquet's tale of Inkle and Yarico offers a sobering precursor to the history of métissage under slavery, insofar as children of mixed race remained symbolic sites for the projection, extension, and displacement of conflicts arising from asymmetrical and exploitative social relations between masters and slaves. Over time, they became the object of new regulations designed to affirm essential differences between slaves and freed persons. No longer physically destroyed or divided, they were made instead to *signify* for colonial power a fictive division, an insurmountable racial distance between "white" and "black."

In this chapter, I sketch the contours and effects of what I call the libertine colony, meaning the system of desire, violence, and exclusion that characterized slave societies in the French Caribbean. This inquiry is driven in part by my effort to establish a relation between two of the most striking characteristics of racial slavery in the French Caribbean: the juridically enforced racial segregation that resulted in an exceptionally rigid three-tiered caste society comprised of whites, free people of color, and slaves; and the persistence of interracial libertinage and concubinage as a social norm in the colonies, particularly among elite white men. Although many members of the white elite themselves accused wayward sexuality of threatening the grounds of colonial authority, they misapprehended, wittingly or unwittingly, the ways in which such sexual indulgences of the ruling elite impacted the discourses and practices of racial exclusion while at the same time shoring up the fragility of white rule. Central to my analysis are the offspring of mixed race, who both rendered palpable the prevalence of interracial desires and became the contested object of colonial miscegenation laws. As such, persons of color figured prominently in discursive and legal attempts to manage sexual relations between masters and slaves. I argue that the law, originally invoked to suppress sexual relations between free persons and slaves, soon functioned to displace responsibility for the taboo act onto slave women and persons of mixed race, thus enabling the continuance of libertinage. In the law and in colonial narratives, free people of color were figured as a congenitally immoral, bastard race that had inherited the moral ills of libertinage and wore the stain of slavery. Legal abrogations of mulatto rights were explicitly informed by such notions, as well as by the fear that white possessions, properties, names, and stature would devolve to nonwhite women and their illegitimate children. Yet, while colonial discourse and social legislation displaced the social stigma of libertinage onto the racial other, colonials in time openly justified métissage as essential to the very preservation of racial slavery and white hegemony. Changing political and economic ambitions of the ruling class had a significant impact on strategies of avowal, disclosure, and repression of colonial libertinage and its reproductive consequences.

In exploring the relationship among desire, miscegenation, and the law in the libertine colony, I am particularly interested in the circumstances of women of color, both slave and free. My analysis illuminates the ways in which they were positioned by economies and rhetorics of desire, and the difference that slavery made in the opportunities they had to participate in, respond to, or resist the exploitative politics of colonial libertinage. For slave women, white male desire represented not only an additional source of physical and psychological oppression but, as importantly, a new set of reproductive demands that inscribed them as the mothers of both slave and free persons in the colonies. Indeed, slave women bore the burden of and paid the price for cross-racial libertinage in the colony, without necessarily reaping any rewards. Why, then, did the discourse of colonial libertinage construct slave women as both objects and subjects of desire, that is, as libidinal adversaries to be coerced, dominated, and in some cases never freed? The circumstances of free women of color pose a different set of questions, for some women of color assumed central roles in the libertine drama, wielding ruses of sexuality and desire to both exploit and compound oppressive colonial hierarchies of race and gender. How is it, then, that the free woman of color emerged in narrative descriptions of Saint-Domingue as a figure for both the repressed sexual anxieties of whites, and their fantasies of moral redemption, sentimental purity, and domestic virtue? What difference did gender make in the ways in which people of color were constructed in and constrained by exclusionary laws?

In what follows, I trace the evolution of legal and narrative discourses of miscegenation in the seventeenth- and eighteenth-century Caribbean colonies, with particular emphasis on Saint-Domingue. These are read against shifts in the social, demographic, and economic condition of the free people of color as colonial segregation reached its apogee. I propose that the law, far from proscribing illicit sexual practices, offered instead strategies of repression and displacement that enabled the continued sexual subjugation of colored women to white men. In this sense, the libertine colony operated to ensure the unperturbed release of white desire across women of all races while at the same time enforcing a racial caste system of unprecedented severity.

Introducing the Taboo: Libertinage, Miscegenation, and the Law

Nowhere are the vagaries of regulations concerning miscegenation more apparent than in the early period of colonization, when missionaries and colonial administrators attempted to define and manage the sexual frontier between a majority white male colonial populace and an increasing number of enslaved African women. Moral, racial, and economic concerns were critically imbricated and often blurred in legislative controls on interracial relationships. Likewise, accepted notions of what constituted an offense, to whom, and on what grounds were remarkably unstable and shifted over time. While discourses of colonial authority constructed figures of deviance in both the free white male and the slave female so as to explain and rationalize the desire between them, early sexual regulations quickly focused on the existence of offspring as a means of both "proving" the crime and exacting a penalty. Debates about interracial libertinage thus took into account the sexual act itself and the possibility of manumission for both the child and the slave woman. Yet, in constructing this morally encumbered filial triangle, colonial legal codes were less effective in suppressing interracial sex than in denying, repressing, and ultimately accommodating the continuance of conflicted intimacies between masters and slaves.[12]

The moral compass for evaluating sexual relations between blacks and whites, masters and slaves, was first set by missionary observers of colonial life in the seventeenth century. In their narrative accounts, missionary writers called the relationship "libertinage," "debauchery," and "detestable abuse," terms that denounced sexually predatory behavior in the male. Yet in making the white male libertine culpable, missionary representations of African women demonstrated a marked ambiguity, such that their innocence was always qualified. The Jesuit priest Pelleprat, traveling through Martinique in 1639, retained a characteristically negative view of colonial libertinage. His narrative was written with the aim of publicizing the Jesuit mission, in particular its efforts to police colonists and indentured servants and convert natives and Africans. Pelleprat's discussion of sexual impropriety thus emphasized the efficacy of baptism on the souls of slaves, as it would inspire the highest codes of chastity. Praising the virtue of slave women who were faced with immoral French men, Pelleprat narrated two instances of female resistance: "A slave who found herself solicited to do evil, by a Frenchman on the island of Saint-Christophe, declared to him that she would rather die than commit such a wicked action, and, unable to defend herself otherwise against this libertine, she struck him so severely with a torch that he was obliged to retire and cease his bad design. The virtue of another slave was no less commendable in the island of Martinique. This one . . . was invited by her own master to do evil, and finding herself forced by his entreaties, gave him a big slap to protect herself from his shameful pursuits." [13] In the name of Christian morality, the Jesuit unequivocally defends the women's use of force to protect their sexual propriety. While the women emerge as heroines for the author's mission, demonstrating the success of proselytism, the master carries the stigma of sexual depravity and libertinage. Yet in suggesting that sexual propriety among slaves is one of the lessons taught by missionaries, Pelleprat's self-referential narrative implies that non-Christian slave women may not be as virtuous and deserving of pity. In addition, the idea that true heroines would rather die than experience a loss of feminine virtue devalues the will to survive of those slave women who struggled unsuccessfully to control their sexuality. Written out of the script of female heroism, the silenced victim-survivor carried a stigma of impurity and, worse, shared the burden of moral responsibility for the crimes committed against her. [14]

Writing in the 1660s, Jean-Baptiste Du Tertre shared Pelleprat's condemnation of libertinage in terms that repeated the Jesuit's qualified defense of slave women. In his ethnographic sketch on slaves, Du Tertre included a chapter entitled "De la naissance honteuse des Mulastres, et de leur condition." Here the author attributes the appearance of mulattoes to a particular kind of "blind love" or "the unruly passion of some of our Frenchmen who are inclined to love their negresses despite the blackness of their face, which renders them hideous, and the intolerable odor that they cast forth, which should in my opinion extinguish the ardor of their criminal fire." [15] This wholesale depreciation of black female slaves appears to dismiss the abuse of power on the part of white men, for merely "loving" such women occasions the priest's unequivocal reprimand. Yet Du Tertre's subsequent critique of male libido denounced free white males, who in his view shamelessly assaulted defenseless black women. Slave women did submit to the master's will but only on account of the enormity of the violence they would otherwise face. He attributed their loss of sexual purity to "fear of bad treatment, the terror of the threats with which they [the masters] frighten them, and the force used by these passionate men to corrupt them." [16]

Although these early missionary observers consistently attributed illicit sexual relations to both white male concupiscence and the abuse of power over slave women's bodies, in each case the grounds for condemnation were confused and the discourses of love, sex, and sin critically unsettled. The question remains: What was considered criminal in the miscegenated rapport—sex outside marriage, sex between persons of different "races," or rape as a means of torture and abuse of slaves? A partial response may be had if we consider that the Compagnie des Isles de l'Amérique initially encouraged white men to marry black and native women. This was consonant with Richelieu's policy of French assimilation in New France, which called for the absorption of natives into French culture, in part through intermarriage and métissage.[17] Pelleprat himself relates the story of a German Protestant minister who, having been expelled from Brazil with the Dutch, moves to Martinique with his black female companion and two children. When converted to Catholicism, he marries the concubine, a fact which absolves him from sin in the eyes of the author.[18] While the story follows up on Pelleprat's missionary auto-justification, it suggests that the crime of miscegenation could be reduced to the lack of conjugality between partners. Likewise, Father Labat stated that he knew of two white colonials who married black women, one of whom did so on the urging of the clergy.[19]

Yet in condemning French colonists as the unjust perpetrators of carnal assault French missionaries were in agreement with colonial law, which criminalized the sexual abuse of black women slaves. The first penal code on the matter was decreed by Lieutenant General Tracy in 1664. It forbade commanders of slaves and indentured servants "to debauch negresses, on pain of twenty lashes of the whip [*liane*], for the first offense, forty lashes for the second, and fifty lashes and the fleur de lis branded on the cheek for the third."[20] The code is remarkable for placing blame on the free male and subjecting him to the same forms of whipping and branding used on slaves, in the worst case imposing a permanent mark of servitude as a means of public humiliation.[21] More importantly, it is the only early law that targeted exclusively the crime of fornication. It is possible that practical rather than moral considerations motivated this law; intimacy, sexual violence, and its attendant jealousies were considered detrimental to the maintenance of "order" on the plantation.[22] Within a few years, however, legislation ostensibly intended to curb sexual relations between free men and slave women began to focus on the problem of bastardy. That is, the illegality of sexual relationships between free men and slave women was increasingly limited to cases in which the women bore illegitimate, mixed-race offspring.

While it could be argued that this shift was merely a practical measure—crimes of fornication were most easily proven in the presence of offspring—the effect was to bring to bear on questions of penalty and compensation a range of considerations tied to the reproduction of labor, thus confounding the issue of transgressive sex. From the inception of slavery, colonists had adopted the Roman legal principle of Partus sequitur ventrem, stipulating that children born to enslaved women would follow the condition of the mother. This custom identified female captives as wombs for slavery, thus enabling the continuous renewal of the labor force within the closed space of the plantation. On the appearance of mixed-race children, however, early colonial magistrates took exception to this rule and declared mulattoes free. The reasons given by Du Tertre are symptomatic of a paradox in antimiscegenation policy: "The Governors took pity on these poor children, for they thought that they were sufficiently unhappy to wear the opprobrium of their birth in the color of their face, without adding slavery to punish a crime of which they are innocent. That is why they did not insist on this legal axiom that renders the child of the condition of the mother who births him, Partus sequitur ventrem, and they declared them free in order to punish the crime of their fathers."[23] Du Tertre's comment established what would be a long-standing colonial attitude toward mulattoes; their very biracial aspect betrayed their origins in a "crime" for which they were ostensibly innocent. Yet as markers of that sexual transgression their legal condition would reflect societal attitudes toward it. The paradox is that freedom for mulattoes became a means both to validate mulatto innocence and to punish the father, who was declared financially responsible for the child in the first twelve years. This notion of punishment assumes that masters would prefer to maintain their own offspring as slaves in order to make up for the expenditure incurred during their upbringing.[24] The requirement that the father/master assume the cost of birth and maintenance of the child also acted as a deterrent to sexual relations between masters and slaves on the plantation.[25] The mulatto was thus defined a priori as outside the bounds of paternal kinship and filial attachment and was used by the state to prosecute the crime of his or her birth.

By focusing on bastardy, colonial legislators sought not only to integrate the mulatto child into the process of penalty, but also to identify the slave mother as a possession to be forfeited. Expressing outrage at the continuance of sexual abuse in spite of legislative action, Lieutenant General De Baas in 1669 instituted new punishments for masters who had children by their own slaves. In this case, the master would not only lose his mulatto child who would be freed, but also his female slave, subject to "confiscation" by colonial authorities.[26] That the slave woman should be thus removed from the master's control seems less a measure of protection than confirmation of her status as chattel whose reproductive destiny was reserved for the production of property. What is clear from this code is that in prosecuting bastardy the law displaced the site of illegality from interracial sex to reproduction, thus implicating both slave women and children in prescriptions of punishment ostensibly directed toward the father.

Thus, for the earliest period on record, legal and narrative documents denounced white male deviance for the sexual pursuit of slave women, often relying on the presence of offspring to prosecute the crime. Overriding the Roman principle that conferred on the child the slave status of the mother, early laws purported to punish the father by freeing the child. In the years leading up to the promulgation of the Code noir, however, a profound change occurred in antimiscegenation discourse and legal codes. Taking the entire illegitimate family triad to task for libertinage, colonial lawmakers revised their assumption that freeing the mulatto was an appropriate form of punishment by considering slave women's interests in the free status of their children. In 1680, the Superior Council of Guadeloupe rescinded the provision for automatic manumission on the grounds that it encouraged the crime by rewarding the mother, whose offspring might be spared a life of slavery. Illegitimate mulattoes born to slave women would henceforth be slaves.[27] For Yvan Debbasch, this change in policy marked the gradual appearance of a segregationist ideology of blood purity, whereby all descendants of African slaves were perpetually excluded from the class of masters.[28] Yet a crucial shift occurred also on the level of the discourse on gender and miscegenation. Whereas in the earliest instances the sexual act was considered a case of moral depravity and abuse of power on the part of the sexually deviant white male, a dissenting view displaced the responsibility onto the figure of the black woman, conceived as a sexual predator who accrues benefits from the pursuit of free lovers.

Latent in the works of Pelleprat and Du Tertre, the trope of the fallen, lascivious woman became prevalent after 1680 in antimiscegenation discourse. It attributed an illicit agency to slave women, abiding in their sexual offerings to those in power. The opinion was reinforced by the appearance of new ways to name the deviant sexual relation, from "debauchery," "libertinage," and "concubinage" to "prostitution," suggesting volition and the calculation of benefits on the part of the woman, even within the constraints of enslavement.[29] This language inexorably altered the grounds for condemning sexual unions between masters and slaves, since placing slave women in the role of prostitute saved masters from the moral burden of coerced sex.[30] The word *prostitution* meant "abandonment to lasciviousness" (*impudicité*), as defined in the 1694 *Dictionnaire de l'Académie Française*. When rape was cast as seduction by a slave woman, she became the locus of deviance, culpability, and threat. This discourse placed male violence under erasure, masked by what Saidiya Hartman has called the "phantasmal ensnaring agency of the lascivious black."[31] The point is not that slave women were unlikely to secure some control over their relations with desiring masters by negotiating advantages but that their actions were always overdetermined by a situation of powerlessness and extreme violence, in which their sexual compliance if not bartered could be commanded.[32] By labeling and then penalizing female slaves as treacherous sexual agents, the colonial power structure succeeded in stripping illicit unions of any form of reciprocity they may have entailed, thus consolidating absolute power over slave women's bodies.

Importantly, however, the discourse of prostitution also aimed to channel the reproductive capacities of slave women for the economic benefit of the master through coupling with slave men. "Prostitution" was to be punished in favor of a sham slave domesticity promoted by the performance of Catholic marriages among them. The 1680 decree by the Superior Council of Guadeloupe stated: "The malice of the slave negresses has gotten to the point where most of the girls despise their equals, refuse to marry them and abandon themselves easily to artisans and domestics, even to the sons of the master's family in hopes of conceiving free mulattoes and not slaves."[33] So great was the anxiety surrounding the sexual desires and reproductive aims of slave women that the issue became a central focus of debates leading up to the creation of the Code noir. When Colbert solicited memoirs from Intendant Patoulet and his successor, Bégon, on the question of "the governance of slaves," both addressed the question of miscegenation in terms that vilified slave women as prostitutes.[34] Bégon summarized the concerns of the Crown with respect to "the extraordinary prostitution that reigns among the negresses" and advocated its prevention with proper marriages between black slaves.[35] In this, he voiced the generalized opinion of the lack of chastity among slave women, which was attributed to their African heritage of polygamy and matrifocality.[36] This proposal was consistent with the view that female slaves were breeders for the colony and the state, whose involvement in libertine affairs impeded the reproduction of labor.

While the implication here is that libertinage bears no fruit for slavery, the new antimiscegenation discourse also placed a burden of immorality on the mulatto offspring of interracial unions. No longer perceived as innocents begotten of sin and marked with the color of servitude, mulattoes were increasingly blamed for the very forbidden desires from which they were presumed to have originated. Patoulet expressed this growing prejudice when he proposed that they remain enslaved so as to prevent the unrestrained libertine behavior they exhibited when free: "Most of them not only prostitute themselves but also assist in the prostitution of the others."[37] In fact, Patoulet justified the new law on the unique basis that mulatto sexual deviance would pose too great a moral threat to free society: "Given the knowledge that I have already of the perverse inclination of mulattoes and mulâtresses, I would think it necessary to retain them in slavery."[38] Seen as necessarily born of an illicit and illegitimate union, inheritors of the libidinal savagery imputed to their mothers, the mulatto became a privileged figure for pathological sexuality and the repressed desires of whites. Not surprisingly, this portrayal was coincident with the growth of the free population of color in the late seventeenth century, whose members aspired to social advancement and economic standing beside whites. The specter of mulatto men taking white women loomed large in the colonial imagination. As Du Tertre pointed out: "There are many of these mulattoes in the islands who are free and who work for themselves; I have seen some rather handsome ones who married French women."[39] The evolving discourse on miscegenation invested both black women and mulatto offspring with the stigma of illicit, adulterous desire, which was capable of disrupting colonial reproductive dynamics and posing a threat to white men. Furthermore, by progressively displacing culpability for the primal scene of interracial sexuality to the slave woman and mulatto child, official discourse not only masked the responsibility of the master but actually promoted métissage. By keeping their children as slaves, masters stood to gain economically from the miscegenated relationships that the law essentially took for granted.

The promulgation of the Code noir in 1685 was a decisive moment in the history of French colonial slavery and miscegenation. In regulating slavery on the part of the state, the Code incorporated the colonies and their inhabitants—slave and free—into the body politic of the ancien régime.[40] Like previous laws, the Code doled out punishment for illegitimate miscegenation and concubinage between slaves and free persons only in the presence of offspring. Article 9 subjected free men who had one or more children with their slave concubines to a hefty fine of two thousand pounds of sugar.[41] The mixed-race offspring would be enslaved, following article 13, which reinstated the Partus sequitur ventrem rule. If the offending male was himself the master of the slave woman, she was to be "confiscated," with the children for the benefit of the colonial hospital, "without ever being able to be freed." In one important respect, however, the Code noir departed from local customs. Rather than castigating slave women for seeking rewards through sex, the Code forgave the "crime" if the master and his slave were married. No penalty would apply when "the man, who was not married to another person during his concubinage with his slave, marries, in the form observed by the Church, his said slave, who be will freed by this means, and the children rendered free and legitimate." Attempts to explain this paradoxical principle have highlighted important precedents in Roman law. Alan Watson explains that according to Justinian's rule: "If an owner had no wife and made his slave woman his concubine, and she remained in that condition at his death, the slave woman became free and their children were freeborn." [42] Scholars have also argued that by encouraging white men to form legitimate bonds with their concubines and children, framers of the Code may have intended to make amends for the lack of French women brought to the colonies in the seventeenth century. [43] What is certain is that this change in policy established a significant opportunity for black female emancipation within the miscegenated relationship. Consistent with the "one blood" policy of colonial assimilation, the Code recognized black women as potential founders of the master class by endorsing métissage within the bounds of marriage. [44] Mixed-race descendents of interracial marriages became legitimate subjects with rights to inheritance and property under the law.

On the other hand, article 9 punished slave women severely if they illegitimately bore children for the master but were not subsequently married. Indeed, the confiscation of those slave women and children, never to be freed, was unprecedented and foreshadowed later prejudices against manumitting slave women. Such extreme punishment signals an unspoken assignation of guilt to those slave women who entered into relationships with their masters but were unsuccessful in securing legitimation through marriage. In addition, for all its liberality on questions of métissage, the Code hardly abandoned earlier concerns with slave domesticity and pronatalism. Consensual, Catholic marriages were encouraged between slaves (articles 10–11), whose "families" were deemed indivisible at the auction block (article 47). [45] Of course, as Joan Dayan reminds us, the Code noir was a "document of limits" whose regulations shored up many areas of flagrant abuse. [46] To legislate proper Christian marriages between slaves was to discourage not only libertinage with white and black men but also the more coercive practices of breeding and sexual violation. The dispute over miscegenation thus amounted to a dispute over the proper use of the slave woman's body, oscillating between two figures of maternity in the colonial economy of reproduction: that of the slave mother of slaves; and that of the free wife of the master, the mother of free colored children. Her illegitimate children of mixed race carried the stigma of a crime committed in the crucible of the slave regime, and, though sons of the masters, they were institutionalized as natural slaves. If legitimized, they became a class unto themselves known by the name of *libres* or *affranchis*.

Theories of Mulattoes

It is possible to read the evolution of a segregationist caste system in the eighteenth-century Caribbean as a protracted and virulent reaction to the mild egalitarianism of the Code, in particular its indifference to racial distinctions between classes—outside of the title, only the juridical terms *slave* and *free*, with a distinction between "naturally free person" (*libre naturel*) and "freed person" (*affranchi*), are invoked—and its allowance of marriage across classes, hence across races.[47] These marriages were later viewed in exclusively racialist terms and redefined as *mésalliance*, a word denoting the principle in French marital law barring the union of persons from different social classes. As colonial racism became the ordering principle of an increasingly stratified society, mésalliance was seen as detrimental to the supremacy of the white elite. Within fifteen years of its passage, significant contestations of the freedom by marriage provision in article 9 were voiced by the courts in Martinique. In 1724, the Superior Councils of the French Caribbean begged the royal authorities for the harsh antimiscegenation provisions contained in the Louisiana Code noir,[48] and in 1727 the intendant requested a royal decree to suppress the second half of article 9, which pressured whites to marry their concubines.[49] Efforts to outlaw mésalliance intensified throughout the eighteenth century, as color prejudice reached its apex and colonial courts implemented a set of racially exclusionary social policies.

Although legislation designed to discourage mésalliance contributed greatly to the establishment of a racially segregationist society, it appears to have had virtually no effect on the now customary practice of interracial libertinage.[50] The outrage over interracial sexual liaisons was perhaps best articulated by the traveler Baron de Wimpffen, who remarked: "When this abuse of intimacy between master and slave would have no other inconvenience than to alter the first principal of any subordination, the respect of the subordinated, it would already be a great evil."[51] Others conceived of an oblique rapport between sexuality and domination, although this view was often suffused with the ideology of the black female sexual savage. Pierre de Vaissière quotes a 1763 memoir to Choiseuil in which the author bemoaned a rather ironic conjunction of desire and the law: "Would you not have difficulty believing that people of every condition, without excepting the interpreters of the laws of the kingdom, prostitute themselves publicly, and even find glory in being in the arms of a vile and impure species to whom, in contempt of the ordinances and most saintly duties, one has often neglected to administer the sacrament of baptism; that they prize the numerous productions that follow from this abominable mixture; and that they do not blush at sending the unhappy ones, upon leaving their bed, to work in their stations under the whip of a commander, a slave like them?"[52] Here the locus of threat equivocates between the slave woman and her master. In the sexual relationship, power is attributed to the slave woman, who is accused of impurity and a libidinal excess that is equated with animality and seen to compel the master's subjection. Yet in projecting white lasciviousness, complicity, and power onto the black the author nonetheless recognizes the master's power to profit from such affairs, through both the resulting offspring and the service that is nonetheless demanded from the lover under the whip. The master's power to dominate and terrorize is thus enhanced by the dramatic and unpredictable reversal of his prior willful sexual subjection to his slave lover.

A similar kind of equivocation between desire and domination was arguably at work in the social and legal division of free society along lines of color. In order to examine the relation among white colonial desire, libertinage, and the politics of racial exclusion, we must reexamine the extent to which sexual taboos existed in colonial slave societies. Freud offers a helpful theoretical perspective on the problem of the taboo, which he defines as something deemed unapproachable or forbidden that is protected against through prohibitions of unknown origin accepted as natural by the community. Since taboos derive from strong, almost instinctual desires shared by the entire group, transgressions are seen to endanger the community and are punished by all members so as to "avert the danger of becoming aware that they all want to do the prohibited thing."[53] In addition to punishing the transgression by means of acts of atonement and purification, the community may regard the perpetrator of the action as taboo as well and thus capable of transmitting the forbidden desire and tempting others to follow his or her example. On the other hand, the enforcement of the prohibition may trigger obsessional acts, or "compromise actions," that both express remorse and find substitutes to "compensate the instinct for what has been prohibited."[54] As we have seen, the relation between desire and the law in French Caribbean slave societies was a vexing one, for the law equivocated between policing white colonial desire and policing desire's effect—the illegitimate child of mixed race. While an initial prohibition made sex between masters and slaves taboo and held free men accountable for transgressions, later laws hesitated to prosecute fornication alone. For most of the history of the French Antilles, interracial libertinage was illegal only between masters and slaves whose unions produced children, who were seized and confiscated on behalf of the colony and later the state. Thus, rather than punishing the free male and making him the new taboo object, the law found substitute culprits in the slave woman and mulatto child. They became the new objects of taboo, considered not only to embody the forbidden desire but to tempt the white community into sexual immorality. As a consequence, the process of communal atonement now occurred through the obsessive persecution of the new taboo objects.[55]

I would argue that throughout the eighteenth century colonial policies codifying exclusionary boundaries and racial hierarchies continued to reflect what white lawmakers thought about the sexual relations between whites and nonwhites and their wishes to safeguard the white community against particular social consequences of those desires, especially where offspring were concerned. As in the above case, these socially sanctioned and legally enforceable restrictions served to redistribute the burden of expiation for sexual transgressions from the dominant to the dominated group, namely, the free people of color. By imputing to this group the desires they refused to suppress in themselves, the whites sought to deny that they continued to do the prohibited thing. Making the racial others taboo meant not only defining them in terms of immorality, concupiscence, and sexual savagery; it also meant making them forbidden, untouchable, and unclean, capable of polluting white society if allowed any elite social privileges, political offices, or conjugal ties to whites. In this sense, I read the escalation of racially segregationist measures and the establishment of a three-tiered caste society in relation to the persistence of interracial libertinage and métissage throughout the eighteenth century. In addition to generalizing the symbolic condition of illegitimacy across the entire population of free people of color, much exclusionary legislation sought to block the social or material enfranchisement of the slave concubines and mixed-race children of white men.

The illegitimate family thus remained the dominant metaphor structuring the attitudes of the colonial elite toward slaves and nonwhites in the colonies. In interpreting the colonial politics of exclusion in terms of interracial sexuality and blood ties, I seek not to minimize the extent to which social, political, and economic conditions influenced the creation of a caste system in Saint-Domingue. I intend, rather, to establish beyond doubt the fundamental role of sexuality in shaping discourses and practices of race and class domination under slavery. I will suggest that social, political, and economic factors provoked important shifts in attitudes toward the illegitimate family and the colonial desires that produced it.

By all accounts, the natural production of mulattoes was undeterred by legislative penalties and moral opprobrium. Traveling in Martinique in the last decade of the seventeenth century, Labat attributed interracial libertinage to the lasciviousness of both black women and white men. Crediting the royal decree of 1685 with partially remedying the problem, he nevertheless denounced the concomitant increase in abortions among slave women anxious to suppress evidence of their affairs.[56] With his characteristic sly wit, the author exposed domestic comedies arising in households where slave concubines shadow legitimate marriages. He noted whimsically the happy alliance between friars eager to receive confiscated human capital at the local hospital and white mistresses who avidly await the chance to denounce their black rivals, "preferring to see them confiscated than to pass up the occasion to avenge themselves." Yet such denunciations were often thwarted by a counteralliance of masters and their slave lovers, whose calculated defense strategies created farcical scenes at the tribunal. Women would commonly deny the affairs, exploiting the near impossibility of proving the paternity of the child. Father Labat described one case in which a master advised his slave concubine to falsely accuse the very clergyman who called her to the tribunal, "such that it was a most comical scene (a priest or a monk would have found this scene miserable) to hear the circumstances that she brought to prove that she had never known another man."[57]

Nowhere was métissage more prevalent than in Saint-Domingue. By 1713, concubinage was said to be generalized, thus arousing concern among administrators, who blamed the lack of white women.[58] That year, an ordinance passed by the colonial administration reaffirmed article 9 of the Code noir and expressed outrage at masters who, "instead of hiding their turpitude, glory in it despite the penalty of fine and confiscation . . . , taking their concubines and the children they have had with them into their homes and exposing them to the eyes of all with as much assurance as if they were begotten of a legitimate marriage."[59] Likewise, in 1724 Intendant Mithon raised the prospect that the French in Saint-Domingue would soon resemble a race of mixed bloods like their Spanish neighbors.[60] The question as to whether the mulatto children of interracial unions would be enslaved or free became an especially contentious issue. On one hand, the prevalence of métissage on the plantation was manifest in the racial division of labor. Over time, mulattoes of both sexes were favored to work in the plantation household, and mulatto women, increasingly prized as sex objects due to their beauty, were placed in the role of concubine.[61] At the same time, métissage contributed to the population of free people of color through the manumission of slave women and mulatto children. Critics attributed the increase in manumissions in the eighteenth century to the persistence of concubinage and métissage.[62] In the latter half of the century, women vastly outnumbered men in the numbers of legally freed slaves and slightly outnumbered men in the population of libres.[63]

Yet the class of free people of color was quite diverse in gender, color, and circumstance. Referred to variously with the terms *mulattoes*, *mixed bloods*, *free people of color*, and *freedmen*, the free people of color included former slaves and their descendants of all skin tones. While their first appearance and early growth had much to do with miscegenation on the plantation, the population grew substantially due to internal reproduction and continued manumission through self-purchase, military service, and other sacrificial deeds, which brought increasing numbers of black men into the freed group. Métissage was always an important cause of growth, though it often occurred in the context of mixed marriages between women of color and European immigrant men, who often profited financially from such unions. On the whole, the free people of color were the group most capable of natural increase in New World slave societies, and they were the only population that was almost entirely native born. They exhibited a far more normal gender balance than did slaves and whites, and they increased far more rapidly, as was apparent in the colony of Saint-Domingue.[64] As the last of the sugar colonies to be populated and cultivated, Saint-Domingue had a free colored population of five hundred in the year 1700, slightly less than that of Martinique. But within a half century the free people of color were three times more numerous in Saint-Domingue than in Martinique for an equivalent white population, amounting to 20 percent of the total free population. Between 1750 and 1789, the numbers of libres increased ten times, such that at the time of the Saint-Domingue revolution they equaled the number of whites, approximately thirty thousand persons.[65]

The free people of color made a strong impact on the island's economy. Having acquired and inherited property as a result of their own labors or from white benefactors, many free coloreds were successful sugar planters, and in particular, they dominated the cultivation of coffee and indigo, crops whose production soared after 1760.[66] The libres were also skilled in a variety of trades and building crafts, and as self-employed merchants many owned a considerable amount of property in the cities. In addition, as Stewart King has shown, many of the free people of color occupied important positions of leadership in the colonial military, thereby forming a subclass within the group.[67] Affluent free people of color achieved a high level of education, often because poor local schooling combined with the discrimination they experienced in Saint-Domingue led them to seek training in France. While abroad, some wealthy, educated mulattoes married into aristocratic French families. Within the colony as well, the wealthier free people of color had strong ties to whites and often traced their wealth to bequests and gifts from white relatives.[68] As slave-owning pseudoelites displaying the material accoutrements of privilege, taste, and wealth, they aspired to join the ruling class of whites. By the end of the century, prominent mulattoes were demanding recognition and integration by means of titles of nobility, military honors, and access to the high offices and social entitlements enjoyed by whites of comparable means.[69]

Over the course of the eighteenth century, however, the colonial order in Saint-Domingue staunchly resisted the social and political rise of the free class. The law intervened as a mechanism of social control, gradually imposing a segregationist regime on the island's population. What is fascinating is that the laws and penalties that codified the restructuring of society along racial lines exhibit many of the same discourses of displacement and projection of sexual deviance apparent in the antimiscegenation discourse of the seventeenth century. In Saint-Domingue, the signifier *mulatto* became synonymous with the entire population of free people of color, as whites constructed the free class in terms of sex between whites and blacks.[70] Authorities justified color prejudice and legal discrimination on the basis of a presumption of moral impurity in free persons of color, who were believed to carry the "original vice" of concubinage between a white master and a black female slave. In 1755, the administrators of Saint-Domingue proclaimed that the people of color, in their pretensions to amass the finest in material possessions and accede to high ranks in the militias and judicial system, demonstrated not only arrogance but the desire to "make others forget the memory of their first origin," hoping that talent could obscure "the vice of their birth."[71] As the scholar Yvan Debbasch has pointed out, "Whoever says *libre* in the society of the whites continues to think instinctively of concubinage, fundamental immorality, familial attachments or relations of affection among the servile mass."[72] That the infamy of an entire class could be reduced to a primal scene of disavowed desire and/or sexual coercion suggests that the response to the free people of color was still a response to métissage and an attempt to control the demographic consequences of white male sexuality.

By the end of the eighteenth century, an imperious regime of color prejudice had installed a barrier to social and political advancement by anyone whose genealogy revealed African ancestry. Hysteria over race and purity of origins coalesced with official policies designed to protect white "blood" and its hold on power at a time when the disproportion between whites and nonwhites was stunning. Yet many laws imposing a segregationist order suggest that rigid distinctions between races were enacted by severing the filial, emotional, and economic ties that linked whites to their mixed-race kin. In particular, legal infringements on masters' rights to free their slaves reflected concerns over the possible social consequences of interracial libertinage and blood bonds between masters and slaves on the plantation. Although article 55 of the Code noir had affirmed the right of masters to manumit their slaves without justification, by the early eighteenth century royal officials were complaining that there were too many affranchis.[73] The earliest restrictions on manumission called for written permission from colonial authorities for the emancipation of slaves, without which their freedom would be nullified. In 1736, a royal ordinance reprimanded cunning masters and their slave concubines who circumvented local authorities by having their illegitimate offspring registered as free by the priest on baptism. In addition to nullifying the freedom given to any child whose mother was enslaved, the ordinance required that the master pay a fine.[74] In a clear attempt to restrict, or, more probably, profit from, the manumission of concubines, a 1775 law imposed a manumission tax for women that was twice the amount for men.[75]

While constraining slave owners' ability legally to manumit their slave lovers and nonwhite children, colonial legislation also blocked avenues by which planter elites had commonly entitled members of their illegitimate families through the transfer of land, money, and material possessions. In 1726, a royal decree banned the extension of patrimony to freed persons by means of "donations." The new policy amended articles 56, 57, and 59 of the Code noir, thus instating for the Antilles a law already in effect in the harsher Louisiana code.[76] Efforts to impede the social uplift of nonwhite kin extended to onomastics as well. On manumission, freed slaves had commonly been given or had assumed the French names of either their former masters or, in the case of mixed-race individuals, their natural fathers or white relatives. In a 1755 decree by the Council of Port-au-Prince, priests were prohibited from registering the name of a free person as the father of an illegitimate child without the master's consent.[77] This provision was followed in 1773 by a much tougher law banning the assumption of any "white" name by nonwhites and imposing African ones instead.[78] In defense of the law, the administrators argued that "the usurped name of a white race can place the status of persons in doubt, throw confusion in the order of successions, and in the end destroy this insurmountable barrier that public opinion has laid down, and that the wisdom of the government maintains between the whites and the people of color."[79] In reinforcing the legally sanctioned color line in Saint-Domingue, laws on onomastics portrayed unmarried women of color as eager to steal the names and patrimony of whites for their illegitimate children. Any free colored person already having "usurped" the name of a white was commanded to rename themselves by the letter of the law within three months or be imprisoned. The 1773 law thus represented a blanket degradation of free people of color by way of a metaphor of disownment and repudiation unmistakably rooted in a consciousness of persistent métissage. The result of the legal protections accorded the name of the father, both real and symbolic, was the codification of assumptions of bastardy in the free population of color.

Of course, the most obvious way of blocking the transfer of names and white privilege was through restrictions on legitimate marriages between whites and free nonwhites. Exhortations to ban interracial marriage focused explicitly on the perceived need to maintain power, privilege, and wealth in white hands. In addition, the possibility of marriage between white men and slave women belied notions of repellent blackness behind which whites concealed their attraction to black women.[80] Marriage debunked the equally pervasive stereotype of black sexual savage and prostitute, thus raising the far more threatening possibility of reciprocity and sentiment between whites and blacks. Still, the royal administration refused to ban interracial marriage in the colonies; it did so only in France in reaction to increasing black immigration from the colonies.[81] The alternative method of discouraging mixed marriage in the Caribbean was through onerous social and political sanctions applied to the white partner. As early as 1703, the Superior Council of Martinique denied titles of nobility to two whites who had married mulatto women.[82] By 1733, misallied whites were excluded from high ranks in the militia as well as from public positions in the colony.[83]

Among the last of the exclusionary measures to be implemented, laws abrogating the civil rights and social freedoms of the free people of color reflect their rising prosperity, social ambitions, and demographic importance in the latter half of the eighteenth century. Through a range of regulations covering public and private life, colonial authorities patronized free people of color on the basis of both race and presumed illegitimacy and immorality. Nonwhites were excluded from the surgical and legal professions on the basis of racially restrictive notions of honorability and trustworthiness.[84] After 1769, free people were also barred from service in the officer corps of the militia.[85] In addition, a vague notion of "disrespect" enabled whites to threaten free individuals with a "return" to slavery if their demeanor was judged too immodest for their condition. Joan Dayan relates the stunning example of two mulatto women, who, accused of insulting two white women, were sentenced to be displayed daily at the "Negro market" with iron collars around their necks.[86] Likewise, the "crime of irreverence" was cited when in 1767 the Council of Port-au-Prince condemned a free mulatto to be "whipped, branded, and sold for the king's profit" for having struck a white.[87] The increasing fragility of freed persons' claims on a qualified freedom was made more apparent when in 1778 they were required to carry their manumission or baptismal acts as proof of their status.[88] The same year a tougher provision insisted that people of color furnish proof not only of their own but also their mother's freedom, once again presuming origins in concubinage on the plantation.[89] Finally, the increasing obsession over racial distinctions among people of color led to a 1773 law requiring them to be designated by racial labels in all notarial documents.[90]

These multiple exclusions and discriminations all point to the extent to which colonial authorities used the law as a means to reassign bodies signifying the libidinal crossing of boundaries into discrete categories of dispossession. In a 1771 letter to colonial administrators, the French minister reiterated the crown's position on the exclusion of *sangs-mêlés* (mixed bloods) from the nobility in the following terms: "[His Majesty] thought that such an honor [*grace*] would tend to destroy the difference that nature has put between whites and blacks, and that political prejudice has taken care to preserve, like a distance which people of color and their descendants should never be allowed to overcome."[91] Repressing the colored person's natural origins in the crossing of races, the law instead invokes nature to justify the artificial social and political distinctions called for by the colonial order. Free people of color in Saint-Domingue were forced through their social devaluation to signify to whites the fiction of the impermeable and essential boundary between masters and slaves, one that their bodies openly challenged, signifying instead sexual proximity and forbidden intimacies. In this sense, the legal codification of the segregationist order may be seen as the effort both to reinscribe through the social what colonial desires had disrupted and to disavow the complicity of the master class in those desires.

Thus, the juridical formation of a caste society cannot be separated from the sexual, social, and filial ambiguities introduced through métissage. The progressive invention of criteria for the separation and containment of free people of color points not only to the political challenge they posed to white rule but more importantly to the very meanings attached to sexual relations in the colonies. Exclusionary legislation aimed to dispossess the human results of libertinage, thus essentially controlling métissage by social means rather than by restricting white colonial desire. As the laws suppressed the economic and political threat they perceived in slave women and mixed-race illegitimates, they also blamed these groups for the moral outrage of colonial libertinage. Yet white attitudes about interracial desire and the illegitimate family were not impervious to changing political and historical circumstances. As the law became the chosen means through which to police, segregate, and dispossess the growing class of free coloreds, this group was judged by elites to be increasingly necessary to the system, an intermediate class that could be manipulated in the interests of either the state or the ruling class in an atmosphere of increasing social and political tension. This was particularly the case after the 1760s, when the colonial autonomist movement gained fervor and mulattoes emerged as the crucial middle ground in a power play pitting white Creoles against the royal administration. During the prerevolutionary conflicts of 1768 and 1769, whites endeavored to take political power from the king's functionaries and economic power from metropolitan merchants and absentee landowners. To achieve these aims, they tried to galvanize the support of the colored class for a general insurrection. In response to this threat, the Duc de Choiseuil, minister of war, marine, and foreign affairs under Louis XV, identified mulattoes as a strategic social barrier to white autonomy and advocated the cessation of mésalliance so as to preclude the libres from joining forces with whites.[92]

A similar notion of the social barrier prevailed among white elites in the colonies, though for quite different purposes. While whites viewed people of color as allies in the fight against ministerial despotism, they also considered them to be a potential bulwark against a more threatening enemy at home. In late Saint-Domingue, the predominant theory of mulattoes rationalized their presence as a necessary protection against the massive and growing servile class.[93] After 1775, a rumor of a widespread slave revolt unleashed a wave of hysteria in the colonial elite,[94] enough to awaken deep insecurities that had thus far been largely displaced onto the free people of color. Some whites publicly advocated what Yvan Debbasch has described as a "moderate segregationism" to appease the mulattoes' demands for integration with the dominant class. Likewise, Intendant Malouet propagated the notion of the "honest affranchi," suggesting that only mulattoes could save whites from a potential slave revolt. His contemporary, the Barré de Saint-Vincent, valued the very numerical force of the intermediate class as a factor preventing the destructive slave rebellions that had already taken place in Jamaica and Surinam.[95] While their proposals were defeated by the more radical faction of white colonials, moderates in Saint-Domingue echoed what royal authorities had also come to realize: mulattoes were essential to the racial balance of power in the colonies.

Thus, as the free class obtained increased economic independence, representatives of colonial power in Saint-Domingue and France responded with a discourse that transformed its potentially subversive ascendance into an instrumental asset. Nowhere is this more apparent than in the entries for the term *mulatto* in the *Encyclopédie* (1765) and the *Supplément de l'Encyclopédie* (1776–77). In the first instance, the mulatto is constructed as the shameful evidence of white "disorder." Reference is made to disciplinary measures proposed in the Code noir to stop the abuse of interracial libertinage. Much of the article is taken directly, sometimes verbatim, from Father Labat's chapter on mulattoes, as both texts state the legal intervention of Louis XIV through the Code noir and then decry such unwanted consequences as an increase in abortions and false testimony at trial.[96] In the *Supplément*, however, the tenor changes dramatically; disdain turns to apology for white male desire for slave women, and the fruit of this union is deemed a valuable acquisition in the colonial contest.

> It would have undoubtedly been desirable, for the benefit of morals and the population of whites in the colonies, that Europeans not feel anything but indifference for the negresses; but it was morally impossible for the contrary not to have occurred. For the eyes are easily accustomed to a difference in color that constantly presents itself, and the young negresses are almost all well made, easy and little interested. One cannot

keep from granting, however, that from this disorder there has resulted some real advantages for the colonies.

1) Manumissions of mulattoes have considerably increased the number of freedmen, and this class is, most certainly, in all times, the whites' surest defense against the rebellion of the slaves. They have some themselves; and if ever they are wealthy, they affect with the blacks the superiority of whites, which they must renounce if the slaves shake off the yoke. And in times of war the mulattoes are a good militia to deploy in defense of the coasts, because they are almost all robust men and better fit to sustain the fatigues of the climate than Europeans. 2) Their consumption of French merchandise, on which they spend all the profit of their labor, is one of the principal resources of the colonial commerce.[97]

Here the absolution of white sexual aggression requires not only that morality be marshaled in the service of libertinage but that the very fact of slavery be suspended, such that female slaves, identified with the ethnic name "negresses," appear as mere anthropological curiosities cut out of any power relation. With this vivid trope of dumb female flesh disinterestedly accommodating the master's desire, the author calculates the advantages of miscegenation, all of which instrumentalize the mulatto class in its numbers, wealth, and utility as soldiers. What is important, above all, is their strategic function within the balance of colonial order: their determined imitation of the white elite through luxury consumption ensures colonial profitability, while their social affect of superiority over slaves affords the whites protection against the masses. The visible shift in discourse on mulattoes between the two editions of the *Encyclopédie* points to the impact of political and historical circumstances on constructions of interracial desire and libertinage in the colony. While the first century of colonization witnessed the continued denial of white desire through figures of black sexual savagery and mulatto delinquency, late Saint-Domingue saw an increasing willingness to valorize both miscegenation and whites' responsibility for it. All of a sudden, the libertine colony took on a sort of political necessity.

Hilliard d'Auberteuil's Saint-Domingue: A Racial Economy of Desire

The paradox of Saint-Domingue's three-tiered caste system is the way in which the "insurmountable distance" repeatedly invoked to characterize racial distinctions was in constant opposition to the continued libidinal crossing of racial boundaries. One may ask, then, in what sense did segregation in the public sphere allow whites to disavow the rampant interracial sexual desires pursued in private? Alternatively, how did the libidinal anxieties of whites influence policies designed to create a racialized caste society? Nowhere is the relationship between colonial desire and regimes of exclusion better illustrated than in Michel René Hilliard d'Auberteuil's *Considérations sur l'état présent de la colonie française de Saint-Domingue*, published in 1776.[98] Born in Rennes in 1751, Hilliard d'Auberteuil came to Saint-Domingue at the age of fourteen to pursue a career in law. During the ten years of his apprenticeship as a legal clerk, he traveled widely throughout the Caribbean, all the while preparing a manuscript, which he published on his return to France in 1776.[99] Historians have regarded Hilliard d'Auberteuil as an agitator for values of economic liberalism and political autonomy for the islands in the face of the allied interests of the royal administration and metropolitan maritime bourgeoisie. The book caused a sensation in the colonies due to its blunt attacks on officials in the colonial administration, as well as numerous intimations of imminent secession, and it was eventually censored.[100] Equally sensational, however, was Hilliard's subtle description of colonial society, in particular his critique of the white population and the controversial reforms he proposed regarding the free people of color. While it is impossible, and indeed misguided, to ascribe a coherent logic to Hilliard's colonial racial fantasmatics, a close look at the major arguments of his social critique reveals a new dimension of the debate on miscegenation in Saint-Domingue at a critical historical juncture. Hilliard's discourse balances an enlightened critique of morals in a slave colony with a proposal for the biological and social engineering of race and class differences for the preservation of slavery.[101] It is this latter goal that brings colonial sexual practices squarely into the realm of social policy. While on one hand Hilliard prescribes the biological reproduction of each caste, he also proposes the juridical means to maintain class distinctions. The most compelling paradox in Hilliard's thought is that the biological and the legal do not coincide where white desire is concerned. Private sexual ethics are not restricted to match the barriers placed between groups in the public sphere; on the contrary, the racial caste system is predicated on the consummation of colonial desire for the racial other.

Ironically, Hilliard identifies libertinage from the start as a central yet undesirable aspect of colonial society. As a representative of reason and the law, the author portrays the social malaise in Saint-Domingue in terms of an excess of passion: "A stay in Saint-Domingue is not at all deadly; it is our vices, our devouring vexations that kill us." (2:24). The inhabitants are "violent and irascible," tormented by a litany of moral weaknesses. The author's description of the planter's malaise abounds with unusual images of violence and morbidity: "Burdened by troubles and work, the colonists again surrender themselves to vice, and death strikes them down like the scythe mows down ears of corn [*comme la faulx renverse les épis*]" (2:25). While Hilliard at times appeals to the theory of climatic determinism to account for the unhealthy "excess of pleasures" in Saint-Domingue, he judges the descent into moral and physical decay to be only furthered by the lack of culture, education, and the arts in the colony. In particular, white Creole women appear as emblematic of a colonial degeneration resulting from a supreme lack of occupation in a society where slave labor renders them all but superfluous. Considered neither intelligent nor beautiful, they are, rather, voluptuous, pursuing their lovers irrespective of race or status (2:31–32). For Hilliard, this luxuriant sensuality signifies the wasteful debauchery of colonial life: "Hours that rapidly slip away in the bosom of pleasure are followed by days of boredom, pain and dejection" (2:33). Yet Hilliard attributes most of the colony's moral temptations not to the white Creoles but to the immigrants arriving daily from Europe. Alongside those of the lowest classes are rebellious bourgeois sons seeking refuge in the colonies, "youth without principles, lazy and libertine, gotten away from the paternal hand that wanted to correct them" (2:33). Migrating to the colony in search of fabled fortunes, they succeed only in polluting the coastal cities with the insalubrious commerce of prostitution. The author judges the conduct of metropolitan officials as hardly an improvement, as they, too, contribute to the moral deficit of colonial life through their haughtiness and reproof of Creole culture.

To rid the colony of the "froth that infects it," Hilliard seeks a remedy in the law: "To contain the passions, it is necessary to use only the eternal power of reason, and in countries where they are the most alive, it is all the more necessary to ensure the empire of Law" (2:38).[102] For Hilliard, law will underwrite a new social order built on a strong white Creole elite. He advocates replacing royal officials and their imported legislation by Creoles practicing a reformed colonial law that gives whites authority over the two other groups in the colony: "There must not be great men, nobles, legions of people; there must only be free people [*ingénus*], slaves and laws" (2:49). The class rhetoric is important here, since in many respects the discourse of colonial racism reproduced older forms of prejudice against nonnobles.[103] Yet in predicating his program of legal and social renewal on the creation of a stronger white Creole class, Hilliard confronts the contentious issue of colonial population management. In fact, his proposals for the reproduction and enfranchisement of the ruling class within the closed space of the colony extend to all colonial subgroups: "We must limit ourselves to encouraging the interior population, and making a lot of Creoles" (2:45). Describing Saint-Dominguan society according to its composite parts (white Creoles, black slaves, and the racially heterogeneous affranchis), he outlines specific policies designed to ensure both the natural reproduction and juridical delimitation of each group.

On slavery, Hilliard is a great apologist. Refusing to engage in moral arguments about its legitimacy, he suggests that better treatment of slaves will render them docile and content. His real objective is to increase the natural reproduction of slaves through a pronatalist politics. The idea was not new, but it had gone out of style since the late seventeenth century. Louis XIV had encouraged Christianizing slaves in large part to facilitate their marriage and reproduction in accordance with Catholic morality, as is apparent in the Code noir.[104] But with the decline in missionary influence and the rise of the slave trade and large-scale plantation agriculture in the eighteenth century colonists treated slaves as expendable units of production to be replaced almost exclusively through the trade.[105] Hilliard's pronatalism follows both from his apparent alarm over the statistical human waste of the slave trade and from his implicit fear of its demise. After the importation of nearly a million people from Africa over the course of a century, he reports that fewer than 290,000 remain, suggesting a near total lack of natural reproduction.[106] The massive export of captives has, in his view, depopulated coastal Africa, causing slavers to move farther and farther inland and resulting in the rising cost and nearing obsolescence of the trade generally. According to the author's estimates, the mortality rate of slaves on arrival in the colonies was 30 percent and the average lifespan of an imported slave was just fifteen years.

In addition to addressing the shortcomings of the slave trade, Hilliard's pronatalism reflects the tendency in the late eighteenth century to attribute the ills of slavery to masters' mistreatment and cruelty. As historians have shown, black women were frequently mutilated and tortured as punishment for their perceived ability to inhibit their reproductive functions. Some colonists viewed pregnancies as liabilities, both in terms of the loss of labor from the mother and the resources and time needed to tend to the child. Those masters who did believe in natural reproduction typically employed brutal tactics to penalize women whose pregnancies did not produce healthy children. Blind to factors such as chronic malnourishment, physical exhaustion, illness, and the violence of slavery itself, masters instead blamed women for their infertility. Abortions were brutally punished by fitting an enormous spiked iron collar around a woman's neck to be worn day and night until she bore a child for the master. Both mothers and midwives were severely whipped when infants were either stillborn or afflicted with common tetanus, known as lockjaw, which colonists attributed to the slaves' practice of witchcraft.[107]

Although Hilliard boldly castigates masters for their brutality toward slave women, his own proslavery humanitarianism translates slave reproduction into the language of capital gain. He blames their "destructive economy" for slave women's low birth rates. In the manner of a physiocratic reformer, he calculates precisely the costs and benefits of a slave woman's pregnancy so as to demonstrate the long-term profit for the master. Abortions, says Hilliard, are caused by their brutal practices and should not be punished: "Only an excess of tyranny can stifle maternal feelings in them.... It would take only feeble encouragements to bring the population of blacks in the colony to the highest level" (2:66). He objects to slave marriages because they impinge on the master's power to dispose of them as he chooses. Like many of his contemporaries, he considered the slave family to be a political unit capable of fomenting resistance and sedition on the plantation: "A conspiracy by two or three families could destroy the largest plantations by fire, poison, revolt."[108]

Yet Hilliard's pronatalism fails to conceive the possibility that infertility was a sign of women's calculated resistance to slavery itself, thus partaking in the very revolt he so feared. Regarding slave women as natural vessels whose reproduction should be a matter of fact, Hilliard imagines the channeling of their sexual potential so as to produce the servile class within the closed space of the colony. He proposes improving living conditions and providing incentives for women to bear children such as child care and preferential treatment. The rationale behind these kinds of reforms was further expounded by Justin Girod de Chantrans, whose *Voyage d'un Suisse dans les colonies d'Amérique* appeared in 1785.[109] Girod's pronatalism rested on assumptions about slave promiscuity and high fertility in women. For him, slaves had a natural penchant for love. They pursued temporary, clandestine affairs as the only free expression of their humanity possible in the plantation system. If these fleeting relationships rarely yielded children, it is, he argues, because children represented an added burden and a painful reminder that slaves have no control over their destiny. Marriage, on the other hand, took away the joys of libertinage. Thus, the author's proposed reforms exploited slave promiscuity by establishing advantages for childbearing, including an annual fertility festival, "fêtes from which sterile women would be excluded, or placed as witnesses in the row of spectators. One would see mothers with their children, assembled at one table, adorned with gifts from the master, exposing to the eyes of others . . . the rewards of wisdom."[110]

Of course, the reforms passed in Saint-Domingue hardly resembled Hilliard's and Girod's pronatalist fantasies. In 1784 and 1785, the law accorded an unofficial form of freedom, called *liberté de savane*, to those slave mothers who bore no less than six children for the master, all of which survived beyond the age of ten. This measure compelled women both to produce children and to ensure their healthy delivery to the killing fields of slave labor. Given the toughened restrictions on manumission generally, childbearing may have been the only way for field slave women to obtain freedom.[111] Hilliard's own proposals cast manumission in predominately masculine terms, reserved for those rare cases in which slaves risked their own lives to save the master. Furthermore, he insists that freedom never be granted to young male slaves, who were liable to procreate with free black women and reproduce their color in the free class. The implications of this proposal point to the gendered terms of Hilliard's proposals for the biomanagement and segregation of the colonial population. Reserving free black women for impregnation by lighter races, he intended to harness white desire and interracial libertinage for the color-coding of the colonial caste system.

In his discussion of "les affranchis," Hilliard outlines the legal policing of the color line, designed to keep all slaves and a defined class of free people of color in perpetual subjugation to the white Creole class. Skin color here becomes the indelible marker of servitude: "Self-interest and security demand that we burden the race of blacks with such contempt that whoever descends from it be covered with an indelible stain until the sixth generation" (2:73). If mulattoes are to be excluded from the legal status of whites, it is on the basis of their racial genealogy of blackness. Hilliard's racial division of society is predicated on a kind of color coding imposed by a set of regulations regarding marriage and reproduction. Taking the mulatto archetype as the racial dividing line between slavery and freedom, he advocates that all persons whose complexions range from mulatto to black be maintained in slavery through severe limitations on manumission. At the other extreme of the color spectrum, he posits the limit of whiteness as the sixth generation of racial amalgamation with whites, "those degrees at which the most active discernment cannot find any difference" (2:83). The possibility of crossing the racial borderline after six generations is central to both Hilliard's color scheme and his reproductive plan for whites, since mixed bloods can eventually become "white." It is in the interval between the two racial essences, white and black, that the affranchi class exists as a phenotype: "This class must be absolutely distinct from the slaves in exterior and individual signs as well as in civil rights. It must therefore be yellow, that is, entirely composed of mulattoes" (2:88).

In defining his three classes in terms of color—black, yellow, and white—Hilliard invokes the principle of the "stain" of blackness and slavery to degrade the freedoms given affranchis in the Code noir. This idea may be traced to article 58 of the code itself. For, while the code accorded to freed slaves all the rights, privileges, and immunities of French "ingénus," it also required that they show their former master a "singular respect . . . so that the offense that they would do to them is punished more grievously than if it had been done to another person." Hilliard radicalizes and racializes this idea, proposing that free people of color be relegated to a juridical limbo between black slaves (nonpersons under the law) and whites. Likewise, he would empower whites to avenge any offense committed against them by a free person of color on the spot by physical assault, without recourse to judicial authority.[112] By the same token, misallied whites would be publicly disgraced by effectively losing all privileges associated with racial whiteness. This social dispossession is figured as a descent into a category even lower than that of affranchis, since even they regard the misallied white as their inferior (2:79).

Most importantly, Hilliard proposes that interracial marriage henceforth be outlawed, citing a French precedent for prohibiting the marriage of persons of different social ranks on the basis of "inequality of condition." The injunction against mésalliance is the essential legal means by which to ensure Hilliard's segregationist order, informed by the specter of black women and mulatto children inheriting the names and wealth of white men. Directly refuting the Code noir on this point, he asks: "How many negresses have not taken advantage of [this law] to usurp all the fortune of their masters, made brutish in their libertinage and incapable of breaking free from its empire over their weak and seduced souls?" (2:81). Hilliard makes little distinction between interracial liaisons on the plantation and in free society; in each case, matrimony with women of color sounds the death knell of white privilege and racial identity in the colony. Only after the sixth generation of métissage, when all traces of color have been removed from the skin of the free woman, can she be made the wife of a white man, "because there is necessarily a term at which it is impossible to prevent the race of blacks from crossing with that of whites" (2:82).

Whereas Hilliard invokes the old myth of the black sexual savage to denounce interracial marriage, sexual liaisons between masters and slaves become indispensable to his colonial biopolitics and system of color casting. For in identifying the mulatto "race" as the crucial intermediary caste in the colonial social structure, Hilliard endorses its creation through métissage. In order to homogenize the existing freed persons into one phenotype, he proposes marrying persons whose skin color differs substantially enough to produce offspring of a uniform color approaching the "yellow" of his imagination: "It is necessary to begin by marrying all free blacks presently existing in the colony to *mulâtresses*, and mulatto men to free negresses." Second, he proposes automatic manumission for all mulattoes born "of the weakness of the colonists, and whom they must love since they produced them (*ils les ont fait naître*)" (2:88). Hilliard's feeble appeal to filial love is superseded by more overtly political and sexual arguments. In order to defend his suggestion that mulattoes be produced on the plantation through "scandalous liaisons," he dwells less on the social advantages of a numerous mulatto class than on the imperious nature of colonial passions; it is "physical and political necessity" that compels the union of whites and blacks. Declaring the ineffectiveness of all colonial laws to prevent it, Hilliard presents an apology for unbridled white colonial desire: "There are physical needs that make themselves felt more urgently in hot countries. The need to love there degenerates into a furor, and it is fortunate that in a colony like Saint-Domingue black women are found to satisfy a passion that without them could cause great devastation" (2:91). Here he invokes the language of climatology and degeneration to figure the white male, who cannot prevent himself from "loving" his slaves, thus transversing a power dichotomy that could not otherwise be transgressed. In his recourse to the language of need, Hilliard essentially declares the sexual violation of slave women to be both a natural and an indispensable means of producing the intermediate class of mulattoes.[113] No longer a taboo, miscegenation is normalized within the logic of colonial population control.

The irony of Hilliard's ideology thus lies in its insistence that all racial caste divisions be summarily violated in private. While lines of exclusion distinguishing race and rights regulate the social sphere, the biological reproduction of the colonial order actually depends on the métissage of white and black.[114] In this sense, Hilliard inscribes a racial economy of desire alongside the juridical surveillance of caste distinctions. But the terms of his argument give pause when one wonders what the real goal of this bio-political schema is: social control through the color-coding of classes or the sexual hegemony of the white elite? It would seem that rather than ridding the colony of irrepressible passions by imposing stricter laws the author is attempting to manage the reproductive potential of colonial libertinage in the interests of social control. In the text, white men are progenitors whose relationships with slave women bring about the racially color-coded class of affranchis, which therefore protects them from the slaves. Whereas previously racial discrimination and segregation had acted to disavow rampant colonial métissage, Hilliard now makes segregation the justification for that same métissage. What enables his rigid class divisions is his attack on mis-alliance, thereby repudiating the Code noir's article 9, which made these relationships potential avenues for black female emancipation and entitlement. While the language of sexual need disavows the possibility of sentiment between white men and slave women, any legal recognition given to them is the ultimate taboo, as it deflects property and inheritance from legitimate white families to "those whose condition is to work persever-ingly" (2:95). The end result of Hilliard's project is to strip the miscege-nated relationship of any trace of female agency, thus transferring the taboo of miscegenation from the slave woman to the mulatto child, the despised object of legal retaliation in the public sphere.

The Other Empire: The Mulatto Woman and the Libertine Colony

By the late eighteenth century, travel writing on the Antilles was no longer exclusively motivated by the concerns of state propaganda, religious zeal, or individual adventure. Travel writing had become, in addition, the chosen genre of scientific explorers seeking to expand their knowledge of physi-cal and moral worlds beyond Europe, as well as satirical critics of colonial manners eager to influence metropolitan opinion on the profligate, bad-mannered planter.[115] The last two decades of the eighteenth century saw the arrival in Saint-Domingue of yet another class of observers, what I will call the traveling philosophes. These individuals brought with them not only an acute awareness of colonial reformism in the metropole but an arsenal of Enlightenment philosophical notions, which, when applied to the colo-nies, often yielded scathing and sententious accounts of colonial life, slavery, and commerce. Two such traveling philosophes were Alexandre-Stanislas de Wimpffen and Justin Girod de Chantrans.

Wimpffen, a minor nobleman from Alsace, arrived in Jacmel on the southern coast of Saint-Domingue in 1788 and traveled throughout the island until 1790, when prerevolutionary unrest precipitated his departure. Although Wimpffen admits to seeking his fortune in Saint-Domingue and appears to have owned a coffee plantation, his epistolary account, *Voyage à Saint-Domingue pendant les années 1788, 1789 et 1790*, reads as an unapologetic yet often superficial critique of the entire colonial enterprise.[116] On one hand, the author approaches the colony with disgust and indignation, using several authorial personae in order to condemn the total vacuum of morals and society, as in a world turned upside down. At times, he is a disinterested, cosmopolitan *homme raisonnable*, a philosopher obliged to judge and correct man's folly. Referred to elsewhere as "voyager," "idle man," or "gardener"—never "master" or "inhabitant"—he poses as an outsider to the system in what would seem to be an overt denial of the territorial and economic motivations of his travels. As a horticulturalist man of thought, Wimpffen extols bucolic values and solitude in nature in a self-conscious repudiation of planter depravity, pretension, and flamboyance.[117] Yet his lengthy proposals for improvements and the reform of slavery, his confused plan to save the colonies in the interests of the state, and his own material investment in a plantation all attest to the interest he had in the colonial system despite its moral and material squalor. His views on slavery suggest this tension. While raising economic and moral objections to the institution (the latter based mainly on his view of its corrupting influence on the masters), he maintains, nevertheless, that slavery is a necessary evil. For Wimpffen, the real slaves are the colonists themselves, who suffer the tyranny of a commercial monopoly: "The Commerce of France is the true owner of Saint-Domingue."[118]

Justin Girod de Chantrans offered a somewhat less equivocal portrait of colonial life. A bourgeois from Besançon, Girod received military training in the corps du Génie and was later schooled by Jesuits, after which he served in the military throughout France. In 1780, he was sent on a military assignment to Saint-Domingue. During his first six months on a sugar plantation outside of Cap Français, he wrote a travel journal, *Voyage d'un Suisse dans les colonies d'Amérique*, which he published anonymously in 1785.[119] Compared to the Wimpffen's *Voyage à Saint-Domingue*, Girod's text displays greater clarity and sincerity of feeling, even as he deplores in similar terms the paltry existence of the colonials he observes. While at times marveling at the activity of the city, Girod also adopts the tone of the Rousseauian *promeneur solitaire*, nostalgic for the exotic, savage nature that "European cupidity" has all but eradicated. His portrait of plantation life is sober at best. Comparing the masters to Montesquieu's oriental despots trapped in a social dystopia, Girod defends the slaves, who, desiring freedom, are not inherently inferior but rather degraded by their condition and lack of education. Demystifying the myth of colonial riches, he blames monopoly commerce for the cycle of debt that further depraves the master class. A sensitive critic of colonial deforestation, environmental mismanagement, and moral decay, he views the European Age of Discovery as "fatal to humanity."

In Girod's and Wimpffen's descriptions of morals and society in Saint-Domingue, sexual relations between masters and slaves receive little direct comment. While both writers critique the generalized libertinage of colonial life, they tend to accept the exploitation of slave women as an inevitable feature of slavery. Girod raises the issue in reference to the intense jealousy felt by slave men against whites who sexually abuse female slaves. Citing the case of repeated poisonings in the region of Cap Français, he blames "the libertinage without bounds and without discretion, of whites with negresses."[120] The criticism is limited, however, to the master's pursuit of slaves in the fields and factory, which Girod considers to be against his self-interest: "Why constantly bring trouble and disorder to an entire plantation solely with a view to satisfying the caprices of the moment?" In contrast, relationships between masters and slaves in the plantation household are explained by "the great facility that [whites] have in finding mistresses without violence or scandal among their domestics."[121] Girod suggests that these seductions caused the masters' wives maddening fits of jealousy.[122]

Baron de Wimpffen is much more emphatic on the question of colonial debauchery and miscegenation, using irony and sarcasm to render the lack of conventional morality in what he calls "an order of things against nature." For this observer, sexual libertinage in the logic of slavery points up the seemingly insoluble dichotomy between metropolitan and colonial morality, demonstrating Saint-Domingue to be a place of obscenities so shocking as to be almost unreal and comical. Miscegenation is thus "the most fatal consequence of slavery," which threatens to subvert white authority: "The colonist who would be ashamed to work alongside his negress, would not blush at living with her in the degree of intimacy that necessarily establishes relations of equality between them, which prejudice would challenge in vain."[123] In particular, the author exposes the depravity of colonists who seek material profit by procreating with their slaves, remarking that "one of the ways to become rich in Saint-Domingue is to make a lot of bastards." Remarking the commodity value of mixed-race slaves, Wimpffen feigns surprise that the metropole has not ventured to monopolize such a commerce, "to encompass in its exclusive privilege even the manufacturing of the human race."[124] Here he ironizes on the metaphor of capital production, which had long been invoked to describe colonists who sired mulattoes in order to sell them as slaves, thus making a profit.[125] The relationship among illicit sex, slavery, and commerce is further borne out by the preponderance of the sex trade in port cities, such that the value of a female slave far exceeded that of a male. According to Wimpffen, slave owners of all races and both sexes commonly send their slaves on nocturnal missions and share in the profits.[126] Even the clergy is implicated in Wimpffen's portrayal of the colonial harem, as the author casts doubt on the origins of so many children populating the cloistered quarters of the parish priest. The "conjectures that public malice allows itself on the children that the parish priest's mulâtresse contributes to the population of the parsonage, follow their course; and as this growth in family represents for the reverend father, and for the rest of the colonists, a considerable increase in fortune, you understand that . . . few people are disposed to believe that he owes it only to the benevolence of his parishioners."[127]

While both Wimpffen and Girod de Chantrans take the master's sexual relations with slaves to be a matter of fact, those between white men and free women of color generate far more complex narrative representations. Despite the exclusionary legislation meant to marginalize the free people of color politically and socially, free women of color in particular retained a particular visibility and influence in colonial society due to their sexual, economic, and domestic associations with elite white men. Likewise, the mulatto woman entered colonial ethnography as one of its most controversial figures. In narrative descriptions of Saint-Domingue by Creoles and metropolitans alike, the free mulatto woman stands as a privileged icon of colonial libertinage, embodying the very nexus of concupiscence, luxury, and consumption that came to signify the Antilles in the French colonial imagination.[128] In her reading of the mulatto woman's elegance, Joan Dayan has characterized her as "a concrete signifier for lust that could be portrayed as 'love,'" inspiring both sensual adulation in white men and brutal displays of jealousy in white women.[129] I would like to expand on her inquiry into tropes of mulatto femininity by examining their function within the system of miscegenation, desire, and exclusion that both sanctioned white colonial desire and enacted social barriers to control its consequences. The mulatto woman represented not only the taboo product of prior miscegenation but a site of continued racial transgression that defied the segregationist boundaries imposed by judicial authority. If the mulatto concubine stood as a social signifier of white male sexual hegemony, she also raised fears of the devolution of white power to the free people of color through mésalliance or other means that could not be controlled by legal codes. Colonial ethnography was thus constrained to explain the imperious attraction between whites and those who were increasingly the object of exclusionary legislation, relegated to a juridical limbo between full rights and servitude. Narrative representations of the mulatto woman grappled ultimately with the problem of rationalizing her attractions in terms of necessity (there are not enough white women) and desire (she is preferred to white women). At the same time, the mulatto woman was portrayed as an agent of colonial excess, a corrupting temptress whose shameless libertinage exonerated white colonials from the responsibility for colonial miscegenation.

In Hilliard d'Auberteuil's account of Saint-Dominguan society, the class of affranchis figured prominently, not least because of its growing size. Hilliard summarized the illicit power of the *mulâtresse* with a paradigmatic ethnographic description: "The mulâtresses are in general much less docile than mulatto men because they have arrogated to themselves an empire over most of the whites, founded on libertinage. They are well made, their movements are guided by voluptuousness; the affectation of their attire does not sit badly with them. They observe high standards of cleanliness and they are sober, avaricious, proud."[130] Here the author outlines what would become the dominant figure of the mulatto woman in colonial narratives: a colored Venus who cultivates beauty, sophistication, and sensuality for the purpose of seducing white men. His impression of her indocile behavior is suggestive of the way in which whites considered mulatto women to transgress the boundaries otherwise placed on those of their race by colonial law. Hilliard recuperates such transgression into a fantasy of desire: she is unruly because white power allows it, submitting to her attractions. Moreau de Saint-Méry, the white Creole author of the exhaustive *Description topographique, physique, civile, et politique de la partie française de Saint-Domingue*, extended this vision of *mulata* agency under colonialism.[131] He read her cult of seduction as her only power in a society that otherwise reviled her race: "The sole occupation of the numerous class of women who are the fruit of the mixture of whites with slave women is to avenge themselves, with weapons of pleasure, for being condemned to abasement."[132] While accepting the mulatto woman's vilification, Moreau identified sexuality as the exclusive domain of mulatto agency in the colony.

In nearly every published description of Saint-Domingue, the mulatto woman was figured primarily as a libertine whose sole occupation was to perfect the art of pleasure. References abounded to figures of sexual excess in the European and Greco-Roman tradition of erotic literature. Portraying her as a devotee of pleasure to rival the *Laïs* and *Phrinés*, Moreau de Saint-Méry marveled in her cult of *volupté*: "There is nothing that the most inflamed imagination can conceive, that she has not foreseen, divined, accomplished. Charming all the senses, surrendering them to the most delicious ecstasies, and suspending them by the most seductive raptures: that is her sole study."[133] Baron de Wimpffen described mulatto women with a mix of Enlightenment and antique allusions: "These mulâtresses . . . are the most fervent priestesses of the American Venus. They have made voluptuousness a kind of mechanical art, that they have carried to the ultimate point of perfection. Next to them Arétin would be but an ignorant, prudish beginner."[134] The reference to Arétin, the hero of a famous but clandestine pornographic text detailing various sexual positions, underscored further a libertine, erotic intertext. Observing a scene of mulatto women dancing in the night, the ethnographer-voyeur invoked the myth of Bacchus to portray their passion as fiery and carnivorous, inciting them to devour the victim of desire. These fantasies of nymphomania, vampirism, and male engulfment were complemented by the trope of autoeroticism in the mulata Venus, whose cultivation of pleasure occurred not only at the expense of but in spite of her lover. References to ecstasy as a mechanical art pointed to what further distinguished the erotic powers of the mulatto woman: she manufactured pleasure from her own resources, independent of her partner. Girod de Chantrans explained this talent as necessary given that excessive libertinage caused the decline of male libido: "Ecstasy has become for them the object of particular study, an art which is both sought after and necessary with worn out or depraved lovers that simple nature can no longer arouse."[135] Moreau de Saint-Méry further reveled in the mulatto woman's ability to feel greater pleasure than her partner, including "some secrets of ecstasy that even Sappho's code did not contain."[136] Of course, these commentaries all beg the question of these writers' personal encounters with mulatto sensuality. As travelers and erstwhile residents of Saint-Domingue, they were members of the privileged white male elite on which the mythologized mulatto women would have unleashed their most deadly weapons of pleasure. The only disclaimer comes from Wimpffen, who notes that he has only indirectly experienced their character and "overabundance of *sensibilité*." As for their sensual allure, the author demurs: "I admit that in this regard I am obliged to refer to the testimony of others" (120).

That mulatto women were so consistently figured as sexually predatory and prone to excess recalls a central trope in the early modern European imaginary of exotic, faraway continents. Unexplored geographies were
imagined as loci of sexual license, idolatry, and cannibalism, entailing the
topsy-turvy conglomeration of feminized men and masculine women. For
Anne McClintock, rituals of conquest entailed an erotics of submersion
within contested zones of barbarous femininity, reflecting the anxiety of
European male travel and "boundary loss." [137] It is not surprising that such
a trope reappeared within the colonial space of eighteenth-century Saint-
Domingue, as racial borders were becoming increasingly blurred, and white
male "travelers" continually sought to reassert their conquest of the contact
zone. Literally submerged among races they demonized, white planters in
particular were consistently portrayed as isolated and bereft of social contact. [138] Monstrous female sexuality offered a way for colonists to resolve the
paradox of transracial desire and racial paranoia into an acceptable fantasy
of their own sexual slavery and submission at the hands of colored womanhood. Recalling the ideology of survival literature and the captivity narrative, the trope of the mulatto Venus provided a safe means by which to
figure the irrepressible reality of interracial sex. [139] At the same time, such
images allowed whites to repress the often drastic power asymmetries that
facilitated their sexual hegemony in the colony.

In other ways, however, colonial figures of mulatto women reflected the
need to justify white attraction for them with comparisons to white women.
Colonial travelers and writers devalued white femininity in their representations of the tropics, as Hilliard d'Auberteuil's description of white female
indolence, sexual fatigue, and physical weakness makes clear. In Wimpffen's
and Girod's accounts, white women are the least discussed figures of colonial society, almost escaping comment entirely. Wimpffen demonstrated a
marked ambivalence toward white Creole women, comparing them nega-
tively to both metropolitan French and mulatto women: "European women
can hardly notice Creoles except to mock them, especially when they have
not been raised in France. The latter consider the former to be nothing
but prudes, whereas the men, who so rarely find the degree of sensitivity
to which mulâtresses pretend, and then only in [European women], allow
them to bemoan the decadence of the old courtesies and the deprivation
of the tastes of our sex." [140] Wimpffen saw the creolization process as puni-
tive to white women, who are represented as envious rivals of their colored
servants. Girod judged white women to undergo the same process of degeneration as men, since tropical climes caused both heightened sexual desire

and a generalized loss of physical vigor.[141] In a more lengthy description, Moreau de Saint-Méry generally concurred; victims of climate and undisciplined passions, white women languished in a state of "idleness," unable to maintain their beauty. Colored women, on the other hand, were positioned as belonging to the hot tropics, thus enjoying "all the perfection that nature has accorded her species."[142] Drawing on theories of climate and human variety, this rhetoric naturalized free women of color as licentious divas whose sensuality derived, furthermore, from their genealogy of blackness.[143] That the mulatto woman was seen as the inheritor of the original sin of the slave mother is made clear in Moreau de Saint-Méry's assumption of her origin in libertinage on the slave plantation.[144] Colonial discourse thus responded to the mulatto woman by reformulating the earlier trope of the black sexual savage, whose unrepentant lasciviousness concealed both white complicity and the unequal power relations in which interracial desires were pursued. Viewed in terms of historic stereotypes of mulattoes in general, the near euphoric celebration of the concupiscent mulatto woman suggested less the subversion than the accommodation of white sexual power in the colonies.

As an independent sexual agent and colonial border figure, the mulatto woman was credited with the power to dominate her lovers, when she did not dispose of them entirely. With the colony's white men at her feet, the stereotyped mulatto courtesan extracted their resources for her own adornment, arrogating to herself an empire of consumption as well as pleasure. This relationship typified a second dominant trope of mulatto femininity, that of the luxury consumer. While all colonial writers delighted in describing their materialism, Moreau de Saint-Méry provided the most ample portrait. He associated mulatto elegance with the urban space of port cities such as Cap Français and Port-au-Prince, whose accelerated growth after 1770 was accompanied by a rising mulatto elite.[145] "This luxury consists," he wrote, "almost entirely in a single object, dress." Contrasting this vestimentary ostentation with the simplicity of her private apartment, which contained only the sparest furnishings and decoration, he pointed out the public nature of mulatto women's elegance and colonial luxury more generally. Both Wimpffen and Moreau described their indulgence in the most sumptuous Indian cloth, noting especially their signature silk head wraps and gold jewelry. Indeed, mulatto women's high taste and consumption of luxury goods caused a scandal in colonial society, especially among white women, who attempted unsuccessfully to copy the fashions of their rivals. This competition was taken by all colonial writers as indicative of the undeniable influence of the latter. Wimpffen noted that European women attempted to imitate the mulata's use of brilliantly colored scarves as head wraps.[146] Just as important are the erotic connotations of such mimicry. Moreau, for one, subtly evoked the homoeroticism arising from white women's excited admiration of colored women: "Who would believe that the careless attire of mulâtresses is often taken as a model for the white women, and there are even some [white women] who have, with the former, conversations in which a displaced curiosity, not free from danger, is satisfied only at the expense of decency!"[147] Here mulatto women constitute a libidinal danger zone not only for their white male lovers but for white women, the unsuspecting victims of their influence. That this admiration could shift to "indecency" further identifies the mulatto woman as a New World Sappho, whose ironic conquest of white women made them the rivals as well as the lovers of white men.

Just as subversive to the colonial order was the perceived effect of the mulatto women's empire of consumption on white men. For Girod de Chantrans, their prodigious luxury showed "the extent of the blindness of men dominated by love and vanity."[148] Likewise, Moreau de Saint-Méry attests: "Everything enters in the toilette of various mulâtresses, according to her reputation and the price that one has paid for her defeat." Yet what typified the stereotyped mulatto woman's material indulgence was not merely her inordinate consumption but her wastefulness and prodigality. "A mulâtresse will hardly ever take a needle . . . to prolong the life of an expensive garment. Her pride tells her that she must replace it with another, and she knows how she acquired the first."[149] In this sense, the mulatto woman stands as a privileged signifier of white colonial libertinage and excessive venality. The stereotype carried particular importance in an era in which luxury was considered by white Creole reformers as a strategy of what they called "ministerial despotism," referring to the connivance of members of the royal administration with the maritime commercial elite to enrich themselves by monopolizing the traffic in elite merchandise sold to colonials at inflated prices. Dedicating an entire chapter to the problem of luxury, Hilliard notes the rise in luxury among the white elite after 1763, and objected that it detracted from capital investment in tropical industries.[150] Ten years later, Girod inserted mulatto women into the debate, suggesting that her extravagance, and, more importantly, colonial libertinage, was the true despot in the colonies: "One often clamors against [mulatto women's] exorbitant spending; but in providing a market for the manufactures of France, they are the useful cause of a voluntary tax that the metropole applies to the libertinage of the colonists. It is thus not from the metropole that they must expect a reform in this regard: let them do it themselves, if they wish it to be done."[151]

Yet the idea of the mulâtresse as an illegitimate subject of colonial consumption, draining the resources of the white elite, was contradicted by the widely held view of colored women as economically prudent, thrifty, and even entrepreneurial. This apparent inconsistency points to a critical split in the image of the mulatto woman between promiscuous sensuality and domestic respectability.[152] As a "*ménagère*" (literally, a housekeeper), the mulatto woman occupied a position in a stable partnership with a white man whose household and economic resources she managed.[153] Girod de Chantrans explained the frequency of the practice: "Not only do domiciled whites consider it necessary to their pleasures and advantageous for their interests to have a woman of this species at the head of their household, it is even a common practice of etiquette and good taste among them."[154] Wimpffen concurred, adding that their sophistication, their good business sense, and the elusive Rousseauian trait of *sensibilité* actually made free mulatto women preferable to white Creole women as domestic partners. What Wimpffen did not mention was that many white immigrants found the advantage of living with, and especially marrying, a free colored woman to be an economic gain. As early as 1734, official correspondence noted the frequency with which newly arrived French settlers sought their fortunes not on the sugar plantation but in marriage with free women of color possessing considerable savings. On average, free women of color were more independent and financially much better off than white women.[155]

Instead, Wimpffen's narrative presents the ménagère as an idealized version of an older trope in literature from the colonial contact zone, that of the nurturing native. "More than one European," he writes, "abandoned by his selfish fellow brothers, has found in [his ménagère] the most tender solicitude, the most constant and generous humanity, without there being mixed any feeling other than benevolence."[156] Here the European appears as a lost, vulnerable subject of empire, soliciting aid, comfort, and love in the arms of a "native" woman. Though of mixed race, her humanity is pure insofar as she gives herself over as an emotional caretaker. Yet, even as she becomes a necessary apparatus of colonial male survival, it is in a rapport that evacuates questions of power and domination. This is a particularly validating fantasy for a slave society, for, as Mary Louise Pratt has argued, scenes of cross-racial affection displaced servitude in sentimental narratives as a means by which the submission of the colonized could be guaranteed.[157]

Indeed, the fact that she asks nothing in return—accepting that she will never be his wife—makes the colored woman ménagère trope an ideal site for the symbolic redemption of white colonists. The assumption that mulatto women prefer whites to men of their own race suggests also the need of the ruling class to be loved by the subalterns. Girod de Chantrans argued, furthermore, that loving a woman of color would invariably result in the master's increased humanity toward slaves, "because it is not natural to mistreat the one who procures for us and shares the greatest of pleasures."[158]

Thus, as a racially hybrid marker of sexual excess, material extravagance, and domestic virtue, the mulatto woman aroused both fear and desire in the ruling class. The popular icon of mulata femininity obscured the frequency of mésalliance between mulatto women and white men, conventional marriages between mulatto women and free men of color, and the economic independence of mulata businesswomen and slave owners. Yet, insofar as whites displaced interracial desires onto women of mixed race, representations of mulatto women offer important insights into white attitudes toward their own sexuality and participation in colonial libertinage. In fact, the question of whether or not the commerce of whites with women of color was advantageous to the colony was rigorously debated by members of the elite.[159] As the historian David Garrigus explains, contemporaries were concerned, in particular, about the "inability of individual colonists to sacrifice their immediate pleasures for the public good." In his view, political fears about the frailty of colonial society as a whole and its lack of a civic spirit and public sphere that would make it truly "French" were linked to the weakness of legitimate bonds and the sexual power of women of color.[160] Yet all too often colonials and observers alike rushed to justify libertinage and concubinage with free colored women as rendered necessary by the very structure of a slave society and for the security of whites. In narrative sources, the position of the mulatto woman concubine was never contested outright but was rationalized as inherent to the system, "a necessary evil," not least because of the numerical insignificance of white women. For Girod, libertinage prevented a huge power differential between those who created the law and those who observed it by forming the critical intermediate class and ensuring its continued alignment with the white elite.[161]

What is fascinating, however, is that despite the prevalence of narrative portraits of colored female desirability and domestic availability, the mulatto woman was increasingly policed by the law in ways that suggest growing anxieties among members of the political elite about colonial libertinage, miscegenation, and luxury. In conformity with the historic strategies of displacement that located vice and immorality on the colored body, the Superior Councils did not hesitate to curb the mulatto woman's influence, using exclusionary legislation to cause her public humiliation. Laws against mulattoes in general proliferated in the last decades of French rule in Saint-Domingue, reflecting, as Garrigus suggests, tensions about the nature of white political power and legitimacy. In addition to requirements that all people of color carry proof of their freedom, restrictions on employment, onomastic controls, and laws prohibiting coloreds from carrying arms, legislation was passed that specifically prohibited people of color from wearing luxurious attire. Attempts to enact a dress code for free people of color had a long history in the colonies to judge from a 1720 law that aimed to prevent them from wearing silk, gold, and lace with the threat of a return to slavery.[162] In 1775, the procurer general of Cap François moved to "restrain the overly flamboyant luxury of the *filles publiques*," many of whom were women of color.[163] Four years later, colonial administrators imposed new standards of "modesty" on the dress of free people of color in language bespeaking a concern with unruly femininity. The law recognized the economic advantages of mulatto elegance but claimed the interest of morality to prevail in imposing a new definition of *respect* for whites: "We expressly forbid [the free people of color] to affect through their clothing, hairstyles, dress or attire, a reprehensible assimilation with the way in which white men and women arrange themselves. . . . Likewise, we forbid them all objects of luxury on their exterior that are incompatible with the simplicity of their condition and origin, on pain of being stripped of them on the spot."[164]

Joan Dayan has argued that laws such as these misapprehended the true subversiveness of the colored woman's taste, for it was not she who assimilated to the whites, but the whites who rushed to copy her. Explains Dayan, women of color "staked their reputation on evading these structures, and even when they acceded to the denuding strategies of the courts (simple coiffure, unadorned dress), this supposed lack became the style imitated by their white rivals."[165] In this sense, legal restrictions on dress represented the effort of colonial authorities to police boundaries of privilege, demonstrating the ways in which, as Ann Laura Stoler and Frederick Cooper would have it, "a grammar of difference was continuously and vigilantly crafted as people in the colonies refashioned and contested European claims to superiority."[166] I would contend that legislation restricting mulatto access to entitlements and privileges was in many ways self-referential, calculated to lessen the demands they made on white men and thus contain the threat posed by the colonial desire for white rule. The agency of the free woman of color exhibited a particular paradox within the colonial regime. Since she was the quintessential object of white colonial desire, the mulatto woman's legal status became a highly charged indicator of official anxieties about the licitness, permissiveness, and effects of such desires. By punishing her displays of luxury and elegance, colonial authorities could indirectly denounce libertinage, even as they made it less onerous for members of the white elite to indulge themselves in it. Only mésalliance, or the establishment of legal filiation, was punishable in the law for white men, bringing on them the same discriminations as those suffered by free coloreds.

What, then, was the relationship between desire and the law in the libertine colony of Saint-Domingue? As I have shown, the functioning of the libertine colony was complex and seemingly contradictory in that it operated to ensure both the social and political subordination of colored races through exclusionary measures and the sexual hegemony of white men. These two trends were intricately related throughout the history of the colonies, as segregation and exclusion followed directly from colonial authorities' efforts to punish, displace, and repress the reality of white male libertinage. What the libertine colony could not do was control the demographic consequences of this desire. Ironically, its very prosecution depended initially on the presence of offspring to prove the "crime." Thus, at the inception of colonialism illicit desires between the masters and female slaves were punishable if they bore fruit—the child of mixed race. Over time, the meanings ascribed to this illegitimate family triad by narrative and legal discourses changed in ways that suggest the gradual accommodation of white male desire and the attendant criminalization of both black slave women and the children of mixed race, who were both held accountable for the crime.

In this sense, the history of colonial desire is inextricably linked to the contested position of the slave woman on the plantation. Whereas slave women's associations with free men on the plantation in some cases resulted in access to better living and working conditions and the possibility of manumission or marriage, eighteenth-century legal measures increasingly acted to eliminate any sexual agency on her part. Thus, slave women were increasingly cloistered and subjugated in absolute terms to white power/ desire, meant to exist both as wombs for more slaves and as sexual objects for their masters. Likewise, exclusionary measures against free people of color acted in part to transfer the anxiety about miscegenation onto the products of mixed race, who were deemed politically dangerous, physically degenerate, and sexually aggressive. The illegitimate child of the sin of the father thus became the victim of exclusionary legislation to be policed in the public sphere. However, as the free population of mixed race imposed itself as a growing presence, colonial discourses revalued the act of miscegenation as a sexual, political, and demographic necessity. While black women were recast as fertile wombs for the production of mulattoes, free women of color became new objects of colonial desire in public. The object of a new discourse celebrating consumerism, luxury, eroticism, and domestic love, the mulatto woman was also interpellated in the law as a threat to public order. Specifically, one of the very attributes that constituted her desirability to white men, elegance in dress, was targeted in the laws against her. Thus, as the mulatto woman was erected into the quintessential figure of colonial libertinage, she was prosecuted for it. This very cycle of displacement and discrimination facilitated the continued libidinal transgression of boundaries of exclusion by desiring white male subjects.

Chapter Five *Race, Reproduction, and*

Family Romance in Saint-Domingue

By the end of the eighteenth century, the Caribbean had become the seat of the most brutal regime of slavery in human history. The French island of Saint-Domingue was, in the language of the day, the pearl of the French empire and the most profitable colony in all the world. Yet profitability, when counted in pounds of sugar produced and reexported by France to its European neighbors, eschewed the incredible human toll of the Old Regime colonial enterprise. Nowhere in the colonial world were people so swiftly driven to death, while being rendered physically and socially incapable of maintaining a positive rate of reproduction.[1] Nowhere did the population of captives so greatly outnumber the "free," sometimes on the order of thirty to one. It was a genocidal state of affairs maintained by an astounding rate of slave consumption; in the last decades of the eighteenth century, the single colony of Saint-Domingue became the largest buyer of slaves in the Northern Hemisphere, importing more than twice as many persons as the rest of North America.[2] If French profits soared during this time, it is because of the extraordinarily violent disciplinary regime, which extracted on average ten to fifteen years of labor from captive men and women before they were driven to death.

In the seventeenth century, when tobacco production was still in full force, slaves were subjected to living and working conditions of a cruelty unimaginable even to the most experienced observers. In a candid disclosure of the lethal effects of the system, Du Tertre confessed: "We feed them however we want, we push them to work like beasts, and with their consent or by force, we draw from them all the service of which they are capable until their death."[3] He marveled at the quantities of sweat pouring from

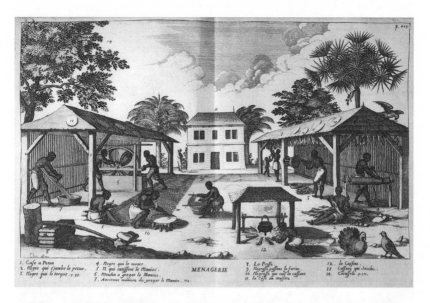

17. "Ménagerie," in Jean-Baptiste Du Tertre, *Histoire générale des Antilles habitées par les François.* Paris, 1667–71. (Reproduced courtesy of the McCormick Library of Special Collections, Northwestern University Library.)

the bodies of working captives. Forced to labor day and night on only a few hours sleep while being driven by callous overseers, they fell dead in the fields from illness or exhaustion.[4] By 1700, slaves were more than twice as numerous as whites in the Lesser Antilles as well as in Saint-Domingue, and their numbers would explode in the eighteenth century. Between 1700 and 1754, the population of slaves in Saint-Domingue increased twentyfold, from 9,000 to more than 172,000.[5] This demographic shift was concomitant with the rise of sugar cultivation on large plantations, the closest thing the early modern period knew to an industrial factory.[6] Because sugar production required prompt and precise cutting, crushing, and processing of the cane in order to preserve its sugar content, the work was literally nonstop and involved hundreds of persons in diverse tasks.[7] They were forced either to perform like machines or die in the process. Such was the fate of fatigued mill feeders, who in a moment of inattention could be swept up, arms first, into the mill. Father Labat's remedy for such deadly "accidents" was not to reduce the eighteen- to twenty-hour work shifts, but to swiftly amputate the limbs of any unlucky slaves before their whole bodies were pressed by the machine.[8] In the fields, the work was no less intense. Girod de Chantrans offered the most vivid, if stylized, eighteenth-century description of working slaves: "The sun struck directly over their heads: sweat flowed from

18. "La Figure des Moulins a Sucre," in César de Rochefort, *Histoire naturelle et morale des iles Antilles de l'Amérique*, Rotterdam, 1681. (Photograph reproduced courtesy of the Newberry Library.)

every part of their bodies; their limbs made heavy by the heat, fatigued by the weight of their pick-axes and by the resistance of the rich soil, which was hardened to the point of breaking the tools, nonetheless made the greatest effort to conquer all of these obstacles."[9]

If the sugar plantations became "killing machines" for thousands of slaves, it is only partly due to the unceasing and strenuous work require-ments.[10] Slavery was accompanied by what C. L. R. James called a "regime of calculated brutality and terrorism" designed to guarantee the hegemony of the whites, themselves secretly terrorized by the power and number of slaves in their midst. For James, Saint-Domingue exhibited the "unusual spectacle of property-owners apparently careless of preserving their prop-erty; they had first to ensure their own safety."[11] Before the passage of the Code noir, the only constraint on colonists' ability to beat their slaves to death was that they do so at night. This was a common punishment for "theft," planter terminology for the unauthorized pursuit of food. Du Ter-tre explained that as an alternate measure colonists would nail their slaves to a wall or a tree by the ear for a few days before cutting it off.[12] Fugitives could be subjected to more prolonged rituals of torture, during which their

19. Allegory of Nature, represented by a white woman nursing a white child and a black child, in Guillaume-Thomas Raynal, *Histoire philosophique et politique . . . des deux Indes*, Paris, 1775. (Photograph reproduced courtesy of the Newberry Library.)

bodies, slashed by the whip, were periodically rinsed in a searing solution of peppers, salt, and lemon juice. Alternatively, they were quartered, burned at the stake, or fitted with iron collars topped with enormous crossing bars such that they would never again be able to take flight. The only thing worse than such punishments was the Catholic mission's sanction of them. Labat almost enthusiastically acculturated to the violence, reassuring his readers that the scars on the backs of slaves "excited the compassion of those who were not accustomed to them; but soon one gets used to them."[13]

In 1685, the ostensibly humanitarian Code noir set no limit on the number of lashes a slave could receive, nor on the length of the workday. Most of its other reforms, including requirements on the provision of food and clothing for slaves and limits on the master's ability to mutilate and murder them, were habitually ignored. The different types of whips and irons and their corresponding tortures only tell part of the story; some colonists amused themselves by inventing variations on familiar tortures, which they named with derisive or trivializing expressions.[14] These acts of cruelty were more likely to attract royal admonition in the eighteenth century, when the Crown acted to rein in the abuses. Yet any attempts to police abusive masters came up against the growing sense, even among royal officials, that the slaves had to be terrorized to be "contained." Hence in 1741, when a rich colonist in Saint-Domingue was charged with murdering two hundred of his own slaves, of which five suffered a "complete mutilation," colonial authorities accepted his proposal that he make a 150,000 pound "gift" to the public works fund. From France, the naval minister advised: "If it is necessary to repress inhuman masters' abuse of their authority, it is also of great consequence to do nothing that could bring the slaves to ignore it and wander from the bounds of dependency and submission."[15]

This kind of thinking would ultimately sabotage the important reforms attempted in the last decades of the eighteenth century. Alarmed by the rising cost of slaves, high rates of mortality, low fertility, and the philosophical offensive against colonial slavery, the royal administration outlawed gratuitous acts of violence. A royal ordinance of 1786 prohibited masters and overseers from "giving more than fifty lashes of the whip, striking them with a bat, mutilating them, or making them perish from different kinds of death."[16] Those who killed their slaves would suffer the death penalty, and masters were forbidden to mistreat slaves who made complaints against them. Yet in one of the most renowned cases of colonial brutality the king's law fell silent. In 1788, a coffee planter from Saint-Domingue named Lejeune murdered four slaves and tortured two others accused of poisonings on his plantation. So heinous was his vengeance—he burned the feet, legs, and thighs of his victims, leaving them to decompose in chains—that fourteen of his slaves charged him before the tribunal. When a commission investigated the allegations, they discovered two torture victims on the verge of death, unmistakable evidence of his guilt. Still, the whites of the town petitioned the governor and intendant on behalf of Lejeune, insisting not only that he be absolved but that his slaves be whipped for having denounced him. The case became a sensational affair, with every political body of any influence providing an opinion. It was as though Lejeune stood for all of white Saint-Domingue and the colonial power structure behind it. When the courts acquitted Lejeune and dropped all charges, it was clear that colonial legitimacy in Saint-Domingue had reached a crisis point. No amount of torture, violence, or murder counted when visited on slaves. Fearing that "insubordination" would result if their complaints were ever prosecuted under colonial justice, the courts chose instead to use the threat of these very acts in order to maintain hegemony. Lejeune lucidly made the case in his own defense: "It is not the fear of the law's equity that prevents the black from stabbing his master, it is the sense of absolute power that [the master] has over his person."[17]

Yet, the increasingly brutal repression of slaves and the protections accorded to delinquent masters must be seen in light of acts of slave resistance that over time eroded whites' sense of legitimacy and security. While armed revolt was uncommon, slaves worked in diverse ways, both individually and collectively, to oppose slavery, improve their well-being, and sabotage colonial interests. Suicide, abortion, poisonings, and *maronnage*, or escape into the hills, were common forms of resistance. The most significant organized resistance movement in the French Caribbean before the Haitian Revolution was the work of Makandal, an African-born slave who turned fugitive and terrorized the whites of Saint-Domingue throughout the 1750s. By the time he was finally arrested in 1757, he had masterminded a conspiracy to poison the water supply of Cap Français and massacre all the whites on the island.[18] Colonial authorities averted the attack, but they could not quell the mythology surrounding Makandal in the minds of slaves, nor the revolutionary consciousness he had inspired. Likewise, white Saint-Domingue for the first time glimpsed the reality of colonial terror in reverse, that is, the genocidal messianism that slavery could ignite in its victims.[19]

Thus, by the onset of the Haitian Revolution, Saint-Domingue had one of the most violent, brutal, and divided societies in human history. Yet this was not always apparent from the colonial narratives produced about it. Indeed, what is fascinating about colonial writings on the French Caribbean generally is the extent to which slaves were made visible less as laborers or tortured bodies than as vital producers of culture. This is especially significant given the perennial indictment of white colonial society precisely on the grounds that it lacked culture and the institutions that could generate it. Slaves, however abused, degraded, and maligned, were nonetheless conceived in terms that valorized the diversity and resilience of the cultural forms they adapted to the colonies. Especially compelling to writers was their ability to synthesize traditions and develop a specifically Creole culture that marked them, in the eyes of the slave owners, as belonging to the colony. Over time, *Creole* became an ideologically charged signifier through which slaveholding elites represented colonial society as a cohesive unit while repressing the institutionalized practices of brutality and racial apartheid through which their hegemony was enforced. Slaves were essential to white Creoles' conceptions of themselves, not merely as a negative self-definition but more importantly as the mirror in which they recognized their own cultural specificity and affirmed their difference from the French.

This chapter will continue the focus of the preceding one on the role of sexuality and desire in colonial discourses and practices of exclusion. Here I will examine the ways in which the same desire comes through in ethnographic representations of Creole society, where the word *Creole* is taken to mean "originating in the colony." In particular, I explore the work of the renowned Creole lawyer and statesman Moreau de Saint-Méry, whose book, *Description de la partie française de Saint-Domingue*, purported to represent the totality of the colonial population on the eve of the Haitian Revolution and drew important distinctions between Creoles, whites, and slaves in the colonies. I argue that the colonial discourse of créolité elaborated in the text is heavily structured by the particular gendered and racialized subject position of its author and those white Creoles for whom he speaks. Moreau eschews much of the brutality and segregationism of slavery in order to present colonial society as being fundamentally unified through culture and, more importantly, links of desire and filiation among masters, slaves, and free people of color. Although common tastes, language, origin, and habits all form the basis of the Creole identity in Moreau de Saint-Méry's writing, it is expressed through a familiar trope in European colonial discourse — the consolidation of white male power through the control of colored women.[20] More than merely describing the population of Saint-Domingue, he tells a story of the attraction of white men for slaves and free people of color, who are markedly feminized through themes of seduction and romance.

Colonial social relations thus appear to be determined not by violence and domination but by reciprocal desire.

This narrative is most explicit in the meticulous racial classification system that serves to define the intermediary class of free people of color in terms of métissage between black and white. I read Moreau de Saint-Méry's racial taxonomy as a sexual allegory whereby whites imagined their own political, racial, and sexual supremacy over nonwhites while at the same time repressing the reproductive consequences of white male libertinage. In this respect, I evoke the "biopolitical" dimensions of Moreau's text, that is, the ways in which it addresses the conflict between the interracial sexual libertinage of the ruling elite and the threat posed by a proliferating mixed-race population that contested white claims to superiority. I argue that Moreau's racial text contains not only a theory of desire through the repeated presentation of interracial couplings but, just as importantly, a theory of reproduction that fantasizes a limit to the procreative effects of this desire. By revising Enlightenment ideas about hybridity, degeneration, and fertility, Moreau portrays the mulatto woman as the imagined endpoint of reproduction, thus relegating interracial reproduction to the primary instance of métissage between white men and black women. This representation installs a powerful logic of filiation according to which white men are the real and symbolic fathers of the subaltern races in the colony. Insofar as it legitimates white political authority in the colonial imagination, the filial allegory constitutes what I call a "family romance" of racial slavery in late-eighteenth-century Saint-Domingue. Pushing the structure of interracial desire to its logical conclusion, I theorize the incestuous dimensions of miscegenation in Saint-Domingue, where white men directed their most frenetic passions toward those mixed-race women they claimed to be their "daughters." In this sense, I take Saint-Domingue to be emblematic of a larger fantasy informing colonial slavery in the Caribbean and elsewhere. By analyzing various colonial narratives in light of Sadean libertinage and modern anthropological and psychoanalytic theory, I argue that incestuous desire both contributed to and was enabled by the social violence of slavery.

Allegories of Desire in Moreau de Saint-Méry's Ethnography of Creole

No writer contributed more to the colonial discourse of creolization than the white Creole magistrate, statesman, and ethnographer par excellence Moreau de Saint-Méry. His writing, remarkable in breadth, detail, and style, raised the social description of the colony to a level of philosophical elegance indicative of his time. Abandoning the generic examples of Du Tertre's natural history and Labat's ambulant and disorganized "*Journal du voyage*," Moreau took as a model the *Encyclopédie* for his two-volume masterwork, *Description topographique, physique, civile, politique et historique de la partie française de l'isle Saint-Domingue.*[21] Although the book was first published in Philadelphia in 1797, it had been prepared over many years as part of a massive project designed to produce a totalizing account of the French Caribbean colonies, Saint-Domingue the principal among them. Completed after several state-funded trips to France and provincial Saint-Domingue, the book reflects the author's direct experience and his unlimited access to public and private archives, including documentation and observations contributed by elite residents of Saint-Domingue. That it appeared so late after its inception is a consequence of the political ferment of two revolutions and the transatlantic peregrinations of an Old Regime colonial statesman.

Médéric Louis Élie Moreau de Saint-Méry was born in 1750 into the white Creole elite of Martinique. He boasted family ties to Martinique's superior judges and Joséphine, the future empress of France. Following in the family tradition, he studied law, mathematics, and astronomy in Paris, receiving the title *avocat du parlement* in just three years. On returning to the colonies, he settled in Cap Français and ascended the ranks of the *magistrature* to become a counselor in the Superior Court in 1785. During the same period, he emerged as an emblematic figure of the colonial Enlightenment. An active freemason, he was a prominent member of the Chamber of Agriculture and the Cercle des Philadelphes, later to become the Royal Society of Arts and Sciences. This organization made Saint-Domingue a major center of learned exchange and scientific debate in the Western Hemisphere, comparable in its time only to Philadelphia and Boston.[22] Moreau's rise in the colonies was concomitant with his growing notoriety on the French political and cultural scene, as he spent a considerable amount of time in Paris working on his research projects. A disciple of Rousseau and Diderot, he was secretary and president of the Musée de Paris and held memberships in the Royal Society of Agriculture and several provincial academies. Soon he became an important consultant to the royal administration on all questions colonial, publishing memoirs on colonial legislation, science, and agriculture. These responsibilities and his research kept him in Paris for much of the 1780s, where he took a leading role in the prerevolutionary assemblies, eventually acting as a spokesperson for the colonial elite in favor of more political and economic autonomy for the colony. He was a proslavery Enlightenment revolutionary, a moderate who wished for a philanthropic, parliamentary revolution that would protect the monarchy. Although his continuing work away from Saint-Domingue led to a loss of prestige in the colony, his reputation grew in the Parisian assemblies. He fought for a new constitution for Saint-Domingue, opposed the extension of rights to free people of color, and polemicized against the Société des Amis des Noirs. Significantly, the address he delivered on May 12, 1791 provoked Robespierre's famous speech calling for the end of the colonies should they compromise revolutionary principles.[23]

Eventually, Moreau was alienated by the radical phase of the French and Haitian revolutions and escaped to Philadelphia, where he opened a small bookstore and publishing house. The shop became a social center for a community of elite émigrés, including Talleyrand, de Noailles, and the Duc d'Orléans. Although he would never return to Saint-Domingue, Moreau was determined to complete and publish his remaining historical works in Philadelphia, drawing on his enormous collection of notes and drafts. Published one year after a similar work on Spanish Santo-Domingo,[24] the *Description de la partie française de l'isle Saint-Domingue* was the belated accompaniment to his other massive work, the six-volume *Loix et constitutions des colonies françaises de l'Amérique sous le vent (de 1550–1785)*, published from 1784 to 1790.[25] Yet, whereas *Loix et constitutions* appeared during the height of Old Regime colonial prosperity, the *Description* was published at a time when the fabric of colonial society the author so exhaustively describes had been torn to pieces in the Haitian Revolution. By 1797, the revolution had reached its radical stage. While the planter class had attempted to wrest economic and political power from metropolitan interests and secure a greater degree of self-governance, the revolution had far greater relevance as a massive civil war that involved all colors and castes of the society, causing a near complete collapse of governmental authority. Most significantly, Toussaint Louverture had risen to the leadership of the most massive slave insurrection in history, one that forced the National Assembly to pass an abolition decree in 1794. Soon thereafter, Toussaint distinguished himself as a general in the French army by successfully defending the island against foreign invasion. By 1797 he had been named commander in chief and governor of the colony.

Although it was published after the beginning of the Haitian Revolution, Moreau's *Description* was never intended as a response to events in the colony. It was, rather, intended to be part of a colonial encyclopedia, the publication of which was stalled due to the upheavals of the French Revolution and in the end never completed. In his *Discours préliminaire*, he refused even to comment on contemporary events, much less admit the potential loss of the colony, insisting instead that his work portrayed the glory of the colony on the eve of the revolution at a time when it was the "Hercules" of the colonial world and a model of plantation governance, agricultural and industrial innovation, and "French genius."[26] Comparing Saint-Domingue to the lost civilizations of Greece and Rome, he regards his text as the virtual preservation of what has been obliterated, a rare and precious blueprint of what once was and possibly could be again if and when France were able to reimpose its authority on the rebels. Hence the work is encyclopedic in scope and rigor, a totalizing account of the topography, history, industries, government, and society of Saint-Domingue. It is comprised of an ethnographic tableau of the colonial society and population, followed by three longer sections containing "topographic" descriptions of each of the three administrative provinces of the island.

Moreau de Saint-Méry's ethnography is unprecedented not only in its descriptive breadth and detail but in the distinctions the author makes within socioracial groupings. First dividing the population into the three standard ethnographic classes—whites, slaves, and affranchis (free non-whites)—the author further divides them on the basis of origin to distinguish persons native to the island from those born elsewhere. Thus, for the first two castes, white and slave, Creole emerges as a cultural identity distinct from those of European and African, and it is shared by both blacks and whites. By defining the affranchi class with an elaborate racial typology to distinguish variations in skin color resulting from métissage, the social, racial, and origin signifiers implicitly collapse together, as though all affranchis are Creole. Thus, the common factor binding the tripartite colonial social structure is the Creole identity. On the basis of this inclusive new sociocultural category, one may read in the text an inchoate theory of creolization as a cultural process linking all three segments of the colonial population. This is significant given that Moreau displays a nationalist enthusiasm for the colony as his "native country (*patrie*)." Like Hilliard d'Auberteuil, he laments the absenteeism and disdain for the colonial "birthplace" that characterized the white Creoles' rise from filibustering to planter wealth. His nationalism is expressed through an idea of creoleness that implies a degree of cultural evolution and unity underlying racial and power dichotomies. He writes: "It would be a false idea indeed to believe that each of these three classes has its own character, which distinguishes it entirely from the other two" (29).

The bulk of the author's ethnographic account is reserved for slaves and displays the author's marked preference for Creoles over Africans.[27] Whereas the creolization process is seen to degrade whites in tastes, habits, and physique, blacks are rather improved in Moreau's estimation. Disparaged in everything from language and religion to physical and moral character, African slaves figure in an ethnographic typology that traces the continental perimeter of Africa, reducing the peoples of entire nations to particular cultural and psychological traits corresponding to their relative value in the European slave trade. While the Senegalese are "similar to whites" in intelligence and morality, the Bambaras and Mandingues are thieves, the Aradas deceitful, Monsombés and Mondongues cannibalistic, the Ibos given to suicide, and so on, complete with Creole nicknames that further deride African national and cultural specificities. Any resistance in Africans is coded as aberrant, almost inexplicable behavior. Attributing Ibo suicides to "the slightest vexation or discontent" (51), Moreau proudly reports the colonial response, which is to mutilate the dead beyond recognition so as to counteract Ibo beliefs in transmigration back to Africa.[28] In such a hell of violence and denial, the Africans considered most valuable and desirable are the Congolese, whose supposedly resilient smiles, singing, dancing, and cheerfulness enliven the environments of both slaves and their masters.

Despite the stereotypical distinctions he draws between African ethnic groups, Moreau theorizes their cultural assimilation in the *nouvelle patrie* through a symbolic personage, "The African made colonial," whose character traits are inexorably altered in the colonial melting pot. This process of cultural transformation is the first step on the way to creoleness, a morally and physically superior standard of blackness. Claiming that "domesticity has beautified the species," Moreau clearly links slavery and "creolization" to the natural historical notion of domestication as theorized by Buffon, one of his greatest influences (59). In describing domestication as the process by which man changes the natural state of animals, Buffon had already made a rather revealing comparison with slavery: "A domestic animal is a slave that one uses, abuses, alters, uproots, and denatures."[29] In the naturalist's grand narrative of "universal man," domestication was a process that "civilized" men first experienced themselves by cultivating the arts, society, and industry and then imposed on others (animals and, evidently, slaves) to complete their conquest of their surroundings. This idea heavily informs Moreau de Saint-Méry's narrative of black creolization. In contrast to Africans, whom he describes as dumbfounded by all manner of colonial industry and material culture, Creole blacks are "intelligent," the signal attribute of the "civilization" they have supposedly witnessed in slavery: "Accustomed, from birth, to the things that announce the genius of man, their spirit is less obtuse than that of the African" (59).

Through such a rhetoric of perfectibility and progress, Moreau both euphemizes and artfully evades the fact that slaves were in fact being sacrificed to the industrial arts of European reason. His argument points above all to the idea of a shared culture and familiarity between Creole slaves and whites, such that "being raised with whites, or under their eyes, the latter attach themselves to them in a more immediate manner" (59). This domestic, physical, and cultural intimacy is the ground on which he will naturalize slavery, establishing an almost filial connection between masters and slaves. This desired filiation, which would transcend and in fact negate the perversity of exploitation, produces rather fantastic illusions in the narrative. The benefits of Creole birth are said to accrue over generations, such that the children of Creole slaves are of even better "quality" than their parents. Furthermore, Creole blacks display less phenotypical difference from the white ideal: "The nose lengthens, the traits soften, the yellow tint of the eyes weakens, as the generations distance themselves from their primitive beginning" (72). In this valuation of native-born slaves, Moreau makes no mention of their station as captive workers without control over the conditions of their existence. The magnitude of this denial comes through in his comment on their eating habits: "Happy with little in his ordinary life, [the slave] is perhaps of all men the one who consumes the least food, especially compared to his work" (61).

When labor is pushed to the far horizon of the ethnographic portrait— even the subsistence labor of the Creole garden is omitted—what emerges instead is an exclusive focus on slave culture and "morals." Although Moreau's discourse of slave creolization affirms the influence of white society and industry on slaves, it is far more significant as an expression of white identification with, and appropriation of, black Creole culture. Nowhere is this more apparent than in the author's description of slave dances such as Calenda, Chica, and most importantly Vaudou. The author follows in a long line of European observers astonished by the slaves' passion for dance and their determination to convene at night despite the most grueling labor demands. Yet, as a powerful cultural form through which slaves both expressed their African origins and forged new cultural alliances, dance posed a threat to colonial authorities, who quickly suppressed it. Article 16 of the Code noir forbade slaves belonging to different masters to assemble, day or night, under any pretext, a measure that undoubtedly targeted dances. Later colonial legislation specifically prohibited slaves from dancing the Calenda and even created a special military division to stop it.[30] The increasing severity of the laws suggests, however, the persistence and flowering of these forms of slave culture, which were tacitly approved by many whites. Moreau exhibited considerable tolerance and an elated admiration for slave dances such as the Chica. "The impression that it causes is so powerful," he wrote, "that the African or the Creole, of whatever shade, who would watch without emotion would be regarded as having lost all but the last sparks of sensitivity" (64). Indeed, dance stirred the bodies and souls of performers and observers alike, thus compounding its subversive potential. Colonial writers in the late eighteenth century increasingly linked dance to African-derived religious practices, funerary rites, and magic.[31] Moreau's text is especially remarkable for providing the first detailed description of the syncretic cult of Vaudou, which combined rituals of divination, sacrifice, and dance.

According to Moreau, Vaudou was a cult of the serpent, embodying the spirit, power, and knowledge of the all-powerful supernatural being "*le vaudou*." The serpent communicated this power through his human representatives, the "grand priest" and "grand priestess," also known as the "king" and "queen." Moreau was acutely sensitive to the syncretic aspect of the sect, noting the influence of African and Creole customs mixed with "European ideas" (65). For the ritual ceremony, Vaudou believers assembled at night in total privacy before the king and queen. After renewing vows of adoration of the serpent, fidelity to the sect, and secrecy, initiates made invocations to a nonvenomous serpent held in a crate. The spirit's responses were communicated by the queen, who, upon mounting the crate, was figuratively penetrated by the serpent and spoke the divine oracle in a state of convulsive ecstasy. After a ceremony of offerings, the entire assembly joined in a possession dance called Vaudoux: Writes Moreau, "Swooning and fainting spells follow for some, and a kind of frenzy for others; but in everyone there is a nervous trembling that they seem unable to subdue" (67). The author also described an analogous possession dance called Don Pèdre, in which liquor and gunpowder provoked a heightened state of delirium.[32]

Modern interpreters of Vaudou contend that what Moreau described was the very form of "sacred marronnage" that would unify and sustain slaves in their freedom fight and remain the foundation of Haitian belief for the next two centuries.[33] The Vaudou initiation ritual represented a literal and figural freedom of the soul, with the neophyte being momentarily traversed and possessed by the Gods during the riveting trance. As though repudiating their condition under colonialism as violated bodies, human property sacrificed for profit in the material world, vaudou dancers became sacred vessels of higher powers that protected as well as dominated them. Essential to this process was the transfer of magical substances deemed powerful in warding off evil designs, accompanied in the ritual by chants sung in Kikongo. Moreau refers cynically to a "packet filled with herbs, animal hair, bits of horn and other equally disgusting things" held by the initiate as he or she dances, and he transcribes the accompanying song with no French translation (67).[34] Yet what bothered him and colonial authorities was less the real affect of magical powers than the seditious potential of Vaudou as a political organization that could invest absolute, metaphysical power in its leaders. Such authority could compete with, and indeed surpass, the temporal authority slave owners derived from the force of the whip. Imputing to the Vaudou queen actions that do not necessarily encourage "good order and public tranquility," Moreau de Saint-Méry denounces her as a charlatan: "She dictates all that pleases her to that assembly of imbeciles, that never raises the slightest doubt before the most monstrous absurdity, and that does nothing but obey what is despotically prescribed" (66). "In a word," he concludes, "nothing is more dangerous, according to all the accounts, than this cult of Vaudoux. It is founded on the extravagant idea, which can be made into a terrible weapon, that the ministers of the said being know and can do anything" (66).

If on one hand Moreau feared the subversive potential of Vaudou, his text is far more remarkable for exposing whites' inclination to partake of its incantatory force. As a respected jurist, high court counselor, and codifier of every colonial law on record, he had personally overseen the passage of prohibitions against slave dance and ritual. It is thus more than ironic that his detailed account of Vaudou exposed both its prevalence in the colony and the excited gaze of the white male participant-observer. His voyeurism is both rewarded and punished by the power of possession: "What is very true and remarkable in Vaudoux is this kind of hypnotism that brings followers to dance to the point of losing consciousness. . . . Whites found spying on the mysteries of the sect and who are touched by one of its members have sometimes begun to dance, and consented to pay the Vaudoux queen to put an end to their chastisement" (68). Far from debunking Vaudou's mystique, Moreau affirms it on the basis of the eyewitness's rapturous delirium. The symbolic importance of this conspicuous spy figure emerges against the backdrop of the author's numerous affirmations of secrecy in Vaudou. He insists that Vaudou is a secret society meeting at night in undisclosed locations, "closed and sheltered from any profane eye." Followers twice take an oath of secrecy on pain of death, and the ceremony proceeds only after it is confirmed that "no curious person has penetrated the enclosure" (65). This insistence on secrecy suggests that Vaudou's threat lay in the concerted attempt by devotees to evade the controlling gaze of colonial authority. If slaves organized fake, public versions of the Vaudou possession dance, it was to camouflage its secret powers and "quiet the alarm that this mysterious cult of Vaudoux causes in the colony" (68). In response, Moreau de Saint-Méry seems intent on accentuating the violence involved in telling the slaves' secrets. In so thoroughly and painstakingly explaining every detail of the Vaudou ritual, the author disclosed all that was most private, hidden, and sacred to the slaves. At the same time, the author as eyewitness betrayed a deep desire among white colonials to participate in and acculturate to black Creole rituals and dance forms. It is as though the campaign to wipe out slave culture was really about appropriating it. How else can we understand white women's frenetic attachment to dance as an almost spiritual rapture? "In short, the dance plunges them into such a delirium," writes Moreau, "that an outside spectator would believe that this pleasure has the greatest command over their souls" (41). In a short work entitled *Dance*, the earliest book on the subject published in the United States, he elaborated a general theory of dance, emphasizing its spiritual and emotional qualities and noting its propensity to sustain crowds all night long, as in a celebratory act of abandon and rejoicing. The essay confirms that in restricted balls the white ladies of Saint-Domingue feverishly danced the Afro-Creole styles of Calenda and Chica.[35]

While the author's positive appraisal of Creole slaves hinges on the ritual unveiling of their secrets and identification with their culture, one cannot fail to observe the gendered implications of that gesture. Consciously and unconsciously, sexuality structures Moreau's statements about all colonial peoples, manners, and customs. Even in the description of whites, moral depravation flows from undisciplined desires and a shocking lack of public decency in the colony. Afflicted with the generalized "taste for dissipation," European whites find Saint-Domingue to be a space of temptations ranging from gambling and sex to overeating and luxury. The stereotypical bourgeois son who ventures to the tropics "at an age at which desires are effervescent" will shorten his life because of them (33). The same is true for young white Creoles, whose poor education leads to a self-destructive search for pleasure: "Thus the Creole, losing sight of all that is not apt to satisfy his penchants, disdaining everything that does not carry the imprint of pleasure. . . . He seems to exist only for voluptuous enjoyment" (37). Less sexually self-indulgent than their male peers, white Creole women still suffer from an insatiable need for love, especially since, as Moreau claims, they habitually find themselves in the unflattering position of being the rivals of their slaves and free women of color.

Although the author lamented the lack of sexual morality among all social classes in Saint-Domingue, desire was nonetheless central to his vision of a socially cohesive Creole populace. Women figured prominently in an allegory of heterosexual desire that framed the legitimacy of white Creole rule in terms of the sexual submission of the enslaved. In fact, Moreau distinguished between African and Creole slave women on the basis of their receptiveness to sexual advances from white men:

> A very distinctive character of the négresses born in Africa is their invincible penchant for black men. Neither their acquaintance with whites; nor the advantages they find with them and that frequently include manumission for [the women] or their children; nor the fear of a punishment that pride and jealousy can render extremely severe; is sufficient to retain them. They fight for a while, or hide more or less happily this inclination which always prevails in the end. The proof is that they openly choose a black whenever an event happens that destroys their relations with white men." (57)

What begins as a commentary on African marital customs quickly devolves into a self-referential discourse of sexual desire, thus exposing the erotic subtext of colonial slavery. Through the voice of the narrator, white colonists appear as suitors in a fantasy of unrequited passion for African slave women. Bribery, promises of freedom, coercion, and brutality figure in the colonial arsenal of seduction, as the male narrator presumes the right to the bodies of slave women. Most surprising is that the ethnic preferences of African women are rationalized in terms of their "primitive education." Judging that African women seek partners with a similar mindset, language, and social status, the author adds the criterion of sexual stamina: "Perhaps also (and I have heard several negresses admit it) the advantage that nature . . . has given to black men over other men in what constitutes the physical agent of love greatly influences the choice for which the white man is but a pitiful competitor" (58).

Such a frank admission of sexual rivalry between white and black men reveals the primacy of sexual politics in the self-conception of white colonists. Moreau offsets the impact of losing the sexual contest by imputing to African men a supersexual urge and power typical of the discourse of the sexual savage. Elsewhere African men are devalued as polygamous, violently jealous, and vengeful. African women, however, are continually identified and judged on the basis of their sexuality. While female domestic slaves were chosen in large part for their attractiveness and desirability as mistresses, Moreau de Saint-Méry's ethnography confirms that *all* slave women were systematically mishandled and examined to determine their sexual worth for white Europeans. He openly discusses genital modifications he attributes to practices of excision in certain African cultures (51–52). His negative appraisal of Arada women supplements character insults with criticisms of a sexual anatomy considered too masculine. The most charitable comment is reserved for the Congolese, whom the author judges to be most accommodating of the sexual advances of the collective white male subject: "In a country where the morals are not of an exemplary purity, the Congolese negresses' penchant for libertinage has . . . increased ours for them" (53).

Predictably, then, the superiority of Creole slaves is figured in terms of seductive femininity and sexual permissiveness. So central is sexual *disponibilité*, or availability, to the ideologically coded definition of *Creole* that Moreau de Saint-Méry finds it incongruous for an African slave woman to both resist white men and emulate Creole slave women. In this sense, the *Description* is reminiscent of the orientalist imaginary of works such as Montesquieu's *Persian Letters* (1721, 1754), in which slavery is sexual and entails erotic reversals of the power dichotomy between ruler and ruled. As though slave women's sole labor is to attract the master's desire, Moreau de Saint-Méry praises their dental hygiene and frequent cold water baths, comparing their health and physical radiance to that of Ethiopian beauties, who far surpass fairer-skinned women's charms in torrid climes (62). He delights further in the exchange of sensual and sumptuary luxury whereby white men serve the slave women they claim to love: "The greatest token of love that one can give a negress is to take her to a merchant to choose the superb Indian and Persian muslins from which she makes her skirts." Here Moreau evokes slave women in the bustling urban centers such as Cap François, where sexual slavery was an open commerce.[36] So strong is their economic and sexual influence over white men that their own status as material possession is conveniently suspended: "How many of them use intrigue to inspire hope in credulous lovers when, having been duped for a long time, they realize that their presents have not gotten them any rights! We have seen negresses who had as many as one hundred negligees, valued at no less than two thousand French écus" (77).

Yet if Moreau models his ideal of Creole slave femininity on the image of the urban courtesan, his representation of plantation life and culture is no less structured by the allegory of white male desire. In scenes of gallantry between slaves in the cane fields, the male characters serve as foils for the author's own persona and that of his class. The slave, unable to contain the pulsing desire in his veins, travels great distances in the night, braving fatigue, geographical obstacles, and the occasional zombi, to reach the arms of his true love. It is a "lovers' audacity" memorialized, says Moreau, in Creole songs (70). This reference to song points to the importance of orality both to slaves and to the masters who reinterpreted slave experience, especially in matters of love. Moreau concludes his segment on Creole slaves with a discussion of the Creole language, whose role in linking radically opposed social groups cannot be overestimated. For, in addition to functioning as a vehicular language for the ethnically diverse population of Africans, Creole provided a means of communication between masters and slaves.[37] Some scholars have argued that masters observed and participated in rituals of storytelling and singing associated with oral slave cultures, such that the subversive aspect of the culture had to be deftly disguised.[38] Almost all previous observers of colonial life had regarded Creole as "gibberish" unworthy of a cultured tongue. Moreau de Saint-Méry refuted this view, taking issue in particular with Justin Girod de Chantrans's condescending assessment in his *Voyage d'un Suisse dans les colonies d'Amérique.*[39] For Moreau, Creole is a language with an inestimable dexterity of expression and intonation, such that "a European, no matter how familiar he may be with [Creole], or how long he has resided in the islands, will never possess its finesses" (81). Moreau asserts that Creoles of all complexions use the Creole language, and the Blacks have no other among them (83).[40] He asserts furthermore that French is actually inadequate to colonial life and culture: "There are a thousand little nothings that one would not dare say in French, a thousand voluptuous images that cannot be rendered with French, but that Creole expresses with infinite grace" (81).

The relationship between Creole and volupté is telling of the male indulgence that typified colonial slavery. To illustrate Creole eloquence, the author inserts a text he describes as "a well known song, which will show whether the Creole language is an insignificant and unsavory language"

(81). The song, known by its first line as "Lisette quitté la plaine," is believed to be the earliest written text in the Creole language, dating from the
mid–eighteenth century.[41] It was composed by Duvivier de la Mahautière, a
member of the Superior Council in Port-au-Prince. The poem in five stan-
zas evokes the story of a slave abandoned by his love, who departs for the
city. Moreau includes the original and a French translation. Translated from
French to English, the first stanza reads as follows.

> Lisette, you've left the plain;
> My happiness has gone away.
> My tears, like two fountains,
> Flow onto your path.
> All the day, harvesting cane,
> I dream of your sweet charms.
> A reverie in my cabin
> At night puts you back in my arms.[42]

Patrick Chamoiseau and Raphaël Confiant have argued that the poem's
images and rhetoric betray the white writer's stylistic imitation of Renaissance poets such as Du Bellay or Ronsard. By invoking classic European
metaphors such as fountains for tears and lamenting that "work calls me
in vain," the speaker suggests a range of experience and choice that a slave
would clearly not have. Chamoiseau and Confiant conclude that the love-
lorn speaker is more likely a white Creole planter lamenting the departure
of his mulatto mistress.[43]

But the text is far more remarkable in its use of Creole to romanticize
the plantation, cane fields, and slave culture as a stage for gallantry and flir-
tation. By composing a song in Creole, the author goes against the more
common literary practice in Saint-Domingue, which was to vent personal
animosities and satirize the lubricity of colonial life in short verse written
in French.[44] The text of "Lisette quitté la plaine" suggests that, in contrast,
the Creole language allowed whites to express themes of love and rural simplicity by beautifying the life of slaves. It was a "frenchified" Creole, to be
sure, one that became known as Salon Creole, as opposed to the *gros créole* spoken by field slaves.[45] Still, by appropriating the slave male voice the
author identifies with key elements of slave culture, including dance and
performance: "My steps, far from Lisette, / stay away from the Calinda; /
And my sash fitted with bells / languishes on my *bamboula*."[46] In typical
pastoral fashion, the speaker contrasts the misery and corruption of the city
with the plantation, where his love, like his speech, is true: "You will find

in the city, / More than one young frivolous suitor, / Their mouth artfully distils / A honey sweet but full of seasoning."[47] As for the love object, the poem is clearly addressed to the black slave woman. Lisette is a negress, a fact that comes through clearly in the Creole original.[48] But what is at the center of the poem is the subjective male experience of love and chagrin. Through an ironic pastiche of the slave's discourse, the author finds a socially acceptable medium in which to express the repressed desire of the masters for enslaved black women. As the earliest example of a literature in Creole produced by white colonials, this poem indicates, furthermore, the extent to which colonial whites relied on black Creole culture to represent themselves. The poem promotes agrarian values in a slave society, suggesting that love will fill the deepest void. But, lest there be any doubt as to the iron limitations placed on the loves, dreams, and desires of actual slaves, Moreau includes one final distinction between Africans and Creoles: "The inhabitants of the French colony have Africans branded on the breast with their name or initials" (83).

Colors of White

As the foregoing analysis has shown, Moreau de Saint-Méry's ethnography posits "Creole" as both a language and a culture that transcends the race and class differences within the colonial population. This unifying cultural identity has a significant erotic underpinning. In feminizing the class of slaves the author constructs an allegory of desire, such that Creole identity is symbolically associated with the sexual coupling of master and slave. The allegory becomes explicit in the description of the last denomination of colonial society, the affranchis (freedmen), also described as gens de couleur (people of color) and sang-mêlés (mixed-bloods). The slippage in terminology points to the conflation of the intermediate category between "free" and "slave" with racial métissage. Moreau's description of the "free" class privileges its racial variety, presenting this group as the umbrella category for the entire racial spectrum of colonial humanity: "The affranchis ... offer a great variety of shades from their mixture with whites, blacks and between themselves" (86). In so privileging racial hybridity as the distinguishing trait of the affranchis, it is as though the author takes them to be the quintessential Creoles, born in the colony from the sexual union of masters and slaves. As such, his description of the affranchis raises the question of the relation between creolization and métissage in the colonial imagination.

The section is undoubtedly the best-known part of Moreau's enormous work, as it is dominated by an extraordinary taxonomy that defines and rationalizes the racial makeup of this class. Undertaking the tabular and arithmetic definition of *nuances de la peau*, the author claims to classify all variations of color in persons belonging to the intermediate class between free and slave, those who bear the trace of blackness in their genealogies if not on their bodies. Unprecedented in scope, this racial science typifies what some critics have termed the "colonial" or "Antillean" Enlightenment. It was inspired by contemporary innovations in algebra and statistics, as well as the Enlightenment anthropology of figures such as Buffon and De Pauw. Yet, whereas the philosophes in Europe theorized the blending of "races" with an empirical immunity that displayed only a naive belief in white supremacy, the colonial practitioners of racial science radicalized this notion, instituting the taxonomy as an instrument of social control.[49] Indeed, Moreau de Saint-Méry's obsessive "calculus of color" posits an "ultimate racial boundary supporting the notion of racial hierarchy" and discriminatory policies in the public sphere.[50] As Joan Dayan has shown, this color classification relies heavily on metaphors of animality and degeneration, as well as a fantasy of blood contagion that added a metaphysical dimension to the "epistemology of whiteness."[51]

Yet insofar as racial thinking fixates on the issue of sexual unions between blacks and whites, theories of race represent, as Robert Young has argued, "covert theories of desire."[52] As theories of desire, they are also theories of sexual power with distinct ideological overtones. In the last chapter, we saw the way in which colonial libertinage was supported by the prohibitive function of the law, which worked to disallow the transfer of power to the illegitimate family triad. The question remained, however, as to the management of white male libido and the demographic consequences of transracial desiring. Ann Laura Stoler and Frederick Cooper clarify the competing interests of colonial sexualities and regimes of power when they point out that "while the colonies were marketed by colonial elites as a domain where colonizing men could indulge their sexual fantasies, those same elites were intent to mark the boundaries of a colonizing population . . . [and] to curb a proliferating mixed-race population that compromised their claims to superiority and thus the legitimacy of white rule."[53] It is fascinating, then, to consider the extent to which the racial taxonomy tells stories not only about sex and the limits of racial purity but also about who has the power to reproduce. This possibility rejoins Foucault's critical insight into the inherent "biopolitical" aspect of discourse about sex, that is, its concern with the regulatory control of populations and biological reproduction.[54] Turning to Moreau de Saint-Méry's racial taxonomy, I will pursue two related questions. How does the racial text rationalize the release of white libidinal energies across the colonial color spectrum while at the same time marking the limits of white racial purity? More importantly, what anxieties does the taxonomy relay about the ability of the white elite to manage the biological reproduction of colonial society so as to ensure its own survival within it?

At its origin, Moreau's classificatory system presupposes a fantasy: that of a white male coupling with a black female, whose offspring begins a chain of successive couplings, always with the same white male factor crossing with the mixed-race female product of his prior union, to the nth degree. Such is the incestuous logic of the first six categories of color between white and black, on which Moreau founds his racial organization of colonial humanity. He names these successive degrees of whiteness *mulâtre, quarteron, métis, mamelouc, quarteronné*, and finally *sang-mêlé*, signaling the last identifiable class before the lineage fades imperceptibly into whiteness. Moreau's chosen terminology considerably expands that of his predecessor, Hilliard d'Auberteuil. Hilliard had named, for the purposes of segregation, four degrees of racial difference, including *mulâtre* and *quarteron* on the side of whiteness and *griffe* and *marabou* on the side of blackness.[55] Moreau expands the range between mulatto and white, recuperating the term, *métis* from its previous usage referring to the first degree of mixture between Europeans and Indians and applying it to a greater degree of whiteness.[56] The word *mamelouc*, etymologically a variation of an Egyptian word meaning "one who is possessed, slave," had been used in Brazil to denote the children of Portuguese men and Indian women.[57] Moreau's emphasis, indeed his obsession, lies on the white side of the archetypal blending of the races, for on the side of blackness he adds but one new racial denominator to Hilliard's griffe and marabou: *sacatra*. As Joan Dayan has shown, these terms referred to the animal world, a clear indicator of the degradation associated with a "descent" into blackness.[58] The foundational table of racial difference thus appears as "Combinations of the White."

D'un Blanc et d'une	Négresse, vient	un Mulâtre
"	Mulâtresse	Quarteron
"	Quarteron	Métis
"	Métive	Mamelouque
"	Mamelouque	Quarteronné

"	Quarteronnée		Sang-mêlé
"	Sang-mêlée	Sang-mêlé, qui s'approche continuellement du Blanc.	
"	Marabou		Quarteron
"	Griffonne		Quarteron
"	Sacatra		Quarteron

(I, 86)

Whereas the first six instances of racial mixing yield varieties approaching whiteness, the last three deviate from this genealogy, involving rather the combination of the white male term with degrees of female blackness. The exercise of racial naming thus reveals eleven terms representing that many points on the racial spectrum from white to black. From these, Moreau de Saint-Méry displays the results of combinations of each term with the other ten, resulting in eleven tabular arrangements of theoretical couplings. Adding East Indians and West Indians as two final categories of race, he identifies "thirteen distinct classes, as for the nuance of the skin, in individuals who form the population . . . of Saint-Domingue" (89).

What is immediately apparent from Moreau de Saint-Méry's racial thinking is the deep anxiety it reveals about the empirical connection between generational alchemies of race worked out on paper and actual human variety in Saint-Domingue. The elaborate taxonomy is founded on a belief in the racial purity of the first two factors—black and white—and a confidence that skin color adequately reflects these and the degrees of mixture between them. Yet at every turn the tabulations seem only to suggest the absurdity of dividing humanity by degrees of skin color, for even Moreau cannot quite decide to what extent heredity drives physical appearance. The initial succession of métissage, tending toward white, obeys what Jean-Luc Bonniol calls a "genealogical principle" of racial classification, whereby the categories ignore physical color to designate instead genealogically determined points on an axis between white and black poles. However, the fact that Moreau de Saint-Méry works with only a limited number of racial signifiers to denote what would be an infinite number of possible genealogies suggests that he prioritizes a phenotypic basis of classification.[59] Thus, in the table, the last two degrees of whiteness combined with white always yields sang-mêlé, and the mixture of white with three varieties of blackness produces a constant quarteron. A further problem arises when he admits degrees of color within each category, stretching the limits of whiteness beyond the imagination. For each step on the way toward white, he devises an inventive poetics with which to render the visible (or invisible) trace of race. Mulattoes, for example, can be two shades, described in the language of alchemy as that of "red copper" and "yellow copper" (90). The white skin of a quarteron is "tarnished by a nuance of a very faint yellow." Métis are very white, but their whiteness is "not at all animated" (91). The color of the mamelouc is "a discolored, matte white, on which one can make out something of a yellowish tint. . . . It lacks elasticity" (92). The terminal category of sang-mêlé signals by its very name the passage from color to blood, as Moreau declares the trace of blackness to be barely detectable to the eye, requiring instead verification with genealogical records. Here race becomes chimerical, a fantasy, as the author seems to admit, of the colonial imagination: "Colonial prejudice has adopted the maxim that however close [in color] the nonwhite woman may be to the white, their procreation would not produce a white" (89).

The author's confidence in categories of color breaks down when he confesses that inconsistencies in actual color cause confusion within classes. He admits, for example, that a person whose parents are of a light complexion may nonetheless be of even darker hue than a person from an "inferior" class (96). In this case, the tables are but a theory of color difference, a hypothetical onomastics of an idealized racial spectrum. Reconfiguring racial being in terms of the fractional composition of 128 genealogical parts, he proposes a mathematical coefficient as a surer way to delimit genetically determined color categories. Each category is given a fractional value corresponding to the proportion of black and white blood; for example, mulattoes range from 49 to 70 parts white, quarterons 71–100, and so on. But this leads the author into ever more fantastic limits of whiteness, as he takes his fractions into the thousands to represent the hypothetical eighth generation of sang-mêlés at 1 part black to 8,191 parts white. At this point, the visible signifier of racial origins is believed to return in uncanny ways: "They say that . . . if the clue is not found in the color, it is in the assemblage of traits, in a flattened nose, in thick lips, that reveal all too well their origin" (100).

One of the most significant conclusions of Moreau's racial taxonomy is his admission that an excess of racial paranoia threatens to consume whites themselves, foreshadowing the emergence of nineteenth-century racisms that would collapse phenotypic and national differences among Europeans. Thus, he cautions the reader against the "eye of prejudice," which, if it strolled across the European continent, would surely find "with this system, the wherewithal to develop a colored nomenclature, because who has not observed, when traveling in this part of the world, rather dark tints and traits that seem to belong to Africa?" Already the fact that the author figures East and West Indians within his taxonomy is suggestive of the totalizing reach of his racial thinking. Most threatening are questions about the purity of colonial whites who fall from grace not by mésalliance but by physical degeneration "in a climate where the skin of the European itself takes on a yellowish tone when exposed for long enough" (100).

On several occasions, then, Moreau de Saint-Méry concludes that there is no sure correlation between genealogy and skin color, thus undermining the utility of both the tabular and fractional classification systems. What remains is the process of racial identification itself: the mathematical attempt to rationalize and map out the human evidence of métissage that imperiled white colonial rule. On one hand, his system reveals the paranoia sweeping the class of masters in Saint-Domingue, insistent on claiming for themselves the right to rule based on their racial purity. The question of just how white is white was contemporaneous with the increase in property ownership and prosperity among free people of color in the late eighteenth century. As early as the 1760s, conflicting opinions were voiced by those in power on the question of admitting "white" sangs-mêlés to the ruling elite. In 1766, the French minister of the navy, the Duke of Praslin, reiterated the principle of race as an "indelible stain" of slavery: "As a consequence, those who descend from [slavery] may never enter into the class of whites. Because, if ever there was a time when they could be reputed to be white, they would enjoy all the privileges of whites, and could, like them, aspire to all offices and dignities, which would be absolutely contrary to the constitutions of the colonies."[60] Hilliard d'Auberteuil judged the sixth generation to be the cutoff point for the category of white, since he considered this degree of nuance to be imperceptible.[61] In 1776 the Chamber of Agriculture at Cap Français recommended that legitimate quarterons born free be considered white.[62] By the time Moreau was writing, however, no compromise seemed possible given the force of "opinion," which, "not admitting the possibility of the total disappearance of the trace of the mixture, consequently wishes a line prolonged until infinity forever to separate the white race [*descendance*] from the other" (99).

Yet, as much as the racial calculus stigmatizes mixed-race persons as forever bound by their putative origins in slavery, it may also be read as a legitimating allegory of elite male sexual power on the island. The notion of an infinitely receding limit of whiteness can only be imagined by representing repeated métissage between white men and nonwhite women. In this respect, the taxonomy reveals what Robert Young has called "an ambivalent driving desire at the heart of racialism: a compulsive libidinal attraction disavowed by an equal insistence on repulsion."[63] In Foucauldian terms, discourse about interracial sex functions less to repress it than to name, define, and validate the very desires that it would seem to prohibit.[64] By conjuring the infinitesimal degrees of whiteness that still bear the trace of blackness, Moreau rehearses the taboo mixing of the races in a phantasm of interracial sex, with the white male term repeatedly crossing with the nonwhite female, never to reproduce itself perfectly. That the colored woman's body mediates the interracial crossing is crucial. Moreau's racial tables certainly allow for the possibility of white females giving birth to mixed-race babies. In the first phase of analysis, the taxonomic tables show a male term from one racial category coupling with females from the other ten categories, including "white." In the next two phases of analysis, however, Moreau fixes the sex of the terms such that it is always the white or colored male who mates with the colored female.[65] This erasure of white womanhood from the final analysis of racial mixture points to the true taboo of colonial métissage. For, if Moreau's obsessive demonstration of interracial sex seems to ratify it as a colonial practice, it does so by repressing white women as partners. Moreau's schema is thus selective in whose desires it normalizes. Dropping out of the allegory of the illegitimate interracial family, the white woman remains the protected domain of white colonial patriarchy.

Yet, whereas Moreau manages to evade the frightening prospect of white women giving birth to colored children and colored women giving birth to white children, his taxonomy cannot but conjure the threatening specter of white racial extinction via the colored woman's body. Ironically, by pushing the boundary between "white" and sang-mêlé to the limits of mathematical reason, the author theorizes the very means by which pure whites would be vastly outnumbered by the products of their sexual encounters. In this sense, the taxonomy confronts what whites could no longer ignore in colonial demographics, for the "bodily legacy of white colonial patriarchy" was the unbounded growth in mixed-race populations.[66] In the two decades prior to the revolution, the numbers of free people of color had increased at nearly twice the rate of whites in the same period, so that the two populations were nearly equivalent at about thirty thousand persons.[67] I would argue that Moreau de Saint-Méry's taxonomy implicitly resolves the conflict between colonial desires and the threat of unlimited métissage for the biological reproduction of colonial society. I read this colonial racial science as an ideology of sexual power, racial supremacy, *and* biopolitics, one that validates the libidinal freedom of the white elite while at the same time fantasizing a limit to its reproductive effects. Even as it seems to posit the eventual disappearance of the white ruling class, Moreau's taxonomy authorizes and prescribes not only whose desires may be fulfilled but also who has the power to reproduce.

We must return to the rhetoric of race and métissage in order to discover how, at the heart of his theory, Moreau de Saint-Méry invokes a discourse of degeneration that forecloses the threat of unlimited growth in the population of mixed race. Indeed, his categories are more than simply degrees of color; they represent steps in a process of physical and moral transformation. The question of degeneration recalls the very origins of the term *mulatto*, which derives from *mule* and implies the crossing of two species to form a hybrid. When first describing mulattoes in the seventeenth century, Father Du Tertre wrote: "These poor children are engendered from a white male and a black female, just as the mule is the product of two animals of different species."[68] The analogy in Du Tertre exploded into a full-scale debate in the following century over races and species. For eighteenth-century philosophers and natural historians, the question of whether blacks and whites belonged to different species was central to debates about the origins and unity of humanity. By the middle of the century, two major schools of thought had emerged: monogenesis, the belief that all humans comprise a single species; and polygenesis, the belief that different races constitute different species.[69]

In his natural historical treatise *De l'homme*, Buffon elaborated the view that all humanity belongs to the same species, defined as "a constant succession of similar individuals who reproduce themselves."[70] For him, differences in the color, physique, and character of the world's peoples merely proved the impact of environment, climate, and food on human beings and did not preclude the joining of the races in fertile unions.[71] Far from being an aberration of nature, the mulatto proved the unity of the human species insofar as he or she could reproduce. Métissage was central to Buffon's idea of natural variety within the species, as it contributed to the continuum of color around the globe.[72] Mulattoes were thus no more degenerate than any other group, since Buffon subjected all people to the possibility of degeneration due to the progressive dispersal of humanity through the ages from its putative origins in temperate climates.[73] Yet a slippage in the naturalist's use of the terms *race*, *species*, and *variety* allowed for ambiguity on the possible degeneration of one species into another, thus of humans into another species.[74] In this respect, Buffon unwittingly left an opening for Voltaire's polygenetic argument. Voltaire contested Buffon's theory of variation within the species, claiming that blacks and whites belonged to different species. In the introduction to his *Essai sur les moeurs*, he presented gory descriptions of blacks dissected by Dutch naturalists to prove that their color reaches their very core. Voltaire had no less disdain for mulattoes, whom he referred to as "animals of their species" and "a bastard race."[75] Elsewhere he obliquely rejected Buffon's inclusive notion of degeneration, which encompassed all races: "Never did a slightly educated man suggest that non-mixed species degenerated."[76]

Nowhere does Moreau de Saint-Méry claim that whites and slaves constitute different species, and throughout the nearly twenty pages of analysis, the word "race" appears only once.[77] That the author uses terms such as "tint," "color," and "nuance" to refer to human variety, rather than "race" or "species," suggests his affinity with Buffon's monogenetic theories of natural variety.[78] In addition, the genealogical principle driving his taxonomy presupposes that the sexual union of whites and blacks forms a fertile population. Yet his animalized racial names and narrative description of each category belie this fact, revealing that he associates the alchemy of color with notable changes in physique, such that continued amalgamation leads to degeneration. What is more, he supposes a degree of sterility in persons of mixed race as they approach white, following from both physiological and moral causes.

The mulatto type emerges, first and foremost, as the most advantageous blend of the author's stereotyped notions of black physicality and white delicacy and intelligence: "He has the strongest constitution, the most analogous to the climate of Saint-Domingue" (90). He exhibits the additional benefit of extended age and attractiveness and is naturalized as the quintessential man of the senses: "He is the man of this climate that burns, of this zone where man seems to be devoted to pleasure" (90). Farther along in the lineage of racial whitening, however, physical abnormalities and weaknesses begin to appear, calling into question the very ability to reproduce. Quarterons display a marked lack of vigor and greater vulnerability to climate than whites do: "The climate of Saint-Domingue being less favorable to children whose color approaches white, quarterons thrive but little" (107). Métifs suffer an even more serious state of physical precariousness. Close to the white in appearance and intelligence, they are weaker, more susceptible to climate, and nearly sterile. Thus, the métif "barely reproduces himself, and they are already a rare thing" (92). For mameloucs, the reproductive prognosis grows ever more severe: "Mameloucs who are the product of the mamelouc with the mamelouque, are perhaps rare enough that one would not find four of them in all the colony, and this fact would not be surprising considering what I said about the degeneration of the people of color, after the quarteron" (92).

Moreau de Saint-Méry was not the only one of his time to posit the declining fertility of mulattoes; he was preceded in this by a white planter from Jamaica, Edward Long, whose best-known work, *History of Jamaica*, was published in 1774. Long maintained that whites and blacks constitute two distinct species, and that the fertility of mulattoes diminished if they joined with other mixed-race hybrids. His belief that their unions with whites continued to be fertile reflected his anxiety about an unlimited racial amalgamation capable of consuming the race of white Englishmen. Long's description of racial contamination is replete with metaphors of metallic impurity and infectious disease: "This alloy may spread so extensively, as even to reach the middle, and then the higher orders of people, till the whole nation resembles the Portuguese and the Moriscos in complexion of skin and baseness of mind. This is a venomous and dangerous ulcer, that threatens to disperse its malignancy far and wide, until every family catches infection from it."[79] Whereas Long sounds a warning for those whites who persist in their interracial sexual relations, thus inflating the population of color, Moreau de Saint-Méry actually denies such consequences. The crucial site of this denial is the colored woman's body. For, while infertility characterizes the third and fourth generation of white métissage (métifs and mameloucs), the infertility hypothesis is most crucial where women of color are concerned, since they are the repeated objects of white colonial desire and bear mixed-race children.

What is fascinating is that in order to call radically into question the fertility of women of color, Moreau relies not solely on genetic-physiological arguments but on moral and social ones. For him, the celebration of luxury, lust, and volupté in women of color was not merely a means of displacing white interracial desire or denying the asymmetries of power that characterize such relationships. Indeed, stereotypes of mulatto women proved to be doubly functional in the colonial racial ideology, as they allowed the white elite to disavow the threat that interracial sexuality posed to colonial demographics. By assigning to free women of color the role of sexual temptress bent on avenging colonial racism with "weapons of pleasure," Moreau suppresses their maternal capacity, thus denying them any role in the biological reproduction of colonial society. His explanation for infertility in "*le sexe coloré*" thus joins social causes to claims of physiological degeneration: "Recall that I mentioned the mulâtresses as the most precocious Creoles. This quality, their natural disposition, the seductions of their fellow men, the effect of a reputation that attaches to the entire class, are so many causes that destine them, early on, for incontinence. You would be sorry to learn to what extent this disorder has increased, and that sometimes the period that separates childhood from puberty and that belongs, so to speak, equally to both, is hardly respected. From that follows all evils, of which the inability to reproduce is not the least, or the coming of offspring who are feeble and weak" (104–5). Moreau's narrative reinscribes the specter of mulatto sterility by emphasizing the premature prostitution of women of color. Ironically, nature explains not the sterility itself but the behaviors and "disposition" that lead to it. The author laments this state of things even as he conceals the role of white colonial desire by positioning mulatto men in place of the white lovers he describes elsewhere in his work. The lack of issue from mulatto women's relations with their men is attributed to their premature bodily corruption and physical rapture. Libertinage, we are told, bears no fruit: "After all, the corruption of morals that leads all vices in its path, makes the mulâtresses fear maternity. Hence the means and perhaps the crimes that protect them from it" (107).

Roger Toumson has argued that the image of a de facto sterility in the mulatto woman acts to restore the supposed natural order of racial separation that was transgressed in producing her.[80] Yet in the opposite sense the trope strongly enables the perpetual libidinal transgression of the color line, liberated from the unconscious fear of increase in the caste of mixed bloods. Furthermore, Moreau de Saint-Méry's figure of mulata sterility recalls tropes in clandestine literature and medical discourse of the eighteenth century, specifically concerning the relationship among sex, pleasure, and fertility. For Moreau, what precludes maternity in mulatto women is the precocity of their sexual affairs, a theme recalling a licentious novel, *Le rideau levé*, published in 1788 and attributed to Mirabeau.[81] In this story, the sexual awakening of the central character and first-person narrator, Laure, is contrasted with that of her friend Rose, whose prepubescent entry into sexual activity leads to a disastrously obsessive sexual appetite, illness, and premature death. In addition to making women languish in a weak, sickly state, precocious sex permanently threatens the reproductive organs.[82] A related idea in early modern sexual ideology supposed that precocity, joined with excessive indulgence in pleasure, leads to degenerate offspring. Nicolas Venette's classic 1687 treatise on sex and marriage, *Tableau de l'amour conjugal*, maintained that while jouissance is a necessary condition of conception, overindulgence in it can debilitate both partners. Furthermore, the insatiable female who engages in repeated intercourse would likely produce a girl child. The implication is that moderation leads to the more perfect male offspring and that sexual excess diminishes the procreative function.[83]

As Nancy K. Miller has argued, the fantasy of libertinism was to imagine that women could play the game as well as men, a fact that required either the denial or the artful evasion of the "rule of consequence."[84] Yet, whereas libertine writers could simply ignore questions of fertility and reproduction, Moreau's particular ideological needs actually *demanded* a theory of female sterility through libertinage. Indeed, the fiction of libertinage, degeneration, and infertility in women of color allowed members of the white elite to deny their colored mistresses any role in the reproduction of colonial society, thereby repressing their anxieties about uncontrolled growth in the free population of color.[85] Far from desiring the eventual extinction of the free people of color, however, Moreau actually delegates responsibility for their production to the primal instance of interracial coupling between the white male and black female. The author is emphatic about what he believes to be the true origins of the mulatto race: "It is the concubinage of whites with negresses, that accounts for why the free mulattoes are so numerous" (107). So convinced is he of this filiation, that he predicts the quick disappearance of the free class without it: "There would thus be no error in maintaining that if the free mulattoes were not recruited from the children of whites and negresses, it would take this class much less time to disappear than was required for it to reach its current level" (108). Left to themselves, persons of mixed race would become extinct, owing, we may presume, to both their defective physiology and their sexually profligate lifestyles. For Moreau, what is necessary for their survival, and by extension the survival of the colony, is the continued consummation of the original desire of masters for their slaves, of white men for black women.

Thus in Moreau's biopolitical fantasy the libertine and sterile mulata represents the endpoint of a previous fertile liaison between white men and black slave women. The author's justification for sordid liaisons on the plantation relies on the supposition of their positive social effects and natural necessity: "It seems that [this illegitimate commerce that offends morality] prevents greater vices: the weakness of masters for slaves causes slavery to be softened. One might go so far as to say that the heat of the climate that irritates desire, and the ease of satisfying it, will always render useless the legislative precautions that one will want to take against this abuse. The law remains quiet where nature speaks imperiously" (107–8). Moreau bases his apology for the transracial desire of his class on an a priori claim to the bodies of black women and on the laws of nature, which make illegitimate sexual relationships an inevitable function of climate and desire. Neutralizing the problem of vice by affirming the positive effects of sex on slavery as an institution, the author suggests that slave women benefit from the "softening" of their masters toward them. Especially remarkable is the language that allows Moreau to claim the fertility of relationships on the plantation. In a passage from the manuscript, he makes clear his belief that offspring follow more naturally from the satisfaction of male sexual "need" than mere libertinage.[86] If such affairs bear fruit, it is because of the natural, instinctual desires that motivate them, in defiance of all social laws. The reference to the Code noir, which punished precisely those interracial sexual liaisons that produced illegitimate mulatto offspring, cannot be missed. Challenging the prohibitive function of the law, Moreau opposes nature as the unassailable foundation of sexual urges and their procreative consequences, thus absolving the colonist from any social or moral wrongdoing.

Two critical implications follow from this stunning admission. On one hand, Moreau's ethnographic allegory suggests that the brutal logic of the colonial economy of reproduction of both enslaved and free people of color hinges on the slave woman's body.[87] The perceived population needs of the colony become a means of rationalizing her continued subjection to the master's desires. Furthermore, by affirming the primacy of the master-slave relation for colonial biopolitics, Moreau constructs a fantasy of white male paternity over the entire class of mulattoes, thus effectively denying them any significant role in the biological reproduction of colonial society. The ideological importance of such a move is unmistakable, for in affirming a paternal filiation with mulattoes the author essentially defines free people of color as the masters' bastards, to be dominated and controlled as such. What we have, then, is a representation of the whole of colonial society on the model of filiation comprised of white master, black female slave, and mulatto offspring. Moreau de Saint-Méry was not alone in invoking a notion of family as a means of consolidating political authority over nonwhites. Colonial claims of white paternity reflect changing attitudes toward the class of mixed race that were bound up in the desire of the white elite to both control and subjugate it. This was especially true after the 1760s, when the numbers and wealth of free people of color increased dramatically and whites tried to attract their support for an insurrection against the metropolitan administration. Hilliard d'Auberteuil argued for the importance of maintaining a viable mulatto class, distinct in its skin color and restricted civil rights.

Like Moreau, he also believed in "producing" this class through the sexual relationships between white men and slave women.[88] Émilien Petit, a member of the Superior Council at Port-au-Prince and a direct predecessor of Moreau de Saint-Méry as codifier of colonial law, wished to capitalize further on the ideological uses of white paternity. In his two-volume treatise on colonial slave law, *Traité sur le gouvernement des esclaves*, Petit proposed that not only should all natural children of the master be freed but they should be recognized and financially supported by him. Petit believed that, in addition to imposing a sort of tax on concubinage, the payments would encourage mulatto political fidelity to the white "father" and, by extension, the entire class of whites.[89]

Moreau de Saint-Méry's own language in the preceding passage on the origins of mulattoes points to the predominant means of exploiting the mulatto population for the maintenance of the colonial social order. By using the military term *recruit* to signify the birth of persons of mixed race, he alludes to the actual militarization of colored men throughout the eighteenth century in Saint-Domingue. As early as 1724, the government had conscripted free blacks into military service to chase fugitive slaves. While most of the century saw the passage of major restrictions on manumission, there were also intentional loopholes that encouraged masters to free mulattoes by conscripting them into the militia for ten years of service.[90] Military service became an easy way for masters to bail their illegitimate sons out of slavery without any bureaucratic or financial hassle. For the administration, free men of color represented an available workforce for policing and defending the colony. Moreau de Saint-Méry explains that the doubling of the affranchi, or "free" population, between 1770 and 1780 was due mainly to filial solicitude and the need to "recruit" members of the *maréchaussée*, or rural police. On the more staggering growth of gens de couleur between 1780 and 1790, he cites, in addition to an increase in mixed marriages, the need to fortify the colony's defenses and infrastructure with revenue from manumission taxes and/or the physical service of the freedmen (85).[91] During this period, mulatto recruits were relegated to special units of the colonial militia and maréchaussée responsible for the pursuit of maroon slaves, vagabonds, and white bandits (holdovers from the days of buccaneering), as well as to a new expeditionary force, the Chasseurs Royaux. The historian Stewart King has suggested that security "may have been the most important function of the class, from the point of view of the colony's leaders."[92] Still, the recruitment of mulattoes into the colonial armed forces did little to improve their social status. On the contrary, concomitant with the increasing reliance on mulattoes to defend the colony, elites in Saint-Domingue excluded military service as a basis of civic virtue.[93]

Consistent with his justification of mulatto population growth in terms of the interests of the colonial elite, Moreau depicts the stereotyped mulatto man as a weak-willed, easily manipulated instrument of colonial power. He reconciles the image of military discipline with that of sloth, selfishness, and lust. Chronically adolescent, the mulatto is at the behest of his pathological craving for *volupté*, even when "made" into an "excellent soldier." Physically well-formed like the black, intelligent and capable of skill in the arts and shop crafts like poor whites, he is perpetually held back by "indolence and love of rest" (103). No mention is made of the entrepreneurial ambition that accounted for mulatto property acquisitions in urban and plantation real estate. Moreau only indirectly recognizes mulatto wealth by mockingly enumerating the fashionable mulatto's wardrobe—"the jacket, the fine-cloth pants, the smart hat, and the kerchiefs at head and neck are dear to him" (104). Still, he is but a mimic, whose love for European finery will not suppress the stain of blackness, which, for Moreau, reappears with a vengeance in old age, bringing about the yellowing of the whites of the eyes—a familiar trope in racial physiognomy—and the appearance of splotches he calls *lotas*, which cause "a change in the skin characterized by ugliness and deformity" (104). His stereotyped mulatto retains atavistic traits of the slave in his appearance as well as his physique, traits to be exploited by the dominant class:

> We make the mulatto into an excellent soldier. . . . In the Torrid Zone, there could not be a more valuable warrior than he who lives on little; who is happy with roots and fruits that the climate produces; who does not fear the sun and who needs no clothes, so to speak; who climbs a mountain with agility; who knows how to get to the top of a tree and who is a sufficiently good hunter that he almost never misses a shot. . . . It is the mulattoes who commonly pursue fugitive slaves, and we judge from that their superiority over all other soldiers; especially since when they take off their shoes, they have the same advantages as the slave who uses his bare feet to climb up on rocks, or go down steep cliffs. (103–4)

The emphasis here is on the *lack* of clothing, the naked foot, the animal-like dexterity, the ability to climb a tree, scale a mountain, and capture a runaway. The old climatic stereotype dies hard and here retains elements of a Carib imaginary, since the mulatto is figured as the quintessential native, naturally able to scavenge off the land. Stepping out of his shoes, symbolic of the trappings of the culture he has illegitimately usurped, the mulatto is but a noble savage set to chase the object of colonial property. What allows for this representation is not merely the consummate racism of a slave society but also the narrative of mulatto bastardy in which the illegitimate mulatto son's service to the master appears as a perpetual yet ultimately futile process of expiation, redemption, and self-sacrifice before the symbolic white father, who refuses him recognition.

Incestuous Fantasies: Colonial Family Romance in Saint-Domingue

For Freud, "family romance" is the child's dream of replacing his or her real parents with imaginary ones with enhanced wealth or social status.[94] As the child gradually discovers that his or her parents are not as powerful, socially privileged, or loving as he or she first imagined them to be, the child fantasizes an alternative family that will satisfy these primary desires. Historians and cultural critics have borrowed from and expanded Freud's notion of family romance in order to account for the collective metaphors of the familial order through which social relationships and forms of political authority are imagined as more natural or just. Whereas the child seeks validation and identity within the nuclear family, political elites and social actors consciously or unconsciously deploy family images so as to justify a desired sociopolitical order.[95]

Strikingly, Moreau de Saint-Méry's ethnography represents colonial society through relations of filiation that bind masters, slaves, and free people of color in a family romance that was not entirely imaginary but rather was rooted in the regime of sexual domination and reproductive violence under slavery. The story unfolds in the very order of the author's ethnographic presentation of stereotyped figures: the whites, figured as predominantly male; followed by the slaves, where females carry the greatest textual and symbolic weight; and finally the class of free nonwhites, who are shown, through a meticulous taxonomy of racial genealogies, to descend from a primal scene of métissage between whites and blacks. Especially significant is Moreau's forceful claim of biological paternity over the class of mixed race. Simone Vauthier has written of plantation societies: "If bastardy is a common enough phenomenon, in no modern society has the silence of the father been to the same extent a factor in the development and structuration of the social organism."[96] In Moreau's colonial imaginary, however, what becomes important is precisely the generic claim of white paternity, a gesture that disgraces the class of free colored people as the masters' bastards. His declaration of filiation thus offers a discursive means by which to co-opt the power of mulattoes and free people of color by claiming responsibility for them. If the riddle of paternity is settled, *patrimony*, or the succession of inheritance, and most of all the name of the father are not tendered, a fact that ensures the desired subordination of the class.

The ideological work performed by Moreau de Saint-Méry's family romance is remarkable considering the historical evolution of white attitudes toward interracial sexuality and the products of those unions in the French Caribbean. As I argued in the previous chapter, the initial stigma that colonial elites attached to the entire class of free people of color was not merely political. Rather, it was heavily inflected by repressed anxieties about their own interracial desires, anxieties that were exacerbated by the numerical increase in the affranchis throughout the eighteenth century. Yet in time, as the free people of color were revalued as a means of protecting the whites from the slaves, the desire for the racial other came out of the closet, so to speak, albeit under the cover of political necessity. Colonial libertinage and white sexual freedom were justified and indeed advocated as the only way both to produce and control the issue of those desires, the population of mixed race. This required an ideology of race and reproduction that would endorse white male sexual hegemony in the colony while at the same time dispelling the threat of unlimited increase in the population of mixed race. Moreau's family romance may thus be read as a timely fantasy of sexual power and population control. The mulata infertility hypothesis is key in this regard, for it posited a stopping point for the proliferation of mixed-race people, thus freeing white male desire for nonwhite women from the rule of consequence. If the intermediary class of free coloreds could be almost entirely attributed to sexual relationships occurring between white men and black women, then whites could imagine themselves to be in control of the demographics of colonial libertinage by virtue of their sexual possession of female slaves. In this sense, Moreau's symbolic representation of the illegitimate family triad underwrites the libidinal freedom of whites and their near exclusive power over the reproductive and sexual resources of the entire colony.

In addition to legitimating white colonial desire, Moreau de Saint-Méry's family romance of Saint-Domingue says a great deal about the kinds of psychosexual fantasies underlying elite male authority in a patriarchal slave society.[97] The family romance of white fathers, slave mothers, and illegitimate mulatto children coexisted with and was often superseded by the representation of amorous relations between whites and mulatto women, free and slave. As we have seen, the stereotyped mulâtresse is almost white but not quite; perceived to possess the charms, intelligence, and sensibility thought to be the sole province of the white race, she avails herself also of the corporeal sensuality that whites associated with blackness. Slaveholder demand for this combination was reflected in the colonial marketplace, for mixed-race females were significantly more costly than black females.[98] In free society, white men sought mulatto women as lovers, concubines, and ménagères—permanent concubines fulfilling all the duties of a wife—and in some cases as legal wives.

Such evidence of white male desire for both black and mulatto women, whom they imagine as their symbolic daughters, raises the possibility of incest in the colonial family romance. An incestuous logic dominates as well Moreau de Saint-Méry's taxonomic representation of racial hybridity in Saint-Domingue. As Werner Sollors suggests in his study of interracial themes in literature, one of the ironies of tabular or mathematical representations of race is that they model racial amalgamation as an allegory of repeated incest.[99] The primary racial table, "combinations of the White," represents a stable white male partner that crosses with successive generations of his own offspring, so as *almost* to reproduce himself as his children become whiter and whiter. Moreau uses the masculine racial term to denote the result of each cross, yet consistently converts that term to the feminine so as to maintain the heterosexual logic of racial reproduction. By repressing the possibility of white women starting interracial families of their own, and protecting them as the sole legitimate wives of the white male elite, his narrative and taxonomic representation posits white men as what Sollors calls the "universal" origin of métissage.[100]

Although Moreau never mentions incest as an actual feature of colonial sexual practices, I would suggest that the allegory is more than an accident of diagrammatic convenience. Considering that mulattoes are both claimed as the illegitimate children of the white master and feminized as his preferred sexual objects, the racial taxonomy would appear to index the unconscious incestuous desires of the white male elite. What we have, then, is a dynamic metaphor of filiation, a mis en abyme of the illegitimate family romance that installs the white father as perpetually in pursuit of his own mixed-race daughter. The pervasiveness and the lure of this fantasy is suggested in colonist Ducoeurjoly's *Manuel des habitans de Saint-Domingue*, a guidebook for new European arrivals that appeared more than a decade into the Haitian Revolution, but which, like Moreau's *Description*, described life in prerevolutionary Saint-Domingue. Warning the male newcomer against running carelessly "from the white woman to the negress, from the negress to the mulâtresse, and successively from the mulâtresse to the different degrees of color," the author complains of the lubricity and maladies of these women while at the same time representing the incestuous pattern of colonial fantasies of métissage.[101] I would like to take seriously the idea of incestuous family romance in relation to white patriarchal identity, sexual hegemony over slaves, and exclusionary practices in French Caribbean slave societies. What makes the incestuous family romance in Saint-Domingue so compelling is that, rather than being a merely imaginary relation superimposed on a desired social reality, incest appears to be itself critically enmeshed in a set of interracial desires, fantasies, and libidinal practices through which whites imagined themselves to have produced the tripartite social order. Several questions thus arise. To what extent does slavery as a social organization foster incestuous desires, and what is the relationship between miscegenation and incest? What meanings can we ascribe to acts and/or fantasies of father/master-daughter/slave incest in Saint-Domingue? What kinds of sexual, racial, or political effects does the incestuous family romance produce that the simple family romance does not?

The coincidence of incest and miscegenation in a slave society might at first appear odd since the two ideas seem to be mutually exclusive. Whereas incest suggests sex within relations of consanguinity—a sort of radical *endogamy*—miscegenation refers to the sexual union of individuals of different "races," hence to a form of *exogamy*. That such radically contradictory practices could and did occur simultaneously in slave societies is one of the most remarkable yet little studied phenomena of this form of social organization. Indeed, the sexual violence and social abjection of slavery is nowhere better reflected than in the fact that slave societies defied not only their own weak prohibition against interracial sex but more importantly what anthropology and psychoanalysis alike have determined to be the most fundamental and universal rule in all human societies—the prohibition against incest. Literary research suggests several ways in which miscegenation, or the taboo against it, leads to incestuous tendencies in racially demarcated societies.[102] Reading the discourse of endogamy by North American white supremacists and Nazi fascists, Werner Sollors has shown that the exaggerated sense of racial threat and vulnerability leads the racist to define the other members of his or her group with metaphors of kinship and family (sisters and brothers) united not only against the other race but, more importantly, against any member who would commit the "horror of horrors," miscegenation. The requirement of marriage within the group thus installs a form of symbolic incest as a "prerequisite" for racial purity, based as it is on notions of blood purity.[103] Yet under slavery, the prevalence of actual interracial sexual relations and rape made incest a likely occurrence due to the very imperative of denial and secrecy that structured slave societies along lines of race. That is, the proliferation of illegitimate and usually unacknowledged mixed-race children among the master's slaves could easily lead to accidental or knowing incestuous encounters between half-siblings, or between the father and daughter.

It comes as no surprise, therefore, that the interlocking themes of miscegenation and incest were common in the legal and cultural discourse surrounding slavery in the United States and became an almost stereotypical feature of much liberal antislavery literature both there and in the Caribbean.[104] In Simone Vauthier's readings of antebellum antislavery novels such as Mary Denison's *Old Hepsy* (1858), the primary repression in a slave society is less the incest taboo than the fact of interracial sexual liaisons that confuse bloodlines and obscure blood relations across the color line. It is the silence of the father about his illegitimate progeny from black and colored slave women, and the subsequent disavowal of nonwhite members of the master's family (forming, rather, a "shadow family"), that undermines norms of kinship and increases the risk of incest. Writes Vauthier: "When refusing to acknowledge his slave son, the father fails to transmit with his surname what Jacques Lacan calls the Name-of-the-Father, i.e. the universal Law that prohibits incest." For Vauthier, this situation illustrates the irrepressible danger to society and the family posed by the radical exclusion of "part of [the] population from onomastic filiation and consequently from the Law, in the psychoanalytic sense of the word."[105]

Vauthier effectively argues that the mixed-race son's incestuous pursuit of his master's white daughter (his half sister) represents a displaced search for social justice and defiance of the father who denied him.[106] The same may be said for Oedipal aggressions toward the father, as displayed by male "tragic mulatto" figures in many U.S. novels of slavery.[107] As Heather Hathaway has argued, the "desire to kill the father for sleeping with the mother is intensified by the rejection of the 'black' son by the 'white' father because of racial 'impurities.'"[108] In cases in which the mixed-race son is free and the mother is not, this hatred also entails a deep resentment toward the father for continuing to possess her as a slave. Yet the very notion of an Oedipal complex is problematic in a slave society, where the family is often cut through with racial and class antagonisms. For white Creole children in particular, the figure of the "mother" is radically split between the white mother and the black slave nurse who breastfeeds them. Moreau de Saint-Méry blames white female frailty for this fact and paints a striking picture of white women's overcompensation for their inability, or refusal, to suckle their children: "Their children are nursed before their eyes, they contend with the nurse for their caresses. . . . In short, the mothers compensate with attention and solicitude, their powerlessness to satisfy a law, the breach of which is sometimes cruelly punished in other climates" (42). While condemning white women's violation of the law of maternity, Moreau indicates the centrality of the slave woman in satisfying the child's earliest needs, superseding the natural mother as an object of desire. For white colonials, the slave nurse thus becomes the site of a nonsexual miscegenation involving the passage of blood and milk, life-giving substances that instantiate an affective and quasi-biological filiation between slave women and white children. So valued was this function that it could lead to the emancipation of slave nurses who had suckled several of the master's children in addition to, or instead of, their own.[109] Terms of filiation such as *frère* and *soeur de lait* (milk brother, milk sister) suggest a natural solicitude for the slave nurse, who is situated with her children on the threshold of the master's family. For some whites, however, the "foreign" milk was but a venomous conduit for the slave woman's essential iniquity and impurity. Accusing the nurse of transmitting with her milk the vices of a "lascivious and burning" temperament, Baron de Wimpffen lamented that she was both the origin of the child's moral corruption and the object of his first aggression: "What can be hoped from the power of education in places where . . . the first words stuttered by the young Creole will be the order to tear up the nurse's breast with blows of the whip?"[110] Here it is on the body of the wet-nurse that the child passes from the state of dependency and obedience to a position of tyranny and domination.

It is easy to imagine how this could hold true for the white male child's sexual development. Quasi-Oedipal, incestuous desires for the black "mother figure"—the male child's first love object—could all too easily be acted on as part of his ability to dominate his slaves.[111] But I would argue that the most important incest fantasy in French Caribbean slave societies involves not the white Creole infant and the black mother figure nor even two half siblings but rather the white father and his mixed-race daughter. In this case, the father's failure to pass on the incest prohibition is due not primarily to his refusal to recognize his mulatto offspring but to his *own*

incestuous transgression. Rather than remaining the repository and potential transmitter of the law against incest, the father becomes himself the
primary instigator of its violation. In antebellum fiction, cases of incest between half siblings occur frequently in the context of a prior or simultaneous
incest threat from the father to the mixed-race daughter. The father thus
emerges as the rival of his daughter's sibling lover in doubly incestuous love
triangles.[112] Yet father/master-daughter/slave incest stands alone as one of
the most endemic and perhaps most silenced abuses in slave societies, to
judge from late-twentieth-century literature by African American women
exploring its consequences for descendants of female slave victims.[113] Reflecting the tendency toward interracial desire, the sexual and reproductive
exploitation of slaves, and the libidinal excesses of the slaveholding elite,
father-daughter incest corresponds as well to the logic of racial taxonomiz-
ing practiced in late-eighteenth-century Saint-Domingue. In the anglophone West Indies, there was even a phrase for it, to judge from the anonymously published 1787 novel *Adventures of Jonathan Corncob*. The expression
"washing the blackamoor white" described the process of incestuous reproduction leading to lighter and lighter shades of progeny. For Werner Sollors,
repeated incest is an extreme "model of colonial family building" focused
on the "racial fantasy world of a self-made patriarch, the 'father of them
all,' whose descendant-counting starts with himself as universal origin."[114]

Hortense Spillers has provocatively argued that, due to the enormous
avoidance, denial, and censorship that historically surrounds father-daughter incest, "it is only in fiction . . . that incest as dramatic enactment and
sexual economy can take place at all."[115] I would contend that, while it
would be misguided and well beyond the scope of this study to attempt to
prove the incidence of incest in Saint-Domingue, the narrative evidence
indicates that the white male fantasy of métissage mirrored in biological
terms a structure of father-daughter incest. Thus, at the subconscious level,
the fantasy of miscegenated father-daughter incest was pervasive in Saint-
Domingue. The question, therefore, becomes, how do we interpret such
fantasies given the particularities of the social context in which they arose?
As the following analysis will show, although none of the most influential
theories of incest, be they anthropological, psychoanalytic, or literary, are
entirely adequate to explain the possible social meanings of miscegenated
father-daughter incest in a slave society, each of them provides valuable insights into the ways in which modern slavery resists analysis through concepts of nature, culture, the family, kinship, and society, on which reflections on incest have been based. Through a critical analysis of three of the

most provocative arguments about incest and its taboo in the Western tradition, I will first construct a theoretical frame through which to understand how slavery as a social system fostered fantasies and practices of incest by the white father/master with mixed-race children. I will argue that more so than the phenomena of brutality, sexual abuse, and "social death" through which slavery's inhumanity has often been understood, it is the enabling of incest in a slave society that epitomizes the radical social violence of the institution. Finally, taking clues from Moreau de Saint-Méry's *Description* and an account of father-daughter incest in Girod de Chantrans's travel journal, I will suggest how the "incestuous family romance" showed up in gendered policies of mastery and social control, as well as sexual ideologies in Saint-Domingue.

In his study of human kinship, Claude Lévi-Strauss theorized that the incest taboo was universal and essential to the foundation of all human societies, culture, and language. For him, the prohibition against incest marks humanity's passage from nature to culture and social organization. The importance and uniqueness of the incest taboo lies in its irreducible duality between nature and culture; a coercive rule that binds members of a culture to established traditions and laws, its universality also attaches it to the domain of nature or common instinct. More than being a mere feature of culture, the incest taboo *is* culture, insofar as it imposes the rule of exchange on the arbitrariness of nature. Following Marcel Mauss, Lévi-Strauss takes kinship systems, like all the social and cultural forms that proceed from them, to be based on a logic of reciprocal exchange requiring the establishment of alliances between individuals and families.[116] By forcing men of the same family to relinquish their daughters and sisters to other men within a certain group, the incest taboo institutes the exchange of women and the creation of social bonds among men: "The law of exogamy . . . is the archetype of all other manifestations based on reciprocity. . . . It furnishes the fundamental and immutable rule which assures the existence of the group as a group."[117]

Slavery as a social system poses a number of problems for this theory of the incest taboo, not least because Lévi-Strauss's claim that the incest prohibition is fundamental to kinship and human society is based on a definition of kinship structures as "systems prescribing marriage."[118] In this respect, he implicitly restricts his definition of incest to marriage between members of the legitimate family, whose belonging within the family is legible in nomenclature and who must be formally exchanged so as to secure social relationships within the group. He is thus powerless to explain whether sex between blood relations would be taboo *outside* of kinship.

If anything, his theory suggests that insofar as natural children born outside of marriage are excluded from the legitimate family and unmarked by the patronymic, the rules of kinship—including the incest taboo—simply would not apply. On the other hand, slavery may be seen to instantiate in the extreme the kind of "ownership" of women that Lévi-Strauss's model of kinship presumes. While feminists first assailed him for a sexist portrayal of women as exchangeable objects, Juliet Mitchell recuperated his analysis as descriptive rather than prescriptive. Women cannot really be reduced to the status of objects, but they are positioned as such within the male-dominated kinship system. They are the equivalent of a sign that is being communicated, as in a language.[119] Yet what Lévi-Strauss's metaphor obscures is the extent to which his theory fails when children actually *are* possessed as saleable commodities.[120] As the perpetual owner of his own offspring, the father/master withholds her from the norms of exchange and reciprocity that are the necessary complements of the incest taboo.[121] Ownership enhances the power differential between father and child and thwarts the operations of kinship, thus placing the master outside of the black family and the mixed-race children outside of the master's family.[122]

Given the psychoanalytic assumptions behind Lévi-Strauss's theory, these conditions would favor the corruption of the incest prohibition as it is conceived in his work. His argument about the universality of the taboo depends on the notion that incest may be the most primal and powerful of human desires and is neither naturally nor morally repugnant: "There is nothing in the sister, nor in the mother, nor in the daughter, that disqualifies them as such. Incest is socially absurd before being morally culpable."[123] In this sense, his entire theory was a rewriting of Freud's psychoanalytic illustration of primal incestuous desire in his highly contentious work *Totem and Taboo*, which also credits the incest taboo with founding the social order.[124] Freud's theory is especially compelling for any consideration of incest and slavery, since it posits a fascinating connection between the physical and sexual domination exercised by the father over subordinates in the patriarchal family. The book also stands as one of the rare occasions on which Freud theorizes incestuous desire in the adult parent rather than the child.[125] Whereas Freudian psychoanalysis typically takes the son's incestuous desires toward the mother as symptomatic of male infantile libido, Freud's own myth of origins presents these desires as responses to a different form of incest, one that was ever more "primitive," ever more "original." Using Darwin's notion of the primal horde, Freud analyzes the conflicts engendered by the violent and jealous father, who amasses wives and female children for his own sexual consumption, driving out all male children on their maturity. The father is the object of a profound ambivalence on the part of the sons; loved and admired, he is at the same time a hated and feared obstacle to the satisfaction of their desires for power and sexual mates. The overthrow of this patriarchal tyranny calls for a revolution: "One day the brothers who had been driven out came together, killed and devoured their father and so made an end of the patriarchal horde."[126] The sons, in killing the father, satisfy their deep hatred of him and at the same time effect an essential identification with him, which is followed by filial guilt and the renunciation of both their act of patricide and the privileges gained from it, hence the institution of prohibitions against incest and the killing of the totem, the displaced emblem of the father. In social terms, the story accounts for the beginning of everything from the social contract to moral restrictions, religion, and culture.

What is most compelling about this narrative of human beginnings is the way in which it theorizes a state of pure origin lacking all social taboos and rules as necessarily both patriarchal *and* incestuous. Thinking backward from the Oedipus complex he observed in his patients, Freud imagined the other side of civilization not as the fulfilled incest wish of the sons for the mother but the previous libidinal supremacy of the *father* over his sons and his taking of his daughters. How fascinating, then, that the figure of the incestuous father would be used to subversive effect in eighteenth-century libertine fictions, which aimed precisely to challenge and radically undermine dominant moral norms, sexual restrictions, and their corresponding social code. The difference is that, whereas Freud's primal father institutes an order of incestuous patriarchy, libertine fiction presents the incestuous father as diametrically *opposed* to the patriarchal norms of eighteenth-century society. In place of the moralizing patriarch, censurer of desire, image of the law, and the symbolic figure for the institution of the family and its prohibitions against nonreproductive sexuality, libertine writers such as Mirabeau and Restif de la Bretonne substitute the father as erotic tutor, initiator, and teacher of his nubile daughters.[127]

At its most radical, the libertine system actually remoralizes paternal incest as a precondition for the daughter's sexual liberation. In Sade's fiction, this is presented as an escape from a male-dominated, patriarchal society into one in which libertinage and prostitution bring about women's economic and sexual independence. In his insightful reading of Sade, Marcel Hénaff explores these social meanings of incest. Following Lévi-Strauss, Hénaff sees the incest taboo as the foundation on which all other forms of exchange, social institution, culture, and language are based. So, while incest represents the male libertine's opportunity for easy sexual gratification, it is especially important as a politically symbolic act: "Institution and culture—language—come at the price of sexual prohibition, but the price is exorbitant, and one should refuse to pay it. The libertine, then, will be the one who does not defer his desire and does not accept its inscription into the exchange system and therefore into the system of relay and redirection. In concrete terms, what incest signifies for Sade is: I am taking the woman closest to me because she is the one I can get to most quickly." [128] In the Sadean imaginary, this ethos of incestuous pillage appears to undermine patriarchal limitations placed on *female* desire and to liberate the woman as a free sexual agent, a prostitute circulating in a libidinal economy outside the bounds of male exchange. [129] Perpetrated by the father or brother, incest abolishes all filial ties linking daughters to the family, thus transforming women into independent desiring subjects on a par with men: "What this multiply overdetermined incest marks . . . is the wrenching away from the maternal sphere of influence, denial of the familial prohibition and destruction of the closure that this prohibition brings about as the necessary order of exchanges and alliances. Through incest, the daughter mutates into a 'girl' in the depraved sense: a loose, unattached woman, free of duties, a vagrant pudendum." [130] Of course, behind the move to redeem incest in the interests of a dubious female liberation, the real objective of the Sadean libertine is to sabotage the system of rules, prohibitions, and kinship regulations that places limits on *male* erotic desires. Libertine fiction operates, then, as a radical attack on the symbolic father and on the social order that he represents.

What meanings, then, can we ascribe to the performance and/or fantasy of paternal incest in a slave society, where there is clearly no move to upset the dominant social order? I would contend that illegitimate father-daughter incest was enabled by the social order of racial slavery, even if it offended the sensibilities of white kinship. Just as the very principle of ownership of persons radically contradicted social meanings of self and personhood in white society, miscegenation under slavery allowed for the eruption of two parallel yet entirely conflicting sets of norms relating to desire and kinship. Whereas the master observed rules of kinship in his white family, in his mixed-race shadow family slavery promoted his treatment of all slave women as his sexual property, irrespective of blood ties. [131] What made sex with the mulatto daughter especially alluring was precisely the presence and residual power of the dominant incest taboo in the white colonial psyche. In the shadow family, the slave master was theoretically "free" from all constraints and social norms governing sexual relations with his legitimate kin and could explore his incestuous desires at will. Added to the power of ownership and the obsession with a woman who was desirable because she was *almost* white was the pleasure of transgression; the mulatto daughter was the daughter that the slave master *could* possess, or so he hoped.[132]

In one of his letters on slave sexuality, the Swiss traveler Girod de Chantrans wrote about the ways in which male slaves avenge the taking of their lovers by rivals, black and white, by poisoning them. Lamenting the "libertinage without bounds and without discretion" of whites on the plantation, he included the following anecdote of a "recent" incident "known by all the colony."

> A white man aged fifty five or thereabouts, unmarried, father of several mulattoes or mulâtresses, had among them a daughter with whom he had fallen in love. He lived on his plantation, in the middle of his already large family, and each day urged his daughter to submit to his wishes; each time he was refused.
>
> First he used caresses; but being unable to vanquish his daughter's repugnance by this means, he tried threats and finished with cruelties.
>
> Nothing could shake the constancy of this unhappy one, all the more moving in the persecutions that she endured, that her good conduct and judgment were praised in all the neighboring parts. Her brothers, witnesses to the horrors of which she was a victim, driven in the end by pity and indignation, strangled the father in his bed. Only they did not think to escape afterwards, and were arrested.
>
> Justice had no trouble getting to the bottom of the mystery of iniquity that had caused this catastrophe: it could not however keep from condemning the guilty to death. All were executed, even the daughter who took part in the plot.[133]

In light of Moreau de Saint-Méry's racial taxonomy and family romance, I read this primal scene of incestuous aggression as a striking illustration of the unconscious incest wish of the white male elite and the most threatening obstacle to that wish. The narrative tone is reminiscent of the sympathy and outrage in early-seventeenth-century accounts of slaveholder concupiscence, but here the woman is seen as heroic in her resistance to her *father*, who has fallen in love with her. What is remarkable about the story, and indeed worth the telling, is not merely the fact of incest but also the powerful vengeance of the brothers, who, rising up against the father, sabotage his wish to sexually possess his daughter. The brothers' revolt, unsuspected by the father, is the effective means by which to punish the incestuous father with death. The ultimate irony, however, lies in the sons' and daughter's fate. The law, by prosecuting them for murder, appears to vindicate the father and condone his crime of incest. Girod de Chantrans himself laments that the laws, so rigorous against the sons' reprisals, are powerless to protect the daughter's outraged virtue and sensibility. The apparent coincidence of the father's actions and colonial law suggests furthermore that the law of the father, understood both as paternal authority and the rule-bound culture that it represents, is no longer marked by the prohibition of incest but rather by its defense.[134] Through the circulation of the story in the colony, the confluence of miscegenation and incest would have been reinscribed within the collective unconscious, along with the frightful revenge of the mulatto sons.

As a theory of miscegenated father-daughter incest and its taboo in a slave society, the anecdote exhibits striking parallels with Freud's story of human beginnings and the incestuous father. In Girod's text, colonial patriarchy resembles the dynamics of the primal horde, in which the powerful patriarch attempts to exert sexual dominance over wives and children. My point is not to posit the incest wish as a conscious impulse manifested in the "real" lives and actions of elites but to demonstrate the ways in which slavery both generated and fostered the consummation of incestuous desires by the slave owner and patriarch. In the colonies, the actual ownership of persons making up the illegitimate interracial family replaces the physical power that maintains the primal father's sexual tyranny in Freud's narrative. The most significant challenge to the white father remains, however, the threat of revenge from the mulatto sons. They seek not to replace him in his position of patriarch with sexual rights over all women but rather to save their sister from his criminal desires. In so violently opposing the white father's willful evasion of the incest taboo, the rebellious sons and daughter affirm that taboo, and in so doing, make a symbolic declaration of belonging to the master's family.

Girod de Chantrans finds comfort in the fact that, whereas the oppressed may never receive justice for sexual crimes committed against them, the story of this incident will at least "put the brakes on their oppressors."[135] He assumes, then, that the father's desire for the daughter will henceforth be forestalled by a latent fear of the mulatto sons' patricidal rebellion. Yet in the opposite sense, the story offers a cautionary tale demonstrating that incestuous desires may only be fulfilled in the *absence* of the mulatto son.

In this respect, the story sheds light on the particular forms of suspicion, sexual competition, and coercion that characterized the rapport between white men and free men of color, who were on the whole considered to be the masters' bastards. I would contend that the father-daughter incest fantasy becomes legible in the specific means by which men of color were treated and contained in Saint-Domingue. In Freud's myth of origins, the incestuous father establishes his tyrannical patriarchy by banishing his sons from the familial horde/harem. In the colonies, what better way to repel the threat the sons pose than the preemptive militarization of mulatto men, whose aggressions were to be exhausted not on the white elite but on fugitive slaves and white vagabonds left over from Saint-Domingue's origins in piratical nomadism? The whites' presumption of sexual dominance over the entire colony, and over women of color in particular, would necessitate the warding off of the menace to that dominance, the vengeance of mulatto men. Coerced and armed to protect the symbolic white father, and furthermore to police the boundaries between white and black, slave and free, mulatto men were made over as the primary defenders of the colonial social order and the law of the incestuous father. This scenario thus presents an inversion of the Oedipal complex, so central to the structuring of personality and human desire in psychoanalysis. Whereas in the Oedipal scenario the father easily imposes his law on the desiring male child by installing the fear of castration, in the colonies the father marshaled his *political* power to eradicate all threats to his sexual/symbolic ascendancy. Desiring to "kill" the son and sleep with the daughter, the father risked judgment and death at the hands of the son, carrier of an incest prohibition linked to a search for legitimation and social retribution.

The man of color thus signified to white colonials not only the repressed primal scene of métissage but more importantly the incest prohibition denied by the white "father" as he desired his mixed-race progeny. The military and socially exclusionary legislation against the mixed-race "son" may thus be read as so many attempts to evade or suppress the primary incest taboo, which would otherwise restrict white male sexual access to colored women. Yet if the incestuous family romance shaped colonial policies and stereotypes of mulatto men in the colonies, it was equally evident in the ways in which colored women came to represent the libertine colony. There is a sense in which the ideology of the mulatto woman voluptuary resonates with the Sadean theory of incest as the absolute severance of women from filial ties and her propulsion into a libertine economy of lust, luxury, and prostitution. Fatherly incest would effect a radical form of what Orlando

Patterson has called "natal alienation," meaning a denial of "all claims on, and obligations to . . . living blood relations."[136] Indeed, in narrative representations, whites imagined women of color to exist entirely outside the bounds of kinship. Icons of sensual pleasures and erotic excess, they do not desire marriage. As Moreau de Saint-Méry writes, "the influence of climate, taste for luxury, and their aversion for husbands from their class, who are the most suspicious and despotic of spouses, everything induces women of color to flee marriage and to give themselves up to a lucrative concubinage, which better satisfies their voluptuous inclinations" (107). In gratifying male sexual fantasies, the ideology of the mulatto woman also justified male wishes by displacing responsibility for the miscegenated relation onto her. In the libertine colonial fantasy, the mulatto woman thus became a free sexual agent in search of the symbolic white "father" over all other men. Finally, in the Sadean imaginary incest represents a direct attack on the mother as a figure for the values of modesty, virtue, and resistance cultivated in the daughter as a rampart against libertinage and masculine desire. In a slave society, the practice of incest with the illegitimate mulatto daughter would mean the further devaluation of the slave mother; while abolishing the filial identity of the daughter, it would undermine whatever power over her the mother may have attempted to salvage.

* * *

Not surprisingly, the white male elite's fantasy of incest and mulatto patricide only partially captured the reciprocal desires and anxieties of elite free people of color prior to the Haitian Revolution. While many did harbor deep resentment of the dominant class of whites, they were far more interested in joining whites as fully endowed members of the political and social elite than in fighting them to the death. What is fascinating is that so central were sexual politics to questions of race and rights in Saint-Domingue that activists of color adopted the dominant script of family romance as a way to legitimate their political demands. By way of conclusion, I cite the case of the leading mulatto intellectual and political spokesperson at the time of the revolution, Julien Raimond. Raimond was a planter from Saint-Domingue's southern province, a center of mulatto activism. He was chosen by the mulatto intelligentsia to plead the case for mulatto rights before the royal government in France. Arriving in France in the 1780s, he became the unofficial spokesperson for the colonial elite of color, addressing several memoirs to the Maréchal de Castries, the minister of navy, and to Louis XVI himself. His best-known published work, *Observations sur l'origine et les progrès du préjugé des colons blancs contre les hommes de couleur* (1791), was written for the French National Assembly at a critical moment in revolutionary debates on the mulatto question.[137] Refuting a proposal by the colonial committee according full rights only to the "whitest" free people of color, Raimond advocated the extension of active citizenship to all free "mixed bloods." He did so, however, by manipulating the dominant discourse of family romance and white anxiety about interracial libertinage to his own advantage. In his revised narrative of race, reproduction, and family romance in Saint-Domingue, mulatto rights actually become the formula for curing the moral depravity of the colony.

Raimond's history of color prejudice affirms everything whites had worked to repress concerning their interracial relationships with slaves and free people of color. In his version of early colonial libertinage between the first white colonists and slaves, white men have hearts and women get rewards. Instead of leaving their concubines and blood children in slavery, white fathers consistently extend freedom and property to them, if they do not altogether legitimate the unions. Yet, if Raimond is determined to reverse the stereotypes of mulatto bastardy and immorality that justified white racism in the dominant narrative of colonial family romance, he does so largely by claiming the legitimacy of relationships between white men and free women of color. These, he argues, became increasingly common as the numbers of mulatto women grew in the first half of the eighteenth century and white men continued to arrive in the colony from France. At the same time, he boldly displaces the stereotype of libertinage and sterility from mulatto women to white women. So morally corrupt was the first batch of white female imports to the colony, he writes, that "their marriages with whites did not have all the fruit that had been promised."[138] Wives of color, on the other hand, ensured white men numerous heirs and had the additional advantage of bringing a significant dowry in land and slaves, thus giving white men a head start in the colonial business.

For Raimond, such openness in matters of love and marriage was synonymous with a total lack of racial prejudice against free people of color. What spoiled this picture of conjugal and political harmony was less white male racism than white female jealousy of colored women. It was a jealousy fueled at midcentury by the enviable culture and probity of the first generation of free colored youth sent by their white fathers to be educated in France: "The talents, qualities, graces and knowledge that most of these young people possess, and that brought condemnation upon the vices and ignorance of island whites, were the very cause of the abasement in which they were thrown."[139] With the growth of the free population, white female envy was translated into racial prejudice and exclusionary policies such as laws discouraging mésalliance. Raimond blames these regulations in particular for expanding interracial concubinage, which was so strongly condemned, though widely practiced, by whites throughout the eighteenth century: "These colored girls who before were the honest rivals of the white girls because they could marry white men, were obliged to prostitute themselves to the whites, with whom they now live in concubinage."[140] He charges, furthermore, that granting rights uniquely to the "whitest" of the free people of color would only *reward* illegitimacy and concubinage, "to the detriment of legitimate children of virtuous fathers and mothers."[141] The only solution, therefore, is immediately to recognize all free sang-mêlés as active citizens. This will result in legitimate métissage, the end to sexual immorality, and the dissolution of prejudice in the colony: "Many whites will no longer be repulsed by marrying colored girls, because these marriages will no longer take offices away from them; hence the colored girls who will expect only their virtue to win their alliance with whites, will practice it."[142]

What is striking about this argument is that the most eloquent mulatto activist of the revolutionary period justifies rights for free people of color not based on an inclusive interpretation of the Declaration of the Rights of Man and Citizen nor even on the more strategic notion of their economic or political indispensability to the colonial elite. Raimond strikes instead at the core of colonial sexual politics, with the full knowledge that the racial prejudice of the white elite is itself rooted in their own attitudes toward interracial sexuality on the island. Raimond's task, then, was to turn white male libertinage to political advantage. While he undermined many of the stereotypes on which whites based their own self-legitimating family romance, however, he posed no serious challenge to white sexual hegemony, seeking only to reinscribe it into networks of kinship linking whites and nonwhites. It is by portraying desiring white males as would-be husbands condemned to concubinage by anti-mésalliance legislation—hence as victims rather than perpetrators of colonial racism—that Raimond masks mulatto rights as white male liberation and the triumph of bourgeois morality in the colony. Free women of color, on the other hand, remain critically disempowered in this narrative of legitimate family romance, their sole right being the power to salve racial divisions through sexual availability, domesticity, motherhood, and conjugal love. If Raimond considers this an improvement over their role as concubines, he discounts the material and social freedoms that some colored women negotiated in their independent sexual relationships with men of all races. It is as though a secondary objective of Raimond's program of legitimate family romance is to discipline the alleged rapacity and excesses of colored female desire, a stereotype that he largely accepts. Made over in the image of bourgeois virtue and domesticity, the mulatto woman would found the new class of masters. Mulatto men, for their part, would also be eligible partners for white women, for only when both white and nonwhite men can legitimately access women of all races will equal rights for mulattoes be secured.

In appealing to a model of legitimate métissage as the means by which to restore moral order to the colonies, while at the same time ending the economic and political disparities between whites and free sang-mêlés, Raimond provided a powerful counterdiscourse to that of Moreau de Saint-Méry. The mulatto activist understood that race was not a "difference" like any other, on which power relations were calibrated and boundaries of exclusion maintained. In the colonial Caribbean, color prejudice and racial identities were never divorced from realities and fantasies of sexuality and desire or from the reproductive consequences they often entailed. Ironically, the same may be said of the postcolonial state of Haiti, in which the masculine heterosexual racial rhetoric of Jean-Jacques Dessalines, the liberator and first emperor of Haiti, reproduced some of the libidinal fantasies of white colonial discourse. In his 1805 constitution for Haiti, Dessalines forbade any white person to set foot in the new territory as a master or property owner (article 12) and redefined all Haitians as "black" regardless of color variations among them.[143] The new emperor nonetheless specified that this article applied neither to white women naturalized as Haitian by the government nor to their present or future children (article 13). Hence, in refashioning blackness as a political identity, Dessalines masked the continuance of métissage on the white woman's body. Expelling the men and naturalizing the women, Dessalines secured the libidinal spoils of "black" racial supremacy.

Conclusion

I began this study with a question—"why do we study texts that degrade our humanity?"—and it is to this question that I return. Phrased in another way, why remember the terror of the past, every miserable act of human indecency, will to domination, and ideological myth on which French Caribbean societies were forged? Why recall slavery, a social and cultural system that in our contemporary moment has been relegated to history, thankfully abandoned, one hopes, in favor of a less terror-ridden model of pluralism and diversity? Why so relentlessly engage, analyze, and critique the logic of gendered violence, rape, and exploitation that for two centuries or more shaped the cultures of the Caribbean and much of the Americas? These questions become more rhetorical with each iteration, for what is striking is less the advantage of forgetting than the need to investigate more fully the first two centuries of Caribbean literary and cultural history. Yet it is impossible to ignore the political implications and intellectual burden of studying the cultures abjected from Western memory. What the postcolonial studies movement has shown is that there *is* a space for memory in the West; yet in taking up the invitation to remember scholars are placed in the uncomfortable position of retelling the abject in ways that reaffirm the former structures of colonial power and recall the abasement of mostly non-European subalterns. The more difficult questions thus remain. For whom do we remember, and whose memory do we claim to represent?

Half a century ago, Frantz Fanon adamantly refused to be constrained by history or to ground his human vocation on his ancestral past, however brutal or glorious. Reacting against what he considered to be the Négritude movement's obsession with history as a means of facilitating racial pride, he pointed to the potential trap of retelling the past as a replacement for concrete political action against ongoing injustice in the present: "Do I not have anything better to do on this earth than to avenge the blacks of the seventeenth century?" Choosing instead to create himself through his acts, present and future, Fanon queries:

> Moral pain before the density of the Past? I am a negro and have been assailed by tons of chains, storms of blows, and rivers of spit, which flow down my shoulders.
>
> But I do not have the right to let myself be anchored . . . , stuck by the determinations of the past.
>
> I am not the slave of slavery which dehumanized my fathers.[1]

Fanon compares the oppressive burden of the past to the immobilizing chains of slavery itself. More recently, Édouard Glissant has suggested that there is a critical difference between the principled refusal to be determined by history and a willful or passive forgetting: "The slave is first one who does not know. The slave of slavery is one who does not want to know."[2] For Glissant, stories about slavery *do* have political significance, not as a means of exposing the barbarism of the former colonial power but as a way of consolidating a sense of lived experience among the people of the Caribbean. According to him, their brutal memories have been replaced by a far more devastating form of cultural amnesia, assisted by assimilationist policies, the virtual lack of indigenous cultural production, and the folklorization of Creole. The will to remember the unspeakable is not, however, without peril. As Toni Morrison's *Beloved* makes clear, freedom from slavery is won not by the legal or physical unburdening of the captive person, or even by the captive's own revolt or planned escape, but rather through the utterly exhausting and death-defying task of encountering the past of slavery in memory and language without being reenslaved by it, without being repossessed or dis-membered by it.[3]

In rereading narratives of colonialism and slavery in the Caribbean, I have been mindful of the risks of remembering slavery there as well as in the United States. Although my sources relate most closely to the beliefs and practices of the colonizing population and in particular its religious and civil leadership, this study invariably reconstructs violent images and figures of abjection among ruler and ruled. The point has been to reinterpret the texts, narratives, and histories that colonials and their representatives told about the cultures arising in their midst and the power relations obtaining therein. Through the exegesis of the poetics of slavery, we do not recover a history of verifiable events but rather a repository of beliefs, values, and images that are relevant to a literary history of French colonialism and offer valuable perspectives on many otherwise irrecoverable aspects of past Caribbean cultures. What we gain is the power to imagine, in the words of Joan Dayan, "what cannot be verified" and what could not have been inscribed on any document held in a historical archive.[4]

In this study, I have imagined the way in which culture flows and contacts—commonly known as creolization—took place under conditions of extreme violence, as well as the relation of these interactions to the social and political structures of domination. At the forefront of my analysis have been the various forms of desire motivating the French colonial endeavor in the Caribbean, and which later impacted the evolving system of slavery. These are not exclusively libidinal but also include the desires created by circumstances of threat, vulnerability, social ambiguity, and confrontation with radical alterity—the desire to be safe, the desire to reinvent, the desire to make and destroy, the desire to claim land and resources, and the desire to possess and to control.

In the encounter between the French and the Caribs, what is fascinating is the complimentarity of violence and desire. For the framers of missionary colonialism, the goal of incorporating the Caribs into Christianity implied the negation of Carib difference, as well as the exchange of land and resources in return for the gift of faith. This imagined reciprocity was enforceable through violence and war. Missionary desire was also fundamentally imbricated with commercial, linguistic, and territorial ambitions, which in turn determined the kinds of stories told about the relation between the French and the Caribs in the early Caribbean. If, according to Emmanuel Levinas, we may be linguistically and cognitively incapable of narrating a cross-cultural encounter in a way that manages more than one point of view, the dictionary as a genre best illuminates the multiple tensions and negotiations of the cross-cultural border by recording the discourses through which they were articulated by both sides.

The world of the spirit supplied a similar medium for the enactment of cross-cultural encounters, as well as the imbrication of violence and desire—spiritual, commercial, and libidinal. In the seventeenth century, the application of missionary and demonological paradigms to the putative spiritual powers of Caribs and Africans legitimated the Christian mission. Yet, if the beating devil was the primary figure whereby missionaries justified their desire for Carib souls, Christians nonetheless embraced the brutality of slavery as the ostensible means of redeeming African souls through the forcible submission of the body. Christian discipline reproduced the dynamic of diabolical servitude by making Africans work for Europeans under the threat of violence. Blessebois's tale suggests, however, that the colonial context was ripe for discourses of body and spirit that eluded and subverted that framework, painting white colonials as idolatrous libertines held in the terror of the zombi. Though he imputed them to diabolical femininity, Blessebois cast libertine desire and occult forms as invariably shared by both women and men, and raised the possibility that the occult beliefs and practices of the elite drew from available spirit beliefs of subordinated Africans and perhaps Caribs as well.

In dealing primarily with narratives of colonialism produced by the French, I have been particularly attentive to transformations occurring within the French settler population, diverse in class, language, ethnicity, and regional origin. Familiar binaries of civility or nobility and savagery, typically assumed to have distinguished colonial Europeans from subjugated groups, were just as commonly deployed to highlight dissidence and deviance among the settlers, so threatening was the self-fashioning process to colonial authorities. In their narratives, colonial writers attempted to shape and reform settlers' desires to abandon their past identities, better their social condition, or liberate themselves entirely from traditional measures of social worth. The desire for nobility was, I believe, the unifying factor in colonial social performance, discernible through the seemingly opposed practices of plantation agriculture and piracy.

Most importantly, this study reconsiders the relation between social violence, colonial racial paradigms, and legal discrimination, on one hand, and rampant interracial libertinage on the other. It is not enough to recognize that slavery was a system of sexual domination; we must investigate the ideas and beliefs that sanctioned specific practices of white sexual and political supremacy. Only by refusing to expose in the greatest possible detail the extent to which white Creole identity was embedded in feelings of sexual entitlement to subjugated persons, as well as the knowledge of filial attachment to them, do we do violence to those abused by slavery in the past. French narratives offer an exceptional view of the fantasies of desire and reproduction whereby whites and Creoles imagined their sexual and political authority. In Saint-Domingue, the system of apartheid developed as a response to and an accommodation of the continued practice of interracial libertinage by making sure that its human products would be subordinated to white power. In late-eighteenth-century colonial texts, the magnitude of

the slaveholders' sexual and reproductive exploitation of captive women became painfully clear, as did the signal importance of ideas about the family
as a means of veiling relations of violence and naturalizing white rule. The
centrality of themes of sexuality and the family in Julien Raymond's vindication of mulatto rights leaves little doubt as to the political potency of
colonial desire in the French Caribbean. Only by exploring and rereading
the libertine colony will scholars, writers, and living communities be able
to recognize and contest its varied legacies in the present.

Notes

Introduction

1 Édouard Glissant, *Le Discours antillais* (1981; reprint, Paris: Gallimard, 1997), esp. 40–140. Citations are to the Gallimard edition.

2 Michel-Rolph Trouillot, *Silencing the Past: Power and the Production of History* (Boston: Beacon, 1995), 95–105.

3 Louis Sala-Molins, *Les Misères des lumières: Sous la raison, l'outrage* (Paris: Éditions R. Laffont, 1992), 147–48, 179. See also his *Le* Code noir *ou le calvaire de canaan* (Paris: Presses Universitaires de France, 1987), 17.

4 Jacques Bouton, *Relation de l'establissement des François depuis l'an 1635 en l'isle de la Martinique, l'une des Antilles de l'Amérique: Des moeurs des sauvages, de la situation, et d'autres singularitez de l'isle* (Paris: Cramoisy, 1640).

5 Francisco Lopez de Gomara, *Histoire générale des Indes occidentales* (1569, 1580, 1584, 1606); Garcilaso de la Vega, *Le Commentaire royal, ou L'Histoire des Yncas, Roys du Peru* (1633, 1704, 1715, 1727, 1737); Antonio de Herrera y Tordesillas, *Description des Indes occidentales qu'on appelle aujourdhuy le Nouveau Monde* (1622); Bartolomé de Las Casas, *Tyrannies et cruautez des Espagnols, perpetrées ès Indes occidentals, qu'on appelle le Nouveau Monde* (1579, 1582, 1620, 1630, 1642). On such publications and the influence of Spanish colonial historiography on early modern French travel writing and antislavery opinion, see Edward D. Seeber, *Anti-slavery Opinion in France during the Second Half of the Eighteenth Century* (Baltimore: Johns Hopkins University Press, 1937).

6 Jacques Cartier, *Brief recit et succinte narration de la navigation faicte es ysles de Canada, Hochelage et Saguenay et autres . . .* (Paris, 1545); Cartier, *Discours du voyage faict . . . aux Terres neufves du Canada . . . et pays adjacents, dite Nouvelle-France . . .* (Rouen: R. Du Petit Val, 1598); Samuel Champlain, *Des sauvages, ou Voyage . . . faict en la France nouvelle, l'an mil six cens trois . . .* (Paris: C. de Monstr'oeil, 1604); Champlain, *Les Voyages de la Nouvelle-France occidentale, dicte Canada . . .* (Paris:

Impr. de L. Sevestre, 1632); Marc Lescarbot, *Histoire de la Nouvelle-France, conte-nant les navigations, découvertes et habitations faites par les Français ès Indes Occi-dentales et Nouvelle-France* . . . (Paris: J. Milot, 1609); Gabriel Sagard, *Le Grand voyage du pays des Hurons* . . . (Paris: D. Moreau, 1632); Gabriel Sagard, *Histoire du Canada* . . . (Paris: C. Sonnius, 1636).

7 Estimates are based on bibliographical information contained in G. Boucher de la Richarderie, *Bibliothèque universelle des voyages*, 4 vols. (Paris: Chez Treuttel et Würtz, 1808); Jacques de Dampierre, *Essai sur les sources de l'histoire des Antilles françaises, 1492–1664* (Paris: A. Picard et fils, 1904); and Régis Antoine, *Les Écri-vains français et les Antilles: Des premiers Pères blancs aux surréalistes noirs* (Paris: G. P. Maisonneuve et Larose, 1978). For a comparison of the numbers of published travel works on the subject in various parts of the world, see David Cohen, *The French Encounter with Africans: White Response to Blacks, 1530–1880* (Bloomington: Indiana University Press, 1980), 7.

8 Gilbert Chinard has shown that traces of influence from the narratives of colo-nization in the Caribbean appeared in exotic, sentimental novels by Gomber-ville and Prévost and in the genre of the "imaginary voyage." Gilbert Chinard, *L'Amérique et le rêve exotique dans la littérature française au XVIIe et XVIIIe siècle* (Paris: Librairie E. Droz, 1934), 59–85, 189–220, 280–82. See also Goeffrey Atkin-son, *The Extraordinary Voyage in French Literature from 1700 to 1720* (Paris: Cham-pion, 1922); and Jean-Michel Racault, *L'Utopie narrative en France et en Angleterre, 1675–1761* (Oxford: Voltaire Foundation, 1991).

9 One only has to refer to the footnotes in Jean-Jacques Rousseau, *Discours sur l'origine et les fondements de l'inégalité parmi les hommes*, edited by Jacques Roger (1755; reprint, Paris: Garnier-Flammarion, 1971) to appreciate the extent to which French colonial impressions of Island Caribs informed the author's notion of "sav-age" man. On the relationship between travel literature and the anthropology of the French philosophes, see Michèle Duchet, *Anthropologie et histoire au siècle des lumières* (1971; reprint, Paris: Albin Michel, 1995); and Numa Bruc, *La Géo-graphie des philosophes: Géographes et voyageurs français au XVIIIème siècle* (Paris: Orphrys, 1975).

10 On the popularity of *Oroonoko* in France, see Seeber, *Anti-slavery Opinion*, 59–60.

11 On Diderot and Raynal's text in relation to colonialism and slavery, see Srinivas Aravamudan, *Tropicopolitans: Colonialism and Agency, 1688–1804* (Durham: Duke University Press, 1999), 289–325; Hans-Jürgen Lüsebrink and Manfred Tietz, eds., *Lectures de Raynal: L'Histoire des deux Indes en Europe et en Amérique au XVIIIe siècle* (Oxford: Voltaire Foundation, 1991); Michèle Duchet, *Anthropologie et his-toire: Diderot et l'Histoire des deux Indes ou l'écriture fragmentaire* (Paris: Nizet, 1978); and Yves Bénot, *Diderot: De l'athéisme à l'anticolonialisme* (Paris: Maspéro, 1970).

12 The journal maintained an antislavery perspective for its duration. For more on antislavery literature and the physiocratic critique of slavery, see Seeber, *Anti-slavery Opinion*, 90–109; and Duchet, *Anthropologie et histoire*, 160–70.

13 In Dobie's assessment of Montesquieu's *De l'esprit des lois*, the issue of colonial-ism is "largely displaced onto the Spanish context, while the attendant problem

of slavery is transposed onto the arena of domestic life in the Orient." Madeleine Dobie, *Foreign Bodies: Gender, Language and Culture in French Orientalism* (Stanford: Stanford University Press, 2001), 39.

14 See ibid., 4–6, 38–43.

15 On antislavery and reformism in eighteenth-century France, see Duchet, *Anthropologie et histoire*, 137–93; Seeber, *Anti-slavery Opinion*; Cohen, *The French Encounter with Africans*, 130–55; Yves Bénot, *La Révolution française et la fin des colonies* (Paris: Éditions La Découverte, 1988), 7–103; Léon-François Hoffmann, *Le Nègre romantique: Personnage littéraire et obsession collective* (Paris: Payot, 1973), 81–99; Sala-Molins, *Les Misères des lumières*; and Roger Mercier, *L'Afrique noire dans la littérature française: Les premières images, XVIIe–XVIIIe siècles* (Dakar: Université de Dakar, Faculté des lettres et sciences humaines, Publication de la Section de langues et littératures, 1962).

16 For extended commentary on Condorcet's text, see Carl Ludwig Lokke, *France and the Colonial Question: A Study of Contemporary French Opinion 1763–1801* (New York: Columbia University Press, 1932), 86–90; and Sala-Molins, *Les Misères des lumières*, 19–73.

17 Guillaume-Thomas Raynal, *Essai sur l'administration de St.-Domingue* (n.p., 1785).

18 Philip Boucher, *Les Nouvelles Frances: France in America, 1500–1815, an Imperial Perspective* (Providence: John Carter Brown Library, 1989), 93.

19 On the formation and goals of the Société des amis des noirs, see Lokke, *France and the Colonial Question*, 90, 119–30; Cohen, *The French Encounter with Africans*, 138–42, 150–53; and Robin Blackburn, *The Overthrow of Colonial Slavery, 1776–1848* (London: Verso, 1988), 169–73.

20 On the impact of the Haitian Revolution on French abolitionism and colonial policy, see Cohen, *The French Encounter with Africans*, esp. 155–79; Lawrence C. Jennnings, *French Antislavery: The Movement for the Abolition of Slavery in France, 1802–1848* (Cambridge: Cambridge University Press, 2000); Philippe Vigier, "La Recomposition du mouvement abolitionniste française sous la monarchie de Juillet," in *Les Abolitions de l'esclavage: De L. F. Sonthonax à V. Schoelcher, 1793, 1794, 1848*, edited by Marcel Dorigny (Paris: L'Organisation des Nations Unies, 1995); and Francis Arzalier, "Les mutations de l'idéologie coloniale en France avant 1848: De l'esclavagisme à l'abolitionnisme," in *Les Abolitions de l'esclavage: De L. F. Sonthonax à V. Schoelcher, 1793, 1794, 1848*, edited by Marcel Dorigny.

21 See the text of the proclamation "Aux cultivateurs esclaves" in Glissant, *Le Discours antillais*, 78–86.

22 On "Schoelcherisme" in French history, see ibid.; Françoise Vergès, "'I Am Not the Slave of Slavery': The Politics of Reparation in (French) Postslavery Communities," in *Frantz Fanon: Critical Perspectives*, edited by Anthony C. Alessandrini (London: Routledge, 1999), 258–75; and Vergès, *Monsters and Revolutionaries*, 1–71.

23 Vergès, *Monsters and Revolutionaries*, 9.

24 Blackburn, *The Overthrow of Colonial Slavery*, 492; Cohen, *The French Encounter with Africans*, 263–70.

25 Stewart Mims, *Colbert's West India Policy* (New Haven: Yale University Press, 1912), 175–76, 225.

26 Boucher, *Les Nouvelles Frances*, 84; Lokke, *France and the Colonial Question*, 16.

27 Paul Butel, "L'Essor antillais au XVIIe siècle," in *Histoire des Antilles et de la Guyane*, edited by Pierre Pluchon (Toulouse: Édouard Privat, 1982), 114.

28 Ibid., 113. For a comparison of French and English colonial sugar production in the eighteenth century, see Robin Blackburn, *The Making of Colonial Slavery* (London: Verso, 1997), 431–36.

29 Charles Frostin, *Les Révoltes blanches à Saint-Domingue aux XVIIe et XVIIIe siècles (Haïti avant 1789)* (Paris: Éditions de l'École, 1975), 63.

30 Ibid., 64.

31 Jules François Saintoyant, *La Colonisation française sous l'Ancien Régime* (Paris: La Renaissance du livre, 1929), 2:345.

32 Blackburn, *The Overthrow of Colonial Slavery*, 169–73; Frostin, *Les Révoltes blanches*, 64.

33 Jean M. Goulemot, editor's preface to *Dialogisme culturel au XVIIIe siècle*, edited by Jean M. Goulemot, *Cahiers d'Histoire culturelle*, vol. 4 (Tours: Université de Tours, 1997).

34 "Presque tous les auteurs ont surtout traité la question de l'abolition de l'esclavage, qui a tant passionné les esprits dans la première moitié de ce siècle." Lucien Peytraud, *L'Esclavage aux Antilles françaises avant 1789: D'après des documents inédits des archives coloniales* (Paris: Librairie Hachette, 1897), x.

35 Ibid.; Pierre de Vaissière, *Saint-Domingue: La Société et la vie créole sous l'ancien régime (1629–1789)* (Paris: Perrin, 1909); Dampierre, *Essai sur les sources de l'histoire antillaise*.

36 Roger Toumson, *La Transgression des couleurs: Littérature et langage des Antilles, XVIIIe, XIXe, XXe siècles* (Paris: Éditions caribéennes, 1990), 23.

37 Antoine, *Les Écrivains français et les Antilles*, 7.

38 Joan Dayan, *Haiti, History, and the Gods* (Berkeley: University of California Press, 1995).

39 Peter Hulme, *Colonial Encounters: Europe and the Native Caribbean, 1492–1797* (London: Methuen, 1986), 8.

40 The expression is that of Emmanuel Levinas. See Robert Young, *White Mythologies* (London: Routledge, 1990), 1–27.

41 In "Orientalism Reconsidered," Said writes, "We cannot proceed unless therefore we dissipate and re-dispose the material of historicism into radically different objects and pursuits of knowledge, and we cannot do that until we are aware clearly that no new projects of knowledge can be constituted unless they fight to remain free of the dominance and professionalized particularism that comes with historicist systems and reductive, pragmatic or functionalist theories." Edward W. Said, "Orientalism Reconsidered," in *Europe and Its Others*, edited by Francis Barker, Peter Hulme, Margaret Iversen, and Diane Loxley (Colchester: University of Essex, 1985), 1:22–23.

42 Gayatry Spivak, *The Post-colonial Critic*, edited by Sarah Harasym (New York:

Routledge, 1990), 19, 20. See also Gayatry Spivak, "Can the Subaltern Speak?" in *Marxism and the Interpretation of Culture*, edited by Cary Nelson and Lawrence Grossberg (Basingstoke: Macmillan Education, 1988), 271–313.

43 Similar criticisms have been voiced by scholars from various disciplinary perspectives. See, for example, Benita Parry, "Problems in Current Theories of Colonial Discourse," *Oxford Literary Review* 9, nos. 1–2 (1987): 27–58; Ann McClintock, "Postcolonialism and the Angel of Progress," in *Imperial Leather: Race, Gender and Sexuality in the Colonial Contest* (New York: Routledge, 1995), 1–17; Carole Boyce Davies, "From Postcoloniality to Uprising Textualities: Black Women Writing the Critique of Empire," in *Black Women, Writing, and Identity: Migrations of the Subject* (London: Routledge, 1994), 80–112; and Frederick Cooper and Ann Laura Stoler, "Between Metropole and Colony: Rethinking a Research Agenda," in *Tensions of Empire: Colonial Cultures in a Bourgeois World*, edited by Frederick Cooper and Ann Laura Stoler (Berkeley: University of California Press, 1997), 1–56. The most controversial attack on postcolonial theory is offered in Aijaz Ahmad, *In Theory: Classes, Nations, Literatures* (London: Verso, 1992).

44 Edward Said, *Orientalism* (New York: Pantheon, 1978), 1–28. For a critique of Said's ahistoricism, see Dennis Porter, "Orientalism and Its Problems," in *The Politics of Theory*, edited by Peter Hulme, Margaret Iversen, and Diana Loxley (Colchester: University of Essex, 1983); and Lisa Lowe, *Critical Terrains: British and French Orientalisms* (Ithaca: Cornell University Press, 1991), 1–29.

45 For a probing discussion of Bhabha's methodological obscurities, see Benita Parry, "Signs of Our Times: Discussion of Homi Bhabha's *The Location of Culture*," *Third Text* 28–29 (1994): 5–24.

46 On debates about the relationship between plantation slavery and capitalist relations of exploitation, see Ania Loomba, *Colonialism/Postcolonialism* (New York: Routledge, 1998), 128–33. For a reading of early modern narratives of colonialism from the English Caribbean that takes account of postcolonial perspectives, see Keith Sandiford, *The Cultural Politics of Sugar: Caribbean Slavery and Narratives of Colonialism* (Cambridge: Cambridge University Press, 2000).

47 Parry, "Problems in Current Theories of Colonial Discourse," 35.

48 Dobie, *Foreign Bodies*, 4.

49 Aravamudan, *Tropicopolitans*.

50 McClintock, *Imperial Leather*, 73.

51 Ibid.

52 Roland Barthes, "Le Discours de l'histoire," in *Le Bruissement de la langue: Essais critiques IV* (Paris: Editions du Seuil, 1984), 163.

53 Hayden White offers an insightful critique of theories of historical representation in "The Question of Narrative in Contemporary Historical Theory," in *The Content of the Form: Narrative Discourse and Historical Representation* (Baltimore: Johns Hopkins University Press, 1987), 26–45. Barthes calls this illusion the "effet du réel." Barthes, "Le Discours de l'histoire," 174–77.

54 Spivak, *The Post-colonial Critic*, 19–20.

55 See Catherine Gallagher and Stephen Greenblatt, *Practicing New Historicism* (Chi-

cago: University of Chicago Press, 2000), 7. Although the critics associated with New Historicism have deliberately avoided articulating an overarching theoretical paradigm, this volume best describes their style of criticism and methodological perspective. See also H. Aram Veeser, ed., *The New Historicism* (New York: Routledge, 1989). For an interesting critique of New Historicism from the perspective of a cultural historian, see Sarah Maza, "Stephen Greenblatt, New Historicism and Cultural History, or, What We Talk about When We Talk about Interdisciplinarity," *Modern Intellectual History*, 1, no. 2 (August 2004): 249–65.

56 Gallagher and Greenblatt, *Practicing New Historicism*, 12.

57 Arun Mukherjee, "Whose Post-colonialism and Whose Post-modernism?" quoted in Davies, *Black Women, Writing, and Identity*, 85.

58 For Kristeva, the abject is a sort of fantasy through which an infant separates itself from the mother by imagining her as an object of horror, distaste, and fear. Julia Kristeva's ideas on abjection are outlined in *Powers of Horror: An Essay on Abjection*, translated by Leon S. Roudiez (New York: Columbia University Press, 1982).

59 Gallagher and Greenblatt, *Practicing New Historicism*, 28.

60 Hulme, *Colonial Encounters*; Dayan, *Haiti, History, and the Gods*; Vergès, *Monsters and Revolutionaries*.

61 Fernando Ortiz, *Cuban Counterpoint: Tobacco and Sugar*, translated by Harriet de Onís (New York: Knopf, 1947), 102–3; Kamau Brathwaite, *The Development of Creole Society in Jamaica, 1770–1820* (Oxford: Clarendon, 1971), 296.

62 Brathwaite, *The Development of Creole Society in Jamaica*, 306.

63 See O. Nigel Bolland, "Creolization and Creole Societies: A Cultural Nationalist View of Caribbean Social History," in *Intellectuals in the Twentieth-Century Caribbean*, edited by Alistair Hennessy (London: Macmillan, 1992), esp. 1:52, 58.

64 Édouard Glissant, *Caribbean Discourse: Selected Essays*, translated, with an introduction, by J. Michael Dash (Charlottesville: University Press of Virginia, 1989), 128. For Glissant's theoretical formulation of creolization, see also his *Poétique de la relation* (Paris: Gallimard, 1990), 77–89, 103.

65 Jean Bernabé, Patrick Chamoiseau, and Raphaël Confiant, *Éloge de la créolité / In Praise of Creoleness*, translated by M. B. Taleb-Khyar (Paris: Gallimard, 1989), 87–88. For an analysis of the francophone creolization thesis in relation to Caribbean literary history, see J. Michael Dash, "Psychology, Creolization, and Hybridization," in *New National and Post-colonial Literatures*, edited by Bruce King (Oxford: Clarendon, 1996), 45–58; and "Textual Error and Cultural Crossing: A Caribbean Poetics of Creolization," *Research in African Literatures* 25, no. 2 (1994): 159–68.

66 Glissant, *Caribbean Discourse*, 64.

67 Derek Walcott, "The Caribbean: Culture or Mimicry?" in *Critical Perspectives on Derek Walcott*, edited by Robert D. Hamner (Boulder: Three Continents Press, 1997), 53.

68 Patrick Chamoiseau and Raphaël Confiant, *Lettres créoles: Tracées antillaises et continentales de la littérature: Haïti, Guadeloupe, Martinique, Guyane, 1635–1975* (Paris: Hatier, 1991), 27.

69 Ibid., 29, 46.

70 Jacques Adélaïde-Merlande, "Le Créole: Aux origines de l'utilisation de ce terme." In *Créoles de la Caraïbe, Actes du colloque universitaire en hommage à Guy Hazaël-Massieux, Pointe-à-Pitre, le 27 mars 1995*, edited by A. Yacou (Paris: Karthala, 1996), 51.

71 Ibid.

72 Labat writes, for example: "Créoles, c'est à dire, nez dans le païs." Jean-Baptiste Labat, *Nouveau voyage aux isles de l'Amérique contenant l'histoire naturelle de ces pays, l'origine, les moeurs, la religion, et le gouvernement des habitants anciens et modernes . . .* (1742; reprint, Fort-de-France Martinique: Éditions des Horizons Caraïbes, 1972), 1:79.

73 *Littré* quoted in Roger Toumson, "'Blancs créoles' et 'Nègres créoles:' Généalogie d'un imaginaire colonial," in Yacou, *Créoles de la Caraïbe*, 110. See also Roger Toumson, *La Transgression des couleurs* (Paris: Éditions Caribbéennes, 1989), 159; and *Mythologie de métissage* (Paris: Presses Universitaires de France, 1998), 119–23.

74 Bolland, "Creolization and Creole Societies," 64.

75 This kind of thinking was perhaps most famously expounded in Gilberto Freyre's classic study of Brazilian slave society, in which he argued that a greater frequency of miscegenation in Brazil led to a much smaller social divide between whites and slaves than existed in other slave societies. Gilberto Freyre, *The Masters and the Slaves: A Study in the Development of Brazilian Civilization*, 2d English-language ed., translated by Samuel Putnam (New York: Knopf, 1971).

76 Brathwaite, *The Development of Creole Society in Jamaica*, 303.

77 Françoise Vergès, "Métissage, discours masculin et déni de la mère," in *Penser la créolité*, edited by Maryse Condé and Madeleine Cottenet-Hage (Paris: Éditions Karthala, 1995), 79–81. In an article entitled "Métissage et créolisation," Glissant conceives of métissage as a meeting of "*lieux communs*" that can no longer be degraded because they are increasingly generalized in what he calls a "*chaos monde:*" "In this context, métissage no longer appears as an accursed given of existence, but more and more like a potential source of richness and opportunity." Edouard Glissant, "Métissage et créolisation," in *Discours sur le métissage, identités métisses: En quête d'Ariel*, edited by Sylvie Kandé (Paris: L'Harmattan, 1999), 49.

78 Glissant, "Métissage et créolisation," 47.

79 Bernabé, Chamoiseau, and Confiant, *Éloge de la créolité*, 29.

80 This criticism rejoins those of a number of scholars who have attacked the theory of créolité for its regressive gender politics. See, for example, A. James Arnold, "The Gendering of Créolité: The Erotics of Colonialism," in Condé and Cottenet-Hage, *Penser la créolité*; and Vergès, "Métissage, discours masculin et déni de la mère." For attacks on créolité as an essentialist cultural discourse, see Chris Bongie, *Islands and Exiles*, 63–65, and Michel Giraud, "La Créolité: Une rupture en trompe-l'oeil," *Cahiers d'Études Africaines* 148, no. 37–4 (1997): 795–811.

81 Angela Yvonne Davis, *Women, Race and Class* (New York: Vintage, 1983), 23–24. See also bell hooks, *Ain't I a Woman: Black Women and Feminism* (Boston: South End, 1981). Davis and hooks are largely responsible for having redirected the study

of slavery toward issues of gender. This work has been continued by Deborah
Gray White, Jaqueline Jones, Jennifer Morgan, Stephanie Camp, Elizabeth Fox-
Genovese, Brenda Stevenson, and Hortense Spillers. For a review of historical
work on women in slavery in the United States, see Debora Gray White, "Revisiting Ar'n't I a Woman," in *Ar'n't I a Woman? Female Slaves in the Plantation South*,
rev. ed. (New York: Norton, 1999), 1–15.

82 Hortense Spillers, "Mama's Baby, Papa's Maybe: An American Grammar Book,"
Diacritics 17, no. 2 (1987): 65–81.

83 Dayan, *Haiti, History, and the Gods*; Saidiya Hartman, *Scenes of Subjection: Terror,
Slavery and Self-Making in Nineteenth-Century America* (New York: Oxford University Press, 1997); Arlette Gautier, *Les Soeurs de Solitude: La Condition féminine
dans l'esclave* [*sic*] *aux Antilles du XVIIe au XIXe siècle* (Paris: Éditions Caribéennes,
1985).

84 Hartman, *Scenes of Subjection*, 81.

85 Ibid., 85. See also Joan Dayan's comments on the proslavery discourse of perfect
submission in *Haiti, History, and the Gods*, 189–99.

86 Gautier, *Les Soeurs de Solitude*, 151–83.

87 Dayan, *Haiti, History, and the Gods*, 56.

88 On Gramsci's ideas on hegemony, see Antonio Gramsci, *Selections from the Prison
Notebooks*, translated and edited by Quintin Hoare and Geoffrey Nowell Smith
(New York: International Publishers, 1971), esp. 180–83, 245–46.

89 On the range of uses to which pyschoanalytic understandings of desire have been
put in colonial studies and the different interpretive possibilities of a Foucauldian
model of desire, see Ann Laura Stoler, *Race and the Education of Desire: Foucault's
History of Sexuality and the Colonial Order of Things* (Durham: Duke University
Press, 1995), 165–95.

90 Freud's ideas on fantasy were developed in numerous works throughout his career.
For a detailed and scholarly discussion of this concept, see the article "Phantasy"
in J. Laplanche and J.-B. Pontalis, *The Language of Psycho-analysis*, translated by
Donald Nicholson-Smith, *The International Psycho-Analytical Library* 94 (London:
Hogarth Press, 1973), 314–19. On the relation between fantasy, politics, and social
reality, see Jacqueline Rose, *States of Fantasy* (Oxford: Clarendon, 1996). For a reading of the intersection between sexual fantasies and colonial ideology, see Susan
Zantop, *Colonial Fantasies: Conquest, Family, and Nation in Precolonial Germany,
1770–1870* (Durham: Duke University Press, 1997).

91 On the history of the French term *libertinage*, see Rosy Pinhas-Delpuech, "De
l'affranchi au libertin, les avatars d'un mot," in *Éros Philosophe: Discours libertins des
lumières*, edited by François Moureau and Alain-Marc Rieu (Paris: Honoré Champion, 1984), 12–20; Raymond Trousson, "Préface," in *Romans libertins du XVIIIe
siècle*, edited by Raymond Trousson (Paris: Robert Laffont, 1993), i–ix.

92 Jacques Bouton, *Relation de l'establissement des François depuis l'an 1635 en l'isle de la
Martinique, L'une des Antilles de l'Amérique: Des moeurs des sauvages, de la situation,
et d'autres singularitez de l'isle* (Paris: Cramoisy, 1640), 96.

93 Ibid.

94 Jean-Baptiste Du Tertre, *Histoire générale des Antilles habitées par les Français* (1667–71; reprint, 4 vols. in 3, Fort-de-France, Martinique: Éditions des Horizons Caraïbes, 1973), 2:399.

95 See, for example, Claude-Prosper-Jolyot Crébillon (Crébillon fils), *Les Égarements du coeur et de l'esprit*, edited by Jean Dagen (1736; reprint, Paris: Flammarion, 1985); and Choderlos de Laclos, *Les Liaisons dangereuses*, edited by Joël Papadopoulos (1782; reprint, Paris: Gallimard, 1972).

96 On libertinage as a philosophy of seduction, control, and manipulation, see Peter Brooks, *The Novel of Worldliness* (Princeton: Princeton University Press, 1969); Nancy K. Miller, *French Dressing: Women, Men and Ancien Régime Fiction* (New York: Routledge, 1995); Catherine Cusset, "Editor's Preface," *Yale French Studies* 94 (1998): 1–16 (special issue, "Libertinage and Modernity"); Michel Delon, *Le Savoir-vivre libertin* (Paris: Hachette Littératures, 2000); and Colette Cazenobe, *Le Système du libertinage de Crébillon à Laclos* (Oxford: Voltaire Foundation, 1991). On the relation of libertine literature to ethics, see Catherine Cusset, *No Tomorrow: The Ethics of Pleasure in the French Enlightenment* (Charlottesville: University Press of Virginia, 1999).

97 Brooks, *The Novel of Worldliness*, 188.

98 Dayan, *Haiti, History, and the Gods*, 213, 214.

99 Marcel Hénaff, *Sade: The Invention of the Libertine Body*, translated by Xavier Callahan (Minneapolis: University of Minnesota Press, 1999), originally published as *Sade: l'invention du corps libertin* (Paris: Presses Universitaires de France, 1978).

100 Ibid., 161.

101 [Justin Girod de Chantrans], *Voyage d'un Suisse dans les colonies d'Amérique* (1785; reprint, with a foreword by Pierre Pluchon, Paris: Librairie Jules Tallendier, 1980), 182.

102 It is important to note, however, that concubinage was criminalized only when it produced offspring. See chapter 4.

103 Alexandre-Stanislas de Wimpffen, *Voyage à Saint-Domingue pendant les années 1788, 1789, 1790* (Paris, 1797), reprinted in *Haiti au XVIIIe siècle*, edited by Pierre Pluchon (Paris: Karthala, 1993), 81.

104 In this project, I am primarily interested in analyzing representations of heterosexual interracial sexual contact between white men and black women with respect to the system of desire and exclusion that ensured white political and sexual hegemony. Although white women reportedly did take part in interracial libertinage, I examine the impact and ideological repercussions of their activities through male-authored colonial discourse, insofar as white female desire for the racial other fueled white male anxieties about their own sexual dominance in the colony.

105 Pierre Ulric Dubuisson, *Nouvelles considérations sur Saint-Domingue, en réponse à celles de M. H.D.* (Paris: Chez Cellot et Jombert, 1780), 2:4.

106 Girod de Chantrans, *Voyage d'un Suisse*, 153.

107 Michel René Hilliard d'Auberteuil, *Considérations sur l'état présent de la colonie française de Saint-Domingue: Ouvrage politique et législatif* (Paris: Chez Grangé, 1776), 2:77.

108 Wimpffen, *Voyage à Saint-Domingue*, 214.

109 In the 1770s and 1780s, the proportion of free people of color in Saint-Domingue (as a percentage of the total free population) was approximately twice that of Martinique and the English islands of Jamaica and Barbados. Only Puerto Rico had a larger percentage of free coloreds. For comparative statistics on free people of color in New World slave societies, see David W. Cohen and Jack P. Greene, introduction to *Neither Slave nor Free: The Freedmen of African Descent in the Slave Societies of the New World*, edited by David W. Cohen and Jack P. Greene (Baltimore: Johns Hopkins University Press, 1972), esp. 10, table 2. See also Jane G. Landers, ed., *Against the Odds: Free Blacks in the Slave Societies of the Americas* (London: Frank Cass, 1996).

110 Stewart King, *Blue Coat or Powdered Wig: Free People of Color in Pre-revolutionary Saint-Domingue* (Athens: University of Georgia Press, 2001), 266.

111 Wimpffen, *Voyage à Saint-Domingue*, 89.

112 Historians may be impeded in part by the lack of documentary evidence of interracial miscegenation. I thank Stephanie McCurry, Dylan Thomas, and Jennifer Morgan for discussing this issue with me.

113 On discriminatory laws against free people of color in Saint-Domingue, see Gwendolyn Midlo Hall, *Social Control in Slave Plantation Societies: A Comparison of St. Domingue and Cuba* (Baltimore: Johns Hopkins University Press, 1971); Gwendolyn Midlo Hall, "Saint-Domingue," in Cohen and Greene, *Neither Slave nor Free*; Léo Elisabeth, "The French Antilles," in Cohen and Greene, *Neither Slave nor Free*; Frostin, *Les Révoltes blanches*, 304–10; John D. Garrigus, "Colour, Class and Identity on the Eve of the Haitian Revolution: Saint-Domingue's Free Coloured Elite as *colons américains*," in Landers, *Against the Odds*, 20–43; and C. L. R. James, *The Black Jacobins: Toussaint L'Ouverture and the San Domingo Revolution*, 2d rev. ed. (New York: Vintage, 1989), 36–45.

114 Jean-Luc Bonniol, *La Couleur comme maléfice* (Paris: A. Michel, 1992), 56–57. See also the earlier and much more extensive study on which Bonniol relies, Yvan Debbasch, *Couleur et liberté: Le jeu de critère ethnique dans un ordre juridique esclavagiste*, vol. 1, Annales de la Faculté de droit et des sciences politiques et économiques de Strasbourg, no. 16 (Paris: Dalloz, 1967).

115 The questions of why and precisely when the association between dark-skinned Africans and slavery was naturalized rather than seen as circumstancial have been very much debated. On the emergence of racial slavery in the Americas, see Blackburn, *The Making of New World Slavery*, 12–20; Kathleen Brown, *Good Wives, Nasty Wenches, and Anxious Patriarchs: Gender, Race, and Power in Colonial Virginia* (Chapel Hill: University of North Carolina Press, 1996); and Winthrop Jordan, *White over Black: American Attitudes toward the Negro, 1550–1812* (Chapel Hill: University of North Carolina Press, 1968), 44–98.

116 Robert Young, *Colonial Desire: Hybridity in Theory, Culture and Race* (London: Routledge, 1995), 9.

117 This idea represents a slight adaptation of Winthrop Jordan's insight into the ambivalence of English colonials, who were "caught in the push and pull of an irrec-

oncilable conflict between desire and aversion for interracial union" (quoted ibid., 149–50).

Chapter One   Border of Violence

1 On the definition of *Carib* since the early colonial period, see Neil Whitehead, introduction to *Wolves from the Sea: Readings in the Anthropology of the Native Caribbean*, edited by Neil Whitehead (Leiden: KITLV Press, 1995), 9–22; Jalil Sued Badillo, *Los Caribes: Realidad o fábula* (Río Piedras, P.R.: Editorial Antillana, 1978); Jalil Sued Badillo, "The Island Caribs: New Approaches to the Question of Ethnicity in the Early Colonial Caribbean," in Whitehead, *Wolves from the Sea*; Louis Allaire, "The Caribs of the Lesser Antilles," in *The Indigenous People of the Caribbean*, edited by Samuel M. Wilson (Gainesville: University Press of Florida, 1997), 179–85; Peter Hulme, "Caribs and Arawaks," in Hulme, *Colonial Encounters*; and Philip Boucher, *Cannibal Encounters: Europeans and Island Caribs, 1492–1763* (Baltimore: Johns Hopkins University Press, 1992), 1–11.

2 My interpretation of Columbus's journal refers to the translated excerpt entitled "The Journal of Columbus (1492–1493)," in *Wild Majesty: Encounters with Caribs from Columbus to the Present Day—An Anthology*, edited by Peter Hulme and Neil Whitehead (Oxford: Oxford University Press, 1992), 17–28. In his journal, the only surviving copy of which is a transcription penned by Las Casas, Columbus designates both the hostile group and its place of origin with the terms *Canibales* and *Caribes*. He writes, for example: "The admiral also says that on the islands he passed they were greatly fearful of *Carib* and on some they called it *Caniba*, but on Españiola, *Carib*" (25). The term *cannibal* eventually passed into other languages with the primary meaning of "man-eater." To their credit, the French distinguished between Island Caribs, whom they called Caraïbes, and mainland Caribs, called Caribes or Galibis. On the continued utility of seventeenth-century French ethnic terminology, see Whitehead, introduction to *Wolves from the Sea*, 17–20.

3 "The Journal of Columbus," 26.

4 On legislation concerning Caribs and their status in early Caribbean history, see Joseph Boromé, "Spain and Dominica 1493–1647," *Caribbean Quarterly* 12 (1966): 30–46; Boucher, *Cannibal Encounters*; Badillo, *Los Caribes*, esp. 86–87; Badillo, "The Island Caribs"; Troy S. Floyd, *The Columbus Dynasty in the Caribbean, 1492–1526* (Albuquerque: University of New Mexico Press, 1973); and Carl Sauer, *The Early Spanish Main* (Berkeley: University of California Press, 1966). On the use of the term *Carib* as a political distinction, see also Hulme, *Colonial Encounters*; Whitehead, introduction to *Wolves from the Sea*; Neil Whitehead, introduction to *Lords of the Tiger Spirit: A History of the Caribs in Colonial Venezuela and Guayana, 1498–1820* (Dordrecht: Foris, 1988).

5 On Carib resistance against the Spanish, see Boromé, "Spain and Dominica"; Boucher, *Cannibal Encounters*, 13–20; Floyd, *The Columbus Dynasty in the Caribbean*, 135; and Badillo, "The Island Caribs."

6 Badillo, "The Island Caribs," 74.

7 The writings of Dominican missionaries contain several transcriptions of speaking natives designating themselves as Caraïbe rather than the self-ascriptions recorded in the first Carib/French dictionary. This narrative evidence will be discussed further below.

8 On French-Carib relations in the first half-century of colonization, see Boucher, *Cannibal Encounters*, 31–61; Hilary Beckles, "Kalinago (Carib) Resistance to European Colonisation of the Caribbean," in *Crossroads of Empire: The European-Caribbean Connection, 1492–1992*, edited by Alan Cobley (Cave Hill, Barbados: Department of History, University of the West Indies, 1994), 23–37; Michael Craton, "From Caribs to Black Caribs: The Amerindian Roots of Servile Resistance in the Caribbean," in *In Resistance: Studies in African, Caribbean, and Afro-American History*, edited by Gary Y. Okiriro (Amherst: University of Massachussets Press, 1986), 96–116; Nellis Crouse, *French Pioneers in the West Indies, 1624–1664* (New York: Columbia University Press, 1940); and Jacques Petitjean Roget, introduction to *Histoire de l'isle de Grenade en Amérique, 1649–1659: Manuscrit anonyme de 1659*, edited by Jacques Petitjean Roget and Élisabeth Crosnier (Montreal: Les Presses de l'Université de Montréal, 1975), 7–35. The best contemporary source is Jean-Baptiste Du Tertre, *Histoire générale des Antilles habitées par les François*, 3 vols. (Paris: Jolly, 1667–71).

9 Caribs still survive on the island of Dominica, where several hundred live on a reserve on the northeastern coast. On the last surviving Island Carib population, see Anthony Layng, *The Carib Reserve: Identity and Security in the West Indies* (Washington, D.C.: University Press of America, 1983).

10 Jean-Baptiste Du Tertre, *Histoire générale des Antilles habitées par les Français* (1667–71; reprint, 4 vols. in 3, Fort-de-France, Martinique: Éditions des Horizons Caraïbes, 1973), 1:535–41.

11 On recent theoretical trends in border studies, see David E. Johnson and Scott Michaelsen, "Border Secrets: An Introduction," in *Border Theory: The Limits of Cultural Politics*, edited by David E. Johnson and Scott Michaelson (Minneapolis: University of Minnesota Press, 1997); Tobias Wendl and Michael Rösler, "Frontiers and Borderlands: The Rise and Relevance of an Anthropological Research Genre," in *Frontiers and Borderlands: Anthropological Perspectives*, edited by Michael Rösler and Tobias Wendl (Frankfurt: Peter Lang, 1999); and Debra Castillo, "Border Theory and the Canon," in *Post-colonial Literatures: Expanding the Canon*, edited by Deborah Madsen (London: Pluto, 1999). On the border as the site of subaltern knowledge production, see Walter Mignolo, *Local Histories/Global Designs: Coloniality, Subaltern Knowledges and Border Thinking* (Princeton: Princeton University Press, 2000).

12 See, for example, Bernabé, Chamoiseau, and Confiant, *Éloge de la créolité*; and Chamoiseau and Confiant, *Lettres créoles*, 15–20.

13 On the establishment of the company, see Du Tertre, *Histoire générale des Antilles habitées par les Français*, 7–14; Jacques Petitjean Roget, *La Société d'habitation à la Martinique: Un demi siècle de formation, 1635–1685*, 2 vols. (Lille: Atelier Reproduction des theses, Université de Lille III, 1980), 1:62–69; and Nellis M. Crouse,

French Pioneers in the West Indies, 1624–1664 (New York: Columbia University Press, 1940), 17–19.

14 Boucher, "The Caribbean and the Caribs," 18.

15 Du Tertre, *Histoire générale des Antilles habitées par les Français*, 9. All subsequent page references to the reprint edition will be included in the text.

16 Marcel Mauss, *The Gift: The Form and Reason for Exchange in Archaic Societies*, translated by W. D. Halls (London: Routledge, 1990), 3.

17 On representations of reciprocity in situations of colonial contact, see also Hulme, *Colonial Encounters*, 147; and Mary Louise Pratt, *Imperial Eyes: Travel Writing and Transculturation* (London: Routledge, 1992), 84.

18 A similar ideology of assimilation was applied in seventeenth-century Canada and eighteenth-century Louisiana, to little effect. See Cornelius Jaenen, *Friend and Foe: Aspects of French-Amerindian Cultural Contact in the Sixteenth and Seventeenth Centuries* (New York: Columbia University Press, 1976), especially 153–85; and Jerah Johnson, "Colonial New Orleans: A Fragment of the Eighteenth-Century French Ethos," in *Creole New Orleans: Race and Americanization*, edited by Arnold R. Hirsch and Joseph Logsdon (Baton Rouge: Lousiana State University Press, 1992), 12–57.

19 The historian Joseph Rennard explains that there were no more than a few secular priests in Saint-Christophe before 1635, when, on the reorganization of the company, two Capuchins were sent there on official duty. See Joseph Rennard, *Histoire religieuse des Antilles françaises des origines à 1914, d'après des documents inédits* (Paris: Société de l'histoire des colonies françaises, 1954), 12; and Guillaume de Vaumas, *L'Éveil missionaire de la France au XVIIe siècle* (Paris: Bloud and Gay, 1959).

20 Jean-Baptiste Du Tertre, *Histoire générale des isles des Christophe, de la Guadeloupe, de la Martinique, et autres dans l'Amérique . . .* (Paris: J. et E. Langlois, 1654), 59.

21 Bouton, *Relation de l'establissement des François depuis l'an 1635 en l'isle de la Martinique*, 133.

22 Mathias DuPuis, *Relation de l'establissement d'une colonie française dans la Gardeloupe, isle de l'Amérique, et des moeurs des sauvages* (Caen: Marin Yvon, 1652), 227–28.

23 On the role of missionary travel relations as colonial propaganda, see Philip Boucher, "The Caribbean and the Caribs in the Thought of Seventeenth-Century French Colonial Propagandists: The Missionaries," in *Proceedings of the Fourth Meeting of the French Colonial Historical Society*, edited by Alf Andrew Heggoy and James J. Cooke (Lanham, Md.: University Press of America, 1978), 17–32; and Gabriel Debien and J. Le Ber, "La Propagande et le recrutement pour les colonies d'Amérique au XVIIe siècle," *Conjonction: Bulletin de l'Institut Française d'Haïti* 12 (1953): 60–90.

24 On Du Tertre's life and work, see Dampierre, *Essai sur les sources de l'histoire des Antilles françaises, 1492–1664*, 108–28.

25 On conventions of humanist historiography, see Erica Harth, *Ideology and Culture in Seventeenth-Century France* (Ithaca: Cornell University Press, 1983), 130–40.

26 Jean-Baptiste Du Tertre, *Histoire générale des isles . . . dans l'Amérique* (Paris: Jacques Langlois, 1654), [ii]. All subsequent page references will be included in the text.

27 Bartolomé de Las Casas did much to disseminate stories of the ruthless massacre of millions of Indians in the Greater Antilles, especially in his *Brevísima relación de la destrucción de las Indias*, first published in Seville in 1552. A French translation appeared in 1579 entitled *Tyrannies et cruautez des Espagnols perpetrées ès Indes Occidentales*, translated by Jacques de Miggrode (Anvers: Chez François de Ravelenghien, 1579). For a modern edition, see Bartolomé de Las Casas, *Très brève relation de la destruction des Indes*, translated by Gonzalez Batlle Fanchita. Paris: La Découverte/Poche, 1996.

28 Mathias DuPuis, *Relation de l'establissement d'une colonie françoise dans la Guadeloupe*; Armand de la Paix, [Raymond Breton], "Relation de l'île de la Guadeloupe" (1647), reprinted in Raymond Breton, *Relations de l'île de la Guadeloupe* (Basse Terre: Société d'histoire de la Guadeloupe, 1978). See also Raymond Breton, *Les Caraibes, La Guadeloupe, 1635–1656: Histoire des vingt premières années de la colonisation de la Guadeloupe d'après les relations du R. P. Breton*, edited, with a preface, by Joseph Rennard (Paris: G. Flicker, 1929).

29 See also Dupuis, *Relation de l'establissement d'une colonie française dans la Gaudeloupe*, 226–27.

30 On the trope of the devil in missionary interpretations of Carib belief systems, see chapter 3.

31 This recognition was codified in a treaty signed by France and England in 1660, which promised that neither nation would settle Dominica and Saint-Vincent. On the status of the "neutral" islands in the seventeenth century, see Joseph Boromé, "The French and Dominica, 1699–1763," *Jamaican Historical Review* 7 (1967): 10–39; and Boucher, *Cannibal Encounters*, 51–52.

32 Whitehead, introduction to *Wolves from the Sea*, 9; Louis Allaire, "The Caribs of the Lesser Antilles," in *The Indigenous People of the Caribbean*, edited by Samuel M. Wilson (Gainesville: University Press of Florida, 1997), 180.

33 For a critique of early modern ethnographies in a New World context, see Peter Mason, *Deconstructing America: Representations of the Other* (London: Routledge, 1990); Rolena Adorno, *The Armature of Conquest: Spanish Accounts of the Discovery of America, 1492–1589* (Stanford: Stanford University Press, 1992); Stephen Greenblatt, *Marvelous Possessions: The Wonder of the New World* (Chicago: University of Chicago Press, 1991); and John Elliott, *The Old World and the New* (London: Cambridge University Press, 1970). On colonial sources relating to Caribs in particular, see Hulme, *Colonial Encounters*; and Badillo, *Los Caribes*.

34 See Hulme, *Colonial Encounters*; José Rabasa, *Inventing America: Spanish Historiography and the Formation of Eurocentrism*, Oklahoma Project for Discourse and Theory, no. 11 (Norman: University of Oklahoma Press, 1993); and Pratt, *Imperial Eyes*.

35 Hulme, *Colonial Encounters*, 52.

36 César de Rochefort, *Histoire naturelle et morale des iles Antilles de l'Amérique* (Rotterdam: Arnout Leers, 1658).

37 On the life and publications of César de Rochefort, see Petitjean Roget, *La Société*

d'habitation à la Martinique, 1:153–55; and Dampierre, *Essai sur les sources des l'histoire des Antilles françaises*, 137–45.

38 "In their language, this Carib word means, 'superfluous people [*gens ajoutez*], who suddenly appear without warning,' 'foreigners,' or 'strong and valiant Men.'" Rochefort, *Histoire naturelle et morale des iles Antilles*, 336.

39 Ibid., 344.

40 See, for example, Du Tertre, *Histoire générale des Antilles habitées par les Français*, 1:323.

41 For two specialist views on the historical evidence of Island Carib cannibalism, see Neil L. Whitehead, "Carib Cannibalism: The Historical Evidence," *Journal de la Société des Américanistes* 70 (1984): 69–87; and Robert A. Myers, "Island Carib Cannibalism," *Nieuwe West-Indische Gids* 58 (1984): 147–84.

42 Breton, *Relations de l'île de la Guadeloupe*, 52. Breton's dominant role as the source of the anonymous manuscript was established by Joseph Rennard in the introduction to his edition of Breton's writings. Rennard notes the existence of two copies of these manuscripts and proposes that Breton wrote the "Parisian" version in order to correct certain mistakes contained in the first, which could be attributable to Armand de la Paix's misreading of Breton's original. See Rennard, introduction to *Les Caraïbes, La Guadeloupe, 1653–1656*, by Raymond Breton, 19–21.

43 Breton, *Relations de l'île de la Guadeloupe*, 53. The correction appears in the editor's footnote.

44 Ibid., 76–77.

45 Pierre Pelleprat, *Relation des missions des PP. de la Compagnie de Jésus dans les isles et à la terre ferme de l'Amérique méridionale* (Paris: Sébastien et Gabriel Cramoisy, 1655), 67–68; Mathias Du Puis, *Relation de l'establissement d'une colonie française dans la Gardeloupe*, 185–87; Du Tertre, *Histoire générale des Antilles habitées par les Français*, 2:340–42. Pelleprat and Du Tertre considered Caribs to be the descendants of the conquering Galibi peoples and their female slaves, the Ignéris. The latter was another contemporary term for the former inhabitants of the Lesser Antilles, who were said to have survived in the mountains.

46 For a structuralist analysis of recorded myths of Carib origins, see C. J. M. R. Gullick, "Island Carib Traditions about Their Arrival in the Lesser Antilles," in *Proceedings of the Eighth International Congress for the Study of the Pre-Columbian Cultures of the Lesser Antilles* (Tempe: Arizona State University Department of Anthropology, 1980), 464–72. Gullick concludes that commonalities between various Carib myths point to the truth of their origins. In my opinion, Gullick is far too accepting of colonial accounts as accurate portrayals of contemporary native beliefs.

47 Breton, *Relations de l'île de la Guadeloupe*, 76–78.

48 Bouton, *Relation de l'establissement des François depuis l'an 1635 en l'isle de la Martinique*, 125.

49 Du Tertre, *Histoire générale des Antilles habitées par les Français*, 2:381.

50 Rochefort, *Histoire naturelle et morale des iles Antilles*, 478–79. On this point, Rochefort was the most reliable of colonial chroniclers, much more so than Du

Tertre, who denied the extent of French treachery with the Caribs. See Petitjean Roget's introduction to *Histoire de l'isle de Grenade en Amérique, 1649-1659: Manuscrit anonyme de 1659*, edited by Jacques Petitjean Roget and Élisabeth Crosnier (Montreal, Les presses de l'Université de Montréal, 1975).

51 Chevillard, *Les Desseins de son Éminence Cardinal Richelieu pour l'Amerique* (1659; reprint, Basse-Terre, Guadeloupe: Société d'histoire de la Guadeloupe, 1973), 129.

52 Rochefort, *Histoire naturelle et morale des iles Antilles*, 381.

53 Johannes Fabian, *Time and the Other: How Anthropology Makes Its Object* (New York: Columbia University Press, 1983), 29. On anthropology's privileging of abstract description over personal and historical narrative, see also Mary Louise Pratt, "Fieldwork in Common Places," in *Writing Culture: Poetics and Politics of Ethnography*, edited by James Clifford and George E. Marcus (Berkeley: University of California Press, 1986); and Gordon M. Sayre, *Les Sauvages Américains: Representations of Native Americans in French and English Colonial Literature* (Chapel Hill: University of North Carolina Press, 1997), 108-9.

54 This view is found in standard reference books and articles on Island Caribs. See especially Irving Rouse, "The Carib," in *Handbook of South American Indians*, edited by Julian H. Steward (Washington, D.C.: Smithsonian Institution, Bureau of American Ethnology, 1949), 4:547-65; and Douglas Taylor, "The Caribs of Dominica," *Bureau of American Ethnology Bulletin* 119 (1938): 109-59. Most modern histories of the colonial French Caribbean also rely on this view, including Petitjean Roget, *La Société de l'habitation à la Martinique*; Lucien-René Abénon, *La Guadeloupe de 1671-1759: Étude politique, économique et sociale* (Paris: L'Harmattan, 1987); Chauleau, *Histoire antillaise*; and Armand Nicolas, *Histoire de la Martinique des Arawaks à 1848* (Paris: L'Harmattan, 1996). An important exception is Boucher's *Cannnibal Encounters*. For a full critique of the persistence of colonial stereotyping in modern anthropological accounts of the native Caribbean, see Hulme, "Caribs and Awaraks."

55 Breton provides an early analysis of the linguistic picture of the native Caribbean in his brief chapter "De leur langue," in *Relations de l'ile de la Guadeloupe*, 55.

56 This explanation points to the variability of ethnic nomenclature across disciplines and historical periods. *Kariña* is the modern anthropological term for the language and peoples of the South American mainland (now Surinam and Guiana) referred to in seventeenth-century French sources as the Galibis or Calibis. Arawakan is the accepted name among modern linguists for a category of Amerindian languages associated with the Lokono peoples of the same region. Ironically, Island Caribs spoke an Arawakan language. See J. A. Mason, "The Languages of South America," in Steward, *Handbook of South American Indians*, 4:157-318. For a clear presentation of the traditional conquest interpretation of the linguistic evidence, see Berend Hoff, "Language Contact, War, and Amerinidian Historical Tradition," in Whitehead, *Wolves from the Sea*, 38-59; and Douglas Taylor and Berend Hoff, "The Linguistic Repertory of the Island Carib in the Seventeenth Century: The Men's Language—a Carib Pidgin?," *International Journal of American Lin-*

guistics 46, no. 4 (1980): 301-12. For a technical description of linguistic borrowings in Island Carib, see Douglas Taylor, *Languages of the West Indies* (Baltimore: Johns Hopkins University Press, 1977).

57 Hulme, *Colonial Encounters*, 57-77.

58 Neil L. Whitehead, "Ethnic Plurality and Cultural Continuity in the Native Caribbean" in Whitehead, *Wolves from the Sea*, 101. For new perspectives on ethnic identity in the native Caribbean, see Whitehead's introduction to *Wolves from the Sea*; Badillo, "The Island Caribs," 9-22, 61-90; Allaire, "The Lesser Antilles before Columbus"; Louis Allaire, "The Caribs of the Lesser Antilles," in Wilson, *The Indigenous People of the Caribbean*; Hulme, *Colonial Encounters*, 73-78; and Boucher, *Cannibal Encounters*, 2-6.

59 Raymond Breton, *Dictionaire caraibe-françois, composé par le R. P. Raymond Breton* (1665; reprint by Jules Platzmann, Leipzig: B. G. Teubner, 1892), 105. All subsequent references to Breton's dictionary will be to this edition.

60 See, for example, Rochefort, *Histoire naturelle et morale des iles Antilles*, 401; and Du Tertre, *Histoire générale des isles . . . dans l'Amérique*, 43.

61 Rochefort, *Histoire naturelle et morale des iles Antilles*, 326.

62 Ibid., 400-401. On the oppositional use of the term *Carib* by Amerindians, see also Badillo, "The Island Caribs," 62, 75; and Whitehead, introduction to *Wolves from the Sea*, 12-13.

63 On the Carib appropriation of European categories, see also Hulme, *Colonial Encounters*, 67-73.

64 Du Tertre, *Histoire générale des isles . . . dans l'Amérique*, 58.

65 Breton, *Relations de la Guadeloupe*, 55.

66 Rochefort, *Histoire naturelle et morale des iles Antilles*, 459.

67 Breton, quoted in Petitjean Roget, *La Société d'habitation à la Martinique*, 1:397.

68 Rochefort, *Histoire naturelle et morale des iles Antilles*, 299-300. Whereas the Carib chief gives up his own son, Aubert offers a servant, who reportedly falls ill shortly thereafter and is returned.

69 Pacifique de Provins, *Brève relation du voyage des îles de l'Amérique* (1643; reprint, in *Le voyage de Perse, et Brève relation du voyage des îles de l'Amérique*, with critical introductions by P. Godefroy de Paris and P. Hilaire de Wingene, Assisi: Collegio S. Lorenzo da Brindisi Dei Minori Cappucini, 1939), 13.

70 Rochefort, *Histoire naturelle et morale des iles Antilles*, 460.

71 Petitjean Roget, *La Société d'habitation à la Martinique*, 1:407.

72 Bouton, *Relation de l'establissement des François depuis l'an 1635 en l'isle de la Martinique*, 138.

73 Ibid., 39-40.

74 Petitjean Roget, *La Société d'habitation à la Martinique*, 1:404-05; Chamoiseau et al., *Éloge de la créolité*, 26-30.

75 Du Tertre, *Histoire générale des isles . . . dans l'Amérique*, 5.

76 Bouton, *Relation de l'establissement des François depuis l'an 1635 en l'isle de la Martinique*, 32-33.

77 Ibid., 136.

78 For a detailed account of the French appropriation of the Carib cassava bread and wine, see Petitjean Roget, *La Société d'habitation à la Martinique*, 1:453–61.

79 In his dictionary, Breton explains: "It is a metal that we sent to France to study and fabricate, but to no purpose. Our Savages always discerned the fraud; even silver and gold do not equal it . . . it is the richest of their gems" (106).

80 Chevillard, *Les Desseins de son Éminence*, 41.

81 Bouton, *Relation de l'establissement des François depuis l'an 1635 en l'isle de la Martinique*, 131.

82 Pelleprat, *Relations des missions des PP. de la Compagnie de Jésus*, 59–60.

83 In two articles, Pietz traces the emergence of the material object as fetish to the intercultural spaces of the West African coast in the sixteenth century, where objects were transvalued across widely divergent social systems. See William Pietz, "The Problem of the Fetish, I," *Res* 9 (1985): 1–15; and "The Problem of the Fetish, II," *Res* 13 (1987): 23–46.

84 Du Tertre, *Histoire générale des isles . . . dans l'Amérique*, 460–61.

85 Ibid., 58.

86 Rochefort, *Histoire naturelle et morale des iles Antilles*, 426.

87 Bouton, *Relation de l'establissement des François depuis l'an 1635 en l'isle de la Martinique*, 109.

88 Chinard, *L'Amérique et le rêve exotique dans la littérature française au XVIIe et au XVIIIe siècles*, 50.

89 Du Tertre, *Histoire générale des Antilles habitées par les Français*, 2:338–39.

90 Ibid., 339.

91 Ibid.

92 Ibid., 340.

93 Rochefort, *Histoire naturelle et morale des iles Antilles*, 341, 297. On the majesty of Amichon, he explains: "The first of those Ambassadors was named Captain Amichon and was well respected among them. He was accompanied by thirty of the most clever and able men of Dominica. Monsieur Auber says that he has never since seen savages more handsome and agile" (297).

94 Ibid.

95 Eric Cheyfitz, introduction to *Poetics of Imperialism* (New York: Oxford University Press, 1991).

96 See, for example, Vincent Crapanzano, "Hermes' Dilemma: The Masking of Subversion in Ethnographic Description," and Talal Asad, "The Concept of Cultural Translation in British Social Anthropology," both in *Writing Culture*, edited by Clifford and Marcus.

97 This is a central argument of David Murray's *Forked Tongues: Speech, Writing and Representation in North American Indian Texts* (Bloomington: Indiana University Press, 1991). See also Cheyfitz, *The Poetics of Imperialism*; and Stephen Greenblatt, "Kidnapping Language," in *Marvelous Possessions* (Chicago: University of Chicago Press, 1991).

98 Dennis Tedlock, *The Spoken Word and the Work of Interpretation* (Philadelphia: University of Pennsylvania Press, 1983), 324. See also George Marcus and Dick Cushman, "Ethnographies as Texts," *Annual Review of Anthropology* 11 (1982): 25–69; and James Clifford, "On Ethnographic Allegory," in *Writing Culture*, edited by Clifford and Marcus, 109.

99 Rochefort's text representation of Carib speech is perhaps the most available to counterhegemonic readings, as has been shown by Keith Sandiford in his chapter, "Rochefort: French Collusions to Negotiate." Sandiford points out Rochefort's inclusion of contestatory speech attributed to Caribs, arguing that this voice "erodes the ethnographer's exclusive power to inscribe." It is not clear how Sandiford views Rochefort's own role in mediating this language, since he regards the inscriptions as the "authentic voice of Carib indigenes." See Sandiford, *The Cultural Politics of Sugar*, 44–45, 54–55.

100 On the translation of native languages in sixteenth-century New Spain, see J. Jorge Klor de Alva, "Language, Politics, and Translation: Colonial Discourse and Classic Nahuatl in New Spain," in *The Art of Translation: Voices from the Field*, edited by Rosanna Warren (Boston: Northeastern University Press, 1989), 143–62; and Shirley Brice Heath and Richard Laprade, "Castilian Colonization and Indigenous Languages: The Cases of Quechua and Aymara," in *Language Spread: Studies in Diffusion and Social Change*, edited by Robert Cooper (Bloomington: Indiana University Press, 1982). On the North American context, see Murray, *Forked Tongues*, 14–22.

101 Raymond Breton, *Dictionaire caraibe-françois, Meslé de quantité de remarques historiques pour l'éclaircissement de la langue* (Auxerre: Gilles Bouquet, 1665). All page references in parentheses will refer to the facsimile edition, *Dictionaire caraibe-français*, reprinted by Jules Platzmann (Lepzig: B. G. Teubner, 1892). See also the newest edition: Raymond Breton, *Dictionnaire caraïbe-français*, edited by Marina Besada Paisa and Jean Bernabé (Paris: Éditions Karthala, 1999). When citing Breton's literal translations of long phrases in Carib (as opposed to his narrative definitions), I have placed the author's French translation in a note so as to preserve the record of the initial translation and the author's particular interpretation of Carib speech. On the significance of Breton's dictionary to linguistic research on the Carib language, see Sylvain Auroux and Francisco Queixalos, "La Première description linguistique des Antilles françaises: Le Père Raymond Breton," in *Naissance de l'ethnologie? Anthropologie et missions en Amérique XVIe–XVIIIe siècle*, edited by Claude Blanckaert (Paris: Éditions du Cerf, 1985); and Hoff, "Language Contact, War, and Amerindian Historical Tradition," 37.

102 A similar argument is made by Klor de Alva in his analysis of the role of Classical Nahuatl in New Spain. See his "Colonial Discourse and Classical Nahuatl," esp. 148–49.

103 Breton, *Relations de l'ile de la Guadeoupe*, 55. The relation between these tongues and the Creole that developed through plantation slavery is in dispute. On the contribution of early colonial contact languages to Creole, see Raymond Relousat,

"La problématique langagière dans le dictionnaire de Breton," in Breton, *Dictionnaire caraïbe-français*, lvix–lxxxvii; and Petitjean Roget, *La Société d'habitation à la Martinique*, 1:447–53.

104 Rochefort, *Histoire naturelle et morale des îles Antilles*, 392.

105 "Pere, . . . moy voulé Chrestienne bonne pour le grand Capitou le Dieu des Chrestiens." Chevillard, *Les Desseins de son Éminence de Richelieu pour l'Amérique*, 133.

106 "O Jacques, France mouche fasché, ly matté Karaibes." Du Tertre, *Histoire générale des isles . . . dans l'Amérique*, 43.

107 Rochefort, *Histoire naturelle et morale des îles Antilles*, 394.

108 Du Tertre, *Histoire générale des isles . . . dans l'Amérique*, 50.

109 Raymond Breton, *Dictionaire français-caraïbe* (1666, reprint by Jules Platzmann, Leipzig: B. G. Teubner, 1900); *Petit Catéchisme, ou sommaire des trois premières parties de la doctrine chrétienne* (Auxerre: Gilles Bouquet, 1664); *Grammaire caraïbe* (Auxerre, Gilles Bouquet: 1667). The manuscripts *Relation de l'île de la Guadeloupe par les missionnaires dominicains à leur général en 1647* and *Brevis Relatio Missionis fratrum praedicatorum in insulam guadelupam* are reprinted in Breton, *Relations de l'île de la Guadeloupe*. On Breton's life and work, see Auroux and Queixalos, "La Première description linguistique"; and articles assembled in the 1999 edition of Breton, *Dictionnaire caraïbe-français*.

110 Clifford, *The Predicament of Culture*, 24.

111 Murray, *Forked Tongues*, 14–31.

112 Breton, *Petit Catéchisme*, 6–7.

113 Petitjean Roget, *La Société d'habitation à la Martinique*, 1:433.

114 This dictionary definition provides the basis for an article by the anthropologist Douglas Taylor, "The Meaning of Dietary and Occupational Restrictions among the Island Carib," *American Anthropologist* 52 (1950): 343–49.

115 The original translation is "Allons à la guerre."

116 A *callebassier* is a species of tree.

117 On the French colonial uses of manioc, see Petitjean Roget, *La Société d'habitation à la Martinique*.

118 "Comment se nomme cela? Corrige mon discourse; Accoustume moy a ton langage."

119 "Je vais diligenter, dépescher d'écrire."

120 "Je reviendray de la Dominique lors que je sçauray si bien la langue que je ne la pourray plus oublier."

121 McClintock, *Imperial Leather*, 28.

122 Mikhail Bakhtin, "Discourse in the Novel," in *The Dialogic Imagination*, edited by Michael Holquist, translated by Caryl Emerson and Michael Holquist (Austin: University of Texas Press, 1981), 349.

123 Murray, *Forked Tongues*, 117.

124 "Les Sauvages de l'Isle de S. Vincent ont repoussez les Chrestiens."

125 "Il n'y a plus qu'une isle où les sauvages n'ayent estez chassez."

126 "Il nous enleve nostre terre."

127 "Vous peuplez plus que nous."

128 "Celuy la est un pirate qui enleve, et met aux fers les Caraibes."

129 "Habite toymesme cette isle."

130 "Je l'ay habité premier que toy."

131 "Les Caraïbes qui viennent des autres isles sont gens de nostre nation."

132 "Ha pourquoy nostre nation est elle si miserable!"

133 "Qui t'amene ici? Pour quel sujet, quelle raison?"

134 "Je suis icy pour vous voir."

135 "Tu es aussi ignorant et mal versé en nostre langue comme je le suis en la tienne."

136 "Nos langages ne se ressemblent pas, nos discours ne se raportent point."

137 "Ne contrefais pas mon parler."

138 "The neutralization of the other who becomes a theme or an object," writes Levinas, "is precisely his reduction to the same." Although Levinas here refers to the relationship with a metaphysical, or absolute, other that is transcendent to the same, his reflections extend metaphorically to the possibility of ethical relations of intersubjectivity. Emmanuel Levinas, *Totality and Infinity: An Essay on Exteriority*, translated by Alphonso Lingis (Pittsburgh: Duquesne University Press, 1969), 43.

139 Ibid.

140 Ibid., 53.

141 See Clifford, *The Predicament of Culture*; and Stephen A. Tyler, "Post-modern Ethnography: From Document of the Occult to Occult Document," in Clifford and Marcus, eds., *Writing Culture*, 126.

142 Marcus and Cushman, "Ethnographies as Texts," 35.

143 Frantz Fanon, "Le Noir et le langage," in *Peau noire, masques blancs* (Paris: Éditions du Seuil, 1952), 13.

Chapter Two   White Noble Savage

1 Gordon Lewis, *Main Currents in Caribbean Thought: The Historical Evolution of Caribbean Society in Its Ideological Aspects, 1492–1900* (Baltimore: Johns Hopkins University Press, 1983), 67.

2 Saint Christopher is located on the northwestern end of the Lesser Antilles and is now known as Saint Kitts. Its placement outside of the ordinary Spanish navigational track made it attractive for northern European refugees. See Boucher, *Cannibal Encounters*, 39.

3 Du Tertre, *Histoire générale des isles . . . dans l'Amérique*, 5–6.

4 According to W. Adolphe Roberts, the accord between d'Esnambuc and Warner was based on a mutual desire to drive out the Caribs and share the island between themselves. Du Tertre's scene of origins is directly followed by an account of hostilities with the natives. On the historical conditions of d'Esnambuc's voyage, see Roberts, *The French in the West Indies*, 31–42; and Petitjean Roget, *La Société d'habitation à la Martinique*, 1:42–61.

5 On the thematic variation and polemical significance of the noble savage trope, see Dickason, *The Myth of the Savage*; Anthony Pagden, *The Fall of Natural Man: The American Indian and the Origins of Comparative Ethnology* (Cambridge: Cam-

bridge University Press, 1982); Duchet, *Anthropologie et histoire au siècle des lumières*; Peter Mason, *Deconstructing America*; and Chinard, *L'Amérique et le rêve exotique dans la littérature française au XVIIe et XVIIIe siècles*. For its antique origins, see Peter Mason, "Classical Ethnography and Its Influence on the European Perception of the Peoples of the New World," in *The Classical Tradition and the Americas*, vol. 1: *European Images of the Americas and the Classical Tradition*, edited by Wolfgang Haase and Meyer Reinhold (Berlin: Walter de Gruyter, 1993). On the attribution of the myth to Rousseau, see Hoxie Neale Fairchild, *The Noble Savage: A Study in Romantic Naturalism* (New York: Columbia University Press, 1983). The anthropologist Ter Ellington extends and greatly expands Fairchild's critique by questioning the extent to which belief in something called the noble savage ever existed. See Ter Ellington, *The Myth of the Noble Savage* (Berkeley: University of California Press, 2001).

6　Hayden White, "The Noble Savage Theme as Fetish," in *First Images of America*, vol. 1, edited by Fredi Chiappelli (Berkeley: University of California Press, 1976). White's argument is marred, however, by his insistence on connecting the critique of inherited power he locates in the contradictory phrase "noble savage" to the political projects of eighteenth-century French writers such as Rousseau and Diderot, who could not possibly have used the English expression.

7　Lescarbot, quoted in Ellington, *The Myth of the Noble Savage*, 22.

8　Ibid., 21–34.

9　The dilemma faced by colonial writers is similar to that encountered later by eighteenth-century novelists, who aspired to represent a range of human behaviors and weaknesses indicative of their times while not encouraging such moral corruption in their readers. See George May, *Le Dilemme du roman* (New Haven: Yale University Press, 1963). On the role of colonial narratives in legitimating Creole society with respect to metropolitan England, see Sandiford, *The Cultural Politics of Sugar*. Sandiford offers an extensive reading of tropes of appeasement and pacification of the native Caribs in Rochefort's *Histoire naturelle et morale des iles Antilles*.

10　In order to encourage overseas commerce, the king decreed in 1629 that commoners who ran ships of over two hundred tons would enjoy noble privileges. See Davis Bitton, *The French Nobility in Crisis, 1560–1640* (Stanford: Stanford University Press, 1969), 70.

11　The letters renewing the contract of the Compagnie de Saint-Christophe in 1642 reserved four letters of nobility for those who "at their own expense occupy and inhabit the said islands and remain there under the authority of the Company for at least two years, with fifty men." Quoted in J. Le Ber and Gabriel Debien, "La Propagande et le recrutement pour les colonies d'Amérique," *Conjonction: Bulletin de l'Institut Française d'Haïti* 12 (1953), 80–81.

12　Bitton, *The French Nobility in Crisis*, 65–75. On the changing basis of claims to noble status in early modern France, see also Donna Bohanan, *Crown and Nobility in Early Modern France* (New York: Palgrave, 2001); G. Chaussinand-Nogaret, *La Noblesse au XVIIIème siècle* (Paris: Hachette, 1976); and Ellery Schalk, *From*

Valor to Pedigree: Ideas of Nobility in France in the Seventeenth and Eighteenth Centuries (Princeton: Princeton University Press, 1986). On literary representations of nobility, see David Posner, *The Performance of Nobility in Early Modern European Literature* (Cambridge: Cambridge University Press, 1999).

13 My discussion of French piracy draws on the following historical works: Janice E. Thomson, *Mercenaries, Pirates and Sovereigns: State-Buiding and Extraterritorial Violence in Early Modern Europe* (Princeton: Princeton University Press, 1994); Jenifer Marx, *Pirates and Privateers of the Caribbean* (Malabar, Fla.: Krieger, 1992); Roberts, *The French in the West Indies*; Lewis, *Main Currents in Caribbean Thought*; Michel Le Bris and Virginie Serna, eds., *Pirates et flibustiers des Caraïbes* (Paris: Éditions Hoëbeke, 2001); and Hugh Rankin, *The Golden Age of Piracy* (Williamsburg, Va.: Colonial Williamsburg Foundation, 1969). For an account of English piracy in the eighteenth century with implications for the French case, see Marcus Rediker, *Between the Devil and the Deep Blue Sea: Merchant Seamen, Pirates and the Anglo-American Maritime World, 1700–1750* (Cambridge: Cambridge University Press, 1987).

14 On the distinction between privateering and piracy in international law, see Thomson, *Mercenaries, Pirates and Sovereigns*, 22–26.

15 Ibid., 42.

16 Alexandre Olivier Oexmelin, *Histoire des aventuriers flibustiers qui se sont signalez dans les Indes: Contenant ce qu'ils ont fait de remarquable depuis vingt années, avec la vie, les moeurs et les coûtumes des boucaniers, et des habitans de S. Domingue et de la Tortue . . .* (Paris: Jacques Lefebvre, 1699). All parenthetical citations will refer to the modern edition: Alexandre Olivier Oexmelin, *Les Aventuriers et les boucaniers d'Amérique par Alexandre Oexmelin, Chirurgien des Aventuriers de 1666 à 1672*, reprint with a preface by Bertrand Guégan (Paris: Éditions du Carrefour, 1930).

17 See *pirate* and *aventurier* in *Dictionnaire de L'Académie française* (Paris, J. P. Coignard, 1694), 1:242, 624. In the *Encyclopédie*, *aventurier* is defined first in commercial terms as "a man without character or home, who boldly involves himself in business, but who cannot be trusted" and then in terms of piracy: "*Aventurier* is also the name given in America to hardy and enterprising pirates who unite against the Spanish and who make raids against them. They are also called buccaneers." See *aventurier* in *Encyclopédie, ou dictionnaire raisonné des sciences, des arts et des métiers* (Paris: Briasson, 1751), 1:869.

18 Petitjean Roget, *La Société de l'habitation à la Martinique*, 1:42. According to Petitjean Roget, the term was used in preference to *corsair* to mean "under the protection of a king." Oexmelin referred to both sanctioned and unsanctioned pirates as *flibustiers*.

19 Evidence of the eventual coalescence of all of these pirate terminologies appears in the definition of *aventurier* in the 1798 *Dictionnaire de L'Academie française*: "The name *aventurier* was given to certain *coureurs de mer* who pirated on the seas of America, otherwise called freebooters and buccaneers." *Dictionnaire de L'Académie française*, 5th ed. (Paris: J. J. Smits, 1798), 108. Oexmelin's book was quoted as the basis for the encyclopedia article "Buccaneer." *Encyclopédie*, 2:348.

20 *Boucan* is a word of *tupi-guarani* origin according to Odile Renault-Lescure. See her "Glossaire français d'origine amérindienne," in Breton, *Dictionnaire caraïbe-français* (1999 ed.), 257.

21 Henceforth my use of the term *pirate* will encompass the meanings of the French terms *flibustiers, boucaniers,* and *corsairs* unless otherwise noted.

22 In private correspondence, the governor of Saint-Domingue, De Cussy, expressed regret at having suppressed filibustering at the behest of the Crown, citing the loss of defensive capacity. Quoted in Vaissière, *Saint-Domingue,* 26, n. 1.

23 Du Tertre, *Histoire générale des isles . . . dans l'Amérique,* 467–68.

24 Du Tertre, *Histoire générales des Antilles habitées par les Français,* 3:188.

25 On the European myth of the wild man, see Mason, *Deconstructing America,* 43–46; and Hayden White, "The Forms of Wildness: Archaeology of an Idea," in *The Wild Man Within,* edited by Edward Dudely and Maximillian E. Novak (Pittsburgh: University of Pittsburgh Press, 1972), 3–37.

26 Du Tertre, *Histoire générale des Antilles habitées par les Français,* 1:179.

27 Du Tertre, *Histoire générale des isles . . . dans l'Amérique,* 467.

28 Du Tertre, *Histoire générale des Antilles habitées par les Français,* 2:418–20.

29 On its founding, the colony of Tortuga was granted equal freedom of conscience for Catholics and protestants. In the 1660s, Saint-Domingue received certain privileges from the company administration under the influential governors Ogeron and De Cussy, such as exemption from paying the head tax and permission to trade with the Dutch. On the sedition of 1670, see Frostin, *Les Révoltes blanches,* 77–118.

30 On the suppression of piracy in the French Caribbean, see Roberts, *The French in the West Indies,* 53–88. The decline of piracy in the French islands was aided by the simultaneous suppression of piracy by the English authorities. From the 1680s onward, England imposed its authority on the islands of New Providence and Fort-Royal, formerly bases of operations for pirates. See Rankin, *The Golden Age of Piracy,* 20–21; and Kris E. Lane, *Pillaging the Empire* (Armonk, N.Y.: M. E. Sharpe, 1998), 164–92.

31 When it was published in England in 1684, Oexmelin's book was an instant success, appearing in two editions in the same year. Contemporary English pirate narratives include one by Basil Ringrove appended to the English edition of Oexmelin's text, J. Esquemeling, *Bucaniers of America, the Second Volume: Containing the Dangerous Voyage and Bold Attempts of Captain Bartholomew Sharp . . .* (London: William Crooke, 1685); and William Dampier's *A New Voyage Round the World* (London: James Knapton, 1697). Despite the fact that Oexmelin's text was a publishing sensation known and read by subsequent English writers of pirate stories, the work has not been examined by English literary scholars, who tend to focus on William Dampier as the major forerunner of the genre of pirate or sea narrative. See, for example, Philip Edwards, *The Story of the Voyage: Sea Narratives in Eighteenth-Century England* (Cambridge: Cambridge University Press, 1994); and Anna Neill, "Buccaneer Ethnography: Nature, Culture, and Nation in the Journals of William Dampier," *Eighteenth-Century Studies* 22, no. 2 (2000): 165–80.

32 More than twenty modern editions of Oexmelin's work in three languages have been published since 1980. Oexmelin's account is the earliest narrative source cited by modern histories of the buccaneer phenomenon in the Caribbean and the chief source of information about this subculture in classic histories of piracy and buccaneering such as Rankin, *The Golden Age of Piracy*; Philip Gosse, *The History of Piracy* (New York: Longmans, Green, 1932); and James Burney, *The History of the Buccaneers of America* (London: Swan Sonnenschein, 1816).

33 Oexmelin's French nationality was established by Vrijman in "L'Identité d'Exquemelin," *Comité des travaux historiques et scientifiques: Bulletin de la section de géographie* 48 (1933): 34–57. The doctoral thesis in medicine is the following: Henri Pignet, *Alexandre-Olivier Exquemelin: Chirurgien des aventuriers 1666–1707 (?)* (Montpellier: Imprimerie de la Presse, 1939). This work's flagrant falsifications have been meticulously refuted by the historian Michel-Christian Camus in "Une note critique à propos d'Exquemelin," *Revue française d'histoire d'outre-mer* 77, no. 286 (1990): 79–90. Historical prefaces and introductions to Oexmelin's work nonetheless continue to repeat elements of Pignet's fabricated narrative. For example, in his preface to a 1996 French edition of Oexmelin, Michel Le Bris reproduces Pignet's falsities via an earlier preface by Francis Lacassin, which he cites liberally. See Michel Le Bris, "Chirurgien de la Flibuste," introduction to A. O. Oexmelin, *Les Flibustiers du Nouveau Monde: Histoire des flibustiers et boucaniers qui se sont illustrés dans les Indes* (Paris: Phébus, 1996); and Francis Lacassin, "Exmelin ou Le docteur Watson au service du crime," in *Histoire des Frères de la Cote, flibustiers et boucaniers des Antilles*, by A. O. Exmelin (Paris: Éditions Maritimes et d'Outre-Mer, 1980).

34 On the life and work of Oexmelin, see Camus, "Une note critique"; and Bertrand Guégan, "Notes sur la vie et les éditions d'Oexmelin," in Oexmelin, *Les Aventuriers et les boucaniers d'Amérique*. For brief interpretations of Oexmelin's work, see Antoine, *Les Écrivains français et les Antilles*, 65–72; and Lewis, *Main Currents in Caribbean Thought*, 79–80.

35 The first sequence of editions is as follows (note the changes in the title and the spelling of the author's name): A. O. Exquemelin, *De Americaensche Zee-Roovers* . . . (Amsterdam: Jan ten Hoorn, 1678); A. O. Exquemelin, *Americanische Seeräuber* . . . (Nürnberg: Durch A. O., 1679); Esquemeling, *Piratas de la America, y luz à la defensa de las costas de Indias Occidentales* . . . (Colonia: Lorenzo Struickman, 1681); J. Esquemeling, *The Buccaneers of America: A True Account of the Most Remarkable Assaults Committed of Late Years upon the Coasts of the West Indies* . . . *Wherein Are Contained* . . . *the Exploits of Sur Henry Morgan, Our English Jamaican Hero* . . . , translated from Spanish (London: William Crooke, 1684); J. Esquemeling, *The History of the Bucaniers, Being an Impartial Relation of All the Battles, Sieges, and Other Most Eminent Assaults* . . . *More Especially the Unparalleled Achievements of Sir H. M.* . . . . (London: Thomas Malthus, 1684); Alexandre Olivier Oexmelin, *Histoire des aventuriers qui se sont signalez dans les Indes* . . . *avec la vie, les moeurs, les coûtumes des habitans de Saint Domingue* . . . (Paris: Jacques Lefebvre, 1686); and

Oexmelin, *Histoire des aventuriers flibustiers qui se sont signalez dans les Indes . . .* (Paris: Jacques Lefebvre, 1699).

36 "The Translator to the Reader," in Esquemeling, *Bucaniers of America*, [iii].

37 "The Publisher to the Reader," in Esquemeling, *The History of the Bucaniers*, [v].

38 [Frontignières], preface to Oexmelin, *Histoire des aventuriers* (1686 ed.), [vii].

39 Ibid., [xxi].

40 Michel-Christian Camus has shown that the text displays historical inaccuracies and differs significantly from the Dutch where matters of national pride were at stake. Camus, "Une note critique," 86–89.

41 [Frontignières], preface to Oexmelin, *Histoire des aventuriers* (1686 ed.), [iii].

42 Ibid., [vi]. Through the trope of the honnête homme, seventeenth-century noble apologists such as Nicolas Faret, author of *L'Honnest homme ou l'art de plaire à la cour* (1630), defended noble status as both hereditary and contingent on the practice of virtue. The honnête homme was a person trained in the arts of conversation and the virtues of nobility. Shalk, *From Valor to Pedigree*, 131–32.

43 On the production of the 1699 edition, see Camus, "Une note critique"; and Bertrand Guégan, "Notes sur la vie et les éditions d'Oexmelin," in Oexmelin, *Les aventuriers et les boucaniers d'Amérique*.

44 Guégan did not resist the temptation to alter Oexmelin's text. He made a number of slight edits to reduce its length. Unless otherwise indicated, all textual citations refer to the modern edition.

45 Frostin, *Les Révoltes blanches*, 47.

46 In *Sodomy and the Perception of Evil* (New York: New York University Press, 1983), B. R. Burg examines the buccaneer communities of the seventeenth-century Caribbean as examples of free homosexual enclaves that evolved with little or no interference from a dominant or repressive heterosexual nation. I reject his argument that homosexual acts were the only form of sexual expression engaged in by buccaneers. Oexmelin's writings show that women were commonly bought, raped, or entertained on land as part of the debauched indulgences of the piratical lifestyle.

47 Hobsbawm, quoted in Rediker, *The Devil and the Deep Blue Sea*, 269. See also Peter Linebaugh and Marcus Rediker, *The Many-Headed Hydra: Sailors, Slaves and Commoners and the Hidden History of the Revolutionary Atlantic* (Boston: Beacon, 2000), 154–67.

48 Thomson, *Mercenaries, Pirates and Sovereigns*, 46. On piracy as social revolt, see also Aravamudan, *Tropicopolitans*, 71–102; and Lewis, *Main Currents in Caribbean Thought*, 78–83.

49 Here I follow Norbert Elias's analysis of the "civilizing process" in the West as intricately tied to the state's repression of affect and control of physical violence, a view that relies on Weber's theory of state formation as a problem of the "monopoly of force." With Elias, I invoke the term *savage* to refer to those forms of violence that exceeded the norms of what was socially acceptable for early modern French subjects. Norbert Elias, *The History of Manners*, vol. 1: *The Civilizing Process* (New York: Pantheon, 1982), xv. On the Weberian concept of the state in relation to the

problem of international violence and piracy, see Thomson, *Mercenaries, Pirates, and Sovereigns*, 7–20.

50 Elias, *The History of Manners*, 191–205.

51 Marc Bloch, *Feudal Society*, translated by L. A. Manyon, with a foreword by T. S. Brown (London: Routledge, 1989), 293. On the relationship between nobility and warfare, see also Bitton, *The French Nobility in Crisis, 1560–1640*; Schalk, *From Valor to Pedigree*, 3–65; Dewald, *Aristocratic Experience and the Origins of Modern Culture, 1570–1715*, 45–69; and J. Q. C. Mackrell, *The Attack on "Feudalism" in Eighteenth-Century France* (London: Routledge, 1973).

52 Mackrell, *The Attack on "Feudalism" in Eighteenth-Century France*, 30–47. See also Sarah Maza, *The Myth of the French Bourgeoisie: An Essay on the Social Imaginary, 1750–1850* (Cambridge, Mass.: Harvard University Press, 2003), 27–36.

53 The pirates accompanying Olonnais on his expedition to Maracaïbo were especially well armed, as each carried a gun, two pistols, and a sabre (111). For more on the pirate arsenal, see Le Bris and Serna, *Pirates et flibustiers des caraïbes*, 130–31.

54 Pierre Goubert, *L'Ancien régime*, vol. 1: *La société* (Paris: Armand Colin, 1969), 154.

55 Based on my reading of Oexmelin, I differ from Srinivas Aramavudan's suggestion of a relation between pirates and anticolonialism when he argues that this liminal subculture had the potential to "mediate between reified oppositions of colonizer and colonized." My interpretation does concur with Aravamudan's reading of the piratical critique of trade. He writes: "If all trade is allegorized by piracy, Defoe's economic writings are scattered with acknowledgments that there is a vast difference between honest men and tradesmen because 'Trade is almost universally founded upon Crime.'" Aravamudan, *Tropicopolitans*, 92–93.

56 The same strategy was pursued by England, as is evident in the famous case of Captain Morgan. After his arrest and repatriation to London, he was knighted and returned to Jamaica as lieutenant governor with a mission to eliminate piracy. Marx, *Pirates and Privateers of the Caribbean*, 133–34.

57 The company had withdrawn from Tortuga in protest of the settlers' violation of its official monopoly, dependent as they were on Dutch and other merchants. Repressing a civil revolt, Ogeron allowed all French merchants to trade providing that they pay an entrance or exit tax of 5 percent. Oexmelin, *Les Aventuriers et les boucaniers d'Amérique*, 43–44.

58 Oexmelin describes in detail Ogeron's participation in a state-sponsored sack of Curaçao, his subsequent shipwreck at Puerto Rico, and his heroic effort to recover French prisoners. Michel-Christian Camus has questioned the authenticity of that anecdote. Camus, "Une note critique," 84–85. It nonetheless represents the editor's will to glorify Ogeron as a heroic leader of the pirates.

59 The extent to which this account is shaped by state interests is evident from modern histories of the siege, which recount the dispute between pirates and the French general Pointis over their share of the booty. Feeling cheated, the pirates sacked Cartagena for a second time so as to ensure themselves of proper compensation. After several more exploits in the colonies, Du Casse was awarded the Golden

Fleece by the king of Spain and was promoted to the highest military rank in France. See Roberts, *The French in the West Indies*, 83–88; and Marx, *Pirates and Privateers of the Caribbean*, 132.

60 For a complimentary perspective on the recivilization and reincorporation of William Dampier, former pirate turned pirate writer, into the English nation, see Neill, "Buccaneer Ethnography."

61 Elias, *The History of Manners*, 202–3.

62 In Old Regime France, the bourgeoisie infiltrated the upper class by investing in offices of the bureaucratic absolutist state and by acquiring landed estates, or fiefs, on which they could live "nobly" and thereby hope to join the upper class after several generations. Yet the "feudalization" of the bourgeoisie in the seventeenth century required the abandonment of commerce. New and aspiring nobles typically adhered to the *loi de dérogeance*, which marked commerce as inimical to the profession of nobility. To "pass" as noble, the enterprising bourgeois had to give up and disavow the very capitalist activity that had enabled him to bid for noble status in the first place. On class mobility and the "feudalization of the bourgeoisie" in seventeenth-century France, see Harth, *Ideology and Culture in Seventeenth-Century France*; Boris Porchnev, *Les Soulèvements populaires en France au XVIIème siècle* (Paris: SEVPEN, 1963); George Huppert, *Les Bourgeois Gentilhommes* (Chicago: University of Chicago Press, 1977); and Jonathan Dewald, *The European Nobility, 1400–1800* (Cambridge: Cambridge University Press, 1996). On the bourgeois investment in nobility as a deterrent to capitalism in France, see Roland Mousnier, *La Vénalité des offices sous Henri IV et Louis XIII* (Rouen: Manguard, 1945).

63 Saint-Christophe, Martinique, and Guadeloupe were sold to the colonial governors Poincy, Du Parquet, and Houel, respectively.

64 Mims, *Colbert's West India Policy*, 70.

65 Newly conquered islands included the dependencies of Guadeloupe; Marie Galante, La Desirade, and Les Saintes; Saint-Martin; Saint-Croix; and Tortuga Island. See Du Tertre, *Histoire générale des Antilles habitées par les Français*, vol. 1; and Roberts, *The French in the West Indies*, 37–41.

66 Rochefort, *Histoire naturelle et morale des iles Antilles*, 36–37. Poincy found his apologist in Rochefort, who received much of his information from the governor's personal papers and thanked him in kind with roaring praise. Rochefort makes of Poincy the incarnation of imperial nobility and elegance, bringing to Saint-Christophe an unprecedented level of civility by building churches, defenses, and public infrastructure; improving the justice system; and attracting settlers. Rochefort also praised Poincy's three-story mansion for its beauty and craftsmanship (see figure 12). Rochefort, *Histoire naturelle et morale des iles Antilles*, 30–31, 284.

67 On the sailors' baptism, see Henning Henningsen, *Crossing the Equator: Sailors' Baptism and Other Initiation Rites* (Copenhagen: Munksgaard, 1961), 147–50; and Rediker, *Between the Devil and the Deep Blue Sea*, 186–90.

68 For other firsthand accounts of the baptismal rite of crossing, see Guillaume Cop-

pier, *Histoire et voyage des Indes Occidentales, et de plusieurs autres regions maritimes et esloignées . . .* (Lyon, Jean Hugueton, 1645), 47–48; and Oexmelin, *Les Aventuriers et les boucaniers d'Amérique*, 16–18.

69 On sea travel as a dangerous space of marginality and transition, see McClintock, *Imperial Leather*, 24–25.

70 *Vaisseau d'hôpital* appears in the *Dictionnaire de L'Académie française* of 1762, meaning "a ship destined for the sick." *Dictionnaire de l'Académie française*, 4th ed. (Paris: Chez la veuve de Bernard Brunet, 1762), 886. On the role of the ship of fools in the historical repression of the mentally ill in early modern Europe, see Michel Foucault, *Histoire de la folie à l'âge classique* (Paris: Librairie Plon, 1961), 10–16.

71 Foucault argues that the seventeenth-century hospital facilitated the internment of the poor in a time of profound economic development and crisis. He discusses, in particular, the edict of 1656, which created the Hôpital général in Paris, whose function was to prevent "beggary and idleness as the source of all disorder." Quoted in Foucault, *Histoire de la folie à l'âge classique*, 77.

72 The hospitals supplied engagés, particularly women, in the early decades of colonization. Du Tertre notes, for example, that the company directors sent a number of "girls" from Saint-Joseph's hospital in Paris. Du Tertre, *Histoire générale des Antilles habitées par les Français*,1:228. In the 1680s, Louis XIV sent hundreds of young women and orphans living in the hospitals to the Caribbean islands. B. David, "Les Origines de la Population Martiniquaise," *Mémoires de la société d'histoire de la Martinique* 3 (1973): 23.

73 In invoking the term *homosocial*, I refer to Eve Sedgwick's analysis of the intense male bonds of friendship, mentorship, identification, and heterosexual rivalry that, though enabling male entitlement in Euro-American societies, often closely resemble "the most reprobated expressions of male homosexual sociality." Eve Kosofsky Sedgwick, *Between Men: English Literature and Male Homosocial Desire* (New York: Columbia University Press, 1985), 89.

74 Du Tertre, *Histoire générale des isles . . . de l'Amérique*, 24–25; Rochefort, *Histoire naturelle et morale des iles Antilles*, 320.

75 Coppier, *Histoire et voyage des Indes Occidentales, et de plusieurs autres regions maritimes et esloignées.*

76 Legislation was passed to thwart the demise of indentured servitude after the conversion to sugar production in the 1640s and 1650s. Colbert reduced the term by half and required all ships to carry servants. Boucher, *Les Nouvelles Frances*, 49.

77 Letter of November 19, 1680, quoted in Chauleau, *Histoire antillaise*, 87.

78 Ibid.

79 For another account of the abduction of young engagés, see Pelleprat, *Relation des missions des R.P. de la compagnie de Jésus*, 21–22.

80 Jean Bernabé, "Présentation," x; "La Créolité: Problématiques et enjeux," in Yacou, *Créoles de la Caraïbe*, 206.

81 See "famille," in *Dictionnaire de l'Académie française* (1694), 436. On the idea of the family in early modern France, see also Jean-Louis Flandrin, *Familles: Parenté,*

maison, sexualité dans l'ancienne société (Paris: Hachette, 1976); and Philippe Ariès, *L'Enfant et la vie familiale sous l'ancien régime* (1965; reprint, Paris: Éditions du Seuil, 1973).

82 On the meanings attached to the Latin *familia* in ancient Rome, see Suzanne Dixon, *The Roman Family* (Baltimore: Johns Hopkins University Press, 1992), 1–6. On patriarchal themes in biblical scripture, see Gerna Lerner, *The Creation of Patriachy* (New York: Oxford University Press, 1986), 162–63.

83 In the 1670s, the ratio of men to women in Guadeloupe and Martinique was approximately two to one, whereas in Saint-Domingue it was as high as eight to one. Gautier, *Les Soeurs de Solitude*, 33.

84 On the circumstances and condition of women engagés in the Antilles who were not part of these large contingents, see Jacques Petitjean Roget, "Les Femmes des colons à la Martinique au XVIIe et XVIIIe siècles," *Revue d'Histoire de l'Amérique française* 19, no. 2 (1955): 176–235; and Gabriel Debien, "Les Premières femmes des colons des Antilles (1635–1680)," *Revue de "La Porte Océane"* 90 (1952): 7–11.

85 On the history of clothing and the vestimentary revolution in seventeenth- and eighteenth-century France, see Daniel Roche, *La culture des apparences: Une histoire du vêtement, XVIIe–XVIIIe siècles* (Paris: Fayard, 1989), translated by Jean Birrell as *The Culture of Clothing: Dress and Fashion in the "Ancien Régime"* (Cambridge: Cambridge University Press, 1994). On the eighteenth-century French critique of luxury, see Maza, *The Myth of the French Bourgeoisie*, 40–68.

86 For an extensive reading of Blessebois's work in relation to colonial libertinage and diabolism, see chapter 3.

87 Jean-Baptiste Labat, *Nouveau voyage aux isles de l'Amérique, contenant l'histoire naturelle de ces pays, l'origine, les moeurs, la religion, et le gouvernement des habitants anciens et modernes . . .* (Paris, 1742; reprint, 8 vols. in 4, Fort-de-France, Martinique: Éditions des Horizons Caraïbes, 1972). All page references in the text will refer to the reprint edition. An earlier edition of the same title was published in 1722. Jean-Baptiste Labat, *Nouveau voyage aux isles de l'Amérique . . .* (Paris: P. F. Giffart, 1722).

88 Antoine-François Prévost, *Histoire générale des voyages, ou, nouvelle collection de toutes les relations de voyages par mer et par terre qui ont été publiées jusqu'à présent dans les différentes langues de toutes les nations connues.* 16 vols. (Paris: Didot, 1759), 15:491.

89 Although it had been quite powerful at the outset of colonial settlement, the Dominican presence in Martinique and Guadeloupe suffered great losses at midcentury when Governor Hoüel of Guadeloupe ousted the order for political reasons. At the time of Labat's arrival, the Dominican holdings on both islands were badly in need of repair. Chauleau, *Histoire antillaise*, 65–68.

90 Petitjean Roget, *La Société d'habitation à la Martinique*, 1:1152–53.

91 Correspondence of Intendants Mithon and Vaucresson, Governor de Machault, and Ministre Pontchartrain, cited in Antoine, *Les Écrivains français*, 78. See also Joseph Rennard, *Histoire religieuse des Antilles françaises des origines à 1914, d'après des documents inédits* (Paris: Société de l'histoire des colonies françaises, 1954), 73.

92 Marcel Chatillon, "Le Père Labat à travers ses manuscrits," *Bulletin de la Société d'histoire de la Guadeloupe* 40-42, 2e-4e trimestres (1979):21-26.

93 Labat's published compilations include *Voyage du Chevalier Desmarchais en Guinée, Isles voisines et à Caïenne* (1730, 1731); *Relation historique de l'Éthiopie occidentale* (1732); *Mémoires du chevalier d'Arvieux, contenant ses voyages dans l'Asie, la Syrie, la Palestine et la Barbarie* (1735); and *Nouvelle Relation de l'Afrique Occidentale* (1728).

94 Additions to the second edition include an extra volume on the history of French colonization and new chapters on tropical products, such that the final work comprised four volumes. Close connections to some in the colonial administration may have facilitated publication of the posthumous edition. Chatillon notes Labat's rapport with André Bruë, director of the Compagnie du Sénégal, whose memoirs he published as *Nouvelle relation de l'Afrique Occidentale* (Paris: Chez G. Cavelier, 1728). Labat's massive output was also connected to colonial propaganda around 1720, the time of Law's speculation in Louisiana. Chatillon, "Le Père Labat à travers ses manuscrits," 27-29.

95 Only the Capuchin order refused to operate plantations due to religious principles, choosing instead to tend modest gardens. See Rennard, *Histoire religieuse*, 80.

96 Sydney Mintz, *Sweetness and Power: The Place of Sugar in Modern History* (New York: Viking, 1985), 48. Stoler and Cooper summarize this thought cogently: "Europe was made by its imperial projects, as much as colonial encounters were shaped by conflicts within Europe itself." Cooper and Stoler, "Between Metropole and Colony, 1.

97 The literary figure of the parvenu was made most famous by Marivaux in his novel *Le paysan parvenu* (1734-35). On Marivaux's critique of hierarchies of rank and appearance and advocacy of merit as a basis for making social distinctions, see Amy Wyngaard, "Switching Codes: Class, Clothing and Cultural Change in the Works of Marivaux and Watteau," *Eighteenth-Century Studies* 33, no. 4 (2000): 523-41.

98 On the relation between merit and nobility in early modern France, see Jay Smith, *The Culture of Merit: Nobility, Royal Service, and the Making of Absolute Monarchy in France, 1600-1789* (Ann Arbor: University of Michigan Press, 1996); Schalk, *From Valor to Pedigree*; and Chaussinand-Nogaret, *La Noblesse au XVIIIème siècle*. Whereas historians have traditionally portrayed merit as an Enlightenment idea informing a bourgeois critique of hereditary nobility, Jay Smith has shown that a certain idea of merit undergirded ideals of aristocratic service. Labat's ideal of nobility is nonetheless at odds with the traditional noble abhorrence of commercial wealth.

99 On the issue of books, Labat advocated the establishment of a colonial publishing house: "For with so many people reading, will they read all of their lives without writing anything? Will they not get the itch to become Authors? . . . It seems to me that many Authors have already come out of our sugar factories and our cocoa storehouses." (2:330). Labat was alone in his judgment of colonial literary ambition. Later historians and travelers to the Antilles noted precisely the *lack* of interest in literary arts, except for the colonial taste for licentious books. According to Baron de Wimpffen, *Margot la Ravaudeuse* was the most common reading in

planter households in late-eightenth-century Saint-Domingue. Wimpffen, *Voyage à Saint-Domingue*, 119.

100　On the function of gifts in securing relations of mutuality and obligation between classes in early modern France, see Smith, *The Culture of Merit*, 24.

Chapter Three　Creolization and the Spirit World

1　On the association between the devil and Native American religiosity in European accounts of the New World, see Fernando Cervantes, *The Devil in the New World: The Impact of Diabolism in New Spain* (New Haven: Yale University Press, 1994); Fernando Cervantes, *The Idea of the Devil and the Problem of the Indian: The Case of Mexico in the Sixteenth Century*, Research Papers, no. 24 (London: University of London, Institute of Latin American Studies, 1991); Sabine MacCormack, "Demons, Imagination, and the Incas," in *New World Encounters*, edited by Stephen Greenblatt (Berkeley: University of California Press, 1993), 101–26; Peter Mason, *Deconstructing America*, 41–68; and Richard Beale Davis, "The Devil in Virginia in the Seventeenth Century," in *Witchcraft, Magic and Demonology*, vol. 8 of *Witchcraft in Colonial America*, edited by Brian P. Levack (New York: Garland, 1992), 361–79. For an analysis of the enduring legacy of diabolism in modern Latin America, see Michael T. Taussig, *The Devil and Commodity Fetishism in South America* (Chapel Hill: University of North Carolina Press, 1980). On the idea of the devil in medieval and early modern Europe, see Jeffrey Burton Russell, *Lucifer: The Devil in the Middle Ages* (Ithaca: Cornell University Press, 1984); and *Mephistopheles: The Devil in the Modern World* (Ithaca: Cornell University Press, 1986).

2　On the discourse of demonology in early modern Europe, see Sophie Houdard, *Les Sciences du Diable: Quatre discours sur la sorcellerie* (Paris: Editions du Cerf, 1992); Stuart Clark, *Thinking with Demons: The Idea of Witchcraft in Early Modern Europe* (Oxford: Oxford University Press, 1997); and Nicole Jacques-Chaquin, ed., *Les Sorciers du carroi de Marlou: Un procès de sorcellerie en Berry (1582–1583)* (Grenoble: J. Millon, 1996).

3　Elaine Scarry, *The Body in Pain: The Making and Unmaking of the World* (New York: Oxford University Press, 1985), 199.

4　On the chastisement of the body in early Christian and medieval Christianity, see, for example, Talal Asad, "Pain and Truth in Christian Ritual," in *Genealogies of Religion: Discipline and Reasons of Power in Christianity and Islam* (Baltimore: Johns Hopkins University Press, 1993), 83–124.

5　On the torture of suspected witches and heretics in early modern Europe, see Nicolau Eymerich and Francisco Peña, *Le Manuel des inquisiteurs*, translated and edited by Louis Sala-Molins (1376; reprint, Paris: Mouton, 1973), 207–12; and Guy Bechtel, *La Sorcière et l'occident* (Paris: Plon, 1997), 312–54.

6　Du Tertre, *Histoire générale des Antilles habitées par les Français*, 2:469.

7　Breton, *Dictionaire caraïbe-français*; Du Tertre, *Histoire générale des Antilles habitées par les Français* and *Histoire générale des isles . . . dans l'Amérique*; Pelleprat, *Relation des missions des PP. de la Compagnie de Jésus*; Sieur de la Borde, *Relation de l'origine*, *moeurs, coutumes, religion, guerres et voyages des Caraïbes sauvages des isles Antilles de l'Amérique*, in *Recueil de divers voyages faits en Afrique et en Amérique, qui n'ont point été encore publié*, edited by Henri Justel (Paris: Louis Billaine, 1674); Rochefort, *Histoire naturelle et morale des iles Antilles*.

8 Du Tertre, *Histoire générale des isles . . . dans l'Amérique*, 405.

9 Ibid., 404.

10 Breton, *Dictionaire caraïbe-français*, 135.

11 Stephen D. Glazier, "A Note on Shamanism in the Lesser Antilles" in *Proceedings of the Eighth International Congress for the Study of the Pre-Columbian Cultures of the Lesser Antilles* (Tempe: Arizona State University, Department of Anthropology, 1980), 449.

12 Jean Bodin, preface to *On the Demon-Mania of Witches*, translated by Randy A. Scott (Toronto: Center for Reformation and Renaissance Studies, 1995), 36–37. See also Johann Weyer, *On Witchcraft: An Abridged Translation of Johann Weyer's De praestigiis daemonum*, translated by John Shea, edited by Benjamin G. Kohl and H. C. Erik Midelfort (Asheville, N.C.: Pegasus, 1998). On the dispute between Bodin and Weyer, see H. R. Trevor-Roper, "The European Witch-Craze," in *Witchcraft and Sorcery: Selected Readings*, edited by Max Marwick (Middlesex: Penguin, 1970), 134–37. The effectiveness of Weyer's argument in effectively undermining witchcraft beliefs has been questioned. See Sydney Anglo, "Melancholia and Witchcraft: The Debate between Wier, Bodin, and Scot," in *Folie et déraison à la Renaissance: Colloque international tenu en novembre 1973 sous les auspices de la Fédération internationale des instituts et sociétés pour l'étude de la Renaissance* (Brussels: Éditions de l'Université de Bruxelles, 1976), 209–28.

13 Du Tertre, *Histoire générale des Antilles habitées par les Français*, 2:349–50.

14 Du Tertre, *Histoire générale des isles . . . dans l'Amérique*, 408.

15 Breton, *Relations de l'île de la Guadeloupe*, 57.

16 Du Tertre, *Histoire générale des isles . . . dans l'Amérique*, 405. An almost identical passage appears in *Histoire générale des Antilles habitées par les Français*, 2:347.

17 Du Tertre, *Histoire générale des isles . . . dans l'Amérique*, 407.

18 La Borde, *Relation de l'origine, moeurs, coutumes, religion, guerres et voyages des Caraïbes*, 12.

19 Breton, *Dictionaire caraïbe-français* (1892 ed.), 216.

20 Ibid., 217–18.

21 See Elaine Scarry's discussion of "God in the scene of hurt as a bodiless voice" in *The Body in Pain*, 200–201.

22 Breton, *Dictionaire caraïbe-français* (1892 ed.), 218.

23 One of the most famous images from the French witch craze appeared in Pierre de Lancre's *Tableau de l'inconstance des mauvais anges* of 1612. It depicts a spectacular scene of a witches' Sabbath feast presided over by Satan himself. Witches and demons partake of the meat of corpses, hanged men, and unclean animals and eat the hearts of unbaptized children. Transposed to the colonial scene, native cannibalism was also compared to the Eucharist but with different consequences. Notably, during the French expedition to Brazil in the mid–sixteenth century, Jean

de Léry's representation of Tupinamba cannibalism relied on metaphorical rhetoric that evoked France's religious wars. On narrative representations of cannibalism in the colonial world, see Pagden, *The Fall of Natural Man*, 80–89; Frank Lestringant, *Le Cannibale: Grandeur et décadence* (Paris: Perrin, 1994), esp. 124–42; W. Arens, *The Man-Eating Myth: Anthropology and Anthropophagy* (New York: Oxford University Press, 1979), 43–80; Hulme, *Colonial Encounters*, chapters 1 and 2; and Mason, *Deconstructing America*, 54–57.

24 Du Tertre, *Histoire générale des Antilles habitées par les Français*, 2:383.

25 Ibid.

26 This trope was likely imported into French colonial discourse from the earlier Spanish American historiography. Philip Boucher credits Antonio de Herrera's history for introducing to French readers "the endlessly quoted anecdote about the Caribs of Dominica who supposedly died after eating a Spanish monk." Boucher, *Cannibal Encounters*, 20.

27 Jean de Léry, *Histoire d'un voyage faict en terre de Brésil* (1580; reprint, with an introduction and notes by Frank Lestringant, Paris: Librairie Générale Française, 1994), 385–86.

28 Bouton, *Relation des François depuis l'an 1635 en l'isle de la Martinique, l'une des Antilles de l'Amérique*, 107.

29 Du Tertre, *Histoire générale des isles . . . dans l'Amérique*, 404.

30 In Pierre de Lancre's account, the devil's mark mimicked God's ritual imprint of his faithful. In an explanation recalling Elaine Scarry's analysis of the significance of the body as a figure for divine power, De Lancre states that through the mark the devil demonstrated his power by exerting control over his purported followers' every physical sensation. See Pierre De Lancre, *Tableau de l'inconstance des mauvaises anges, ou il est amplement traité des sorciers et de la sorcellerie* (1610; reprint, with notes and an introduction by Nicole Jacques-Chaquin, Paris: Aubier, 1992), 179–80.

31 Breton, *Dictionaire caraibe-français* (1892 ed.), 341. Later in the passage, when describing the care he gave to Caribs trembling with fear of the devil, Breton insinuates that they did in fact dream that the devil was beating them: "They willingly fell to their knees before me to thank me for protecting them (they said) from *mapoya*, who was beating them."

32 La Borde, *Relation*, 15; Breton, *Dictionaire caraibe-français* (1892 ed.), 341.

33 Rochefort, *Histoire naturelle et morale des iles Antilles*, 420.

34 Ibid., 422.

35 Pelleprat, *Relation des missions des PP. de la Compagnie de Jésus*, 60.

36 Pelleprat seems to overestimate the population of slaves at 12,000 to 13,000 persons. Historians estimate that the population could not have exceeded 2,700, which is the number recorded by the first census in 1664. B. David, "Les Origines de la Population Martiniquaise," *Mémoires de la société d'histoire de la Martinique* 3 (1973): 17; Patterson, *Slavery and Social Death*, 480.

37 Pelleprat, *Relation des missions des PP. de la Compagnie de Jésus*, 61.

38 Sala-Molins, *Le Code noir ou le calvaire de Canaan*, 60.

39 Jean-Baptiste Labat, *Nouveau voyage aux isles de l'Amérique contenant l'histoire naturelle de ces pays, l'origine, les moeurs, la religion, et le gouvernement des habitants anciens et modernes* (1742; reprint, Fort-de-France, Martinique: Éditions des Horizons Caraïbes, 1972), 2:387.

40 Pelleprat, *Relation des missions des PP. de la Compagnie de Jésus*, 55–56.

41 Du Tertre, *Histoire générale des Antilles habitées par les Français*, 2:469.

42 Sala-Molins, *Le Code noir*, 90. Sala-Molins undertakes an exhaustive reading and contextualization of the Code noir. For additional commentary, see Dayan, *Haiti, History, and the Gods*, 199–212; Joseph Roach, "Body of Law: The Sun King and the Code Noir," in *From the Royal to the Republican Body*, edited by Sara E. Melzer and Kathryn Norberg (Berkeley: University of California Press, 1998); Joseph Roach, *Cities of the Dead* (New York: Columbia University Press, 1996), 55–63; Peytraud, *L'Esclavage aux Antilles françaises*, 143–66; Elsa Goveia, *The West Indian Slave Laws of the Eighteenth Century* (Barbados: Caribbean Universities Press), 35–50; and Alan Watson, *Slave Law in the Americas* (Athens: University of Georgia Press, 1989), 83–90.

43 Orlando Patterson, *Slavery and Social Death: A Comparative Study* (Cambridge: Harvard University Press, 1982), 5.

44 On subsistence gardens and slave markets in the French Antilles, see Peytraud, *L'Esclavage aux Antilles françaises*, 218–19.

45 This article was mitigated somewhat by article 29, which recognized the practice of giving slaves small allowances and permitting them to work on their own account, collecting part of the proceeds. In addition, article 30 acknowledged that slaves were often made to represent the master as his agent in certain administrative or commercial affairs.

46 On justifications for slavery from classical to modern times, see Blackburn, *The Making of New World Slavery*, 10–72; and Sala-Molins, *Le Code noir*, 20–72.

47 Articles 55–59 outline the relatively liberal policy on manumissions. For more on manumissions and the status of *affranchis*, or freed persons, see chapter 4.

48 Peytraud, *L'Esclavage aux Antilles françaises*, 181–94. Planter hostility to organized religion reached its height in the mid–eighteenth century, when the Jesuit missionaries were expelled from Saint-Domingue, suspected, among other things, of providing slaves with poison. On the church and the Christian mission in eighteenth-century French Caribbean slave societies, see Debien, *Les Esclaves aux Antilles françaises*, 268–95.

49 Homi Bhabha, *The Location of Culture* (New York: Routledge, 1994), 86–87.

50 Dayan, *Haiti, History, and the Gods*, 205.

51 It is, however, possible to construe the subjection of slaves to criminal trials as a means of protecting them, for in addition to requiring the presentation of evidence slaves as defendants had the right to appeal. In 1711, this right was restricted to capital cases and sentences of hamstringing. Goveia, *The West Indian Slave Laws*, 41.

52 On Labat's literary persona and travel writing about the Antilles, see Antoine, *Les Écrivains français et les Antilles*, 73–90; Lafcadio Hearn, *Two Years in the French West Indies* (New York: Harter and Bros., 1890), 148–83; and Friedrich Wolfzettel,

Le Discours du voyageur: Pour une histoire littéraire du récit de voyage en France, du Moyen âge au XVIIIe siècle (Paris: Presses Universitaires de France, 1996), 260–66.

53 Labat, *Nouveau voyage aux isles de l'Amérique*, 1:96. Further page references to this work will appear in the text in parentheses.

54 See Robert Mandrou, *Magistrats et sorciers en France au XVIIème siècle: Une analyse de psychologie historique* (Paris: Plon, 1968), 437–45.

55 Pierre Pluchon, *Vaudou, sorciers, empoisonneurs de Saint-Domingue à Haïti* (Paris: Karthala, 1987), 15–16.

56 The creolization of traditional African healing practices and knowledge of spells now survives in Martinique and Guadeloupe by the name of *quimbois*. Over time, this practice incorporated European myths of magic and witchcraft and evolved a literate underpinning, such that the modern *quimboiseur* uses magic books and Western techniques of magnetism, hypnotism, and so on. Gerson Alexis, *Vodou et quimbois: Essai sur les avatars du vodou à la Martinique* (Port-au-Prince, Haiti: Éditions Fardin, 1976), 57.

57 Pluchon, *Vaudou, sorciers, empoisonneurs*, 144; Gabriel Debien, *Les Esclaves aux Antilles françaises aux XVIIe–XVIIIe siècles* (Basse-Terre, Guadeloupe: Société d'Histoire de la Guadeloupe et de la Martinique, 1974), 400.

58 Many of the same stories are preserved in the Creole oral traditions of the French Caribbean. See, for example, Patrick Chamoiseau, *Au temps de l'antan: Contes du pays Martinique* (Paris: Hatier, 1988).

59 See, for example, Pierre de Lancre, *Tableau de l'inconstance des mauvais anges*, 179–80.

60 See, for example, Rochefort, *Histoire naturelle et morale des iles Antilles*, 495; and Du Tertre, *Histoire générale des isles . . . dans l'Amérique*, 413–14.

61 On this subject, Du Tertre writes: "They practice such frightening austerities, such painful fasts, such strange mortifications, and effusions of blood that are so cruel, that many Saints who possess glory have never born similar rigors in this life." Du Tertre, *Histoire générale des Antilles habitées par les Français*, 2:389.

62 Other than references to policing the spirit world, scenes of violence toward slaves are limited in Labat's narrative. He is careful to point out, however, that responsibility for acts of disciplinary violence on the plantation was often doled out to other slaves or free blacks, creating a chain of black on black violence. Labat, *Nouveau voyage aux isles de l'Amérique*, 2:288.

63 The obsession with the mutilated black body recurs in nonmissionary writing as well, in ways that confirm the function of the body as a fetish for colonial authority. One notable example is in the proreformist novel by Jean-François Saint-Lambert called *Ziméo*, in which the title character leads a slave revolt to contest bad treatment by masters in Jamaica. While the story ostensibly protests barbarous conditions on the plantation, it recasts the desecration of the black body as a rite performed by slaves themselves as a way of attesting their love for more "humane" masters. The scene occurs during a revolt by maroon slaves, when the faithful slaves of one Wilmouth demonstrate that automutilation is the ultimate gesture of love and recognition: "There are those who give themselves great blows

of the knife deep into the flesh in order to prove to us how little it costs them to shed their blood for us." Here sentiment is equated with bodily desecration. What humanizes the slave, making him worthy of pity and reform, is his willingness to reify his own mutilation in devotion to the master. Jean-François Saint-Lambert, *Ziméo*, in *Les Saisons, poëme* (Amsterdam, 1773), 59. Representations of slaves' automutilation return in Moreau de Saint-Méry's 1797 *Description de la partie française de l'isle Saint-Domingue*, in which slaves dismember themselves to express chagrin.

64 Labat spoke of slaves from the "*côte de la Mine*" in particular, saying: "They despair, hang themselves, and cut their throats without ceremony for the least cause, most often to cause their masters pain, being advised that they will return to their country after their death." Labat, *Nouveau Voyage aux isles de l'Amérique*, 1:227.

65 Du Tertre, *Histoire des Antilles habitées par les Français*, 2:422.

66 Guillaume Apollinaire, introduction *L'Oeuvre Pierre-Corneille Blessebois*, by Pierre-Corneille Blessebois (Paris: Bibliothèque des curieux, 1931), 5–6. In addition to *Le Zombi du Grand-Pérou*, Apollinaire's edition includes two other novellas, *Le Rut ou la pudeur éteinte* and *Histoire amoureuse de ce temps*. *Le Rut* was reprinted with a preface by Jacques Cellard in *Oeuvres érotiques du XVIIème siècle*, L'enfer de la Bibliothèque Nationale 7 (Paris: Fayard, 1988). A separate edition of *Le Zombi du Grand-Pérou* appeared in 1997, with a preface by Jean-Paul Bouchon (Poitiers: Paréiasaure Édition, 1997). All parenthetical references to the text will refer to this edition. For a complete list of Blessebois's works, see Frédéric Lachèvre, *Le Casanova du XVIIème siècle: Pierre Corneille Blessebois* (Paris: Librairie ancienne Honoré Champion, 1927), 81–92.

67 Lachèvre, *Le Casanova du XVIIème siècle*, 11. In addition to Lachèvre's exhaustive study, my biographical information on Blessebois draws on the following sources: Marcel Chatillon, "Pierre-Corneille Blessebois, le poète galérien de Capesterre," *Bulletin de la Société d'histoire de la Guadeloupe*, 4th trimestre (1976): 15–42; and Bouchon, preface to Blessebois, *Le Zombi du Grand-Pérou*, 1–8. See also Apollinaire, introduction to Blessebois, *L'Oeuvre Pierre-Corneille Blessebois*.

68 Implicated persons included members of the nobility; celebrities, including Jean Racine (his charges were later dropped); and members of the king's circle, including his former mistress, the marquise de Montespan. After 1680, the scope of the investigation was extended to witchcraft when priests were implicated for having performed black masses in association with La Voisin. All told, hundreds of people were interrogated over the course of the affair, which led to one hundred sentencings and thirty-six executions. Interrogated and often tortured, accused persons had no chance for appeal. The event caused such a scandal that it was recorded on the literary record, most notably in the correspondence of Mme. de Sévigné, and in the play *La Devineresse* (1680) by Jean Donneau de Visé and Thomas Corneille, which represented La Voisin as its main character. See François Ribadeau Dumas, *Histoire de la Magie* (Paris: Les productions de Paris, 1961), 435–45; Mandrou, *Magistrats et sorciers*, 427–32; and Russell Hope Robbins, *The Encyclopedia of Witchcraft and Demonology* (New York: Crown, 1959), 80–84.

69 Chatillon, "Pierre-Corneille Blessebois," 21; Lachèvre, *Le Casanova du XVIIème siècle*, 48.

70 Chatillon, "Pierre-Corneille Blessebois," 27; Lachèvre, *Le Casanova du XVIIème siècle*, 52. It is not clear from the secondary literature what Blessebois was charged with, but all indications point to witchcraft.

71 In discussing Blessebois's text. I retain the original French spelling of the term "zombi" because, as I argue, this work contains the earliest appearance of the spiritual concept in a European language and its meanings in Blessebois's story differ significantly from definitions normally attached to the word "zombie" in English.

72 Notably, the dedication to a ship's captain was taken as evidence of Blessebois's previous life as a galley slave. Nodier is quoted in Lachèvre, *Le Casanova du XVIIème siècle*, 56–57.

73 Ibid., 49–53. Lachèvre later credited Pierre Louÿs with first discovering the identities of central characters such as Félicité de Lespinay. In order to highlight Louÿs's original research on *Le Zombi du Grand-Pérou* and its influence on Loviot, Lachèvre published extracts from Louÿs's private correspondance and other documents in Pierre Louÿs and Frédéric Lachèvre, *Pierre Louÿs et l'histoire littéraire* (La Roche-sur-Yon: Imprimerie centrale de l'ouest, 1928), 57–79.

74 Quoted in a letter by Pierre Louÿs in Louÿs and Lachèvre, *Pierre Louÿs et l'histoire littéraire*, 74–75.

75 Chatillon, "Pierre-Corneille Blessebois," 26.

76 Trousson, "Préface," ix–x.

77 Joan Dejean, *Libertine Strategies: Freedom and the Novel in Seventeenth-Century France* (Columbus: Ohio State University Press, 1981), xi.

78 The French dictionary *Petit-Robert* indicates that the word first appeared in French in 1832. The *Oxford English Dictionary* moves the word's first appearance back to 1819, the date of publication of Southey's *History of Brazil*, in which the word is defined as the name of an Angolan deity (Nzambi) but refers to the chief of the Brazilian natives. The word "Zombi" appeared in travel literature and histories recounting a slave revolt in the Brazilian province of Fernanbouc between 1620 and 1630, the leader of which was called Zombi. It is plausible that this name in time became a general term for chief, as indicated by the *OED*. Abbé Grégoire discusses the revolt in his 1808 work, *De la littérature des nègres*, and cites as his source Sebastião da Rocha Pita, *Historia da America Portugueza* (Lisboa Occidental, J. A. da Sylva, impressor da Academia real: 1730). Grégoire indicates that the name Zombi meant "powerful." See Abbé Henri Grégoire, *De la littérature des nègres* (reprint, with introduction and notes by Jean Lessay, Paris: Perrin, 1991), 163–65.

79 While the phenomenon has often been characterized as a supernatural theft of the soul by the houngan, who gains complete control of the victim's body, a scientific explanation maintains that the sorcerer's supposed powers derive from the use of hallucinatory and poisonous substances on a live person. Following interment, the houngan digs up the body and administers more drugs, which have the effect of

transforming the victim into an automaton. The idea that zombification is artificially induced is supported by article 249 of the criminal code in Haiti, which qualifies as murder the use of substances designed to bring on a prolonged lethargic slumber in people. On zombi beliefs in Haiti, see C. H. Dewisme, *Les Zombis ou le secret des morts-vivants* (Paris: Grasset, 1957); Laënnec Hurbon, *Le Barbare imaginaire* (Paris: Éditions du Cerf, 1988), 124; Wade Davis, *Passage of Darkness: The Ethnobiology of the Haitian Zombi* (Chapel Hill: University of North Carolina Press, 1988); Hans-W. Ackermann and Jeanine Gauthier, "The Ways and Nature of the Zombi," *Journal of American Folklore* 104 (1991): 467–69; Métraux, *Le Vaudou haïtien*, 249–52; Jean Kerboull, *Le Vaudou: Magie ou religion* (Paris: Laffont, 1973), 137–48, 272; and Maximilien Laroche, "The Myth of the Zombi," in *Exile and Tradition: Studies in African and Caribbean Literature*, edited by Rowland Smith (London: Dalhousie University Press, 1976), 44–61.

80 In Senegal and Benin, apparent death caused by the sorcerer leads to the sale of the body or servitude in a faraway land. In Cameroon, the victim is made to work on banana plantations. In Congo, stolen souls are said to be sold to a master or shipped to America to be put to work in factories making textiles and automobiles. Most researchers of the zombi phenomenon do not attempt to estimate the precise historical emergence or evolution of the living beliefs they study. On the variations of beliefs in the exploitation of bodies devoid of souls in Africa, see Ackermann and Gauthier, "The Ways and Nature of the Zombi"; Wyatt MacGaffey, *Religion and Society in Central Africa* (Chicago: University of Chicago Press, 1986), 162; and Hurbon, *Le Barbare imaginaire*, 292–95.

81 This is, notably, the first definition of the word given in the 1996 *Nouveau Petit Robert* dictionary.

82 Revert, *La Magie antillaise*, 131–34. Revert relates a curious incident in which some policemen hired a special watchperson to keep away a zombi that had been banging on their kitchen door at night. Jamaica has a notion of malevolent spiritual entities that gather near houses, make strange noises, and attack people. See also Ackermann and Gauthier, "The Ways and Nature of the Zombi," 484.

83 Although Fathers Du Tertre, Labat, and Moreau de Saint-Méry remain standard references on Creole religion in the colonial period, Pierre-Corneille Blessebois has been almost entirely overlooked. No reference is made to him in Revert, *La Magie antillaise*; Christiane Bougerol, *Une Ethnographie des conflits aux Antilles: Jalousie, commérages, sorcellerie* (Paris: Presses Universitaires de France, 1997); or Ary Ebroin, *Quimbois, magie noire et sorcellerie aux Antilles* (Paris: Jacques Grancher, 1977). The significant exception is the historian Pierre Pluchon, who devotes a few lines to Blessebois in *Vodou, sorciers, empoisonneurs*, 32–33. The only other published reference to a zombi in the colonial period dates from late-eighteenth-century Saint-Domingue and also strongly suggests the meaning of nighttime ghost or spirit rather than the flesh and blood zombi known to postcolonial Haiti. When speaking of the courage of slaves who steal away at night, braving "ghosts, specters and werewolves," to see their lovers on faraway plantations, Moreau de Saint-Méry

writes: "A young beauty the color of ebony, whose every limb trembles at a tale of a zombi, watches out for him [her lover] and opens the door . . . without making a sound. Her only fear is to be deceived in her expectation." Moreau de Saint-Méry, *Description de la partie française de Saint-Domingue*, 1:70.

84 Dumas, *Histoire de la magie*, 283–84, 353.

85 For stories of magical transport and invisibility in learned demonology, see Lancre, *Tableau de l'inconstance des démons, magiciens et sorciers*, 131–40; and Bodin, *On the Demon-Mania of Witches*, 112–19.

86 Ackermann and Gauthier, "The Ways and Nature of the Zombi," 468, table 1; Davis, *Passage of Darkness*, 57; MacGaffey, *Religion and Society in Central Africa*, 135–68; J. Van Wing, *Études bakongo: sociologie—religion et magie*, 2d ed. (Louvain: Desclée de Brouwer, 1959), 284–89.

87 While records from the seventeenth-century slave trade to Guadeloupe are scarce, the most active Dutch, English, and French trading posts of the century were concentrated in the region of Benin, Nigeria, and Ghana, particularly around the cities of Elmina (Ghana), Whydah, and Ardra (Dahomey). Persons from this region comprised the greatest proportion of slaves from Africa in the early part of the trade, to be surpassed in the eighteenth century by Bantu peoples from western Central Africa. On the seventeenth-century slave trade and the ethnic composition of slaves in the French Caribbean, see Debien, *Les Esclaves aux Antilles françaises*, 39–68; David Geggus, "The Demographic Composition of the French Caribbean Slave Trade," in *Proceedings of the 13th/14th Meetings of the French Colonial Historical Society*, edited by Philip Boucher (Lanham, Md.: University Press of America, 1990), 14–29; Howard Sosis, "The Colonial Environment and Religion in Haiti," Ph.D. diss., Columbia University, 40–62; David Geggus, "Haitian Voodoo in the Eighteenth Century," *Jahrbuch für Geschichte von staat, wirtschaft und gesellschaft Lateinamerikas* 28 (1991): 21–51; and Petitjean Roget, *La Société d'habitation à la Martinique*, 1:1432–53.

88 Max-Auguste Dufrénot, *Des Antilles à l'Afrique* (Abidjan: Nouvelles éditions africaines, 1980), 104–07. See also D. Westermann, *Gbesela Yeye or English-Ewe Dictionary* (Berlin: Dietrich Reimer, 1930).

89 Kunzi, a catechist who wrote for the missionary Laman in the early twentieth century, produced one of the earliest descriptions of Nzambi written by a Kongolese. In it, he transcribed age-old prayers requesting the deity to perform actions of this kind. An excerpt from his writings is contained in John M. Janzen and Wyatt MacGaffey, eds., *An Anthology of Kongo Religion: Primary Texts from Lower Zaïre*, University of Kansas Publications in Anthropology 5 (Lawrence: University of Kansas, 1974), 71–72. On Nzambi's significance in Congolese language and religion, see also Van Wing, *Études bakongo*, 296–307; MacGaffey, *Religion and Society in Central Africa*, 78–79; and K. E. Laman, *Dictionnaire Kikongo-Français* (1936; reprint, Ridgewood, N.J.: Gregg Press, 1964), 821.

90 See Revert, *La Magie antillaise*, 134–49.

91 On the regional origins of immigrants to the Antilles, see Gabriel Debien, *Le*

Peuplement des Antilles Françaises au XVIIème siècle: Les engagés parties de la Rochelle, 1683–1715 (Cairo: Presses de l'Institut français d'archéologie orientale du Caïre, 1942); and Abénon, *La Guadeloupe*, 43–50. On the popular culture, folklore, and occult beliefs of early modern provincial France and colonial Canada, see Robert Muchembled, *La Sorcière au village* (Paris: Éditions Julliard/Gallimard, 1979); Robert Muchembled, *Popular Culture and Elite Culture in France, 1400–1750*, translated by Lydia Cochrane (Baton Rouge: Louisiana State University Press, 1985); and Robert-Lionel Séguin, *La Sorcellerie au Québec du XVIIe au XIXe siècle* (Ottawa: Les Éditions Lemeac, 1971).

92 Credit for tracing tropes of "sadism" to their antecedents in colonial discourse and practices goes to Joan Dayan, who posits slavery in the French Antilles as the "living model for *The Hundred and Twenty Days of Sodom*." Dayan, *Haiti, History, and the Gods*, 212–14.

93 On the devil as a master illusionist, see Houdard, *Les Sciences du diable*, 36–42; and Marianne Closson, *L'Imaginaire démoniaque en France: Génèse de la littérature fantastique* (Geneva: Droz, 2000), 25–35.

94 Charles Sorel, *Le Berger extravagant* (Paris: Toussaint du Bray, 1627–28). On Sorel's parody and use of illusion, see Harth, *Ideology and Culture in Seventeenth-Century France*, 48–67; Closson, *L'Imaginaire démoniaque*, 318; and Jean Serroy, *Roman et réalité: Les histoires comiques au XVIIe siècle* (Paris: Librairie Minard, 1981), 299–300.

95 Dejean, *Libertine Strategies*, 109–18. The charlatan trope was also employed by the seventeenth-century playwrights Gillet de La Tessonerie (*La Comédie de Francion*, 1642) and Thomas Corneille (*Le Feint astrologue*, 1648). On the charlatan trope in classical theater, see Closson, *L'Imaginaire démoniaque*, 148–52.

96 Dejean, *Libertine Strategies*, 117.

97 See especially Bodin, *On the Demon-Mania of Witches*, 49; and Jacques Sprenger and Henry Institoris, *Malleus Malleficarum* (1487; translation, with an introduction, bibliography, and notes, by Montague Summers, New York: Benjamin Bloom, 1928). See also Houdard, *Les Sciences du diable*, 40–53.

98 Writes De Lancre: "They went there and saw all these execrations with an admirable volupté, and an enraged desire to go there and be a part of it." De Lancre, *Tableau de l'inconstance des mauvais anges et démons*, 192.

99 Closson, *L'Imaginaire démoniaque*, 331–52.

100 Alfred Métraux, *Le Vaudou haïtien* (Paris: Gallimard, 1958), quoted in Laroche, "The Myth of the Zombi," 50.

101 Dayan, *Haiti, History, and the Gods*, 36.

102 Traveling to Martinique in the 1890s, Lafcadio Hearn described the Labat legend as the most impressive in Martinican folkore. See Hearn, *Two Years in the French West Indies*, 148–83. A recent book by Aurélia Montel entitled *Le Père Labat viendra te prendre* (Paris: Maisonneuve et Larose, 1996) ironizes the Labat mystique in contemporary Creole cultures. The book itself is a novelistic rewriting of the author's journal.

Chapter Four The Libertine Colony

1 See Frank Felsenstein's scholarly anthology of the Inkle and Yarico story entitled *English Trader, Indian Maid: Representing Gender, Race, and Slavery in the New World* (Baltimore: Johns Hopkins University Press, 1999). See also Hulme, *Colonial Encounters*, 225–65. Ligon's text was reprinted in 1673. A French translation entitled *Histoire de l'isle des Barbades* appeared the following year in the collection *Receuil de divers voyages faits en Afrique et en Amérique*, edited by Henri Justel (Paris: Louis Billaine, 1674).

2 Zantop explains that later colonial romances privileged plots of love and marriage over ingratitude and abandonment so as better to justify long-term colonial ventures. She analyzes the trope of "virtuous conquest," whereby the male conqueror abandons his motherland for a conjugal union with his native lover in the context of the American Revolution and subsequent independence of the British colonies of North America, as well as the threatened fragmentation of the Spanish colonial empire. Suzanne Zantop, *Colonial Fantasies*, 123. See also Hulme, *Colonial Encounters*, 136, 223.

3 See Werner Sollors's interpretation in *Neither Black nor White yet Both: Thematic Explorations in Interracial Literature* (New York: Oxford University Press, 1997), 196–97.

4 Jean Mocquet, *Voyages en Afrique, Asie, Indes Orientales et Occidentales, faits par Jean Mocquet, garde du Cabinet des singularitez du Roy aux Tuileries Divisez en six livres et enrichis de figures* (Paris: Jean de Heuqueville, 1617).

5 Ibid., 150.

6 While Gilbert Chinard assumed an intertextual relationship, Peter Hulme maintains that the internal similarities point to common colonialist topoi governing the representation of sentiment on the colonial frontier. Hulme, *Colonial Encounters*, 255–59.

7 See ibid., 258, for a comparison of Inkle's violation of Yarico's hospitality with Aeneas's treatment of Dido in the legend of the Aeneid.

8 This reading of the earlier version of the Inkle and Yarico story illuminates as well the meanings attached to the absent miscegenated body in later English editions. By either suppressing the possibility of reproduction or representing the couple's unborn child as a future unit of labor for slavery, English versions of the story make legible the persistence of anxieties associated with miscegenation while at the same time displacing the power to victimize the offspring from the Indian woman to the European man.

9 Du Tertre, *Histoire générale des Antilles françaises habitées par les François*, 1:105, 2:356.

10 Breton, *Dictionaire caraïbe-français* (1892 ed.), 228.

11 While Breton's dictionary contains no terms for the métissage between French and Indian, it does have translations for Carib words for Carib-black and white-black mixtures. Breton defines the term *cachionna* as "child engendered by a white man

and a black woman" and *yaboúloupou* as "children engendered from savages and negresses, who are named thus." Ibid., 13, 99.

12 My discussion draws on and extends previous scholarship on colonial miscegenation laws in the seventeenth-century French Caribbean. See Debbasch, *Couleur et liberté*, 22–33; Gautier, *Les Soeurs de Solitude*, 152–58; Peytraud, *L'Esclavage aux Antilles françaises*, 195–208; Léo Elisabeth, "The French Antilles," in Cohen and Greene, *Neither Slave nor Free*, 139–45; and Bonniol, *La Couleur comme maléfice*, 55–63.

13 Pelleprat, *Relation des missions des PP. de la Compagnie de Jésus*, 65–66.

14 Here my interpretation concurs with Foster's reading of the ways in which the ideology of "true womanhood" in antebellum southern literature devalued slave women who survived sexual violence. The woman's "ability to survive sexual degradation was her downfall. As victim she became assailant, since her submission to repeated violations was not in line with the values of sentimental heroines who died rather than be abused." Frances Smith Foster, *Witnessing Slavery* (Westport, Conn.: Greenwood Press, 1979), 131–32.

15 Du Tertre, *Histoire générale des Antilles habitées par les Français*, 2:477–78.

16 Ibid., 478.

17 According to the historian Bernard Moitt, in the late 1660s the company gave a material bonus to men who established households either by bringing wives with them to the islands or marrying African or Native American women there. Bernard Moitt, *Women and Slavery in the French Antilles, 1635–1848* (Bloomington: Indiana University Press, 2001), 12. See also Johnson, "Colonial New Orleans"; and Roach, "Body of Law."

18 Pelleprat, *Relation des Missions des PP. de la Compagnie de Jésus*, 28–29.

19 Labat's explanation of the affair certainly reflects another qualification of black female virtue, as the author attributes to the black woman a supersexual urge: "His parish priest placed so many scruples into his soul, that he was obliged to marry a certain negress named Jeanneton Panel, who would have had more husbands than the Samaritan if all those to whom she had abandoned herself had married her." Labat, *Nouveau Voyage aux isles de l'Amérique*, 1:307.

20 "Règlement de M. De Tracy, Lieutenant Général de l'Amérique, touchant les Blasphémateurs et la police des Isles," in Médéric Louis Élie Moreau de Saint-Méry, *Loix et constitutions des colonies françaises de l'Amérique sous le vent de 1550 à 1785* (Paris: Chez l'auteur, 1784–90), 1:117–22.

21 Penalties for rape in early modern France were even more harsh. The Edict of Blois of 1580 defined rape as seduction of a minor below the age of twenty-five, notwithstanding the consent of the minor, and stipulated a penalty of death for the offending male. For two contrasting views on the Edict of Blois and French legislation on marriage in early modern France, see Sarah Hanley, "Engendering the State: Family Formation and State Building in Early Modern France," *French Historical Studies* 16, no. 1 (1989): 4–27; and James Traer, *Marriage and the Family in Eighteenth-Century France* (Ithaca: Cornell University Press, 1980).

22 For this reason, Father Labat warned against hiring whites as domestics: "It happens often that they begin affairs with the negresses, which causes great disorder, and sometimes the death of both them and the others." Labat, *Nouveau voyage aux isles de l'Amérique*, 2:292.

23 Du Tertre, *Histoire générale des Antilles habitées par les Français*, 2:478–79.

24 It is interesting to compare this notion of punishment with a similar convention in France regarding illegitimate children of nobles. An edict issued in 1600 officially denied noble status to bastards of nobles. The convention of barring illegitimates from the nobility was explained by François L'Alouëte, author of a sixteenth-century treatise on nobility, as a measure intended to punish the father and discourage him from this "vile sin." Later Florentin de Thierriat advocated that bastards not be barred entirely from the nobility but simply demoted to a lower level. The parallels with the colonial case are striking. On the question of bastardy and nobility, see Bitton, *The French Nobility in Crisis*, 92–110, 146, n. 5.

25 Du Tertre explains: "So that [these poor children] will not remain without assistance, Justice condemns the father to take care of the child until the age of twelve." Du Tertre, *Histoire générale des Antilles habitées par les Français*, 2:479. The master/father was also made to pay a fine. If the father was not the master of the slave woman, he would have to pay a fine to the master in addition to taking responsibility for the child's upkeep. Debbasch points out a variation on the law. Sometime after 1664, mulattoes were enslaved by the mother's master until the age of twenty. This enslavement was a way of reimbursing the master for losses associated with the mother's childbearing and child rearing, which were most likely assumed by the mother or other women on her plantation. Debbasch, *Couleur et liberté*, 23; Peytraud, *L'Esclavage aux Antilles françaises*, 197. For an analysis of the prosecution of bastardy cases involving female slaves and indentured servants in colonial Virginia, see Brown, *Good Wives, Nasty Wenches, and Anxious Patriarchs*, 187–211.

26 "Ordonnance de M. de Baas, touchant les Religionnaires, les Juifs, les Cabaretiers, et les Femmes de mauvause vie," in Moreau de Saint-Méry, *Loix et constitutions*, 1:180. The relevant passage reads: "In regard to masters who abuse their negresses, from this time forward we declare the said negresses confiscated for the benefit of the poor, and their children free." While it is conceivable that the courts could have used this law to confiscate abused slave women who had *not* had children by their masters, I interpret it as targeting bastardy, since it implies that the confiscated slave women do in fact have children. Offending males who were not the masters of the slaves they abused were required to pay a fine of four thousand pounds of sugar.

27 Cited in Debbasch, *Couleur et liberté*, 25. See also Chauleau, *Histoire antillaise*, 100.

28 Debbasch, *Couleur et liberté*, 27.

29 Reference to prostitution appears in the text of the 1680 law as well as in later arguments of the colonial intendant, Bégon. Ibid., 25; Peytraud, *L'Esclavage aux Antilles françaises*, 198.

30 As bell hooks has argued: "As long as the white slaveowner 'paid' for the sexual services of his black female slave, he felt absolved of responsibility for such acts." hooks, *Ain't I a Woman*, 25. Arlette Gautier notes a similar move to attribute sexual

aggression to slave women in the eighteenth-century discourse of writers such as Jean-Baptiste Leblond and the administrator Victor Malouet. Gautier, *Soeurs de Solitude*, 160–61.

31 Hartman, *Scenes of Subjection*, 80–82, 87. On the displacement of responsibility for the sexual oppression of black women in the U.S. antebellum context, see also Hazel Carby, *Reconstructing Womanhood: The Emergence of the Afro-American Woman Novelist* (New York: Oxford University Press, 1987), 28.

32 Some scholars passionately refute the notion that black women could have been complicit in their own sexual victimization, while others grant that some calculation was necessary for the sake of survival. A famous example from the United States is that of Linda Brent, the protagonist of Harriet Jacobs's slave narrative *Incidents in the Life of a Slave Girl* (1861), who takes a white lover in hopes of deflecting the incessant sexual advances of her master and more easily securing her freedom. Yet, while many slave women expected and received something in return for their sexual availability, this must be seen in a context of universalized sexual oppression, wherein women were valued for their attractiveness, they were unable to refuse, and rape could be a means of inflicting terror. In the French colonies, the gains won by sexual means were paltry. Few slave concubines received freedom, and usually the most they could hope for was better food or clothing. For feminist perspectives on rape and miscegenation under slavery, see hooks, *Ain't I a Woman*, 26; Davis, *Women, Race, and Class*, 18–30; Carby, *Reconstructing Womanhood*, chapters 1 and 2; White, *Ar'n't I a Woman*, chapter 1; and Darlene Hine and Kate Wittenstein, "Female Slave Resistance: The Economics of Sex," in *The Black Woman Cross-Culturally*, edited by Filomina Chioma Steady (Cambridge: Schenkman, 1981), 289–98. On the limited benefits of libertinage for slave women in the French Caribbean, see Gautier, *Les Soeurs de Solitude*, 158–80; and Debien, *Les Esclaves aux Antilles françaises*, 376.

33 Quoted in Chauleau, *Histoire antillaise*, 100.

34 Ibid., 94.

35 Quoted in Peytraud, *L'Esclavage aux Antilles françaises*, 241.

36 Ibid., 238.

37 Quoted in Gautier, *Les Soeurs de Solitude*, 155.

38 Quoted in Debbasch, *Couleur et liberté*, 26.

39 Du Tertre, *Histoire générale des Antilles habitées par les Français*, 513.

40 Roach, "Body of Law," 113.

41 I estimate that this was greater than the price of three male slaves based on the 1715 price of six hundred pounds of sugar. François Girod, *La Vie quotidienne de la société créole: Saint-Domingue au XVIIIe siècle* (Paris: Hachette, 1972), 117–18. All of my citations refer to *Code noir, ou recueil d'édits, déclarations, et arrêts concernant les esclaves nègres de l'Amérique* (Paris: Librairies Associez, 1743), a reprint of the 1685 edition with notes and amendments.

42 Watson, *Slave Law in the Americas*, 87–88. See also Peytraud, *L'Esclavage aux Antilles françaises*, 199–201.

43 Arlette Gautier explains that at the time of the Code noir the ratio of French men

to French women was two to one in Martinique. In Guadeloupe, there were five men to two women, and in Saint-Domingue the ratio was eight to one in 1681. By 1700, this ratio had declined to two to one. Gautier, *Les Soeurs de Solitude*, 32–33.

44 On the "one blood policy" in seventeenth-century French colonial ideology, see Johnson, "Colonial New Orleans," 18–24.

45 In article 47, children are only protected against separation from the family until puberty, after which they may be sold freely.

46 Dayan, *Haiti, History, and the Gods*, 203.

47 Debbasch, *Couleur et liberté*, 19; Bonniol, *La Couleur comme maléfice*, 60–61.

48 Article 6 of the Louisiana code is remarkable for explicitly penalizing both interracial marriage *and* concubinage between blacks and whites: "We forbid our white subjects of one and the other sex to contract marriage with blacks, on pain of an arbitrary punishment and fine; and all parish priests, priests, or missionaries, secular or regular, and even ship chaplains, to marry them. We also forbid our said white subjects, even blacks freed or born free, to live in concubinage with slaves." Sala-Molins, *Le Code noir ou le calvaire de canaan*, 109. The law is paradoxical, however, as it goes on to repeat verbatim the prescription in article 9 of the 1685 decree, which allowed white fathers to marry the mothers of their illegitimate children. In 1777, the proslavery reformer Emmanuel Petit lamented that the Louisiana law was too weak, since it punished interracial marriage without banning it entirely. Emmanuel Petit, *Traité sur le gouvernement des esclaves* (Paris: Knapen, 1777), 2:81.

49 Debbasch, *Couleur et liberté*, 45–46; Elisabeth, "The French Antilles," 154.

50 In the North American colonies as well, statutes prohibiting interracial marriage had little impact on the incidence of nonmarital sex, coerced or uncoerced, between whites and blacks. On the contrary, antimiscegenation laws were principally directed at black men suspected of having relationships with white women. Regardless of the circumstances, sex between white men and black women fell outside legal definitions of criminality and rape. For an analysis of miscegenation law and interracial sexual practices in colonial and antebellum America, see A. Leon Higginbotham Jr. and Barbara K. Kopytoff, "Racial Purity and Interracial Sex in the Law of Colonial and Antebellum Virginia," and Eva Saks, "Representing Miscegenation Law," both in *Interracialism: Black-White Intermarriage in American History, Literature, and Law*, edited by Werner Sollors (New York: Oxford University Press, 2000), 81–139, 61–81, respectively; Brown, *Good Wives, Nasty Wenches, and Anxious Patriarchs*, 187–212; Martha Hodes, *White Women, Black Men: Illicit Sex in the Nineteenth-Century South* (New Haven: Yale University Press, 1999); and Martha Hodes, ed., *Sex, Love, Race: Crossing Boundaries in North American History* (New York: New York University Press, 1970).

51 Wimpffen, *Voyage à Saint-Domingue*, 214.

52 Mémoir to M. de Choiseuil, Minister and Secretary of State in the Departments of War and Navy, by M. Bacon de la Chevalerie, Fontainebleau, October 13, 1763. Quoted in Vaissière, *Saint-Domingue*, 215.

53 Sigmund Freud, *Totem and Taboo*, in *The Standard Edition of the Complete Psycho-*

logical Works of Sigmund Freud, translated by James Strachey (New York: Norton, 1950), 41.

54 Ibid., 38.

55 Examining a different context, Heather Hathaway reaches a similar conclusion about the mechanism of transference whereby mixed-race babies become "tabooed objects" in racist societies. See her reading of Langston Hughes's short story "Father and Son" in " 'Maybe Freedom Lies in Hating': Miscegenation and the Oedipal Conflict," in *Refiguring the Father: New Feminist Readings of Patriarchy*, edited by Patricia Yaeger and Beth Kowaleski-Wallace (Carbondale: Southern Illinois University Press, 1989), 153–67.

56 For Labat, the appearance of mulattoes proves indisputably the role of the male in reproduction. While marveling at how mulattoes physically instantiate the "happy medium" between two races, he also offers a lesson on how to tell the difference between a black and a mulatto newborn. The trace of blackness is said to abide at the fingernails and in the "natural parts," a euphemism for the sex organs. Labat, *Nouveau voyage aux isles de l'Amérique*, 1:305.

57 Ibid., 304. Evidently, Labat places himself among the laity in his enjoyment of the scene.

58 A 1713 letter by the administrators Blénac and Mithon cites this lack as the primary cause for the public nature of concubinage between whites and black or mulatto women. Vaissière, *Saint-Domingue*, 75, n. 2. The proportion of white men to white women in 1681 was an astounding eight to one. Gautier, *Les Soeurs de Solitude*, 32–33; Vaissière, *Saint-Domingue*, 74.

59 "Ordonnance des Administrateurs, concernant le concubinage avec les esclaves., du 18 Décembre, 1713," in Moreau de Saint-Méry, *Loix et constitutions*, 2:406.

60 Vaissière, *Saint-Domingue*, 75.

61 Debbasch, *Couleur et liberté*, 58–59; Gautier, *Les Soeurs de Solitude*, 160.

62 Debien, *Les Esclaves aux Antilles françaises aux XVIIe–XVIIIe siècles*, 376.

63 Stewart King gives exact figures based on a sample of notarial records from Cap-Français between 1776 and 1789. See his *Blue Coat or Powdered Wig*, 44; David Geggus, "Slave and Free Colored Women in Saint-Domingue," in *More Than Chattel: Black Women and Slavery in the Americas*, edited by Barry Gaspar and Darlene Clark Hine (Bloomington: Indiana University Press, 1996), 268; and Gautier, *Les Soeurs de Solitude*, 172.

64 On the gender ratio, population trends, and fertility rates among free people of color in late-eighteenth-century Saint-Domingue, see King, *Blue Coat or Powdered Wig*, 40–45, 180–201. For a comparative context, see Cohen and Green, introduction to *Neither Slave nor Free*, 3.

65 I am comparing the census figures provided by Léo Elisabeth in "The French Antilles," 148, and by Charles Frostin in *Les Révoltes blanches*, 304. See also Robin Blackburn, *The Overthrow of Colonial Slavery, 1776–1848* (London: Verso, 1988), 163; and Debbasch, *Couleur et liberté*, 79. The official 1788 census counted 21,813 free persons of color compared to 27,723 whites, but, as Stewart King explains, these

figures undercounted the number of free persons living in rural areas. King, *Blue Coat or Powdered Wig*, xv–xvi, 43–44.

66 Frostin, *Les Révoltes blanches*, 38, 305.

67 King devotes his book *Blue Coat or Powdered Wig* to studying the internal differences and divisions between what he calls the military leadership and the planter elite within the class of free people of color in Saint-Domingue.

68 Ibid., 206, 270.

69 On the economic, social, and political status and activism of the free colored community in Saint-Domingue, see ibid.; Debbasch, *Couleur et liberté*; Garrigus, "Colour, Class and Identity"; Hall, "Saint-Domingue"; Elisabeth, "The French Antilles"; Frostin, *Les Révoltes blanches*, esp. 304–10; Dayan, *Haiti, History, and the Gods*; Bénot, *La Révolution française et la fin des colonies*; and James, *The Black Jacobins*, esp. 36–45.

70 Evidence of the generic use of *mulatto* to refer to any free person of color abounds in colonial narratives. The eighteenth-century travel writer Baron de Wimpffen uses the term to refer to the class in which he groups persons of color tending toward white, defined as "mulattoes, quadroons, half-quadroons, and métis." Moreau de Saint-Méry and Hilliard d'Auberteuil both collapse the subtle racial distinctions they work out in the class of affranchis into the generic term *mulatto*.

71 "Mémoire des administrateurs de Saint-Domingue au Ministre, du 14 mars 1755," quoted in Vaissière, *Saint-Domingue*, 223.

72 Debbasch, *Couleur et liberté*, 101.

73 Elisabeth, "The French Antilles," 140.

74 "Ordonnance du Roi, concernant l'Affranchissement des Esclaves des Isles et Ordonnances des administrateurs en conséquence, du 15 juin 1736," in Moreau de Saint-Méry, *Loix et constitutions*, 3:453.

75 "Ordonnance du Roi, touchant le gouvernement civil, du 2 mai 1775," ibid., 5:577–87. Gabriel Debien explains that manumission taxes were imposed in a previous 1745 law for Martinique. Debien, *Les Esclaves aux Antilles françaises aux XVIIe–XVIIIe siècles*, 374. He insists, however, that libertinage was not a significant cause of affranchissement. For more historical analysis of manumission laws in Saint-Domingue, see Elisabeth, "The French Antilles"; Hall, "Saint-Domingue"; and Peytraud, *L'Esclavage aux Antilles françaises*, 401–35.

76 "Déclaration du Roi, touchant les Libres qui recèlent des Esclaves, et les Donations faites aux Gens de Couleur par les Blancs," in Moreau de Saint-Méry, *Loix et constitutions*, 3:159–60. Yvan Debbasch, after Moreau de Saint-Méry, notes that, while the 1726 declaration was not sent to Saint-Domingue, authorities there instituted the restrictions on donations between concubines by way of common law measures. In the latter half of the eighteenth century, the courts relaxed such restrictions in view of what it considered to be the abusive use of usufruct and feoffment of trust (*fidéicommis*) by colonists wishing to endow their concubines and natural children. Debbasch, *Couleur et liberté*, 84–85. See also Hall, *Social Control in Slave Plantation Societies*, 143.

77 "Arrêt du Conseil du Port-au-Prince, touchant le baptême des enfans légitimes, du 14 Novembre, 1755," in Moreau de Saint-Méry, *Loix et constitutions*, 4:174.

78 "Règlement des Administrateurs concernant les Gens de Couleur libres, du 24 Juin et du 16 Juillet, 1773," in Moreau de Saint-Méry, *Loix et constitutions*, 4:448. For more on restrictions on naming and the response of the free people of color, see King, *Blue Coat or Powdered Wig*, 166–67; Dayan, *Haiti, History, and the Gods*, 226–27; and Élisabeth, "The French Antilles," 157–58. On colonial practices of naming slaves, see Debien, *LesEsclaves aux Antilles françaises aux XVIIe–XVIIIe siècles*, 72–73.

79 "Reglement des Administrateurs concernant les Gens de Couleur libres, du 24 Juin et du 16 Juillet 1773," in Moreau de Saint-Méry, *Loix et constitutions*, 5:448.

80 Here I concur with Robert Young's view of the equivocation of desire for and denigration of black women under slavery: "The white male's ambivalent axis of desire and repugnance was enacted through a remarkable ideological dissimulation by which, despite the way in which black women were constituted as sexual objects and experienced the evidence of their own desirability through their own victimization, they were also taught to see themselves as sexually unattractive." Young, *Colonial Desire*, 152.

81 A decree of 1778 prohibited whites from contracting marriage with "blacks, mulattoes, or other people of color." Peytraud, *L'Esclavage aux Antilles françaises*, 469.

82 "Lettre du Ministre au Gouverneur-Général des Isles, touchant les Titres de Noblesse des Sangs-Mêlés, du 26 Décembre, 1703," in Moreau de Saint-Méry, *Loix et constitutions*, 1:716.

83 "Lettre de M. le Général au Gouverneur du Cap, touchant les Sang-mêlés et les Mésalliés, du 7 Décembre 1733," ibid., 4:174.

84 Debbasch, *Couleur et liberté*, 102.

85 Garrigus, "Colour, Class and Identity," 26, 32.

86 Dayan, *Haiti, History, and the Gods*, 222.

87 "Arrêt du Conseil du Port-au-Prince," in Moreau de Saint-Méry, *Loix et constitutions*, 5:84.

88 "Arrêt du Conseil du Port-au-Prince, touchant les Actes qui concernent les Gens de Couleur se disant libres, du 13 mars 1778," ibid., 5:817.

89 "Arrêt du Conseil du Port-au-Prince, touchant les Actes qui concernent les Gens de Couleur se disant libres, du 9 Janvier, 1778," ibid., 5:807–8.

90 Moreau de Saint-Méry, cited in Garrigus, "Colour, Class and Identity," 28.

91 "Lettre du Ministre aux Administrateurs, sur les Sangs-mêlés, du 27 Mai, 1771," in Moreau de Saint-Méry, *Loix et constitutions*, 5:356.

92 Frostin, *Les Révoltes blanches*, 303–4.

93 Ibid., 64.

94 Peytraud, *L'Esclavage aux Antilles françaises*, 490.

95 Debbasch, *Couleur et liberté*, 111–14.

96 "Mulâtre," in *Encylopédie, ou dictionnaire raisonné des sciences, des arts et des métiers* (Neufchâtel: Samuel Faulche, 1765), 10:853. On the ideological implications of the

passage, see also Béatrice Didier, "Le Métissage de l'Encyclopédie à la Révolution," in *Métissages: Littérature et Histoire*, edited by Jean-Claude Carpanin and Jean-Michel Racault (Paris: L'Harmattan, 1992), 1:11–24.

97 "Mulâtre," in *Supplément à l'Encyclopédie* (Amsterdam: M. M. Rey, 1776–77).

98 Michel René Hilliard d'Auberteuil, *Considérations sur l'état présent de la colonie française de Saint-Domingue: Ouvrage politique et législatif, presenté au ministre de la marine*, 2 vols. (Paris: Chez Grangé, 1776). Page references in the text will refer to this edition.

99 On the details of Hilliard's life and publications, see Gene E. Ogle, " 'The Eternal Power of Reason' and 'The Superiority of Whites': Hilliard D'Auberteuil's Colonial Enlightenment," *French Colonial History* 3 (2003): 35–50; and Lewis Leary, introduction to *Miss McCrea: A Novel of the American Revolution*, by Michel René Hilliard d'Auberteuil, facsimile reproduction with a translation from the French by Eric Laguardia (Gainesville, Fla.: Scholars Facsimiles and Reprints, 1958). Hilliard was an astute and sympathetic observer of the American cause during the Revolutionary War. Other major works attributed to him include two volumes on Anglo-American politics — *Essais historiques et politiques sur les Anglo-Americains* (1781) and *Essais historiques et politiques sur la révolution de l'Amérique Septentrionale* (1782) — and an expanded translation of a work in English, *Histoire de Lord North . . . et de la guerre de l'Amérique Septentrionale jusqu'à la paix* (1784).

100 Lewis, *Main Currents in Caribbean Thought*, 129–36, 248–50; Frostin, *Les Révoltes blanches*, 21, 302–3. Gene Ogle has challenged previous historical judgments of the author's sympathies with the planter elite and the principles of parliamentary resistance, stressing instead the idiosyncratic nature of his reform program, which cannot be reduced to any single cause. See Ogle, " 'The Eternal Power of Reason," 46.

101 In his reading of the *Considérations*, Gene Ogle calls attention to what he calls Hilliard's "internal reform project," noting his proposals concerning social and political relationships within the colony, including the racial engineering of the class of free coloreds. While I concur with Ogle's remarks on the importance of color to Hilliard's hierarchy of rank, I am particularly interested in how such engineering implicated colonial sexuality and reproductive dynamics and the relation between this program of miscegenation and Hilliard's segregationist proposals.

102 In championing the law as a means of ensuring the sociopolitical, economic, and moral health of the colonies, Hilliard joined two other contemporary critics of French colonial jurisprudence: Émilien Petit and Moreau de Saint-Méry. All of their writings attest to the strong influence in the colonies of Montesquieu's injunction that laws be adapted to local circumstances, climate, and manners. On the colonial reception of Montesquieu's *De l'esprit des lois*, see Malick Ghachem, "Montesquieu in the Caribbean: The Colonial Enlightenment between the Code Noir and the Code Civil," *Historical Reflections/Réflexions historiques* 25 (1999): 183–210.

103 The similarity between the discourses of nobility and race are apparent from discussions in eighteenth-century France regarding gradual entry into the nobility

through the attainment of high office. There were degrees of nobility corresponding to generations in office. It was stipulated, for example, that even when a person
was appointed to an ennobling position, it would take several generations of service
in that position to "ascend" to full nobility. See Chaussinand-Nogaret, *La noblesse
au XVIIIème siècle*, 40–50.

104 Articles 10–12. Article 11 of the code specifically forbade masters to force their
slaves to marry against their will.

105 Gautier, *Les Soeurs de Solitude*, 62–63, 92–93.

106 David P. Geggus has shown that fertility levels in Saint-Domingue were among the
lowest in all American slave societies. Geggus, "Slave and Free Colored Women,"
260.

107 On planter pronatalism and slave reproduction, see Moitt, *Women and Slavery in
the French Antilles*, 80–100; Debien, *Les Esclaves aux Antilles françaises aux XVIIe
et XVIIIe siècles*, 343–69; and Gautier, *Les Soeurs de Solitude*, esp. 108–14.

108 Hilliard d'Auberteuil's rebuttal of the Code noir's provision on this point is part
of a general diatribe against Jesuit priests, whom he attacks for using religion as a
way to interfere with the masters' rights. Hilliard d'Auberteuil, *Considérations sur
l'état présent de la colonie française de Saint-Domingue*, 2:67–68.

109 Girod de Chantrans, *Voyage d'un Suisse dans les colonies d'Amérique*, edited by Pierre
Pluchon (1785; reprint, Paris: Librairie Jules Tallendier, 1980), 136.

110 Ibid., 137.

111 Debien, *Les Esclaves aux Antilles françaises aux XVIIe–XVIIIe siècles*, 384; Gautier,
Les Soeurs de Solitude, 111–12.

112 As we have seen, many of these provisions had already been codified in Saint-
Domingue. On the "respect" doctrine, Joan Dayan notes that by the 1770s "any
dispute between a white and a person of color could be settled—meaning whites
would be exonerated—if the white simply said: '*Le mulâtre m'a manqué*' (The mulatto has been disrespectful to me)." Dayan, *Haiti, History, and the Gods*, 223.

113 The concept of physical need would be invoked by later colonial writers such as the
Martinican Dessalles, who wrote in 1786: "Most unmarried masters live in concubinage with their slaves. There are physical needs that make themselves felt in hot
climates more than anywhere else; they must be satisfied." Quoted in Gautier, *Les
Soeurs de Solitude*, 166.

114 This prospect was controversial insofar as it entailed the liberation of mulattoes.
Hilliard's proposals for social reform were angrily refuted by the Creole Pierre Ulric
Dubuisson in his *Nouvelles considérations sur Saint-Domingue*, published in 1780.

115 See, for example, Thibault de Chanvalon, *Voyage à la Martinique* (Paris: J. B.
Bauche, 1761); and P. J. B. Nougaret, *Voyages intéressants dans différentes colonies
françaises, espagnoles, anglaises* (London: J. F. Bastien, 1788).

116 The work was first published anonymously as *Voyage à Saint-Domingue pendant les
années 1788, 1789, et 1790* (Paris: Chez Cochéris, 1797). All page citations in the text
will refer to the modern reprint, edited by Pierre Pluchon, entitled *Haïti au XVIIIe
siècle*. Wimpffen's economic motivations for travel to the colonies are partially revealed in a comment in one of the last letters in the book, which reads: "I had come

there with the noble ambition of occupying myself solely with my fortune" (254). His remarks on coffee production are limited to a brief passage on the arrangement of coffee plants, contained in letter 19. Otherwise, he reveals his lordship over slaves in a passage recounting his practice of eavesdropping on their nighttime parties in order to hear their secret judgments of his conduct (letter 25). For additional commentary, see Pluchon, introduction to Wimpffen, *Haïti au XVIIIème siècle*; Lewis, *Main Currents in Caribbean Thought*, 123–27; Dayan, *Haiti, History, and the Gods*, chapters 3–4; and Antoine, *Les Ecrivains français et les Antilles*, chapter 3.

117 See letters 16–18, in Wimpffen, *Voyage à Saint Domingue*, 134–49.

118 Ibid., 104.

119 On the life and writings of Girod de Chantrans, see Pierre Pluchon's foreword to Girod, *Voyage d'un Suisse dans les colonies d'Amérique*, 9–107.

120 Girod de Chantrans, *Voyage d'un Suisse dans les colonies d'Amérique*, 139.

121 Ibid., 140.

122 Ibid., 189.

123 Wimpffen, *Voyage à Saint-Domingue*, 214.

124 Ibid., 220.

125 Hilliard d'Auberteuil explicitly defended his proposal to free mulattoes by suggesting that it would prevent the indecency of masters who produce children for profit: "The natural manumission of mulattoes would put a restraint on the avarice of some men, who seem to have in their homes mulatto factories (*fabriques de mulâtres*), and who, laying under contribution those who have become the fathers due to weakness, authentically engage in the most despicable of all forms of commerce imaginable." Hilliard d'Auberteuil, *Considérations sur l'état présent de Saint-Domingue*, 2:94–95. Incidentally, Hilliard's own proposal retains the notion of production and commodification by placing a social value on the freedom of mulatto children.

126 For a fascinating analysis of colonial pimping as an expression of the narcissism and self-promotion of white men, see Dayan, *Haiti, History, and the Gods*, 198. On the interests of slave women in rituals of prostitution, see Gautier, *Les Soeurs de Solitude*, 164–65.

127 Wimpffen, *Voyage à Saint-Domingue*, 223.

128 Here I use the terms *mulatto*, *mulata*, and *mulâtresse* to refer to the racially heterogeneous category of free people of color described by colonial ethnography as both a race and a class. This is not to erase phenotypical differences in this group but to gesture to the symbolic significance of an archetypal racial hybrid that became synonymous with the class of libres.

129 Dayan, *Haiti, History, and the Gods*, 56. Dayan links the stereotyped mulatto woman courtesan to figures of luxury, love, and possession that persist in the spiritual imaginary of Haitian Vaudou. In particular, she views the vaudou goddess of love, Ezili, as an appropriation and reformulation by slaves of the strange marriage of lubricity and grace personified by the mulatto woman, suggesting the possibility of "the transcending of violation and whoring through infinite love" (58). For more on the mulatto woman in Saint-Domingue, see Dayan's chapters 3–4; Vais-

sière, *Saint-Domingue*, 334–50; Geggus, "Slave and Free Colored Women in Saint-Domingue"; Susan M. Socolow, "Economic Roles of the Free Women of Color of Cap Français," in Gaspar and Hine, *More Than Chattel*, 259–78, 279–98; Gautier, *Les Soeurs de Solitude*, 165–81; and Jean Fouchard, *Plaisirs de Saint-Domingue: Notes sur la vie sociale, littéraire et artistique* (Port-au-Prince, Haiti: Imprimerie de l'État, 1955), 37–49.

130 Hilliard d'Auberteuil, *Considérations sur l'état présent de Saint-Domingue*, 2:77.

131 Textual references are to the modern edition: Moreau de Saint-Méry, *Description topographique, physique, civile, politique, et historique de la partie française de l'isle Saint-Domingue: Nouvelle édition entièrement revue et complétée sur le manuscrit suivie d'un index des noms de personnes*, vol. 1 (1797; reprint, edited, with a biography, bibliography, and notes, by Blanche Maurel and Étienne Taillemite, Paris: Société de l'histoire des colonies françaises, 1958). For a more ample reading of this text and its racial fantasmatics, see chapter 5.

132 Ibid., 1:77.

133 Ibid., 104.

134 Wimpffen, *Voyage à Saint-Domingue*, 120.

135 Girod, *Voyage d'un Suisse dans les colonies d'Amérique*, 153.

136 Moreau de Saint-Méry, *Description de la partie française de Saint-Domingue*, 1:104.

137 McClintock, *Imperial Leather*, 20–25. On monstrous female sexuality in sixteenth-century English representations of the New World, see Louis Montrose, "The Work of Gender in the Discourse of Discovery," in *New World Encounters*, edited by Stephen Greenblatt (Berkeley: University of California Press, 1993), 177–217.

138 Girod de Chantrans summed up this "monotone life" as follows: "Imagine an unmarried man, the only white in his country house, surrounded by a more or less considerable troop of blacks and negresses who are his domestics, his slaves, consequently his enemies. A mulâtresse manages his household; in her resides all his confidence." On the poverty of social existence outside the plantation, the author remarks: "Liaisons of friendship are otherwise so rare among them, that most individuals must suffice to themselves." Girod de Chantrans, *Voyage d'un Suisse dans les colonies d'Amérique*, 130–31.

139 See Mary Louise Pratt's interpretation of the role of transgression in the survival literature of the eighteenth century in *Imperial Eyes*, 87.

140 Wimpffen, *Voyage à Saint-Domingue*, 118.

141 Girod de Chantrans, *Voyage d'un Suisse dans les colonies d'Amérique*, 175–77.

142 Moreau de Saint-Méry, *Description de la partie française de Saint-Domingue*, 1:152.

143 On this point, we have only to refer to the naturalist Comte de Buffon, whose *Histoire naturelle* described black women of the Hottentot nation as the lowest form of humanity, capable of mating with monkeys. G.-L. L. Buffon, *Histoire naturelle* (1749), edited by Jean Varloot (Paris: Gallimard, 1984), 220.

144 See the discussion in chapter 5.

145 Moreau de Saint-Méry, *Description de la partie française de Saint-Domingue*, 1:105.

146 In her discussion of luxury, dress, and imitation in Saint-Domingue, Joan Dayan has stressed the ways in which colonial historians inscribed the imitation of blacks

by white women in terms of infection and disease, "as if they were too weak-willed or amoral to resist the contagious attractions of loose living, scanty dress, and langorous talk." Dayan, *Haiti, History, and the Gods*, 178.

147 Moreau de Saint-Méry, *Description de la partie française de Saint-Domingue*, 1:108–9.

148 Girod de Chantrans, *Voyage d'un Suisse dans les colonies d'Amérique*, 154.

149 Moreau de Saint-Méry, *Description de la partie française de Saint-Domingue*, 1:106.

150 Hilliard d'Auberteuil, *Considérations sur l'état présent de Saint-Domingue*, 2:97–113.

151 Girod de Chantrans, *Voyage d'un Suisse dans les colonies d'Amérique*, 154.

152 The oscillation of the mulatto woman between two diametrically opposed figures—sexual savage and chaste caregiver—is a familiar feature of the poetics of nineteenth-century Cuban nationalism, to judge from Vera Kutzinski's reading of the discourse of *mestizaje*. In this uniquely Cuban brand of multiculturalism, espoused by writers, mass culture, and the elite of the tobacco and sugar industries, the mulatto woman emerged as the eroticized, racialized symbol of an evolving national identity. Yet she is also figured as the patron saint of the island nation, as the iconic Virgen de la Caridad de Cobre, the Virgin of Charity. In Cuba, the mixed-race sexual relationship remained semantically linked to adultery, as demonstrated by the definition of the verb *mestizar* contained in the 1964 edition of the *Pequeño Larousse*. The first definition given is *adultar*, meaning "to commit adultery." Vera Kutzinski, introduction to *Sugar's Secrets: Race and the Erotics of Cuban Nationalism*. New World Studies (Charlottesville: University Press of Virginia, 1993), 201, n. 3.

153 It is important to note that historically, the *ménagère* was not always a free woman. Frequently she was a slave concubine, who, after many years of service, had a good chance of gaining freedom from the master. See Debien, *Les Esclaves aux Antilles françaises aux XVIIe–XVIIIe siècles*, 376.

154 Girod de Chantrans, *Voyage d'un Suisse dans les colonies d'Amérique*, 153.

155 See letter of M. de la Rochalar, the governor of Saint-Domingue, quoted in Vaissière, *Saint-Domingue*, 76. See also Gautier, *Les Soeurs de Solitude*, 157. According to David Garrigus: "In the 1760s women of color brought an average of 35 percent more property than their spouses to formally contracted marriages while white brides brought slightly less property than their grooms." Garrigus, "Sons of the Same Father," 149. Independent of their relations with men, mulatto women owned rural and urban property, businesses, and slaves. On the economic status of free women of color, see Geggus, "Slave and Free Colored Women in Saint-Domingue"; Socolow, "Economic Roles of the Free Women of Color of Cap François"; and Peytraud, *L'Esclavage aux Antilles françaises*, 251–52.

156 Wimpffen, *Voyage à Saint-Domingue*, 120.

157 Pratt, *Imperial Eyes*, 97. The creation of the ménagère role for native women would remain as a technique of empire in later colonial ventures as well. On the "reeducation" of native and métis women as wives and domestic servants of French men in late-nineteenth-century Indochina, see Ann Laura Stoler, "Sexual Affronts and Racial Frontiers: European Identities and the Cultural Politics of Exclusion in

Colonial Southeast Asia," in *Tensions of Empire*, edited by Frederick Cooper and Ann Laura Stoler (Berkeley: University of California Press, 1997), 208.

158 Girod de Chantrans, *Voyage d'un Suisse dans les colonies d'Amérique*, 155.

159 Ibid.

160 By extending the feminized, sexual stereotype to all free people of color, whites further justified their exclusion from "rational" public life. Garrigus, "Sons of the Same Father," 147–50.

161 Girod de Chantrans, *Voyage d'un Suisse dans les colonies d'Amérique*, 155.

162 "Ordonnance Des Administrateurs des isles du Vent, sur le Luxe des Esclaves et Gens de Couleur. 1720, 4 Juin," in Émilien Petit, *Traité sur le gouvernement des esclaves* (Paris: Knapen, Imprimeur, 1777), 1:83.

163 Dubuisson, *Nouvelles Considérations*, quoted in Debbasch, *Couleur et liberté*, 96.

164 "Règlement provisoire des Administrateurs, concernant le Luxe des Gens de Couleur, du 9 Février, 1779," in Moreau de Saint-Méry, *Loix et constitutions*, 5:855–56.

165 Dayan, *Haiti, History, and the Gods*, 227–28.

166 Cooper and Stoler, "Between Metropole and Colony," 3–4.

Chapter Five Race, Reproduction, Family Romance

1 It is estimated that as many as one-third to one-half of all captives brought to the French Antilles died within the first five years, not counting the mortality rate on the slave ships, which was as high as 25 percent. Debien, *Les Esclaves aux Antilles françaises*, 343–64; Moitt, *Women and Slavery in the French Antilles, 1635–1848*, 90–91; Gautier, *Les Soeurs de Solitude*; Fick, *The Making of Haiti*, 26–27; Fouchard, *Les Marrons de la liberté*, 106, 119–29; Rogozinski, *A Brief History of the Caribbean*, 122–39.

2 According to Philip Curtin's influential study of 1969, Saint-Domingue imported 481,000 people while the rest of North America imported 187,400 (to the British colonies, the United States, and French Louisiana) during the period 1761–1810. Curtin's figures are cited in Rogozinski, *A Brief History of the Caribbean*, 124.

3 Du Tertre, *Histoire générale des Antilles habitées par les Français*, 2:462.

4 Ibid., 2:489.

5 Statistics cited in Frostin, *Les Révoltes blanches*, 28–29; and Patterson, *Slavery and Social Death*, 480.

6 Rogozinski, *A Brief History of the Caribbean*, 128–38; Mintz, *Sweetness and Power*, 48–55.

7 Mintz, *Sweetness and Power*, 46–50; Fick, *The Making of Haiti*, 28–30; Moitt, *Women and Slavery in the French Antilles*, 34–56.

8 Labat, *Nouveau voyage aux isles de l'Amérique*, 2:192.

9 Girod de Chantrans, *Voyage d'un Suisse dans les colonies de l'Amérique*, 148.

10 Rogozinski, *A Brief History of the Caribbean*, 138.

11 James, *The Black Jacobins*, 13.

12 Du Tertre, *Histoire générale des Antilles habitées par les français*, 2:494–95.

13 Labat, *Nouveau voyage aux iles de l'Amérique*, 1:51.

14 For a detailed account of colonial cruelties, see Vaissière, *Saint-Domingue*, 189–95.

15 Response of the naval minister to colonial administrators in Saint-Domingue, July 27, 1741, quoted in Gisler, *L'Esclavage aux Antilles françaises*, 108.

16 Royal ordinance of October 15, 1786, quoted in Vaissière, *Saint-Domingue*, 185–86.

17 Lejeune's testimony is quoted in Gisler, *L'Esclavage aux Antilles françaises*, 121 (and see pages 117–27). See also Vaissière, *Saint-Domingue*, 186–89; and James, *The Black Jacobins*, 22–23.

18 On the Makandal conspiracy, see Moreau de Saint-Méry, *Description de la partie française de Saint-Domingue*, 2:631; Fick, *The Making of Haiti*, 59–75; and Vaissière, *Saint-Domingue*, 236–39.

19 Despite the terror Makandal inspired in white Saint-Domingue, his image was fetishized by whites. Moreau de Saint-Méry reported that portraits of Makandal were sold in Paris and that he acquired one at Versailles. Moreau de Saint-Méry, *Description de la partie française de Saint-Domingue*, 2:631.

20 On the gendered politics of colonial rule, see, for example, McClintock, *Imperial Leather*; Zantop, *Colonial Fantasies*; Stoler, "Sexual Affronts and Racial Frontiers"; and Ann Laura Stoler, "Making Empire Respectable: The Politics of Race and Sexual Morality in Twentieth-Century Colonial Cultures," *American Ethnologist* 16, no. 4 (1989):634–60.

21 All references will be made to the modern edition: Médéric Louis Élie Moreau de Saint-Méry, *Description topographique, physique, civile, politique, et historique de la partie française de l'isle Saint-Domingue: Nouvelle édition entièrement revue et complétée sur le manuscrit suivie d'un index des noms de personnes*, 3 vols. (1797; reprint, edited, with a biography, bibliography, and notes, by Blanche Maurel and Étienne Taillemite, Paris: Société de l'histoire des colonies françaises, 1958). My discussion of Moreau de Saint-Méry's life relies on Blanche Maurel and Étienne Taillemite's extensive biographical and historical introductions to their edition of the *Description*, as well as the following sources: James E. McClellan, *Colonialism and Science: Saint-Domingue in the Old Regime* (Baltimore: Johns Hopkins University Press, 1992); Ivor D. Spencer, introduction to *A Civilization That Perished: The Last Years of White Colonial Rule in Saint-Domingue*, by Médéric Louis Élie Moreau de Saint-Méry, translated and edited by Ivor D. Spencer (Lanham, Md.: University Press of America, 1985); Lewis, *Main Currents in Caribbean Thought*; Stewart Mims, introduction to Moreau de Saint-Méry, *Moreau de St.-Méry's American Journey*, translated and edited by Kenneth Roberts and Anna M. Roberts (New York: Doubleday, 1947); and Anthony Louis Elicona, *Un colonial sous la Révolution en France et en Amérique: Moreau de Saint-Méry* (Paris: Jouve, 1934).

22 McClellan, *Colonialism and Science*, 4–5.

23 Elicona, *Un colonial sous la révolution*, 109–10.

24 Moreau de Saint-Méry, *Description de la partie espagnole de l'Isle Saint-Domingue*, 4 vols. (Philadelphia, 1796).

25 The books were initially intended to be part of the same multivolume work, as announced in the title of the first volume of the *Loix et constitutions*: *Loix et con-*

stitutions des colonies françaises de l'Amérique sous le vent de 1550 à 1785, suivies 1. D'un tableau raisonné des différentes parties de l'administration; 2. D'observations sur le climat, la population de la partie française de Saint-Domingue; 3. D'une description physique, politique et topographique de cette même partie, le tout terminé par l'histoire de cette isle. Of the projected subsections of the encyclopedic work, the tableau of the administration and the history of Saint-Domingue were never completed. The 1797 edition of the *Description* was printed in a run of one thousand copies and was translated into Dutch the following year. With the exception of an abridged version published in 1875, no new editions appeared until that of Maurel and Taillemite in 1958. For a full bibliography of works by Moreau de Saint-Méry, see Blanche Maurel, "La *Description*, ses sources, sa portee, son interpretation," in Moreau de Saint-Méry, Description de la partie française de l'isle Saint-Domingue, 1:xxxviii–xlviii. All citations refer to the 1958 edition, and all translations are mine.

26 Moreau de Saint-Méry, *Description de la partie française à Saint-Domingue*, 1:5. Subsequent page references to the first volume of the *Description* will be indicated in the text in parentheses.

27 Moreau estimates that one-third of the population of slaves is Creole, or born in the colony, the other two-thirds having been brought from Africa (ibid., 44).

28 For a similar perspective on this passage, see Dayan, *Haiti, History, and the Gods*, 247.

29 Buffon, *Histoire naturelle*, 51. This stunning passage indicates the formative impact of colonialism and slavery on Enlightenment theories of "universal" human nature.

30 Several important eighteenth-century laws pertained to dance gatherings. In 1704, the governor of Saint-Domingue prohibited slaves from meeting for nocturnal dances. In 1765, Calenda dancing was mentioned by name, and a special division of the *maréchaussée*, or rural police, set out to dissipate it. The general administration renewed the interdiction against slaves dancing Calenda in 1772. Moreau de Saint-Méry, *Lois et constitutions*, cited by Pluchon in *Vaudou, sorciers, empoisonneurs*, 57–64.

31 Pierre Pluchon cites a number of narrative sources that support this claim. Note a 1765 description of a slave funeral by Père Monnereau in which dance plays a central role. Writing in the 1790s, the emigré writer Descourtilz also directly associated Calenda with funeral rites. Most compelling is a 1786 edict in which authorities prohibited anyone having African blood from performing "magnetism," which resembles the kind of convulsive abandon scholars now associate with spirit possession. Pluchon, *Vaudou, sorciers, empoisonneurs*, 74–77. See also Gabriel Entiope, *Nègres, danse et résistance: la Caraïbe du XVIIe au XIXe siècle* (Paris: L'Harmattan, 1996), 190–96. In my view, Pluchon exaggerates the extent to which earlier dance forms were perceived as expressions of slave religion, projecting back onto the whole of colonial legislation against slave "riots" (*attroupement*) a concern to wipe out what he somewhat anachronistically calls "vaudou." Historian David Geggus mentions that it was only during the revolution that Vaudou meetings were specifically outlawed by name, first by Sonthonax in 1797, then by Toussaint in 1800. Geggus, "Haitian Voodoo in the Eighteenth Century," 47.

32 Alfred Métraux, author of the seminal modern ethnographic study of Haitian vaudou, praised Moreau de Saint-Méry's account for its accuracy, taking issue only with his characterization of Vaudou as merely a cult of the serpent and noting that "the serpent-god, a divinity from Dahomean mythology, is far from being the only great 'vaudou.'" According to Métraux, Moreau de Saint-Méry was influenced by contemporary prejudice and generalized the practices of the numerous slaves from the Ouidah region. The custom of venerating serpents disappeared in the nineteenth century. Métraux, *Le Vaudou haïtien*, 30.

33 On Moreau's account and the history of vaudou in the colonial period, see Métraux, *Le Vaudou haïtien*, 28–32; Pluchon, *Vaudou, sorciers, empoisonneurs*, 92–95; Geggus, "Haitian Voodoo in the Eighteenth Century"; Dayan, *Haiti, History, and the Gods*, 242–67; Léon-François Hoffman, "Vodou sous la colonie et pendant les guerres d'indépendance," *Conjonction: Le Bulletin de l'Institute Français d'Haïti* 173 (1987): 109–35; Michel S. Laguerre, *Voodoo and Politics in Haiti* (New York: St. Martin's, 1989), 22–38; Jean Price-Mars, *Ainsi Parla l'oncle*, edited by Robert Cornevin (1928; reprint, Ottawa: Éditions Leméac, 1973), 165–77; and Carolyn Fick, *The Making of Haiti: The Saint-Domingue Revolution from Below* (Knoxville: University of Tennessee Press, 1990), 40–60.

34 The historian David Geggus has insightfully argued that far from comprising an anticolonial death threat to whites, as it was often interpreted to be, this chant was meant to activate magical substances, thereby ensuring divine protection against several potential enemies, including whites, blacks, and sorcerers. However, by including this aspect, as well as reference to the Petro dance in his account, Geggus argues that Moreau documents the significant Congo or Bantu contribution to rituals that were long believed to derive predominantly from the Aja-Fon ethnic group from Dahomey, called Arada in the colonies. See Geggus, "Haitian Voodoo in the Eighteenth Century."

35 This text was originally published as *Danse: Article extrait d'un ouvrage de M. L. E. Moreau de Saint-Méry ayant pour titre—répertoire des notions coloniales, par ordre alphabétique* (Philadelphia: published by the author, 1796). It was intended to be part of Moreau's projected colonial encyclopedia. I cite the modern English translation of the text, *Dance*, by Lily Hastings and Baird Hastings (Brooklyn: Dance Horizons, 1975). Note Moreau's comment on Chica, the more sensual of the slave dances: "The Chica is no longer danced at the balls of the white ladies, and only occasionally is it performed on the spur of the moment at certain parties where the small and select society reassures the ladies" (63–64). On whites' obsession with dance as entertainment, see Fouchard, *Les Plaisirs de Saint-Domingue*, 130–40. On whites' and blacks' appropriations of each other's dance forms, see Dayan, *Haiti, History, and the Gods*, 178.

36 The system of sexual slavery that existed in late-eighteenth-century Cap-François was described by Baron de Wimpffen as a form of prostitution controlled largely by the slave women themselves: "Here a negress asks to sleep with such and such white man; and as she is, in many households, expected to pay her mistress a certain fee on the price of her nocturnal work, you can imagine that the prude who, by

a principle of honesty, would refuse such permission, would expose herself to the very serious reproach of bad finances, given that most of the black servants cannot cover their nudity except with what they can gain from trafficking in their charms." Wimpffen, *Voyage à Saint-Domingue*, 220–21.

37 As Albert Valdman points out, the acquisition and use of Creole by the European settler group was one of the distinctive characteristics of the linguistic situation in the French Caribbean colonies, as opposed to the anglophone islands. On the role and development of Creole in the colonial period, see Albert Valdman, "Creole, the Language of Slavery," in *Slavery in the Caribbean Francophone World: Distant Voices, Forgotten Acts, Forged Identities*, edited by Doris Y. Kadish (Athens: University of Georgia Press, 2000); Mervin C. Alleyne, "Acculturation and the Cultural Matrix of Creolization," in *Pidginization and Creolization of Languages*, edited by Dell Hymes (Cambridge: Cambridge University Press, 1971); and Yacou, *Créoles de la Caraïbes*.

38 This is a central tenet of the créolité writers Patrick Chamoiseau and Raphaël Confiant's characterization of orality in the colonial period. Following the historian Jean Petitjean Roget, they distinguish between the "plantation" and the "habitation," the latter denoting a small operation in which the master was "omnipresent" and lived in close proximity to the slaves. In their poetic vision of Antillean literary history, the master shared in the cultural values of slaves and authorized the speech of the storyteller, even though he may not have understood it. Chamoiseau and Confiant, *Lettres creoles*, 59.

39 Girod de Chantrans degraded Creole as an infantilized, simplified version of French invented for the use of Africans: "The insipid turns of Creole come perhaps from the stupidity that the first colonists presupposed in blacks. Thus, when they wanted to make them understand to go somewhere, they told them, I want that you go there (*moi vouloir que tu aller là*)." Girod de Chantrans, *Voyage d'un Suisse dans les colonies d'Amérique*, 158. Remarkably, the view of Creole as a reduced form of French remained dominant in twentieth-century Bloomfieldian linguistics. Refuting this position, Alleyne richly documents the extent to which, on the contrary, not only was French used in its full morphological complexity in the contact situation but the Creole verbal system may have expanded that of French. See Alleyne, "The Cultural Matrix of Creolization," 172–73.

40 Although Moreau de Saint-Méry acknowledges the syncretic aspect of Creole, Africa is conspicuously absent from the linguistic mix: "It is a corrupt French mixed with several frenchified Spanish words, and where marine terms also have a place" (80).

41 Chamoiseau and Confiant, *Lettres créoles*, 74. For an extensive reading of "Lizette quitté la plaine," see Deborah Jenson, "Mimetic Mastery and Colonial Mimicry in the First Franco-Antillean Creole Anthology," *The Yale Journal of Criticism*, 17.1 (2004): 83–106. Unfortunately, this article appeared too recently to be considered in my analysis of the song.

42 The original Creole and Moreau de Saint-Méry's French translation of this stanza are as follows:

Lisette quitté la plaine	Lisette, tu fuis la plaine,
Mon perdi bonher à moué:	Mon bonheur s'est envolé;
Gié à moin semblé fontaine,	Mes pleurs, en double fontaine,
Dipi mon pas miré toué.	Sur tes pas ont coulé.
La jour quand mon coupé canne	Le jour, moissonnant la canne,
Mon fongé zamour à moué;	Je rêve à tes doux appas;
La nuit quand mon dans cabane,	Un songe dans ma cabane,
Dans dromi mon quimbé toué.	La nuit te met dans mes bras.

43 Chamoiseau and Confiant, *Lettres créoles*, 73–74. The authors explain that because of its European attributes this text, the first ever written in Creole, was rejected by Haitians, who "refuse to see in it the birth of their literature in the vernacular."

44 Jean Fouchard refutes the long-standing claim that there was no culture among whites in Saint-Domingue by exhaustively surveying the evidence of literary production in the newspapers of Saint-Domingue, the first of which appeared in 1764. So great was the response that by 1769 some in the colony dreamed of creating a literary academy. Fouchard, *Plaisirs de Saint-Domingue*, 67–100. Fouchard has also single-handedly surveyed and documented the thriving theater scene in late-eighteenth-century Saint-Domingue in his book, *Le Théâtre à Saint-Domingue*. He demonstrates that, not only were popular plays by French masters such as Voltaire, Molière, and Rousseau performed in Saint-Domingue, but a number of plays produced on the Saint-Dominguan stage were written by authors residing there, a few of which were dramas in Creole. Though none of these colonial plays appears to have survived intact, Fouchard reconstructs the theatrical scene in Saint-Domingue based on exhaustive archival research. Fouchard, *Le Théâtre à Saint-Domingue* (Port-au-Prince: Imprimerie de l'État, 1955). The only other evidence of literary production in Creole is a song and verse compendium edited by an anonymous Saint-Domingue refugee entitled *Idylles et chansons ou essais de poésie créole, par un habitant d'Hayti* (Philadelphia: J. Edwards, 1818). Valdman, "Creole, the Language of Slavery," 156–57. On colonial attitudes toward Creole, see also Lambert-Félix Prudent, *Des baragouins à la langue antillaise* (Paris: L'Harmattan, 1999), 27–35.

45 On the distinction between varieties of Creole in the colonial and postcolonial periods, see Valdman, "Creole, the Language of Slavery," 157.

46 "Mes pas, loin de la Lisette; / S'éloignent du Calinda; / Et ma ceinture à sonnette / Languit sur mon bamboula." According to Moreau de Saint-Méry, the bamboula was the smaller of two drums used to acompany the Calenda. It was made from carved wood covered with sheepskin or goatskin (63).

47 "Tu trouveras à la ville, / Plus d'un jeune freloquet, / Leur bouche avec art distille / Un miel doux mais plein d'apprêt."

48 The French translation suppresses the racial identity of the love object of the speaker. The Creole verse "Quand mon contré laut' négresse, / Mon pas gagné pour li" is translated as "Mon oeil de toute autre belle, / N'apperçoit plus le souris." I thank Stéphanie Silvestre for pointing out this revealing disparity.

49 Michèle Duchet offers a useful discussion of the racial taxonomies of Enlightenment figures such as De Pauw and Buffon. She emphasizes the theoretical, experimental nature of De Pauw, who lacked a practical motivation for his speculations. See Michèle Duchet, "Du noir au blanc, ou la cinquième génération," in *Le Couple interdit: Entretiens sur le racisme*, edited by Léon Poliakov (Paris: Mouton, 1977), 178.

50 Sollors, *Neither White nor Black*, 115. Jean-Luc Bonniol reads Moreau de Saint-Méry's text as indicative of the move to install a color line between whites and non-whites through a sort of "binary reduction of extreme phenotypical diversity" (66). Bonniol, *La couleur comme maléfice*, 64–72. Roger Toumson views colonial thinking on race and métissage in terms of Freudian notions of totem and taboo and discusses Moreau de Saint-Méry's taxonomy as an attempt to naturalize racial segregation. Roger Toumson, *Mythologie du métissage*, Ecritures francophones (Paris: Presses Universitaires de France, 1998), 100–116. See also Claudine Cohen, "Taxinomie et ségrégation sociale: 'L'Anthropologie' de Moreau de Saint-Méry," in *La Période révolutionnaire aux Antilles: Images et résonnances*, edited by Roger Toumson and Charles Porset (Fort-de-France, Martinique: Actes du Colloque Internationale Pluridisciplinaire, 1986).

51 Dayan, *Haiti, History, and the Gods*, 231. Dayan regards the text as "the first attempt to theorize color as part of a uniquely Antillean enlightenment" (228). For her incisive reading of Moreau de Saint-Méry under the influence of Buffon, see *Haiti, History, and the Gods*, 228–37.

52 Young, *Colonial Desire*, 9.

53 Cooper and Stoler, "Between Metropole and Colony," 5.

54 Referring to the Enlightenment's obsession with population dynamics, the public good, and power over life (*le pouvoir sur la vie*), Foucault maintains that the will to knowledge about sex became closely linked to a concern with reproduction. Thus, the era of "biopower," synonymous with the growth of capitalism, supposed the "controlled insertion of bodies into the machinery of production and the adjustment of the phenomena of population to economic processes." Michel Foucault, *History of Sexuality*, translated by Robert Hurley (New York: Pantheon, 1987), 1:141.

55 Hilliard, *Considérations sur l'état présent de Saint-Domingue*, 2:83.

56 The racial connotations of the word *métif* (or *métis*) originated in Spanish America, where it referred to children born to an Indian and a Spaniard. This definition appeared in the *Dictionnaire de l'Académie française* (1694). The word *mulâtre* appeared in French to define the racial cross between Europeans and Africans beginning in 1604, and it persisted in this meaning, as evidenced in the *Encyclopédie*. On the terminology of métissage, see Béatrice Didier, "Le Métissage de l'Encyclopédie à la Révolution" in *Métissages*, vol. 1: *Littérature-Histoire*, edited by Jean-Claude Carpanin Marimoutou and Jean-Michel Racault (Paris: l'Harmattan, 1992), 11–24; and Toumson, *Mythologie du métissage*, 90–91.

57 Michèle Duchet, "Esclavage et préjugé de couleur," in *Racisme et Société*, edited by Patrice de Comarmond and Claude Duchet (Paris: Maspéro, 1969), 125. See also

translator's n. 55 in Gilberto Freyre, "Preface to the First Brazillian Edition," in *The Masters and the Slaves: A Study in the Development of Brazilian Civilization*. 2d English-language ed , translated by Samuel Putnam (New York: Knopf, 1971), xliii.

58 Dayan, *Haiti, History, and the Gods*, 232.

59 Bonniol, *La Couleur comme maléfice*, 66, 68.

60 Quoted in Peytraud, *L'Esclavage aux Antilles françaises*, 423.

61 Hilliard d'Auberteuil, *Considérations*, 2:82.

62 King, *Blue Coat or Powdered Wig*, 158, 305, n. 3.

63 Young, *Colonial Desire*, 149.

64 Here I follow Butler's interpretation of Foucault's notion of desire in the first volume of *The History of Sexuality*. See Judith Butler, *Subjects of Desire* (New York: Columbia University Press, 1987), 218.

65 Moreau de Saint-Méry claims that his choice to fix the gender variable merely reflects his desire to simplify matters, the important point being the demonstration of racial mixture: "The mulatto is produced in twelve ways; for in this case, as in all the others, I count as only one combination that of the mulatto with a white female and that of a white male with a mulâtresse, since only the sex changes" (90). While the author recognizes the possibility of white women being partners in métissage, I would argue that the representation of white and colored males in the role of progenitor corroborates his repeated defense of white male libertinage with nonwhite women and the sense of sexual intimidation and rivalry between white and nonwhite men that is evident elsewhere in his text.

66 Young, *Colonial Desire*, 102.

67 Frostin, *Les Révoltes blanches*; King, *Blue Coat or Powdered Wig*, xv–xvi.

68 Du Tertre, *Histoire générale des Antilles habitées par les Français*, 2:478.

69 For a comparison of the views of these two thinkers on the question of race and species, see Duchet, *Anthropologie et histoire*, 294–302; and Didier, "Le *Métissage* de *l'Enclyclopédie à la Révolution*," 14–16.

70 Buffon, *Histoire naturelle*, 196.

71 Ibid., 198.

72 Didier, "Le *Métissage*," 15. Buffon offers no comment on the mixed populations of French slave colonies in the Americas, as his descriptions of America focus mainly on Amerindian peoples. Buffon, *De l'homme*, 301.

73 Buffon's monogenetic notion of "race" presupposed a degree of degeneration from a common origin, whereby physical and moral traits would be altered by changes in climate, culture, and environment. The singular origin presupposed by Buffon's monogenesis is the European situated in temperate climates between the fortieth and fiftieth degrees of latitude. Buffon, *De l'homme*, 319–20.

74 On the overlap between Buffon's notions of species, race, and human variety, see Duchet, *Anthropologie et Histoire*, 229–80; Michèle Duchet, preface to Buffon, *De l'homme*; Jean Varloot, preface to Buffon, *Histoire naturelle*; and Patrick Graille, "Portrait scientifique et littéraire de l'hybride au siècle des lumières," *Eighteenth Century Life* 21, no. 2 (1997): 73–74.

75 François Marie Arouet de Voltaire, *Essai sur les moeurs* (1775; reprint, with intro-

duction, bibliography, variants, and notes, by René Pomeau, Paris: Garnier, 1963),
1:6.

76 From *La Russie sous Pierre le Grand*, quoted in Didier, "Le *Métissage*," 15.

77 Moreau makes one reference to "these racial crosses" (90).

78 On the meanings of *race* in the Enlightenment, see Nicholas Hudson, "From
'Nation' to 'Race': The Origin of Racial Classification in Eighteenth-Century
Thought," *Eighteenth Century Studies* 29, no. 3 (1996): 242–64; and Emmanuel
Chukwudi Eze, ed., *Race and the Enlightenment* (Cambridge, Mass.: Blackwell,
1997).

79 Edward Long, *Candid Reflections upon the Judgment Lately Awarded by the Court of
King's Bench . . . On What Is Commonly Called the Negro Cause, by a Planter* (London,
1772), quoted in Young, *Colonial Desire*, 150.

80 Toumson, *Mythologie du métissage*, 114–15.

81 Alexandrian has disputed the authorship of the text, attributing it to the Marquis
de Sentilly. Alexandrian, *Histoire de la littérature érotique* (Paris: Éditions Seghers,
1989), 182.

82 In the novel, Laure's father explains that women "deprive their blood of a vehicle
meant to produce their periods at the usual age, and in an advantageous way, or
they are finally subject . . . to uterine fevers [*des fureurs utérines*]." Similarly, sex with
multiple partners in quick succession causes "uterine ulcers." Honoré-Gabriel de
Riquetti Mirabeau, *Le Rideau levé*, in *Oeuvres érotiques de Mirabeau*, L'Enfer de la
Bibliothèque nationale 1 (Paris: Fayard, 1984), 338.

83 Nicolas Venette, *De la génération de l'homme, ou, tableau de l'amour conjugal* (Co-
logne: Claude Joly, 1696). On Venette's views on fertility and pleasure, see Jean
Mainil, *Dans les Règles du plaisir . . . : Théorie de la différence dans le discours ob-
scène romanesque et médical de l'Ancien Régime* (Paris: Éditions Kimé, 1996), 119–40;
Aram Vartanian, "La Mettrie, Diderot, and Sexology in the Enlightenment," in
Essays on the Age of Enlightenment in Honor of Ira O. Wade, edited by Jean Macary
(Geneva: Librairie Droz, 1977), 347–67. Female sterility is rare in the libertine
tradition, the most notable sterile female characters being Bois-Laurier of Boyer
d'Argen's *Thérèse Philosophe* (1748) and La Durand of Sade's *Juliette* (1797). See
Anne Richardot, "*Thérèse Philosophe*: Les charmes de l'impénétrable," *Eighteenth
Century Life* 21, no. 2 (1997): 89–99.

84 Nancy K. Miller, "Libertinage and Feminism," *Yale French Studies* 94 (1998): 17–28.

85 The fantasmatic nature of Moreau's proposition of mulatta sterility is striking given
that fertility rates among women of color were significantly higher than those for
whites and ensured a strong rate of natural reproduction for the class as a whole.
Stewart King, *Blue Coat or Powdered Wig*, 43–44.

86 On the question of "the masters' weakness," Moreau adds that "the population
benefits from it because it is less libertinage than need that governs these illicit
unions" (107).

87 Black women were symbolically the mothers of all the races, since they were
often used as wet-nurses for white children. Likewise, Moreau credits Creole slave
women with a remarkable propensity for motherhood: "Never have children, those

feeble creatures, had more assiduous care; and that slave who finds the time to bathe her children each night and to give them white linens, is a respectable being" (60).

88 Hilliard d'Auberteuil, *Considérations sur l'état présent de Saint-Domingue*, 2:88–91.

89 In desiring to establish claims of white paternity through the payment of benefits, Petit's position clearly articulates what was a growing anxiety about the economic independence of free people of color, as well as the desire of white colonials to limit and control their resources: "The freedman who is supported by his master, or his patron will not easily have himself deprived of it. One would have found fewer guilty persons among the mulattoes if they had something to lose." Petit makes subtle reference to "the enterprises that one could have mulattoes to blame for," that is, the instances in which mulattoes protested their exclusion from the white elite or allied themselves with the petits blancs, the other sworn enemies of the white landowning and commercial elite. See Petit, *Traité sur le gouvernement des esclaves*, 2:75.

90 In 1740, the defense of the colony momentarily became a justification to increase the manumission of slaves. On the involvement of free blacks and gens de couleur in the colonial military, see King, *Blue Coat or Powdered Wig*, 52–77; Hall, "Saint-Domingue," 174–75; Frostin, *Les Révoltes blanches*; and Garrigus, "Colour, Class and Identity."

91 Moreau de Saint-Méry explains the pressure to manumit as "the force of the opinion that the white, father of a child of color, should look to procure his freedom" (85). The marriages envisioned by the author thus suppose the union of a white man with a slave woman. Revenue from the sale of manumissions supported repairs to the infrastructure. In his description of the capital, Cap François, Moreau de Saint-Méry refers to a fund called *la caisse des libertés*, which was used to pay for city landfills (312).

92 King, *Blue Coat or Powdered Wig*, xiii. Moreau credits the formation of the special corps, the Chasseurs Royaux, to an additional increase in the population of affranchis after 1779, noting the participation of this legion of soldiers in the siege of Savannah that same year (85).

93 During the Haitian and French revolutions, free people of color based demands for equal rights and citizenship on their steadfast military service to the patrie. Garrigus, "Sons of the Same Father," 150–51; King, *Blue Coat or Powdered Wig*, 75–77.

94 Sigmund Freud, "Family Romances (1909) [1908]," in *The Standard Edition of the Complete Works of Sigmund Freud*, translated by James Strachey (London: Hogarth, 1959), 9:237–41.

95 The historian Lynn Hunt invokes the idea of family romance to explore the "collective political unconscious" of the French Revolution. Lynn Avery Hunt, *The Family Romance of the French Revolution* (Berkeley: University of California Press, 1992), xiii. Françoise Vergès devised the term *colonial family romance* to refer to the symbolic metaphors of filiation that suffused French colonial discourse on Reunion Island. She analyzes, further, the ways in which such myths were appropriated and

transformed by the revolutionary political discourse produced by Reunion's own racially diverse population. Vergès, *Monsters and Revolutionaries*, 8.

96 Simone Vauthier, "Of African Queens and Afro-American Princes and Princesses: Miscegenation in Old Hepsy," in *Regards sur la littérature noire américaine*, edited by Michel Fabre (Paris: Conseil Scientifique de la Sorbonne nouvelle, 1980), 91.

97 My use of the term *patriarchal* follows the definition of *patriarchy* given by Kathleen M. Brown in her historical study of the role of gender in the creation of racial slavery in colonial Virginia. According to Brown, patriarchy is "rooted in [the father's] control over labor and property, his sexual access to his wife and dependent female laborers, his control over other men's sexual access to the women of his household, and his right to punish family members and laborers." Brown, *Good Wives, Nasty Wenches, and Anxious Patriarchs*, 4.

98 Gautier, *Les Soeurs de Solitude*, 160.

99 In an exhaustive study of what he calls "interracial literature," Sollors points out the incestuous organizing principle behind Thomas Jefferson's "racial calculus," which presumed that the fourth generation of racial whitening was equivalent to the original (white) blood. Sollors associates this kind of taxonomic allegory with stories of interracial incest that appeared in antislavery literature such as the anonymously published *Adventures of Jonathan Corncob* (London, 1787). Sollors, *Neither White nor Black*, 114–16, 288–89.

100 Ibid., 289.

101 S.-J. Ducoeurjoly, *Manuel des habitans de Saint-Domingue, Contenant un précis de l'histoire de cette île depuis sa découverte* (Paris: Lenoir, 1802), 64.

102 In addition to Sollors, *Neither White nor Black*, see Vauthier, "Of African Queens," 65–107; Simone Vauthier, "Jeux avec l'interdit: La sexualité interraciale dans le roman de Joseph H. Ingraham, The Quadroone," *RANAM* 11 (1978): 133–46; and Richard King, *A Southern Renaissance: The Cultural Awakening of the American South, 1930–1955* (New York: Oxford University Press, 1980), esp. 111–21. For a sociological perspective, see Max Weber, *Economy and Society*, quoted in Sollors, *Neither White nor Black*, 322.

103 Sollors, *Neither White nor Black*, 320. In antebellum slave societies, frequent inbreeding among whites provides the practical corollary to the racist's discourse of radical endogamy. Ironically, in proslavery racist discourse the charge of incest is often invoked to characterize the "crime" of miscegenation, the ultimate taboo for the racially endogamous group. Werner Sollors explains this slippage as a metaphorical association made between one fundamental crime against the blood— incest—and what in racist societies becomes equally aberrant: "Viewed as incest, interracial sexual alliances may be considered a perversion of nature, the violation of a primary cultural taboo—resulting in degenererate offspring, sterility, feebleness, effeminacy" (320). The illogical nature of such an association points to the ironic admission that racist discourse makes when it affirms that miscegenation is incest; in fact, in many cases it *was* incest, due to the prevalence of unacknowledged blood ties on the plantation.

104 Ibid., 287; Vauthier, "Jeux avec l'interdit," 143. Perhaps the best-known example from the Caribbean is the Cuban writer Cirilo Villaverde's novel *Cecilia Valdés*, written between 1839 and 1882. For an interesting take on the centrality of themes of incest and miscegenation to the antislavery politics of the novel, see Sibylle Fischer, introduction to Cirilo Villaverde, *Cecilia Valdés*, translated by Helen Lowe, with an introduction by Sibylle Fischer (New York: Oxford University Press, 2004).

105 Vauthier, "Of African Queens," 90–91.

106 The argument is in reference to the novel *Old Hepsy* (1858) by Mary Denison.

107 In nineteenth-century antislavery literature, the tragic mulatto constantly struggled with the supposed contrariness of his or her makeup, divided between qualities of physical beauty and intellectual sophistication presumed to derive from racial whiteness and the baser instincts of the flesh attributed to blackness. This internal biological and emotional conflict was reflected in tragic predicaments in which the mulatto was destroyed by racial forces he or she could neither control nor overcome. For a detailed genealogy of this trope, see Sollors, *Neither White nor Black*, 220–45.

108 Hathaway notes an important difference between literary images of male and female tragic mulatto figures: "In most cases, male mulattoes are represented . . . as violent, dynamic, and vengeful, while female mulattoes 'tragically' reject their ambiguous relationship to family and race through suicide." Hathaway, "Maybe Freedom Lies in Hating," 154, 155.

109 Émilien Petit, in his *Traité sur le gouvernement des esclaves*, followed Roman slave law in advocating the manumission of slave women who had "milked" their masters or three of the masters' children. In the event of her death, the master's frère or soeur de lait would be freed in her place. (70)

110 Wimpffen, *Voyage à Saint-Domingue*, 215–16.

111 In a different context, the implications of the nursemaid for Freudian theories of the Oedipal stage are insightfully worked out by Ann McClintock in *Imperial Leather*. Looking at the case of women in domestic service in nineteenth-century Europe next to Freud's own "unpublishable" revelations from his own childhood, she suggests that the intimacy between nursemaids and their male charges brought about a male sexual fantasy of seduction by the mother/nurse. Seeing the nursemaid as having both the power of social punishment and the power to evoke sexual desire, McClintock argues that by eliding her the Oedipal theory assigns her roles to the father and mother. The result is to "safeguard the male's historical role as sexual agent" and purify the family romance of class differences. McClintock clearly emphasizes the "formative power of the working-class nurse in the sexual development of the child." McClintock, *Imperial Leather*, 88. My point is to suggest that any male fantasy of seduction or sex with the nursemaid would be, under slavery, easily transposed into the sexual domination of her and that such an act represents, as Jane Gallop has suggested, something between incest and exogamy. Jane Gallop, cited in McClintock, *Imperial Leather*, 94.

112 Sollors discusses two novels in particular: *The Slave* (1836), by Richard Hildreth, and *Adela, the Octoroon* (1860), by Hezekiah Lord Hosmer. See Sollors, *Neither White nor Black*, 288–98.

113 See, for example, Gayl Jones's novel, *Corregidora* (Boston: Beacon Press, 1975), which recounts the efforts of three generations of women to preserve the evidence of the incestuous crimes of their white ancestor; and Carolivia Herron's *Thereafter Johnnie* (New York: Random House, 1991), which examines the relationship between interracial father-daughter incest in slavery and a father-daughter incest pathology in a late-twentieth-century African American middle class family, mounting in the process a devastating critique of American and Western culture as a culture of incest. For a compelling reading of the incest theme in this text, see Arlene Keizer, "The Geography of the Apocalypse: Incest, Mythology, and the Fall of Washington City in Carolivia Herron's *Thereafter Johnnie*," in *Black Subjects: Identity Formation in the Contemporary Narrative of Slavery* (Ithaca: Cornell University Press, 2004), 125–63; and Brenda Daly, "Whose Daughter Is Johnnie? Revisionary Myth-Making in Carolivia Herron's *Thereafter Johnnie*," *Callaloo* 18, no. 2 (1995): 475–91.

114 Werner Sollors comments on a chapter in the novel entitled "The West-Indian Way of White-Washing, or Rather the True Way of Washing the Blackamoor White." In the U.S. context as well, father-daughter incest occurs in various antislavery novels of the nineteenth century. Two novels that attract Sollors's attention are Richard Hildreth's *Archy Moore, the White Slave* (1856), and Hezekiah Lord Hosmer's *Adela, the Octoroon* (1860). Sollors, *Neither White nor Black*, 288–97.

115 Hortense Spillers, "The Permanent Obliquity of an In(pha)llibly Straight: In the Time of the Daughters and the Fathers," in *Black, White and in Color: Essays on American Literature and Culture* (Chicago: University of Chicago Press, 2003), 231. For an interpretation of incest in William Faulkner's fiction with implications for the present argument, see Spillers's "Notes on an Alternative Model—Neither/Nor," in *Black, White and in Color*, 301–18. For a psychoanalytic interpretation of Western cultural myths of father-daughter incest, see Otto Rank, *The Incest Theme in Literature and Legend*, translated by Gregory C. Richter (Baltimore: Johns Hopkins University Press, 1992), 300–338.

116 On the nature of the reciprocity he envisions in the incest taboo, Lévi-Strauss writes: "As opposed to exogamy, exchange can be neither explicit nor immediate; but the fact that I can obtain a woman is, in the last analysis, the consequence of the fact that a brother or a father renounced her." Claude Lévi-Strauss, *Les Structures élémentaires de la parenté* (Paris: Presses Universitaires de France, 1949), 79.

117 Ibid., 596.

118 Ibid., ix.

119 Lévi-Strauss explains his system this way in the essay "Structural Analysis in Linguistics and Anthropology," in *Structural Anthropology*, translated by Claire Jacobson and Brooke Grundfest Schoepf (New York: Basic Books, 1963), 31–55. See also Juliett Mitchell, *Psychoanalysis and Feminism* (1974; reprint, with a new introduction, New York: Basic Books, 2000), 371.

120 Although the Code noir created legal impediments to the prospect of masters owning their own children, the laws of slavery were rarely observed, particularly in matters of reproduction. Article 9 essentially forbade the master to create illegitimate

families with slave concubines by stipulating that any illegitimate children born to him would be confiscated with their mother. The punishment could be avoided if the master married his slave concubine, who would be freed with her children by the act. In addition to prohibiting concubinage and illegitimate reproduction, this article ensured that a master would not be in legal possession of his own offspring. Previous laws, however, stipulated that illegitimate mulatto children should be enslaved so as to punish the slave mother, in which case it is possible to imagine a legal sanction for the master's ownership of illegitimates. See the previous chapter for a fuller discussion of laws regulating concubinage and reproduction.

121 This point relates to the feminist contention that even within kinship systems the prohibition against incest is weakest between the father and daughter. In her study of father-daughter incest, Judith Herman has shown that the rule that prohibits a male from having sex with female relatives is reinforced by the claims of other men on those women. Incest with a sister is forbidden because it interferes with the father's rights, as does incest with the mother. Incest with the cousin or aunt is forbidden because they belong to the uncle. Only in the case of the daughter is the father's right uncontested: "The man who has the power to give a woman away also has the power to take her for himself. . . . No kinsman, and certainly no man outside the family, is in a position to challenge a father's power over his daughters. Thus the rule of the gift is breached most commonly where it is least capable of enforcement, that is, in the relationship between fathers and daughters." Judith Herman and Lisa Hirschman, *Father-Daughter Incest* (Cambridge: Harvard University Press, 1981), 62. In their study, Herman and Hirschman compile an impressive amount of evidence to prove that father-daughter incest occurs more frequently than any other form of incest.

122 On this point, see also Hortense Spillers's discussion of the father function under slavery in "The Permanent Obliquity" and the commentary by Arlene Keizer in "Geography of the Apocalypse."

123 Lévi-Strauss, *Les Structures élémentaires*, 601.

124 Given the proximity of their thought, it is surprising that Lévi-Strauss acknowledges Freud's influence only at the conclusion of his enormous volume. The anthropologist objects that Freud's work is plagued by contradiction: "In seeking to explain why incest is consciously condemned, he explains why incest is consciously desired." Ibid., 609. For a comparison of the two works, see Mitchell, *Psychoanalysis and Feminism*, 370–98.

125 Freudian theory is of especially limited utility for thinking about the incestuous desires of the father for his daughter. One of the most devastating critiques of Freudian psychoanalysis charges that Freud himself perpetuates a silence about parent-child incest and in particular father-daughter incest. The argument maintains that Freud abandoned the "Seduction Theory" of female hysteria, which attributes hysteria to childhood sexual abuse by adults (including fathers), after he had essentially been sanctioned by the entire psychoanalytic profession for suggesting it. In defiance of the testimony of countless women patients who had recounted their

memories of childhood sexual abuse, Freud eventually endorsed the more socially palatable position that patients' reports of sexual abuse were the untrue expressions of the female infant's imagination and fantasy life. See Jeffrey Moussaieff Masson, *The Assault on Truth: Freud's Suppression of the Seduction Theory* (New York: Ferrar, Strauss and Giroux, 1984); Herman and Hirschman, *Father-Daughter Incest*, 7–12; and Keizer, "Geography of the Apocalypse."

126 Freud, *Totem and Taboo*, 176.

127 On figures and meanings of paternity in eighteenth-century French literature, see Jean-Claude Bonnet, "La Malédiction Paternelle," *Dix-huitième siècle* 12 (1980): 195–208. The incestuous father is a main character in *L'Anti-Justine* (1798), by Restif de la Bretonne, and Mirabeau's *Le Rideau levé, ou l'éducation de Laure*. Mirabeau draws a contrast between the unsound erotic education of Rose, who is corrupted by her brother before puberty, and the apparently more fortunate Laure, who is "educated" by a more cautious and knowing father figure, who awaits her maturity before initiating her himself. The author thus recuperates and refigures paternal authority in the interests of libertinage, as the father satisfies both his own and his daughter's desires. Yet, *bienséances*, or standards of decorum, may have been taken into account in his representation of libertine incest. The father is not biologically related to Laure—who is the child of her mother's former lover—and he claims never to have consummated his marriage with Laure's mother. The father (named only "Papa" or "my father" in the novel) actually defends his actions toward Laure on the basis of the lack of consanguinity between them: "This child, who is become so dear to me, is not at all my daughter by nature: absolutely foreign to me, she is my daughter by affection only. The interior scruple can therefore not exist, and any other consideration is indifferent to me, with prudence" (333). This self-conscious rebuttal of the horror of incest is but an ironic nod to conventional morality, however, since in every way the father is Laure's primary caregiver and the mother's untimely death makes possible both the father's central parental role and his incestuous pursuit. Mirabeau, *Le Rideau levé*, 301–446. On incest themes in eighteenth-century literature and culture, see Georges Benrekassa, "Loi naturelle et loi civile: L'idéologie des lumières et la prohibition de l'inceste," in *Le Concentrique et l'excentrique: Marges des lumières* (Paris: Payot, 1980), 183–209; and T. Nelson, "Incest in the Early Novel and Related Genres," *Eighteenth Century Life* 16 (1992): 127–62.

128 Hénaff, *Sade*, 326–27.

129 Hénaff's explanation of the transformation of the girl into a prostitute concurs, though in a different vein, with psychotherapeutic interpretations of the destructive effects of father-daughter incest. Judith Herman and Lisa Hirschman argue that "the father, in effect, forces the daughter to pay with her body for affection and care which should be freely given. In so doing, he destroys the protective bond between parent and child and initiates his daughter into prostitution." Herman and Hirschman, *Father-Daughter Incest*, 4.

130 Hénaff, *Sade*, 271.

131 I thank Mary Weismantel for her discussion on this point.

132 Yet at this point incest as a concept may appear to be a rather unsatisfactory way of explaining the sexual possession and reproductive violation of slave women by the master irrespective of blood ties between them. This is because modern scholarship (in psychoanalysis and anthropology) has explained the tendency toward incest by recourse to assumptions of sentimental attachments within the nuclear family that can border on the amorous, thus arousing sexual desire. One might ask, then, to what extent it is still relevant to speak in terms of kinship and incest in a case in which relationships of sentimental attachment between members of the mixed-race clan were not necessarily the norm. By maintaining incest as an analytic concept applied to sexual relations on the plantation, I am not supposing that the master/father was simply acting as his own stud, inseminating all the women on the plantation merely to produce progeny. Rather, I contend that the slave master's knowing pursuit of his biological daughter must be understood with respect to his knowledge of norms of kinship and family in white colonial society. Even if she is in the category of slave/thing/commodity, she is for the knowing master/father much more than that. She is a daughter available for the taking, all the more desirable because of her mixed race. We are thus left with a paradox: If incest is fundamental to the logic of slavery as a social organization, slavery at the same time exposes the inadequacy of the psychoanalytic and anthropological models we have available for understanding incest and its supposed prohibition. I thank Srinivas Aravamudan for his suggestive discussion on this matter.

133 Girod de Chantrans, *Voyage d'un Suisse dans les colonies de l'Amérique*, 141.

134 Note Werner Sollors's very different conclusion regarding incest in proslavery ideology, that it is the exaggeration of endogamy. Sollors, *Neither White nor Black*, 322.

135 Girod de Chantrans, *Voyage d'un Suisse dans les colonies de l'Amérique*, 141.

136 Patterson, *Slavery and Social Death*, 5. Unfortunately, Patterson does not consider the ways in which sexual aspects of slavery impacted the social alienation experienced by slaves in the Americas.

137 M. Raimond, *Observations sur l'origine et les progrès du préjugé des colons blancs contre les hommes de couleur; sur les inconvénients de le perpétuer; la nécessité, la facilité de le détruire; sur le projet du Comité colonial, etc.* (Paris: Chez Bellin, Desenne, Bailly, 1791). On the political activism and writings of Julien Raimond, see Debbasch, *Couleur et liberté*, 118–25; King, *Blue Coat and Powdered Wig*, 75, 158–60, 195; Hall, "Saint-Domingue," 189; and James, *The Black Jacobins*, 77.

138 Raimond, *Observations sur l'origine et les progrès du préjugé des colons blancs contre les hommes de couleur*, 4.

139 Ibid., 7.

140 Ibid., 12.

141 Ibid., 18.

142 Ibid., 21.

143 "Constitution d'Haïti" (1805), in Thomas Madiou, *Histoire d'Haïti*, (Port-au-Prince, Haiti: Éditions Henri Deschamps, 1989), annexe, 3:545–53.

Conclusion

1 Fanon, *Peau noire, masques blancs*, 186.
2 Glissant, *Le Discours antillais*, 222.
3 Toni Morrison, *Beloved* (New York: Penguin, 1987).
4 Dayan, *Haiti, History, and the Gods*, xvii.

Works Cited

PRIMARY SOURCES

Armand de la Paix [Raymond Breton]. "Relation de l'île de la Guadeloupe." 1647. Reprinted in Raymond Breton, *Relations de l'île de la Guadeloupe*. Basse Terre, Société d'histoire de la Guadeloupe, 1978.

Blessebois, Pierre-Corneille. *L'Oeuvre Pierre-Corneille Blessebois*. Edited by Guillaume Apollinaire. Paris: Bibliothèque des curieux, 1931.

———. *Le Rut ou la pudeur éteinte*. In *Oeuvres érotiques du XVIIème siècle*. Enfer de la Bibliothèque nationale 7. Paris: Fayard, 1988.

———. *Le Zombi du Grand-Pérou ou la comtesse de Cocagne*. 1697. Reprint, with a preface by Jean-Paul Bouchon, Poitiers: Paréiasaure Édition, 1997.

Bouton, Jacques. *Relation de l'establissement des François depuis l'an 1635 en l'isle de la Martinique, L'une des Antilles de l'Amérique: Des moeurs des sauvages, de la situation, et d'autres singularitez de l'isle*. Paris: Cramoisy, 1640.

Breton, Raymond. *Les Caraïbes, La Guadeloupe, 1635-1656: Histoire des vingt premières années de la colonisation de la Guadeloupe d'après les relations du R. P. Breton*. Edited, with a preface, by Joseph Rennard. Paris: G. Ficker, 1929.

———. *Dictionnaire caraïbe-français (avec cédérom)*. 1665. Reprint, edited by Marina Besada Paisa and Jean Bernabé with introduction, articles, and notes by members of the Centre d'études des langues indigènes d'Amérique and Le Groupe d'études et de recherches en espace créolophone. Paris: Éditions Karthala, 1999.

———. *Dictionaire caraibe-français, composé par le R. P. Raymond Breton*. 1665. Reprint by Jules Platzmann, Leipzig: B. G. Teubner, 1892.

———. *Dictionaire français-caraibe, composé par le R. P. Raymond Breton*. 1666. Reprint by Jules Platzmann, Leipzig: B. G. Teubner, 1900.

———. *Dictionaire caraibe-françois, Meslé de quantité de remarques historiques pour l'éclaircissement de la langue*. Auxerre: Gilles Bouquet, 1665.

———. *Grammaire caraibe*. Auxerre: Gilles Bouquet, 1667.

————. *Petit catéchisme, ou sommaire des trois premières parties de la doctrine chrétienne.* Auxerre: Gilles Bouquet, 1664.

————. *Relations de l'île de la Guadeloupe.* 1647. Reprint, Basse-Terre, Guadeloupe: Société d'histoire de la Guadeloupe, 1978.

Chanvalon, Thibault de. *Voyage à la Martinique, contenant diverses observations sur la physique, l'histoire naturelle, l'agriculture, les moeurs et les usages de cette isle, faites en 1751 et dans les années suivantes* . . . Paris: J. B. Bauche, 1763.

Charlevoix, Pierre-François-Xavier de. *Histoire de l'isle espagnole ou de S. Domingue, écrite particulièrement sur des mémoires du P. Jean-Baptiste Le Pers* . . . 2 vols. Paris: F. Didot, 1730–31.

Chevillard, André. *Les Desseins de son Éminence Cardinal Richelieu pour l'Amerique.* 1659. Reprint, Basse-Terre, Guadeloupe: Société d'histoire de la Guadeloupe, 1973.

Colbert. *Code noir, ou receuil d'édits, déclarations et arrêts concernant les esclaves nègres de l'Amérique.* 1685. Reprint, with additions and amendments, Paris: Libraires Associez, 1743.

Columbus, Christopher. "The Journal of Columbus (1492–1493)." In Hulme and Whitehead, *Wild Majesty.*

Coppier, Guillaume. *Histoire et voyage des Indes Occidentales, et de plusieurs autres regions maritimes et esloignées* . . . Lyon: Jean Hugueton, 1645.

Dubuisson, Pierre Ulric. *Nouvelles considérations sur Saint-Domingue, en réponse à celles de M. H .D.* 2 vols. in 1. Paris: Chez Cellot et Jombert, 1780.

Du Tertre, Jean-Baptiste. *Histoire générale des Antilles habitées par les François.* 3 vols. Paris: Thomas Jolly, 1667–71.

————. *Histoire générale des Antilles habitées par les Français.* 3 vols. 1667–71. Reprint, 4 vols. in 3, Fort-de-France, Martinique: Éditions des Horizons Caraïbes, 1973.

————. *Histoire générale des isles des* [sic] *Saint-Christophe, de la Guadeloupe, de la Martinique, et autres dans l'Amérique* . . . Paris: J. et E. Langlois, 1654.

DuPuis, Mathias. *Relation de l'establissement d'une colonie française dans la Gardeloupe, isle de l'Amérique, et des moeurs des sauvages.* Caen: Marin Yvon, 1652.

Esquemeling, J. *Bucaniers of America, the Second Volume: Containing the Dangerous Voyage and Bold Attempts of Captain Bartholomew Sharp* . . . London: William Crooke, 1685.

————. *Bucaniers of America: A True Account of the Most Remarkable Assaults Committed of Late Years upon the Coasts of the West Indies* . . . *Wherein Are Contained* . . . *the Exploits of Sir Henry Morgan, Our English Jamaican Hero* . . . London: William Crooke, 1684.

————. *The History of the Bucaniers, Being an Impartial Relation of All the Battles, Sieges, and Other Most Eminent Assaults* . . . *More Especially the Unparalleled Achievements of Sir H. M.* . . . London: Thomas Malthus, 1684.

Girod de Chantrans, Justin. *Voyage d'un Suisse dans différentes colonies d'Amérique pendant la dernière guerre, avec une table d'observations métérologiques faites à Saint-Domingue* . . . Neuchatel: Imprimerie de la Société Typographique, 1785.

————. *Voyage d'un Suisse dans les colonies d'Amérique.* 1785. Reprint, with a foreword by Pierre Pluchon, Paris: Librairie Jules Tallendier, 1980.

Hilliard d'Auberteuil, Michel René. *Considérations sur l'état présent de la colonie française de Saint-Domingue: Ouvrage politique et législatif, presenté au ministre de la marine.* 2 vols. Paris: Chez Grangé, 1776.

La Borde, Sieur de. *Relation de l'origine, moeurs, coutumes, religion, guerres et voyages des Caraïbes sauvages des isles Antilles de l'Amérique.* In *Recueil de divers voyages faits en Afrique et en l'Amérique, qui n'ont point été encore publiés.* Edited by Henri Justel. Paris: Louis Billaine, 1674.

Labat, Jean-Baptiste. *Nouvelle relation de l'Afrique occidentale . . .* Paris: Chez G. Cavelier, 1728.

———. *Nouveau voyage aux isles de l'Amérique, . . .* Paris: P. F. Giffart, 1722.

———. *Nouveau voyage aux isles de l'Amérique, contenant l'histoire naturelle de ces pays, l'origine, les moeurs, la religion, et le gouvernement des habitants anciens et modernes . . . 1742.* Reprint, 8 vols. in 4, Fort-de-France, Martinique: Éditions des Horizons Caraïbes, 1972.

Mocquet, Jean. *Voyages en Afrique, Asie, Indes Orientales et Occidentales, faits par Jean Mocquet, garde du Cabinet des singularitez du Roy aux Tuileries Divisez en six livres et enrichis de figures.* Paris: Jean de Heuqueville, 1617.

Moreau de Saint-Méry, Médéric Louis Élie. *Dance.* Translated by Lily Hastings and Baird Hastings. 1796. Reprint, Brooklyn: Dance Horizons, 1975.

———. *Danse: Article extrait d'un ouvrage de M .L. E Moreau de Saint-Méry ayant pour titre — répertoire des notions coloniales, par ordre alphabétique.* Philadelphia: published by the author, 1796.

———. *Description topographique, physique, civile, politique, et historique de la partie française de l'isle Saint-Domingue: Nouvelle édition entièrement revue et complétée sur le manuscrit suivie d'un index des noms de personnes.* 3 vols. 1797. Reprint, edited, with a biography, bibliography, and notes, by Blanche Maurel and Étienne Taillemite, Paris: Société de l'histoire des colonies françaises, 1958.

———. *Loix et constitutions des colonies françaises de l'Amérique sous le vent de 1550–1785.* Paris: Chez l'auteur, 1784–90.

Oexmelin, Alexandre Olivier. *Les Aventuriers et les boucaniers d'Amérique, par Alexandre Oexmelin, Chirurgien des Aventuriers de 1666 à 1672.* 1699. Reprint, with a preface by Bertrand Guégan, Paris: Éditions du Carrefour, 1930.

———. *Histoire des aventuriers qui se sont signalez dans les Indes, contenant ce qu'ils ont fait de plus remarquable depuis vingt années, avec la vie, les moeurs, les coûtumes des habitans de Saint-Domingue . . .* Paris: Chez Jacques Lefebvre, 1686.

Pacifique de Provins. *Brève relation du voyage des îles de l'Amérique. 1643.* In *Le voyage de Perse, et Brève relation du voyage des îles de l'Amérique.* Reprint, with critical introductions by P. Godefroy de Paris and P. Hilaire de Wingene, Assisi: Collegio S. Lorenzo da Brindisi Dei Minori Cappucini, 1939.

Pelleprat, Pierre. *Relation des missions des PP. de la Compagnie de Jésus dans les isles et à la terre ferme de l'Amérique méridionale.* Paris: Sébastien et Gabriel Cramoisy, 1655.

Petit, Émilien. *Traité sur le gouvernement des esclaves.* 2 vols. Paris: Knapen, Imprimeur, 1777.

Raimond, M. *Observations sur l'origine et les progrès du préjugé des colons blancs contre les hommes de couleur; sur les inconvénients de le perpétuer; la nécessité, la facilité de le détruire; sur le projet du Comité colonial, etc.* Paris: Chez Bellin, Desenne, Bailly, 1791.

Rochefort, César de. *Histoire naturelle et morale des iles Antilles de l'Amérique.* Rotterdam: Arnout Leers, 1658.

Wimpffen, Alexandre-Stanislas de. *Voyage à Saint-Domingue pendant les années 1788, 1789 et 1790.* Paris, 1797. Reprinted in *Haiti au XVIIIe siècle,* edited by Pierre Pluchon. Paris: Karthala, 1993.

SECONDARY SOURCES

Abénon, Lucien-René. *La Guadeloupe de 1671 à 1759: Étude politique, économique et sociale.* Vol. 1. Paris: L'Harmattan, 1987.

Abénon, Lucien-René, and John A. Dickinson. *Les Français en Amérique: Histoire d'une colonisation.* Lyon: Presses Universitaires de Lyon, 1993.

Ackerman, Hans W., and Jeanine Gauthier. "The Ways and Nature of the Zombi." *Journal of American Folklore* 104 (1991): 467–69.

Adélaïde-Merlande, Jacques. "Le Créole: Aux origines de l'utilisation de ce terme." In Yacou, *Créoles de la Caraïbe.*

Adorno, Rolena. *The Armature of Conquest: Spanish Accounts of the Discovery of America, 1492–1589.* Stanford: Stanford University Press, 1992.

———. "Literary Production and Suppression: Reading and Writing about Amerindians in Colonial Spanish America." *Dispositio* 11, nos. 28–29 (1986): 1–25.

Adventures of Jonathan Corncob, Loyal American Refugee, Written by Himself. 1787. Boston: D. R. Godine, 1976.

Affergan, François. *Exotisme et altérité.* Paris: Presses Universitaires de France, 1987.

Ahmad, Aijaz. *In Theory: Classes, Nations, Literatures.* London: Verso, 1992.

Alegria, Ricardo. "The Study of Aboriginal Peoples: Multiple Ways of Knowing." In Wilson, *The Indigenous People of the Caribbean.*

Alexandrian. *Histoire de la littérature érotique.* Paris: Éditions Seghers, 1989.

Alexis, Gerson. *Vodou et quimbois: Essai sur les avatars du vodou à la Martinique.* Port-au-Prince, Haiti: Éditions Fardin, 1976.

Allaire, Louis. "The Caribs of the Lesser Antilles." In Wilson, *The Indigenous People of the Caribbean.*

———. "The Lesser Antilles before Columbus" In Wilson, *The Indigenous People of the Caribbean.*

Alleyne, Mervyn C. "Acculturation and the Cultural Matrix of Creolization." In *Pidginization and Creolization of Languages,* edited by Dell Hymes. Cambridge: Cambridge University Press, 1971.

Anglo, Sydney. "Melancholia and Witchcraft: The Debate between Wier, Bodin, and Scot." In *Folie et déraison à la Renaissance: Colloque international tenu en novembre 1973 sous les auspices de la Fédération internationale des instituts et sociétés pour l'étude de la Renaissance.* Brussels: Éditions de l'Université de Bruxelles, 1976.

Antoine, Régis. *Les Écrivains français et les Antilles: Des premiers Pères blancs aux surréalistes noirs.* Paris: G. P. Maisonneuve et Larose, 1978.

Apollinaire, Guillaume. Introduction to *L'Oeuvre Pierre-Corneille Blessebois*, by Pierre-Corneille Blessebois. Paris: Bibliothèque des curieux, 1931.

Aravamudan, Srinivas. *Tropicopolitans: Colonialism and Agency, 1688–1804*. Durham: Duke University Press, 1999.

Arciniegas, Germán. *America in Europe: A History of the New World in Reverse*. Translated by Gabriela Arciniegas and R. Victoria Arana. San Diego: Harcourt Brace Jovanovich, 1986.

Arens, W. *The Man-Eating Myth: Anthropology and Anthropophagy*. New York: Oxford University Press, 1979.

Ariès, Philippe. *L'Enfant et la vie familiale sous l'ancien régime*. 1965. Reprint, Paris: Éditions du Seuil, 1973.

Arnold, A. James. "The Gendering of Créolité: The Erotics of Colonialism." In Condé and Cottenet-Hage, *Penser la créolité*.

Arzalier, Francis. "Les mutations de l'idéologie coloniale en France avant 1848: De l'esclavagisme à l'abolitionnisme." In *Les Abolitions de l'esclavage: De L. F. Sonthonax à V. Schoelcher, 1793, 1794, 1848*, edited by Marcel Dorigny. Paris: L'Organisation des Nations Unies, 1995.

Asad, Talal. "The Concept of Cultural Translation in British Social Anthropology." In Clifford and Marcus, *Writing Culture*.

———. "Pain and Truth in Christian Ritual." In *Genealogies of Religion: Discipline and Reasons of Power in Christianity and Islam*. Baltimore: Johns Hopkins University Press, 1993.

Atkinson, Geoffroy. *The Extraordinary Voyage in French Literature from 1700 to 1720*. Paris: Champion, 1922.

———. *Les Nouveaux horizons de la renaissance française*. Paris: E. Droz, 1935.

———. *Les Relations de voyages du XVIIe siècle et l'évolution des idées: Contribution à l'étude de la formation de l'esprit du XVIIIe siècle*. Paris: É. Champion, 1924.

Atkinson, Paul. *The Ethnographic Imagination: Textual Constructions of Reality*. London: Routledge, 1990.

Auroux, Sylvain. "La Première description linguistique des Antilles françaises: Le Père Raymond Breton." In *Naissance de l'ethnologie? Anthropologie et missions en Amérique XVIe–XVIIIe siècle*, edited by Claude Blanckaert. Paris: Éditions du Cerf, 1985.

Auroux, Sylvain, and Francisco Queixalos. "La Première description linguistique des Antilles françaises: Le Père Raymond Breton." In *Naissance de l'ethnologie? Anthropologie et missions en Amérique XVIe–XVIIIe siècle*, edited by Claude Blanckaert. Paris: Éditions du Cerf, 1985.

Badillo, Jalil Sued. *Los Caribes: Realidad o fábula*. Río Piedras, P.R.: Editorial Antillana, 1978.

———. "The Island Caribs: New Approaches to the Question of Ethnicity in the Early Colonial Caribbean." In Whitehead, *Wolves from the Sea*.

Bakhtin, Mikhail. *The Dialogic Imagination*. Edited by Michael Holquist. Translated by Caryl Emerson and Michael Holquist. Austin: University of Texas Press, 1981.

———. "Discourse in the Novel." In Bakhtin, *The Dialogic Imagination*.

Barker, Francis, Peter Hulme, and Margaret Iversen, eds. *Colonial Discourse, Postcolonial Theory*. Manchester: Manchester University Press, 1994.

Barthes, Roland. *Le Bruissement de la langue: Essais critiques IV*. Paris: Editions du Seuil, 1984.

———. "Le Discours de l'histoire." In Barthes, *Le Bruissement de la langue*.

Bechtel, Guy. *La Sorcière et l'occident*. Paris: Plon, 1997.

Beckles, Hilary. "Kalinago (Carib) Resistance to European Colonisation of the Caribbean." In *Crossroads of Empire: The European-Caribbean Connection, 1492–1992*, edited by Alan Cobley. Cave Hill, Barbados: Department of History, University of the West Indies, 1994.

Bénot, Yves. *Diderot: De l'athéisme à l'anticolonialisme*. Paris: Maspéro, 1970.

———. *La Révolution française et la fin des colonies*. Paris: Éditions La Découverte, 1988.

Benrékassa, Georges. "Loi naturelle et loi civile: L'idéologie des lumières et la prohibition de l'inceste." In *Le Concentrique et l'excentrique: Marges des lumières*. Paris: Payot, 1980.

Bernabé, Jean. "La Créolité: Problématiques et enjeux." In Yacou, *Créoles de la Caraïbe*.

———. "De la négritude à la créolité: Éléments pour une apprôche comparée." *Études françaises* 28, nos. 2–3 (1992–93): 23–28.

———. "Présentation." In Breton, *Dictionnaire caraïbe-français*, 1999 ed.

Bernabé, Jean, Patrick Chamoiseau, and Raphaël Confiant. *Éloge de la créolité. In Praise of Creoleness*, translated by M. B. Taleb-Khyar. Paris: Gallimard, 1989.

Bernard, Carmen, and Serge Gruzinski. *De l'idolâtrie: Une archéologie des sciences religieuses*. Paris: Editions du Seuil, 1988.

Berthiaume, Pierre. *L'Aventure américaine au XVIIIe siècle: Du voyage à l'écriture*. Ottawa: Presses de l'Université d'Ottawa, 1990.

Bhabha, Homi. *The Location of Culture*. London: Routledge, 1994.

Bitton, Davis. *The French Nobility in Crisis, 1560–1640*. Stanford: Stanford University Press, 1969.

Blackburn, Robin. *The Making of New World Slavery*. London: Verso, 1997.

———. *The Overthrow of Colonial Slavery, 1776–1848*. London: Verso, 1988.

Blanckaert, Claude, ed. *Naissance de l'ethnologie? Anthropologie et missions en Amérique, XVIe–XVIIIe siècle*. Paris: Les Éditions du Cerf, 1985.

Bloch, Marc. *Feudal Society*. Translated by L. A. Manyon, with a foreword by T. S. Brown. London: Routledge, 1989.

Bluche, François. *Dictionnaire du grand siècle*. Paris: Fayard, 1990.

Bodin, Jean. *On the Demon-Mania of Witches*. Translated by Randy A. Scott. Toronto: Center for Reformation and Renaissance Studies, 1995.

Bohanan, Donna. *Crown and Nobility in Early Modern France*. New York: Palgrave, 2001.

Bolland, O. Nigel. "Creolization and Creole Societies: A Cultural Nationalist View of Caribbean Social History." In *Intellectuals in the Twentieth-Century Caribbean*, edited by Alistair Hennessy. Vol. 1. London: Macmillan, 1992.

Bongie, Chris. *Islands and Exiles: The Creole Identities of Post/Colonial Literature*. Stanford: Stanford University Press, 1998.

Bonnet, Jean-Claude. "La Malédiction Paternelle." *Dix-huitième siècle* 12 (1980): 195–208.

Bonniol, Jean-Luc. *La Couleur comme maléfice.* Paris: A. Michel, 1992.

———. "Le Métissage entre social et biologique: L'Exemple des Antilles de colonisation française." In Kandé, *Discours sur le métissage, identités métisses.*

Boromé, Joseph. "The French and Dominica, 1699–1763." *Jamaican Historical Review* 7 (1967): 10–39.

———. "Spain and Dominica, 1493–1647." *Caribbean Quarterly* 12 (1966): 30–46.

Boucher, Philip P. *Cannibal Encounters: Europeans and Island Caribs, 1492–1763.* Baltimore: John Hopkins University Press, 1992.

———. "The Caribbean and the Caribs in the Thought of Seventeenth-Century French Colonial Propagandists: The Missionaries." In *Proceedings of the Fourth Meeting of the French Colonial Historical Society,* edited by Alf Andrew Heggoy and James J. Cooke. Lanham, Md.: University Press of America, 1978.

———. *Les Nouvelles Frances: France in America, 1500–1815, an Imperial Perspective.* Providence: John Carter Brown Library, 1989.

Boucher de la Richarderie, G. *Bibliothèque universelle des voyages.* 4 vols. Paris: Chez Treuttel et Würtz, 1808.

Bouchon, Jean-Paul. Preface to *Le Zombi du Grand-Pérou* by Pierre-Corneille Blessebois. Poitiers: Paréiasaure Éditions, 1997.

Bougainville, Louis-Antoine de. *Voyage autour du monde, par la frégate du roi La Boudeuse, et la flûte L'Étoile; en 1766, 1767, 1768 and 1769.* Paris: Saillant and Nyon, 1771.

Bougerol, Christiane. *Une Ethnographie des conflits aux Antilles: Jalousie, commérages, sorcellerie.* Paris: Presses Universitaires de France, 1997.

———. "Sorcellerie, malédiction et justice divine à la Guadeloupe." *Ethnologie française* 10, no. 2 (1990): 169–76.

Brathwaite, Kamau. *The Development of Creole Society in Jamaica, 1770–1820.* Oxford: Clarendon, 1971.

Brooks, Peter. *The Novel of Worldliness.* Princeton: Princeton University Press, 1969.

Brown, Kathleen. *Good Wives, Nasty Wenches, and Anxious Patriarchs: Gender, Race, and Power in Colonial Virginia.* Chapel Hill: University of North Carolina Press, 1996.

Bruc, Numa. *La Géographie des philosophes: Géographes et voyageurs français au XVIIIème siècle.* Paris: Orphrys, 1975.

Buffon, G.-L. L., Comte de. *Histoire naturelle.* 1749. Edited by Jean Varloot. Paris: Gallimard, 1984.

———. *De l'homme.* Edited by Michèle Duchet. Paris: François Maspero, 1971.

Burg, B. R. *Sodomy and the Perception of Evil.* New York: New York University Press, 1983.

Burney, James. *The History of the Buccaneers of America.* London: Swan Sonnenschein, 1816.

Burton, Richard D. E. *Afro-Creole: Power, Opposition, and Play in the Caribbean.* Ithaca: Cornell University Press, 1997.

Butel, Paul. "L'Essor antillais au XVIIe siècle." In Pluchon, *Histoire des Antilles et de la Guyane.*

Butler, Judith. *Subjects of Desire*. New York: Columbia University Press, 1987.

Camus, Michel-Christian. "Une note critique à propos d'Exquemelin." *Revue française d'histoire d'outre-mer* 77, no. 286 (1990): 79–90.

Carby, Hazel. *Reconstructing Womanhood: The Emergence of the Afro-American Woman Novelist*. New York: Oxford University Press, 1987.

Cartier, Jacques. *Brief récit et succinte narration de la navigation faicte es ysles de Canada, Hochelage et Saguet . . .* Paris, 1545.

———. *Discours du voyage faict aux Terres neufves du Canada . . . et pays adjacents, dite Nouvelle France . . .* Rouen: R. Du Petit Val, 1598.

Castillo, Debra. "Border Theory and the Canon." In *Post-colonial Literatures: Expanding the Canon*, edited by Deborah Madsen. London: Pluto, 1999.

Cavendish, Richard, and Brian Innes. *Man, Myth and Magic: The Illustrated Encyclopedia of Mythology, Religion and the Unknown*. New ed. New York: Marshall Cavendish, 1995.

Cazenobe, Colette, *Le Système du libertinage de Crébillon à Laclos*. Oxford: Voltaire Foundation, 1991.

Certeau, Michel de. *L'Ecriture de l'histoire*. Paris: Gallimard, 1975.

Cervantes, Fernando. *The Devil in the New World: The Impact of Diabolism in New Spain*. New Haven: Yale University Press, 1994.

———. *The Idea of the Devil and the Problem of the Indian: The Case of Mexico in the Sixteenth Century*. Research Papers, no. 24. London: University of London, Institute of Latin American Studies, 1991.

Chamoiseau, Patrick. *Au temps de l'antan: Contes du pays Martinique*. Paris: Hatier, 1988.

Chamoiseau, Patrick, and Raphaël Confiant. *Lettres créoles: Tracées antillaises et continentales de la littérature—Haïti, Guadeloupe, Martinique, Guyane, 1635–1975*. Paris: Hatier, 1991.

Champlain, Samuel. *Des sauvages, ou Voyage . . . faict en la France nouvelle, l'an mil six cens trois . . .* Paris: C. de Monstr'oeil, 1604.

———. *Les Voyages de la Nouvelle-France occidentale, dicte Canada . . .* Paris: Impr. de L. Sevestre, 1632.

Chatillon, Marcel. "Le Père Labat à travers ses manuscrits." *Bulletin de la Société d'histoire de la Guadeloupe* 40–42, 2e–4e trimestres (1979): 6–42.

———. "Pierre-Corneille Blessebois, le poète galérien de Capesterre." *Bulletin de la Société d'histoire de la Guadeloupe*, 4e trimestre (1976): 15–41.

Chauleau, Liliane. *Histoire antillaise: La Martinique et la Guadeloupe du XVIIe à la fin du XIXe siècle—Éléments d'histoire antillaise*. Encyclopédie antillaise, no. 5. Fort-de-France: É. Gros Desormeaux, 1973.

———. *Dans les îles du vent: La Martinique (XVIIe–XIXe siècle)*. Paris: L'Harmattan, 1993.

———. *La Société à la Martinique au XVIIe siècle (1635–1713)*. Caen: Impr. Ozanne, 1966.

Chaussinand-Nogaret, G. *La Noblesse au XVIIIème siècle*. Paris: Hachette, 1976.

Cheyfitz, Eric. *Poetics of Imperialism*. New York: Oxford University Press, 1991.

Chinard, Gilbert. *L'Amérique et le rêve exotique dans la littérature française au XVIIe et au XVIIIe siècle*. Paris: Librairie E. Droz, 1934.

Clark, Stewart. *Thinking with Demons: The Idea of Witchcraft in Early Modern Europe.* Oxford: Oxford University Press, 1997.

Clifford, James. "On Ethnographic Allegory." In Clifford and Marcus, *Writing Culture.*

———. *The Predicament of Culture: Twentieth-Century Ethnography, Literature, and Art.* Cambridge: Harvard University Press, 1988.

Clifford, James, and George E. Marcus, eds. *Writing Culture: The Poetics and Politics of Ethnography.* Berkeley: University of California Press, 1986.

Closson, Marianne. *L'Imaginaire démoniaque en France: Génèse de la littérature fantastique.* Geneva: Droz, 2000.

Cohen, Claudine. "Taxinomie et ségrégation sociale: 'L'anthropologie' de Moreau de Saint-Méry." In *La Période révolutionnaire aux Antilles: Images et résonnances,* edited by Roger Toumson and Charles Porset. Fort-de-France, Martinique: Actes du Colloque Internationale Pluridisciplinaire, 1986.

Cohen David. *The French Encounter with Africans: White Response to Blacks, 1530–1880.* Bloomington: Indiana University Press, 1980.

Cohen, David, and Jack P. Greene, eds. *Neither Slave nor Free: The Freedmen of African Descent in the Slave Societies of the New World.* Baltimore: Johns Hopkins University Press, 1972.

Cohen, William B. *The French Encounter with Africans: White Response to Blacks, 1530–1880.* Bloomington: Indiana University Press, 1980.

Condé, Maryse. *La Civilisation du bossale: Réflexions sur la littérature orale de la Guadeloupe et de la Martinique.* Paris: l'Harmattan, 1978.

Condé, Maryse, and Madeleine Cottenet-Hage, eds. *Penser la créolité.* Paris: Éditions Karthala, 1995.

Cooper, Frederick, and Ann Laura Stoler. "Between Metropole and Colony: Rethinking a Research Agenda." In Cooper and Stoler, *Tensions of Empire.*

Cooper, Frederick, and Ann Laura Stoler, eds. *Tensions of Empire: Colonial Cultures in a Bourgeois World.* Berkeley: University of California Press, 1997.

Crapanzano, Vincent. "Hermes' Dilemma: The Masking of Subversion in Ethnographic Description." In Clifford and Marcus, *Writing Culture.*

Craton, Michael. "From Caribs to Black Caribs: The Amerindian Roots of Servile Resistance in the Caribbean." In *In Resistance: Studies in African, Caribbean, and Afro-American History,* edited by Gary Okiriro. Amherst: University of Massachusetts Press, 1986.

Crébillon, Claude-Prosper-Jolyot (Crébillon fils). *Les Égarements du coeur et de l'esprit.* Edited by Jean Dagen. 1736. Reprint, Paris: Flammarion, 1985.

Crouse, Nellis M. *French Pioneers in the West Indies, 1624–1664.* New York: Columbia University Press, 1940.

———. *The French Struggle for the West Indies, 1665–1713.* New York: Columbia University Press, 1943.

Cusset, Catherine. "Editor's Preface." *Yale French Studies* 94 (1998): 1–16. Special issue: "Libertinage and Modernity."

———. *No Tomorrow: The Ethics of Pleasure in the French Enlightenment.* Charlottesville: University Press of Virginia, 1999.

Cyrano de Bergerac, Savinien de. *Les Etats et empires de la lune et du soleil.* Edited by Jean-Paul Collet and Madeleine Alcover. Paris: Librairie Larousse, 1968.

Daly, Brenda. "Whose Daughter Is Johnnie? Revisionary Myth-Making in Carolivia Herron's *Thereafter Johnnie.*" *Callaloo* 18, no. 2 (1995): 475–91.

Dampier, William. *A New Voyage Round the World.* London: James Knapton, 1697.

Dampierre, Jacques de. *Essai sur les sources de l'histoire des Antilles françaises, 1492–1664.* Paris: A. Picard et fils, 1904.

Dash, J. Michael. "Psychology, Creolization, and Hybridization." In *New National and Post-colonial Literatures,* edited by Bruce King. Oxford: Clarendon, 1996.

———. "Textual Error and Cultural Crossing: A Caribbean Poetics of Creolization." *Research in African Literatures* 25, no. 2 (1994): 159–68.

David, B. "Les Origines de la Population Martiniquaise." *Mémoires de la société d'histoire de la Martinique* 3 (1973).

Davies, Carole Boyce. *Black Women, Writing, and Identity: Migrations of the Subject.* London: Routledge, 1994.

———. "From Postcoloniality to Uprising Textualities: Black Women Writing the Critique of Empire." In Davies, *Black Women, Writing, and Identity.*

Davis, Angela Yvonne. *Women, Race, and Class.* New York: Vintage, 1981.

Davis, Richard Beale, "The Devil in Virginia in the Seventeenth Century." In *Witchcraft, Magic and Demonology.* Vol. 8 of *Witchcraft in Colonial America,* edited by Brian P. Levack. New York: Garland, 1992.

Davis, Wade. *Passage of Darkness: The Ethnobiology of the Haitian Zombi.* Chapel Hill: University of North Carolina Press, 1988.

Dayan, Joan. "Codes of Law and Bodies of Color." In Condé and Cottenet-Hage, *Penser la créolité.*

———. *Haiti, History, and the Gods.* Berkeley: University of California Press, 1995.

Debbasch, Yvan. *Couleur et liberté: Le jeu de critère ethnique dans un ordre juridique esclavagiste.* Vol. 1. Annales de la Faculté de droit et des sciences politiques et économiques de Strasbourg, no. 16. Paris: Dalloz, 1967.

Debien, Gabriel. *Les Esclaves aux Antilles françaises aux XVIIe–XVIIIe siècles.* Basse-Terre, Guadeloupe: Société d'histoire de la Guadeloupe et de la Martinique, 1974.

———. *Le Peuplement des Antilles françaises au XVIIIe siècle: Les engagés partis de la Rochelle, 1683–1715.* Cairo: Presses de l'Institut français d'archéologie orientale du Caire, 1942.

———. "Les Premières femmes des colons des Antilles (1635–1680)." *Revue de "La Porte Océane"* 90 (1952): 7–11.

Debien, Gabriel, and J. Le Ber. "La Propagande et le recrutement pour les colonies d'Amérique au XVIIe siècle." *Conjonction: Bulletin de l'Institut Française d'Haïti* 12 (1953): 60–90.

Dejean, Joan. *Libertine Strategies: Freedom and the Novel in Seventeenth-Century France.* Columbus: Ohio State University Press, 1981.

Delon, Michel. *Le Savoir-vivre libertin.* Paris: Hachette Littératures, 2000.

Dewald, Jonathan. *The European Nobility, 1400–1800.* Cambridge: Cambridge University Press, 1996.

Dewisme, C. H. *Les Zombis ou le secret des morts-vivants*. Paris: Grasset, 1957.

Dickason, Olive Patricia. *The Myth of the Savage and the Beginnings of French Colonialism in the Americas*. Edmonton: University of Alberta Press, 1984.

Dictionaire de L'Académie française. Paris: J. P. Coignard, 1694.

Dictionaire de L'Académie française, 4th ed. Paris: Chez la veuve de Bernard Brunet, 1762.

Dictionaire de L'Académie française, 5th ed. Paris: J. J. Smits, 1798.

Diderot, Denis. *Supplément au voyage de Bougainville*. Paris: Garnier-Flammarion, 1972.

Didier, Béatrice. "Le Métissage de l'Encyclopédie à la Révolution." In *Métissages*, vol. 1: *Littérature-Histoire*, edited by Jean-Claude Carpanin Marimoutou and Jean-Michel Racault. Paris: L'Harmattan, 1992.

Dixon, Suzanne. *The Roman Family*. Baltimore: Johns Hopkins University Press, 1992.

Dobie, Madeleine. *Foreign Bodies: Gender, Language and Culture in French Orientalism*. Stanford: Stanford University Press, 2001.

Doiron, Normand. *L'Art de voyager: Le déplacement à l'âge classique*. Sainte-Foy, Q.C.: Presses de l'Université Laval, 1995.

Duchet, Michèle. *Anthropologie et histoire: Diderot et l'Histoire des deux Indes ou l'écriture fragmentaire* (Paris: Nizet, 1978).

———. *Anthropologie et histoire au siècle des Lumières*. 1971. Reprint, Paris: Albin Michel, 1995.

———. "Esclavage et préjugé de couleur." In *Racisme et société*, edited by Patrice de Comarmond and Claude Duchet. Paris: Maspéro, 1969.

———. "Du noir au blanc, ou la cinquième génération." In *Le couple interdit: Entretiens sur le racisme*, edited by Léon Poliakov. Paris: Mouton, 1977.

Ducoeurjoly, S.-J. *Manuel des habitans de Saint-Domingue, Contenant un précis de l'histoire de cette île depuis sa découverte*. Paris: Lenoir, 1802.

Dufrenot, Max-Auguste. *Des Antilles à l'Afrique*. Abidjan: Nouvelles éditions africaines, 1980.

Dumas, François Ribadeau. *Histoire de la magie*. Paris: Les productions de Paris, 1961.

Duviols, Jean-Paul. *L'Amérique espagnole vue et rêvée: Les livres de voyage de Colomb à Bougainville*. Paris: Promodis, 1985.

Ebroin, Ary. *Quimbois, magie noire et sorcellerie aux Antilles*. Paris: Jacques Grancher, 1977.

Eccles, W. J. *France in America*. East Lansing: Michigan State University Press, 1990.

Edwards, Philip. *The Story of the Voyage: Sea Narratives in Eighteenth-Century England*. Cambridge: Cambridge University Press, 1994.

Elias, Norbert. *The History of Manners*. Vol. 1: *The Civilizing Process*. New York: Pantheon, 1982.

Elicona, Anthony Louis. *Un colonial sous la Révolution en France et en Amérique: Moreau de Saint-Méry*. Paris: Jouve, 1934.

Elisabeth, Léo. "The French Antilles." In Cohen and Greene, *Neither Slave nor Free*.

Ellington, Ter. *The Myth of the Noble Savage*. Berkeley: University of California Press, 2001.

Elliott, John. *The Old World and the New*. London: Cambridge University Press, 1970.

Encyclopédie, ou dictionnaire raisonné des sciences, des arts et des métiers. Paris: Briasson, 1751–72.

Encylopédie, ou dictionnaire raisonné des sciences, des arts et des métiers. Neufchâtel: Samuel Faulche, 1765.

Entiope, Gabriel. *Nègres, danse et résistance: la Caraïbe du XVIIe au XIXe siècle*. Paris: L'Harmattan, 1996.

Eymerich, Nicolau, and Francisco Peña. *Le Manuel des inquisiteurs*. Translated and edited by Louis Sala-Molins. 1376. Reprint, Paris: Mouton, 1973.

Eze, Emmanuel Chukwudi, ed. *Race and the Enlightenment: A Reader*. Cambridge, Mass.: Blackwell, 1997.

Fabian, Johannes. *Time and the Other: How Anthropology Makes Its Object*. New York: Columbia University Press, 1983.

Fairchild, Hoxie Neale. *The Noble Savage: A Study in Romantic Naturalism*. New York: Columbia University Press, 1983.

Fanon, Frantz. "Le Noir et le langage," In *Peau noire, masques blancs*. Paris: Éditions du Seuil, 1952.

Felsenstein, Frank. *English Trader, Indian Maid: Representing Gender, Race, and Slavery in the New World*. Baltimore: Johns Hopkins University Press, 1999.

Fick, Carolyn E. *The Making of Haiti: The Saint Domingue Revolution from Below*. Knoxville: University of Tennessee Press, 1990.

Fischer, Sibylle. Introduction to Cirillio Villaverde, *Cecila Valdés*. Translated by Helen Lowe, with an introduction by Sybille Fischer. New York: Oxford University Press, 2004.

Flandrin, Jean-Louis. *Familles: Parenté, maison, sexualité dans l'ancienne société*. Paris: Hachette, 1976.

Floyd, Troy S. *The Columbus Dynasty in the Caribbean, 1492–1526*. Albuquerque: University of New Mexico Press, 1973.

Foster, Francis Smith. *Witnessing Slavery*. Westport, Conn.: Greenwood Press, 1979.

Foucault, Michel. *Histoire de la folie à l'âge classique*. Paris: Librairie Plon, 1961.

———. *History of Sexuality*. Vol. 1. Translated by Robert Hurley. New York: Pantheon, 1987.

Fouchard, Jean. *Les Marrons de la liberté*. Paris: Éditions de l'Ecole, 1972.

———. *Plaisirs de Saint-Domingue: Notes sur la vie sociale, littéraire et artistique*. Port-au-Prince, Haiti: Imprimerie de l'État, 1955.

———. *Le Théâtre à Saint-Domingue*. Port-au-Prince: Imprimerie de l'État, 1955.

Fournier, Paul. *Voyages et découvertes scientifiques des missionnaires naturalistes français à travers le monde pendant cinq siècles, XVe à XXe siècles*. Paris: Lechevalier, 1932.

Freud, Sigmund. "Family Romances (1909) [1908]." In *The Standard Edition of the Complete Works of Sigmund Freud*. Vol. 9. Translated by James Strachey. London: Hogarth, 1959.

———. *Totem and Taboo*. In *The Standard Edition of the Complete Psychological Works of Sigmund Freud*. Translated by James Strachey. New York: Norton, 1950.

Freyre, Gilberto. *The Masters and the Slaves: A Study in the Development of Brazilian*

Civilization. 2d English-language ed. Translated by Samuel Putnam. New York: Knopf, 1971.

———. "Preface to the First Brazillian Edition." In Freyre, *The Masters and the Slaves.*

Frostin, Charles. *Les Révoltes blanches à Saint-Domingue aux XVIIe et XVIIIe siècles (Haïti avant 1789).* Paris: Éditions de l'École, 1975.

Gallagher, Catherine, and Stephen Greenblatt. *Practicing New Historicism.* Chicago: University of Chicago Press, 2000.

Garrigus, John David. "Colour, Class and Identity on the Eve of the Haitian Revolution: Saint-Domingue's Free Coloured Elite as *colons américains.*" In Landers, *Against the Odds.*

———. "Sons of the Same Father: Gender, Race, and Citizenship in French Saint-Domingue." In *Visions and Revisions of the Eighteenth Century*, edited by Christine Adams, Jack R. Censer, and Lisa Jane Graham. University Park: Pennsylvania State University Press, 1997.

Gaspar, David Barry, and Darlene Clark Hine, eds. *More Than Chattel: Black Women and Slavery in the Americas.* Bloomington: Indiana University Press, 1996.

Gautier, Arlette. *Les Soeurs de Solitude: La condition féminine dans l'esclave [sic] aux Antilles du XVIIe au XIXe siècle.* Paris: Editions caribéennes, 1985.

Geggus, David. "The Demographic Composition of the French Caribbean Slave Trade." In *Proceedings of the 13th/14th Meetings of the French Colonial Historical Society*, edited by Philip Boucher. Lanham, Md.: University Press of America, 1990.

———. "Haitian Voodoo in the Eighteenth Century." *Jahrbuch für Geschichte von staat, wirtschaft und gesellschaft Lateinamerikas* 28 (1991): 21–51.

———. "Slave and Free Colored Women in Saint-Domingue." In Gaspar and Hine, *More Than Chattel.*

Gerbi, Antonello. *The Dispute of the New World: The History of a Polemic, 1750–1900.* Revised and enlarged ed. Translated by Jeremy Moyle. Pittsburgh: University of Pittsburgh Press, 1973.

Ghachem, Malick. "Montesquieu in the Caribbean: The Colonial Enlightenment between the Code Noir and the Code Civil." *Historical Reflections/Réflexions historiques* 25 (1999): 183–210.

Giraud, Michel. "La Créolité: Une rupture en trompe-l'oeil." *Cahiers d'Études Africaines* 148, no. 37-4 (1997): 795–811.

Girod, François. *La Vie quotidienne de la société créole: Saint-Domingue au XVIIIe siècle.* Paris: Hachette, 1972.

Gisler, Antoine. *L'Esclavage aux Antilles françaises (XVIIe–XIXe siècles): Contribution au problème de l'esclavage.* Paris: Karthala, 1981.

Glazier, Stephen D. "A Note on Shamanism in the Lesser Antilles." In *Proceedings of the Eighth International Congress for the Study of Pre-Columbian Cultures of the Lesser Antilles.* Tempe: Arizona State University, Department of Anthropology, 1980.

Glissant, Édouard. *Caribbean Discourse: Selected Essays.* Translated, with an introduction, by J. Michael Dash. Charlottesville: University Press of Virginia, 1989.

———. *Le Discours antillais.* 1981. Reprint, Paris: Gallimard, 1997.

———. "Métissage et créolisation." In Kandé, *Discours sur le métissage.*

————. *Poétique de la relation.* Paris: Gallimard, 1990.

Godbeer, Richard. "Chaste and Unchaste Covenants: Witchcraft and Sex in Early Modern Culture." In *Wonders of the Invisible World, 1600–1900*, edited by Peter Benes and Jane Montague Benes. Boston: Boston University Press, 1992.

Goubert, Pierre. *L'Ancien régime.* Vol. 1: *La société.* Paris: Armand Colin, 1969.

Goulemot, Jean M., ed. *Dialogisme culturel au XVIIIe siècle.* Cahiers d'Histoire culturelle, Vol. 4. Tours: Université de Tours, 1997.

Gosse, Philip. *The History of Piracy.* New York: Longmans, Green, 1932.

Goveia, Elsa. *The West Indian Slave Laws of the 18th Century.* Barbados: Caribbean Universities Press, 1970.

Graille, Patrick. "Portrait scientifique et littéraire de l'hybride au siècle des lumières." *Eighteenth Century Life* 21, no. 2 (1997): 73–74.

Gramsci, Antonio. *Selections from the Prison Notebooks.* Translated and edited by Quintin Hoare and Geoffrey Nowell Smith. New York: International Publishers, 1971.

Greenblatt, Stephen. "Kidnapping Language." In *Marvelous Possessions.* Chicago: University of Chicago Press, 1991.

————. *Marvelous Possessions: The Wonder of the New World.* Chicago: University of Chicago Press, 1991.

Greenblatt, Stephen, ed. *New World Encounters.* Berkeley: University of California Press, 1993.

Grégoire, Abbé Henri. *De la litterature des nègres.* 1808. Reprint, with an introduction and notes by Jean Lessay. Paris: Perrin, 1991.

Guégan, Bertrand. "Notes sur la vie et les éditions d'Oexmelin." In Oexmelin, *Les Aventuriers et les boucaniers d'Amérique. Guide des Sources de l'Histoire de l'Amérique Latine et des Antilles dans les Archives Françaises.* Paris: Archives Nationales, 1984.

Gullick, C. J. M. R. "Island Carib Traditions about Their Arrival in the Lesser Antilles." In *Proceedings of the Eighth International Congress for the Study of the Pre-Columbian Cultures of the Lesser Antilles.* Tempe: Arizona State University, Department of Anthropology, 1980.

————. *Myths of a Minority: The Changing Traditions of the Vincentian Caribs.* Studies of Developing Countries, no. 30. Assen, Netherlands: Van Gorcum, 1985.

Hall, Gwendolyn Midlo. "Saint-Domingue." In Cohen and Greene, *Neither Slave nor Free.*

————. *Social Control in Slave Plantation Societies: A Comparison of St. Domingue and Cuba.* Baltimore: Johns Hopkins University Press, 1971.

Hanley, Sarah. "Engendering the State: Family Formation and State Building in Early Modern France." *French Historical Studies* 16, no. 1 (1989): 4–27.

Harouel, Jean-Louis. "Le Code noir." In *Abolition de l'esclavage: Mythes et réalités créoles.* Paris: Centre culturel du Panthéon, 1998.

Harth, Erica. *Ideology and Culture in Seventeenth-Century France.* Ithaca: Cornell University Press, 1983.

Hartman, Saidiya. *Scenes of Subjection: Terror, Slavery and Self-Making in Nineteenth-Century America.* New York: Oxford University Press, 1997.

Hathaway, Heather. "Maybe Freedom Lies in Hating: Miscegenation and the Oedipal

Conflict." In *Refiguring the Father: New Feminist Readings of Patriarchy*, edited by Patricia Yaeger and Beth Kowaleski-Wallace. Carbondale: Southern Illinois University Press, 1989.

Hazard, Paul. *The European Mind: The Critical Years, 1680–1715.* New York: Fordham University Press, 1990.

Hearn, Lafcadio. *Two Years in the French West Indies.* New York: Harter and Bros., 1890.

Heath, Shirley Brice, and Richard Laprade. "Castilian Colonization and Indigenous Languages: The Cases of Quechua and Aymara." In *Language Spread: Studies in Diffusion and Social Change*, edited by Robert L. Cooper. Bloomington: Indiana University Press, 1982.

Hénaff, Marcel. *Sade: The Invention of the Libertine Body.* Translated by Xavier Callahan. Minneapolis: University of Minnesota Press, 1999.

Henningsen, Henning. *Crossing the Equator: Sailors' Baptism and Other Initiation Rites.* Copenhagen: Munksgaard, 1961.

Herman, Judith, and Lisa Hirschman. *Father-Daughter Incest.* Cambridge: Harvard University Press, 1981.

Herrera y Tordesillas, Antonio de. *Description des Indes occidentales qu'on appelle aujourdhuy le Nouveau Monde.* Amsterdam: M. Colin, 1622.

Herron, Carolivia. *Thereafter Johnnie.* New York: Random House, 1991.

Herskovitz, Melville. *The Myth of the Negro Past.* Boston: Beacon Press, 1990.

Hine, Darlene, and Kate Wittenstein. "Female Slave Resistance: The Economics of Sex." In *The Black Woman Cross-Culturally*, edited by Filomina Chioma Steady. Cambridge: Schenkman, 1981.

Hodes, Martha. *White Women, Black Men: Illicit Sex in the Nineteenth-Century South.* New Haven: Yale University Press, 1999.

Hodes, Martha, ed. *Sex, Love, Race: Crossing Boundaries in North American History.* New York: New York University Press, 1970.

Hodgen, Margaret T. *Early Anthropology in the Sixteenth and Seventeenth Centuries.* Philadelphia: University of Pennsylvania Press, 1964.

Hoff, Berend. "Language, War, and the Amerindian Historical Tradition: The Special Case of the Island Carib." In Whitehead, *Wolves from the Sea.*

Hoffmann, Léon-François. *Le Nègre romantique: Personnage littéraire et obsession collective.* Paris: Payot, 1973.

———. "Vodou sous la colonie et pendant les guerres d'indépendance." *Conjonction: Le Bulletin de l'Institute Français d'Haïti* 173 (1987): 109–35.

hooks, bell. *Ain't I a Woman: Black Women and Feminism.* Boston: South End, 1981.

Houdard, Sophie. *Les Sciences du Diable: Quatre discours sur la sorcellerie.* Paris: Editions du Cerf, 1992.

Hudson, Nicholas. "From 'Nation' to 'Race': The Origin of Racial Classification in Eighteenth-Century Thought." *Eighteenth Century Studies* 29, no. 3 (1996): 242–64.

Hulme, Peter. "Caribs and Arawaks." In Hulme, *Colonial Encounters.*

———. *Colonial Encounters: Europe and the Native Caribbean, 1492–1797.* London: Methuen, 1986.

Hulme, Peter, and L. J. Jordanova. *The Enlightenment and Its Shadows*. London: Routledge, 1990.

Hulme, Peter, and Neil L. Whitehead, eds. *Wild Majesty: Encounters with Caribs from Columbus to the Present Day—An Anthology*. Oxford: Oxford University Press, 1992.

Hunt, Lynn Avery. *The Family Romance of the French Revolution*. Berkeley: University of California Press, 1992.

Huppert, George. *Les Bourgeois Gentilshommes*. Chicago: University of Chicago Press, 1977.

Hurbon, Laënnec. *Le Barbare imaginaire*. Paris: Éditions du Cerf, 1988.

Hyam, Ronald. *Empire and Sexuality: The British Experience*. Manchester: Manchester University Press, 1991.

Idylles et chansons ou essays de poésie créole, par un habitant d'Hayti. Philadelphia: J. Edwards, 1818.

Jacques-Chaquin, Nicole, ed. *Les Sorciers du carroi de Marlou: Un procès de sorcellerie en Berry (1582–1583)*. Grenoble: J. Millon, 1996.

Jaenen, Cornelius J. *Friend and Foe: Aspects of French-Amerindian Cultural Contact in the Sixteenth and Seventeenth Centuries*. New York: Columbia University Press, 1976.

James, C. L. R. *The Black Jacobins: Toussaint L'Ouverture and the San Domingo Revolution*. 2d rev. ed. New York: Vintage, 1989.

Janzen, John M., and Wyatt MacGaffey, eds. *An Anthology of Kongo Religion: Primary Texts from Lower Zaïre*. University of Kansas Publications in Anthropology 5. Lawrence: University of Kansas, 1974.

Jennings, Lawrence C. *French Antislavery: The Movement for the Abolition of Slavery in France, 1802–1848*. Cambridge: Cambridge University Press, 2000.

Jenson, Deborah. "Mimetic Mastery and Colonial Mimicry in the First Franco-Antillean Creole Anthology." *The Yale Journal of Criticism* 17.1 (2004): 83–106.

Johnson, David E., and Scott Michaelsen. "Border Secrets: An Introduction." In Johnson and Michaelsen, *Border Theory*.

Johnson, David E., and Scott Michaelsen, eds. *Border Theory: The Limits of Cultural Politics*. Minneapolis: University of Minnesota Press, 1997.

Johnson, Jerah. "Colonial New Orleans: A Fragment of the Eighteenth-Century French Ethos." In *Creole New Orleans: Race and Americanization*, edited by Arnold R. Hirsch and Joseph Logsdon. Baton Rouge: Louisiana State University Press, 1992.

Jones, Gayle. *Corregidora*. Boston: Beacon Press, 1975.

Jordan, Winthrop D. *White over Black: American Attitudes toward the Negro, 1550–1812*. Chapel Hill: University of North Carolina Press, 1968.

Kandé, Sylvie, ed. *Discours sur le métissage, identités métisses: En quête d'Ariel*. Paris: L'Harmattan, 1999.

Keizer, Arlene. "The Geography of the Apocalypse: Incest, Mythology, and the Fall of Washington City in Carolivia Herron's *Thereafter Johnnie*." In *Black Subjects: Identity Formation in the Contemporary Narrative of Slavery*. Ithaca: Cornell University Press, 2004.

Kerboull, Jean. *Le Vaudou: Magie ou religion*. Paris: Laffont, 1973.

King, Richard. *A Southern Renaissance: The Cultural Awakening of the American South, 1930–1955.* New York: Oxford University Press, 1980.

King, Stewart. *Blue Coat or Powdered Wig: Free People of Color in Pre-revolutionary Saint-Domingue.* Athens: University of Georgia Press, 2001.

Klor de Alva, J. Jorge. "Language, Politics, and Translation: Colonial Discourse and Classic Nahuatl in New Spain." In *The Art of Translation: Voices from the Field,* edited by Rosanna Warren. Boston: Northeastern University Press, 1989.

Kopytoff, Barbara K. "Racial Purity and Interracial Sex in the Law of Colonial and Antebellum Virginia." In *Interracialism: Black-White Intermarriage in American History, Literature, and Law,* edited by Werner Sollors. New York: Oxford University Press, 2000.

Kristeva, Julia. *Powers of Horror: An Essay on Abjection.* Translated by Leon S. Roudiez. New York: Columbia University Press, 1982.

Kupperman, Karen Ordahl. *America in European Consciousness, 1493–1750.* Chapel Hill: University of North Carolina Press, 1995.

Kutzinski, Vera M. *Sugar's Secrets: Race and the Erotics of Cuban Nationalism.* New World Studies. Charlottesville: University Press of Virginia, 1993.

La Roncière, Charles de. *Histoire de la marine française.* Vol. 4. Paris: Plon, 1910.

Labat, Jean Baptiste. *The Memoirs of Père Labat, 1693–1705.* Translated by John Eaden. [London]: F. Cass, 1970.

———. *Nouvelle relation de l'Afrique occidentale contenant une description exacte du Senegal et des pais situés entre le Cap-Blanc et la rivière de Serrelionne . . . : L'Histoire naturelle de ces pais, les différentes nations qui y sont répandues, leurs religions et leurs moeurs avec l'état ancien et présent des compagnies qui y font le commerce.* Paris: Chez G. Cavelier, 1728.

Lacassin, Francis. "Exmelin ou Le docteur Watson au service du crime." In *Histoire des Frères de la Cote, Flibustiers et boucaniers des Antilles,* by A. O. Exmelin. Paris: Éditions maritimes et d'Outre-Mer, 1980.

Lachèvre, Frédéric. *Le Casanova du XVIIe siècle: Pierre-Corneille Blessebois.* Paris: Librairie ancienne Honoré Champion, 1927.

Laclos, Choderlos de. *Les Liaisons dangereuses.* Edited by Joël Papadopoulos. 1782. Reprint, Paris: Gallimard, 1972.

Laguerre, Michel S. *Voodoo and Politics in Haiti.* New York: St. Martin's, 1989.

Laman, K. E. *Dictionnaire kikongo-francais.* 1936. Reprint, Ridgewood, N.J.: Gregg Press, 1964.

Lancre, Pierre de. *Tableau de l'inconstance des mauvaises anges, ou il est amplement traité des sorciers et de la sorcellerie.* 1610. Reprint, with notes and introduction, by Nicole Jacques-Chaquin. Paris: Aubier, 1992.

Landers, Jane G., ed. *Against the Odds: Free Blacks in the Slave Societies of the Americas.* London: Frank Cass, 1996.

Lane, Kris E. *Pillaging the Empire.* Armonk, N.Y.: M. E. Sharpe, 1998.

Laplanche, J. and J.-B. Pontalis. *The Language of Psycho-analysis.* Translated by Donald Nicholson-Smith. *The International Psycho-Analytical Library* 94. London: Hogarth Press, 1973.

Laroche, Maximilien. "The Myth of the Zombi." In *Exile and Tradition: Studies in African and Caribbean Literature*, edited by Rowland Smith. London: Dalhousie University Press, 1976.

Las Casas, Bartolomé de. *Tyrannies et cruautez des Espagnols, perpétrées ès Indes occidentales, qu'on appelle le Nouveau Monde*. Anvers: François de Ravelenghien, 1579.

Layng, Anthony. *The Carib Reserve: Identity and Security in the West Indies*. Washington, D.C.: University Press of America, 1983.

Le Bris, Michel. "Chirurgien de la Flibuste." In *Les Flibustiers du Nouveau Monde: Histoire des flibustiers et boucaniers qui se sont illustrés dans les Indes*, by A. O. Oexmelin, edited by Michel Le Bris. Paris: Phébus, 1996.

Le Bris, Michel, and Virginie Serna, eds. *Pirates et flibustiers des Caraïbes*. Paris: Éditions Hoëbeke, 2001.

Leary, Lewis. Introduction to *Miss McCrea: A Novel of the American Revolution*, by Michel René Hilliard d'Auberteuil. Facsimile reproduction, with a translation from the French, by Eric Laguardia. Gainesville, Fla.: Scholars Facsimiles and Reprints, 1958.

Lerner, Gerda. *The Creation of Patriarchy*. New York: Oxford University Press, 1986.

Léry, Jean de. *Histoire d'un voyage faict en la terre du Bresil . . . 1580*. Reprint, with preface and notes, by Frank Lestringant. Paris: Librairie Générale Française, 1994.

Lescarbot, Marc. *Histoire de la Nouvelle-France, contenant les navigations, découvertes et habitations faites par les Français ès Indes Occidentales et Nouvelle-France . . .* Paris: J. Milot, 1609.

Lestringant, Frank. *Le Cannibale: Grandeur et décadence*. Histoire et décadence. Paris: Perrin, 1994.

Lévi-Strauss, Claude. "Structural Analysis in Linguistics and Anthropology." In *Structural Anthropology*. Translated by Claire Jacobson and Brooke Grundfest Schoepf. New York: Basic Books, 1963.

———. *Les Structures élémentaires de la parenté*. Paris: Presses Universitaires de France, 1949.

Levinas, Emmanuel. *Totality and Infinity: An Essay on Exteriority*. Translated by Alphonso Lingis. Pittsburgh: Duquesne University Press, 1969.

Lewis, Gordon K. *Main Currents in Caribbean Thought: The Historical Evolution of Caribbean Society in Its Ideological Aspects, 1492–1900*. Baltimore: Johns Hopkins University Press, 1983.

Ligon, Richard. *Histoire de l'isle des Barbades*. In *Receuil de divers voyages faits en Afrique et an Amérique*, edited by Henri Justel. Paris: Louis Billaire, 1674.

Linebaugh, Peter, and Marcus Rediker. *The Many-Headed Hydra: Sailors, Slaves, Commoners, and the Hidden History of the Revolutionary Atlantic*. Boston: Beacon, 2000.

Lionnet, Françoise. *Autobiographical Voices: Race, Gender, Self-Portraiture*. Ithaca: Cornell University Press, 1989.

Lokke, Carl Ludwig. *France and the Colonial Question: A Study of Contemporary French Opinion, 1763–1801*. New York: Columbia University Press, 1932.

Loomba, Ania. *Colonialism/Postcolonialism*. London: Routledge, 1998.

Lopez de Gómara, Francisco. *Histoire generalle des Indes occidentales et terres neuves, qui jusques à présent ont esté descouvertes*. Paris: Michel Sonnius, 1569.

Louÿs, Pierre, and Frédéric Lachèvre. *Pierre Louÿs et l'histoire littéraire*. La Roche-sur-Yon: Imprimerie centrale de l'ouest, 1928.

Lowe, Lisa. *Critical Terrains: British and French Orientalisms*. Ithaca: Cornell University Press, 1991.

Lüsebrink, Hans-Jürgen, and Manfred Tietz, eds. *Lectures de Raynal: L'Histoire des deux Indes en Europe et en Amérique au XVIIIe siècle*. Oxford: Voltaire Foundation, 1991.

MacCormack, Sabine. "Demons, Imagination, and the Incas." In *New World Encounters*, edited by Stephen Greenblatt. Berkeley: University of California Press, 1993.

MacGaffey, Wyatt. *Religion and Society in Central Africa*. Chicago: University of Chicago Press, 1986.

Mackrell, J. Q. C. *The Attack on "Feudalism" in Eighteenth-Century France*. London: Routledge, 1973.

Madiou, Thomas. *Histoire d'Haïti*. 3 vols. Port-au-Prince, Haiti: Éditions Henri Deschamps, 1989.

Mainil, Jean. *Dans les Règles du plaisir . . . : Théorie de la différence dans le discours obscène romanesque et médical de l'Ancien Régime*. Paris: Éditions Kimé, 1996.

Mandrou, Robert. *Magistrats et sorciers en France au XVIIe siècle: Une analyse de psychologie historique*. Paris: Plon, 1968.

Marcus, George, and Dick Cushman. "Ethnographies as Texts." *Annual Review of Anthropology* 11 (1982): 25–69.

Marx, Jenifer. *Pirates and Privateers of the Caribbean*. Malabar, Fla.: Krieger, 1992.

Mason, J. A. "The Languages of South America." In *Handbook of South American Indians*, vol. 4, edited by Julian H. Steward. Washington, D.C.: Smithsonian Institution, Bureau of American Ethnology, 1949.

Mason, Peter. "Classical Ethnography and Its Influence on the European Perception of the Peoples of the New World." In *The Classical Tradition and the Americas*. Vol. 1: *European Images of the Americas and the Classical Tradition*, edited by Wolfgang Haase and Meyer Reinhold. Berlin: Walter de Gruyter, 1993.

———. *Deconstructing America: Representations of the Other*. London: Routledge, 1990.

Masson, Jeffrey Moussaieff. *The Assault on Truth: Freud's Suppression of the Seduction Theory*. New York: Ferrar, Strauss and Giroux, 1984.

Maurel, Blanche. "La *Description*, ses sources, sa portée, son interpretation." In Moreau de Saint-Méry, *Description de la partie française de l'isle Saint-Domingue*, Vol. 1.

Mauss, Marcel. *The Gift: The Form and Reason for Exchange in Archaic Societies*. Translated by W. D. Halls. London: Routledge, 1990.

May, George. *Le Dilemme du roman*. New Haven: Yale University Press, 1963.

Maximilien, Louis. *Le Vodou haïtien*. 2d ed. Port-au-Prince, Haiti: Imprimerie de l'état, 1945.

Maza, Sarah, *The Myth of the French Bourgeoisie: An Essay on the Social Imaginary, 1750–1850*. Cambridge, Mass.: Harvard University Press, 2003.

———. "Stephen Greenblatt, New Historicism, and Cultural History, or, What We

Talk about When We Talk about Interdisciplinarity," *Modern Intellectual History*, 1.2 (August 2004): 249–65.

McClellan, James E. *Colonialism and Science: Saint-Domingue in the Old Regime*. Baltimore: Johns Hopkins University Press, 1992.

McClintock, Anne. *Imperial Leather: Race, Gender, and Sexuality in the Colonial Contest*. New York: Routledge, 1995.

———. "Postcolonialism and the Angel of Progress." In McClintock, *Imperial Leather*.

Mercier, Roger. *L'Afrique noire dans la littérature française: Les premières images, XVIIe–XVIIIe siècles*. Dakar: Université de Dakar Faculté des letters et sciences humaines. Publication de la Section de langues et literature, 1962.

Métraux, Alfred. *Le Vaudou haïtien*. Paris: Gallimard, 1958.

Meyer, Jean, and Jacques Thobie. *Histoire de la France Coloniale*. Vol. 1. Paris: Armand Colin, 1991.

Mignolo, Walter. "Colonial and Postcolonial Discourse: Cultural Critique or Academic Colonialism." *Latin American Research Review* 28, no. 3 (1993): 120–31.

———. *Local Histories/Global Designs: Coloniality, Subaltern Knowledges and Border Thinking*. Princeton: Princeton University Press, 2000.

Miller, Christopher L. *Nationalists and Nomads: Essays on Francophone African Literature and Culture*. Chicago: University of Chicago Press, 1998.

Miller, Nancy K. *French Dressing: Women, Men and Ancien Régime Fiction*. New York: Routledge, 1995.

———. "Libertinage and Feminism." *Yale French Studies* 94 (1998): 17–28.

Mims, Stewart L. *Colbert's West India Policy*. New Haven: Yale University Press, 1912.

———. Introduction to *Moreau de St.-Méry's American Journey*, by Médéric Louis Élie Moreau de Saint-Méry. Translated and edited by Kenneth Roberts and Anna M. Roberts. New York: Doubleday, 1947.

Mintz, Sidney Wilfred. *Sweetness and Power: The Place of Sugar in Modern History*. New York: Viking, 1985.

Mirabeau, Honoré-Gabriel de Riquetti, Comte de. *Le Rideau levé*. In *Oeuvres érotiques de Mirabeau*. L'Enfer de la Bibliothèque nationale 1. 1786. Reprint, Paris: Fayard, 1984.

Mitchell, Juliett. *Psychoanalysis and Feminism*. 1974. Reprint, with a new introduction. New York: Basic Books, 2000.

Moitt, Bernard. *Women and Slavery in the French Antilles, 1635–1848*. Bloomington: Indiana University Press, 2001.

Montaigne, Michel de. *Essais de Michel de Montaigne*. Edited by André Tournon. Paris: Imprimerie Nationale Éditions, 1998.

Montel, Aurelia. *Le Père Labat viendra te prendre*. Paris: Maisonneuve et Larose, 1996.

Montesquieu, Charles de Secondat. *De l'esprit des lois*. 2 vols. Paris: Garnier, 1973.

———. *Lettres persanes*. 1721. Reprint, Paris: Garnier, 1960.

Montrose, Louis. "The Work of Gender in the Discourse of Discovery." In *New World Encounters*, edited by Stephen Greenblatt. Berkeley: University of California Press, 1993.

Moreau de Saint Mery, M. L. E. *A Civilization That Perished: The Last Years of White*

Colonial Rule in Saint-Domingue. 1797. Reprint, translated and edited by Ivor D. Spencer. Lanham, Md.: University Press of America, 1985.

Morrison, Toni. *Beloved.* New York: Penguin, 1987.

Moureau, François. *L'Ile, territoire mythique.* Paris: Aux amateurs du livre, 1989.

Mousnier, Roland. *La Vénalité des offices sous Henri IV et Louis XIII.* Rouen: Manguard, 1945.

Muchembled, Robert. *Popular Culture and Elite Culture in France, 1400–1750.* Translated by Lydia Cochrane. Baton Rouge: Louisiana State University Press, 1985.

———. *La Sorcière au village.* Paris: Éditions Julliard/Gallimard, 1979.

Murray, David. *Forked Tongues: Speech, Writing and Representation in North American Indian Texts.* Bloomington: Indiana University Press, 1991.

Myers, Robert A. "Island Carib Cannibalism." *Nieuwe West-Indische Gids* 58 (1984): 147–84.

Neill, Anna. "Buccaneer Ethnography: Nature, Culture, and Nation in the Journals of William Dampier." *Eighteenth-Century Studies* 22, no. 2 (2000): 165–80.

Nelson, T. "Incest in the Early Novel and Related Genres." *Eighteenth Century Life* 16 (1992): 127–62.

Nicolas, Armand. *Histoire de la Martinique des Arawaks à 1848.* Paris: L'Harmattan, 1996.

Noougaret, P. J. B. *Voyages intéressants dans différentes colonies franaises, espagnoles, anglaises.* London: J. F. Bastier, 1788.

Ogle, Gene E. "'The Eternal Power of Reason' and 'The Superiority of Whites': Hilliard D'Auberteuil's Colonial Enlightenment." *French Colonial History* 3 (2003): 35–50.

Ortiz, Fernando. *Cuban Counterpoint: Tobacco and Sugar.* Translated by Harriet de Onis. New York: Knopf, 1947.

Pagden, Anthony. *The Fall of Natural Man: The American Indian and the Origins of Comparative Ethnology.* Cambridge: Cambridge University Press, 1982.

Parry, Benita. "Problems in Current Theories of Colonial Discourse." *Oxford Literary Review* 9, nos. 1–2 (1987): 27–58.

———. "Resistance Theory/Theorising Resistance or Two Cheers for Nativism." In Barker, Hulme, and Iversen, *Colonial Discourse, Postcolonial Theory.*

———. "Signs of Our Times: Discussion of Homi Bhabha's *The Location of Culture.*" *Third Text* 28–29 (1994): 5–24.

Patterson, Orlando. *Slavery and Social Death: A Comparative Study.* Cambridge: Harvard University Press, 1982.

Pauw, Cornelius de. *Recherches philosophiques sur les Américains.* Edited by Michèle Duchet. 2 vols. Paris: Jean Michel Place, 1990.

Petit, Emmanuel. *Traité sur le gouvernement des esclaves.* 2 vols. Paris: Knapen, 1777.

Petitjean Roget, Jacques. "Les Femmes des colons à la Martinique au XVIIe et XVIIIe siècles." *Revue d'Histoire de l'Amérique française* 19, no. 2 (1955): 176–235.

———. *La Société d'habitation à la Martinique: Un Demi siècle de formation, 1635–1685.* 2 vols. Lille: Atelier Reproduction des thèses, Université de Lille III, 1980.

Petitjean Roget, Jacques, and Élisabeth Crosnier, eds. *Histoire de l'isle de Grenade en*

Amérique, 1649–1659: Manuscrit anonyme de 1659. Montreal: Presses de l'Université de Montréal, 1975.

Peytraud, Lucien. *L'Esclavage aux Antilles françaises avant 1789: D'après des documents inédits des archives coloniales.* Paris: Librairie Hachette, 1897.

Pietz, William. "The Problem of the Fetish, I." *Res* 9 (1985): 1–15.

———. "The Problem of the Fetish, II." *Res* 13 (1987): 23–46.

Pignet, Henri. *Alexandre-Olivier Exquemelin, Chirurgien des aventuriers 1666–1707 (?)* Montpellier: Imprimerie de la Presse, 1939.

Pinhas-Delpeuch, Rosy. "De l'affranchi au libertin, les avatars d'un mot." In *Éros Philosophe: Discours libertins des lumières*, edited by François Moureau and Alain-Marc Rieu. Paris: Honoré Champion, 1984.

Pluchon, Pierre. *Vaudou, sorciers, empoisonneurs de Saint-Domingue à Haiti.* Paris: Karthala, 1987.

Pluchon, Pierre, ed. *Haïti au XVIIIe siècle.* Paris: Karthala, 1993.

———. *Histoire des Antilles et de la Guyane.* Toulouse: Privat, 1982.

Pluchon, Pierre, and Denise Bouche, eds. *Histoire de la colonisation française.* Paris: Fayard, 1991.

Poliakov, Léon. *Le Couple interdit: Entretiens sur le racisme—la dialectique de l'altérité socio-culturelle et la sexualité.* Paris: Mouton, 1980.

Porchnev, Boris. *Les Soulèvements populaires en France au XVIIème siècle.* Paris: SEVPEN, 1963.

Porter, Dennis. "Orientalism and Its Problems." In *The Politics of Theory*, edited by Peter Hulme, Margaret Iversen, and Diane Loxley. Colchester: University of Essex, 1983.

Posner, David. *The Performance of Nobility in Early Modern European Literature.* Cambridge: Cambridge University Press, 1999.

Pratt, Mary Louise. "Fieldwork in Common Places." In Clifford and Marcus, *Writing Culture.*

———. *Imperial Eyes: Travel Writing and Transculturation.* London: Routledge, 1992.

Prévost, Antoine-François. *Histoire générale des voyages, ou, nouvelle collection de toutes les relations de voyages par mer et par terre qui ont été publiées jusqu'à présent dans les différentes langues de toutes les nations connues.* Vol. 15. Paris: Didot, 1759.

Price-Mars, Jean. *Ainsi Parla l'oncle.* Edited by Robert Cornevin. 1928. Reprint, Ottawa: Éditions Leméac, 1973.

———. *Une étape de l'évolution haïtienne.* Port-au-Prince, Haiti: La Presse, 1929.

Prudent, Lambert-Félix. *Des baragouins à la langue antillaise.* Paris: L'Harmattan, 1999.

Rabasa, José. *Inventing America: Spanish Historiography and the Formation of Eurocentrism.* Oklahoma Project for Discourse and Theory, no. 11. Norman: University of Oklahoma Press, 1993.

Racault, Jean-Michel. *L'Utopie narrative en France et en Angleterre 1675–1761.* Oxford: Voltaire Foundation, 1991.

Raimond, M. *Observations sur l'origine et les progrès du préjugé des colons blancs contre les hommes de couleur; Sur les inconvénients de le perpétuer; la nécessité, la facilité de le détruire; sur le projet du Comité colonial, etc.* Paris: Chez Belin, Desenne, Bailly, 1791.

Rank, Otto. *The Incest Theme in Literature and Legend.* Translated by Gregory C. Richter. Baltimore: Johns Hopkins University Press, 1992.

Rankin, Hugh. *The Golden Age of Piracy.* Williamsburg: Colonial Williamsburg Foundation, 1969.

Raynal, Guillaume-Thomas. *L'Anticolonialisme au XVIIIe siècle: Histoire philosophique et politique des établissements et du commerce des Européens dans les deux Indes.* Edited by G. Esquer. Paris: Presses universitaires de France, 1951.

———. *Essai sur l'administration de St.-Domingue.* N.p., 1785.

———. *Histoire philosophique et politique des établissemens et du commerce des européens dans les deux Indes.* 10 vols. Neufchatel: Libraires associés, 1783.

Rediker, Marcus. *Between the Devil and the Deep Blue Sea: Merchant Seamen, Pirates and the Anglo-American Maritime World, 1700–1750.* Cambridge: Cambridge University Press, 1987.

Relousat, Raymond. "La Problématique langagière dans le dictionnaire de Breton." In Breton, *Dictionnaire caraïbe-français,* 1999 ed.

Renault-Lescure, Odile. "Glossaire français d'origine amérindienne." In Breton, *Dictionnaire caraïbe-français,* 1999 ed.

Rennard, Joseph. *Histoire religieuse des Antilles françaises des origines à 1914, d'après des documents inédits.* Paris: Société de l'histoire des colonies françaises, 1954.

Revert, Eugène. *La Magie antillaise.* Paris: Annuaire international des Français d'outre mer, 1977.

Richardot, Anne. "*Thérèse Philosophe*: Les charmes de l'impénétrable." *Eighteenth-Century Life* 21, no. 2 (1997): 89–99.

Roach, Joseph. "Body of Law: The Sun King and the Code Noir." In *From the Royal to the Republican Body,* edited by Sara E. Melzer and Kathryn Norberg. Berkeley: University of California Press, 1998.

———. *Cities of the Dead.* New York: Columbia University Press, 1996.

Robbins, Russell Hope. *The Encyclopedia of Witchcraft and Demonology.* New York: Crown, 1959.

Roberts, Walter Adolphe. *The French in the West Indies.* Indianapolis: Bobbs-Merrill, 1942.

———. *Sir Henry Morgan: Buccaneer and Governor.* New York: Covici, Friede, 1933.

Roche, Daniel. *La culture des apparences: Une histoire du vêtement, XVIIe–XVIIIe siècles.* Paris: Fayard, 1989. Translated by Jean Birrell, *The Culture of Clothing: Dress and Fashion in the "Ancien Régime."* Cambridge: Cambridge University Press, 1994.

Rogozinski, Jan. *A Brief History of the Caribbean: From the Arawak and the Carib to the Present.* New York: Meridian, 1994.

Rose, Jacqueline. *States of Fantasy.* Oxford: Clarendon, 1996.

Rosello, Mireille. *Littérature et identité créole aux Antilles.* Espace caribéen. Paris: Éditions Karthala, 1992.

Rouse, Irving. "The Carib." In *Handbook of South American Indians,* Vol. 4, edited by Julian H. Steward. Washington, D.C.: Smithsonian Institution, Bureau of American Ethnology, 1949.

Rousseau, Jean-Jacques. *Discours sur l'origine et les fondements de l'inégalité parmi les hommes*. Edited by Jacques Roger. 1755. Reprint, Paris: Garnier-Flammarion, 1971.

Russell, Jeffrey Burton. *Lucifer: The Devil in the Middle Ages*. Ithaca: Cornell University Press, 1984.

———. *Mephistopheles: The Devil in the Modern World*. Ithaca: Cornell University Press, 1986.

Sagard, Gabriel. *Le Grand voyage du pays des Hurons . . .* Paris: D. Moreau, 1632.

———. *Histoire du Canada . . .* Paris: C. Sonnius, 1636.

Said, Edward W. *Orientalism*. New York: Pantheon, 1978.

———. "Orientalism Reconsidered." In *Europe and Its Others*, edited by Francis Barker, Peter Hulme, Margaret Iversen, and Diane Loxley. Colchester: University of Essex, 1985.

Saint-Lambert, Jean-François. *Ziméo*. In *Les Saisons, poëme*. Amsterdam, 1773.

Saint-Pierre, Bernardin de. *Paul et Virginie*. Edited by Robert Mauzi. 1796. Reprint, Paris: Garnier-Flammarion, 1992.

Saintoyant, Jules François. *La Colonisation française pendant la révolution*. Paris: La Renaissance du Livre, 1930.

———. *La Colonisation française sous l'Ancien Régime (du XVe siècle à 1789)*. 2 vols. Paris: La Renaissance du Livre, 1929.

Sala-Molins, Louis. *Le* Code noir *ou le calvaire de canaan*. Paris: Presses Universitaires de France, 1987.

———. *Les Misères des Lumières: Sous la raison, l'outrage*. Paris: Éditions R. Laffont, 1992.

Saks, Eva. "Representing Miscegenation Law." In *Interracialism: Black-White Intermarriage in American History, Literature, and Law*, edited by Werner Sollors. New York: Oxford University Press, 2000.

Sanchez, Jean-Pierre. "Myths and Legends in the Old World and European Expansionism on the American Continent." In *The Classical Tradition and the Americas*. Vol. 1: *European Images of the Americas and the Classical Tradition*, edited by Wolfgang Haase and Meyer Reinhold. Berlin: Walter de Gruyter, 1993.

Sandiford, Keith. *The Cultural Politics of Sugar: Caribbean Slavery and Narratives of Colonialism*. Cambridge: Cambridge University Press, 2000.

Sauer, Carl. *The Early Spanish Main*. Berkeley: University of California Press, 1966.

Sayre, Gordon M. *Les Sauvages Américains: Representations of Native Americans in French and English Colonial Literature*. Chapel Hill: University of North Carolina Press, 1997.

Scarry, Elaine. *The Body in Pain: The Making and Unmaking of the World*. New York: Oxford University Press, 1985.

Schalk, Ellery. *From Valor to Pedigree: Ideas of Nobility in France in the Seventeenth and Eighteenth Centuries*. Princeton: Princeton University Press, 1986.

Seabrook, W. H. *The Magic Island*. New York: Literary Guild of America, 1929.

Sedgwick, Eve Kosofsky. *Between Men: English Literature and Male Homosocial Desire*. New York: Columbia University Press, 1985.

Seeber, Edward D. *Anti-slavery Opinion in France during the Second Half of the Eighteenth Century*. Baltimore: Johns Hopkins University Press, 1937.

Séguin, Robert-Lionel. *La Sorcellerie au Québec du XVIIe au XIXe siècle*. Ottawa: Les Éditions Lemeac, 1971.

Serroy, Jean. *Roman et réalité: Les histoires comiques au XVIIe siècle*. Paris: Librairie Minard, 1981.

Sharpley-Whiting, T. Denean. *Black Venus: Sexualized Savages, Primal Fears, and Primitive Narratives in French*. Durham: Duke University Press, 1999.

Smith, Jay. *The Culture of Merit: Nobility, Royal Service, and the Making of Absolute Monarchy in France, 1600–1789*. Ann Arbor: University of Michigan Press, 1996.

Socolow, Susan M. "Economic Roles of the Free Women of Color of Cap Français." In *More than Chattel*, edited by David Barry Gaspar and Darlene Clark Hine. Bloomington: Indiana University Press, 1996.

Sollors, Werner. *Interracialism: Black-White Intermarriage in American History, Literature, and Law*. New York: Oxford University Press, 2000.

———. *Neither Black nor White yet Both: Thematic Explorations of Interracial Literature*. New York: Oxford University Press, 1997.

Sommer, Doris. *Foundational Fictions: The National Romances of Latin America*. Berkeley: University of California Press, 1991.

Sorel, Charles. *Le Berger extravagant*. Paris: Toussaint du Bray, 1627–28.

Sosis, Howard. "The Colonial Environment and Religion in Haiti." Ph.D. diss., Columbia University, 1971.

Spencer, Ivor D. Introduction to *A Civilization That Perished: The Last Years of White Colonial Rule in Saint-Domingue*, by Médéric Louis Élie Moreau de Saint-Méry. Translated and edited by Ivor D. Spencer. Lanham, Md.: University Press of America, 1985.

Spillers, Hortense. "Mama's Baby, Papa's Maybe: An American Grammar Book." *Diacritics* 17, no. 2 (1987): 65–81.

———. "Notes on an Alternative Model: Neither/Nor." In *Black, White and in Color: Essays on American Literature and Culture*. Chicago: University of Chicago Press, 2003.

———. "The Permanent Obliquity of an In(pha)llibly Straight: In the Time of the Daughters and the Fathers." In *Black, White and in Color: Essays on American Literature and Culture*.

Spivak, Gayatry. "Can the Subaltern Speak?" In *Marxism and the Interpretation of Culture*, edited by Cary Neslon and Lawrence Grossberg. Basingstoke: Macmillan Education, 1988.

———. *The Post-colonial Critic*. Edited by Sarah Harasym. New York: Routledge, 1990.

Sprenger, Jacques, and Henry Institoris. *Malleus Malleficarum*. 1487. Translation, with an introduction, bibliography, and notes, by Montague Summers. New York: Benjamin Bloom, 1928.

Stepan, Nancy. "Biological Degeneration." In *Degeneration: The Dark Side of Progress*, edited by J. Edward Chamberlain and Sander L. Gilman. New York: Columbia University Press, 1985.

Steward, Julian H., ed. *Handbook of South American Indians*, Washington, D.C.: Smithsonian Bureau of American Ethnology, 1949.

Stoler, Ann Laura. "Carnal Knowledge and Imperial Power: Gender, Race and Morality in Colonial Asia." In *Gender at the Crossroads of Knowledge: Feminist Anthropology in a Postmodern Era*, edited by Micaela di Leonardo. Berkeley: University of California Press, 1991.

———. "Making Empire Respectable: The Politics of Race and Sexual Morality in Twentieth-Century Colonial Cultures." *American Ethnologist* 16, no. 4 (1989): 642–58.

———. *Race and the Education of Desire: Foucault's History of Sexuality and the Colonial Order of Things*. Durham: Duke University Press, 1995.

———. "Sexual Affronts and Racial Frontiers: European Identities and the Cultural Politics of Exclusion in Colonial Southeast Asia." In Cooper and Stoler, *Tensions of Empire*.

Supplément à l'Encyclopédie. Amsterdam: M. M. Rey, 1776–77.

Taussig, Michael T. *The Devil and Commodity Fetishism in South America*. Chapel Hill: University of North Carolina Press, 1980.

Taylor, Douglas. "The Caribs of Dominica." *Bureau of American Ethnology Bulletin* 119 (1938): 109–59.

———. *Languages of the West Indies*. Baltimore: Johns Hopkins University Press, 1977.

———. "The Meaning of Dietary and Occupational Restrictions among the Island Carib." *American Anthropologist* 52 (1950): 343–49.

Taylor, Douglas, and Berend Hoff. "The Linguistic Repertory of the Island Carib in the Seventeenth Century: The Men's Language—a Carib Pidgin?" *International Journal of American Linguistics* 46, no. 4 (1980): 301–12.

Tedlock, Dennis. *The Spoken Word and the Work of Interpretation*. Philadelphia: University of Pennsylvania Press, 1983.

Thomas, Nicholas. *Colonialism's Culture: Anthropology, Travel, and Government*. Princeton: Princeton University Press, 1994.

Thomson, Janice E. *Mercenaries, Pirates and Sovereigns: State-Building and Extraterritorial Violence in Early Modern Europe*. Princeton: Princeton University Press, 1994.

Tondriau, Julien L., and Roland Villeneuve. *Dictionnaire du diable et de la démonologie*. Marabout université, no. 154. Verviers: Gérard, 1968.

Toumson, Roger. "'Blancs créoles' et 'Nègres créoles': Généalogie d'un imaginaire colonial." In Yacou, *Créoles de la Caraïbe*.

———. *Mythologie du métissage*. Paris: Presses Universitaires de France, 1998.

———. *La Transgression des couleurs: Littérature et langage des Antilles, XVIIIe, XIXe, XXe siècles*. Paris: Éditions Caribéennes, 1989.

Traer, James. *Marriage and the Family in Eighteenth-Century France*. Ithaca: Cornell University Press, 1980.

Trevor-Roper, H. R. "The European Witch-Craze." In *Witchcraft and Sorcery: Selected Readings*, edited by Max Marwick. Middlesex: Penguin, 1970.

Trouillot, Michel-Rolph. *Silencing the Past: Power and the Production of History*. Boston: Beacon, 1995.

Trousson, Raymond. "Préface." In *Romans libertins du XVIIIe siècle*, edited by Raymond Trousson. Paris: Robert Laffont, 1993.

Trousson, Raymond, ed. *Romans libertins du XVIIIe siècle*. Paris: Robert Laffont, 1993.

Tyler, Stephen A. "Post-modern Ethnography: From Document of the Occult to Occult Document." In Clifford and Marcus, *Writing Culture*.

Vaissière, Pierre de. *Saint-Domingue: La société et la vie créole sous l'ancien régime (1629–1789)*. Paris: Perrin, 1909.

Valdman, Albert. "Creole, the Language of Slavery." In *Slavery in the Caribbean Francophone World: Distant Voices, Forgotten Acts, Forged Identities*, edited by Doris Y. Kadish. Athens: University of Georgia Press, 2000.

Van Wing, J. *Études bakongo: sociologie—religion et magie*. 2d ed. Louvain: Desclée de Brouwer, 1959.

Vartaniam, Aram. "La Mettrie, Diderot, and Sexology in the Enlightenment." In *Essays on the Age of Enlightenment in Honor of Ira O. Wade*, edited by Jean Macary. Geneva: Librairie Droz, 1977.

Vaumas, Guillaume de. *L'Éveil missionaire de la France au XVIIe siècle*. Paris: Bloud and Gay, 1959.

Vauthier, Simone. "Of African Queens and Afro-American Princes and Princesses: Miscegenation in Old Hepsy." In *Regards sur la littérature noire américaine*, edited by Michel Fabre. Paris: Conseil Scientifique de la Sorbonne nouvelle, 1980.

———. "Jeux avec l'interdit: La sexualité interraciale dans le roman de Joseph H. Ingraham, *The Quadroone*." RANAM 11 (1978): 133–46.

Veeser, H. Aram, ed. *The New Historicism*. New York: Routledge, 1989.

Vega, Garcilaso de la. *Le Commentaire royal, ou L'Histoire des Yncas, Roys du Peru*. Paris: Augustin Courbé, 1633.

Venette, Nicolas. *De la génération de l'homme, ou, tableau de l'amour conjugal*. Cologne: Claude Joly, 1696.

Vergès, Françoise. "'I am Not the Slave of Slavery': The Politics of Reparation in (French) Postslavery Communities." In *Frantz Fanon: Critical Perspectives*, edited by Anthony C. Alessandrini. London: Routledge, 1999.

———. "Métissage, discours masculin et déni de la mère." In Condé and Cottenet-Hage, *Penser la créolité*.

———. *Monsters and Revolutionaries: Colonial Family Romance and Métissage*. Durham: Duke University Press, 1999.

Vigier, Philippe. "La Recomposition du mouvement abolitionniste française sous la monarchie de Juillet." In *Les Abolitions de l'esclavage: De L. F. Sonthonax à V. Schoelcher, 1793, 1794, 1848*, edited by Marcel Dorigny. Paris: L'Organisation des Nations Unies, 1995.

Villaverde, Cirillio. *Cecila Valdés*. Translated by Helen Lowe, with an introduction by Sibylle Fischer. New York: Oxford University Press, 2004.

Voltaire, François Marie Arouet de, and René Pomeau. *Essai sur les moeurs*. 2 vols. Reprint, with introduction, bibliography, variants, and notes by René Pomeau. Paris: Garnier frères, 1963.

Vrijman,——. "L'Identité d'Exquemelin." *Comité des travaux historiques et scientifiques. Bulletin de la section de géographie* 48 (1933): 34–57.

Walcott, Derek. "The Caribbean: Culture or Mimicry?" In *Critical Perspectives on Derek Walcott*, edited by Robert D. Hamner. Boulder: Three Continents Press, 1997.

Watson, Alan. *Slave Law in the Americas.* Athens: University of Georgia Press, 1989.

Wendl, Tobias, and Michael Rösler. "Frontiers and Borderlands: The Rise and Relevance of an Anthropological Research Genre." In Wendl and Rösler, *Frontiers and Borderlands.*

Wendl, Tobias, and Michael Rösler, eds. *Frontiers and Borderlands: Anthropological Perspectives.* Frankfurt: Peter Lang, 1999.

Westermann, D. *Gbesela Yeye, or English-Ewe Dictionary.* Berlin: Dietrich Reimer, 1930.

Weyer, Johann. *On Witchcraft: An Abridged Translation of Johann Weyer's De praestigiis daemonum.* Translated by John Shea, edited by Benjamin G. Kohl and H. C. Erik Midelfort. Asheville, N.C.: Pegasus, 1998.

White, Debora Gray. *Ar'n't I a Woman? Female Slaves in the Plantation South.* Rev. ed. New York: Norton, 1999.

———. "Revisiting Ar'n't I a Woman." In White, *Ar'n't I a Woman?*

White, Hayden. *The Content of the Form: Narrative Discourse and Historical Representation.* Baltimore: Johns Hopkins University Press, 1987.

———. "The Forms of Wildness: Archaeology of an Idea." In *The Wild Man Within*, edited by Edward Dudely and Maximillian E. Novak. Pittsburgh: University of Pittsburgh Press, 1972.

———. "The Noble Savage Theme as Fetish." In *First Images of America*, Vol. 1, edited by Fredi Chiappelli. Berkeley: University of California Press, 1976.

———. "The Question of Narrative in Contemporary Historical Theory." In White, *The Content of the Form.*

———. *Tropics of Discourse: Essays in Cultural Criticism.* Baltimore: Johns Hopkins University Press, 1985.

Whitehead, Neil L. "Carib Cannibalism: The Historical Evidence." *Journal de la Société des Américanistes* 70 (1984): 69–87.

———. "Ethnic Plurality and Cultural Continuity in the Native Caribbean." In Whitehead, *Wolves from the Sea.*

———. *Lords of the Tiger Spirit: A History of the Caribs in Colonial Venezuela and Guyana, 1498–1820.* Dordrecht: Foris, 1988.

Whitehead, Neil L., ed. *Wolves from the Sea: Readings in the Anthropology of the Native Caribbean.* Leiden: KITLV Press, 1995.

Williams, Eric Eustace. *Capitalism and Slavery.* Chapel Hill: University of North Carolina Press, 1994.

Williams, Patrick, and Laura Chrisman, eds. *Colonial Discourse and Post-colonial Theory: A Reader.* New York: Columbia University Press, 1994.

Wilson, Samuel M., ed. *The Indigenous People of the Caribbean*. Gainesville: University Press of Florida, 1997.

Wolfzettel, Friedrich. *Le Discours du voyageur: Pour une histoire littéraire du récit de voyage en France, du Moyen âge au XVIIIe siècle*. Paris: Presses Universitaires de France, 1996.

Wyngaard, Amy. "Switching Codes: Class, Clothing and Cultural Change in the Works of Marivaux and Watteau." *Eighteenth-Century Studies* 33, no. 4 (2000): 523–41.

Yacou, A., ed. *Créoles de la Caraïbe: Actes du Colloque universitaire en hommage à Guy Hazaël-Massieux, Pointe-à-Pitre, le 27 mars 1995*. Paris: Karthala, 1996.

Young, Everild, and Kjeld Helweg-Larsen. *The Pirates' Priest; The Life of Père Labat in the West Indies, 1693–1705*. [London]: Jarrolds, 1965.

Young, Robert J. C. *Colonial Desire: Hybridity in Theory, Culture and Race*. London: Routledge, 1995.

———. *White Mythologies*. London: Routledge, 1990.

Zantop, Susan. *Colonial Fantasies: Conquest, Family, and Nation in Precolonial Germany, 1770–1870*. Durham: Duke University Press, 1997.

Index

Breton, Raymond (*continued*)
78–79; witnesses Carib rites, 153–54. *See also* Dictionaire caraïbe-français

Brooks, Peter, 26

Buccaneers, 100, 101, 112, 323 n.32

Buffon, Georges Louis Leclerc, 4, 251, 261, 267–68, 359 n.49, 360 n.73

Burg, B. R., 324 n.46

Burton, Richard, 192

Calenda, 252, 253, 355 nn.30–31

Cannibalism, 39–40, 46, 62, 154–55, 300 n.9, 331 n.23

Capuchin order, 49, 329 n.95

Carib language. *See* Dictionaire caraïbe-français

Caribs: anthropophagy and, 39–40, 46, 62, 154–55, 300 n.9; Arawaks, 62, 63, 64, 154–55; botany and, 83; capacity of, for suffering, 170; as colonizers, 62, 65; definitions of, 39, 65, 309 nn.1–2; facility of, with French language, 77; French hostilities with, 62–63; intelligence exchanges of, 68; land ownership of, 62; massacre of, 53–56; opposition of, to Spanish incursions, 40; resistance of, to enslavement, 42, 49; supernatural beliefs of, 56, 57, 149–57; warfare with, 6–7. *See also* Creole; Creolization; *Dictionaire caraïbe-français*; Free people of color; Slave headings

Chamoiseau, Patrick, 19, 22, 259, 357 n.38

Chemin (Chemÿn), 151

Chevillard, André, 63, 69

Cheyfitz, Eric, 75

Chica dance, 255, 356 n.35

Childbearing, 208, 210, 222, 223, 345 n.56

Children, mixed-race: colonial identity of, 127; commodity value of, 228–29, 283; enfranchisement of, 209–10; enslavement of, 207, 365–66 n.120;

financial support of, 213, 224, 273, 346 n.76; incest and, 277–78; legal status of, 197, 201, 206; manumission of, 206, 213; morality of, 216; mother's marital status and, 206; naming of, 214; Partus sequitur ventrem and, 202, 203; as taboo objects, 209, 345 n.55

Chinard, Gilbert, 9, 71, 300 n.8

Choiseuil, Duc de, 216

Christianity: as bestowing virtue, 200; Caribs and, 40, 56, 295; colonial self-interest and, 160–62; conversion to, 47–48, 72, 77–79; libertinage and, 190; pain and, 168–69, 170–72; salvation and, 160–62, 170; slavery and, 157–59, 161–62, 164, 170, 190, 221

Clifford, James, 79

Climatology, 225, 232–33, 268, 271, 274, 349 n.113

Closson, Marianne, 188

Code noir: black female reproduction in, 206–7; children in, 205, 365 n.120; Christian salvation and, 160–62; class distinctions in, 207; on concubinage, 28, 204–6; on corporal punishment, 244; criminality and, 162–63; humans as movable objects in, 159; on inter-racial libertinage, 217; in Louisiana, 207, 213, 344 n.48; on manumission, 213; Partus sequitur ventrem and, 205; Sadism and, 26, 339 n.92; slavery in, 159–62, 163–64, 253, 355 n.30

Colonization: acculturation and, 68–69; Carib resistance to, 3, 42, 49, 301 n.20; Caribs as sources of intelligence and, 68; Creole language and, 18, 247–48, 258, 357 nn.37–40; founding fiction of, 94, 319 n.4; massacre of Caribs and, 53–56; Spain and, 40, 42, 52, 55, 57, 104. *See also* Creole; Creolization; *Dictionaire caraïbe-français*; Missionaries; Mulatto headings; Pirates and piracy; Saint-Domingue; Slave headings

Columbus, Christopher, 39–40, 41, 59, 309 n.2
Compagnie de Saint-Christophe, 46, 121
Compagnie des Indes Occidentales, 122
Compagnie des Isles de l'Amérique, 121, 201
Concubinage: Code noir on, 28, 203, 205–7, 344 n.48; colonists' endowments to, 213, 346 n.76; enfranchisement of concubines and, 209–10; manumission from, 211, 213, 273; mulatto women and, 211, 235–38. *See also* Mulatto women
Confiant, Raphaël, 19, 22, 259, 357 n.38
Considérations sur l'état présent de la colonie française de Saint-Domingue (Hilliard d'Auberteuil), 219
Cooper, Frederick, 237, 261
Corsaire, 100, 321 n.18
Crébillon, Claude-Prosper-Jolyot, 26
Creole: *créoliste* writers and, 19; identity, 20, 246, 250; language, 18, 247–48, 258, 357 nn.37–40; slave women, 256, 361 n.87
Creolization, 17–22, 250–59, 305 nn.75, 77. *See also* Description topographie, physique, civile, . . . ; Du Tertre, Jean-Baptiste; Labat, Jean-Baptiste; Pirates and piracy; Slave headings; Social class; White men
Curtin, Philip, 353 n.2

Dampierre, Jacques de, 9
Dance gatherings, 252–55, 355 n.30, 355 n.31, 356 n.35
Davis, Angela, 22, 305 n.81
Dayan, Joan: on anti-colonial narratives in Caribbean rituals, 192; on Code noir, 206; on color classification, 261, 262, 359 n.51; on cult of desire, 23; on libertinage in Saint-Domingue, 30; on literary fieldwork, 10, 17; on luxury, 237, 351 n.146; on mulatto women, 22, 215, 229, 237, 350 nn.128–29; on

Sadism, 26, 339 n.92; on slaves' will, 163
De l'Esprit des lois (Montesquieu), 4, 300 n.13
De Pauw, Cornelius, 261, 359 n.49
De Vaissière, Pierre, 9
Debbasch, Yvan, 31, 203, 213, 217, 342 n.25
Debien, Gabriel, 346 n.75
Dejean, Joan, 177, 185
Demonology, 146, 154, 187–88, 190
Description topographie, physique, civile, politique et historique de la partie française de l'isle Saint-Domingue (Moreau de Saint-Méry): animalized racial names and, 262, 268; background of, 247–48; Buffon's monogenic theories and, 247–48; on colonial law reform, 348 n.102; on Creole language knowledge, 247–48, 357 n.37; on creolization, 247–48; family romance in, 275–76; incest fantasies in, 276–77; morality of Saint-Domingue in, 255–56; mulatto defined by, 346 n.70; on mulatto women, 231, 233–34; nationalism of, 250–51; racial taxonomies of, 250, 260–64, 359 n.54; on skin colors, 260–61; on slave women and reproduction, 34, 256–57, 271–72; Vaudou in, 254–55, 356 nn.32, 34–35; on white male desire, 270–72; on white women's indolence, 233; on zombies, 337 n.83
Desire, 22–27, 34, 155, 214, 215, 237, 256, 260
D'Esnambuc, Pierre, 45, 94, 126–27
Dessalines, Jean-Jacques, 292
Devils, 150, 151, 166, 184–85. *See also* Beating devil
Dictionaire caraïbe-français, 78–80; botanical descriptions in, 82, 83, 86; boyé sings to make his gods descend in, 153; Carib in, 65, 89–91; chemign (god) in, 151; colonial ethnography in, 75–76;

of, 362 n.89; French names assumed
by, 214, 237; interracial marriages and,
30; legitimacy of, 32; manumission
and, 211, 218; métissage and, 211, 260;
military service and, 215, 273–74, 288;
mulattoes identified with, 212, 346
n.70; growth of population of, 266,
267, 271, 273; racial engineering of,
348 n.101; as racial intermediaries, 33,
216–18, 276; restrictions on, 30, 212–
13, 215, 237; in Saint-Domingue, 8,
212; slave ownership of, 30; whitening
of, 223–24

Free women of color, 197, 229, 269–70,
291

French language, 10, 77, 258, 357 n.39

Freud, Sigmund, 208, 275, 283, 287, 364
n.111, 366 nn.124–25

Freyre, Gilberto, 305 n.75

Frostin, Charles, 110

Fugitive slaves, 102, 242–44, 253–54, 273,
274

Gallagher, Catherine, 15, 16

Garrigus, David, 236

Gautier, Arlette, 22, 23, 342 n.30,
343 n.43

Geggus, David P., 349 n.106, 355 n.31,
356 n.34

Girod de Chantrans, Justin: on colonists'
indolence, 227; on Creole language,
357 n.39; on environmental mismanagement, 228; on incest, 286–87; on
master's love of a mulatto, 236; on
monopoly commerce, 228; on mulatto
women's erotic powers, 231; on pronatalism of, 222; on slave sexuality, 286;
slaves defended by, 228

Glazier, Stephen D., 151

Glissant, Édouard, 3, 18–19, 22, 294,
305 n.77

Gramsci, Antonio, 23

Greenblatt, Stephen, 15, 16

Guadeloupe, 7, 19, 42, 49, 50, 53–56

Guégan Bertrand, 107, 324 n.44

Gullick, C. J. M. R., 313 n.46

Haitian Revolution, 3, 245–46, 249, 289,
301 n.20

Hartman, Saidiya, 22, 23, 204

Hathaway, Heather, 279, 345 n.55,
364 n.108

Hénaff, Marcel, 26–27, 284–85, 367 n.129

Herman, Judith, 366 n.121, 367 n.129

Hilliard d'Auberteuil, Michel René: on
biological reproduction of mulattoes,
225–26; on colonial law reform, 220,
348 n.102; on colonial population
management, 221; on colonists' indolence and extravagance, 220, 234–35;
on interracial marriage, 225; on libertinage, 219–20, 224; on manumission,
223, 350 n.125; on mulattoes, 29, 225,
230, 272–73, 346 n.70; racial taxonomy
of, 262, 265; on stain of blackness, 223,
224; on white Creole elites, 220–21

Hirschman, Lisa, 366 n.121, 367 n.129

*Histoire des aventuriers flibustiers qui se
sont signalés dans des Indes* (Oexmelin):
Amerindians in, 108–9; buccaneer
culture in, 108–9; on colonial industries, 138; European imagination of
the Americas and, 118–19; filibuster
piracy in, 110; French nationalization
of Oexmelin in, 105, 107; as history of
piracy, 103–4, 323 n.32; matelotage in,
109, 110–11, 324 n.46; as moral history,
105; Oexmelin as honest man *(honnête
homme)* in, 105, 324 n.42; on pirate
violence, 112–14, 144; on pirates and
nobility, 115, 116; popularity of, 103–4;
publication history of, 104–7; white
savagery in, 103, 109; state interests
reflected in translations of, 103–5, 323
n.32; on state's repression of piracy,
117–19; translations of, 104, 105, 322
n.31, 323 n.32

Histoire des deux Indes (Raynal), 4–5

Histoire des voyages (Prévost), 4

Histoire générale des Antilles habitées par les François (Du Tertre), 50, 71–74, 121–30, 240–41. *See also* Du Tertre, Jean-Baptiste

Historicism, 11–15, 302 n.41, 303 n.44

Hobsbawm, Eric, 111

Hooks, Bell, 22, 305 n.81, 342 n.30

Hospitals of Paris, 125, 327 nn.70–72

Hulme, Peter, 11, 15, 17, 59, 64

Hunt, Lynn, 362 n.95

Husson, Louis Thomas, 6

Icheïri, 151

Incest, 34; African American women and, 281, 365 n.113; fathers and, 277–79, 281, 365 n.113, 365 n.114, 366 n.121, 367 nn.127, 129; interracial sexual alliances and, 279, 363 n.103; miscegenation and, 278, 279, 281, 285, 287; slavery and, 34, 278–81, 285–86, 368 n.132. *See also* Libertinage

Indentured servitude, 109, 110–11, 126–28, 324 n.46, 327 n.73

Inkle and Yarico legend, 194, 195

Jamaica, 5, 18, 100, 217, 300 n.13

James, C. L. R., 242

Jordan, Winthrop, 308 n.117

King, Stewart, 212, 273, 345 n.65, 346 n.67

Kongolese occult systems, 181–82

Kristeva, Julia, 16, 304 n.58

Kutzinski, Vera, 352 n.152

Labat, Jean-Baptiste: on African witchcraft, 165–66; on Creole society, 140; *créole* used by, 20; culinary experiences of, 134–35, 142–43; on filibusters of Saint-Domingue, 142–43; in folklore, 192–93, 339 n.102; on island nature, 13, 135–36; on literacy, 142, 329 n.99; on luxuries, 141–42; self-descriptions

of, 131–32; as slave owner, 165; on slavery and Christianity, 158; on slaves' resistance to pain, 170–72; on social advancement, 140–42, 329 n.98; on sugar production, 136–40; travel writing of, 131–32; tropical illnesses described by, 134; on violence toward slaves, 168–70

Lacan, Jacques, 279

Laclos, Choderlos de, 26

Lancre, Pierre de, 168

Laplace, Pierre Antoine de, 4

Las Casas, Bartolomé de, 52, 312 n.27

Léry, Jean de, 156, 331–32 n.23

Lescarbot, Marc, 95

Levinas, Emmanuel, 35, 90, 295, 319 n.138

Lévi-Strauss, Claude, 282–83, 365 nn.116, 119

Libertinage, 199, 207, 344 nn.48, 50; caste system and, 29; Christianity and, 190; community atonement for, 208–9; defined, 24–25; desire and, 26–27; free women of color and, 28, 236–39; Hilliard d'Auberteuil on, 219–20, 224–25; impurity of, 211, 269; legal attempts to restrict, 200–207, 209; manumission and, 213; as political necessity, 218; mulatto female sterility and, 270–71; of de Sade, 26–27, 284–85; between races, 199, 203, 204–5, 207, 209–10, 213, 217, 218, 236–38; relation of, to segregationism, 32–33, 197–98, 225–26, 238–39; shortage of white women and, 206, 210, 345 n.58; three-tiered caste system and, 209; white male apologies for, 217–18, 225–26, 236, 272–73, 276

Ligon, Richard, 194, 195

"Lisette quitté la plaine," 259–60, 357 n.42

Loix et constitutions des colonies française de l'Amérique sous le vent (Moreau de Saint-Méry), 249

Long, Edward, 269
Louverture, Toussaint, 249

Maboya, 150–51, 152, 153, 156
Magic, 165, 167, 185
Makandal conspiracy, 245
Mameloucs, 268–69
Manumission: childbearing and, 223;
    Code noir on, 213; concubinage
    and, 211, 213, 273; free people of
    color and, 211, 218; French names
    assumed by freed slaves upon, 214;
    Hilliard d'Auberteuil on, 223, 350
    n.125; legislation restricting, 213; lib-
    erté de savane and, 223; by military
    conscription, 273; of mulattoes, 202,
    203, 218, 225, 349 n.114, 350 n.125; of
    slave women, 206
Maronnage, 245
Marriage: Catholicism and, 206; child-
    bearing and, 206; domesticity and,
    127; indentured servants and, 128;
    legitimization of black women by,
    214, 347 n.80; libertinage and, 222–
    23; between races (*mésalliance*), 207,
    212, 214–15, 224, 235; racial borderlines
    of, 224; slave marriages, 204, 206,
    222; of white men with mothers of
    their illegitimate children, 344 n.48,
    365–66 n.120
Martinique: Carib-French violence on,
    42, 57–58; colonization of, 7; *créole* on,
    19; ethnic borders on, 58; free people
    of color population on, 211, 345 n.65;
    French colonization of, 53; immoral
    behavior on, 25; Jesuits on, 49; settlers'
    acculturation on, 68–69
Matelotage, 110–11, 126, 137, 324 n.46,
    327 n.73
Mauss, Marcel, 47, 66
McClintock, Ann, 13–14, 87, 232,
    364 n.111
Métraux, Alfred, 192, 356 n.32
Military service, 215, 273–74, 288

Miller, Nancy, 271
Mintz, Sydney, 137
Miscegenation: colored population and,
    22; creolization and, 21–22, 305 nn.75,
    77; incest and, 278; Inkle and Yarico
    legend and, 194, 195, 340 n.8; legis-
    lation controlling, 2, 202–7, 216, 344
    nn.48, 50; manumission and, 211;
    metaphor of disownment by white
    father and, 214; mixed-race progeny
    and, 196, 197; by mulatto men and
    white women, 205; population control
    by, 225, 271; racial taxonomy and, 265;
    sexual reproduction and, 196; skin
    colors and, 250; subversion of white
    authority and, 228; three-tiered caste
    system and, 209. *See also* Children,
    mixed-race; Free people of color;
    Incest
Missionaries: on cannibalism, 155;
    Capuchin order of, 49, 329 n.95; Carib
    gods and, 151; colonialism of, 44,
    47–48, 50, 59, 61, 70–71, 74, 77–79;
    conversions of slaves by, 157; corpo-
    ral punishment sanctioned by, 244;
    deaths of, 49; ethnographic writings
    of, 58; French settlers and, 49; gift
    giving of, 47–48, 59, 61, 66, 70–71;
    Jesuits, 49; mercantilism and, 69–
    71; on sexual immorality, 25. *See also*
    Du Tertre, Jean-Baptiste; Labat,
    Jean-Baptiste
Mitchell, Juliet, 283
Mocquet, Jean, 195
Montesquieu, Charles de Secondat, 9,
    257, 348 n.102
Moreau de Saint-Méry, M. L. E. *See*
    Description topographie, physique,
    civile, . . . (Moreau de Saint-Méry)
Morgan (pirate), 114, 115, 325 n.56
Morrison, Toni, 294
Mukherjee, Arun, 15
Mulatto men, 274, 287–90, 292
Mulatto women: domesticity of, 235–36,

Mulatto women (*continued*)
352 n.138, 361–62 n.87; economic independence of, 235, 236; fantasies about,
230–31, 233–34, 288–89; fertility and
sterility of, 34, 37, 269, 270–71, 276,
361 nn.85, 87; material extravagance
of, 234–35, 237, 351 n.146; morality of,
29; mythologies of, 230–31; privilege
of, 229–31, 350 n.129; sexual savage-
chaste caregiver binary, 235, 352 n.152;
spiritual imaginary of Vaudou and,
350 n.129; white men and, 28–29, 230–
31, 232, 235, 259, 351 n.138; whiteness
of, 277; white women and, 28–29, 229,
230, 235. *See also* Children, mixed-
race; Concubinage; Incest; Mulatto
men; Mulattoes
Mulattoes: in American fiction, 279, 364
nn.107–8; commodity value of, 229;
definition of, in encyclopedias, 217;
enslavement of, 203, 211, 342 n.25;
fathers' obligations toward, 202–3,
342 nn.24–25; financial independence
of, 274; fugitive slaves pursued by,
273, 274; intermediary role of, 216–
18, 223–24; legal status of, 33, 202;
manumission of, 202, 203, 218, 225,
349 n.114, 350 n.125; military service
and, 215, 273–74, 288; monogenesis
and, 267; physical qualities of, 263–
64, 268, 274; reproduction and, 267,
269, 345 n.56, 360 n.65; restrictions
on, 215, 237; sexual deviance of, 205;
skin color of, 263–64; white anxieties
about interracial libertinage and, 32,
204–5, 212; white male paternity and,
272, 275–76. *See also* Free people of
color; Mulatto men; Mulatto women
Murray, David, 88

Names, 66, 214, 224, 237, 262, 268
National Convention 1794, 3
Naturally free person (*libre naturel*), 207,
212, 213

New Historicism, 11–12, 15–16
Nine Years' War, 118
Nobility. *See* Social class
Noble Savage, 94, 95
Nouveau voyage aux isles de l'Amérique
(Labat). *See* Labat, Jean-Baptiste
Nursemaids, 280, 364 n.111
Nzambi, 181–82, 338 n.89

Oedipal complex, 286–87, 288
Oexmelin, Alexandre Olivier. *See*
Histoire des aventuriers flibustiers
qui se sont signalés dans les Indes
(Oexmelin)
Ogéron, 115, 118
Ogle, Gene, 348 n.101
Olive, Charles Liénard, Sieur de L',
53–54, 55
Olonnais (pirate), 112–14, 325 n.53
The 120 Days of Sodom (de Sade), 26–27
Orientalism, 11, 12, 13, 302 n.41, 303 n.44
Oritz, Fernando, 18

Pain, 147, 148, 168–69, 170–72
Parry, Benita, 13
Partus sequitur ventrem, 202, 203, 205
Paternity, 210–11, 272, 275–76, 283–84,
367 n.137
Patterson, Orlando, 160, 288–89,
368 n.136
Pelleprat, Pierre, 150, 157, 158, 199–200
Petit, Émilien, 2, 273, 348 n.102, 362
n.89, 364 n.109
Peytraud, Lucien, 9, 302 n.34
Pietz, William, 70, 316 n.83
Pirates and piracy: anti-colonialism
and, 117, 325 n.55; aventuriers, 100,
113, 321 n.17; buccaneers, 100, 101,
112, 323 n.32; Carthagena mission
(1697) and, 118; character of, 99–100;
colonies' relations with, 100–101;
corsaires, 100, 321 n.18; decline of,
103, 322 n.30; filibusters (flibustiers),
100, 104, 110–11, 112, 142–43, 321

Schoelcher, Victor, 6

Sea travel, 100, 123–25, 167–68, 327 n.70

Sedgwick, Eve, 327 n.73

Sexual reproduction: capital gain and, 222; Christianization of slaves and, 221; corporal punishment of black women slaves and, 221; of free people of color, 225–26, 271–73; free women of color and, 269–70; infant mortality and, 221–22; legislation of, 221; racial taxonomies and, 250, 260–66, 359 n.54; slave fecundity and, 223; slave pregnancies as liability for masters, 221–22; sterility of mulatto women and, 269–70; white male sexual satisfaction and, 225, 272; women slaves as breeders, 204. *See also* Libertinage; Miscegenation; Mulatto headings

Sexual slavery, 229, 257, 350 n.126, 356 n.36

Shamans, 150, 152, 153–54, 169–70

Slave masters: Catholicism of, 161; concubinage and, 205–6; corporal punishment of slaves by, 242, 244, 245; Creole language spoken by, 258, 357 n.37; financial support of family members of, 213, 224, 273, 346 n.76; manumission and, 213, 273; marriages of, to slave women, 206, 224; paternity of, 272, 275–76; racial paranoia of, 264–65; respect shown by slaves to, 224, 349 n.112; sexual relations of, with slave women, 199–206, 225–26, 271–73; slave culture and, 258, 357 n.38; spiritual authority of, 169–70; Vaudoo and, 253–54; on women's infertility, 221–22. *See also* Code noir; *Description topographie, physique, civile, . . .* (Moreau de Saint-Méry); Libertinage; Mulatto headings; other Slave headings

Slave rebellions, 217, 218, 245

Slave ships, 167–68, 353 n.1

Slave women: abortion and, 210, 222; colonial economy of reproduction and, 206–7, 272; commodity value of, 229; desire of, 23, 256, 257; manumission of, 206; marriage and, 204, 206; material extravagance of, 257–58; morality of, 216; as nursemaids for white children, 280; ownership of, 283; Partus sequitur ventrem, 202, 203; projection of white anxieties onto, 32–33, 203–4, 238; rape of, 22, 204, 343 n.32; resistance of, 199–200, 222, 341 n.14; sexual reproduction and, 204, 206–7, 221–22; sexual subjection to masters, 225–26, 271–72; as taboo objects, 200, 208, 209, 226. *See also* Concubinage; *Description topographie, physique, civile, . . .* (Moreau de Saint-Méry); Libertinage; Miscegenation; other Slave headings; Violence

Slaves: beating devil, 156–57, 158–59, 164; Christianity and, 157–59, 161–62, 190, 221; colonists as, 227; commodity value of, 160–61, 188, 221, 228–29, 241–42; corporal punishment of, 163, 167–69, 171–72, 242, 244, 334 nn.63–64; Creole language spoken by, 246, 258, 357 n.37; dances of, 254–55; demographics of, 221, 240–41, 349 n.106, 353 n.2; escape of, 273, 274; marriages of, 204, 206, 222; medical care for, 166, 334 n.56; mortality rates of, 241–42; occultism of, 166–67; regional origins of, 181, 338 n.87, 338 n.91; representations of, 245–47; respect doctrine of, 224, 349 n.112; self-flagellation of, 171, 334 n.63; sugar cane sales and, 160; whitening of, 223–24. *See also* Code noir; Concubinage; *Description topographie, physique, civile, . . .* (Moreau de Saint-Méry); other Slave headings; Violence

Smith, Jay, 329 n.98

Social class: aristocratic privilege and, 26–27; clothing and, 128–30, 237;

engagés, 126–27; freed person (affranchi), 207, 213, 217, 223, 224, 346 n.70; interracial marriage and, 32–33, 214–15; invention of, 125, 189, 212; land ownership and, 128–29; matelotage and, 110–11, 126, 324 n.46; mercantilism and, 96; mulatto elite, 233; names and, 66, 214, 224, 237, 262, 268; naturally free person (libre naturel), 207, 212; of pirates, 101, 110, 115, 117–18, 119, 325 n.56; sang mêlé, 215, 262, 264; three-tiered caste system and, 32, 209; trademarks of nobility and, 120, 128–30, 212, 326 n.62; whiteness and, 214, 224, 265; women and social mobility, 128–30

Société des amis des noirs, 5

Sollors, Werner, 277, 278, 363 nn.99, 103

Sorel, Charles, 185

Spain, 40, 42, 52, 55, 57, 104

Spillers, Hortense, 22, 281, 365 n.115

Spivak, Gayatry, 11–12, 14

Steele, Richard, 194, 195

Stoler, Ann Laura, 237, 261, 352 n.157

Sugar production, 7, 8, 131, 136–37, 137–40, 241

Surinam, 5, 217, 300 n.13

Taboos: incest, 279, 283, 284–85; mixed-race children as, 209, 345 n.55; sexual, 208–9, 363 n.103; slave women and, 209, 226

Taylor, Douglas, 64

Tedlock, Dennis, 75

Thomson, Janice, 111

Tobacco cultivation, 7, 98, 240

Tortuga, 8, 100, 101, 102, 105, 109, 117

Toumson, Roger, 10, 270, 359 n.50

Travel writing, 3–4, 300 nn.6, 8, 9. *See also* Girod de Chantrans, Justin; Wimpffen, Alexandre-Stanislas, Baron

Trouillot, Michel-Rolph, 3

Trousson, Raymond, 176

Tyler, Stephen A., 91

Vaissière, Pierre de, 208

Valdman, Albert, 357

Vaudou: chants of, 254, 356 n.34; as cult of the serpent, 253; dances of, 254–55, 356 n.35; initiation ritual of, 254–55; sacred marronnage and, 253–54; secrecy in, 255; social power of, 253–54

Vauthier, Simone, 275, 279

Vergès, Françoise, 6, 17, 362 n.95

Violence: of beating devil, 156–57, 158–59, 164; carnal pleasure in *Le Zombi du Grand-Pérou* (Blessebois) and, 184; corporal punishment of slaves and, 163, 167–69, 171–72, 221, 240–46, 334 nn.62–63; engagés abuse and, 126–27; in French-Carib relations, 53–58; Lejeune affair and, 244–45; pain and, 147, 148, 168–69, 187–88; of pirates, 111–16, 144, 324 n.49; rape, 22, 204, 343 n.32, 344 n.50; scars of, 156–58; sexual submission and, 200; torture and, 244–45; zombie as symbol of, 192

Voltaire, 9, 267–68

Voyage à Saint-Domingue pendant les années 1788, 1789 et 1790 (Wimpffen), 227, 349 n.116

Voyage d'un Suisse dans différentes colonies d'Amérique (Girod de Chantrans, Justin), 227

Voyages en Afrique, Asie, Indes orientales et occidentales (Mocquet), 195

Walcott, Derek, 19

Watson, Alan, 206

Weyer, Johann, 151, 152

White, Hayden, 14, 95, 320 n.6

White men: African slave women and, 256; black men's rivalry with, 256–57, 288, 360 n.65; black nursemaids' influence on, 280–81, 364 n.111; black women's desirability for, 214,

Doris Garraway is assistant professor of French at
Northwestern University.

* * *

Library of Congress Cataloging-in-Publication Data
Garraway, Doris Lorraine
The libertine colony : creolization in the early French
Caribbean / Doris Garraway.
p. cm.
"A John Hope Franklin Center Book."
Includes bibliographical references and index.
ISBN 0-8223-3453-4 (cloth : alk. paper) —
ISBN 0-8223-3465-8 (pbk. : alk. paper)
1. Creoles—West Indies, French—History.
2. Slavery—West Indies, French—History.
3. Libertinism—West Indies, French—History.
4. Culture diffusion—West Indies, French—History.
5. Acculturation—West Indies, French—History.
6. Intercultural communication—West Indies,
French—History. 7. West Indian literature (French)—
History and criticism. 8. West Indies, French—Race
relations—History. 9. West Indies, French—Ethnic
relations—History. 10. West Indies, French—Social
conditions—History. I. Title.
F2151.G247 2005
305.8'0097297'6—dc22   2004028773